The Baltic

The Baltic

A New History of the Region and its People

ALAN PALMER

THE OVERLOOK PRESS
Woodstock & New York

First published in the United States in 2006 by
The Overlook Press, Peter Mayer Publishers, Inc.
New York and London

NEW YORK:
Overlook
141 Wooster Street
New York, NY 10012
www.overlookpress.com

LONDON:
Duckworth
90-93 Cowcross Street
London EC1M 6BF
www.ducknet.co.uk

Originally published in the United Kingdom as *Northern Shores*.

Cataloging-in-Publication Data is available from the Library of Congress

Manufactured in the United States of America
ISBN 978-1-58567-863-1 (US)
ISBN 978-0-71563-968-9 (UK)
2 4 6 8 10 9 7 5 3 1

Contents

Preface   vii

Maps   ix

Author's Note   xiv

Alternative Place Names   xv

1. Sentinels Above the Sound   1
2. Peoples on the Move   15
3. The Viking East   20
4. Pagans and Piasts   30
5. Holy Warriors and Hanse Merchants   38
6. The Rise and Fall of Marienburg   51
7. Ships, Pirates and Adventurers   58
8. The Chimera of Kalmar   65
9. Muscovy and Wittenberg   77
10. Lion of the North   96
11. Nemesis at Poltava   115
12. Imperial Russia in the Ascendant   137
13. Thunder from the South   157
14. Peaceful Change?   183
15. Black, Red and Gold   198
16. Bombarding Bomarsund   206
17. Finns, Poles and Danes   215
18. Towards Democracy   225
19. National Pride   230
20. The Last Years of the Long Peace   241

21. Emperors at War, 1914–17   252
22. Revolution and Independence   271
23. Nine Nations and a Free City   293
24. Hitler's Challenge   310
25. Nazi–Soviet Partnership   326
26. Nazi–Soviet War   349
27. Tragedy of Victory   375
28. Baltic Way   393

Royal Chronology   407
Notes and Select Bibliography   412
Index   429

Preface

A generation ago English-language histories of Europe neglected the Baltic past. Some names were sure of a few paragraphs: Gustavus Adolphus, for leading a Protestant army into Germany and perishing in the hour of victory; Peter the Great, for opening Russia's window to the West; Copenhagen as the city on which Nelson belligerently turned a blind eye; and, in passing, the Hanseatic League, though rarely with mention of its origins in the inland sea. Over recent years, however, interest in the Baltic and its peoples has grown rapidly. Several universities have departments specializing in Baltic studies, if only at post-graduate level. Penguin Classics in translation introduced Thomas Mann's Lübeck and Theodor Fontane's Kessin, a thinly disguised Swinemünde, to a new reading public. In 1980 Eric Christiansen's *The Northern Crusades* stimulated interest in a forgotten chapter of mediaeval history while, in *God's Playground*, Norman Davies recorded the glory, anarchy and tragedy of Poland, the continent's most resilient nation. A decade later Dr David Kirby's two volumes *The Baltic World 1492–1772* and *The Baltic World 1772–1993* examined half a millennium in scholarly detail. I remain grateful to all these authors.

Northern Shores was conceived back in the early 1970s when, aboard a Soviet ship bound for Leningrad, I saw for the first time the sentinel castles that form a seagate for the Baltic. A sense of the past always enhances the pleasures of travel. Was there, I wondered, scope for a narrative account of the region's history from the Vikings to the present day? I began to consider the form of the book, deciding early on to exclude Norway, as a land that looked to the Atlantic rather than to the inland sea. Next year, with my late wife Veronica, I took the car across to Esbjerg. We ferry-hopped through much of Denmark, southern Norway and Sweden. On other journeys we visited Finland and saw a little of East Germany and Poland. But there was no way we could travel freely through the occupied Baltic republics. Notes for the projected book were put aside in favour of topics that interested me elsewhere.

By the end of the century the face of Europe had changed completely and I remembered my discarded notes. The whole region was more accessible. Regular cruise ships sailed from Dover. The 2,000 kilometre flight from Heathrow to St Petersburg took little more than three hours; Stockholm's Arlanda airport, 1,500 kilometres distant, could be reached in two, and I found that, by changing at Copenhagen, Vilnius was only four hours away. I travelled to the Baltic in four successive years. It was pleasant to go by bus from Vilnius across much of the three independent Baltic republics and gratifying to find so many people willing to talk to me. From sixteen-year-olds to an 'over-eighty', I heard reminiscences of the past and speculation on the present and the future. Unfortunately we never got on surname terms and so I cannot thank them individually.

There are, however, many friends whose help it is a pleasure to acknowledge by name. The then Hungarian ambassador to Sweden, Laszlo Szöke, his wife Judit and his daughters Diana and Beata entertained me in Stockholm; I much appreciated Laszlo's guidance on so many informative excursions. I remember with delight a car journey around the Øresund with Christopher and Charmian Johnson, Miranda and Sebastian; Chris has also spent patient hours as my computer mentor. Sir Martin Gilbert enlightened me on many facets of twentieth century history. Sinclair Third generously allowed me to use disks of his notes on the movements of German warships. Aleksas Vilčinskas clarified aspects of Lithuanian history for me and provided information for the chronology of Lithuanian rulers at the back of the book. Reija Fanous kindly answered questions on Finland and the Finnish language. For the loan of books, maps, photographs and pamphlets my thanks go to Clare and Robert Brown, Miranda Jones, Elizabeth Maylor and Sean Lang.

The staffs of the London Library and the Bodleian Library have, once again, helped me with great efficiency. I am grateful to John McLaughlin, most sympathetic of literary agents, and to my patient publishers both at Albemarle Street and Euston Road, with especial thanks to Gordon Wise and Catherine Benwell. I also appreciate the skills of Anne Boston, the cartographer Martin Collins and Douglas Matthews, the doyen of indexers.

Eight of the people whose help I acknowledge by name come from the congregation of St Mary Magdalen, Oxford, the church where I have long been a communicant, and it is with gratitude that I dedicate this book to the many friends at 'Mary Mag's' who, over the years, have given me so much active support and encouragement.

Alan Palmer
Woodstock, January 2005

Maps

1. The Baltic in 2004   x
2. The Baltic in the Early Middle Ages   xii
3. Sweden, Prussia and Russia, 1645–1772   xiii

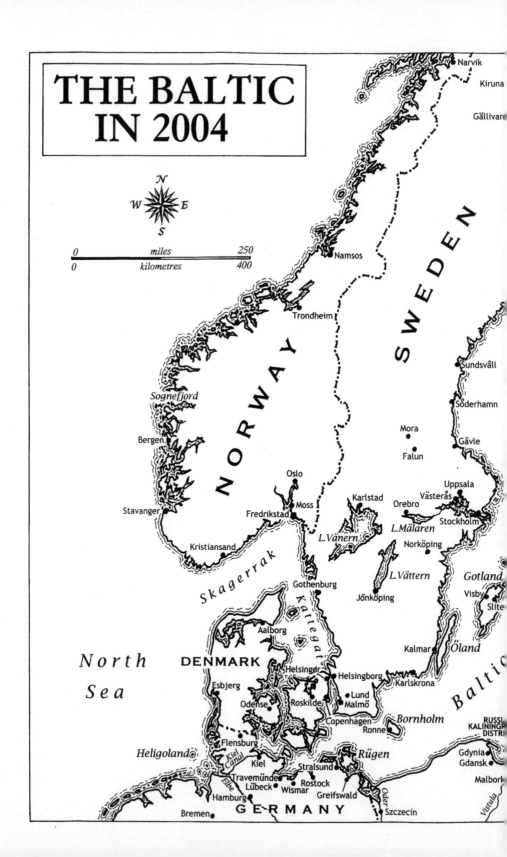

THE BALTIC IN 2004

0 miles 250
0 kilometres 400

Narvik
Kiruna
Gällivare
Namsos
Trondheim

SWEDEN

NORWAY

Sundsvåll
Söderhamn
Mora
Falun
Gävle
Oslo
Karlstad
Uppsala
Västerås
Orebro
Moss
Fredrikstad
Stockholm
L.Vänern
L.Mälaren
Norköping
Kristiansand
L.Vättern
Gotland
Sognefjord
Bergen
Stavanger
Skagerrak
Gothenburg
Jönköping
Visby
Slite
Kattegat
Aalborg
Kalmar
Öland
North
Sea
DENMARK
Helsingør
Helsingborg
Esbjerg
Karlskrona
Lund
Odense
Roskilde
Malmö
Baltic
Copenhagen
Bornholm
RUSSI
KALININGF
DISTR
Ronne
Heligoland
Flensburg
Rügen
Gdynia
Gdansk
Kiel
Canal
Kiel
Stralsund
Malbork
Travemünde
Rostock
Lübeck
Wismar
Elbe
Hamburg
Greifswald
Oder
Vistula
Bremen
GERMANY
Szczecin

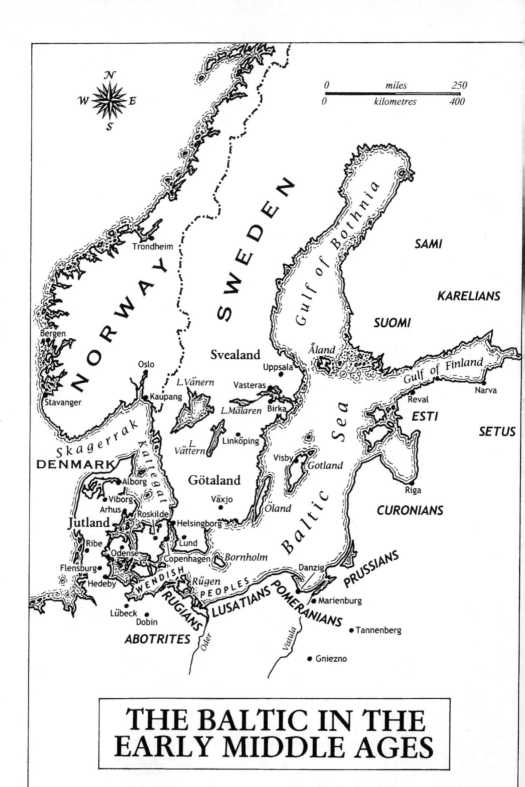

N
W E
S

0   miles   250
0   kilometres   400

Gulf of Bothnia

SAMI

KARELIANS

SUOMI

NORWAY

SWEDEN

Trondheim

Bergen

Oslo

Stavanger

Kaupang

Svealand

Uppsala

Vasteras

L. Vänern

L. Mälaren

Birka

Åland

Gulf of Finland

Narva

Reval

ESTI

SETUS

L. Vättern

Linköping

Visby

Gotland

Riga

Skagerrak

Kattegat

DENMARK

Götaland

Växjö

Öland

Baltic Sea

CURONIANS

Alborg

Viborg

Arhus

Roskilde

Helsingborg

Jutland

Ribe

Lund

Odense

Copenhagen

Bornholm

Danzig

PRUSSIANS

Flensburg

Hedeby

WENDISH

Rügen

PEOPLES

Marienburg

Lübeck

Dobin

RUGIANS

LUSATIANS

POMERANIANS

Tannenberg

ABOTRITES

Oder

Vistula

Gniezno

THE BALTIC IN THE
EARLY MIDDLE AGES

MC

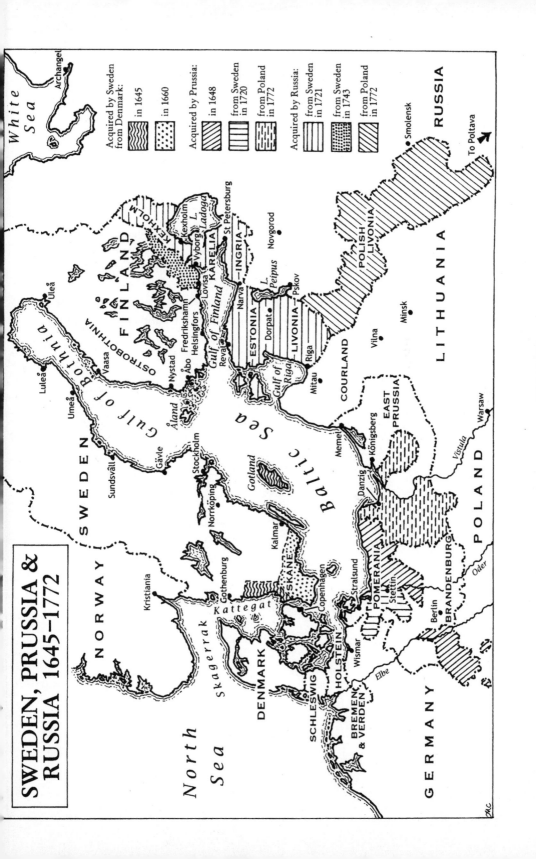

SWEDEN, PRUSSIA & RUSSIA 1645–1772

Acquired by Sweden from Denmark:
- in 1645
- in 1660

Acquired by Prussia:
- in 1648
- from Sweden in 1720
- from Poland in 1772

Acquired by Russia:
- from Sweden in 1721
- from Sweden in 1743
- from Poland in 1772

White Sea

Archangel

North Sea

NORWAY

Kristiania

SWEDEN

Sundsväll
Gävle
Norrköping
Stockholm
Kalmar
Gothenburg

Luleå
Umeå
Uleå
Uleå

Gulf of Bothnia

OSTROBOTHNIA

Vaasa
Nystad
Åbo
Fredrikshamn
Helsingfors

FINLAND

KEXHOLM

Kexholm
Vyborg
L. Ladoga
St Petersburg
INGRIA
Novgorod

KARELIA

Lovisa
Gulf of Finland
Narva
Revala
ESTONIA
Dorpat
L. Peipus
Pskov

LIVONIA

Riga
Gulf of Riga
Mitau

COURLAND

Åland

Baltic Sea

Gotland

Kattegat

Skagerrak

DENMARK

Copenhagen
SKÅNE

SCHLESWIG
HOLSTEIN
Wismar
Stralsund
BREMEN & VERDEN
Elbe

Stettin
POMERANIA
Berlin
BRANDENBURG

Danzig
Meme
Königsberg
EAST PRUSSIA
Vistula
Warsaw

GERMANY

POLAND

Oder

Vilna

Minsk

LITHUANIA

POLISH LIVONIA

RUSSIA

Smolensk

To Poltava

alc.

Author's Note

Unless otherwise stated, all dates are given in the Gregorian calendar, common to Western Europe but not adopted in Russia until after the Bolshevik Revolution. Personal names have been anglicized, except where indicated. Distances are expressed in kilometres and metres rather than miles and yards. For those who, like the author, think more naturally in the old system it may be convenient to remember that 8 kilometres are approximately 5 miles.

Alternative Place Names

Current name is printed first. Abbreviations used: D Danish; E Estonian; F Finnish; G German; La Latvian; Li Lithuanian; P Polish; R Russian; S Swedish; U Ukrainian. If no abbreviation is given, the form of the place name is English.

Cēsis (La)	Wenden (G)		
Daugava river (La)	Düna (G)	Dvina (P)	
Daugavpils (La)	Dvinsk (P)	Dünaburg (G)	
Elblag (P)	Elbing (G)		
Gdańsk (P)	Danzig (G)		
Hamëenlinna (F)	Tavasterhus (S)		
Hamina (F)	Fredrikshamn (S)		
Helsinki (F)	Helsingfors (S)		
Helsingør (D)	Elsinore		
Jelgava (La)	Mitau (G)		
Kaliningrad (R)	Königsberg (G)		
Kaunas (Li)	Kovno (G)	Kowno (P)	
Klaipėda (Li)	Memel (G)		
Kolobrzen (P)	Kolberg (G)		
Kurzeme (La)	Kurland (G)	Courland	
Lviv (U)	Lwow (P)	Lvov (R)	Lemberg (G)
Liepāja (La)	Libau (G)		
Malbork (P)	Marienburg (G)		
Nemanas river (Li)	Niemen		
Oltsztyn (P)	Allenstein (G)		
Øresund (D)	The Danish Sound		
Oslo	Christiania		
Oulu (F)	Uleaborg (S)		
Pärnu (E)	Pernau (G)		
Peipsi lake (E)	Chud (R)	Peipus	
Porvoo (F)	Bogå (S)		

Poznań (P)	Posen (G)	
Saaremaa (E)	Ösel (G/S)	
St Petersburg	Leningrad	Petrograd
Sigulda (La)	Segewold (G)	
Stebak (P)	Tannenberg (G)	
Suomenlinna (F)	Sveaborg (S)	
Suursari (F)	Hogland	
Świnoujście (P)	Swinemünde (G)	
Szczecin (P)	Stettin (G)	
Tallinn (E)	Reval (G)	
Tampere (F)	Tammerfors (S)	
Tartu (E)	Dorpat (G)	
Toruń (P)	Thorn (G)	
Turku (F)	Åbo (S)	
Uuskaupunki (F)	Nystad (S)	
Vaasa (F)	Vasa (S)	
Valga (E)	Walk (G)	
Ventspils (La)	Windau (G)	
Vilnius (Li)	Wilno (P)	Vilna
Vyborg (R)	Viipuri (F)	
Žemaitija (Li)	Samogitia	
Zemgale (La)	Semigallia	

I

Sentinels Above the Sound

———————◇◇◇◇———————

FOR MORE THAN six centuries, navigators sailing southwards into the Baltic have watched the Kattegat narrow until a channel lies defined before them. Blurred smudges on either shore sharpen into the clear image of castles brooding beside the sea. To port the stub of Kärnan, last bastion of a fourteenth century keep, stands at the edge of a low plateau beside Swedish Helsingborg. To starboard, five kilometres away on a promontory at the water's edge, is Kronborg, built as a stronghold to guard Danish Helsingør but transformed into a royal residence and looking less of a fortress than a palace. Even now, with thriving towns sprawled around them, the towers catch the eye. Back in the sixteenth century when both shores were under Danish sovereignty and the twin castles of equal extent, they made the Sound a fine seagate for the Baltic. Fynes Moryson, the Cambridge traveller whose *Itinerary* anatomized so much of the continent in the closing years of Elizabeth I's reign, was impressed by them. 'These castles keep the Strait,' he wrote, looking out from the Kronborg's windows in August 1593; 'Because a great store of ships pass this way in great fleets, the prospect is most pleasant to all men; but most of all to the King, seeing so many ships whereof not one shall pass, without adding to his treasure.' The tolls thus levied 'surpass all the revenues of this kingdom' of Denmark, he noted.

Earlier visitors than Moryson had anglicized Helsingør's name to Elsinore. Twice a troupe of English actors came to entertain the Danish Court there, and the players' tales of the richly furnished Renaissance castle above the Sound gave Shakespeare his setting for *Hamlet*; Elsinore's lasting fame was assured. But to mariners in 'the great fleets' Elsinore was a familiar name for another reason: Kronborg's central spire served as a landmark enabling a navigator to set his course through the busiest channel in northern Europe. Further down the Sound, off the fortified 'merchant's port' of Copenhagen, the coastline fell away again, broad waters opened up and the ships' masters put the helm down. If they were following the southern shore, they sought a fair wind for Rostock or Danzig, or on to Riga, Reval, even to Narva, some 1,300 kilometres to the east. It was not a difficult sea to navigate, for at no point was a ship more than 130 kilometres from land. In early summer the prevailing winds were easterly; from July onwards they came from the west, bringing rain in September. But, whatever their direction, every sea-captain knew he must sail for home before fogs and a crust of ice began to wrap trading cities in frozen hibernation. It was essential to settle toll dues and have the sentinel castles receding to stern by the end of October.

The Øresund, as the channel between Helsingør and Helsingborg is called locally, remains the principal entry to the Baltic, though the obligation to pay shipping dues to the Crown was finally ended by treaty in the heyday of Free Trade, a century and a half ago. But with nine countries having ports around the inland sea, the Sound still carries a 'great store of ships'. In size and character they vary greatly: tankers, elongated container vessels, small freighters, cruise liners with buxom upperworks, trim and unobtrusive warships, fishing boats, racing yachts (especially in high summer) and occasionally the proud elegance of square-rigged 'tall ships', handing down to a new generation the skills of seamanship under sail. But most numerous of all are the ferries: small diesel runabouts several times an hour between the Danish and Swedish shore; bigger, bustling carriers of cars for similar short crossings; speedy 'Sound Bus' hydrofoils serving coastal commuters and casual holidaymakers; and, to link the Scandinavian ports, overnight floating hotels with a maze of cabins and lounges, shops and restaurants, saunas and casinos. Beyond Danish coastal waters more ferries criss-cross the sea. Cars are now carried the length of the Baltic from Kiel to St Petersburg – almost 1,600 kilometres – in 53 hours. Catamarans and conventional vessels draw together Malmö, Travemünde, Gdańsk, Świnoujście, Klaipėda, Tallinn, Stockholm, Helsinki and smaller ports, too. The annual freeze is less restrictive than in Moryson's time, for climatic change in the southern Baltic limits icing to an average three days on the Schleswig coast, rising to three weeks at Stralsund. Farther to the north and east powerful icebreakers keep vital channels open during the long nights and short days of winter. With Great Power rivalry finally in decline, the ferries help to ensure that the inner Baltic is a sea of contact, a potential source of unity for Europe rather than division.

This interdependence of Baltic shores was further strengthened at the start of the new millennium. For, in July 2000, the Øresundforbindelsen (the Sound Fixed Link) was opened, bringing closer together Copenhagen and Malmö, the third largest city in Sweden and the most cosmopolitan. The emergence of road and rail links from tunnels on to an artificial island and up to a two-level bridge 8 kilometres long is a triumph of innovative civil engineering, completed in less than five years of work. To sail south from Copenhagen with, to starboard, the lights of Kastrup airport runway and, more distantly to port, the sight of cars slipping down to a submerged motorway provides an interesting – and slightly unnerving – contrast to the historic approach to the Baltic between the sentinel castles 55 kilometres to the north.

Off the Spanish and Moroccan coasts, ships coming in from the Atlantic follow a passage similar to the Øresund to enter Europe's greater inner sea. Between Tangier and Tarifa the Strait of Gibraltar offers a distant sighting of the Mediterranean, much as does the Sound of the Baltic. Yet there is a difference between the two unfolding scenes. It is not simply that the Pillars of Hercules provide a more imposing gateway than Helsingborg and Helsingør: beyond Gibraltar a prospect of spaciousness opens up, challengingly unconfined. The Mediterranean, more than seven times as big as the Baltic, is a proud sea; by name it affirms mastery over the land of which the Romans made it the centre; and no language in modern Europe disputes this classical Latin claim. By contrast, the northern sea seems modestly apologetic over its shape and its contours. Fynes Moryson, seeking the origin of the word 'Baltic' four centuries ago, wrote that 'it is so called because it is compressed with the land as if it were a girdle'. That at least was the explanation accepted by Tudor seamen, and they may well have been right. When in the eleventh century the monk and pioneer geographer Adam of Bremen first described the northern sea as the *Mare Balticum*, he had in mind the Latin word *balteus,* a girdle around the waist. But the image has not appealed to Adam's compatriots in later years: for to Germans the Baltic is the 'East Sea' (*Ostsee*), as it is also to Swedes (*Östersjön*) and to the Finns (*Itämeri*). Interestingly, while the Russian, Latvian and Lithuanian languages employ variants of the word 'Baltic', the outward looking Estonians call the waters of the Gulf of Finland the 'West Sea' (*Läänemeri*).

Adam of Bremen's girdle was shaped by geological upheaval many millennia back in time. In about 6600 BC melting glaciers from the final Ice Age left northern-central Europe covered by a huge tract of fresh water, known to pre-historians as Lake Ancylus. It was bordered by extensive marshland and fed by rivers flowing northwards from what are now the Harz mountains and the Carpathians. About 4500 BC the spreading waters of Ancylus seeped through natural outlets in southern Scandinavia and mingled with the North Sea, the Atlantic Ocean's junior partner. One channel became the Øresund, but there was also a second channel between the Danish islands of Zealand and Funen, forming the Great Belt (*Store Bælt*) and the Little Belt. For ships trading with the main Baltic ports the voyage through the Belts has always taken longer, though in earlier times some captains tried to evade the Sound tolls by creeping through the islands when there was a sea mist, despite the certainty of losing their cargoes if caught. More recently, in the Second World War, the German battleships *Scharnhorst, Gneisenau* and *Bismarck* headed through the Belts when they left Kiel to attack convoys in the North Atlantic. But the Belts and the Sound are not only important as waterways. Their main significance is oceanographic and dates from their inception, for they served as Nature's in-pipes, gradually broadening and letting the heavily saline Atlantic infiltrate Ancylus, to turn what had been a fresh water lake into an inland sea.

Not that Ancylus and the marshlands around the edge of the lake were ever entirely swamped. The access from the ocean was so narrow that it restricted how much water could enter the Baltic within any six-hour tidal period, while the amount discharged by rivers like the Oder and Vistula made the prevailing current within the Sound and the Belts flow towards the north-west. The shores of western Denmark and Norway were kept ice-free by the comparatively warm Atlantic, but the influence of the Gulf Stream was too weak to check the powerful north-west current from the Baltic and could not penetrate the inland sea, which remains virtually tideless – 'sluggish and hardly moving' (*pigrum ac prope inmotum*), Tacitus asserted, some 1,900 years ago. It is a shallow sea, with an average depth of 36 fathoms (65 metres), and the lack of free-flowing water has kept salinity low. 'The water of the sea' is not 'anything so salt as otherweares', Moryson observed in his *Itinerary* after a voyage down the Sound, 'the ships sailing therein do sink deeper at least three spans than in the German Ocean [North Sea], as manifestly appears by the white sides of the ships above the water when they come out of the sea and enter the said Ocean.'

One legacy of Ancylus – or of a far more distant interglacial era – remains on sale today in towns along the southern shore from the Kattegat to St Petersburg, as well as in all the Baltic capitals. Genuine amber is the petrified resin excreted by pine trees lost long ago beneath the waters of the inland sea. Nowadays people are fascinated by fossilized evidence of insect life and of plants trapped within the resin while it was liquid. In earlier times they were content to marvel at its changing beauty – from brownish yellow through a warm tawniness to the golden translucence seen in fine Tokay wine. A continental river trade in amber flourished long before anyone attempted to map the Baltic's shores. It was prized in classical Greece as a gem of Nature from the 'Amber Coast', the distant rim of a legendary northern sea. Schliemann, digging at Mycenae 130 years ago, unearthed amber beads dating from about 1550 BC in the first Shaft Graves he excavated there. Similar finds were made at neighbouring Tiryns, on Rhodes and Cos, and at Saggara in Egypt. Archaeologists studying the 'Wessex Culture' of Late Iron Age England found Baltic amber in the barrows they opened up, and amber beads were among artefacts in votive hoards in several widely separated sites across Europe, from Brittany to the Harz mountains of old Saxony. Yet, as late as AD 100, Tacitus could treat amber as if it were a recent, fashionable discovery. In the penultimate chapter of the *Germania* he writes disparagingly of a northern barbarian tribe who long regarded amber as mere refuse thrown up by the sea; they neglected it until the coming of the legions when, he claims, the Roman delight 'in luxury made its reputation'.

That reputation was to outlive the Roman Empire and the dynastic empires of more recent centuries, too. In the High Middle Ages ships of the Hanse included amber as a luxury commodity in cargoes they carried westwards; and when, in 1717, the king of Prussia wished to impress Tsar Peter he presented him with amber panels which later brought lustre to the finest room in Catherine the Great's palace at Tsarskoye Selo. Along the coast near Königsberg heavy seas washed so many fragments ashore that the Hohenzollern kings made this most ancient of Nature's jewels a royal monopoly, and until 1918 the Prussian royal coffers benefited from the mine at Palmnicken, 50 kilometres to the west of the city. Today, with Königsberg known as Kaliningrad and Palmnicken as Yantarny, the mine is still the greatest single source of amber in the world. The workings remain a state monopoly, though 'the State' today is no longer German but Russian, with its capital city nearly 1,600 kilometres away. Poland has an 'Amber Coast' stretching eastwards from Świnoujście to Kolobrzeg, with amber workshops in Gdańsk, while Denmark's amber beaches are in north-western Jutland. Lithuania, which experienced an 'amber rush' to the Curonian spit in the 1850s, has an amber museum among the pinewoods of Palanga and even an 'amber gallery' in Vilnius, more than 240 kilometres from the nearest shore. Every summer Latvia hosts a young people's 'festival of amber' at Liepāja in August.

There are many other legacies from the Baltic's glacial pre-history, though none with such romantic associations as amber. The northern fringe of the receding waters left a rim of gravel and sand which was to harden into ridges and provide the only routes through forested lakeland in Sweden and, more especially, in eastern and central Finland; and much of the political and commercial history of the Baltic's southern shores was determined

by the survival of rivers that once flowed into Lake Ancylus. Over the centuries the Vistula and its tributaries the Bug and the Narew formed the axis
around which the Polish nation developed, although they are not in themselves impressive waterways. Nor is the Oder and its main tributary, the
Warta, another route to the sea that helped determine Poland's destiny. All
the rivers bring with them such sediment of sand, silt and detrita from the
forests that they meander to the sea around mud-banks and gravelly islets.
More recently they have served as polluted overflow pipes for the industries of northern central Europe.

Neither the Oder nor the Vistula sweeps down to the sea in magnificent estuaries, like the Garonne or the Tagus. The Oder reaches the Baltic
through a long lagoon with three main outlets and so many reedy channels that the historic port of Stettin – now Poland's Szczecin and chief city
of western Pomorze (Pomerania) – lies 65 kilometres upstream. The
mouths of the Vistula have changed many times: as late as 1840 the river
cut a new channel through sand dunes at Neufahr, leaving a fifteenth-
century lighthouse and fortress which commanded entry into Danzig literally high and dry, some distance to the south.

This southern shoreline of the Baltic is low lying, at least as far as the Gulf
of Riga. Danish Jutland has the best arable land in Scandinavia, capable of
supporting pastoral farming down the centuries. At Marielyst in the
Danish island of Falster comes the most western of many fine beaches of
white sand that recur along the littoral of five countries. Most beaches end
in scrub broken by dunes, which in the west are sometimes 60 metres high,
and by clusters of pine trees. Occasionally marshes lie close to the shore,
so treacherous around the Bay of the Vistula that the whole area is virtual
fenland. Deceptive spits of land enclose lagoons, sometimes with deep
deciduous forests as a backcloth. Now and again the faint outline of a cliff,
greyish-brown in the west, can be seen from a ship heading eastwards. But
on the German island of Rügen the chalk cliffs of Cape Arkona are reminiscent of Dover, and an almost continuous limestone ridge crosses what
is now north-eastern Estonia. Farther inland are the last offspring of lost
Ancylus: lakes Peipsi (*aka* Peipus or Chud) and Võrtsjärv in the eastern
wetlands; and the reed-fringed lakes of Masuria and Mecklenburg amid the
sandiest soil of the north German plain.

Between the Gulf of Riga and Tallinn Bay are hundreds of offshore
islands. Along the coast any good solid rock sprouted a town, like the
highly defensible craggy granite of Toompea, around which Tallinn clusters, but most early cities were river-ports, trading posts established some

distance from the sea to protect them from coastal raiders. Thus Riga's three steeples welcomed incoming ships from 15 kilometres up the Daugava, or 'western Dvina' as the river was called when Latvia was under tsarist rule. Narva lies 13 kilometres upstream from the Gulf of Finland with two fortresses facing each other across the river and recalling the region's frontier past: Hermann Keep, built by the Teutonic Knights, is on the west bank; Ivangorod Castle, built by Tsar Ivan IV, on the east bank. More than 950 kilometres south of Narva, the historic centre of Rostock crowns a hill above the left bank of the river Warnow. Although 13 kilometres from the sea, the 133 metre tower of Rostock's St Peter's Church was so dominant that on clear days mariners would set their course for it from 50 kilometres out in the Baltic. Even Hanseatic Lübeck, for three centuries the pre-eminent commercial centre of northern Europe, lies 22 kilometres up the river Trave.

Across the Baltic, north of the lakes and rolling farmland in Sweden's once Danish provinces of Skåne (Scania) and Blekinge, the shoreline is different. This is a wilder and grander coast. Features shared with southern and eastern shores seem magnified: the forests become thicker, with birch and conifer predominant farther north; sandy beaches become longer and rarer, often overlaid with pebbles; lagoons are replaced by deep inlets and granite cliffs. Instead of offshore shoals the waters lap half-submerged rocks. The Gulf of Bothnia carries the Baltic 800 kilometres up to the approaches to Lapland and the reindeer herds of the Sami people. At its northern point, where a bridge links the older Finnish town of Tornio with Swedish Haparanda, the river Tornionjoki gives the Baltic an Arctic douche. Farther south several rivers have cut valleys eastwards from the mountains that form the spine – or, as the Viking seafarers called it, the keel – of the Scandinavian peninsula. But these rivers are too fast-flowing to carry silt or sludge to the sea. Finland's longest river, the Kemijoki, brings timber floating down from upper Lapland to enter the Gulf of Bothnia a few miles south of Tornio. On both sides of the Gulf a string of lakes perpetuates the handiwork of glacial moulding. They cover 8 per cent of the surface of Sweden, in area the fifth largest country in Europe, and 10 per cent of Finland, Europe's seventh.

There are more islands than off the Baltic's south-western coast. Bornholm, though ruled from Copenhagen since 1660, lies closer to Sweden, Germany and Poland than to Denmark and shares features from both Baltic shores; long stretches of fine-grained white sand backed by pines in the south; cliffs and a rocky shoreline farther north; and, an hour's sailing away, the granite Ertholmene archipelago around the fortress islet of Christiansø. Sweden's Gotland has more uniformity of character than the other islands. Although only a third the size of Crete or Corsica in the Mediterranean, it is the largest in the northern sea, 120 kilometres long and 90 kilometres wide. It is a mid-Baltic gem, rich in Viking and Hanseatic history and, with its fossilized limestone 'cairns' (*raukar*), in pre-history too. Farther south, Öland confounds any easy generalization about the north-western shoreline: it forms a long spit, made vivid in the spring by a bright tapestry of wild flowers. The island delights windmill spotters, rune readers and migratory bird watchers. From the twelfth to the fifteenth centuries the islanders benefited from a thriving fisheries industry, paying their sole annual tax to successive Swedish kings in herring. Stretches of stone wall from sixteen fortified townships survive from an even earlier era; Öland was probably at its best in the Iron Age.

The approaches to Sweden's capital form an enchanted seascape. Thousands of wooded rocky islets are strewn along the Saltsjö, the winding 70-kilometre waterway up to Stockholm, which is itself a city spread over fourteen islands. Many more hundreds of islets are in less frequented channels entering lake Mälaren from north and south. Estimates of the precise number in the archipelago differ widely: a French geographer concedes 10,000, while enthusiastic local guides have been known to boost that figure ten times over. Some 24,000 islets would seem a reasonable estimate. With such a ring of defensive moats it is small wonder that Stockholm is today the one capital on Europe's continental mainland not to have fallen to a foreign enemy during the past two centuries. The last enemy presence – a Danish attempt to perpetuate Scandinavian unity – came as long ago as 1520–21, more than a century before the city was recognized as the seat of government. But Stockholm's fortunate immunity from occupation owes as much to the shrewd policies of Sweden's rulers and statesmen as to geography.

Along with four-fifths of the kingdom's 7,250-kilometre coastline, Stockholm faces east. Ferries regularly cross the entrance to the Gulf of Bothnia to reach Mariehamn in the Åland archipelago in six hours and on to the Finnish coast at Turku in another five, or to Helsinki in nine. Mariehamn is the home port for almost all the ferries and, with a population of 11,000, is the largest settlement in the Ålands. Most of the archipelago's 6,000 islands remain uninhabited. Often they are no more than verdant rocks sprouting a few trees. The archipelago is a stepping-stone, if not to modern Russia, at least to the Russia of Peter the Great, Alexander I and both the Tsars Nicholas. Fourteenth century Kastelholm Castle, 19 kilometres north of Mariehamns and nineteenth century Bomarsund, 11 kilometres farther east, became Russian fortresses after the annexation of Finland in 1809. They emphasize the islands' strategic importance and recall a turbulent history. For in tsarist times the Ålands were the front paw of the Russian bear. Although clipped by enforced demilitarization after the Crimean War, as late as August 1914 the paw figured in Russian naval plans for a pre-emptive strike against allegedly pro-German Sweden.

This tsarist past intrudes persistently among the skerries and red granite cliffs of the southern Finnish coast. At Porvoo, a small cathedral city hemmed in by woods, Tsar Alexander I confirmed the privileges of the Grand Duchy he had newly acquired. In a bay east of Hangö Peter the Great's infant navy gained its first victory against the Swedes (July 1714); and off the coast between Kotka and Hamina in 1789–90 the Russians won one naval battle with the Swedes and lost another within eleven months. A succession of Swedish/Russian fortresses culminated in Sveaborg, a citadel originally spread over seven islands, but now contracted into five and known as Suomenlinna ('Finland's Castle'). It is a World Heritage Site protecting the natural harbour of Helsinki, the most northern capital in the world apart from Reykjavik.

Dominating the Helsinki skyline even today are two cathedrals redolent of old rivalries. The Lutheran Tuomiokirkko, approached up forty-five granite steps, presides over Senate Square. The cathedral, built between 1830 and 1852 and tactfully dedicated to the patron saint of the reigning tsar, is crowned with five turquoise domes, an unexpected adornment for a Protestant church in northern Europe. In Unioninkatu, behind the Tuomiokirkko, nestles a delightful Orthodox church. It is as old as any place of worship in the city, but too modestly compact to satisfy the rulers of Holy Russia. Their creation stands 400 metres away, raised on a grassy hillock behind the port; the red-brick Uspensky Cathedral, consecrated on 25 October 1868 and built to rival the Tuomiokirkko and assert the primacy of Russian Orthodoxy. More than eighty years after tsardom withered away, the sun still glints on the Uspensky's thirteen gilded crosses in a prosperous and independent Finland, but it is the great dome and columns of the Tuomiokirkko that appeal to camera-clickers, amateur and professional alike.

Across the Gulf, 90 kilometres to the south, Tallinn also has its Orthodox cathedral, dedicated to St Alexander Nevsky at the very end of the nineteenth century. To witness the church's ceremonial Liturgy on a great religious festival is still, visually and aurally, a memorable experience. Many Estonians find mock-Moscow cupolas out of place among the tapering spires and solid towers of Lutheran Tallinn and resent the continuing presence of a Russian basilica on the highest eminence of their capital city. Yet the twin Orthodox cathedrals of Helsinki and Tallinn, on either side of the Gulf, are as symbolic as the sentinel castles of the Sound, 1,300 kilometres to the west. They herald the approach of a cultural divide which marks off the old Hanseatic Baltic from a Petrine Baltic created at the beginning of the eighteenth century, when the first 'Emperor of All Russia' opened a window to the west – and made certain bolts were in place on its shutters. From 1715 to 1917 Peter the Great's city was capital of the Russian empire.

St Petersburg is as far from the Danish Sound as Gibraltar from Plymouth. Ships heading eastwards from Tallinn or Helsinki still have 260 kilometres to sail before the waters of the Gulf begin gradually to narrow. Along the indented northern shore larch and pine survive, although the woods were far thicker a century ago and there was more heather and swamp before a strongly fortified frontier line crossed the Karelian isthmus after the First World War. The southern coastline of the upper Gulf is higher, with a long ridge about a kilometre inland cleared by Tsar Peter's serfs to provide terraced fountains and parkland for their emperor and his most favoured lieutenants. This elegant frieze of palaces and villas is still visible on the horizon from ships sailing up the Gulf, a hazy crenellated line from Oranienbaum through Petrodvorets (Peterhof) to the outer fringe of the old imperial capital itself.

Serf labourers were also put to work on the island of Kotlin, just north of Petrodvorets. For Peter had the fortress of Kronstadt built on Kotlin, to form the outer bolt on entry to his city, some 30 kilometres to the east. By the coming of the First World War Kronstadt had grown to become a town of 65,000 inhabitants with two Orthodox cathedrals, one (newly completed) serving as the principal place of worship for the navy. Secrecy prevailed, and it was intensified after the Revolution. Thirty years ago, when Kronstadt was still the main base for the Baltic fleet, Leningrad-bound vessels were kept as far from the roadstead as the shallow waters of the southern shore permitted and passengers were not encouraged on deck. Today, the fortress city is a museum-piece waiting to be catalogued: ships pass close inshore and cameras focus with impunity on orange painted ice-breakers at quays where grey heavy cruisers and submarines so recently awaited their crews.

The Finnish word '*neva*' is translated as 'mud', and the earliest travellers to Tsar Peter's city entered a river flanked by gloomy woods and receding marsh and mudbanks. Count Francesco Algarotti, making the journey in

1739, was amazed to find 'the scene changing in an instant as at an opera' revealing 'on either shore sumptuous edifices grouped together' in neo-classical grandeur. Nineteenth-century industrialism replaced the marsh and forest with dockyards, factory chimneys and cramped suburbs, but to move slowly up 27 kilometres of canalized waterway beyond Kronstadt to a quay within sight of the Admiralty spire and the dome of St Isaac's Cathedral remains an exhilarating experience even today. It is almost as fine as sailing in from the Adriatic and watching the Doge's Palace come into view.

Images of Venice spring naturally to mind, for the two artificial cities built on swamps around headwaters of an inland sea have much in common. Yet, though engineering enterprise enabled St Petersburg to envelop a hundred islands in the Neva delta, the city never became internally dependent on water transport, as Tsar Peter had assumed. Five main canals were dug, but with such appalling loss of life among the labourers that plans for a network of twenty ancillary canals were abandoned. The Nevsky Prospekt, a street a kilometre longer than Venice's Grand Canal, became the new capital's main artery. But the pumping heart of St Petersburg, giving the city its life-blood, has always been the river itself. The first religious festival of the year was the Blessing of the Waters at Epiphany, when amid the splendour of Orthodox ceremonial a hole was cut through the thick ice and (as a Scottish traveller noted in the 1770s) 'all who were present had the happiness of being sprinkled with the water thus consecrated and rendered holy'.

The Neva is deceptive, perhaps because it is not so much a conventional river as a 65-kilometre channel linking the sea to Ladoga, the largest lake fully in Europe. In October early frosts followed by a thaw have been known to bring miniature icebergs swiftly down from Lake Ladoga, and the waters become fast flowing again when the ice of the frozen river melts in the spring. South-westerly autumn gales, coming in from the Baltic, make the waters storm-tossed and more than once have flooded the city: 'In the space of one hour the square in front of the Winter Palace, the boulevard and the streets which lead to the Palace showed a terrible sight of a raging sea with waves and eddying water,' wrote the Tsar's sister Grand Duchess Anna Pavlovna in November 1824, when half the capital was awash. Protective measures were taken, and at high summer the Neva now languidly laps stone embankments along the quays, like the Seine in Paris, though far wider. The muddiness has gone, though on cloudy days the water looks grey, oily and polluted. Under sunshine it brightens to greenish-blue and in the clear light of a summer evening becomes reflectively beautiful. On a mist-free morning, before traffic clogs the bridges, the flow of the Neva between the fortress of St Peter and St Paul and the long facade of the Winter Palace is imperiously majestic.

'What a city! Magnificent beyond description or imagination,' the soldier Sir Robert Wilson roundly declared on arriving in St Petersburg early in the Napoleonic Wars. Yet several visitors have soon been disillusioned. 'When we were in Petersburg, we no longer found it so superb as it seemed to us from a distance,' wrote Algarotti a quarter of a century after the city's foundation; the Russian nobility, he explained, 'had built out of obedience rather than choice. Their walls are all cracked, quite out of perpendicular, and ready to fall.' Ninety years later the Scottish physician, Robert Lee, was worried by 'the damp and unwholesome state of the lower parts of the houses' and Martha Wilmot, writing in the city's centenary year, thought the Winter Palace 'magnificent, boundless and comfortless'. Soon afterwards Robert Johnson, a pioneer tourist, found St Petersburg lacking in harmony: 'A mixture of splendid barbarism and mighty rudeness,' he declared with robust prejudice. Later critics complained that the city was too big, industrialized and claustrophobic: far too many families cramped in far too few apartments. That social problem is unresolved today.

The transference of government to Moscow in 1918 downgraded St Petersburg. In *Theatre Street* the ballerina Tamara Karsavina describes how on returning home from Kiev that autumn she found her native city enveloped by 'a pathetic majesty of desecrated pomp'. In 1924 Peter's creation became Leningrad, honouring the revolutionary who spent no more than a hundred weeks of his fifty-four-year life in its streets, palaces and prison cells. On the fall of communism the imperial name was restored by popular vote. Fittingly, in May 2003, when President Putin led the celebrations of St Petersburg's tercentenary, Russia's head of state was once more by birth a native of the city.

Three other countries with a Baltic coastline have inland capitals: Germany, Poland and Lithuania. Berlin is closest to the sea, little more than 130 kilometres from the up-river port of Stettin (Szczecin), even if 160 from the nearest beaches of contemporary Germany. Although Berlin was once a member of the Hanse, the city turned its back on the Baltic after 1709 when it became capital of Prussia. 'Berlin's position is distinctly that of a city set upon a small river and its marine suburb, Stettin, also lies unfortunately on a blind Baltic alley,' the liberal German historian, Veit Valentin, could write shortly before the Second World War. Yet if you travel northwards towards Wismar or Stralsund, the Baltic scene gradually encroaches on you. Geographically, the lakes around Schwerin and, farther to the east, the Uckersee at Prenzlau recall the lakeland of Sweden and Finland, though without the lush forests of the North. Much of this fertile farmland formed Swedish Pomerania in the late seventeenth and eighteenth centuries. Anklam, on the river Peene 30 kilometres south of Greifswald, remained a strategically important frontier town until the Napoleonic Wars. If Berliners sometimes call the region *Südschweden* (South Sweden) they are not necessarily being ironic.

Warsaw, home of Poland's royal court from the late sixteenth century, is a city of the great Eurasian plain, farther than Berlin from the dunes and spits of the continent's northern shores. Traditionally Poland's rulers looked eastwards or southwards for expansion, to the Ukraine or Silesia; none had ambitions to make the Baltic a Polish lake. But from the Piasts of the 960s to the communist Gomulka a thousand years later, all have accepted that their country's wellbeing depends on safeguarding the mouth of the Vistula, the 1,050-kilometre river that has held the nation together, linking the sea not only to the capital but also to historic Cracow and the great estates of Galicia, far to the south. Paradoxically, it could be argued that Poland's decline as a Great Power began when the hero-king John Sobieski gave the nation its greatest military triumph, the lifting of the Turkish siege of Vienna in 1683; for in marching an army to the Danube, Sobieski relaxed Poland's watch on the Pomeranian seaboard; and Prussia-Germany was the ultimate beneficiary.

Vilnius, Lithuania's capital, is set among wooded hills on both banks of the river Neris, a tributary of the Nemanus (Niemen), and is even deeper inland than Warsaw. Despite dark shadows lingering from the years of German and Russian occupation, it is an attractive city, so tranquil that it might well claim to have the least noisy Friday rush hour of any capital in Europe. There are Soviet housing blocks north of the Neris, but when you look down from the Hill of the Three Crosses you see beneath you the red roofs, yellow-ochre walls and balustraded church towers of Jesuit Catholic culture. This town, you feel, is archetypal Habsburg; it might be Graz in Austrian Styria, though Cracow springs naturally to mind. Yet, like so much about Vilnius's past, this is a misleading impression. For though ten dynasties ruled the region, the Habsburgs were never among them; and, though a Jesuit university was built to power the Counter-Reformation, it won renown for specifically Polish learning and as a seed-plot of Romantic nationalism.

When you walk the city the architecture continues to tease and confound. You expect a baroque cathedral and find a classical temple, with a frontage of six Doric columns and a detached, unadorned campanile. Go up-river for two kilometres and you are surprised by the church of St Peter and St Paul, austerely bland outside, but filled with hundreds of white-stucco figures, animals and foliage, sculpted by Italians four centuries ago to the glory of God and of a Lithuanian noble patron. Then, satiated with Mediterranean rococo, you retrace your steps, come across St Anne's in the Old Town and have no doubt that you are still in Baltic Europe; for, like the Lutheran Marienkirche at Gdańsk, Uppsala cathedral and the Orthodox Uspensky in Helsinki, pocket-sized St Anne's was built with red Baltic bricks, here shaped to accommodate Gothic curves and pinnacles.

Vilnius remains a northern bastion of Catholic Christendom, with churches founded by four different religious orders and a sixteenth-century Lutheran church within a short distance of each other. It is still a western outpost of Russian Orthodoxy and, less than a century ago, was accepted as 'the Jerusalem of the North', the principal home of Yiddish as a written and printed language. No other Old Town in Europe became so faith eclectic.

To land at Vilnius airport today, as do so many visitors to Lithuania from the West, is to slip into the Baltic world through a half-forgotten garden gate. No 'great store' of commerce ever enriched the valley of the Neris, and Vilnius's two castles were built above each other on a hill, protecting a track through dense forest, rather than on opposite shores like the sentinels beside the Danish Sound. The very name *Koben-havn*, 'merchant's port', perpetuates Denmark's historic role as monitor of maritime trade with the West. Vilnius, by contrast, turned inland and through six centuries percolated to the Baltic region the cultural essence of central Eastern Europe. As keys to understanding the past and the future of the Baltic peoples, Copenhagen and Vilnius complement each other.

2

Peoples on the Move

L ITTLE IS KNOWN about the earliest people to settle beside the Baltic. Archaeologists have discovered tantalizing evidence of human habitation from the Ancylus era and even earlier, especially in Götaland (southern central Sweden). In Stockholm's Historiska Museet is displayed the well-preserved skeleton of a mother of several children found at Bäcaskog, east of Kristiansand in Skåne province, dating back 9,000 years. The bodies of early sacrificial victims have been found in Danish peat-bogs, no less well preserved, and in 1999 constructors working on approach roads to the Øresund fixed link bridge to Denmark unearthed a large megalithic settlement east of Malmö. These Baltic Scandinavian aboriginals may be ancestors of the Sami people, who still retain a reindeer culture in Finnish Lapland. But in Copenhagen's Nationalmuseet the 3,500-year-old bronze 'Sun Chariot', ploughed up by a South Zealand farmer before the First World War, and bronze musical horns almost as old, suggest that in Bronze Age Denmark life was already more sophisticated.

There can be no certainty about the origins of any tribal community that evolved around the northern shores. Modern genetic research, following the unravelling of the DNA code, seems to confirm a closer relationship with early farming peoples of the main continental land-mass than was accepted a hundred years ago. Rock carvings of figures fishing from a boat with hook and line found in Bohuslän, the Swedish province with a Skagerrak littoral, indicate common cultural bonds uniting Scandinavia and the rest of Europe 3,000 years back in time. The discovery on Gotland of several hundred ship graves show that by the Bronze Age the islanders were accustomed to sea voyages in craft using oars rather than paddles. Even so, some memorial representations may be fancifully ahead of their time, like the boat with 124 oarsmen pulling hard for Valhalla carved beneath graves on a cliff face at Thorsbo, north of Gothenburg.

Farther east the earliest people to reach the Baltic shore came from central Asia. Before 1400 BC tribes of Finno-Ugrian hunters moved westwards from the forests and steppe lands of what is now Siberia. They settled in present-day Estonia and around Riga – the Liv (Livonian) region of Latvia – forcing out primitive Stone Age folk, of whom even less is known. About 500 BC these Fenns crossed the Gulf into geographical Finland, finally driving the indigenous Sami people into the Arctic North. Eventually the tribes developed different characteristics, determined by their environment: the Tavastians around the lakes of middle Finland long retained primitive hunting skills; the Karelians were thinly spread across forest clearings between Lake Ladoga, the White Sea and the head of the Gulf of Bothnia; and on the more rewarding soil of the south-west between modern Turku and Hämeenlinna were the Suomi, who were soon tilling fields as well as fishing off the skerries and in lake and river. This was the region most open to migration from Sweden, and over the centuries pressure from the west increasingly forced the so-called 'True Finn' Suomi back along the southern coast to merge with the Karelians.

Neither anthropology nor philology is an exact science and few today would follow the nationalistic scholars of the nineteenth century who equated race and language when seeking the origin of a country. But new techniques can revive familiar speculation while mellowing past prejudice. In the early 1980s the Finnish historian Matti Klinge argued that research into hereditary blood groups showed that three-quarters of the Finnish population were of western descent and only a third of eastern origin. He pointed out, however, that the linguistic structure of the Finnish language has remained more markedly eastern in character than western. Is this perhaps because the Finns and their kinsfolk south of the Gulf in Estonia are peoples with traditions of folk epic handed down orally? Their languages were shaped before the coming of written words. Finland's *Kalevala* and Estonia's *Kalevipoeg* survived as tales of patriot derring-do in taming both the forces of Nature and the evil spirits conjured up in a primeval wilderness of lake and forest.

By the end of the Scandinavian Bronze Age (*circa* 500 BC) other migrants felt drawn towards the setting sun, like the Finno-Ugrians before them. They came mainly from the south-east, to form compact units along the Baltic's southern shores, with their communities set apart by forests, bogs and rivers. Among them were Prussian tribes astride the Vistula, the Polanie on the Warta (farther inland, around modern Poznań) and a group of Lithuanian tribes around the river Niemen (Nemanus) and its tributaries. Over the following centuries tribal chiefs, seeking effective means to defend their homesteads, created what were in effect embryonic nations across these marchlands. Some tribes, like the Salic Franks and the Burgundians, provided a nucleus for historic kingdoms established after the collapse of the

Roman Empire in the West. Others bore names that recur in successive periods of northern Europe's history. Thus the Cours (or Curonians), a tribe who lived in the peninsula between the central Baltic and the Gulf of Riga, survived as a separate people until the late thirteenth century and gave their name to the Duchy of Courland (Kurzeme, or in German Kurland) which between 1561 and 1795 enjoyed semi-independence within the Polish Commonwealth. The Cours' neighbours, the Zemgal tribe (Semigallians), also maintained a distinctive corporate existence until 1290, farming the low-lying region west of the Daugava river that later formed the eastern part of the Courland Duchy.

Both Kurzeme and Zemgale are back on the map in today's atlases: they form administrative divisions in modern Latvia. Three of the Western Slav peoples survive as member states of the European Union: Poland; the Czech Republic; Slovakia. Other tribes, once famed and feared for their fighting qualities, have sunk without trace. Among them were most of the Wends, the Western Slavs who settled between Kiel Bay and the Vistula Spit and may themselves be subdivided into Wagrians, Abotrites, Polabians and Rugians. But two of the 'lost' Wendish peoples are still extant, though few in number: some 50,000 Sorbs of Lusatia now live between the Oder and the Elbe and there is an even smaller community of Kashubs, Pomerania's original 'dwellers by the shore'. Like the people of Wales, Cornwall, Brittany and Provence, the Sorbs and Kashubs owe their linguistic survival to academics in the nineteenth and early twentieth centuries who defied the exclusiveness of master nations to fire the embers of a dying culture. By contrast, the Setus, a Finno-Ugrian people who settled around Lake Peipsi, were too isolated to find scholarly champions in the West. No more than 7,000 Setu survive, their communities separated today by the geographically ill-defined border that provides a frontier between Estonia and Russia.

The first recorded contact between the peoples of Europe's southern and northern seas goes back to 330 BC when Pytheas, from the Greek colony of Marseilles, sailed for six days beyond British shores reconnoitring new routes for the trade in tin and amber. Pytheas may have been carried to Iceland, but more probably he made a landfall in the Norwegian fjords; he noted the lack of sun during long winter days, natives who lived on millet and berries, and a vista of mountainous coast and distant frozen sea. Yet though he reached Scandinavia he did not enter the Baltic. It was Tacitus who, in AD 98, first attempted to anatomize the tribes of northern Germany and, in his *Germania*, to record the customs of the folk who lived by 'the Suebian sea' (*Mare Suebicum*). But Tacitus never travelled in the region himself; he wrote from

17

what he learnt from returned veterans, and too much has been read into some passages in the later chapters of his work: to identify 'Suiones' with the Swedes of Svealand or the 'Gothones' on the Vistula with the people of Götaland is dubious. The warlike, cudgel-brandishing Aesti 'on the right shore of the Suebian sea' may or may not be proto-Estonians. Today's Finns might – should they so wish – claim descent from Tacitus's Fenni, an 'unbelievably wild and horribly poor' tribe, who tipped their arrows with bones, travelled fast on foot, slept on the ground and clothed themselves in skins. Yet it is all too easy to slip into faulty assumptions from spotting half-familiar names in a classical text.

Three passages in Tacitus's account carry an authentic ring: the surprise of 'the barbarians' at prices fetched by selling amber; Roman awe at a setting sun with a radiance that lingered until dawn; and – in Chapter 44 – the unusual ships, with a prow at both ends, no sails, and no fixed rowing position along the gunwales. Oars, he said, 'may be moved from one side to the other, as need requires'. Add a snarling dragon-head carved on the prow, a steering paddle on the starboard quarter, a mast with a menacingly decorative square sail, and we could have a description of a Viking vessel seven and a half centuries later. Unfortunately the only known Baltic ship contemporaneous with Tacitus's *Germania* is far less sophisticated: a dugout canoe with a plank across it, found on Björkö island in Lake Mälaren near the Iron Age burial ground at Birka.

The Roman Empire was at its fullest extent some twenty years after Tacitus completed his work. Despite expeditions as far as the Elbe the legions never established towns north or east of the Rhine, the Neckar valley and the Taunus mountains. None of the northern shores came under Roman rule. But trade tentacles reached the Baltic and beyond. From 'Scania' the Romans brought fur, amber and slaves. The evidence of burial sites suggest they offered in return silver coins, jewellery and glass; there may well also have been perishable products, including woollen goods from Britain. The Empire in the West was weakened by bubonic plague (brought to Rome by soldiers from the East in AD 166), by pressure from 'barbarians' beyond the Danubian frontier, by unchecked inflation, and in particular by indiscipline and emperor-making within the legions. In the fourth century the thrust of the Huns and other peoples from the East had a knock-on effect for earlier migrants to the central European plain. They moved westwards across the Rhine and around the Adriatic, outflanking the Alps and in a position to pillage Italy. From 394 the Roman world was permanently divided, with a beleaguered Western court at Rome (or in refuge at Ravenna) and the Eastern Emperors at Byzantium, the city

Constantine the Great founded seventy years earlier on the Bosphorus. By 476 there was no longer a Roman Empire in the West.

Historians once assumed that this partition of the continent left northern Europe isolated. In reality it stimulated trade initiative within Scandinavia and, after the rapid spread of Islam around the Mediterranean, a search for new routes to the Caspian caravans of the Caliph and to Asia's fabled markets. In central Sweden the Vänern and Vättern lake region of Götaland and the Mälaren region of Svealand enjoyed relative prosperity during the three centuries that followed the division of the classical world. From about 550 iron ore, dredged from the shallow lakes or found in the red earth from which the waters had long receded, was used productively and shaped by craftsmen into axes and swords with mounting sophistication. Ship-burials excavated at Vendel, north of Stockholm, in the 1880s revealed finely decorated helmets, swords and carved ornaments dating back to the sixth century. In succeeding decades digs elsewhere in Uppland province unearthed other pre-Viking treasures, including sword-hilts and axes embellished with gold and silver. These discoveries were almost certainly relics of a royal court, strengthening the belief that a Vendel dynasty ruled a Svear kingdom north of Lake Mälaren before the end of the eighth century. There is written evidence that as early as 720 a Dane, Angantyr, was the sovereign ruler of Jutland, but it is not clear if the Götars of Sweden had kings too.

During the First World War Dr Sune Lindqvist supervised the digging of a trench on a mound near the first excavations at Vendel. To his surprise the mound yielded not only ornaments similar to the earlier discoveries, but evidence of trade with Byzantium in the late fifth century. Among the artefacts was a gold pendant coin struck for Emperor Basiliscus, whose brief reign in Constantinople during 475–6 enabled it to be dated with a precision rare in the Baltic's early history. Treasures from the same period were found at other Swedish sites, too. In Västerland province and on the island of Øland highly skilled goldsmiths had created multi-ringed necklaces from both Byzantine and Western Roman coins. Finally, in the 1950s, excavation at Helgö, on Lake Mälaren 27 kilometres west of Stockholm, revealed the outline of a trading port dating back to the fifth century, with workshops and a collection of goods from far beyond the Baltic's eastern shores. They included a bronze Buddha from the Indian sub-continent. Arabic sources confirm that Scandinavian pioneers were on the move eastwards, following the caravan routes of the Slav heartlands. Even before the coming of the Vikings they would bring 'furs of beavers and black foxes as well as swords from most distant parts' to the Black Sea, or by way of the Don and the Volga to the Caspian and on by camels to Baghdad.

3

The Viking East

THE VIKINGS WERE sea warriors from all three Scandinavian shores. Their skill in developing new techniques of boat building enabled them to exploit the political turmoil across Christian Europe, which intensified during the eighth century with the Muslim challenge swiftly spreading from North Africa to southern France and Spain. Originally the Vikings were little more than pirates who went a–plundering (*i-viking* in Old Norse) from personal greed. Yet the Viking phenomenon anticipated, in many respects, the impelling motives of late Victorian imperialism: a search for new markets and new sources for raw materials; the need to satisfy the call to leadership of younger sons with no skills other than in warfare; and the atavistic zeal of a muscular religious faith. The Vikings became colonizers, creating kingdoms outside Scandinavia and settlements well beyond Baltic shores. Sometimes the trading posts were too primitive or badly sited to flourish; a few reverted to their original purpose and long survived as pirate havens, notably in the Orkneys and, in the Baltic, along the coast of Pomerania. But at its zenith the Viking trading empire extended from Greenland and Iceland to the Black and Caspian Seas.

The longship, with which the Viking seamen are always associated, was basically a large galley with high double prows, fore and aft. It was built in clinker style, so that the lower edge of each plank overlapped the one below it, and it was propelled by up to fifty oarsmen, though more often there were between twenty-four and thirty-two in a crew. Three innovations set longships apart from earlier vessels in northern waters: a retractable mast carrying a single rectangular sail with no boom; a steering oar on the right, 'starboard' (i.e. steer-board) side, virtually a rudder; and bowlines and spars enabling the sail to be held taut and as close as possible to the wind, thus giving the craft more speed and the ability to work to windward. The longships were of shallow draught, with no deck and only a rudimentary oaken keel, giving them a depth of two metres from gunwale downwards; some river raiders had a draught of only half a metre. By the eleventh century dragon-style super-longships were 30 metres from prow to prow, but earlier vessels rarely exceeded 20 metres (the length of a cricket pitch). They needed no harbour: they were landing craft to be beached swiftly, for Viking tactics relied on speed, surprise and the avoidance, if possible, of any pitched battles. The smaller warships – about 17 metres – could be sailed to up-river cities or hauled overland. Trader Vikings developed the knorr (or knarr), a vessel that followed similar principles of clinker design but had a lower prow, a broader beam and a deeper hull, so as to provide cargo space. Knorrs were sailing ships, about 16 metres long, and manned by much smaller crews; oars were used only in harbour or close inshore.

Both longships and knorrs hugged the coast where possible, taking soundings to avoid rocks and shoals. Voyages across the open sea were made during the long days of summer. Compasses were unknown, but Viking captains possessed sufficient skills in navigation to set a course from the position of the sun or the stars at night; like all experienced seamen they could read the sky to forecast the weather.

In England the Viking Age began dramatically on 8 June 793 when heathen Norsemen, their square-rigged craft sweeping in like 'dragons flying in the air', destroyed the abbey church on Lindisfarne, a centre of learning famous across the continent. Monks were killed in the abbey itself, thrown into the sea to drown, or carried away as slaves, along with the church treasures. Three Viking ships had beached in Portland Bay four years previously, their crews killing the Wessex posse sent to take them captive, but the incursion may have been a trading expedition that went wrong rather than a piratical raid. Lindisfarne was different. The devastation of Northumbria's Holy Island shocked and alerted the royal Courts of Europe. 'Never before has such an atrocity been seen,' declared the Northumbrian scholar, Alcuin of York. More than any other single event, the attack on Lindisfarne demonized perception of the Vikings for the next eleven or twelve centuries. Not until the 1890s did scholars outside Scandinavia begin seriously to reassess the achievements of the Vikings, recognizing the artistry of their craftsmen, their technological skills, and the seamanship that carried them to the heart of the Mediterranean and on from Iceland to Greenland and Labrador. Even today their commercial empire-building in the East receives scant attention in our histories.

No dramatic scene comparable to the Lindisfarne raid marks the opening of the Viking Age across the Baltic. The sacking by Danes of the Abotrite town of Reric (between Wismar and Rostock) in 808 was an isolated act of vengeance on the Wends for supporting Denmark's Frankish enemies rather than the start of an era of eastward expansion. That began some twenty years later, with the longship captains following the traders in search of booty and arable land on which to settle. Sweden's coastline looked towards the east, and it was natural for Viking vessels from Gotland and the islands of Lake Mälaren to turn in the first instance to familiar trading shores. Remains of a Viking settlement have been found at Grobina, up-river from Liepāja on the amber coast of Latvian Kurzeme, but no attempt was made to penetrate the forests or wetlands of the interior. The Åland Islands and the Finnish archipelago had more to offer, as stepping-stones from Svealand to the Karelian isthmus and beyond. By 855 Viking warriors had made their way up the Neva to Lake Ladoga.

Already there was a trading post at Starya Ladoga, where the river issues from the lake. Swedish merchants had long visited it; some had travelled on southwards, mainly by river to the Black Sea and Constantinople. Their Finnish neighbours called the Swedish merchants 'Rus', and the name stuck, although confusingly it was soon also applied to the local indigenous Slavs, while the Viking Swedes later became more generally known as 'Varangians'. Their leader Rurik – who may have come from eastern Jutland rather than Sweden – used Starya Ladoga as a base for pushing 160 kilometres south-westwards, following traditional trade routes along the river Volkhov, which flows into Lake Ilmen. There in 862 – says the *Russian Primary Chronicle*, compiled *c.* 1110 – Rurik was invited by Slav settlers to establish a 'New Town' (Novgorod). By the early twelfth century Rurik's creation had become a princely republic, officially styled 'Lord Novgorod the Great' and straddling Europe's borderlands from the White Sea to the upper Volga.

Other Swedish Vikings, needing good agricultural land to support a rapidly expanding population, sought more distant objectives than Novgorod, establishing tribute-raising chieftaincies as they moved southwards. Some followed the trade route from the Volkhov down the river Lovat. A third group of Vikings seem to have crossed directly from south-eastern Sweden to Truso, on the western coast of the Gulf of Riga. They then sailed up the river Daugava, reaching the Lovat route among the network of small streams that flow down from the low-lying Valdai hills, the source of many great rivers, including the Volga. From there, two Viking earls (*jarls*), Askold and Dir, supervised portage of ships to the upper waters of the Dnieper, down which they rowed for some 300 kilometres until they reached a point where wooded heights rose abruptly above a river crossing. There the Vikings fortified the township of Kiev, already serving as a western outpost of Khazaria, the confederacy of semi-nomadic tribes of nominally Jewish faith which had spread across the steppe land between the Dnieper and the Volga delta on the Caspian Sea.

The Khazars were content with revenue from taxes imposed as tributes on traders crossing their lands: Askold and Dir had greater ambitions. In the late spring of 860 they sailed down the Dnieper, going over or around 65 kilometres of granite ridges that caused nine rapids in the lower reaches of the river. Within little more than a month their fleet of longships was hugging the coast of the Black Sea. On 18 June 860, while the Byzantine navy was in the Mediterranean fighting the Arabs and Emperor Michael III was with his army in Cappadocia, some 200 Viking vessels appeared unexpectedly off the Bosphorus. 'Like a thunderbolt from heaven', the Patriarch Photius declared, the 'merciless barbarians' ravaged the shores, spreading terror among the Greeks of inner Constantinople. Then, like early Vikings in the west, the raiders turned away, sailing back to their Dnieper stronghold bloated with booty.

Rather surprisingly, normal trade was soon resumed along the old routes from the Baltic to the Black Sea. Seven years later Photius, a vigorous missionizer, could even rejoice that some Rus from the Dnieper had abandoned their 'godless religion for the pure and unadulterated faith of the Christians', and in 874 his successor, Patriarch Ignatius, sent an archbishop to Kiev. The embryonic Christian Varangian community on the Dnieper did not last long, though a vestigial faith may have lingered after its collapse. In 881–2 Oleg, Rurik's successor as prince in Novgorod, advanced deeper into the steppe land than his predecessor had contemplated. Askold and Dir's Kiev was seized by the newcomers, refounded and elevated in status. 'May this be the mother of Russian cities,' Prince Oleg proclaimed – or so a chronicler at the Pecherskii Lavra, Kiev's Monastery of the Caves, patriotically wrote more than two centuries later.

For twenty-five years merchants peacefully made the hazardous journey down the Dnieper each summer and along the Black Sea coast to the metropolis they called Mikligadur, the 'Great City'. Then, in 907, Prince Oleg planned another attack on Constantinople, a sustained assault rather than a second Viking raid. He sought tribute (protection money) from the Byzantine emperor but, more especially, safeguards for his Rus merchants and special terms for the mounting trade they conducted between the Black Sea and Baltic lands. It was not in Oleg's interest to breach the walls of Byzantium and sack the commercial heart of the city.

The *Russian Primary Chronicle* gives the only account of the expedition, which is passed over rapidly in Byzantine sources. The chronicler, who is thought to have been a monk named Nestor, based his narrative on Viking sagas and set down a tale burnished through many generations. He cannot be regarded as a reliable primary source but much of his chronicle corresponds so closely to Viking practice elsewhere that it seems to carry a stamp of authenticity. From Kiev, Nestor relates, 'Oleg sallied forth by horse and by ship, and his vessels numbered two thousand . . . and there were forty men to a ship.' The voyage must have taken six or seven weeks, but no warning of invasion alerted the Byzantine authorities. As in 860 the Rus fired 'palaces and churches' on the upper Bosphorus until, when they approached the Golden Horn, they found the seaway blocked by iron chains secured by cage-shaped buoys. But the Vikings were accustomed to beaching vessels for portage; they had done so many times on the journey south from Kiev; and the ships were duly hauled on rollers past the iron barrier and across the Galata peninsula. At that point Emperor Leo VI wisely sued for peace and, without the means of scaling the walls of the Great City, Prince Oleg no less wisely agreed.

Sparse Byzantine references to the campaign confirm that Oleg achieved his war aims, though it is the *Primary Chronicle* that details the gains: payment of a massive tribute; a monthly allowance of food and wine (together with free baths) for his merchants, so long as they stayed for not more than six months in a designated quarter of the city and entered and left it through a specified gate; the provision of supplies for their homeward journey; and the right 'to conduct as much trade as they need without paying taxes'. The final terms were left for envoys to settle over the next two years. Once a provisional treaty was agreed, Oleg hung his shield on the gate – traditional Viking symbolism for ending a campaign, commentators on Nestor's chronicle point out. For the Kievan monk, however, Oleg's gesture was a token of victory: the prince led the fleet up the Bosphorus and back across the Black Sea, his ships loaded with 'gold, silk fabrics, fruit, wine and all manner of finery'. The wind filled new sails supplied by the Greeks: plain canvas was good enough for the Slav auxiliaries from Novgorod; only silk brocade satisfied Swedish Varangian pride.

Five years later the prospect of new prizes in the East tempted the Vikings out again. In 912 the Rus left the upper waters of the river Don on a raid about which there is little evidence, although it is clear the venture ended in disaster. By agreeing to share booty with the Khakan (the ruler of the Khazars) the Vikings were allowed to cross the portage area from the Don to the lower Volga in the heart of his territories. After negotiating 650 kilometres of reeds and sandbanks the fleet sailed into the Caspian Sea and set course southwards to menace the Silk Road of the Abbasid Caliphate in Baghdad. The raiders seem to have had no difficulty in scattering the caliph's small fleet and they found the Persian coast virtually undefended.

They torched Muslim towns and plundered holy sites without restraint. But tales of heathen Viking sacrilege – and almost certainly a suspicion of double-dealing – enraged the Khakan: he ordered destruction of the homeward-bound fleet. In the early summer of 913 the Rus expedition was ambushed at Itil, the Khazar capital in the Volga delta, and virtually wiped out. Never again did Baltic-style longships raid Caspian shores.

After Oleg's death in 913 the Rus threatened Constantinople again twice during the tenth century. Both incursions were beaten off, in 941 by the defenders perfecting the wall of flame, that dreaded 'Greek fire' which consumed vessels and crews alike. After each campaign the Rus lost some of the privileges Oleg had won for them. Yet a strange relationship bound the Byzantine Greeks and the Norsemen. Though they were feared as pagan raiders and suspect as rival traders, the Norse served loyally as Varangian mercenaries in a Byzantine 'Foreign Legion'. Swedes, Norwegians, Danes – even some Vikings from Iceland – hacked their way bloodily forward in expeditions that ravaged Crete, Armenia, Syria, Bulgaria and Sicily.

Later in the century a greater military honour came their way: they formed an élite corps, the Varangian Guard, that between about 980 and 1090 was responsible for protecting the Emperor's person. 'With their broad and double-edged battle axes on their shoulders they attended the Greek emperors to the temple, the senate and the hippodrome,' wrote Gibbon in *The Decline and Fall of the Roman Empire*. 'The keys of the palace, the treasury and the capital were held by the faithful hands of the Varangians.'

Marginal illustrations in Byzantine manuscripts show blond giants, some in chain-mail and holding round shields with an iron boss, others in scale armour with lozenge-shaped shields. They carry heavy axes, knives or a long spear with double-edged blade, as menacing as a sword. Warriors woven into church tapestries in Norway are similarly accoutred, artistic testimony to forgotten bonds that linked Europe's northern and southern seas in the so-called Dark Ages.

A bloodier bond was Harald Hardrada, the only officer from the Varangian Guard familiar by name to readers of English history. Harald Hardrada, King of Norway, was killed at Stamford Bridge outside York on 25 September 1066 leading an invading army against Harold of England (who was himself the grandson of a Viking). As a young prince, Harald had been forced to flee Scandinavia for Novgorod, Kiev and Byzantium. Six of his fifty-one years were spent in the Varangian Guard. There were campaigns along the Euphrates, in southern Italy and the Balkans; protection – at a price – for pilgrims to Jerusalem and for craftsmen restoring the Church of the Holy Sepulchre; promotion to commander of the Guard; and the steady acquisition of riches in coin and plundered treasure at a time when the value of Arabic silver was highly inflated. Year by year Harald entrusted his gains for safe keeping to Yaroslav the Wise, Grand Prince of Kiev, whose daughter Elizabeth he was pledged to marry. Two sources suggest that in 1044 Harald left Byzantium without imperial permission, but with one last hoard of local booty. His crew are said to have hurriedly slid the treasure chests from stern to bow so as to rock their longship across the iron chain positioned to block him from the open sea. They reached Kiev, where Harald seems to have stayed for some months and collected his bride and his fortune. By 1046 he was in Sweden, almost certainly the wealthiest man around northern shores. He had no difficulty in raising an army that won him the mastery of much of Norway and for eighteen years he ravaged Funen and North Zealand in attempts to seize Denmark as well. Finally in the summer of 1066 came that bid for the English crown, the disastrous gamble that left the war veteran from the Euphrates dead beside Yorkshire's river Derwent.

The cognomen Hardrada ('harsh ruler') evokes an image of the ruthless barbarity with which he waged war. Some Vikings, travelling between Gotland, Novgorod, Kiev and Constantinople, acquired a veneer of neo-classical culture. But not King Harald; he gloried in his reputation, fighting beneath a banner that proclaimed the one word *Landeydan* ('land-ravisher'). Yet he brought back to the Baltic one fitting legacy from his days in Constantinople. When he needed to finance the Danish wars, his mint carefully replicated the style of Byzantium's silver and copper coinage. There was plenty in circulation for the mintmen to copy.

The full travels of other Vikings who went east are unknown to us. Who scratched runes on the marble lion at Piraeus that Venetian invaders carried back to their arsenal in the eighteenth century? What was he doing in Athens? Had a knorr sailed the waters off Salamis, bringing to Attica exotic merchandise or wretched slaves from the north? We can only speculate. Did Halfdan, whose runic graffito was found cut into the polished stonework of Istanbul's St Sophia in 1959, serve in the Varangian Guard? Or was he a Viking merchant who wandered into the domed basilica and, sensing the permanence of the marble balustrade, carved his name into immortality? At Kyrkstigenin in Swedish Oppland a runic inscription commemorates Ragnvald, an officer of the Varangian Guard. Other graves in Oppland and on Gotland recall young adventurers from central Sweden who sailed eastwards to trade with 'the Greeks' as well as to fight. Halfdan may have come from Sweden like Ragnvald or he may have come from Denmark, as his name suggests. Did he, one wonders, like Hardrada, find his way back from the Golden Horn to his native shore?

If so, he would have had a choice of several thriving ports for a landfall. There were trade staging-posts in western Finland, up the Aura river near Turku and the Uskela river near Salo. Most likely he would have made for Gotland, the centre of Viking Baltic trade. A cluster of settlements sprang up along the island's west coast, where the Hanse port of Visby was founded in the twelfth century. There are traces of landing piers at Paviken and near Västergarn and, on the east coast, near Slite. Hoards of treasure have been unearthed on so many sites that Gotland seems to have been primarily an offshore financial centre, serving late ninth century Sweden much as Hong Kong served late twentieth century China. Collections in Visby's museums hold more Arab silver dirhems than any other currency, but there are also thousands of coins from the Frankish lands and from Anglo-Saxon England.

For almost 200 years the principal port in Svealand was Birka, 29 kilometres to the west of Stockholm. Birka may have been founded by foreign traders who, in about 790, sought a more defensible site for a settlement than neighbouring Helgö. The island had a cliff on which it was possible to build a small castle protecting quays, storage shed and piers, and remains have been found of a beacon, to serve either as a warning signal or a lighthouse visible in the night sky from the outer archipelago. By 830 Birka was the northern terminus for the silver trade route from the East. 'There are many rich merchants in Birka and all types of goods, money and articles of value,' noted a Christian missionary monk a few years later. But the prosperity could not last. By the close of the next century the sea was receding from the foot of the cliffs. New merchant ships, with deeper draught than knorrs, had difficulty coming close inshore. There may, too, have been mounting competition from Hedeby, in Denmark. About 970 Birka, like Helgö before it, was abandoned. Sigtuna, 15 kilometres to the north, became Svealand's chief trading port.

Some treasures from the East were found by Norwegian archaeologists who excavated Kaupang, a settlement near the mouth of Oslo fjord, where the Viking equivalent of an international trade fair met before the coming of winter. Pottery from the Rhineland, farming tools from England, and Arabic silver coins show the extent of Kaupang's commercial network. But most trade was with the Faeroes, Scotland, Ireland, Iceland and possibly, after 1000, with the pioneer adventurers in Greenland. Ribe, in southwestern Jutland, though an important trading settlement, had even less contact with the East than Kaupang.

Greatest of all merchant communities – and in 950 the largest town in the Baltic world – was Danish Hedeby (now Haithabu in Germany, east of the E45 autobahn, a few kilometres south of the town of Schleswig). There was a settlement at Hedeby many years before the Viking raids began, for it stood at a key geographical position, astride the main artery from the south in north-western Europe and at the centre of the narrowest isthmus between the Baltic and the North Sea. Hedeby faced north-east, down the winding Schlei fjord and about 38 kilometres from the open sea, a port far enough inland to receive warning of approach by pirates or enemies. West of Hedeby a mere 16 kilometres of moorland provided easy portage to the Eider, a short river that flows into the North Sea at Tönning, with an upstream quay at Hollingstedt. A ditch-and-embankment rampart, known as the 'Danewirke' and built in the eighth century, afforded Hedeby protection from Frankish incursions. The Danish King Godfred extended the rampart and encouraged merchants to settle in Hedeby in 808, after the raid in which his warriors sacked the Abotrite port of Reric, some 190 kilometres along the Mecklenburg coast. Yet, though ninth century Hedeby had the makings of a commercial port, it also served as a hideout for raiders who returned home with booty and slaves from Frisia, the Netherlands and England. The growing trade with the East transformed the town: Hedeby's greatest prosperity came at the middle of the tenth century, the years of Varangian commercial ascendancy at Constantinople.

A Moorish merchant from Cordoba, visiting Hedeby about 975, was far from impressed. The town was too big, he thought; it was not, by his reckoning, rich; a high birth rate prompted families to throw unwanted babies into the Schlei; the main food was fish, because there was so much of it; and Viking singing was dreadful. It was a growling from the throat, 'worse even than the barking of dogs', he grumbled. There must have been a touch of the Wild North about Viking Hedeby. Yet archaeological evidence, from three major digs in the last seventy years, suggests that life in the port at its prime anticipated the commercial bustle of Thames-side London nine centuries later: ship repairing workshops; craftsmen tapping away at silver, bone or amber jewellery; potters, weavers, carpenters and leather-workers; and all the banter of barter in markets where bargains were struck for furs from the Lapps, soapstone from the Swedes, and wax, silk, spices and honey from the East.

Ironically Hedeby, the port that prospered most from the luxury trade with Novgorod and Kiev, was razed to the ground by the one Viking warrior known to have amassed a fortune in the East. For, in his attempt to add Denmark to his Norwegian kingdom, Harald Hardrada led a fleet up

Schlei fjord in the summer of 1049 to destroy his enemy's commercial capital. Nine hundred years later underwater exploration by divers and frogmen revealed that he had employed a tactic favoured by the Byzantines. Harald might not possess the secret of 'Greek fire', but he knew the panic a floating inferno would cause among the Danish defenders. At least one fireship – and probably more – bore down on a wooden barrier outside Hedeby's harbour. Soon the whole town was ablaze. The stock of goods in the warehouses must have fed the flames.

Hedeby was rebuilt; but in vain. Seventeen years after Hardrada's raid it was sacked for a second time, by Wendish pirates. The town never recovered the commercial eminence of the mid-tenth century. Like Birka the approaches to the port were too shallow for the newer merchant ships, with their cargoes of timber rather than luxury goods. No doubt the sunken hulk of the fireship made passage of a narrowing channel even harder. Just as, in Svealand, Sigtuna replaced Birka at the end of the tenth century, so a hundred years later the trade of Hedeby passed rapidly to neighbouring Schleswig. The town remained 'lost' until the 1930s, when the site was rediscovered by archaeologists. Thirty years later Hedeby was excavated thoroughly by a team from the Landesmuseum at Schloss Gottorp.

For a few years early in the eleventh century Hedeby was a trading port in the empire of Canute the Great. Politically Hedeby was linked with Ribe, Kaupang, Trondheim, Lund, Southampton, Ipswich and London in the most extensive of all Viking commonwealths. King Canute is a half-legendary figure in British history, ruler of Northumbria from the spring of 1015 and of all England from the following autumn until his death in 1035, at Shaftesbury in Dorset. By 1019 he was also King of Denmark and for the last seven years of his life titular King of Norway, too. During most of his reign he remained in England, but he was twice forced to campaign in Scandinavia. He suffered defeat in 1026 by a combined Swedish-Norwegian army at Helgö (north of the southern Swedish town of Växjö), though he was able to consolidate his position in western Norway two years later. In England Canute was respected as the strongest king in more than a century and he sought to export to Denmark some of the centralized institutions he inherited. But he was a warrior, not a constructive creative statesman. The maritime empire lacked cohesion. On Canute's death it fell apart. A century and a half elapsed before an empire of commerce linked the North Sea, the Baltic and the rivers of Russia. That interdependence was achieved, not by a latter-day Viking sovereign, but by the informal federation of merchants known as the Hanse.

4

Pagans and Piasts

CHRISTIANITY WAS SLOW to take root on northern shores. In England there had been Christian churches for almost a hundred years before the Roman legions left, and when Augustine arrived at Canterbury in 597 his mission was as much concerned with replanting or pruning Celtic foliage as with sowing the faith in pagan soil. But around the Baltic conditions were different: the Roman Empire stopped well short of the Elbe and there was no vestigial Christianity on which to draw. In Scandinavia, and among tribal communities in the dense forests of the southern Baltic hinterland, Christian monotheism offered no challenge to nature worship until the last decades of the ninth century. Even 300 years later Uppsala's shrine of Frey, the god of health and fertility, was still receiving offerings after weddings in central Sweden. On the southern shore the Wends of Rügen prostrated themselves before Svantovit, their four-headed idol above Cape Arkona, well into the second half of the thirteenth century. The Wendish tribes – Wagrians, Abotrites, Rugians – were led in public worship by a pagan priesthood officiating in temples and they respected the sacred character of particular groves, springs and rocks. Scandinavian peoples, on the other hand, accepted the lead of kings or chieftains who sought by sacrifice and ritual to placate a range of deities, each concerned with a different aspect of human life. Odin was the god of warriors, a deity whose handmaidens welcomed those who fell in battle to Valhalla. The red-bearded and hammer-wielding Thor, who could strike with thunder and lightning or bring rain to the crops and fair weather to garner the harvest, was popular with tillers in the field. Loki was perverse and treacherous, a god to be feared and placated, though more a mischievous Puck than a diabolical Satan.

Scandinavian merchants encountered Christianity, with its unexpected faith in a prophet who rose from the dead, in the lands where commerce carried them. They became familiar with the Christian form of worship, a few perceived that the Church in the West was a pillar of orderly royal government. Some accepted provisional baptism as an act of convenience, a requirement for permission to trade. Others, like Oleg's envoys to Constantinople in 911, were awed by the majesty of 'true religion'. Occasionally fugitives at the Frankish court were baptized, either from sincerity of belief or political expediency. Among these fugitives, at Ingelheim in 826, was Harald Klak, the exiled king of Denmark. When two years later Klak returned home to re-claim his throne he brought with him the first Christian mission to the Baltic, led by Anskar, the 'Apostle of the North', a monk born and schooled near Amiens.

It was a cautious enterprise: Augustine had come to Canterbury with vigorous backing from Pope Gregory the Great and forty monks to support him; Anskar landed at Hedeby in 828 with nothing more instructive than a prayerful commendation from Pope Eugenius II and a single companion, a monk also from Picardy. Within a few months King Harald was forced back into exile, leaving the French missioners stranded and in some danger. With considerable courage they took ship for Birka but were intercepted by pirates. They lost their books and very nearly lost their lives, too. Eventually they reached Birka on foot and were well received by King Bjorn of Svealand. He was not baptized though he was prepared to accept the 'white God' as a deity to be set in the pantheon beside Odin, Thor and Frey. Conservative Swedes saw no reason to give up worshipping the old gods under whom they had prospered. The mission flourished for some eighteen months before Anskar was recalled by Emperor Louis I and consecrated first Archbishop of Hamburg. In 832 he visited Rome and was appointed legate of the Holy See for Scandinavia and for the missions to the Western Slavs.

There followed, however, the two most intensive decades of Viking raids. Hamburg was itself sacked in 845, and Anskar was again fortunate to escape with his life. Yet in 850, at the age of fifty-two, he came back to Hedeby, this time as Primate of a unified archdiocese of Bremen and Hamburg, and with a band of missionary monks to support him. Before he returned to Bremen (where he died in 865) Anskar had the satisfaction of seeing churches founded and flourishing in Hedeby, Ribe and Birka. Christian symbols on rune stones, and an exquisitely crafted late ninth century silver crucifix found at Birka, testify to Anskar's achievements and the gradual infiltration of Latin European culture into the pagan folklore of the North.

For more than 200 years the archbishops of Hamburg and Bremen exercised spiritual authority over Scandinavia and the south-western shores of the Baltic. By the year 1000 Christian missions from Saxony were seeking to convert the Abotrites and the Wagrians; there was even a Saxon bishop at Oldenburg, a Wagrian pirates' haven on the river Brockhau, in the peninsula separating Kiel Bay from Lübeck Bay. Across the Baltic, Olof Skötkonung – the earliest Swedish king historians can clearly identify – was baptized in 1006 at Husaby and built a wooden cathedral on the site of a temple to Freya at Skara. But few Swedes followed the lead of their king. When Olof died in 1022 his son, Anund Jakob, reverted to traditional paganism. Viking dragons envelop the standing stones at either end of Olof's tomb in Husaby Cathedral. Christianity survived in Sweden as the faith of rival chieftains competing for the throne. Priests were appointed by chiefs or even elected by peasant communities. Local variations perplexed legates sent from Rome.

In all these Scandinavian lands central authority, whether spiritual or lay, was weak. Clan freedom and old loyalties persisted. Strong-willed rulers in Denmark and Norway realized they needed the moral backing and administrative structure of the Church to consolidate the unity of their kingdoms and help curb the power of local chieftains in what were still elective monarchies. In both kingdoms the churchmen, too, continued to seek help; royal patronage gave them land and protected their foundations. Within a hundred years of Anskar's death the first partnership of Crown and Mitre was forged in Denmark. It was copied north of the Skagerrak when in 1035 Norway achieved united independence under Magnus I the Good. In Sweden, however, struggles for the succession retarded the growth of a unified monarchy and bolstered the territorial authority of local chieftains (Jarls) who, in the eleventh and early twelfth centuries, tended to be inward looking. Eastward-facing Stockholm was not founded until the turn of the thirteenth century. By 1289 it was described as the biggest town in Sweden but only in 1634 was it officially recognized as the nation's capital city.

Throughout the Middle Ages some regions of Sweden retained considerable independence. The people of Gotland, for example, took little interest in mainland politicking. They were both farmers and commercial middle-men intent on keeping open the historic Varangian trade route to Novgorod, bringing furs, wax and Middle Eastern luxuries westwards and carrying cloth, iron and copper eastwards. Only gradually were these farmer merchants, prospering in the limestone houses they built for themselves across the island, challenged by foreign traders who settled on the west coast, transforming Visby into a town of their own.

Along the Baltic's southern shore different conditions prevailed. These were Marcher borderlands, with sovereignty contested by German-speaking Saxons and Holsteiners, and by Danes and indigenous Wends. By 1070 the German Christian missions planted at the start of the century had succumbed to pressure from Wendish princes who with a few exceptions lapsed into paganism. Piracy flourished once more at Oldenburg, where the ancient deities were worshipped in a temple built on high ground, above the charred ruins of the proto-cathedral.

In Denmark, however, kingly Christianity had come to stay. Harald Bluetooth, who reigned from 958 to 987 and was baptized in 960, was the first Scandinavian ruler to promote Christianity with genuine conviction. His father Gorm the Old, king in north Jutland, had encouraged the setting up of bishoprics at Aarhus and Ribe, though not himself a Christian. To Harald, who claimed the overlordship of coastal Norway as well as southern Sweden, the spread of the new faith served as a way of binding his kingdom together. Unique testimony to his convictions may still be seen in central Jutland. At Jelling he built a wooden church outside of which he ordered two rune stones to be placed. On one side of the smaller stone a serpent is entwined around a mythological creature from the old religion, while the obverse shows the figure of Christ. A runic inscription proclaims 'Harald king bade this be ordained for Gorm his father and Thyra his mother, that Harald who won for himself all Denmark and Norway and who made the Danes Christian'. Fittingly the church, the runic stones and two adjacent burial mounds now form a World Heritage Site.

Only the palest radiance of holiness emanates from Denmark's earliest Christian rulers. In 1026 the revered empire-builder Canute the Great lost his temper with his brother-in-law, allegedly over a game of chess, and had him killed in the wooden church at Roskilde, built by Harald Bluetooth forty years previously. Three generations later, Canute II (reigned 1080–86) was a harsh ruler who introduced a primitive poll tax levied at the point of the sword by warriors under royal command. Most repellent of all was Eric II (1134–37) who had his cousin, eight nephews and nieces and probably his brother put to death, after having killed King Niels and at least five bishops to secure the throne. His reign ended with assassination in the council chamber. With bland discretion the monastic scribes dubbed him 'Eric the Unforgettable': he had, after all, given land to the Church at Lund and Ringsted.

Almost every mediaeval kingdom had a ruler whom a pope would later canonize. Remarkably, it was the tyrannical Canute II who became Denmark's only royal saint. He had met his death when an angry mob broke down the doors of the church of St Alban at Odense and stabbed the king and his brother as they knelt at prayer. Murder at the altar made Canute II a martyr to the Faith. Despite his record of brutality, in 1101 he was canonized by Pope Paschal II. Odense gained a cathedral ('Sankt Knuds'): the Church in Denmark as a whole gained even more. For in 1103 the diocese of Lund – in Swedish Skåne today but then within the Danish kingdom – became a Metropolitan See, independent of the archbishops of Bremen and Hamburg and controlled by a formidable succession of warrior prelates. The Scandinavian Church had at last distanced itself from a specifically Germanic Christendom.

As yet, however, it was not autochthonous. The influence of churchmen from England and France remained strong, culminating in the achievements in Sweden and Norway of the papal legate, Cardinal Nicholas Breakspear (later Pope Hadrian IV), born in Hertfordshire and schooled at Avignon. In 1153 Breakspear presided over the Synod of Linköping where, in the presence of King Sverker and the leading jarls, the backsliding Swedish Church was formally received into Catholic Christendom. Eleven years later the first Archbishop of Uppsala was also English by birth. But the principal missioners of these decades across both Sweden and Denmark came from France: white monks of the Cistercian Order, with their mother house at Cîteaux, on the borders of Brittany and Maine. The Cistercians soon spread as far east as Gotland. Their monastery at Roma in the interior of the island was planted in 1164, the same year that the Order reached central Wales and founded Strata Florida Abbey.

Beyond the headwaters of the Gulf of Finland the Greek Orthodox rite flourished: the doctrines and practices of Byzantine Christendom bolstered the secular power of the Grand Prince of Kiev and his satellite ruler, the Prince of Novgorod. In about 988, more than a century after Patriarch Ignatius first sent an archbishop to the middle Dnieper, Prince Vladimir of Kiev embraced Christianity. Pagan idols from the surrounding hills were cast into the river and his subjects ordered to accept baptism by total immersion in its muddy waters; sundry concubines were discarded, and the Princess Anna, sister of the Emperor Basil II, became Vladimir's sole wife. This dramatic revolution from above had lasting consequences for all eastern Europe. The Kievan State soon assimilated the political ideology, forms of worship and social code of Byzantium, with the prince seeking to fulfil the autocratic responsibilities of the emperor. Within half a century a stone cathedral was built at Novgorod and dedicated to Holy Wisdom (St Sophia) in emulation of the mother church at Constantinople. Orthodox Christianity had spread from the Black Sea to the Baltic hinterland: Grand Prince Yaroslav the Wise, who ruled in Kiev from 1019 to 1054, could claim sovereignty over the southern coast of the Gulf of Finland up to the river Narva, virtually the frontier line between the republics of Russia and Estonia today. By 1136, when Novgorod became completely independent and Kiev passed into decline, there was an Orthodox cathedral of the Holy Trinity as far west as Pskov, south of Lake Peipsi. Traces of one or more early eleventh century Orthodox churches have been found in Gotland, no doubt built to meet the spiritual needs of the many Novgorod merchants trading fur, mead, honey and wax in the central and western Baltic.

Paganism persisted beyond the western limits of 'Lord Novgorod the Great'; customary reverence was offered to deities with unfamiliar names responsible for natural phenomena and the shaping of human behaviour. Towns were slow to develop. On the site of modern Tallinn's harbour there was a trading-post called Lidna or Lidinisse ('stronghold') by the Estonians and Reval by German-speakers as early as the eleventh century; and at least one primitive track ran through thick woodland to a settlement that the Germans knew as Dorpat – Tartu today. In both places there were markets for furs and slaves, shipped to Gotland or to Schleswig. But Reval (Tallinn) was only urbanized after Estonia passed under Danish sovereignty in the thirteenth century. Around the mouth of the river Dvina – the Daugava in today's Latvia – fishing villages were scattered, possibly as far upstream as Riga, and there were similar settlements in Courland at Windau (Ventspils), Libau (Liepāja) and Memel (Klaipėda). Near the coast the Couronians and Semigallians farmed arable areas. Inland, across a 500-kilometre swathe of lake, marsh and forest, a virtual wilderness perpetuated tribal divisions and kept settlements compact and isolated. Only when chance produced tribal chieftains who were skilled warriors and charismatic leaders do we find stirrings of national identity. So it was to be, as early as the turn of the tenth century, with the Poles.

The Polanie tribe settled on the fringe of the Eurasian plain in the basin of the river Warta during the Bronze Age migrations. For twelve or thirteen centuries they left no mark, political or cultural, on Europe's history. Then, as the millennium was coming to an end, their leading family, the Piasts, leapt from pagan obscurity to dynastic eminence within forty years. Legend maintains that *circa* 960 Lech, the chief (*knez*) of the Polanie, was hunting on the eastern edge of the Warta forests when he found the nest of a white eagle in a hilltop clearing and gave orders for a settlement to be built there, which soon became the town of Gniezno. Although the Piasts were to remain the ruling house of Poland for 400 years, little is known about Lech or his forebears; it seems likely he already had a power base at Posen (Poznań), 50 kilometres east of Gniezno, at the confluence of the rivers Warta and Cybina and astride a historic amber route from the coast into central Europe. Even today the vast and rather dreary plain around Poznań forms a region known as Old Poland (Wielkopolska). But tradition and sentiment favour Gniezno rather than Poznań as the cradle of the nation: a white eagle has remained the Polish emblem down the centuries, in 1295 becoming a crowned eagle; and the Archbishop of Gniezno is recognized as Primate of Poland, still senior churchman in today's deeply Catholic country.

If Catholicism came with the Piast dynasty, so too did Poland's access to the Baltic. Lech's son, Mieszko I, was baptized in Gniezno in 966, a year after he married Dobrava, the daughter of the duke of Bohemia. As a Catholic duke Mieszko played an astute role in the power struggle between the Saxon 'Ottonian' dynasty of Holy Roman Emperors and the papacy. His strategic plan was to secure control of the Oder and the Vistula, the two great rivers that flowed into the Baltic. He almost succeeded. By the time of his death his warriors had thrust forward up the Warta to its confluence with the Oder and taken Cüstrin (Kostrzyn). Other Polish foot-soldiers cut their way through forests 'no mortal man had been able to penetrate' to reach the Vistula and follow a second amber trail to the Baltic coast. It is probable that Mieszko I founded Danzig (Gdańsk); a hagiography of St Adalbert, written about 1000, mentions a town with 1,200 inhabitants established where the Vistula flows into the sea.

Mieszko's son, Boleslaw I the Brave, who reigned from 992 to 1025, was the first Polish ruler crowned as king, though not until a few months before his death. He secured Metropolitan status for the archdiocese of Gniezno in the hope of sealing the close partnership of Church and State. His territorial gains look impressive on the map: expansion in the south and east to include Cracow and, briefly, much of Moravia and Bohemia; and the acquisition of the Pomeranian coastline westwards from Danzig to the approaches to Stettin, the Wendish fortress commanding the mouth of the Oder. But the Greater Poland of the early Piasts proved as ephemeral as the empire of Canute: Mieszko II (reigned 1025–37) had to abandon much of the coast and footholds in Bohemia and Moravia. Although his son Casimir I (1038–58) held the nascent kingdom together, fierce fighting in the Warta borderland made him move his capital away from Gniezno in Old Poland eastwards to Cracow, in Little Poland (Malopolska). Some of the fighting was in response to a Bohemian (Czech) invasion, but there were also local rebellions, with tribal chiefs exploiting pagan resentment caused by sword-point conversions.

Under Casimir's successor, Boleslaw II (1058–79), the Piast Church–State partnership faltered. Although he was a consistent supporter of Pope Gregory VII's attempts to enhance the mystique of the papacy, Boleslaw II suspected treason among the religious hierarchy and in 1078 he had Bishop

Stanislaw of Cracow hacked to death. The Church was unforgiving: Boleslaw was deposed, Stanislaw hailed as a martyr and eventually canonized. The Church was also, politically, a beneficiary: for (as in Sweden) problems of disputed succession in an elective monarchy left the bishops as arbiters between castle-holding warlords. During the twelfth century Piast Poland became fragmented, with only the Church preserving a sense of nationhood. By 1250 there were nine Piast duchies across the realm; the loosest of links bound the ruler in Cracow to distant kinsmen seeking to maintain ducal authority along the Pomeranian shore. The first King Boleslaw had been 'the Brave'; the second was 'the Bold'; by the 1270s the fifth and last was 'Boleslaw the Bashful' – 'the Chaste' to scribes at work in the kindlier monasteries.

Yet the Piast dynasty enjoyed one final flourish of national fulfilment under Casimir III the Great (1333–70). The frontier was advanced eastwards. Legal codes were drawn up and foreign traders were encouraged to settle. Among them were 'wandering' Jews, who were allowed courts of their own and became the forefathers of the largest and most concentrated Jewish community in Europe. New towns were founded; old cities embellished with 'brick Gothic'; and Cracow was given a university and much else of architectural distinction, too. But this 'Golden Age' shone only briefly, and with less lustre along the Baltic coast than in Malopolska. Casimir's failure to produce a son allowed the crown to pass to his nephew, King Louis of Hungary, an absentee ruler. He, too, had no sons and conceded tax privileges to Poland's territorial magnates (the *szlachta*) in return for an undertaking that they would ensure his newly-born daughter Jadwiga was elected and crowned 'king' of Poland on his death. This agreement (the Privilege of Kosice, 1374) had momentous consequences for Europe from the Baltic to the Black Sea (*see p. 54*). The power of the Polish nobility to determine their nation's future was confirmed.

5

Holy Warriors and Hanse Merchants

THE EARLIEST COLONIZERS of the west Baltic hinterland were German-speaking pioneers. They crossed from Holstein into Wendish Wagria at the turn of the eleventh century, seeking arable land or new pastures. About 1140 the German thrust – a largely spontaneous movement at first – became systematic: Count Adolf II of Holstein, a vassal of Duke Henry of Saxony, organized well-armed expeditions to appropriate territory for the landowners of Lower Saxony, who protected their gains with small forts and stockades. In the wake of the soldiery came peasants freed from manorial bonds and encouraged by Count Adolf to farm the land and clear the forests. Trading settlements were set up – or revived – on promising sites beside the rivers. As if to acknowledge an ever expanding Baltic frontier, the restored see of Oldenburg was in 1160 moved 50 kilometres east to Lübeck, which Adolf II had founded in 1143 around an island hill at the confluence of the Trave and Wakenitz, upstream from a Wendish riverside settlement. Increasingly the Saxon drive to the east became identified with a Holy War against pagan nature worshippers. Ecclesiastical power and temporal lordship advanced together.

It was the spirit of the age. These were years when across much of western Europe kings, barons and knights responded to the calls by successive popes for a crusade against the Seljuk Turks and the Muslim caliphate. Poles, Saxons, Danes and a few Norwegians and Swedes were among the 100,000 warriors persuaded to take the cross and head for Jerusalem. The First Crusade (1096–99) was a success: Jerusalem was freed from Islamic rule, a Christian Kingdom established, and the Christian principality set up at Antioch and Edessa in northern Syria. But the sanctified land-grabbing of the Crusaders revived the fighting qualities of the Muslims. In 1145 Pope Eugenius III appealed for a new army to check the resurgence of 'infidel' power. In France and southern Germany the knights again responded enthusiastically. By contrast the people of Lower Saxony were reluctant to look to the Middle East. Their perceived enemy lay closer to home; for them the western Slavs along the Baltic shores formed a heathen challenge more immediately compelling than the threat from Islam. The Danes and the Poles, though mistrusting Saxony's Duke Henry the Lion, were willing to join any assault on these pagans of the North, provided Pope Eugenius sanctioned the enterprise. On 13 April 1147 his Bull *Divina dispatione* authorized a crusade against the Wendish Slavs: any man who took the cross might display on his armour similar insignia to the Crusaders in the Holy Land; and like them he could be certain of spiritual indulgence, on Earth and in Heaven.

The first northern crusade was a total failure. Prince Nyklot, warrior chief of the Abotrites, proved a wiser strategist than his adversaries. He launched a pre-emptive strike into Wagria and overran the new Saxon settlements on the right bank of the river Trave within eight weeks of the Papal Bull, well before the improvised coalition could confront him. By midsummer Henry the Lion and his Danish ally were ready; the Poles prepared a diversion in Pomerania; a Danish war fleet hugged the Baltic coast; and 160 kilometres inland no fewer than seven bishops converged on Crusader headquarters at Magdeburg, on the Elbe. Their heavily armed contingents came from as far west as Mainz and as far south as Olmütz (Olomouc) in Moravia.

Nyklot won the only battle of the 1147 war by separating Danes from Saxons in front of Dobin, his island hideout amid the lakes and marshes of Mecklenburg. Wends from Rügen surprised the Danish fleet in Wismar Bay. From Magdeburg the army of the Seven Bishops advanced some 160 kilometres northwards for an unrewarding siege of Demmin, Nyklot's effective capital. They razed to the ground a heathen temple at Malchin, and then swung north-east, encouraged by two rapacious Saxon landowners tempted to seize the rich prize of Stettin. But coalition intelligence – if it existed – was faulty: Stettin was a trading centre which already housed some German merchants and was in contact with both Gotland and Novgorod; and the ruling Pomeranian prince was no pagan, but a baptized Christian with a resident bishop, who was scathing in condemning the newcomers: 'If they had come to strengthen the Christian faith,' Bishop Albrecht said of his episcopal colleagues, 'they should do so by preaching, not by arms.' Stettin was spared an assault. The chastened Crusaders turned away from walls draped with banners displaying a cross.

Peace came that same year, ahead of winter. Nyklot could not launch a counter-offensive against so many enemies and he agreed to terms that cost him little. He lost no territory, though in Wagria his army fell back from the Trave. One crusader objective was, in theory, attained: Nyklot accepted baptism, along with all his warriors. 'Let the God who is in Heaven be our

God and it will suffice,' Nyklot assured Duke Henry. 'You may worship whom you choose; we will worship you.' To be free from crusader encroachment was worth a phrase of flattery and a sprinkle of holy water. Once the invader was gone, his people reverted to paganism. Over the next two centuries other native peoples followed their precedent.

There were no more papal-sponsored crusades against Baltic pagans until the pontificate of Innocent III, half a century later. The struggle for control over the river estuaries and Mecklenburg coast continued in a succession of short campaigns. Sometimes King Valdemar I of Denmark and Henry the Lion fought each other, with the Saxons enlisting covert aid from Nyklot, who had a profitable understanding with Pomeranian pirates. But the two rulers fought as allies in 1160 in a campaign which saw Nyklot killed and the Abotrite lands distributed among the victors. Generous shares went to Lund's successive militant archbishops Eskil and Absalon (who built the stone cathedral at Roskilde and – in 1167 – founded Copenhagen). Danish power, based on naval command of inshore waters, was in the ascendant. After Valdemar I invaded and captured Rügen (1168), the responsibility for converting the island's pagans was assigned by the pope to the diocese of Roskilde, and both the king and Absalon built and endowed churches, to be served by a Danish priesthood. When in 1180 political machinations within the empire deprived Henry the Lion of the Duchy of Saxony, Denmark was the chief beneficiary along the Baltic coast, although Nyklot's Christian grandson was recognized as the first Prince of Mecklenburg. King Valdemar's son, Canute VI, accumulated lands from Schleswig to the mouth of the Oder, absorbing most of the German 'colonies' established earlier in the century. Only towns that could count on imperial protection retained some independence.

Unlike later wars, or the fighting in Old Poland a hundred years previously, these campaigns were too limited in scope to devastate the region. If the thrust to the East destroyed the outward symbols of pagan culture, it advanced the border of 'civilized', and predominantly urban, Latin Christendom. Towns like Lübeck and Schwerin and, after the turn of the century, Rostock and Stralsund, grew rapidly. By 1150, within eight years of its foundation, the new Lübeck was protected by a stone wall and had the beginnings of a port, with a quay and warehouses on the site of the Wendish settlement. Count Adolf II, the city's founder, offered special concessions to attract merchants to Lübeck from the Rhineland, Westphalia and the Netherlands.

But Lübeck's earliest years proved stormy. A contemporary account, written about 1170 by a parish priest from Holstein named Helmond, describes the pressure Henry the Lion put upon his vassal, the enterprising Adolf II. In 1152, so Helmond relates, the duke protested to Count Adolf that 'our town of Bardowick [on the lower Elbe, a few miles north of Lüneburg] was losing its citizens as a result of trade in Lübeck, for all the traders and merchants are setting up there. Likewise the people of Lüneburg are complaining that our salt-mines are running down since you opened one at Oldesloe. I ask you therefore to let us share in your town of Lübeck and your salt-mines . . . If not,' Duke Henry warned, 'We forbid all further trading at Lübeck.'

Adolf II refused and the duke carried out his threat. The merchants backed their count and stayed on; they did not wish to leave their newly built expensive houses. But Adolf and his merchants had bad luck: in 1157 a great fire swept through the narrow streets, destroying everything in its path. 'Now that our homes have been razed to the ground . . . find us a place where we can set up a town,' the merchants petitioned the duke. Henry obliged; a site was chosen nearby on the river Wakenitz and named Löwenstadt (Lion's Town) in his honour. There, however, the water proved too shallow for successful trading. At last the duke persuaded the count to let him have the burnt-out shell of the old town. According to Hermond, 'the merchants and traders at once returned with joy, leaving behind them the unwanted new town and started to rebuild the town's churches and walls. The duke sent messengers into the northern towns and states, Denmark, Sweden, Norway and Russia, offering them peace and free right of access through his town of Lübeck.'

By the end of the century merchant families from Lübeck were helping to create the port of Riga; and in 1226 Emperor Frederick II made Lübeck a free city, endowed with municipal and commercial rights. Some of these privileges survived until the coming of the Weimar Republic after the First World War. There was no other chartered Imperial City east of the Elbe. A year later Lübeck merchants provided ships and men to fight at Bornhöved, the battle in which the North German towns defeated King Valdemar II's attempts to substitute Danish hegemony for Imperial rule along the shores of Mecklenburg and Pomerania.

During the years Adolf II was building his haven for merchants at Lübeck, German-speaking entrepreneurs at Visby, in Gotland, were seeking ways to protect their interests and their ships. They were already sailing to English east coast ports – Hull, Boston, Lynn among them – and there was a steady trade between Visby and Novgorod, where a 'Gotland quarter' came into being in the second half of the twelfth century, with a church dedicated to St Olaf. It was essential to keep the East–West trade route open, free from increased lawlessness on land and piracy at sea. The Visby merchants' solution was to forsake their own rivalries: in 1161, with backing from Duke Henry the Lion, the German-speaking merchants who used Gotland formed a communal association, 'The United Gotland Travellers of the Holy Roman Empire'. Visby was transformed into a walled city, with thirty towers defending the accumulated riches of its warehouses and banking institutions; and for more than a hundred years the 'Gotland Community' flourished.

It was not, however, an association of native-born Swedish Gotlanders. The walls of Visby were designed as much to keep out the original merchant-farmers of the island as to fend off raids from foreign invaders. Among the founding fathers were Danes, Saxons and Frisians eager to open up Baltic trade. The 'United Travellers' shaped events far beyond the island of Gotland. Other trading towns came together; a league of Wendish merchants sponsored by Lübeck, Wismar and Rostock in the middle years of the thirteenth century soon gained the adherence of Stettin, Stralsund and Greifswald. But it was the commercial association of Gotland that from the turn of the twelfth century became a prototype for the 'Hanse', a term in use in Hamburg by 1266 to describe the business federation linking these 'free cities of the sea'.

The federation was never a single Hanseatic League (as it is so often called). In origin the Hanse was an alliance of convenience, bringing together the leagues of several trading towns (Wendish, Westphalian, Saxon and later Prussian). At its peak the federation included almost 200 ports or inland towns, as far apart as Cracow, Stockholm, Berlin, Riga and Arnhem. The strength of the Hanse came from the size of its mercantile marine and the privileges it won for the trading enclaves (*Kontors*) which it was allowed to establish and administer in Bergen, London, Bruges and Novgorod. Within thirty years of its creation the Hanse had a virtual monopoly of the carrying trade around Europe's northern shores. Only at the close of the fifteenth century was the monopoly loosened; even then the Hanse enjoyed another 150 years of influence in the power politics of Germany and the Baltic lands.

As the Hanse's tentacles spread outwards to the Rhineland, the Low Countries and Britain, so the importance of Gotland declined. Cologne, Brunswick, Dortmund, Bremen and Hamburg joined the Wendish ports and Danzig, Thorn and Elbing as specifically German trading cities to challenge Visby's pioneer initiative. In 1293 joint action by representatives of the North German ports secured the transfer of Visby's right to negotiate with Novgorod to Lübeck; and five years later the seal of the Gotland Community was used for the last time. Visby remained a Hanse town even after Gotland was seized by Denmark in 1361, but its merchants had little influence on general trade policy. The Hanse Diet generally met at Lübeck, although in 1367 it convened as far from the Baltic as Cologne. Perhaps it was inevitable that a mainland city like Lübeck should supplant off-shore Visby as dominant partner in this earliest of Europe's commercial empires.

Trade expansion and colonization of the southern Baltic shore continued into the thirteenth century and beyond. The holy wars of the north were resumed, though with different objectives and in a new form. Innocent III, the most statesmanlike of mediaeval popes, authorized a crusade in the Eastern Baltic soon after his election in 1198, with the immediate objective of converting the Livs and their neighbours; and in 1217 his successor, Honorius III, called for a crusade against the 'heathen' Prussians, the westernmost Baltic tribe, who were settled between the lower Vistula and the Niemen. In Livonia the effective leader of Innocent III's crusade was Albert von Buxhoevden, Bishop of Uxhüll, acting under the patronage of Archbishop Hartwig of Bremen and Hamburg. In 1201 Albert sailed up the Dvina river with a fleet of 23 ships carrying 500 heavily armed Crusaders; they landed at a Liv fishing village 15 kilometres from the sea. With Hartwig's support and backing from the merchants of Lübeck, Bishop Albert founded there the port of Riga, with a riverside quay and the beginnings of a town to attract German traders. Solidly constructed churches held promise of fulfilling the papal mission. A fort offered protection to converts, settlers and bankers alike. Within a year Albert's see was transferred from Uxhüll to his newly founded city.

To safeguard Riga, in 1202 Bishop Albert established the earliest military monastic order in northern Europe, the Knighthood of Christ in Livonia. The Sword Brothers, as they were generally called, were a mounted and well-armed élite of tough Germans who, like the Templars and Hospitallers in the Holy Land, took vows of monastic commitment and obedience. There were never many of them, probably no more than 120 monk knights at any one time. They lived in fortified 'convents' rather than in camps or castles, and they wore white tabards, with a red sword and a small cross emblazoned on their left shoulders, as did the Templars. Militarily they were kept primarily in reserve, defending settlements in winter, but ready in summer to move forward in support of the advancing crusaders when they encountered stiff resistance.

43

The knight-brothers were battle-hardened warriors: they conquered most of Livonia brutally but effectively. By 1210, the Livs and their neighbours in the upper Dvina valley were under the authority of Bishop Albert; the Catholic see of Riga and the Orthodox archdiocese of Novgorod shared a common frontier for the first time. Each settlement on the Dvina was protected by a castle, around which a chartered town developed, where German colonists were encouraged to make a new home; traces of the castles survive at Koknese and Krustpils. There was, however, mounting suspicion between the bishop and his empire builders. It was agreed that north-east of Riga the river Gauja should form a demarcation line between Albert's lands and those of the Order, and here too, among the woodland that covers the steep limestone slopes from Sigtuna to Cēsis, castles abound today. Most face each other across the valley, with the bishop's line of fortresses on the right bank keeping watch on the Order's activities along the left.

The Sword Brothers needed careful scrutiny; their conduct fell short of the ideals they professed. Although religious fanaticism fired some knight brother pioneers with zeal to bring heathen souls to God, after a few summers of campaigning the Order became greedy for land, booty and slaves, the human trophies of war. The Sword Brothers had been promised a third of any territory they won, and when disputes arose over the distribution of spoils all discipline collapsed. Their harsh treatment of the peasants prompted a series of revolts; they began to impose tolls of their own on goods conveyed down the Dvina; they launched unauthorized campaigns, notably against the Danish settlement of Estonia; they even held captive a papal legate whom Gregory IX dispatched to the Baltic in the wildly optimistic belief that the knight-brothers could be shamed into observance of the vows they had forsaken.

Thirty years after their foundation the Sword Bearers were arrogant and over-confident. They sought to recruit a crusading army to carry the war into north-western Lithuania, the region then known as Samogitia (Žemaitija today). Few responded to their call, and the enterprise proved their undoing. For in Grand Prince Mindaugas the Lithuanians had found a natural leader who was both a ruthless fighter and a skilful politician. In the summer of 1236 nemesis struck the Sword Brothers at Saulė, a place name honouring the sun goddess of Lithuania's pagan pantheon. A raiding party of knight-brothers loaded with booty was trapped on the edge of a bog and destroyed by Mindaugas's light cavalry supporting Samogitian bowmen who knew their forest and its swamps. Some fifty knight-brothers were slain that day. The occasion was full of portent: Saulė was the first major defeat inflicted on German invaders by native Balt peoples. In 1986

the Lithuanian Soviet authorities marked the 750th anniversary of this forgotten battle by erecting a huge commemorative sundial, surmounted by
a statue of an archer, in the neighbouring city of Šiauliai.

Not that the crusades in the East Baltic were ever solely German undertakings. The Swedes backed missions to secure Christian footholds in
Estonia and in southern Finland, where in 1222 one Swedish king, John
Sverkersson, was killed in a skirmish. Valdemar II, King of Denmark
1202–42, demonstrated the effectiveness of sea power by sending a fleet of
deep-draught warships to seize the Estonian offshore island of Saaremaa in
1206, establishing a base from which he mounted an invasion of northern
Estonia thirteen years later. On that occasion Valdemar came as a crusader
and was accompanied by the Archbishop of Lund, two other bishops and
their chaplains.

The campaign is steeped in legend. The formidable army that landed at
Reval was thrown into confusion by an Estonian attack from the hill of
Toompea. When the fighting became desperate the archbishop is said to
have knelt in prayer, with hands raised in supplication: a red flag with a
white cross upon it floated down from heaven, in token of God's blessing
on the Danish cause; and beneath the banner, Valdemar's army went on to
gain a historic victory. The emblem of Denmark today is still this *Dannebrog*,
the oldest national flag in the world. And Estonia is the only republic with
a capital named after the foreign invaders who made it a city; for the word
Tallinn derives from the Estonian for 'Danish Town' (*Tanni linn*).

Soon Reval/Tallinn did indeed become in every sense a Danish town,
founded little more than forty years after Copenhagen itself. A cathedral,
eight churches, a nunnery and a Dominican abbey, all planted from
Denmark, were grouped around the castle and royal treasury on Toompea
hill, where the king's lieutenant resided. Between Toompea and the quayside everything essential to administer a distant dependency was concentrated – an arsenal, commercial warehouses, stables with horses kept ready
for any expeditionary force from the homeland. It was, however, a curious
form of 'colonization'. After Valdemar completed a land settlement in 1242
the Danish kings never intervened in Estonian affairs. There was virtually
no centralized control; nominal vassals enjoyed a rare independence on
their territorial fiefs. The treasury remained in Danish hands but there were
many months when the Sword Brothers were virtual masters of the growing city. Yet, despite these obstacles, during a 120-year period thirteen successive rulers of a country 1,300 kilometres west of Estonia could count
on steady revenue from the tolls, tithes and taxes of their overseas colony.

★

Danes and Sword Brothers were still contesting Estonia and Livonia when the first attempts were made to answer Pope Honorius's call for a crusade against the Prussians, farther west. Once again the fighting began badly, with the Prussians wiping out a force of Germanic and Polish knights at Kulm (Chelmno) in 1222, as they were still being formed into an invading army. Yet another order of military monks was established to provide support for the crusaders: the Knights of the Bishop of Prussia, a small body of men, more generally known as the Knights of Dobrin (Dobrzyń), after the fort on the Vistula that served as their headquarters. Duke Konrad of Masovia, the Piast vassal prince who had suffered the heaviest losses from the Prussian incursion in 1222, was unimpressed. He sought stronger protection than Dobrin could offer. In 1225 Duke Konrad looked to the crusaders of the east and approached Hermann of Salza, the Grand Master of the Teutonic Order of the Hospital of St Mary in Jerusalem, the only one of the three military monastic brotherhoods whose knights and priests came almost entirely from the same nation.

Konrad's initiative had momentous consequences for northern Europe. Hermann of Salza was a great potentate, a knight from Thuringia created a Prince of the Holy Roman Empire by Frederick II, the ambitious Sicilian Hohenstaufen emperor; but Hermann was so independently minded that he could bargain with Frederick's papal adversaries. The Teutonic Knights – whose headquarters were then at Acre – formed a collectively rich brotherhood, respected in Palestine for their valour, their skill in building castles, and their genuine piety. They had already shown willingness to defend Christendom in Europe as well as fight in the Holy Land. In the second decade of the century they came to the assistance of Andrew II of Hungary when his Transylvanian lands were threatened by the vanguard of the Mongol Horde, but the knights received scant recognition or reward from the Hungarian king for their fourteen years of hard campaigning. This Transylvanian experience made Grand Master Hermann delay acceptance of Duke Konrad's invitation. He only agreed to send a detachment under a Provincial Master to the Vistula after Frederick II and the duke guaranteed that all territorial conquests would remain under control of the Order. At the same time the grand master curried favour with the papal Curia.

He won all he sought. In the winter of 1229–30 Gregory IX formally authorized the Teutonic Knights to conquer the 'heathen' Prussians, confirmed the grand master's autonomy and the authority in the field of his provincial master, and recognized the Order as the recruiting agency for the coming campaign. The Dominicans preached a crusade, to which the

Order's wealth and prestige ensured a ready response; in modern parlance, the Prussian Crusade became a multi-national operation co-ordinated by successive provincial masters. Over the next three decades Polish dukes, German margraves and landgraves, Swedish jarls and feudal magnates from across central Europe advanced the frontiers of northern Christendom. In one instance the international character of the armies left an ironic mark on history: for crusaders led by King Ottokar II of Bohemia fought with such tenacity at the mouth of the Pregel river in 1254–5 that in his honour the Order called the fortress founded there Königsberg. But the city became associated with a different line of kings, for from 1701 to 1861 the Hohenzollern rulers of Prussia were crowned in Königsberg. The name survived until 1946, when it was changed to honour a lightweight figure who had never come within 800 kilometres of the city, the wartime Soviet president, Mikhail Kalinin.

By the time King Ottokar was fighting his way to the mouth of the Pregel, the crusade was in its twenty-fifth year. It was in 1230, at ill-fated Kulm on the Vistula, that Provincial Master Balk established the knights' first field headquarters. He immediately sent a force upriver to forestall a second Prussian incursion by building the fort which became the castle of Thorn. Next year the knights began a methodical advance north-west down the Vistula in partnership with the Poles. The knights were formidable fighters, superior armed horsemen in themselves and supported by cross-bowmen able to concentrate the firepower of their weapons so skilfully that arrows became as deadly as artillery. Like the Sword Brothers before them, the Order colonized their conquests, building stone castles around which they developed chartered towns like Elbing, a port on the easternmost outlet of the Vistula which was founded in 1237 with financial backing from the Hanse merchants in Lübeck. Several new towns – Frauenburg (Frombork), Marienwerder (Kwidzyn) and Marienburg (Malbork), the most impressive of all – honoured the patron of the Order, the Virgin Mary; for, despite the rich pickings of conquest, in those years the military monks dutifully sought to fulfil their religious obligations and devotions.

Pope Gregory IX continued to favour the Order. In May 1237, less than a year after the disaster at Saulė, he dissolved the Knighthood of Christ in Livonia, and assigned the surviving Sword Brothers and their lands to the Teutonic Order of St Mary (who soon afterwards also took over the Knights of Dobrin). Within ten years of reaching northern Europe the Teutonic Knights appeared to be masters of western Prussia and much of Livonia. They controlled the littoral of the Gulf of Riga, the whole of the river Dvina and the lower Vistula, apart from Danzig itself.

The Order achieved this supremacy without a single defeat and with few battle casualties.

Wise statecraft would have consolidated such gains, concentrating on the development of the profitable links with the Hanse and the promotion of East–West trade. Instead, the Order overstretched its resources and accepted commitment to Pope Gregory's grand strategy of Crusade – not only against Islam, heretics and pagan nature worshippers, but also against the Greek Orthodox schismatics, and in particular 'the Patrimony of St Sophia', as Novgorod was occasionally styled. At the same time the Teutonic Knights met increasing resistance in eastern Prussia and Livonia. Moreover, from 1242 onwards, they were attacked by the hardened warriors and river fleet of Duke Svantopolk of Danzig, an ex-ally who resented trade competition from Elbing and the other newly founded towns. It took forty years for the knights to round off their conquests of Prussia and Livonia. They did not enter Danzig until 1308; and Samogitia was only briefly in their hands at the start of the following century.

The war against schismatic Novgorod was at first waged on two uncoordinated fronts, either side of the Gulf of Finland. The Swedes, who coveted the rich yield in fur and fish from Novgorod's northern territories, were willing to join a crusade against their proto-Russian trade rivals. In June 1240 a Swedish war fleet sailed into the mouth of the Neva to attack Novgorodian settlements around Lake Ladoga. It was an ill-planned undertaking; the invaders were defeated beside the river by Alexander, the young Prince of Novgorod, who was known thereafter as Alexander Nevsky in recognition of his victory. Three months later, far to the south of the Gulf, the Teutonic Knights began their campaign beyond Lake Peipus by taking the fortress of Izborsk and the trading city of Pskov. In the following summer the knights struck eastwards from Dorpat, with support from their Estonian vassals. After initial gains, they were thrown back again.

A renewed offensive next spring ended in disaster. On 5 April 1242 Alexander Nevsky's army trapped the knights and the Estonians on the southern shore of Lake Peipus and inflicted a heavy defeat. It was much too early in the year for a set-piece battle in such treacherous terrain. Chroniclers recall 'the crash of shattering spears and the sound of clashing swords'. They relate how 'the frozen sea moved', cracking under the weight of armed horsemen; and 'the ice could not be seen, for all was covered with blood', many Germans perishing in the waters of the lake.

Alexander Nevsky became the earliest, and most durable, Russian patriot hero. His defiance of German invaders was vividly evoked in 1938 by the innovative montage of Eisenstein's famous Soviet film. Almost certainly, the chroniclers – and Eisenstein with them – exaggerated both the scale of the battle and the Prince's tactical ingenuity, for the Novgorodian force may well have outnumbered the knights by three to one. But the victory beside the lake had a lasting significance. It imposed an enduring boundary between Latin Christendom and Orthodoxy. Although raiding parties of knights from Livonia made forays around the lake in the fifteenth century, no Teutonic invaders crossed the frontier in strength until the Bolshevik Revolution.

The character of the northern crusades changed in the second half of the thirteenth century. Pope Alexander IV assigned prime responsibility for waging war against Novgorod's schismatics to the kings of Sweden, leaving the Teutonic Order to concentrate on the war with the heathens of the southern Baltic shore. Birger Jarl Magnusson, virtual ruler of Sweden at mid-century, was the first soldier of eminence to respond to the Pope's call. He encouraged colonization of southern Finland eastwards along the coast from Åbo to Porvoo, mounted a second abortive attack on the Novgorodian line along the Neva (1249), and effectively conquered central Finland, building the first inland castle guarding the lakes, a red-brick mediaeval barracks at Tavesterhus.

Later in the century Birger Jarl's kinsman Tyrgils Knutson, the biggest landowner in central Sweden, countered Novgorodian raids into Finland by leading a crusade to clear the Karelian coast of 'heathen pirates'. In 1293 Tyrgils founded a fortress city at Vyborg that was to serve as the key to the Karelian isthmus through six and a half centuries of conflict. Eight years later he renewed the war with Novgorod, seeking to establish a permanent Swedish presence on Lake Ladoga. Remarkably, the Swedes succeeded in building the fort of Landskrona in the muddy marshland where the Neva flows into the sea, but the isolated outpost was untenable and it was evacuated in 1301 after a short siege. More than 400 years elapsed before Peter the Great dragooned his serfs into creating a city close to Tyrgils's chosen site.

Border warfare in Karelia continued well into the fourteenth century. When stubborn defence denied the Swedes access to Ladoga's southern settlements, they made repeated attempts to reach the lake's northern shore, but they were again beaten off. The Novgorodians, strengthened by dynastic links with the new principality of Moscow, responded to these attacks by sending an army westwards, south of the Finnish lakes. The army besieged Tavesterhus and in 1318 reached the Gulf of Bothnia, where the cathedral at Åbo was burnt to the ground. Eventually, in 1323, a truce of exhaustion was followed by the peace treaty of Nöteborg (Orekhov). The

Swedes were confirmed in possession of all south-western Karelia, including Vyborg. Novgorod received vast territories in eastern Finland, an ill-defined forest region stretching to the reindeer grazing grounds of Lapland and the fur trappers' Eldorado of the frozen North, and on to Arctic waters, where a rich yield from sea and river was disputed with the fishermen of Norway as well as with the Swedes.

South of the Gulf of Finland the Teutonic Knights were challenged by the rising power of Lithuania. Mindaugas, the Grand Prince whose horsemen helped the Samogitians humiliate the Sword Brothers at Saulė, unified Lithuania, endowing his new fortress city of Vilnius with strong walls and well sited towers. Like Nyklot of the Abotrites, Mindaugas accepted Christian baptism as a political act. In 1253 he even received the crown of a king from Pope Innocent IV, but the need to prosecute a counter-crusade against the Order made him revert to paganism before his death ten years later. In the east the Lithuanians pushed back the Tartars and acquired vast territories in what are now Belarus and the Ukraine, extending to the river Dnieper. At the same time, under Mindaugas's successors both the Teutonic Knights and the Lithuanian warriors made raids and forays along the rivers Niemen and Dvina. Eventually in 1323 Lithuania's outstanding ruler, Gediminas (Grand Prince, 1315–41), led his army through Samogitia to seize the port of Memel, devastating the 'amber coast' and sweeping inland to destroy the fort at Dobrin in September. Twenty years of uneasy peace were followed by even fiercer fighting at mid-century. Samogitia remained a region of great strategic importance, the last segment of Baltic coast separating conquered Prussia from conquered Livonia.

6

The Rise and Fall of Marienburg

THE TEUTONIC ORDER that waged unrelenting war against the Lithuanians in the fourteenth century was very different from the military monastic brotherhood Grand Master Hermann originally sent to the Vistula. The fall of Acre to the Mamelukes in 1291 put an end to crusading in the Holy Land; the Order moved headquarters to Europe, first to Venice and in the autumn of 1309 to Marienburg where the existing castle of the knights was converted into a citadel and *Residenz* for the grand master.

Marienburg, only 60 kilometres inland from Danzig and 138 kilometres from Thorn, soon became in effect a capital city, compact in size but with an authoritative voice in Europe's affairs. For the Order claimed complete sovereignty over a Teutonic Prussia and a Teutonic Livonia that, at its zenith, stretched along southern Baltic shores from the mouth of the Vistula to the Narva. The rights of the Archbishop of Riga and his three suffragan bishops were (grudgingly) acknowledged and token respect given to the statutes of the Lübeck merchants. But the grand master was, in all but name, doge of the Baltic throughout the fourteenth century; he was at the same time master of a religious order, a commercial magnate, head of a well-ordered administrative system, and commander of a highly efficient war machine.

The Teutonic Order owned more ships in the Hanse than any individual merchants or association and retained a monopoly of the lucrative amber trade well into the fifteenth century. There was a huge granary within the eastern walls of Marienburg Castle, for the Prussian plains produced a fine harvest of rye and barley. Most of the grain brought good returns to the Great Treasury when exported from Danzig, along with timber and strangely contrasting cargoes of pitch and tar, furs and wax. The six Prussian towns affiliated to the Hanse – Danzig, Elbing, Braunsberg (Braniewo) and Königsberg on the sea and the river ports of Kulm and Thorn – were completely under the grand master's control; he supervised their city assemblies and determined how they should vote at the Hanse Diet. The grand master was the only territorial ruler granted *ex officio* membership of the Hanse, which remained technically a federation of free cities. Small wonder if occasionally English merchants referred to the grand master as *caput Hansae* (Head of the Hanse).

While Marienburg was the new Prussia's administrative centre, management of the economy was shared with officials at Königsberg, home of the Order's Great Treasury. The provincial master in Riga was in effect governor of Livonia and its dependencies. He had an unenviable task, calling for rare diplomatic tact. He was obliged to conform to general policy laid down in Marienburg while accommodating the needs of Riga's patrician merchants and preventing simmering disputes with the archbishop and his suffragans from coming to the boil. In practice, the provincial masters rarely settled Riga's own affairs, but they presided over a well constructed administrative system based upon fifteen geographical districts, each controlled by a functionary of the Order. After the purchase of Estonia from the Danes in 1346 the masters brought good government to a land accustomed to weak rule, working with, rather than against, the knights of the Harrien and Wierland districts, who had won lordly privileges from the Danish Crown.

In both Prussia and Livonia generous grants of land and initial exemption from payment of tithes encouraged migration. Among those who headed east were knights from the Rhineland and enterprising merchants, frustrated by patrician exclusiveness of burghers in their home towns. Tillers of the soil from Holstein, Saxony and Westphalia found that even a peasant could count on receiving the equivalent of 20 hectares. All settlers, whether in the towns or the countryside, were obliged to render military service when war came to their region. A colonial caste system evolved, in which the original knight-brothers became territorial magnates, rarely mindful of their monastic vows. A lower baronage of later migrants had sufficient status to rank as manorial feudatories. Native-born 'Old Prussian' tribal leaders who were willing to be baptized and co-operate with their Christian overlords were allowed to retain land.

Some native Old Prussians, Letts and Estonians remained free peasants. Most, however, were treated as underdogs, lesser breeds within the feudal law, closely bound in service to their new masters. When they rose in revolt, a terrible vengeance fell on the Teutonic colonialists; and the retributive punishment subsequently inflicted on the rebels was correspondingly harsh. 'Savagery, cruelty and tyranny' marked the Order's conduct of the wars, the Archbishop of Riga told Pope Boniface VIII at the turn of the century. His complaint had no effect. The knights continued to mould their northern domains with an iron hand. Such is the way of empire builders.

★

The outstanding soldier-statesman of the Teutonic Order was Winrich von Kniprode, in the 1340s military commander along the Niemen and from 1352 to 1382 grand master at Marienburg. In a decade of campaigns in the eastern Baltic he learnt the need for strongly fortified winter-quarters and for a patient field diplomacy that in later years enabled him to conclude expedient alliances with disgruntled factions in the enemy camp, notably the lesser Lithuanian princes. Even before becoming grand master he had encouraged his two predecessors to advance the considerable sum to the provincial master in Riga to purchase Estonia from the king of Denmark, thus allowing Estonia to become a dependency of the Livonian Knights in a loose feudal confederation that survived for two centuries. But Kniprode's most enduring achievement was a defensive barrier in depth west of the Masurian lakes to protect newly colonized Prussia. Sixteen forts or castles commanded every route emerging from the forests or from the marshland that made the region so treacherous. Shortly before his death in 1382 he approved plans to convert the grand master's *Residenz* at Marienburg into a magnificent palace, a grandiose concept that took seventeen years to fulfil.

In his forays (*reyse*) up the Niemen and Vilija, Grand Master von Kniprode was as brutal as his contemporary Edward of Woodstock – the Black Prince – whose raids (*chevauchées*) systematically devastated the heart of France during the second phase of the Hundred Years War. Like Edward, von Kniprode was criticized for the cost of his palace building and the extravagant splendour of the entertainment he provided during the long periods of inactivity between the *reyse*. But the money was well spent. In the wake of the Black Death, the plague that weakened armies in the field in 1350–51, the grand master's style of campaigning bolstered the Order's military effectiveness by attracting new, short-term knight recruits, anxious to fulfil crusading vows as a form of atonement but welcoming a companionship in arms known to be far from penitential.

Some came from England, where the Hanse Steelyard beside the Thames acquainted Londoners with 'Easterling' traders. (Cannon Street Station stands on the site today.) Geoffrey Chaucer – controller of customs in the port of London in the 1370s, the years when he is thought to have devised the *Canterbury Tales* – tells us in the Prologue that his knight fought for the Order: 'In Lettow [Lithuania] hadde he reysed and in Ruse'. So did many of Edward III's knights and squires, when not rampaging through France. As early as Michaelmas 1349, for example, we hear of forty English knights building a castle and chapel to receive converted Lithuanians; and one of the earliest Knights of the Garter, John Montague (later third Earl of Salisbury), fought in Prussia during Winrich von Kniprode's grand mastership.

But after Kniprode's death did campaigning in the Baltic hinterland fall short of expectation? The Black Prince's nephew, Henry, Earl of Derby (later King Henry IV), sailed from Boston in Lincolnshire on 19 July 1390 with a party of eleven knights, twenty-seven esquires and all the backing that 110 servants, grooms and minstrels could provide and funds from his father, John of Gaunt, sustain. On leaving Danzig the expedition headed for the Niemen, to support the Teutonic Knights as they ousted the Lithuanians from Kaunas. The combined army then turned south-east and tried to fight its way into Vilna, with Derby's men capturing one of the western forts. But this was all that the expedition achieved. Bouts of sickness, and tension with their German hosts, induced Derby to take his men back to the Vistula in October. There they lingered through the winter, mostly at Danzig. With the coming of spring they sailed back home.

Undaunted, Derby drummed up support for a second expedition. In July 1392 he set out again, this time with some 250 crusaders. They never took the field. On reaching Königsberg Derby found the Order had no need of his services. Most of his men seem to have been left to make their own way back to England. The Earl, with a retinue of fifty, spent ten months on a Grand Tour of the European courts; he even took ship from Venice for the Holy Land, though as a pilgrim rather than a crusader.

By the closing years of the century there was doubt, not least in Rome, if any campaign of the knights constituted a crusade. For in a marriage contract concluded at Krevo in August 1385 the Grand Duke Jogaila of Lithuania undertook 'to join his lands . . . to the crown of the kingdom of Poland for all time'; and on 15 February 1386 he was duly baptized in Cracow Cathedral. As King Wladislaw II Jagiello he shared the throne of Poland with his twelve-year-old wife, Jadwiga. She was Casimir the Great's great-niece and, in accordance with the Privilege of Kosice (*see p. 37*), had been elected 'king' by the Polish nobles two years previously. Jogaila's conversion, and the astonishing dynastic union that followed it, made Lithuania like Poland, a 'Christian' rather than a 'heathen' land. With what was presumably a gesture of goodwill between Catholic neighbours, Grand Master Zöllner, Kniprode's successor, was invited to become Jagiello's godfather. The honour was declined.

The war with Lithuania continued. Grand Masters Wallenrod and Conrad von Jungingen insisted that, since Jagiello recruited schismatic Russians and 'godless' Tartars from the Crimea, the knights were justified in going into battle beneath the Cross of Catholic Christendom. By playing off rival factions in Lithuania and Poland, Jungingen was able in 1405 to conquer Samogitia without Jagiello's intervention. The land link between Prussia and Livonia seemed finally achieved.

Two years later Conrad von Jungingen was dead, and the electoral conclave of the Order agreed to accept his brother Ulrich as the new grand master. It was a fatal choice. Ulrich had none of Conrad's military prestige or natural authority: the Samogitians revolted, the burgomasters of the Hanse ports of Thorn and Danzig sought to shake off the Order's shackles and join the Polish kingdom, and the rival Lithuanian factions at once ended their quarrels. Even though the grand master's diplomacy failed to win him a reliable ally, he was determined on a preventive war against Poland.

The initiative, however, was seized by Jagiello. Early in July 1410 the king massed an army of 34,000 Poles, Lithuanians and Tartar, Russian and Czech mercenaries on the lower Vistula. Most of the army was mounted on good horses and could move swiftly. Jagiello headed north-west, so as to slip behind Kniprode's line of forts, with Marienburg itself as his objective. On 15 July the invaders found the knights, under the grand master's command, holding the crest of a ridge between the villages of Grunwald and Tannenberg, 100 kilometres south-east of Marienburg. Ulrich von Jungingen had hastily mobilized almost as many men as Jagiello, including Swiss and Westphalian volunteers. The knights may well have been over-confident, as one contemporary suggested. They were veterans, better armed and in a good defensive position. They could even count on the support of bombards, primitive cannon.

The battle lasted six hours. It began with the ritual discharge of shot from the bombards, a noisy overture rather than an effective repellent. Attacks by the Tartar horsemen and later by Lithuanian cavalry were repulsed with little difficulty. The knights then gave pursuit, charging cumbersomely forward at the centre of the line. At once, like the French at Agincourt five years later, they ran into difficulties. As they moved down to the soft, sandy terrain they were impeded by the weight of their heavy armour and found themselves checked by Russians fighting on foot. The Poles, lighter armed and with smaller horses, then struck decisively from the right flank, toppling the knights. Tartar horsemen gave support. In the general mêlée all the senior officers of the Order were killed, including the grand master and his deputy. Four hundred knight-brothers and an unknown number of auxiliaries perished at Tannenberg.

The Poles and Lithuanians also suffered heavy casualties. It was some days before Jagiello could resume his advance on Marienburg, eager to consummate his victory by taking the Order's headquarters. By 25 July

Marienburg was encircled and the Poles brought up cannon to lob stone shot into the newly completed palace. But the solid walls of the town and castle remained inviolate, while a full granary ensured that the defenders could not be starved into submission. Dysentery broke out in the Lithuanian camp and there was a whiff of mutiny among mercenaries eager to be paid off before the coming of winter. On 19 September Jagiello raised the seven-week siege and began peace negotiations.

A treaty was concluded at Thorn in February 1411: the Order kept all conquests prior to 1409 except for Dobrin, which passed to Poland, and Samogitia, which was to be held jointly for life by Jagiello (who died in 1434, aged eighty-two) and his cousin, Grand-Duke Vytautas. The Order had to pay a huge sum to Jagiello as ransom money for the return of prisoners. Perhaps the greatest losers by the treaty were the Hanse patricians in Danzig and Thorn, who hoped to gain more commercial independence under Polish rule than the Order permitted. Once peace was concluded, the new grand master ordered the execution of the burgomasters in both cities.

The Teutonic Order never recovered from defeat at Tannenberg. The knights lost prestige and credibility. Few foreign volunteers answered calls for crusades against schismatic Russians, Lithuanian crypto-pagans or – a new enemy – the Hussite heretics of Bohemia. In tussles of diplomacy the popes now backed Jagiellonian Catholic Poland. Grand masters could no longer dictate terms to the Hanse and their share of the association's trade dropped dramatically; in 1440 Grand Master von Russdorf ruefully admitted that the revenue received by the Order from commerce was less than a tenth its value before Tannenberg.

Eventually in 1453 Danzig, Elbing and Thorn joined the Poles in a war against the Order that dragged on for thirteen years. With the Livonian Order – as the knight-brothers based in Riga were now generally called – forced to look to the protection of the eastern borders against a new threat from Russia, the knight-brothers of Prussia were left to fend for themselves. In June 1457 the Poles entered Marienburg Castle, handed over to them by mercenary auxiliaries whose demands for overdue back pay the Order could not meet. In October 1466 the second Treaty of Thorn confirmed Polish suzerainty over the Order's best farming land along the lower Vistula and over the west Prussian Hanse ports. For more than 300 years these Polish lands were known, slightly confusingly, as 'Royal Prussia'. Danzig became a 'Free City', also under the protection of the kings of Poland.

The knights retained only Königsberg, which became the Order's final headquarters, together with the amber coast northwards to Memel and the rump of east Prussia. Even for these territories – known at first as 'Eastern Prussia' and from 1525 to 1772 as 'Ducal Prussia' – the grand master took an oath of fealty to the Polish king. The Order still had a role to play in the eastern Baltic, particularly in Livonia and in shaping the character of Prussia, but the years of crusading conquest were at an end.

7

Ships, Pirates and Adventurers

DESPITE ALMOST CONTINUOUS warfare around northern shores, ships plied the waters of the Baltic in ever-increasing numbers throughout the later Middle Ages. Burgeoning commerce, handled almost exclusively by the Hanse, demanded bigger and better vessels. When trading began from Lübeck in the 1160s goods were still mainly loaded into knorrs, the modified Viking longships with a cargo capacity rarely exceeding 20 tons. By the end of the century, however, the shipwrights were turning out a superior vessel, the cog, a ship originating in the northern Netherlands and carrying eight times as much as any predecessor. Cogs were clinker-built, rounded at the bow and stern, about 28 metres long and 6 metres in the beam, with fore and aft 'castles', a single heavy and cumbersome sail and a rudder. They seem generally to have had crews of ten or twelve. In good weather a cog sailed at 5 knots, rising to 10 knots with a following wind; a voyage from Lübeck to Danzig would normally take four days, with five more days needed to reach Riga.

The cog became the archetypal Hanse ship. It was depicted on official seals of cities and appears in many paintings of the time. But within the Baltic it was superseded late in the fourteenth century by the hulk, a flat-bottomed and broader-beamed vessel, able to carry more than 300 tons, but less manoeuvrable. For longer voyages out into the ocean, the Danzig shipyards built carracks, three-masted ships closer in size and design to the caravels with which Columbus, Diaz and Magellan opened up the new world. The Hanse merchant fleet – some 750 vessels at the close of the fifteenth century – included sailing ships smaller than cogs, intended for deep sea voyages but later employed on the broader rivers and for coastal trade. Galleys or longships with a sail penetrated the Elbe south of Hamburg and the upper Vistula, Niemen and Dvina, if the chronic fighting along their banks permitted. During the Thirteen Years War between Poland and the Teutonic Knights (1454–66) trains of as many as a hundred barges filled with grain were escorted down the Vistula to reach the granaries and roadstead of Danzig.

The prime objective of the Hanse was to keep trade moving, for that was the surest way to maintain commercial prosperity. Into the Baltic, Hanse vessels brought cloth and wool from England, cloth from Flanders, tin from Cornwall, lamb-skins and coney-skins from Scotland, wine from France and, increasingly in the later Middle Ages, salt from the Bay of Bourgneuf, south of the Loire estuary, and from Portugal. Salt, of course, was essential in the markets of northern Europe as the only way to preserve the food yield of summer and autumn for consumption in the ice-bound months of winter.

Out of the Baltic the ships carried furs, flax and wax from Novgorod and Livonia; amber from Königsberg; timber, pitch and resin from the forests of Lithuania and the Vistulan basin; furs from northern Sweden in ships from Lübeck; rye, wheat and barley from the plains of Prussia and Poland; and minerals and metal from Sweden and the outer ranges of the Carpathians, south of Cracow. Some cargoes served markets within the Baltic, notably butter from Stockholm and cattle from Kalmar. The Wendish towns were also markets for surplus butter and for oxen from Jutland, but agrarian Denmark, for the most part, held little interest for the Hanse.

The burghers of Lübeck were Sweden's principal entrepreneurs. From 1347, when a charter was granted specifically to the free miners of Falun, the merchants benefited in particular from the regular transport of copper through Stockholm and Lübeck itself to Flanders. Lübeck, too, played a central role in the Norwegian fish industry: dried cod and herring origi-nally loaded in Bergen were packed into barrels and either sent in bigger vessels to other ports or transported overland to the cities of inner Germany and Austria. Some Lübeck ships would take flour to Bergen, cross the North Sea with Norwegian cod for Boston, and return to their home port with bales of cloth from Stamford or Lincoln or Nottingham.

The fur trade was always lucrative, but for English consumers the most valuable imports were timber for their ships and wax for their candles. The Hanse kept their monopoly of wax longer than for any other commodity. Baltic wax was still giving light to England's monastic cathedrals and abbeys during the first twenty years of Henry VIII's reign. Protestantism forced the trade into recession. In 1528–9, the last twelve months before the English Reformation began in earnest, Hanse merchants brought 344,080 kilos of wax into the kingdom. For 1540–44, the five years following Henry's final dissolution of the monasteries, wax imports were down to an annual average of only 83,337 kilos.

Between the ending of the Crusades and the expansion of the Ottoman Turks within Europe, trade in silk, carpets and other luxuries from the eastern Mediterranean brought wealth to Venice, Genoa, Pisa and Ragusa (Dubrovnik). But riches from the East still followed a familiar trail to the Baltic, boosting commercial enterprise in Reval, Danzig and Stettin, especially after the union of Lithuania and Poland. Some Hanse ports had local specialities. As late as 1368 Lüneburg salt was the main export from Lübeck, although the merchants had diversified and the city's prosperity was not by then dependent on the yield of the salt-pans; 680 ships entered or left the port that year. Wismar rather than Lübeck became the leading beer town of the Baltic, even though there were hop-gardens beside the Trave. In 1460 Wismar had 200 breweries and a brewers' majority on the city council, and was exporting beer around the inland sea as well as to Bergen and Flanders. But Bremen and Hamburg, Hanse ports serving North Sea trade rather the Baltic, were the main suppliers of beer to the Netherlands and to Germany as a whole.

The most concentrated specialization of all was in Skåne, the centre of Europe's herring industry at the turn of the fourteenth and fifteenth centuries. Ships from Lübeck would bring Lüneburg salt, together with flour and beer, to Skanör, Malmö and Falster. They would return to Lübeck laden with salted herring – in 1400 some 65,000 barrels in a single year. The herring trade declined in the following century, partly because the fish migrated to the more saline North Sea, but also because of Dutch competition. At the same time, the yield of salt from Lüneburg lessened year by year. By 1450 the trade in both salt and herrings was in reverse; much more salt was brought into the Baltic from France and Portugal than left Lübeck.

Trade disputes between the Hanse and foreign rivals were generally settled by embargoes, blockade or the closure of ports. But from 1227 until 1566 there were skirmishes at sea, and occasional battles, in which Hanse vessels participated. No ships were built specifically for warfare until the sixteenth century. Fighting men embarked in cogs to serve as boarding parties; archers manned the 'castles', fore and aft. By the late fifteenth century light cannons (culverins), cast in bronze like church bells, could be placed aboard hulks, carracks and upriver barges. From about 1350 ships began to sail in convoy, with at least two escorts carrying men-at-arms. This protection was as much to fend off pirates as to counter enemy action; twenty years later, when the Hanse towns were at war with Norway and Denmark, the number of escorts was considerably increased.

There was, however, no Hanse Navy. Significantly the armed escorts were called, not warships, but 'peaceships' (*vredenschepe*). Wars with the Dutch (1438–41) and the English (1470–74) were, on both occasions, precipitated by the seizure of Hanse ships and cargoes at sea in response to trade restrictions imposed on foreign vessels in the Baltic ports. For offensive operations the Hanse merchants resorted to privateering: they commissioned privately owned armed vessels to intercept and seize enemy ships. The captain and owners of a privateer shared the value of the captured goods and any ransom money received for the release of worthies taken captive.

Some of these Hanse sea-dogs passed into legend. Among them was a Danzig privateer and city councillor named Pawest, who sailed a captured French ship on raids down the Channel as far west as Ushant. Better known, however, is Paul Beneke, whose operations were backed by Danzig's Guild Fraternity of St George. Beneke left the Baltic and sailed English waters during the 1470s, a time when rumbling disputes with London erupted into open warfare. On one occasion Beneke took prisoner the Earl of Salisbury, for whom a good ransom was paid. Early in 1471 he captured the Caen-owned *Le Cygne,* as she crossed the Channel with no less a dignitary than the Lord Mayor of London aboard.

An even more rewarding prize came his way two years later, a ship crossing from Flanders to England on the first stage of a homeward voyage to the river Arno and Florence; she carried a rich cargo of alum, silks, brocades, tapestries – and Hans Memling's new triptych, *The Last Judgement.* Beneke was not avaricious; the trappings of luxury in the cargo guaranteed good money for the owners and pickings for his crew, and he could afford to be generous with another man's munificence. Agnolo Tani, the Medici agent in Bruges, had commissioned the triptych to present to a church in Florence, at a time when the city basked under the princely rule of Lorenzo the Magnificent. Instead, Beneke presented it to the Marienkirche, Danzig's red-brick basilica, then nearing completion.

The Medici would not let Beneke's actions go unchallenged. Forty years of litigation won some compensation, long after Agnolo Tani, Beneke and Lorenzo were dead. But, apart from a Napoleonic interlude at the Louvre, the Memling remained in the Marienkirche. It was still there early in the Second World War, before being removed to safety ahead of the Russian invaders. They found it, however, hidden in a mine at Halle, and for ten years the triptych was again on display as a trophy of war, this time at Leningrad. At last in 1956 it was handed to the Poles, to become a showpiece of Gdańsk's National Museum. One day perhaps it may return to the chapel at the foot of the tower of the Marienkirche, where a copy now stands. Memling portrayed Agnolo and his wife on the wings of the triptych. If they look bewildered, it is small wonder.

*

Piracy – as distinct from legalized privateering in time of war – was endemic to the Baltic. It was as natural a vocation for Wendish Abotrites in Prince Nyklot's time as for seafarers along the coasts of Devon or Fife 300 years later. The scourge became especially bad in the closing years of the fourteenth century, when the Dukes of Mecklenburg – lineal descendants of Nyklot – reverted to family practice and (like Warwick the Kingmaker in England) harnessed piracy to dynastic ambition. The Hanse in the Mecklenburg ports of Rostock and Wismar connived at these activities, for self-protection and in some instances for personal gain. The island of Bornholm was seized and raids made on distant ports, from Norway round to Finland. On 22 April 1393, so an English merchant records, 'several wrongdoers and bandits from Wismar and Rostock in the Hanse sailed in a large ship to the town of Bergen, took the town by storm, seized the merchants and goods there, set fire to their houses, and demanded a huge ransom from the inhabitants'. Vyborg had already suffered similar treatment, and Malmö became the target later in the year.

The 'wrongdoers' were not smash-and-grab raiders, acting independently. In the Baltic even piracy had an embryonic trading association, the Vitalien Brotherhood (*Vitalienbrüder*). The chief lair of the Brothers was the inlet of Vivesholm on Gotland, 30 kilometres down the coast from Visby. By 1397 they formed so grave a menace that all the year's exports from the Prussian ports were sent westwards in no more than three convoys. Next summer conditions were even worse: only one heavily escorted convoy from Danzig and Elbing was able to pass safely through the Øresund with cargoes for the West.

The merchants looked for alternative routes. Use was made of the 65-kilometre, centuries-old overland trail from Lübeck to Hamburg, part of the salt road from Lüneburg; and in 1398 a canal with locks was completed to link the river Stecknitz, a Trave tributary, with the Delvenau, a tributary of the Elbe. Some goods could now be carried by water from the Baltic to the North Sea. But the waterway – which took eight years to construct – was not an embryonic Kiel Canal. Only narrow barges could pass the locks. As a commercial venture, the value of the pirate-free route was slight. Moreover both the road link and the canal only handled goods that passed through Lübeck. Ships with cargoes from Danzig and the eastern Baltic still had to run the gauntlet of pirates lurking in the sandy bays along Mecklenburg's indented coast.

By the spring of 1399 it was clear that mass piracy threatened the prosperity of the Teutonic Order's 'colonies' in Prussia and Livonia. In exasperation, Grand Master Conrad von Jungingen marshalled the knights to resolve the problem. Four thousand men-at-arms were assigned to a fleet of eighty-four ships assembled at Danzig. A second, smaller fleet gathered in the Trave to embark soldiers at Lübeck. The Danzig fleet landed on Gotland, where the knights attacked and destroyed the brotherhood's lair at Viveholm, while the Lübeckers denied them shelter along the Wendish coast. Klaus Störtebeker, the most impudent and enterprising of Vitalien raiders, escaped to the North Sea, probably through the Great Belt, and began to threaten the Frisian Islands; but in 1401 he was captured and, along with his followers, beheaded in Hamburg. For a few years the Baltic remained pirate free.

Piracy was, of course, also a menace to ships from non-Hanse ports. Not that there were many of them in the Baltic at the end of the fourteenth century. The Hanse fraternities were jealously exclusive. English and Dutch ships are first known to have penetrated the Baltic about 1250, braving navigational hazards along the Jutland coast before sailing down the Kattegat to trade at the annual salt fish fair at Skanör. The English sold woollen goods and cloth and returned home with herrings, salt and hides. But threats from the Hanse towns that they might suspend all trade with England put an end to these visits; any general embargo would cause a slump in the wool trade. Not until the cloth boom of Edward III's reign were English vessels again seen in the Baltic, and then only fleetingly.

For much of the 1350s the merchant adventurers unloaded cloth and took aboard grain, timber and copper at Danzig, Elbing and Stralsund. Several of the adventurers even rented houses and shops and English registered ships are known to have sailed from Danzig to Hull, Boston, Ipswich and down the Channel to round Land's End and land the last of their cargo at Bristol or at Newport, where customs duty was lower. But outside competition – whether English, Dutch or Novgorodian Russian – alarmed the Hanse, and by 1357 Danzig and Elbing were again closed to foreigners, though the English connection with Stralsund lasted longer. There was a brief thaw when English knights arrived to support the Teutonic Order in Lithuania and by 1390, the year that Derby's expedition reached Danzig, the merchant adventurers were allowed to elect a governor who controlled business with the Hanse in the port. Friction between grand masters and merchants hampered the English traders. They found themselves challenged by new regulations that changed the sizes in which cloth might be cut, forbade wives and families from joining them in Danzig, and prevented the governor from convening assemblies to assist him. Not until 1579 were merchants from the newly chartered Eastland

Company allowed to settle and establish a depot, and then at Elbing rather than Danzig. Even this concession was of limited value, for the working of the port was already hampered by silt brought down-river by the Vistula and its tributaries. 'Our ship passed through the mud like a plough upon land,' wrote Fynes Moryson, disembarking at Elbing fourteen years after the company began trading there.

The Dutch had greater success than the English in challenging the Hanse hold on Baltic trade. By 1497 more ships registered in the Netherlands were passing through the Øresund than from any other country. Seventy years later, on the eve of the Dutch revolt, nine in every ten ships leaving Danzig was a Hollander. There were five reasons for Dutch success: good seamanship; the building of ships especially suited for Baltic conditions; a willingness to meet market demands by undercutting rivals and bringing cheap salt from the Bay of Bourgneuf and cloth from both Flanders and England; new shipboard techniques of gutting and preserving herring; and sheer enterprise and persistence – Dutch traders reached Novgorod as early as 1432, purchasing flax and wax there. Moreover, after 1466 the Dutch were the first people to take advantage of Danzig's new status as a Free City in special relationship with the Polish Crown. The Polish landowners sent their grain to the port for shipment to Zeeland, Holland and Flanders. During the summer of 1471 1,000 ships left Danzig with corn for the cities of the Netherlands. A hundred years later more than 2,000 ships headed westwards through the Danish Sound in the seven months that the sea was free from ice. The Baltic, so often perceived as a backwater, remained a thriving waterway for Europe's commerce, even though by then the navigators of Portugal had opened up new routes to more distant shores.

8

The Chimera of Kalmar

A S MASTERS OF the Øresund and the Belts the political vagaries of Denmark's kings were a matter of prime concern to all who traded in the Baltic. So, too, were the affairs of neighbouring Sweden, where the ambition of patriarch landowners and the persistence of narrowly regional loyalties had delayed the emergence both of centralized royal government and of a unified economy. The possibility of a Scandinavian empire or confederation seemed remote. Disunion benefited the Hanse. No trading league within the inland sea wished to see entry into the Baltic monitored by a single unified power.

Few Danish kings in the late Middle Ages ruled with character or determination. The challenge of Valdemar II, who had understood sea power and planted the Danish colony in Estonia, was checked in 1227 after the battle of Bornhöved, although in the last year of his reign he fitted out a fleet to support the Teutonic Knights and his colonial vassals in their war with Novgorod. His five successors were hampered by internal conflict between crown, bishops and baronage and it was not until the early fourteenth century that a combination of shrewd diplomacy and blatant aggression allowed Eric VI to seize and briefly hold Lübeck, Wismar, Rostock and Stralsund. But on Eric's death in 1319 Denmark lapsed once more into anarchy, with the elective character of the monarchy exploited by neighbouring princes in northern Germany. Three claimants jostled for the Danish throne: each was deposed – two of them twice over – before an eight-year interregnum brought a pause in the wearisome game of crown grabbing. Only in 1340 was Denmark's decline arrested, with the accession of Valdemar IV, the most far-sighted of Eric VI's many nephews. 'Another day (*Atterdag*) will come,' the young king reputedly declared, confident he could restore Denmark's unity and authority; and it is as 'Valdemar IV Atterdag' that Danes remember him.

The young Atterdag was a patient ruler, not prepared to risk war to restore Denmark's authority until his finances and his army were in good order. Crown lands appropriated during twenty years of anarchy were redeemed, and the kingdom gained a judicature and a state council (Rigsrad). Over-mighty subjects lost their castles, if not their heads. Atterdag had no grand design for making the Baltic a Danish lake. His earliest initiative in foreign affairs was to pull back from the Gulf of Finland, handing Estonia to the Teutonic Order for a good price. He was content to see his neighbour King Magnus II Eriksson of Sweden look to the East, committing his resources to crusades against Novgorod's Orthodox schismatics. Atterdag's ambitions lay nearer home. He was determined to recover Helsingborg, the fortified port across the Sound from Helsingør. Magnus Eriksson had purchased Helsingborg as recently as 1331, as part of a dubious deal, brokered by the Church, which ceded to Sweden the provinces of Skåne and Blekinge. Ironically the burden of debt incurred by this purchase and the campaigns in the East provoked a rebellion in southern Sweden, supported by Magnus's younger son, and in 1358 the Swedish king was forced to seek assistance from Denmark. Atterdag's price for aid was the retrocession of Helsingborg. When, a year later, the son died and the rebellion petered out, the Danes kept Helsingborg, as a foothold from which to step deeper into Sweden should Magnus's kingdom continue to fall apart.

Magnus Eriksson is one of Europe's unluckiest kings. He was elected to the Swedish throne in July 1319, two months after inheriting Norway's (non-elective) throne from his maternal grandfather, Haakon Longlegs; Magnus was then a child of three. Twelve years elapsed before he could be declared of age and during this minority his hands were effectively tied by Sweden's self-perpetuating oligarchy, the Council of the Realm (Riksrad). Even so, Magnus's personal rule began well. Marriage to Blanche of Namur was followed by the birth of two sons and in 1335 a royal proclamation abolishing the last vestiges of serfdom in Sweden. Nearly twenty years later he approved a Land Law, which set down a basic legal code for all Sweden and established the important constitutional principle that the Riksrad was a council responsible to the community as a whole rather than to the king. But Magnus's debts mounted year by year, despite the short-term palliative of negotiating loans from his brother-in-law, the Duke of Mecklenburg. The Council of the Realm complained at the lease of crown castles to Germans as security for the loans, and the councillors also mocked the king's liking for the company of pages and stable-boys. One young favourite was even created a duke. In England, only a few years previously, such conduct had culminated in King Edward II's deposition and brutal murder.

Magnus's lifestyle stirred the wrath of a virtuous and formidable member of his court. Birgitta Gudmarsson, daughter of one landed magnate and wife of another, was the queen's chief lady-in-waiting. In 1399, eighteen years after her death, Birgitta was canonized as St Bridget; and she is rightly revered as a visionary mystic and as the founder of the Order of St Saviour, the Brigittines. But the living Birgitta must have been, literally, a holy terror. She verbally lashed moral laxity at court and encouraged Magnus's crusading ventures. To the good fortune of all visitors to Sweden she also browbeat him into surrendering a royal palace for her beautifully sited abbey of Vadstena. In widowhood the future of her Order shaped her thoughts and her actions, and in 1349 she left Sweden for Rome to begin a long fight for papal backing.

As if to give terrible point to St Bridget's moral strictures, her departure was followed by the coming of the Black Death later in the year. Bubonic plague spread rapidly across the kingdom, apparently brought to Scandinavia in a ship from England. By the end of 1350 the Black Death may have killed as many as 200,000 of Magnus Eriksson's subjects, about 30 per cent of the population. Quite apart from the human suffering, the plague was a social and economic disaster. Shortage of men left farms abandoned, cut crown revenue and made it harder for the king to raise an army.

The plague swept over Denmark, too, but with less intensity. Valdemar IV Atterdag was able to assemble a powerful force at Helsingborg with which in 1359–60 he recovered the remainder of Skåne, together with neighbouring Blekinge and Halland. In July 1361 he sailed northwards on a more ambitious expedition, the invasion of the Swedish island of Gotland. Magnus Eriksson was taken by surprise and was not ready to plunge into a war. Atterdag had little difficulty in defeating the native-born and poorly armed small farmers in a battle fought outside the walls of Visby. It is not clear how much support the Gotlanders received from the Hanse traders, whose relations with their extra-mural neighbours remained strained. When mass graves beside the battlefield were excavated almost a hundred years ago, good quality armour was found, as well as leather fragments from peasant clothing; but one of Europe's finest walled cities had surrendered without resisting for a single day of siege. Was there collusion? If so, it did not save all the warehouses. Booty was loaded aboard the ships, with Viking zeal. The richest haul was reputedly lost in a storm at sea, a fate that also had Viking precedence.

Atterdag confirmed Visby's chartered Hanse privileges. South of the Baltic, however, the merchants saw his invasion as a challenge to their commercial hegemony. Next spring they belatedly came to Magnus Eriksson's support. A fleet of more than fifty ships set out from the Wendish ports, under the command of Burgomaster Wittenborg of Lübeck, with

Copenhagen as his main objective. But the Burgomaster was a poor strategist or a poor navigator – or both. He sailed past Copenhagen and landed troops to besiege Helsingborg, thus giving Atterdag an opportunity to intercept the fleet. Danish boarding parties captured twelve of the largest ships. The remainder limped back to Lübeck, the unfortunate Burgomaster Wittenborg with them. He was later executed.

The Danish successes exasperated the Swedish nobles, many of whom had by now despaired of Magnus. Another rebellion challenged what little remained of the king's authority. So desperate was his plight that he sought sanctuary at the Danish court and again called on Atterdag for help. On this occasion Denmark's price was a marriage contract. At Roskilde in 1363 Atterdag's ten-year-old daughter Margaret (Margrete) married Magnus's surviving son, twenty-three-year-old King Haakon VI, in whose favour in 1355 Magnus had abdicated as ruler of Norway. For the first time in 300 years there was a faint prospect of an eventual Nordic dynastic union.

The Swedish rebels were outraged by the marriage. They mistrusted Haakon, who a few months earlier had supported their rebellion and even briefly held his father captive before the marriage project was mooted. The Council of the Realm deposed Magnus and, despite their earlier hostility to German influences, elected his nephew, Albert of Mecklenburg, to succeed him. With support from both Atterdag and Haakon, Magnus Eriksson fought to recover his Swedish throne, but he lost a battle at Gataskogen and was taken prisoner. King Albert held his uncle in harsh confinement at Stockholm for several years until Haakon raised the money to ransom him. Misfortune dogged poor Magnus to the end. In 1374, at the age of sixty-eight, he drowned in Norway.

After 1361 the Gotlanders reviled Atterdag as 'Valdemar the Wicked'. Within Denmark, however, his subjects thought highly of him: he ruled wisely, constant in his resolve to preserve orderly government. But over-confidence made him a rash military leader in his later years. Though still at war with Albert of Mecklenburg, he seized ships sailing through the Sound with grain from the Prussian Hanse ports and thereby made Grand Master Kniprode a personal foe. At the same time he sought to impose new tolls on the Dutch. By 1369 Denmark faced a formidable coalition of enemies. While their king was skirmishing with Holsteiners beyond the Jutland border, landing parties from Dutch and Hanse ships seized Copenhagen. They fired the port and demolished the fortress that Bishop Absalon had built at Slotsholmen when the city was founded.

It was now Atterdag's turn to acknowledge defeat. In May 1370 he accepted humiliating peace terms in the Treaty of Stralsund: the fortresses of Helsingborg, Falsterbo, Skanör, and Malmö were to be held for fifteen years by the Hanse, who would receive two-thirds of the revenue of their ports; no successor to Atterdag could be elected by the Danish Rigsrad without the Hanse Diet's consent. Never before had the Hanse wielded such power.

To outsiders familiar with the seafaring republics of the Mediterranean and Adriatic it seemed as if the merchants of Lübeck could convert their trading empire in the Baltic into a political commonwealth if they wished. But the Hanse remained a commercial association; its business was trade busy-ness, not territorial administration. The fortresses were never regarded as possessions; they were sureties for commercially good behaviour by the sovereign master of the Øresund.

In 1370, when Queen Margaret was seventeen, she gave birth to her only child, Olav. The Hanse raised no objection to his election as King of Denmark by the Rigsrad in 1376, a few months after his grandfather's death. Unexpectedly Haakon VI died four years later and, through right of primogeniture, the ten-year-old Olav succeeded him as King of Norway; the two Scandinavian crowns were thus linked in a personal union that lasted until the close of the Napoleonic Wars. Unfortunately the royal mortality rate remained high; Olav was a frail lad, and in 1387 he too died. His mother Margaret possessed a strong personality – her childhood governess had been a daughter of St Bridget. Already she was *de facto* ruler of the two kingdoms and in Copenhagen the Rigsrad duly proclaimed her Regent and Steward of Denmark. Norway accorded her similar status.

'Margrete Valdemarsdotter? A king without trousers!' scoffed Albert of Mecklenburg in Stockholm. The jibe rebounded, for Margaret's statecraft – aided by the infinite capacity of Sweden's nobility for political intrigue – soon left Albert a king without a crown. He made two fatal mistakes. He appointed loyal Germans to lucrative stewardships; and at the same time he allowed the wealthy magnate, Bo Johansson Grip, to dominate the Council of the Realm and acquire strategically important castles, first in Finland and later in central Sweden. On Grip's death the councillors interpreted his will as leaving his estates to Margaret; in 1389 they invited her to become Mistress and Lord of Sweden.

An anti-German rising in support of the Council's coup d'état induced King Albert to lead his mercenaries into Dalarna, Sweden's main copper-mining district. Near Falen they suffered a heavy defeat, the weight of armour trapping their horses in a marshy swamp. Albert was captured and held prisoner for five years until a good ransom was paid. Some of his

German baronage held out in Stockholm until 1395; other supporters went to Gotland to swell the numbers of the Vitalien Brotherhood. Ex-king Albert returned to Rostock and lived for another seventeen years in ducal Mecklenburg. The despised 'Margrete Valdemarsdotter' was mistress of all Scandinavia, from the North Cape to the Holstein border and from the islands off Bergen eastwards to Vyborg and Karelia.

Tradition and prejudice were against the crowning of a woman, and Margaret was too much of a realist to challenge convention. But who should rule this sprawling empire? The death of Olav not only left Margaret child-less; it also ended the male line for all the Scandinavian dynasties. Margaret's immediate problem was to find a successor acceptable as a joint sovereign and young enough to be prepared for the tasks awaiting him. There were few suitable candidates. Eventually Margaret chose her great-nephew, Boleslaw of Pomerania, who as Atterdag's great-grandson had good Danish genes in his blood. Hastily his name was de-Polonized to Eric, and he crossed from Stettin to Sweden. In May 1397 delegates from the councils of the three kingdoms gathered at Kalmar, the nearest Swedish fortified port to the Danish-held province of Blekinge. There, on Trinity Sunday, twelve-year-old Erik was crowned King of Denmark, Norway and Sweden in a ceremony of great state. A Letter of Homage was signed and sealed by the seventeen councillors that same day. There seemed every prospect that the fifteenth century would see a dynastic union in the western Baltic to match the new and unexpected Poland-Lithuania union in the east.

Yet the Union of Kalmar rested on the thinnest of parchment. Apart from similarity of language, no common bond kept the peoples together. Danes and Swedes fought each other as readily and as bloodily as English and Scots. The mountain keel separating Norway and Sweden was both a physical obstacle hampering internal travel and a political-economic divide: Norway looked mainly to the North Sea and the Atlantic, Sweden to Finland and, apprehensively, to the rising challenge of Muscovy in the east. The rulers of Denmark, though holding the keys to the Baltic, looked also to the bolts on their backdoor, the peninsula from Jutland into the con-tested duchy of Schleswig and Holstein.

Doubts over the union emerged within a week of Eric's coronation. A charter, drafted at Kalmar, provided for what today would be called a joint foreign and defence policy, while guaranteeing the existing laws and cus-toms of each country. Copies of seals from the Letter of Homage appear to have been attached to the draft. But only three of the six delegates from Denmark put a signature to the charter, and not one of the Norwegians.

Margaret remained in effect ruler of the three kingdoms. She was an astute Regent. At a Diet in Nyköping she recovered for the Crown most of the estates earlier filched by the Swedish nobility. As in Denmark, she even succeeded in the needle's-eye task of extracting money from the Church, though the burden of some taxes fell ultimately on the peasantry. Rightly she saw the need for commercial allies to offset the stranglehold of Lübeck and, like her father, she dabbled in marriage diplomacy. In 1406 the pliant Erik was married to Philippa, daughter of England's King Henry IV, but the Hanse threat of an embargo on English cloth weakened the budding entente. Despite her age, Margaret continued to make sea-crossings between the three kingdoms, and in September 1412 it was aboard a ship in Flensburg fjord that she died. King Eric VIII was by then twenty-seven, old enough to identify the dangers that threatened the Union of Kalmar.

There was little he could do to counter them. He saw the union through Danish eyes, spending much of his reign in Copenhagen, although Queen Philippa lived mainly in Sweden. Eric desperately needed taxes for the chronic war he was forced to wage in defence of his Schleswig frontier; the Swedes resented their king's preoccupation with German affairs and sought once again to hold the castles and estates Margaret had recovered from them. To check their intrigues and to exact revenue from a reluctant peasantry Eric fell into Albert's ways: he brought reliable stewards across from Denmark and even from Pomerania, rekindling embers of Swedish xenophobia. At the same time merchants and manufacturers were badly hit by debasement of the coinage. In 1426 Eric took a decisive initiative: a royal decree let Europe's traders know that in future every ship passing through the Øresund must pay a toll to the Danish crown. The Hanse regarded the toll as a direct challenge to their commercial supremacy.

But if Eric had learnt nothing from past mistakes, neither had the people of Lübeck. A Wendish fleet, commanded by their leading citizen, again sailed westwards into the Sound: again it was defeated; and the axe fell on yet another burgomaster's neck. This time, however, the Hanse-Danish war dragged on for nine years; and it was the other two kingdoms of the Kalmar Union that suffered most distress. Bergen's trade dwindled and no Hanse ships called at Stockholm or Kalmar itself. When Eric ordered the seizure of the saline fleet inward-bound from Bourgneuf, all the salt was retained in Denmark (including Blekinge, Halland and Skåne). By 1434 Sweden's inland province of Dalarna, which included the copper and iron mines of the Bergslagen district, was short of food and deeply resentful of new taxes imposed by a Danish royal steward. The miners rose in revolt and were supported by the free peasantry. Their leader, Engelbrekt

Engelbrektsson, who was a member of the lower nobility as well as a mine-owner, became Sweden's first people's hero.

The Council of the Realm, meeting hurriedly at Vadstena, was in a quandary: the higher nobility loathed the royal stewards but feared peasant excesses. While the Councillors were still deliberating, Engelbrekt and the vanguard of his followers reached Vadstena, burst into the council chamber and demanded the king be deposed. The council played for time: a decree deposing Eric was drafted but it was not implemented. A few months later (January 1435), a Diet convened at Arboga recognized Engelbrekt as captain-general of the army, gave him custody of Örebro castle and its domains, and began negotiations with Eric to save the union. In the early summer the king crossed to Kalmar, where he was confronted both by Engelbrekt and by a new and ambitious spokesman for the nobility, Karl Knutsson Bonde, who was appointed Earl Marshal. Eric agreed to abolish the hated taxes and replace the stewards by Swedes. By January 1436 it was clear that he would do neither; and the rebellion was renewed. This time, however, the pace of events was set, not by Engelbrekt and the peasantry, but by the ruthless Earl Marshal. Ominously, in the first week of May Engelbrekt was murdered, struck down by an axe when he stepped forward to greet a close supporter of Knutsson as he landed on an island in Hjälmaren lake, near Örebro. The Swedish resistance movement was far from united.

Even so, it was strong enough to prevent Eric from waging his war with the Hanse effectively. He was forced to make peace on unfavourable terms: all ships from Wendish ports were exempted from payment of the Sound toll; and the Hanse monopoly on trade from Bergen was re-affirmed. The Danish nobility now joined the Swedes in seeking the king's deposition, a feat achieved in 1439, although with a last gesture of defiance, Eric seized the island of Gotland and established himself in Visby. Thereafter, for ten years, the first crowned ruler of the triple kingdom subsisted as a pirate chief. Eventually, the third union king, Christian I, persuaded Eric to accept a pension and retire to Denmark, where in 1459 he died, aged seventy-four.

It is surprising that there was even a second union king, let alone a third, fourth and fifth. For Karl Knutsson was not content to remain earl marshal. In 1439 he became Protector of the Realm and he barely troubled to hide greater ambitions. Within the council a pro-union faction emerged: better a weak absentee king in Copenhagen than a greedy tyrant on hand in Stockholm. After deposing Eric, the Danes, Norwegians and Swedes agreed to offer the throne to his nephew, Christopher of Bavaria, who was duly elected king in the autumn of 1440 and crowned next year. Karl Knutsson was, for the moment, outplayed; inappropriately he became Lord

Chief Justice of Sweden; and, like Grip in King Albert's reign, he began to collect strategic castles and fiefdoms in Finland. King Christopher emphasized that each of the three kingdoms should manage its own affairs. Genuine union seemed more and more a chimera.

Sweden's history over the next eight decades is depressingly repetitive and includes thirteen years of chronic warfare with Denmark. The score line of the elective monarchy for the period 1440–1521 reads: kings or regents deposed, 7; restored, 4. When Christopher of Bavaria died young (in 1448), Danes and Norwegians accepted the accession of his fifth cousin, Christian of Oldenburg, the dynasty that was to rule in Copenhagen for 400 years. King Christian I was primarily interested in Denmark's southern border His lasting achievement was the attachment (in 1460) of the 'indivisible' duchies of Schleswig and Holstein to the Danish realm, although the precise character of their 'indissoluble union' long remained a matter of contention.

The Swedes went their own way after Christopher of Bavaria's death. Karl Knutsson filled Stockholm with soldiery and induced the council to elect him Regent. Three years later he acceded as Charles I Knutsson. Soon other great landowners followed the path Knutsson had trod; many held castles in Finland, while some had manors in Denmark, too. This clique of closely related magnates – Vasas, Oxenstiernas, Trolles, Totts, Axelssons – packed the council. Twice, when courtly extravagance led to new taxes, they forced Knutsson into exile and tolerated the rule of King Christian I until he, in turn, made them dig even deeper into their pockets. The peak of Riksdag power came with the Kramar Recess of 1484, which gave the councillors rights of unmolested refuge and sanctuary in their fortified manors and acknowledged their authority as 'kings over their own peasants'.

Yet the free peasantry – who collectively owned more land in Sweden than the lay magnates or the Church – were articulate: they had a few spokesmen in the Riksdag, making it a forerunner of parliament; and they gave enthusiastic backing to Sten Sture, the demagogue who secured the regency after the death in 1470 of Charles I Knutsson, his uncle by marriage. Sture 'the Elder' was the first soldier-statesman to bang the drum of patriotism, rallying the Swedes to gain a famous victory over Christian I's army, beneath the slopes of Brunkeberg (13 October 1471). The battlefield lay almost in the shadow of Stockholm's walls, though the site is now within the central city, much of it covered by the Konserthuset and the twin Kungstoren towers to its east.

Sture the Elder was regent for twenty-eight years in all, a span interrupted by a brief return to the union fold between 1497 and 1501 under the portly and profligate King Hans (*aka* John II). Sture, in contrast to the ineffectual ruler, travelled through much of Sweden, seeking solutions for peasant grievances and reviving the mining industries of Dalarna. His diplomatic skills and patience contained the growing threat from Ivan III of Muscovy, but he suffered constantly from the intrigues of the episcopate, protective of the Church's wealth and privileges. Perhaps it is ironic that Sture's outstanding cultural legacy should dominate a great church, Stockholm's Storkyrkan. The regent commissioned *St George and the Dragon*, an equestrian masterpiece in oak and elk-horn, sculpted by the Lübeck-born Bernt Notke to commemorate Brunkeberg. It was completed eighteen years after the victory: St George is poised to thrust his sword into the writhing Danish dragon as it lurches towards a maidenly crowned Sweden, on her knees in prayer. Is there a finer example of Gothic visual propaganda anywhere in Europe?

But the dragon was not slain. The war was resumed by a later generation. Christian II (King of Denmark 1513–23) was determined to avenge his grandfather's defeat and force the recalcitrant Swedes back into the Union of Kalmar. The Unionists were supported by Archbishop Trolle of Uppsala. Soon after his accession the king sailed up the Saltsjö with a large fleet, but he was rebuffed. In 1517 a second attempt to invade ended in defeat by Sture 'the Younger's' peasant army at Brannkyrka. On this occasion Christian II held as hostages six envoys he had invited aboard ship to discuss a truce. Among them was a young member of the Vasa clan, Gustav Eriksson, who after two years of detention in Denmark managed to escape to Lübeck.

Early in 1520 Christian II launched a third attack. He led a well-equipped mercenary army north-eastwards from Halland through the frozen lake district to take Västerås and Uppsala and come down on Stockholm from the north. Sture the Younger was fatally wounded in a battle on the ice near Ulricehamn, but his widow put the massive keep at Stockholm in a state of defence and defied the invaders through four months of siege. Early in November the king accepted homage from the Swedish nobility, assembled on the former battlefield of Brunkeberg. He was then crowned by Archbishop Trolle and presided over a coronation banquet to which all the great families were invited, in an apparent gesture of reconciliation. Three days later, with the families again assembled in the great hall of the castle, the king called on the archbishop to read out a list of all nobles, churchmen and burghers who had favoured his deposition. Eighty-two men were then seized, led away in chains, and declared guilty of heresy in defying the will of the church.

All eighty-two were executed in Stortorget, the market square where the stock exchange was later built. Among those beheaded were two bish-ops and three brothers of Sture the Younger. It was raining heavily that day, and rivers of blood ran down the steep alleys of the old town to darken the waters of the Saltsjö. Five centuries later the Stockholm Bloodbath of 1520 remains as vivid in Swedish images of the past as does the Massacre of St Bartholomew's Day 1572 for the people of Paris.

Before the end of the year a second Swedish legend was in the making. Gustav Eriksson, one of the few nobles absent from the bloodbath, made his way home secretly from Lübeck and sought to kindle rebellion among the miners and peasants of Dalarna by recounting what had happened in Stockholm. Yet though Gustav, like both of his Sture kinsmen, was a nat-ural demagogue, he failed to convince his audience: a rallying call to arms outside Mora church after Mass on Christmas morning was, perhaps, inju-diciously timed. Disconsolately, Gustav trudged off into the forested mountains, seeking exile amid the solitude of Norway.

Hardly had he left Mora when reports reached local communities con-firming Gustav's account and bringing news of fresh killings of revenge as the king made his coronation progress through the provinces. At once skiers set out in a bid to persuade Gustav to return and put himself at the head of national resistance. Near the village of Sälen, 90 kilometres into the mountains, the skiers caught up with him. He turned again; and Sweden's fate turned with him. Gustav became Captain-General of Dalarna by acclamation. Soon other provinces backed the peasant-miners' hero. A long struggle lay ahead. At last, in the spring of 1523 came news that the Danish nobility, tired of Christian II's extortions, had deposed him in favour of his uncle, Frederick. Three months later, on 6 June 1523, Gustav rode ceremonially into Stockholm, the first king of the Vasa dynasty. The Union of Kalmar was ripped apart.

So at least legend recounts, and it is not far from the truth. Over the fol-lowing third of a century Gustav became the unifying sovereign that Sweden had lacked, instituting hereditary monarchy, centralizing the administration and moulding the Riksdag into a parliament of four Estates. He made it possible for Sweden to emerge as the Great Power of northern Europe in the reign of his grandson, Gustavus Adolphus. To honour Gustav Vasa's memory young skiers still enter the *Vasaloppet* each year, a 90-kilometre race in the steps of his snow-shoes from Mora to Sälen.

But Gustav did not triumph through any spontaneous explosion of national will. Good generalship, personal charisma and the patience of the peasantry ensured his final victory. He could not, however, have put a well-equipped mercenary army into the field, and hired Finnish privateers to support it, without the subsidy of 114,500 silver marks advanced by Lübeck merchants who had been angered by a sudden rise in Christian II's Sound toll. For the first nine years of his reign Gustav struggled to loosen the merchants' grip on the economy. Not until 1534 did shrewd diplomacy and the Reformation zeal that purged the Church of 'superfluous' wealth finally lift the burden of annual payments to Lübeck. Sweden was at last a genuinely independent kingdom.

9

Muscovy and Wittenberg

———◦◦◦———

THE KALMAR EXPERIMENT in union coincided with momentous changes along the Baltic's eastern and southern shores. Moscow, which in the 1350s had been a principality of no more than 10,000 square kilometres, defied the onslaught of Mongols and Tartars to form, by the 1470s, the nucleus of a Russian empire. By shrewd diplomacy and adroit use of his military levies against the Golden Horde, Ivan the Great – Ivan III, Great Prince of Moscow and Vladimir from 1462 to 1505 – became the first Russian ruler free to look to the West for expansion since Michael of Novgorod sent raiding parties into Finland at the start of the previous century.

Novgorod itself was Ivan's first objective. Gone were the days of the city's warrior princes. 'Lord Novgorod the Great' was now an urban republic, governed by an oligarchy of magnates drawn from competing merchant guilds. Through the enterprise of boatmen-adventurers whom they employed, the magnates acquired a colonial river empire of pine forest, stretching northwards to the Arctic. But the city of Novgorod was vulnerable, a plum so over-ripe with wealth that it would fall at the first shaking. For protection against the encroaching power of Muscovy the Novgorod oligarchs turned to Ivan III's rivals and sought alliance with Greater Lithuania. But in vain: Ivan struck first, with willing help from Pskov, a province independent of Novgorod for the past 120 years. Before the coming of winter in 1471 Novgorod's militia were overpowered and the city occupied. In 1478, when Ivan felt his authority securely established, he formally annexed the republic; the great 'veche' bell, symbol of Novgorod's independence, was carried away as a trophy for the Kremlin that Ivan was building beside the Moskva river.

A major blow to Novgorod's economy followed. In 1494 Ivan ordered the arrest of Germans trading in the city and the withdrawal of Hanse privileges. Forty-nine merchants, several of them from Riga and Reval, were held captive for three years, only to perish on their journey home. Twenty years later Ivan's son, Vasily III, granted the Hanse a new charter, but

Novgorod's days of prosperity were over. The Livonian and Swedish-Finnish ports benefited from Novgorod's lost trade.

Under Ivan III, Muscovy gained a strip of Baltic coast for the first time, as well as a long land frontier with Swedish Finland. The Russian challenge prompted immediate reaction from Sweden, then under the regency of Sten Sture. The defences of Vyborg were strengthened and in 1495, with help from an intensely cold winter, they repelled a Russian assault. A granite fortress was built at Olavinlinna, to give its name to the 'new castle' town of Nyslott and dominate Finland's central lakeland, where it still presides in fine tranquillity today; and in 1496 a surprise Swedish amphibious attack was launched up the Narva river to seize the equally new Muscovite frontier castle of Ivangorod. In this enterprise the Swedes had support from the Teutonic Knights. Wolter von Plettenberg, provincial master of the Livonian Order from 1494 to 1535, collaborated closely: Ivangorod faced the knights' Estonian castle of Narva across the river and when the Swedish raiders left they handed over their conquest to the Order. Desultory skirmishing between knights and Muscovites continued along the border for several years.

Though born in Westphalia, Master von Plettenberg had spent almost all his life with the Livonian Order, mostly at Narva. In 1489, when he was in his mid-thirties, he became commander of the Order's military forces, but he was also a worldly-wise statesman, in the tradition of the fourteenth century grand masters. His diplomacy sought to create a coalition of Swedes, Danes, knights and Lithuanians to keep the Russians away from the Baltic and ultimately from the cereal yielding farmland of the Vistula basin. For eight years his envoy in Rome persistently petitioned Alexander VI for a crusading Bull to allow Latin Europe to unite against the Orthodox schismatics. But a Rome basking in the glory of the Renaissance was unlikely to respond to such outdated concepts. Realistically, the pope wished for good relations with the Russians to help curb Turkish power, now that Constantinople was in Ottoman hands. Each of Plettenberg's potential allies had problems of their own: Danes and Swedes fought each other; the Grand Prince of Lithuania needed to tighten the dynastic bond with Poland. Even in Riga the master found it hard to raise funds from the merchants or the archbishopric; the Estonian marchland seemed far away. Only after November 1501, when invading Russians swept aside a small army of knights and six raiding columns devastated central Livonia, did the burghers of Riga hurriedly provide the war credits and local levies that the Order needed. More than 3,000 experienced mercenaries arrived by sea from Lübeck. By the following autumn a new army, equipped with field guns, was ready to set out from Wenden and hold the line of the Narva.

Plettenberg's troops met the Russians at Lake Smolina, south of Pskov, on 13 September 1502. The battle was no great clash of arms; both sides pulled away badly mauled, and it is hard to say who won. Yet Smolina was negatively decisive. Early next year the Russians and the Order reached a settlement at Pskov, virtually reimposing the thirteenth century border that separated Livonia and Estonia from Novgorod. Vasily III incorporated Pskov in Muscovy in 1510, and the Russians turned their armies against the Lithuanian empire in the steppe-lands, in 1514 capturing Smolensk, key city of the central Dnieper. But along the Narva there was, once again, only occasional skirmishing for more than half a century.

Smolina was the last set-piece battle of the Teutonic Knights. Soon a more insidious threat challenged the structure and faith of monastic knighthood, in both Prussia and Livonia. In the year that Smolina was fought, Emperor Maximilian granted a charter for a university at Wittenberg, a small town on the Elbe in Saxony. The university's rapid rise to fame is central to Europe's general history. For in 1508 Martin Luther, an Augustinian monk newly ordained priest, began teaching philosophy and the scriptures there, winning renown as a critic of fund-raising that fudged the faith. In October 1517 he nailed ninety-five 'theses' to the door of the castle church. In these statements of personal conviction he condemned the sale of indulgences to raise money for the building of St Peter's in Rome. A restless people, angered by the greed of the Church hierarchy, welcomed Luther's denunciation of the papacy's worldly concerns. Over the following three years he developed the theology that his opponents found heretical: justification by faith alone; the primacy of the Bible as the source of belief; the wrongfulness of 'superstitious' practices; and a different understanding of the nature of the consecrated elements in the Eucharist.

Luther's general appeal rested less on his doctrinal teachings than on his national assertiveness and his command of the German language. He won support from rulers seeking independence from pope and emperor, particularly his sovereign lord, the Elector of Saxony. The princes' protection saved him from death at the stake in 1521 after he defended his views courageously and defiantly at the Diet of Worms. In these early years of fame he was popular with the peasantry, who assumed that reform of the church would free them from social bondage and the payment of tithes. Politically, however, Luther's thought was always conservative, never revolutionary: the people had a duty to obey their princes. When, for the sixth time in fifty years, the German peasants rose in revolt in 1524–5, Luther denounced their presumption in offering a challenge to ordered society.

By 1520 printing was well established at Wittenberg, its craftsmen thriving on Luther's words. Four thousand copies of his treatise 'To the Christian nobility of the German Nation' were sold within five days of publication that year; and between 1522 and 1524 his translation of the New Testament appeared in fourteen approved editions, as well as at least sixty-six pirated versions. It was the printing press that carried Luther's teaching northwards and along the Baltic's southern shore. At the University of Rostock and in Lübeck long disputes with traditionalists were finally resolved in favour of the reformers. In Riga, Reval and Dorpat the outcome was less clear; hostility to episcopal authority was strong, but there were doubts over Luther's doctrinal teachings. The strangest phenomenon was a wave of mob iconoclasm. At Riga, in 1524, a wooden statue of the Virgin Mary – to whom the cathedral was dedicated – was solemnly denounced as a symbol of witchcraft and hurled into the river. As it floated, it was deemed guilty and carried off to the Kusberg, the mound for burning witches, and there the flames consumed it. A year later, at Dorpat, a mob vented its anger on the ikons of an Orthodox church.

Some religious houses – notably the Premonstratensians at Treptow's Marienkirche, in Pomerania – forged close links with Wittenberg. But the most surprising response of all came at the heart of eastern Prussia where, in 1521, Bishop George Polentz invited Johann Briesmann, a close colleague of Luther, to preach in Königsberg cathedral. Polentz subsequently declared himself convinced by the claims of the new 'heresy'. Some leading Teutonic Knights shared the bishop's convictions; and in the following year Grand Master Albert von Hohenzollern, who was a cousin of the Margrave of Brandenburg, travelled to Wittenberg to consult Luther over the future of the knight-brothers. By now, only fifty-five remained in Prussia; was there a role for the Order in a reformed ecclesiastical structure?

Luther considered the monastic ideal discredited and outmoded: Albert should secularize eastern Prussia and the Order itself, urging the knight-brothers to renounce their vows and marry, on the understanding they retained their property. The advice coincided with the grand master's inclinations; he was already contemplating a revolution from above. He could count on support from the bishop and the burghers' Estates, and he had left senior posts in the Order unfilled. On returning to Königsberg he renounced his vows and married. He also began negotiations with Sigismund I of Poland (reigned 1506–48) to revise the feudal obligations prescribed in the second Treaty of Thorn (*see p. 36, above*). In 1525 Albert travelled to Cracow to do homage to the King of Poland as Duke of Prussia. A conclave of knight-brothers accepted secularization. Some genuinely welcomed the change; some were intimidated by a mob that forced them to remove the cross from the habits they wore. One knight-brother, Philip von Kreutz, commander of the fortress at Insterburg, wrote frankly: 'Now all the estates had done their homage, and I saw no means by which the dirty deal could be changed, I did homage too, in order to save my property thereby, for I had a large sum of money in my employment, more than any other Teutonic lord.' But several knights with lands elsewhere in Germany continued to give military support to Emperor Charles V and the Catholic cause: the crusading cross remained an emblem of battle.

By 1526 the towns and villages of newly enfeoffed Ducal Prussia had become Lutheran, thus creating the earliest established evangelical church. By contrast, within Lithuania there was no accepted leadership or co-ordination and by mid-century thirty-four individual sects were competing in self-righteous rivalry. In Polish Royal Prussia, particularly at Elbing and Danzig, the reformers won early converts. But the Vistula swept through lands much varied in character and social structure. At Cracow King Sigismund I's Jagiellonian Catholicism was enlightened by a humanist education and the influence of his Milanese queen, Bona Sforza; their castle above the great river was an Italianate palace, where a Renaissance court flourished. There was a rich diversity of faith across Poland and more concern at Cracow over ways of checking Turkish and Muscovite incursions along far-flung frontiers than with the religious disputation that excited Ducal Prussia. Königsberg, as a port, was a better centre for spreading the new religion than inland Wittenberg, although the city had to wait until 1544 before a Protestant university was established there.

Most former knight-brothers were content to concentrate on increasing the grain yield from their lands in Ducal Prussia. In this task they succeeded. So too did their neighbours along the Vistula: cereal exports from Königsberg, Danzig and Elbing remained high throughout the half-century that followed the Reformation. Conditions of work on demesne land varied considerably. In some instances the landowners treated the peasants as villeins and kept them in bondage. Elsewhere, the peasants were accepted as tenants, with a right to inherit or sell their farms. But the decades of warfare that lay ahead were to cause such widespread devastation and deprivation that the legal status of the peasantry declined, particularly in the east.

In 1525 the septuagenarian Wolter von Plettenberg still held office as

Master of the Livonian Order, presiding over an administration that controlled the Baltic shore from Courland to Narva. Grand Master Albert von Hohenzollern advised Plettenberg to follow his example and secularize the Livonian Order. The master was under pressure from the Archbishop of Riga and leading landowners to rule as a lay Duke of Livonia, a move they believed would forestall more radical social changes advocated by anti-clerical merchants in the city. Plettenberg hesitated. He agreed to serve as sole temporal lord over Riga, confirming the city's privileges and permitting the free exercise of Lutheran practices in its churches. But he would not rule as a sovereign prince; he was too old to trim his ways, too loyal to his vows for a 'dirty deal', too worldly wise to hear in Riga's clamour the demands of the province as a whole. The heresies of Wittenberg and the despoiling of altars and holy chapels appalled him, but these were matters for the secular church authorities, he believed. The first duty of the Order was military, to defend the border of Catholic Christendom against the schismatics of the east. In this task a master needed the independence to turn to any ruler with the will and power to offer aid. Significantly in 1526 Emperor Charles V bestowed on Wolter von Plettenberg and his successors as master the status of an imperial prince. Livonia's Baltic shore became, briefly, the north-eastern frontier of the Holy Roman Empire.

Lutheranism was carried sea-borne to both Denmark and Sweden. As early as 1520 Christian II invited a group of Luther's closest colleagues to travel to Roskilde but their mission failed to kindle excitement. They returned to Wittenberg, soon followed by the exiled king himself. This unfortunate association of Lutheranism with an unpopular and discredited ruler may have delayed acceptance of the reformed faith in Scandinavia. In north and central Germany and along the southern Baltic coast the new religion stimulated use of the vernacular; by contrast, the first Danish language Bible was printed and circulated as late as 1550 and literate Swedes and Finns had to wait even longer for a full translation. In Frederick I's reign Skåne was strongly Protestant at an early stage, with a Mass-book in Danish printed in 1529 at Malmö. Until the Thirty Years War Denmark remained, in general, a tolerant kingdom: the Diet of Odense formally proclaimed religious freedom in 1527, a right scrupulously observed for almost a century.

There was, however, a brief rebellion in the following decade. When Frederick I died in 1533 the Catholic nobility in the Council of the Realm blocked the accession of his eldest son, Prince Christian: he had attended the Diet of Worms where Martin Luther's courage and sincerity impressed him; and thereafter he was sympathetic to Wittenberg teachings. The peasants, as in so much of Germany, favoured the reformed movement, believing it would give them greater social freedom, and they rose in rebellion against the Rigsrad, firing many manor houses in Jutland. The rising coincided with an external challenge, generally known as the Count's War (*see below, p. 85*). With alarm the Catholic councillors consulted their collective conscience, swallowed their pride and crowned Prince Christian, but the rebellion continued. The veteran general Johan Rantzau led an army that prevented the rebels receiving aid from Lübeck and swept aside all opposition in Jutland. Copenhagen endured a siege for over a year before surrendering in the summer of 1536 on generous terms.

The protest enabled Christian III to replenish the Crown's coffers by confiscating episcopal and monastic land. Lund, for so long the ecclesiastical capital of Scandinavia, lost some of its twenty-five churches and eight monasteries, their stones carted 24 kilometres away to complete a new castle at Malmö. But the king retained his genuine interest in Luther's teachings. In 1537 he invited the Wittenberg pastor, Johann Bugenhagen, to travel to Copenhagen to reorganize ecclesiastical affairs on a Protestant structure. Bugenhagen duly 'consecrated' seven pastors as superintending 'bishops', introduced a new liturgy, approved the theology being taught at the University of Copenhagen, and then went back home to Wittenberg. Monastic schools continued to flourish; the gentry expected Christian III to make certain there were enough nunneries in Jutland for the education of their daughters; and he did not fail them. Despite the social upheaval of 1535–6 and the king's sincerity it is hard to escape an impression that Denmark embraced the Reformation not so much warmly as casually, and almost absent-mindedly.

In Stockholm the gospel of Wittenberg was assessed with calculated shrewdness. By temperament Gustav Vasa was no more inclined to theological speculation than Sigismund of Poland. But experience steeled an inherent anti-clericalism. For the king and the nobility, Archbishop Trolle's treachery at the Stockholm Bloodbath branded the hierarchy as pro-Danish and unpatriotic. A fifth of Sweden's agricultural land was held by the bishops or the monasteries and was exempt from any form of taxation: as in Denmark, any attack on the tithe-collecting Church would be popular. Relations with Rome were formally cut in 1524 and the pope's newly nominated archbishop left Sweden. Olaus Petri, a schoolmaster from Örebro who had spent several years at Wittenberg, was welcomed at court and headed a movement of reform within the Church.

In the kingdom as a whole the level of literacy was low and printing made slow progress. Ideas were spread orally. In June 1527 Olaus Petri was invited to clarify Luther's teachings to the Riksdag, convened as a Diet at Västerås. After listening to Petri, Gustav roused the nobility with a stirring speech on the corrupting influence of ecclesiastical greed. The Riksdag took their cue from the king and gave his anti-clericalism their backing.

Within a few months Gustav was plundering the Church on a scale that makes Henry VIII seem a hurried bag-snatcher. All church property, and not merely the monasteries, was 'nationalized', all decorative 'superfluous' wealth, from eucharistic ornaments to ornate bells, confiscated. There were as usual exceptions: St Bridget's abbey at Vadstena, for example, survived until the end of the century. But when Gustav died in 1560 he was richer than any Swedish sovereign, before or since. Not that all the money remained in his exchequer. Fourteen schools were founded; roads and bridges built to open up the country. Sweden gained a navy and, more remarkably, in 1544 the earliest modern national army based upon a system of conscription. When faced by major rebellions in Dalecarlia and Småland Gustav had the money to pay for the cannon and troops who restored order. He redeemed and recovered lost fiefs, scattering the country with royal manors run efficiently by chosen bailiffs who held their lord in awe. His wealth enabled the king to rule independently of any Council of the Realm, though he worked in partnership with the Riksdag when popular endorsement would strengthen an innovation with the durability of law. By 1544 Gustav was sufficiently sure of his authority to secure from the Riksdag a Succession Pact: henceforth Sweden would be a hereditary monarchy.

As a ruler Gustav was paternalistic, hot tempered, imperious and ruthless. At times the Vasas resemble their contemporaries the Anglo-Welsh Tudors, another dynasty of upstarts. There is a similar search for good, centralized administration under a new class of royal servant and similar patronage of parliament, Gustav bolstering the Riksdag of four Estates while Henry VIII encouraged the Commons to underwrite his new order. It was left to Gustav's eldest son, Eric XIV, to set up the Royal Commission, a conciliar court to check over-mighty subjects as the Court of Star Chamber did in Tudor Westminster. Parallels cannot, of course, be carried too far. Gustav's marriage in 1531 to a Protestant princess, Katherine of Sachsen-Lauenburg, made political good sense. He treated her unsympathetically and in 1535 she died, at twenty-two, having given birth to Eric two years earlier. Like Henry VIII, Gustav then turned to an up-and-coming family for a second queen, Margaret Leijonhuvud, the mother of his remaining ten children. When Queen Margaret too died the fifty-six-year-old widower married her niece, forty years his junior. But none of Gustav's wives faced trial and execution for treason, nor did the king's sexual appetite directly influence the unravelling of Sweden's Reformation.

The calls of Olaus Petri and other reformers for changes in ritual and worship had been heeded soon after the Diet of Västerås dispersed. In 1531 – the year in which Laurentius Petri, Olaus's brother, began forty-two years in office as the first Protestant Archbishop of Uppsala – an experimental Swedish-language Mass-book appeared, but its strictures were not uniformly imposed. When Olaus Petri and the evangelical Dean of Uppsala presumed to lecture their sovereign on the need to press ahead with a revised church order, they were seized and charged with high treason; characteristically, King Gustav restored their freedom on payment of heavy fines. Wittenberg dogma and Catholic rites continued in Sweden and in Finland; the Church only officially acknowledged its Lutheran grounding in the closing years of the century. Yet, curiously, the king was incensed at not being invited to join the Schmalkaldic League of German Protestant princes when, in February 1531, they formed a defensive alliance to resist Charles V. Although Gustav was admitted to the league in 1542 he never became a whole-hearted supporter of German Protestantism.

There remained unfinished business to safeguard the throne. In 1534 Sweden achieved the rarity of an alliance with Denmark, in order to forestall attempts by the deposed Christian II to recover his Scandinavian crowns. The discredited king had support from ambitious factions among the burghers of Copenhagen and Malmö and more formidable aid from Lübeck, commanded by Count Christopher of Oldenburg (from whose activities the Count's War takes its name). The conflict coincided with the upsurge of peasant discontent within Denmark (*see above p. 83*). Most of the fighting was in Jutland and Skåne, although a Danish expeditionary force landed at the mouth of the river Trave, causing great alarm in Lübeck, not far upstream. This setback was compounded in the summer of 1535 by naval defeat from a combined Swedish-Danish fleet. The episode proved a turning point in Hanse affairs. Although Lübeck's merchant community continued to prosper, and from time to time backed privateers and hired mercenaries, the city worthies never again sought to impose their will as political arbiters of the Baltic world.

In foreign affairs Gustav avoided rash adventures, sparing his kingdom and the new army of conscripts the strain of a protracted war. His good, clear military mind concentrated on defence, guarding against any further attempts to restore the union. It was on his initiative that salt was stockpiled to counter a possible blockade in a war that would prevent Dutch suppliers reaching Swedish ports. His enduring legacy, however, was a

chain of fortresses, some of which were modified in his sons' reigns to survive as late Renaissance palaces. In 1548 prisoners were set to work on
Vaxholm Fortress, island guardian of the Stockholm shipping lane. Old castles like Stockholm's Tre Konor and Kalmar were converted into effective
citadels, while new fortresses commanded strategic routes between the
forests or along the indented coast.

The most striking castle intact today is Gripsholm, a thick-walled
three-storeyed hexagon, 50 kilometres west of the capital, with four
copper domes crouching on red brick towers that, from across the waters
of Mälaren, rise like stumpy mooring posts at the edge of the lake. Gustav
laid the foundation stone of Gripsholm in 1537, allowing his stonemasons
to raid the walls of the neighbouring demolished convent of Pax Mariae.
There were many other new castles, too: at Borgholm a ruined shell of
limestone walls still stands gauntly on the cliffs of Öland; at Uppsala the
Chamber of State of Gustav's castle survives, despite a great fire in 1702;
at Vadstena a keep was planned during Gustavus's reign but not completed
– in Dutch Renaissance style – until long after his death. Yet the stone
walls that left the deepest imprint on Sweden's history straddle rocky
Älvsborg, a small island at the mouth of the Göta älv, guarding 18 kilometres of littoral that formed the kingdom's sole outlet to the Kattegat.
During the half-century after Gustav's death, the cost of preventing Älvsborg from passing permanently into Danish hands dug deeply into
Sweden's reserves of silver; but without the castle there could have been
no port of Gothenburg to profit from trade across the oceans in the centuries to come.

Another major port, too, owes its inception to Gustav's far-sightedness.
In 1550 the king sought the establishment in Finland of a trading rival to
challenge Reval and Narva, on the Gulf's southern shore. A site was chosen
at the innermost point of a bay formed by the mouth of the river Vantaa:
settlers were ordered eastwards from the trading post of Borga (Porvoo) to
create a town and harbour there. A service of pilots was established for ships
sailing along the southern Finnish coast and through the Stockholm and
Åbo archipelagos; moored barrels guided vessels into the Vantaa sea lane.
But Helsingfors, as the Swedes called the place, failed to prosper. The inner
bay was too densely silted and shallow to provide a safe anchorage. After
eighty years of neglect a new site was chosen 5 kilometres nearer the sea,
but it did not receive civic status until 1651. Even then, Helsinki remained
primarily a garrison town rather than a trading port until Finland passed
under Russian rule in the nineteenth century.

★

A surprise twist in Baltic politics may have contributed to Helsingfors's early neglect: for the Swedes were suddenly offered a rich trading prize only 80 kilometres across the Gulf. Russia's desire for open access to the west had again posed the Baltic Question. In January 1558 Ivan IV – *Ivan groznyi*, Ivan the Terrible or Ivan the Awesome, the first prince crowned as Tsar – sent a Russian army across the river Narva in strength. The Livonian Order was too depleted and internally divided to stem the invasion; none of Plettenberg's successors had his military skill or gifts of leadership. The town and fortress of Narva fell on 11 May, Dorpat on 30 July. A second invasion a year later swept aside all resistance. Surviving commanders of the knight-brother garrisons and guilds in the trading cities sought help from Emperor Ferdinand or from Baltic rulers, including Poland's Sigismund II Augustus – who in a letter to the Queen of England warned her of 'the Muscovite, enemy to all liberty under the heavens'. Reval's garrison, poised loftily over the city from within Toompea castle, negotiated with Denmark, which had recovered a footing in Livonia by purchasing from the Bishop of Wieck extensive territories, including his palatial castle above the sea at Haapsalu and offshore islands in the Gulf of Riga. But the burghers of downtown Reval thought otherwise: Denmark was too distant for effective help and its ruler, the young and cultivated Frederick II, too personally acquisitive for the good of their commerce. The city council turned, instead, to Sweden and in the summer of 1561 invited King Eric XIV to take Reval under his protection ahead of the Danes. Reval thus became a keystone of Sweden's future empire south of the Baltic.

By now the Livonian Order was passing into history. The last provincial master, Gotthard Keppler, negotiated a settlement with King Sigismund II Augustus in March 1562 by which the knight-brothers were finally secularized. Keppler himself became hereditary Duke of Courland, ruling Latvia's peninsula from his castle at Mitau (Jelgava). Together with the archbishop and the landed nobility in Wenden and Wolmar the duke did homage to the Polish Crown, like Albert von Hohenzollern thirty-seven years previously. The burghers of Riga, who had recognized each master since Plettenberg as a temporal lord, clung to their independence for twenty more years before they, too, acknowledged Polish suzerainty.

The Livonian Order withered away not simply because the knight-brothers could no longer hold the Narva line against Tsar Ivan, but because other Baltic rulers coveted its possessions. War ravaged Livonia and Estonia almost continuously from 1558 until 1583 and intermittently for another forty years thereafter. Earlier attempts to confront Muscovy with a united front gave way in the 1560s to an anti-Swedish coalition that carried the conflict to the western Baltic and Scandinavia, while giving Ivan the Terrible an opportunity to push back the frontier of Greater Lithuania farther south before re-entering the general conflict at the end of the decade.

The Livonian Wars provide scant military interest. The greatest 'innovation' was Ivan's use of *gulaigorod*, a tactic in which advancing troops consolidated their positions by hurrying wagons forward to provide improvised forts; but similar defensive circles were familiar to Caesar and, more recently, to the knights after Tannenberg-Grünwald. Probably the worst agrarian devastation was caused by Danish and Swedish armies living off the land in south-western Estonia. Trade from the Livonian ports suffered although Danzig and Elbing, farther to the west, benefited.

So, more remarkably, during the late 1560s did Russian-held Narva; for Tsar Ivan insisted, as a guarantee of his neutrality in the second phase of the wars, that ships using Narva should cross Baltic waters unhindered, thus boosting the port's trade in flax and hemp. Richard Chancellor's discovery of the White Sea route to Muscovy in 1553 opened up an alternative to the Baltic for both English and Dutch seamen, but Archangel was not founded for another thirty years, and it was too remote to attract merchants northwards. The littoral of the Gulf of Finland, from the mouth of the Neva westwards through the region of Ingria and on to Narva and across Estland to the Gulf of Riga, became a cherished objective of Russian policy, with Reval remaining the best trading port on the open sea. During the third phase of the wars, Reval withstood a Russian siege of more than seven months in the winter of 1570–71 and again for seven weeks in 1577: six cannonballs from this second siege lie embedded like a row of studs in the thick wall of Kiek in de Kök, the intriguingly named 'Peep into the cookhouse' bastion, from which visitors may still look down on Tallinn's eating-places and on much else, too, in the city below.

The second phase of conflict had begun in May 1563 when an absurd fret over naval courtesy signals led to a brief clash off the island of Bornholm in which the Danish admiral was captured by a Swedish flotilla. Indignantly, the Danes responded with a full-scale war that dragged on for seven years and in which Poland and Lübeck sided with Denmark. A surprise assault on Älvsborg Castle by Danish mercenaries cost the Swedes their outlet to the Kattegat. Next summer Eric XIV countered with a march across the mountainous keel of Scandinavia that took the Swedes to the Norwegian coast at Trondheim, but their supply line could not be held through the winter. The Swedes had more success in Halland where, by capturing the fortress of Varberg in 1565 and holding it for three years, they reasserted their presence on the Kattegat; Varberg, however, was too sandy to develop as a port. There was a curious lack of foresight in both armies. The ablest Danish general, Daniel Rantzau, was unable to mount an invasion of Sweden in 1567 until the autumn, far too late in the year for a decisive victory. Linköping was put to the torch but he had penetrated no farther than Norrköping when winter swept down, forcing his mercenary army into a retreat whose rigours read like an advance notice for 1812 in Russia. The only commander to emerge from the war with credit was the Swedish admiral, Klas Horn, who defeated a combined fleet (mainly Danish) off Bornholm and again off Öland. Eventually the Emperor Maximilian II put forward a peace plan that served as a basis for the Treaty of Stettin (1570): the main participants renounced conflicting territorial claims; Maximilian imposed partition on Livonia (subsequently rejected by Sweden) and, as he hoped for Ivan's military aid against the Turks, insisted on continued free trade with Narva. The harshest clause in the treaty committed Sweden to paying Denmark 150,000 *riksdaler* for the recovery of Älvsborg. The sum demanded was more than a third of Sweden's annual revenue; it required the levying of a special tax, much resented by both the nobles and the peasantry.

Poland, though allied to Denmark, took little part in this Baltic Seven Years War, except for disputing Swedish possession of several castles in Livonia. Sigismund II Augustus, who succeeded his father in 1548, shared his parents' Renaissance humanism and acceptance of religious diversity, but he knew that the magnificence of the Polish Court rested on shaky foundations. His failure to father a male heir foreshadowed a disputed succession, with the crown likely to be kicked around by the *szlachta* nobility and the gentry. At the same time Ivan the Awesome's armies ravaged Lithuania's eastern marchlands. In 1563 they caused consternation by capturing Polotsk, a fortress on a ridge above the upper Dvina (Daugava) guarding historic trade routes to Riga and Vilna. To strengthen military links between the Grand Duchy and the Polish 'crownland' (*Korona*), the king formally annexed the vast Lithuanian palatinates in the Ukraine and along the upper Dniester.

Sigismund Augustus also initiated a constitutional revolution without precedent. He began talks with the Polish and Lithuanian nobility to tighten the loose bonds that had associated Cracow and Vilna since 1386 and create a dual state. At Lublin in July 1569 the king proclaimed the union of Poland and Lithuania in The Commonwealth of the Two Nations (*Rzeczpospolita Obojga Narodów*), the largest unified kingdom in Europe. Joint government was executed by a common elective monarchy and a central Diet (Sejm) that was effectively controlled by the *szlachta* from regional assemblies. Senators from Royal (i.e. Polish) Prussia and the great landowners from the Grand Duchy sat with the Polish nobility in the Sejm. Warsaw's position on the middle Vistula made the city an administrative centre even though Cracow was the royal capital for another forty-two years. Lithuania retained its own administration, laws and army but opened its territories to magnates from the Polish heartland, who could now further enrich themselves by acquiring new estates and local power in the east. Both Danzig and Riga jealously protected their privileges; the Danzig senators, for example, strongly resisted the king's plans for a joint fleet in the Baltic, fearing it might harm the city's trade.

The Sejm needed peace, time and patience to complete the constitutional structure of the union. Accordingly in June 1570 Sigismund Augustus agreed on a three-year truce with Ivan the Awesome, even though it left Polotsk in Russian hands. But the king was a sick man: when he died in July 1572 it was left to a 'Convocation Sejm', meeting in the following January at Warsaw under the presidency of the Archbishop of Gniezno, to settle procedure for electing a successor. The convocation agreed that all nobles were entitled to vote in person and that a prince from any land could be a candidate for the throne provided he undertook to observe certain fundamental articles. The Confederation of Warsaw, as the articles are generally called, committed an elected king to keep peace between contending religious faiths; to summon the Diet for at least six weeks in every two years and not impose extraordinary taxes without its consent; and not to interfere with the jurisdiction of the nobles over their peasantry.

The first foreign prince, Henry, Duke of Anjou, was elected on 10 May 1573, largely through the canvassing of his mother, Catherine de Medici. King Henry's knowledge of Polish affairs was negligible and remained so. He accepted the Confederation and was duly crowned in Cracow but he was puzzled at the multiplicity of religious creeds in the country and mistrusted the nobility. After thirteen months of wrangling with the Sejm, Henry heard that his elder brother, King Charles IX of France, had died. He slipped away from Cracow at the first opportunity, hurrying back to Paris to claim a throne unfettered by constitutional checks: Warsaw seemed well worth a miss.

The Sejm tried again; and in 1575 chose Stephen Batory, the ruling Prince of Transylvania, who was Sigismund II Augustus's brother-in-law. Batory was a good soldier and an adroit politician, willing to observe the restraints of the Confederation of Warsaw. He tactfully accepted Poland's commitment to religious toleration although he was a good Catholic who encouraged Jesuit educational enterprise at Riga and Dorpat. He was also a skilled diplomat. By 1578 Poles and Swedes were fighting, side by side, against Ivan the Terrible, fording the river Gauja under darkness in late October to surprise the Muscovite troops besieging Wenden Castle, the former stronghold of the Order. The victory is rightly celebrated at Cēsis (Wenden's modern name) as the turning point of the wars: Batory's army rolled back the invaders, recovering Polotsk and by the autumn of 1581 besieging Pskov.

At the same time, totally independently, the Swedes launched an offensive in Finland, capturing Kexholm on Lake Ladoga. More remarkably in January 1581 the French 'soldier of fortune', Pontus de la Gardie, led an invasion force 80 kilometres across the frozen Gulf before thrusting inland to seize the castle at Wesenberg (Rakvere), halfway between Reval and Narva. This largely forgotten success enabled de la Gardie eight months later to march eastwards and secure for Sweden the prize of Narva itself. The Poles agreed on a truce with the tsar in 1583, the Swedes following suit the following summer. After a twenty-five year struggle Ivan the Terrible was forced to accept King Stephen Batory as master of Livonia and John III of Sweden as master of Estonia. Around the Baltic all the bloodshed and suffering of Ivan IV's wars gained Russia nothing.

While Poland-Lithuania was being reshaped constitutionally, Vasa Sweden became the shuttle in a fratricidal power game. Like Charles V, Henry VIII and Sigismund Augustus, Eric XIV (reigned 1560–69) was an intelligent Renaissance Prince – the first Swedish king to rule in splendour and fill his court at Kalmar with artists and musicians. Almost certainly he was also the first European king to own an organ that he played himself. Any chronicle of his nine-year reign is full of promising initiatives left unfulfilled: a naval shipbuilding programme; efforts to increase the yield of customs tolls; changes in military training that would have anticipated many of Gustavus Adolphus's reforms. By temperament, however, Eric was unstable and he hankered for royal absolutism too blatantly. Not without reason, he was deeply suspicious of his half-brothers, especially the eldest, Duke John, who in 1562 married Sigismund II Augustus's sister Catherine – a devout Catholic – without the Swedish king's permission. Foolishly, and somewhat blatantly, John began an intrigue intended to make him an independent ruler in Finland. King Eric's guards surrounded Åbo castle and carried the recently-weds off to Gripsholm, where they were imprisoned in apartments on the first floor. Duke Karl's Chamber retains painted wooden panelling and across its plastered walls a trailing plant pattern on which John and Catherine's eyes must have focused for five weary years. A son was born soon after their incarceration at Gripsholm, reputedly in the chamber that is so well preserved today. He was named Sigismund, to honour his Polish grandfather.

In May 1567 King Eric totally lost all self-control. His finely-tuned mind snapped while he was in residence at Uppsala. He stabbed his kinsman Nils Sture, one of several nobles cast into the castle dungeons, ordered the immediate killing of the other eminent prisoners held there, and ran off into the forest mentally unhinged. Even so, apparent sanity returned, and soon afterwards he married his young mistress, Karin Mansdotter, daughter of a peasant soldier. In 1568 Eric proposed that Karin be crowned, with all the ceremonies that he loved. A coronation was more than his half-brothers could stomach: they rose in revolt; there was a brief civil war; Eric surrendered; and in February 1569 he was deposed. The Riksdag hailed his eldest half-brother as King John III. The tragic Eric spent the remaining eight years of his life being moved from prison to prison, probably dying in the end from poison in his soup. Queen Karin, with the two children she had borne him, was shipped into exile but as a widow allowed back into Finland, where she lived until 1612. Her black alabaster sarcophagus is in Turku cathedral.

John III (reigned 1569–92) resumed his father's practice of building castles, but he also shared Eric's cultural instincts. The dominant figure at court, however, was Queen Catherine, who clung tenaciously to her Catholicism: Jesuits were welcomed in Stockholm; the young Sigismund received a Counter Reformation upbringing; and John issued the so-called Red Book, emphasizing a continuity of worship with Rome. In his tenth year on the throne John III appears to have been received into the Catholic church by the queen's Jesuit confessor. From 1579 onwards John's brother Duke Charles of Södermanland – Gustav Vasa's youngest son – became the champion of Lutheranism. A crisis loomed in 1587, when the Polish Sejm elected Sigismund to succeed Stephen Batory as king. From a Polish standpoint the election made good sense. Sigismund was a descendant of the Jagiellonians; he was a Catholic; and it was hoped in Warsaw that, as heir-apparent in Stockholm, he might add Estonia to Poland's gains in Livonia. The Riksdag, with John III's approval, took counter measures: the Statute of Kalmar emphasized that Estonia was a Swedish possession and that the kingdom was Protestant in faith. When John died in 1592 Duke Charles convened a synod in Uppsala at which the clergy reaffirmed their Lutheran commitment before Sigismund could cross from Poland and claim his inheritance. But he came, none the less.

A curious situation then arose. For seven years Sigismund ruled in Poland with Jesuit backing and in Sweden as the sole Catholic permitted to hold public office in a Lutheran state. When the king was summoned back to the Vistula to attend to the problems of his elected monarchy, Duke Charles encouraged Swedish and Finnish defiance of 'the Pole', although the leading magnates remained loyal to Sigismund once he had accepted an Accession Charter pledging to respect their traditional rights. A series of revolts flared up, most seriously in Finland. Sigismund returned to Kalmar and in 1598 a full-scale civil war in southern Sweden culminated in the battle of Stångebro, near Linköping, in which the king was defeated and held captive by his uncle, Duke Charles. A year later he was deposed from the Swedish throne, though he continued to reign in Poland as Sigismund III. On the duke's order the loyalist Councillors of the Realm were arraigned and executed in what became known as the Bloodbath of Linköping; Eric Sparre, the outstanding champion of aristocratic constitutionalism, was among the victims. At first the duke ruled Sweden as Protector of the Realm, fearing that an apparent usurpation might rekindle the civil war, but in 1604 he acceded, at the age of fifty-four, as King Charles IX.

His coronation three years later was celebrated with a costly splendour at variance with his natural parsimony but matching his pride in an almost imperial monarchy: Europe must know him as sovereign lord from Kalmar up to the Arctic. No ruler before or since included 'King of the Lapps in the North Country' among his titles. Charles IX did indeed possess many kingly qualities. He tamed the magnates on the Council of the Realm, although they never willingly co-operated with him and tended to absent themselves from court, fearing they might suddenly fall foul of his Vasa temper. He was a good administrator, ruling in his father's style, with bailiffs supervising the kingdom as though it were a private estate. Like Gustav Vasa, too, he could kindle support from the commonalty by the spoken word, for he enjoyed a demagogue's fluency of speech. He founded new towns: the prefix in Smealand's 'Karlstad' and in 'Karlskoga' preserve his memory; and he pressed ahead with the settlement at Gothenburg, encouraging Dutch merchants to migrate there. The legal system was reformed, even though the King's personal reputation remained stained by the Linköping Bloodbath. He promoted industry, setting up mills, developing the copper mines of Falun, and ensuring the iron foundries of central Sweden were at work again.

There was, however, a fundamental weakness in Charles's style of government. His foreign policy was dangerously ambitious. Expeditions were mounted against Russian settlements around the White Sea, too distant and remote to be controlled from Stockholm. In Poland an over-confident campaign led to one of Sweden's worst defeats, at Kirkholm in 1605, when Polish lancers routed an army 10,500 strong. But Charles was looking even farther east: in 1610 Jacob de la Gardie led a Swedish force into Moscow during the 'time of troubles' that weakened Russia after Ivan IV's death; briefly it seemed possible a Swedish nominee might reign as tsar. Yet this bold enterprise, too, proved disastrous: mercenaries mutinied for lack of pay; the Swedish auxiliary force was exposed to attack by a Polish-Lithuanian army and in June 1610 it was defeated at Klushino. Intervention in Russia brought no lasting gains and left the homeland denuded at a time when Denmark again posed a threat to Sweden's growing authority, both within the Baltic and in Scandinavia.

Denmark – still in dynastic union with Norway – seemed in many ways a fortunate kingdom. Only two reigns spanned almost ninety years, and both monarchs were able and sane. Frederick II was on the throne from 1559 until 1588 when Christian IV acceded at the age of ten; he lived to reach seventy. Frederick had begun badly: he plunged into the Baltic Seven Years War in 1563 only to find the cost of campaigning so high that he had to borrow extensively from his in-laws in Saxony. At that point he recognized the true skills of his treasurer, Peder Oxe, who had been under a cloud of disapproval. In 1566 Oxe changed the basis of assessing the Sound Dues, so that the toll would be levied on the weight of cargo carried rather than on the ship itself. The money came flowing in, and within twelve months the revenue from the Dues trebled. Frederick was able to clear his debts and throughout his later years keep a splendid court at Kronborg, his castle beside the Sound at Helsingör.

Frederick's son Christian IV shared his father's liking for opulent ornamentation of palaces, preferring a gold motif and plaster cherubs, plump and tinted pink. But he was a builder as well as a decorator. He transformed Frederiksborg, the castle in which he was born, and planned Rosenborg as a summer palace. In his northern kingdom he built Christiania as a fortified administrative capital beside the straggling settlement of Oslo and he created Kristiansand as a fortified port on the Skagerrak. In what is today the Swedish county of Skåne he left a permanent 'Danish' mark on his new town of Kristianstad, with levelled ramparts and moats that provide a tree-lined girdle and a magnificent church dedicated to the Holy Trinity. Within Copenhagen he also gave his patronage to buildings that served more general needs: the Rundetårn observatory; the naval and commercial quarter of Christianshavn, with canals in the Amsterdam fashion; and the red brick Børsen. He was a patron of science as well as of the arts, and a scholar capable of exchanging letters in Latin with his tediously pedantic brother-in-law, James VI & I, of Scotland and England. Yet in many ways Christian IV was a hearty extrovert: hard-riding, hard-drinking and hard-wenching, he reputedly fathered more bastards than any royal contemporary.

Politically Christian suffered from the grumbling appendix of elective monarchy, a Council of the Realm highly protective of its rights. His councillors were suspicious of any royal initiative in foreign affairs, particularly one that might cause them to dig deeply in their pockets. For Christian was eager to restore Denmark's command of the sea before Sweden's new settlement on the Göta älv gave Charles IX trade benefits in the Kattegat and beyond. Moreover he was increasingly disturbed by Swedish activities in northern Norway. Yet by late 1610 the temptation to seek swift victories while Sweden was already at war on three fronts was irresistible; even the Council of the Realm concurred. In April 1611 Denmark again went to war with the old enemy.

Charles IX of Sweden was taken by surprise. He could, at that moment, count on a mere 472 mercenaries to supplement the limited reserves of the home army. Within a month the Danes once more held the island fortress of Älvsborg and had overrun the vaunted defences of Kalmar castle. In fury at what seemed like a stab in the back King Charles, though sick and ailing, challenged Christian IV to resolve the disputes between them in single combat. Christan's response seemed to him so impertinent that he suffered an apoplectic stroke, the second within a year. By the end of October Charles was dead. The throne and a host of problems at home and abroad passed to his son Gustav II Adolf, a lad of sixteen, better known across Europe as Gustavus Adolphus.

10

Lion of the North

G USTAVUS ADOLPHUS BECAME Europe's outstanding warrior king, a soldier of courage who was also a strategist and reformer, a model for later commanders from Marlborough to Napoleon. The many threads of his life form a warp around which legends were readily woven. He was tall and broad-shouldered with short-cropped light brown hair and a tuft of tawny beard; it was natural for him to be hailed as the Lion of the North. His physical endurance and resilience inspired the troops who served under him. Thirteen times he was wounded, on two occasions severely: in later years the pain from scars and bruises made him reject even the lightest protective body armour. Within weeks of his accession he survived being thrown by his horse through the thin ice of a frozen river and at a critical moment in a later campaign he remained in the saddle for sixteen hours without a break. He favoured a war of movement, expecting his men on occasions to march more than 320 kilometres in a week; but in the one siege of his military career – at Riga in 1621 – he was ready to step down and add his muscular strength to their digging of trenches. War encompassed his reign: when his father died he was with the army in Ostergotland; twenty-one years later he was himself killed at Lützen, leading his horsemen to a sixth victory in the open field.

Gustavus's military genius was complemented by the contrasting skills of his chief minister Axel Oxenstierna, and of the Dutch-born financier, Louis de Geer. Oxenstierna, a natural diplomat from one of the historic noble families, was appointed chancellor early in 1612 at the age of twenty-nine and still presided over the chancery, at least in name, when he died forty-two years later. He was in effect foreign minister, principal internal administrator and finance minister, as well as regent from 1632 to 1644 during the minority of Queen Christina. His leadership contented the fractious nobility: their privileges were formally confirmed by charter; they were recognized as an Estate in the Riksdag, rewarded with land in Livonia, consulted on the Council, given departmental responsibilities over expenditure and the administration of the army and navy; they had the appearance of governing; and the reformed Riksdag met for eleven 'parliamentary' sessions during the reign. Yet, though Gustavus regularly tuned his persuasive oratory to please the Estates and listened to their response, all power and initiative rested with the king, the chancellor and his nominees. The Oxenstierna system hardly made for a balanced constitution, but it gave Sweden greater political cohesion during Gustavus's years of territorial expansion than in the previous half-century of chronic war and confusion.

Louis de Geer, a far less famous figure than Oxenstierna, was among many Dutch merchants and bankers attracted to Charles IX's new town of Gothenburg. He became the greatest Swedish entrepreneur of the pre-industrial age. In Gustavus's early years, when copper was challenging silver as Europe's metal of currency, de Geer helped the king establish a trading company to supply Europe with copper from the Falun mine. By 1626 when the price of copper fell dramatically, de Geer was concentrating on the iron industry of central Sweden, using imported techniques of smelting and forging to give Gustavus the weapons of war he needed. Without the cannon forges at Finspång and the muskets from Norrköping there could have been no Swedish empire created along the southern coast of the Baltic.

Gustavus's military education began in the last years of his father's reign, with skirmishes to preserve the Swedish hold on Estonia. But the first task after his accession was to check the Danish advance into the homeland. Here he was helped by King Christian IV's limited objective. The Danes did not seek territorial expansion; they wanted to safeguard their control over entry to the Baltic by keeping the Swedes away from the Øresund and the Kattegat. The War of Kalmar, as the conflict was called, dragged on indecisively for two years. The new settlement at Gothenburg was destroyed during the fighting and there was widespread devastation across three provinces. Yet it was a strange war; the Danish navy ruled the narrow seas, but neither king was willing to commit troops to a pitched battle. At last, through English mediation, peace terms were agreed in the summer of 1613 and a treaty signed at Knäred. The Swedes surrendered a fortress on Oesel island (Saaremaa), off the north of the Gulf of Riga, and abandoned claims to the Arctic coast of Norway. The most contentious issue was the future of Älvsborg. Christian himself wished Denmark to annex the fortress and deny Sweden access to the Kattegat. His councillors dissuaded him; they feared that annexation would lead to further wars that Denmark could not afford. A compromise settlement left the fortress in Danish hands for six years until the Swedes paid an indemnity of a million *riksdaler* in silver coins.

This crippling sum was, in 1613, three times as high as Sweden's annual revenue and almost seven times the ransom imposed by the Treaty of Stettin forty-three years previously. As on the earlier occasion, a tax was levied on the whole population of Sweden and Finland, about 1.2 million people. For the first time the tax was scaled according to social standing: the king handed over a fifth of his personal annual income; a bishop 50 *riksdaler*. Small sums were levied from peasants and labourers. Even a serving maid was assessed at half a *riksdaler*. Money was also raised by the sale of Falun copper at a peak price in Amsterdam, Europe's leading commodity market and financial centre throughout the century. By 1619 the ransom was paid off and the Danish garrison left. Ships could move freely along the Göta älv river. Gothenburg began to rise again from the ashes, a well-planned port that owed much to the influence of the Dutch – including an inner network of canals. In 1621 Gothenburg was re-founded as a city by royal charter.

The threat from Russia receded during the 'Time of Troubles' (1604–13), the period of anarchy following the end of the Rurik dynasty that had ruled Muscovy for seven centuries. The chief beneficiary from Russia's civil wars was Poland-Lithuania; Polish troops occupied Moscow from 1610 to 1612 and held Smolensk for more than half a century (1611–67). The Swedes had more limited objectives than the Poles: Gustavus was a realist, seeking control of trade routes and the tolls that went with them rather than striking eastwards into the Russian steppeland. Novgorod was taken by a Swedish army under Jacob de la Gardie in July 1611, though the city was restored to Russia six years later by the Peace of Stolbova. Gustavus suffered a personal military setback in 1614 when he failed to capture the citadel of Pskov, but the Stolbova settlement brought him almost all he wanted. The frontier in the east was advanced around the Gulf of Finland, giving Sweden the whole of Karelia, the mouth of the Neva, some two-thirds of the shore of Lake Ladoga and the coast of Ingria and providing a land bridge from Vyborg round to Narva. Now no Russian ship could sail the Baltic without Sweden's permission, Gustavus Adolphus proudly assured the Riksdag in Stockholm.

Throughout his reign Gustavus Adolphus was either fighting a war or shaping up for the next one. Stolbova brought Sweden a truce. The king took the opportunity to reform the army in anticipation of renewed struggle against a more formidable adversary, his cousin Sigismund III of Poland. Oxenstierna devised a system of conscription, through which one male in ten over the age of fifteen was called up for twenty years' service in a field army, with a guarantee of receiving free landed property as a 'pension' if he survived. The serving soldier could expect to receive good and regular pay. His status in society was raised; he was disciplined in mind and purpose by a Lutheran ideology that exacted loyalty: prayers were held twice daily, and in his campaigns he carried with him a book of psalms and simple hymns suitable for battle. In theory, Gustavus could rely on at least 30,000 experienced troops to augment his mercenaries (who were, for the first time, organized in regiments, named after primary colours). Tactics were modified, notably in the offensive use of pikemen. He revived the threat of a cavalry charge with the sword, using lighter horses, little body armour, and practising co-ordination with the artillery. Over the next ten years Gustavus constantly changed the army's structure and training, improving the mobility of cannon, and the fire-power of musketeers in a search for the perfect fighting force.

By 1620 this new professional army, though not yet at its peak, was ready to take the field against Poland. Like so many conflicts, the war was fought for creed and greed. Sigismund's Catholicism, nurtured by Jesuit tutors during his boyhood in Sweden, brought Counter Reformation Baroque to Warsaw. By Swedish reckoning, it threatened the purity of Stockholm's Protestantism, too, for Sigismund had never abandoned hope of recovering the Vasa throne. But, though Gustavus Adolphus was inspired by a genuine sense of mission, his prime objective in fighting Sigismund was to control Livonia's ports and rivers. Early in the autumn of 1621 he took advantage of Sigismund's preoccupation with the Turkish menace on Poland's southern borders to launch an offensive around the Gulf of Riga. On 15 September 1621 his army entered the Hanse city itself after a short siege, levelling the main bastion by the firepower of his new mobile 4-pounders and sending his horsemen to storm through gaps in the walls that Teutonic Knights had thrown around Riga in the pre-cannon era.

A four-year truce followed. When the struggle for Livonia began again in June 1625 the Swedes captured Dorpat, where a Lutheran university was to receive its foundation charter a few months before Gustavus's death. He had yet to win a victory in the open field. It came against the Polish cavalry at Wallhof early in 1626, a battle fought in snow and ice on a short January day. The king then carried the war into Lithuania and southwards towards the lower Vistula, suffering a defeat at Hammerstein in May 1627 but sealing his success in August with a second major victory, at Dirschau, where he was fortunate to survive a wound in the neck. Elbing fell and Danzig was threatened. Eventually, in September 1629, under French mediation, the Poles accepted the Truce of Altmark. Poland acknowledged Sweden's paramount position in 'Livland' (central and northern Livonia, including

Estonia); and for six years the Poles surrendered all rights and dues in the ports and harbours of the Prussian coast as far south as Memel. Next year Oxenstierna negotiated a treaty with the Free City of Danzig that assigned most of the shipping tolls imposed in the port to the Swedish treasury.

The supreme prize remained Riga. A governor-general took up residence in the castle beside the Daugava and ensured that the conquered provinces and the Swedish homeland were integrated; the high nobility received fiefs in Livland although Gustavus Adolphus respected the chartered rights of his new subjects. The three hundred merchant families and forty-three brotherhoods (trade guilds) of Riga were highly suspicious of Oxenstierna's mercantilism and jealously guarded their privileges, but the city of Riga was a pillar of Sweden's Baltic empire through nine decades. Today the Swedish Gate, the one surviving archway in the restored section of the walls, is all that reminds the visitor of these years, though it dates from the end of the century.

By 1629 England and Scotland were looking to the Baltic for material to fit out ships and the stores to keep them at sea. The hulls might as ever be hewn from the best English oak but the upper works came, for the most part, from northern shores. Flax, hemp and timber commodities headed Riga's exports; the city's sawmills specialized in shaping ships' masts and deck boards. The trade was a steady source of revenue for Gustavus Adolphus and his successors. Sweden could also count on good rewards from the commerce of Narva, Reval, Memel, Elbing and Danzig; and there were, too, the customs duties levied on the grain trade along the rivers Vistula, Daugava and Niemen. The king of Sweden seemed assured of a higher income from these tolls than the king of Denmark from his lucrative Sound Dues: the customs duties yielded half a million *riksdaler* in 1629 alone. In practice, however, the income proved lower than anticipated. Baltic trade was cut by two developments. Bubonic plague, a pandemic in 1625, lingered or resurfaced in particular ports, forcing other towns to impose quarantine on their vessels. But, above all, the earliest of the great European wars encroached increasingly along Baltic shores and trade routes.

The first and last shots of the conflict that began in May 1618 and ended in November 1648 were fired in Prague. Central Europe was the principal arena of battle and, in theory, the acceptance or rejection of Protestantism the main issue separating the combatants. But the Thirty Years War enveloped many quarrels: the balance between the territorial princes of the empire; control of mountain passes across the Alps; Spain's determination, after half a century of conflict, to beat down the Dutch and retain a hold on the Netherlands; and, more especially, the power struggle between the two great Catholic dynasties, the Bourbons in Paris and the Imperial Habsburgs in Vienna and Madrid. There was a lack of unity among the Protestants: during the first phase of the war the Lutherans of Germany stayed neutral, leaving the more radical Calvinists of Bohemia, Transylvania and Hungary to defy Emperor Ferdinand II and the Counter Reformation. Provided the Habsburgs were not tempted to send armies to the northern shores, there was no reason why Denmark, Sweden or any other Baltic power should enter the war.

By 1625 the Imperialists were in the ascendant. The Spanish general Spinola had cut the Protestant supply line through the Rhineland and captured the Dutch fortress of Breda. Spinola's one-time deputy, Tilly, was master of Bohemia, Moravia and the Austrian lands; and the Emperor Ferdinand II had growing support from the ambitious but highly skilled mercenary general Albrecht von Wallenstein, a landed magnate from Moravia, able to raise a new army at his own expense. By contrast the level of generalship among 'Protestant' commanders ranged from the brutal mediocrity of Mansfeld (another soldier of fortune) to the incompetence of minor princes with titles easily forgotten. The two outstanding Lutheran kings, the Baltic rivals Christian IV and Gustavus Adolphus, continued to stand on the sidelines, mutually suspicious. Briefly in 1624–5 there seemed a faint prospect they might act together, but it soon became clear that they were only prepared to consider alliance if one conceded supreme command to the other. Neither would give way.

Gustavus was absorbed in his duel with Sigismund of Poland, who received financial backing from Emperor Ferdinand II. In the king's absence, Oxenstierna was left to put the Swedish economy on a war footing, delegating responsibility for keeping the foundries firing to De Geer and for building up a modern navy to Klas Fleming the Younger. Christian IV, however, was already heavily committed in Germany as sovereign Duke of Holstein. The War of Kalmar had shown the effectiveness of his fleet in protecting the Øresund and Denmark's long, vulnerable coast. Christian was a courageous soldier, but he was no strategist and he lacked good military counsellors. Other rulers found much to say in Christian's favour, encouraging him to go to war: fair words saved them from active and expensive commitment. Mistakenly he believed he could count on subsidies from the English and the Dutch. In 1625 he came forward as champion of the Protestant cause and invaded Germany. It was a rash decision, ultimately responsible for expanding the theatre of war so as to include Europe's northern periphery.

Christian struck southwards down the Weser in an inclement June. Snow fell on the town of Hamelin; his horse stumbled, and the heavily built king was thrown some 25 metres down a steep slope. Miraculously he survived, relatively unscathed. A good portent, his men believed. They were wrong: nine months of marching and counter-marching were followed in 1626 by a disastrous campaign. There was little co-ordination between Mansfeld (who was defeated by Wallenstein at Dessau in April), the main Danish army and a third, ineffectual Protestant force, led by the Prince of Brunswick, who was terminally ill and died in June. The Danes fought valiantly but were outnumbered by the emperor's veterans and broken by Tilly at Lutter in August. Christian IV, having lost half his army and had his horse shot under him, retired prematurely to winter quarters at Stade, on the western side of the Elbe estuary. He was still there a year later, without reliable allies inside or outside Germany and unable to raise enough troops to resist Wallenstein who, having already overrun Brandenburg, swept northwards into Holstein and Jutland.

The Duke of Friedland, as Wallenstein styled himself, became the richest of warlords. He delighted in his independence of Emperor Ferdinand (who was heavily in debt to him) and of the Catholic princes and their generals. As his army reached the coast of Jutland, his world vision broadened. Wallenstein's chosen newest title, General of the Oceanic and Baltic Seas, gave notice of ambitions flaunted with an arrogance three centuries ahead of the age. Wismar, he thought, had potential as a naval base and once he secured Holstein there was even talk of digging a Kiel canal.

These naval plans received warm backing from distant Madrid, where Spain's chief minister, Olivares, had long contemplated sending a fleet into northern waters to destroy the Dutch carrying-trade in the Baltic. The perceived threat of Habsburg galleons on the coast of Pomerania stimulated shipbuilding in both Copenhagen and Stockholm. The emphasis was on heavily armed, all-cannon three-masters rather than on shallow-draught vessels better suited for the shallows around the Gulfs of Finland and Riga or the sandy indentures of the Prussian littoral.

At high summer in 1628 Wallenstein began a new offensive to clear north German shores. He massed his army in Mecklenburg and mounted a siege of Stralsund, a superbly sited port linked to the mainland by only three causeways and protected from sea-raiders by the island of Rügen, 3 kilometres across a strait. The Danes and Swedes responded vigorously, but independently. In Copenhagen a resilient Christian IV prepared an invasion fleet to land south-east of Rügen and isolate Wallenstein. Meanwhile, on 3 July the burghers of Stralsund concluded a treaty with Sweden by which Gustavus Adolphus undertook to protect the port for thirty years, provided he could establish and maintain a base there. By the last week in the month Wallenstein could see the masts of both a Danish and a Swedish fleet off Rügen. Twice he attempted to break into Stralsund, having boasted that he would take the city 'even were it chained to heaven', but he could make no impression on its solid walls. On 3–4 August he pulled his troops back. Stralsund's siege was at end; the chain was rattled but not severed and sound Lutheran Swedes were soon to arrive and solder any imperfections in its links. The Stralsunders convinced themselves that 12,000 besiegers lay dead. Protestant Europe rejoiced in a victory for 'the Cause', although the extent of Wallenstein's immediate discomfiture was much exaggerated.

In Stockholm plans were completed for a show of strength: Stralsund must be made to serve the Vasas as Calais had served Edward III and his successors in the Hundred Years War. Alexander Leslie from Blair Atholl, who had fought for Sweden for the past twenty years, was confirmed as Stralsund's Governor and garrison commander. An expeditionary corps massed at Älvsnabben, to the south of the Stockholm archipelago, ready to back up Leslie; frigates and transports awaited the newest addition to the fleet, the most powerful and ornate warship afloat. The *Vasa* was 45 metres long and 11 metres wide; at Älvsnabben she would embark 300 troops to join 150 seamen and gunners already aboard. She would then, it was assumed, cross to Stralsund, bearing down on the German coast with the wind filling 1,300 square metres of sail. For the royal ship *Vasa* was designed to impress: a carved springing lion, 4 metres long and weighing 350 kilograms, was shaped as her figurehead, and gilded lions surmounted the gunports. The *Vasa* could roar, too, for her two gun-decks housed 64 bronze cannon, giving her heavier firepower than any other ship of her displacement. There were several hundred figures carved in pinewood or oak around the decks, including Roman emperors, biblical characters, Greek gods and goddesses and Swedish royal heroes. Her mainmast stood 52 metres high, a sturdy spire for the flagship of the new fleet.

The *Vasa* duly sailed for Älvsnabben from the naval yard in central Stockholm on 10 August 1628, with a light wind blowing. About 100 metres off the southern tip of Djurgården island, a sudden gust filled her sails. Well-wishers around Stockholm's inner bay saw her begin to slip away to starboard and were horrified that she could not be righted. After a maiden voyage of 1.3 kilometres, the *Vasa* capsized and sank in the waters of the Saltsjö. Some fifty seamen and gunners went down with her; about a hundred were saved. More than fifty of the cannon whose weight was held to have caused the disaster were salvaged before winter ice sealed the wreck.

None of the *Vasa*'s sculpted figures was seen again until the spring of 1961 when a team led by the underwater archaeologist Anders Franzen slowly raised her hull from 30 metres of mud and water. Careful conservation and meticulous restoration work allowed the ship and many varied artefacts to be housed in an attractive museum, opened in the summer of 1990 and standing less than two kilometres from where she sank. The Vasamuseet is a tribute to German, Dutch and Swedish woodcarvers of the seventeenth century and to marine scientists of the twentieth. It also reveals more of Gustavus's grandeur and folly than even the finest equestrian statues can convey.

The loss of the *Vasa* was followed within a month by disaster for the Danes in Pomerania. Christian IV had landed some 50 kilometres southeast of Stralsund and seized the small town of Wolgast on the river Peene, where it is said the beer was to his liking. He lingered there, rather than marching into Mecklenburg. At last, on 2 September, his Danish army emerged, only to be intercepted a few kilometres outside the town by Wallenstein's vanguard and speedily defeated. King Christian was fortunate to escape to his ships. The fleet turned westwards and headed for the Øresund. Three months later he sued for peace. The war seemed about to end in decisive victory for the Habsburgs.

Gustavus Adolphus had discussed intervention with his council early in the year, before negotiating with the burghers of Stralsund. An invasion of Germany was out of the question so long as the Polish war continued, but the French-sponsored Truce of Altmark of September 1629 relieved pressure in the east. While the terms of a possible truce were still under consideration, the king sought the backing of his council for a campaign in Pomerania and Mecklenburg. Intervention was agreed in principle as early as 8 January 1629, although the councillors accepted the king's decision that no invasion could be mounted for another eighteen months. Unlike Christian IV, Gustavus Adolphus would not plunge into war prematurely.

A month later the kings of Sweden and Denmark came together for the only face-to-face discussion of their reigns. Christian IV accepted an invitation to meet his old enemy in the village of Ulvsbäck, at the home of the Lutheran pastor. Defeat at Wolgast had left him demoralized: peace talks with Wallenstein were already well advanced, though the terms were harsh; Jutland remained in enemy occupation; Denmark could not afford the material or financial burdens of further campaigning. Gustavus, hoping as much for ships as for troops, appealed in vain to the spirit of Protestant union. Tempers rose, and nothing was achieved. Christian IV made peace with Wallenstein and his imperial master at Lübeck in June; he recovered his occupied lands but lost hereditary rights over two German bishoprics and he had to acknowledge imperial sovereignty over Holstein. Gustavus, meanwhile, urged Oxenstierna to press Cardinal Richelieu, as a lasting enemy of the Imperialists, to provide subsidies to maintain the army with which he proposed to cross the Baltic.

At Ulvsbäck Christian IV had asked his host, 'What business has Your Majesty in Germany?' Gustavus Adolphus parried the question, perhaps because he was no surer of the answer then than generations of historians since. In Holland, England and Scotland popular sentiment credited him with the highest motives: he came, it seemed, to save Protestantism in the land of its birth; and it was easy for Gustavus to convince himself that his hymn-singing army was marching to protect the church from its enemies. Yet the record of his exchanges with Oxenstierna shows that he had realistic, attainable objectives. Sweden's future – militarily, politically and commercially – depended on naval command over the inland sea. In the past, Sweden's rulers were concerned with the fate of the Narrows, either in the Øresund or at the head of the Gulf of Finland. Their rivals at sea were, for the most part, Danes, Lübeckers and latterly Poles. By 1626 the king believed he had found ways to counter the danger in the eastern and central Baltic: from Narva to Elbing the Swedes held firm footholds on the southern shore. But in 1629 a new threat emerged. The trouncing of Christian IV brought the prospect of a Habsburg naval presence in the Baltic closer, with shipwrights in Wismar already using their skills to fulfil Wallenstein's orders. In the western Baltic Sweden needed to hold, not simply a string of bases along the littoral, but territory in depth to support them, using the hinterland as a defensive glacis. Gustavus's first 'business in Germany' was to clear the Catholic Imperialists from Baltic shores. He had no ambition to become a Charlemagne of the North; Sweden lacked the manpower and the money to found and sustain a territorial empire stretching across the continent. In essence all the campaigns of Gustavus's reign had a similar war aim: to capture and hold the commercial cities along the southern Baltic shore and make certain that the customs dues imposed on their upriver trade swelled the Swedish exchequer. If fortune favoured his enterprise in Germany he might later create a Protestant confederation under Swedish presidency. That, in itself, would be a revolutionary achievement. Never before had a kingdom of the North moved centre stage in Europe.

On 4 July 1630 the king landed at Peenemünde, a fishing village at the tip of Usedom island and beside the most western of several 'mouths' of the river Oder. Thunder and lightning added to the drama of this seventeenth century D-Day. Offshore lay sixty vessels, protective warships covering the disembarkation and transports that were loaded with infantry, sixteen troops of horse, and the best field artillery in Europe. It was a relatively small invasion force, no more than 13,000 men, but the king was confident of an early link with General Leslie's garrison at Stralsund, barely 65 kilometres to the west.

Surprisingly the invaders faced no opposition. Wallenstein, who in May had planned to concentrate 30,000 men along the Pomeranian shore, was out of favour with Emperor Ferdinand II. His arrogant megalomania infuriated even his patrons in Madrid. Ferdinand, who thought little of the Swedish threat, assigned Wallenstein's best troops to Italy. Under pressure from the Electors, he was about to dismiss him from his command. Instead of confronting the King of Sweden on the coast – as he had the King of Denmark in neighbouring Wolgast two years previously – Wallenstein was forced to wait on events in Bavaria, his life protected by his personal guardsmen.

From Peenemünde Gustavus Adolphus had no difficulty in pushing forward up the Oder basin. On 20 July his army took Stettin, the capital of Pomerania, whose ruling duke was cajoled into becoming Gustavus's first territorial ally in Germany. But Duke Bogislav carried little weight in German affairs. No electoral prince welcomed the Swedish presence at this stage. After twelve years of war the most influential – John George, Elector of Saxony, and George William, Elector of Brandenburg – were seeking an early peace and a compromise settlement. They echoed Christian IV's doubts: why should an outsider from across the East Sea meddle in the business of the Holy Roman Empire?

Like Richelieu, Gustavus Adolphus valued manipulative propaganda, and he sent ahead of him into Germany an able diplomat and budding spindoctor. Johan Adler Salvius was to ensure that every move by the king was seen in the best light. From Salvius Europe learnt, by two printed handouts in five languages, that Gustavus Adolphus held German liberties in great respect and was deeply committed to the Protestant cause. He was, he claimed, acting in self-defence: Ferdinand had supported Sigismund of Poland and threatened Sweden's 'mastery (*dominium*) of the Baltic Sea'. The manifesto did not impress the Electors, but Salvius's activities fed the 'corantos', the forerunners of newspapers that were increasingly circulating in German towns remote from the war and in Amsterdam and London (where the autocratic government of Charles I sought to ban reports of Swedish victories in case they gave heart to the Puritan opposition). Salvius was ready with follow-up news releases, the raw material of legend. When Gustavus, who was notoriously short-sighted, disembarked at Peenemünde he stumbled on a narrow gangway made slippery by heavy rain and was seen to sink to his knees. It was an accident less humbling than Christian IV's dramatic unsaddling at Hamelin and the chance that he fell forwards was put to good use. Soon Protestants across the continent could hear from pastors in the pulpit that their liberator king knelt in prayer at the moment he set foot on German soil. And perhaps he did, for public prayer became his practice before each major battle of the campaign. He needed every aid that powers spiritual or temporal could offer.

But it was from a prince of the Catholic Church that Gustavus received the money to keep his armies in the field. In January 1631, as he headed southwards towards Frankfurt-on-the-Oder he paused in the small town of Barwalde. There emissaries from Cardinal Richelieu were on hand with a treaty, already agreed with Oxenstierna, by which France assigned Sweden twice-yearly subsidies sufficient to keep an army of 30,000 infantry and 6,000 horsemen on active service against the emperor for five years. Gustavus undertook to uphold freedom of worship in Germany, for Catholics and Protestants alike, and agreed not to invade Bavaria, whose ambitious ruler, Duke Maximilian, was a potential French ally. The Treaty of Barwalde was no secret accord: Gustavus insisted the alliance be made public, partly to hold the French to their commitment, but also to boost Sweden's military prestige among the German princes: they must understand that, though Ferdinand II might think little of the Swedes, Cardinal Richelieu knew better.

By the end of the year no one could doubt Gustavus's military genius. In the spring of 1631 he thrust deeply into the German lands, capturing Frankfurt-on-the-Oder in mid-April before heading westwards to occupy Berlin. The army pursued Tilly around Mecklenburg until, desperate to replenish his food stocks, he made the political mistake of invading unravaged Saxony, thus cementing an alliance between Gustavus and Elector John George. On 17 September their combined armies – 30,000 under the King of Sweden, 10,000 under the Elector – cornered Tilly at Breitenfeld, in rolling hill-country 8 kilometres north of Leipzig. The Saxons, forced back into conventional defensive positions by Tilly's cavalry, lost nearly a third of their men; but the Imperialists were taken in the flank by the Swedish light horsemen and musketeers, with Gustavus himself leading the infantry to capture more then twenty of Tilly's cannons, which were then turned on the imperialist army. Tilly retreated westwards across the river Weser, leaving Gustavus free to head into the Catholic heartland of the

Main. The prince-bishop's citadel in Würzburg was stormed on 14 October; six weeks later the Swedes were in Frankfurt-on-Main; by Christmas they were at Mainz. It seemed likely that in the coming summer Gustavus would advance down the Danube on Vienna.

Gustavus's queen, Maria Eleonore, a sister of the Elector of Brandenburg, joined him in the southern Rhineland in February for a brief interlude of festive celebration. They had married in 1620, when Gustavus hoped for Brandenburg's diplomatic support over Polish affairs. He had also hoped in those days for a son; but Queen Eleonore gave birth to only one child, Maria Christina, who was too young to make the winter journey southwards with her mother; she never saw her father after her fourth birthday, on the eve of his departure for the German campaign.

The winter pause in the fighting gave the king and his chancellor an opportunity to formulate peace plans. Gustavus revised a programme of 'future action', drafted in consultation with Oxenstierna in the previous May. He now proposed changes in the structure of the empire: a Protestant inner council – *Corpus Evangelicorum* – would with Swedish participation protect the status and freedom of Lutherans and Calvinists; Sweden expected monetary compensation for participation in the war and a general recognition of Sweden's right to control Germany's Baltic coast.

Peace was not, however, yet in sight. With the coming of spring the Swedes and their German Protestant allies were again on the march eastwards. The army crossed the Danube at Donauwörth and on 14 April encountered Tilly's main force covering the river Lech from high ground on the far bank. That night the king supervised the building of a bridge of boats and, early in the morning, sent several hundreds of his best Finnish troops to prepare the way for the artillery to follow. In the ensuing battle Tilly was wounded. Before the end of the month he was dead.

By then, however, Gustavus faced a new commander. Wallenstein was back in the field, the desperate emperor having bought his services on terms never revealed. The armies clashed at Nuremberg in the first week of September but the Swedes could not dislodge Wallenstein from carefully fortified hill positions. Two months of pursuit from Bavaria back to the crucible of Saxony culminated on 16 November 1632 in a decisive battle at Lützen, a cluster of houses, farmsteads and a church 24 kilometres west of Leipzig.

A misty day was made darker by smoke from the burning village, for it lay to windward of the Swedish lines. In mid-morning the king successfully led a light cavalry charge on the imperial horsemen, taking them by surprise and capturing their supporting cannon, as at Breitenfeld. By noon reinforcements allowed the imperial cuirassiers to launch a fierce counter-attack. In the confused fighting of the next hour the imperial cavalry commander, Pappenheim, was mortally wounded. Soon afterwards the King of Sweden's horse was seen heading across the field injured, panic-stricken and, ominously, riderless. Victory at Lützen went to the Swedes that afternoon but at an incalculable cost. No one had seen Gustavus fall; his body, stripped naked by scavengers and hacked by vengeful sword-thrusts, was found after nightfall, covered by corpses in a ditch. He died from a shot through the head, still only in his thirty-eighth year. At that age Marlborough had yet to fight a major battle, Washington was in the colonial militia, and Cromwell had five years to go before taking command of his first troop of horse.

Nearly a quarter of a century after Gustavus's death, Lord Protector Cromwell vividly recalled to a Swedish envoy his deep sorrow on hearing the 'heavy tidings' from Lützen. Few figures in history – and none from the Baltic – have seemed to contemporaries to be driven by such spiritual power imparted by God. This charisma burnished the reputation of his kingdom and his subjects abroad: Sweden, until now no more than one among many trading partners in the Baltic, was hailed by Puritan apocalyptics as the land chosen by the Almighty to purge Europe of Habsburg rule and Papist idolatry. Early in 1632 a London printer defied the government by bringing out the *Swedish Intelligencer,* a means of keeping the English abreast of news from the continent. For several years after Lützen the *Swedish Intelligencer* continued to appear, describing the new style of warfare brought to the continental mainland by the Lion of the North and bolstering Sweden's prestige in the West.

That, however, became increasingly difficult. Chancellor Oxenstierna, who shaped policy during the twelve years of Queen Christina's minority, accepted that much of Sweden's apparent power was illusory. Gustav's highly trained professionals formed less than 18 per cent of the anti-Imperialist army, and by now heavy casualties had thinned their best brigades. Lines of communication with the coast were vulnerable and, across the Baltic, the homeland could not be denuded for fear that Ladislav IV (who succeeded his father, Sigismund III, in 1632) would seek to reassert the Polish dynastic claim to the Swedish throne.

Oxenstierna remained south of the Baltic until 1636 and cobbled together an alliance with the Protestant princes, the League of Heilbronn (April 1633), but he hoped for an early end to the war in Germany on advantageous terms. Meanwhile, for Sweden and all her Baltic possessions he instituted a shared regency government of five Councillors of the

Realm (the Lord Treasurer, the Earl Marshal of the army, the Admiral of the fleet, the Chief Justice, and himself as Chancellor). At first the system worked well and there were no signs of domestic unrest: Gustavus had made the war pay for itself, mainly through the subsidies from Richelieu, forced contributions from German rulers he assisted, and protection money from German cities threatened with destruction (Munich among them). Oxenstierna was even able to lighten the tax burden at home in the first year of the regency.

In February 1634 the chancellor learnt that Wallenstein was dead, stabbed in the Bohemian town of Eger by an Englishman, an agent of the Imperialists whose cause the super-mercenary was about to betray. Wallenstein's removal gave the surviving Imperial commanders more freedom of manoeuvre, and in the following August they were able to dispel the myth of Swedish invincibility. At Nördlingen, in the Black Forest, Sweden's General Gustav Horn and his ally, Bernard of Saxe-Weimar, engaged a combined Spanish and Imperial army and were heavily defeated. Almost half the Swedish troops perished on the battlefield; Horn and Bernard together lost 14,000 men and all their cannon. The League of Heilbronn virtually disintegrated: Oxenstierna was compelled to realign Sweden's forces. He travelled to Paris and negotiated a new treaty with Richelieu that brought France openly into the war, with responsibility for general strategy in southern Germany.

A Swedish army remained active in Brandenburg under Johan Baner and the great 'father of artillery', Lennart Torstensson. An Imperial threat to the Swedish bases along the Pomeranian coast in October 1636 was countered by their joint victory at Wittstock. In the later stages of the war Torstensson advanced to within 40 kilometres of Vienna, and in November 1642 he won the second battle of Breitenfeld in familiar open country outside Leipzig. Torstensson's tactical improvisation, and particularly his imaginative siting of cannon, restored Sweden's high military reputation.

Yet even before the German campaigns came to an end Denmark posed the Baltic Question again. Christian IV was by now in his late sixties and short of cash. For eighty years Peder Oxe's revised scheme for levying tolls on shipping in the Øresund had financed his wars, patronage of the arts and personal extravagance. But he needed a new source of revenue, and in 1643 he sought to levy similar tolls at the mouth of the Elbe while also raising the Sound Dues. At the same time Christian negotiated anti-Swedish alliances with the Poles and also with his nominal enemy, Emperor Ferdinand III. But Danish diplomacy was heavy-footed. The new Sound Dues angered the Dutch, who remained the most active traders in Baltic waters; and Oxenstierna soon realized the purpose of the alliance building. In response he ordered a pre-emptive strike. Torstensson invaded Jutland from the south, but he could not cross to Funen and Zealand and threaten Copenhagen before an Imperial army attacked his positions in Germany, forcing him on to the defensive. The Danes had some success at sea until in a running fight off Kolbberger Heide (1 July 1644) four Swedish vessels bore down on the royal flagship, *Trefoldighe*, wounding Christian IV so seriously that he lost the sight of an eye. At this point a Dutch fleet sailed down the Kattegat to enter the Baltic and tilt the balance of naval power strongly against the unfortunate king.

Reluctantly Denmark accepted peace terms at Brömsebro (August 1645). Sweden gained the islands of Gotland and Ösel (at the northern entry to the Gulf of Riga) as well as two Danish-Norwegian counties, Jämtland and Härjedalen, and the right to hold the province of Halland, on the eastern shore of the Øresund, for thirty years. The Danes were also forced to make drastic concessions over the levying of tolls, not only on Swedish vessels but on Dutch and English ships too. The war that Christian IV had hoped would raise Denmark's revenue left the kingdom in even deeper financial crisis. Danes and Swedes were to fight each other on six more occasions in the following century and a half, but Denmark had by now lost all prospects of primacy in northern Europe's affairs.

That status was enjoyed over the next seventy years by Sweden. For, by the comprehensive peace settlement of Westphalia in 1648, the Swedes secured almost all that Gustavus Adolphus sought when he first intervened in Germany. No Habsburg ships of war would sail the Baltic for more than 200 years, and then only briefly. The Swedish negotiators – Oxenstierna's son and the far from popular careerist Salvius – gained possession of western Pomerania (including Stettin and Stralsund and the mouth of the Oder), the port of Wismar and an outlet to the North Sea in the bishopric of Bremen-Verden (though not the free Hanse city of Bremen). These German acquisitions automatically made the ruler of Sweden a prince of the Holy Roman Empire, with the right to participate in meetings of the Imperial Diet. At the same time, the Swedes negotiated a final agreement on war debts: their garrisons would remain in Germany over the next three years until the empire collectively raised the money to settle outstanding claims for compensation. In effect the Germans were paying the Swedes to take their army back home again.

Sweden was at peace for the first time in half a century. The novelty was short-lived, a pause lasting a mere seven years, but it was in many respects a fruitful interlude. On 18 September 1644 Queen Christina had become, at eighteen, the kingdom's active sovereign. The Councillors of the Realm expected her to marry early and give birth to an heir: they never understood the complexities of her character and – apart from Oxenstierna – they undervalued the quality of her mind. She respected the memory of her father and rewarded the returned veterans with land. Her inclination favoured peace and the enjoyment of a cultured society. By 1649 she had decided not to marry, partly because she was bisexual, but also because she rebelled against the fetters of royal motherhood. The Riksdag accepted that, if she died without a legitimate child, the succession should pass to her first cousin, Charles Gustavus of the Palatinate, the son of Gustavus Adolphus's sister, Catherine. He had already distinguished himself in the final campaigns of the Thirty Years War.

In taste and temperament Christina seems at times a throwback to her great-uncle, Eric XIV. She read widely and studied deeply, and she appreciated good art, particularly the works of Titian and Raphael. Under her patronage, in 1652, Italian singers brought opera to Stockholm for the first time (more than a century ahead of popular taste, it would seem). She cultivated intellectual hedonism and encouraged scholars from France and the Netherlands to make journeys to Stockholm, even if they were physically ill-suited to the rigours of the north. The jurist and theologian Grotius came at the start of her reign. Although he hurried back to Holland at the first icy blasts from the Arctic in 1645, he died on the way home. At the queen's request the fifty-three-year-old philosopher René Descartes gave her tutorials three times a week at five in the morning, until he was trapped by the Swedish winter of 1649–50; he caught pneumonia and did not live to see the spring. Very sensibly, Blaise Pascal resisted the siren call from the north, limiting himself to an exchange of letters and the dedication to his 'incomparable Princess' of a calculating machine. He was still in good health when the queen laid down her crown.

Christina took the business of government seriously, playing politics astutely until, at the age of twenty-four, the game began to bore her. Money matters were beyond her comprehension, but she understood the importance of trade and of building up a Swedish mercantile fleet. She supported two short-lived overseas ventures: Louis de Geer founded a West African slave trading company that sought, unsuccessfully, to hold part of the coast of Ghana; and Oxenstierna planted a colony at the mouth of the Delaware River. In the 1640s some Swedes were encouraged to cross the Atlantic to people 'Fort Christina' but it proved impossible to defend New Sweden from the more determined and systematic

Dutch colonizers to the north. Fort Christina is now, more prosaically, known as Wilmington.

Yet the queen's political objectives lacked clarity of purpose, apart from a general wish to create a new nobility to help the Crown recover powers lost to the Council of the Realm. In this she succeeded. At her accession there were some 295 noble families in the kingdom: by the end of the reign the total reached 767, enough to swamp the old aristocracy – although, in fact, only twenty-two families were great and wealthy landowners, with estates in Sweden, Finland and Livonia. The queen possessed the characteristic Vasa glibness of speech. When she addressed the Riksdag in 1650 the commonalty backed their sovereign, seeing her as a protector of the poor, someone who would lift the burden of taxation while curbing the privileges of the territorial magnates. This was an illusion. Unwisely, crown estates continued to be sold off, or donated, indiscriminately to the old and new nobility. It would seem that land ownership changed more extensively in Christina's reign than at any other time in Swedish history. Royal revenue was cut, falling by 43 per cent during the nine years of her full sovereignty, and heavier taxes were needed to replace the loss. Small wonder that in 1650 the free peasantry, on whom the greatest burden fell, became restless. But at no time did they show hostility to the queen in person. Had Christina called on them to march against Poland or Russia, they would have followed her lead.

Instead, by 1652, Christina had made up her mind to abdicate. She chose to go into exile for personal reasons, not political. At her request the Pope had secretly sent to Stockholm in 1651 two Jesuit scholars, who were both physically and mentally tough. Catholic metaphysics challenged her mind; the prospect of travelling abroad, of seeing for herself the artistic treasures and antiquities of the South, stimulated her senses. Despite her personal extravagance – court expenses rose from 3 per cent of royal revenue in 1635 to 20 per cent at the height of her reign – the councillors sought for two years to dissuade her from stepping down, but in June 1654 she convened the Riksdag to gather in the Chamber of State at Uppsala Castle. There, shortly after her twenty-eighth birthday, she ceremonially laid down her crown before the assembled Estates. Her cousin from the Palatine succeeded to the throne as Charles X Gustav.

Christina travelled in some pomp to Brussels and on to Innsbruck, where in November 1655 she was received into the Catholic Church. Shortly before Christmas she made a formal entry into Rome on horseback, her manner defiantly individualistic rather than penitential or devotional. Although she paid two brief visits to Sweden and travelled to Paris and Naples, she lived in exile for thirty-four more years, titillating the prurient by her ways but also giving her patronage to the composers Scarlatti and Corelli and supporting Bernini at a time when the master of Roman Baroque was out of favour with the Papacy.

There is little trace of Queen Christina around Baltic shores: a fine portrait at the age of twenty-four by David Beck in Stockholm's Nationalmuseum (where her collection of Cranach paintings is also housed); more portraits at Gripsholm; a sixth century German *Codex* at Uppsala University; the silver throne that catches the eye in the Hall of State of Stockholm's royal palace; a replica of her coronation carriage at Ulriksdals Slott; and, more personally evocative, her stone summer house off the north-western side of the Kungsträdgården, in her day an Italianate royal garden. Only bills of account and old etchings recall the masques and pageantry with which she set out to brighten a drab court. But Christina's influence was pervasive. A nobility eager to prove its social standing through fine living commissioned town palaces and country homes of elegance and fashion. Out at Läckö, on Lake Vänern, Christina's favourite general, de la Gardie, completed a Renaissance palace of 250 rooms and then built a second lakeside home at Karlberg on Lake Mälaren, that has long served as a military academy. The third de la Gardie palace, Jakobsdal, was on headland less than 8 kilometres north of Stockholm and was the starting point for Christina's coronation procession; it later became a royal palace and was renamed Ulriksdal and greatly transformed. Also on Mälaren, Oxenstierna had a Dutch Baroque villa at Tidö and Marshal Wrangel (of Danish-Estonian descent) could retire to Skokloster, northeast of Sigtuna. These palaces were intended as havens of peace, not castles. They survive today to reflect the pride and self-confidence of a victorious officer corps.

I I

Nemesis at Poltava

AFTER THE LIVONIAN wars and the marches and counter-marches of Danish, Imperialist and Swedish armies across the German plains the Baltic region needed an era of calm and stability, an opportunity to graft a culture of its own on to the profits of thriving maritime trade and new industries. But that ideal proved unattainable for at least a century and a half. Instead, within a few months of the final peace settlement of Westphalia, a minor dispute between Polish colonialists and a Cossack Hetman east of the river Dnieper gave notice of an even longer cycle of conflict ahead, generally known as the two Northern Wars. By the time the cycle ended in 1721 Russia and Prussia had replaced Sweden and Denmark as the Baltic's leading powers, and Royal Poland seemed set in terminal decline.

The Polish-Lithuanian Commonwealth – the *Rzeczpospolita* – kept free from entanglement in the Thirty Years War. It could not, however, relax its vigilance; there was too much uncertainty around the frontiers, especially in the east. Under Michael Romanov the Russians attempted in 1632–34 to recover Smolensk and other lands lost to the Poles during the 'Time of Troubles', but they failed disastrously. Rightly King Ladislav IV assumed that the tsar or his successor would strike again once Muscovy recovered from defeat. He therefore modernized his own army, ready either to renew the conflict with the Russians or make a bid to recover Livonia from the Swedes. In this venture he found the *szlachta* gentry unwilling to support him; they feared that any war would devastate their estates. Ladislav then resorted to the dangerous device of making a secret deal with the Cossacks of the Ukraine, whom he planned to use as mercenaries against the Commonwealth's perpetual enemy in the south-east, the Ottoman Turks. The plan misfired calamitously: in May 1648 resentment at the arrogance of Polish officialdom prompted the field commander of the Cossacks, Hetman Khmelnitsky, to lead a full-scale revolt of Cossack warriors and Ukrainian peasant frontiersmen. By chance, the insurrection coincided with the sudden death of King Ladislav IV. Chaos followed. By September Polish colonizers and thousands of Jews who controlled the commerce of the Ukrainian towns were fleeing westwards. Not until the summer of 1651 did Ladislav's elected successor – his Vasa half-brother, John II Casimir – check the Cossack incursion with a victory at Berestechko.

Even so, the revolt rumbled on for eight more years. Although the epi-centre may have been a distant outpost of the Polish Commonwealth, shock waves spread from east to west around Baltic shores. In January 1654 Tsar Alexis responded favourably to an appeal from Hetman Khmelnitsky to take the Orthodox peoples of the Ukraine under Holy Russia's protec-tion. By the summer Russian troops had recovered Smolensk from the Poles and were advancing in strength through present-day Belarus, threat-ening trade along the upper waters of the river Dvina. In Stockholm King Charles X Gustav could no longer stand aside. The Swedish position in Livonia had to be defended. Plans were completed to intervene in Poland, initially by an invasion from Pomerania.

In July and August 1655 three Swedish armies invaded the Polish heart-land and Lithuania. The campaign revived memories of Gustavus Adolphus's triumphant progress from Stralsund to Mainz, for the Swedes met little opposition as they advanced up the Vistula. By the end of the first week in September Warsaw had surrendered. The main Polish army was defeated at Żarnów soon afterwards. Charles X Gustav entered Cracow after an eight-week siege and went into residence at Wavel Castle, while Poland's John Casimir found shelter in Silesia.

By now Charles X had convinced himself that the Commonwealth of the Two Nations was disintegrating. The earlier, limited war aim of safe-guarding Swedish mastery of the Baltic littoral gave way to more ambitious plans that would have reduced Poland to a Swedish dependency. He was, however, faced by mounting opposition from other powers with Baltic interests. The Dutch – still the sea's principal traders – were opposed to any extension of Sweden's hold on key ports along the southern shores. So too was Brandenburg-Prussia, now ruled by Frederick William (the Great Elector, 1640–88). By the Westphalian peace settlement Frederick William had received eastern Pomerania, thanks largely to the force of 8,000 men he raised and led in the last campaigns of the long war. In 1653 he created a standing professional army, the nucleus of the formidable Prussian war machine of later centuries. If the Commonwealth of the Two Nations was falling apart, the Elector coveted Poland's Royal Prussia. And while the Swedes remained heavily engaged in the heart of Poland, it was tempting to make a bid to seize Stettin and western Pomerania, too. Frederick William believed himself in a strong position.

But Charles X Gustav was no fool. He was aware of the Elector's ambitions and well informed of secret negotiations he had undertaken with the Dutch. In October 1655, rather than risk being cut off by Frederick William's army, Charles X left Field Marshal Arvid Wittenberg to hold southern Poland and surprised the Elector by a rapid march back up the Vistula. As winter closed in on Königsberg, so too did the Swedes. By Christmas Frederick William was under siege in his most profitable port and capital. Hurriedly he sought terms from Charles. In January 1656 he formally recognized the King of Sweden rather than the King of Poland as his overlord in Ducal Prussia. At the same time, he assigned 1,500 auxiliary troops to support Sweden's campaign against the Poles and pledged half of Brandenburg-Prussia's customs dues to the Swedish exchequer. These were terms Gustavus Adolphus and Oxenstierna might well have imposed.

Charles's lightning warfare outpaced Sweden's resources. Arvid Wittenberg could not hold down the Poles. Guerrillas began to harass the Swedish lines of communication. To the north-east of Cracow the limestone uplands known as the Polish Jura stretch as far as Częstochowa. The town is dominated by the Paulite monastery of Jasna Góra, home of the Black Madonna, an ikon venerated by Catholic pilgrims for at least two centuries before the Swedish invasion. In 1620–21 a Dutch military engineer had been engaged by the prior to protect the monastery with a ring of fortifications. So effective were these defences that in this autumn of 1655 they withstood ten weeks of siege by Swedish mercenaries, who were eventually forced by the coming of winter to retire. Jasna Góra's proud defiance of the invader fired national enthusiasm and passed into patriotic legend; it was immortalized towards the end of the nineteenth century by Henryk Sienkiewicz in *The Deluge*, the second novel of an epic trilogy set in this First Northern War. To Catholic contemporaries the Black Madonna's victory left no doubt that the angels were on the side of Poland. A century earlier Poland had been a tolerant 'state without stakes', accepting Lutheran, Calvinist and even Unitarian believers, though its kings never wavered from the Catholic faith. Decades of defence against Sweden's militant Lutheranism changed the spirit of the nation. Now John II Casimir returned from Silesia to join the Archbishop of Gniezno in dedicating Poland to the Blessed Virgin Mary. Rome rejoiced that the Counter Reformation had found a new militant champion in eastern Europe. Henceforth Polish patriotism and the Catholic faith were inseparable partners, each gaining strength from the other.

Charles X failed to capture Lvov or Lublin and he lost Warsaw. Soon he was forced on the defensive by a three-pronged invasion by Tsar Alexis's army in the East. During the summer and autumn of 1656 the Russians captured Dorpat in Estonia, penetrated westwards into Finnish Karelia and, most dangerously of all, advanced down the river Dvina. By the end of August Riga itself was under siege. Elector Frederick William, eager to shake off the shackles so recently imposed by Sweden, excelled himself in diplomatic duplicity. An envoy met the tsar outside Riga and offered neutrality if the Russians would give assurances that his lands would not be invaded. At the same time the elector himself agreed to help Charles X break Polish resistance in return for territorial gains on the middle Vistula and recognition of Frederick William's full and independent sovereignty over Ducal Prussia. Well-trained Prussian troops fought alongside the Swedes for three bloody days in July 1656 and recovered Warsaw. But Frederick William could never be a reliable partner in the field. By the following autumn he had struck a bargain with John Casimir and duly changed sides. 'Alliances are all very well but forces of one's own are better still' (*Alliancen seindt zwar gutt, aber eigene Krefte noch besser*). The words are the elector's, written in 1667; they might well have been Bismarck's two centuries later.

Not that Charles X ever looked on Brandenburg as a stanchion of his grand design. He could have no illusions over the general hostility aroused by the Swedes' continued presence south of the Baltic. Poles and Russians agreed on a truce in order that both armies could engage the common enemy. Emperor Ferdinand III offered to supply John Casimir with good Austrian troops to oust the Swedes from Royal Prussia. And it was almost inevitable that Frederick III of Denmark should make ready to take advantage of Sweden's apparently rapid decline.

King Frederick, personally as courageous as his father and politically more astute, possessed many admirable qualities. A grasp of military strategy was not among them. He was hampered by constant friction with the nobility who controlled the Council of the Realm, were slow to provide essential supplies and mistrusted the generals to whom the king entrusted command. Frederick needed the war to be short and victorious. His best hope was to revive the opening gambit Christian IV employed in 1611 and strike for Kalmar and central Sweden while the main enemy army was south of the Baltic. Instead, in June 1657, Frederick sent his ablest commander to mop up the isolated Swedish enclave of Bremen-Verden. A second army gained some success in Halland, threatening Gothenburg. But Frederick himself went to sea with his fleet. The Danish navy was, at this time, superior in numbers and quality to the Swedish and patrolled the western Baltic, justifiably confident it could prevent Charles X bringing an army back to the homeland.

That, however, was an operation Sweden's king was far too canny to attempt. He chose to follow the example set by Torstensson and return to the western theatre of war overland. On hearing that Denmark had joined his enemies Charles broke off his campaign in Poland, leaving his generals to hold Royal Prussia as best they could while he led yet another long and rapid march from his field headquarters across Pomerania and into Holstein with an army of 9,000 veterans. By the autumn they controlled almost all the Jutland peninsula. The winter of 1657–8 proved as cold as any then on record; and across Poland and Livonia the guns seemed frozen into silence. But Charles X made winter his ally. At the end of January 1658 his huge army crossed the frozen Little Belt to occupy Funen: two troops of cavalry horse were lost when the ice cracked after the passage of the cannons; and the king himself had a fortunate escape when the royal sledge disappeared into the waters soon after he had vacated it. Despite these hazards the winter march continued. Hard frozen ground enabled wagons and cannons to move more speedily than in a wet autumn or a spring thaw. On 6 February Charles X and his army began the even longer crossing from Langeland over the Great Belt to Lolland. The army swung northwards into Zealand to threaten Copenhagen from the south. Charles X was at Koge, with the smudge of the Skånian coast visible across the waters of the bay, when Frederick III sued for peace.

A preliminary truce was agreed only a fortnight after the crossing of the Great Belt and a peace treaty was concluded in the former Danish capital of Roskilde on 26 February. Denmark surrendered the provinces of Blekinge, Bohusland, Halland, and Skåne (with its fine annual yield of corn), the island of Bornholm and the Norwegian county and city of Trondheim. Frederick had also to provide two thousand cavalry for the Swedish army and accept the presence of Swedish troops on Danish soil until detailed disputes between the two countries were settled. For Frederick the terms were harsh: he lost a third of his kingdom and, indirectly, much revenue, too. Outsider owners of ships trading in the Baltic – mainly Dutch and English, but a few French – were well satisfied: for the first time two independent kingdoms would share control of the Øresund, making it harder for any one ruler to close the Baltic to foreign vessels or impose exorbitant tolls.

The ambition of Charles X was not, however, satiated. In the previous year he had contemplated the destruction of Poland: now he envisaged a Three Crown Union, dominated by Sweden, with Denmark and Norway as dependent on Stockholm as Livonia. In August 1658 – less than six months after the Peace of Roskilde – he made Danish delay in executing detailed provisions of the treaty an excuse for ordering resumption of the war. Copenhagen and Christiania (Oslo) were to be occupied and Denmark subjugated. As a first step, the Swedes crossed the Sound to Helsingør and in September seized the fortress-palace of Kronborg from which they subsequently removed any treasures of value.

Such blatant aggression was a major military and diplomatic blunder. The townsfolk of Copenhagen, already angered by the Council of the Realm's persistence in maintaining exemption of the nobility from taxation, now loyally backed King Frederick in resisting the Swedish assault on the capital. Christian IV had made Copenhagen a fortified city, protected by a rampart, moats and bastions, with four gates commanding entry to the inner town. The Swedish army could no more penetrate these defences than it had the monastic fortifications at Jasna Góra. Moreover, by taking Kronborg Sweden alienated all those nations eager to prevent any one country from acting as master of the Øresund. Frederick III suddenly found that, from a mixture of motives, he had acquired powerful allies. A Dutch fleet forced its way through the Sound to relieve Copenhagen from siege and Dutch troops landed on Funen to help Danish guerrillas against the Swedish army of occupation. That supreme opportunist, Elector Frederick William, entered Holstein in strength, with another 20,000 men held in reserve either in Brandenburg or the Hohenzollern enclaves in the Rhineland; and Austrian Imperialist troops and the Poles kept up the pressure on the Swedish outposts in Pomerania.

Even republican England, so long a supporter of Sweden, sent General-at-Sea Mountagu with a fleet to the Sound to bolster the Danes – and make certain they did not become too dependent on the nation's Dutch rivals. Young Samuel Pepys crossed the North Sea in a ketch with despatches for his kinsman Mountagu and dined aboard the flagship *Naseby* off Elsinore. But the fleet's presence in Baltic waters was brief. Across England and Scotland it was a time of troubled doubts and rekindled loyalties. By August 1659 the *Naseby* was back in the Thames. Nine months later, rechristened *Royal Charles*, she brought Charles II home from The Hague to Dover.

To the Great Powers peace in northern Europe became an urgent necessity. The Baltic trade could survive separate campaigns but not the disruption of long and general war. Yet Charles X was obstinately disinclined to give up the contest. He summoned the Riksdag to meet at Gothenburg but in February 1660, before the first session opened, the thirty-seven-year-old king suddenly fell ill. Within a few days he was dead, apparently from pneumonia.

Peace talks began almost immediately, with the French and Dutch for once acting in concert as mediators. The Roskilde terms were reimposed on the two main combatants, although by the Treaty of Copenhagen Denmark recovered Trondheim in Norway and Bornholm, where the islanders placed themselves directly under the king rather than accept administration by the despised Council of the Realm. Sweden was confirmed in possession of her natural geographical limits within Scandinavia.

French diplomacy was largely responsible for a broader settlement, agreed at the Oliva monastery, outside Danzig, in May 1660; peace was restored between Sweden, Poland, Brandenburg and the Emperor Leopold I (who had succeeded Ferdinand III two years previously). The loser by the Oliva Treaty was Poland: John II Casimir recognized the sovereignty of Sweden over Livonia and of Brandenburg over East Prussia, as well as formally renouncing his dynastic claims in Sweden. The Russian threat, so alarming to the Swedes four summers back in time, failed to materialize, largely through the instability of Tsar Alexis's throne in Moscow and raids from the tartars of the Crimea. A peace treaty concluded at Kardis in 1661 restored the frontiers that existed before the war: the bear ambled back from Livonia and Estonia to his den.

Across the rich steppe lands of the Ukraine, however, Poles, Russians and Cossacks continued the fighting until 1667, when in exhaustion they agreed on a thirty-year cessation of hostilities, the Truce of Andrusevo. Smolensk, Kiev and the east bank of the Dnieper passed under Russian rule; but the west bank of the river remained Polish. Alexis's foreign minister, Ordyn-Naschokin, favoured a realignment of foreign policy, by which Russia and Poland would jointly stand on the defensive against Turkey and concentrate on driving the Swedes out of their Baltic provinces. As yet the proposal was too revolutionary for the tsar, but it remained an alternative concept that was to attract his youngest son, Peter the Great.

The First Northern War left deep scars on the economy of the lands it ravaged. The passage of the armies reduced the yield from some of the most fertile fields of Europe, especially in central Poland. Warsaw was burnt by the invaders and its palaces pillaged. Elsewhere many small peasant farms were abandoned, particularly in Estonia and Livonia, either directly from the effects of the fighting or because the land was seized by the invaders and awarded (or sold) to Swedish noble families. Poland also suffered from the decline of the Baltic grain trade in the second half of the century. More cereal was being grown in other parts of Europe and many landowners ceased to sow and plough, finding dairy-farming potentially more profitable.

Forests, too, were thinned in some areas, temporarily cutting the timber trade down the Dvina and Niemen. In the Dalecarlia region of unravaged Sweden and in parts of Finland the government intervened, anxious to control the felling of trees in order to conserve future supplies. No such curbs checked the mounting prosperity of Gothenburg, however. On 21 July 1664 Samuel Pepys noted with great satisfaction in his diary that he had placed an order for 1,000 masts from Gothenburg, 'the biggest [order] that ever was made in the Navy and wholly of my composing, and a good one I hope it is for the King'. But for hemp and flax the Royal Navy still looked in the first instance to Riga.

The later stages of the war strangled one potential rival to Riga. From 1642 to 1681 the Duchy of Courland and Semigallia was ruled by Jacob Kettler, a grandson of the last grand master of the Livonian Order, who became the first Duke in 1561 as a nominal vassal of the Polish king. Remarkably the earliest campaigns of the century left the Courland peninsula relatively unscathed, although Gustavus Adolphus invaded Semigallia in force, taking the duchy's capital, Mitau, in 1621 and again four years later. But Polish preoccupation with the Ukraine and Swedish commitments in the Thirty Years War enabled Duke Jacob to develop Windau (Ventspils), an ice-free port with extensive pine forests in the hinterland. By 1645 the shipyards of Windau were building merchant vessels for Courland traders with astonishing speed; soon men-of-war were on the stocks, too. When the Thirty Years War ended Duke Jacob had his own navy and a merchant fleet that exported pine masts to English ports and even to Venice and sailed the wider oceans. Tobago became briefly Duke Jacob's colony and possession of an island at the mouth of the river Gambia gave the merchants of Mitau and Windau a prospect of wealth from the African-Caribbean slave trade. Duke Jacob encouraged a glass-making industry and the setting up of an iron foundry. Windau, only 200 kilometres from Riga and facing the western Baltic, was becoming a serious competitor to the second city of Charles X's extended realm. In the 1658 campaign a Swedish invasion spared neither Mitau nor Windau. For two years Duke Jacob was held captive; he lost much of his merchant fleet and virtually all his navy. The nascent industries were destroyed, while the two overseas colonies fell prey to piracy and to Dutch and British empire builders. Although Jacob Kettler ruled the duchy for another twenty years, the would-be masters of the Baltic had cut Courland's ambitions down to size.

In the aftermath of the war there was widespread political uncertainty. The two royal 'losers', John II Casimir of Poland and Frederick III of Denmark, both sought to strengthen the authority of the Crown and make kingship hereditary rather than elective. In Poland the Sejm protected its rights and sought to counter any royal initiative. A major rebellion instigated by a section of the landed magnates led to a battle at Matwy in July 1666 in which the royal army suffered heavy casualties and was defeated. John Casimir remained king on sufferance until, two years later, the last of the Polish Vasas abdicated and settled for a quiet life in France.

Literally tens of thousands of *szlachta* – one account says 80,000 – converged on Warsaw for the election of John Casimir's successor. They chose one of their own number, Michael Wisniowecki, a compromise candidate of no distinction. Political power in the Commonwealth of the Two Nations continued to be exercised not by the Crown, nor by any other central authority, but by local assemblies dominated by the landowning nobility, who formed as much as 10 per cent of the population. Michael was followed by John Sobieski (reigned 1674–96), who in 1683 became the saviour of Turkish-besieged Vienna. Yet even this glorious feat of Polish arms did nothing to unify the country and check the centrifugal authority of the provincial diets. Ominously, in 1697 the *szlachta* again looked abroad and chose the wealthy and manipulative Elector of Saxony, who reigned as King Augustus II. In 1668 John Casimir had warned the nobility that, unless the system was changed, Poland-Lithuania would be partitioned by its neighbours. His prophecy went unheeded.

By contrast, in Denmark Frederick III was remarkably successful in his attempts to assert the authority of the Crown. The partnership he achieved with the defenders of Copenhagen in 1658–9 outlasted the war. With considerable patience Frederick waited until he had complete backing from the city's burghers before carrying through a royal coup in two stages, on both occasions protected by a regiment of German mercenaries under a trusted general. In October 1660 he convened the Diet to meet in the capital and induced the non-noble estates to propose that the monarchy be made hereditary, a measure that became law three months later. By the summer of 1661 he felt sufficiently strong to trim the privileges of the Estates and impose royal absolutism on the kingdom. A Royal Law, drawn up in 1665, shaped the form of enlightened absolutism that prevailed until 1848, when Frederick VII summoned a constituent assembly. The burghers of Copenhagen, who had hoped for a system of consultative decision-making as in Sweden, were disappointed. Nor were they pleased by Frederick III's determination to build the Kastellet, a citadel on the Copenhagen waterfront designed to overawe the capital, like the Tower of London beside the Thames. But there was no stirring of revolt within Denmark.

★

Political change in Sweden was delayed by the need to impose a second twelve-year regency, for Charles XI was only four when his father died. Magnus de la Gardie, the chancellor, was no Oxenstierna. He owed his influence in the realm to competent generalship, landed wealth and a tempestuous liaison with the young Christina followed by marriage to her cousin, Charles X Gustav's sister. He was therefore the boy king's uncle. As a connoisseur of the arts, benefactor to Uppsala University and devotee of French culture, de la Gardie was an aristocrat who exuded magnificence. By contrast Charles XI grew up bigoted, unprepossessing, unimaginative and tongue-tied; 'That young lout,' his uncle Magnus dubbed him at the age of twenty. The comment was unfair. Charles XI was a conscientious hard-worker hampered by dyslexia, and he became the most innovative Swedish king since Gustav Vasa.

The chancellor governed by grace of the Council of State (Riksråd, or Råd), a self-indulgent oligarchy. De la Gardie proved a bumbling statesman. So great was his admiration for Louis XIV's France that in 1672 he persuaded the Råd to accept a treaty of alliance that would guarantee Sweden annual French subsidies. Rather curiously, he seems to have thought Sweden could avoid fighting in Louis's wars simply by mobilizing an army in Pomerania to threaten the North German princes should they wish to aid the emperor or the Dutch against France. But Elector Frederick William was far from intimidated; in 1675 he raised an army of 45,000 men, determined to seize Swedish Pomerania. The Swedes were defeated at Fehrbellin and found themselves at war not only with Brandenburg-Prussia but also with the Netherlands, Emperor Leopold I and, yet again, Denmark. By the summer of 1676 the Danes had recovered all of Skåne except for Malmö. In June a joint Dutch-Danish fleet defeated the Swedes off the southernmost tip of Öland. A chance shot ignited the powder magazine of the flagship *Kronan*, sending a second decorative 'pride of the Swedish navy' to the bottom of the Baltic. In 1980 marine archaeologists brought to shore cannons, carved wooden figures and silver coins scattered from the wreck. Within a few years they went on display in the Kalmar Region Museum, testimony to the destructive power of seventeenth century explosive. The Danish admiral, Niels Juel, inflicted a second defeat on a Swedish squadron that entered Køge Bay.

In a last attempt to save the southern provinces Charles XI – who was by now sovereign in his own right – led his troops westwards into Skåne and on 3 December 1676 surprised the Danish army outside Lund with a ferocious assault across a frozen river. The battle rolled on through the brief daylight hours until the king himself recklessly led a charge to break the centre of the Danish lines. So intense was the fighting that half the combatants were left dead on the battlefield. Technically Lund was a Swedish victory and it was followed in the new year by a campaign that forced the Danes back across the Sound. But forest fighters (*snapphanar*) waged a guerrilla resistance movement for two years. Fortunately for Sweden the war went well for Louis XIV farther south in Europe and in 1679 he dictated peace for the North at Fontainebleau: Sweden – France's only ally – retained the provinces ceded at Roskilde and recovered most of Pomerania from Elector Frederick William.

For the remainder of his reign Charles XI kept his troops on the alert. In 1680 he founded Karlskrona as a naval port in Blekinge, at the head of an archipelago not far from where the *Kronan* sank. Yet never again did he go to war. Reconciliation was a necessity. Charles married a Danish princess, of whom he became extremely fond and who bore him a son and two daughters before dying pathetically young. In public affairs he encouraged the foundation at Lund of Sweden's second university, in the hope of winning the loyalty of the next generation of Skånians and Blekingans.

The interlude of peace allowed him to concentrate on long-neglected abuses in government and, in particular, the danger that the high nobility would bind the peasantry in latter-day feudal servitude, as in Poland. The Riksdag of 1680 was presented with a royal reform programme. Incompetent or corrupt officials under the regency, already blamed for the low level of military preparedness, were brought before a parliamentary court that 'ransacked' (confiscated) their properties. Grants of land in both Sweden and the Baltic Provinces given by the Crown – notably by Queen Christina – as fiefdoms or pledges to the new nobility in the past half-century were subject to 'reduction' (handed back to the Crown), a process to recover lost revenue that had begun under Charles X but was abandoned by the regency. Crippling confiscations made the great landowners bewail their impoverishment; Magnus the Magnificent was left with only one palace. 'Even so,' Michael Roberts has pointed out, 'it was not de la Gardie, but his faithful archivist, who actually starved to death.'

The Riksdag of 1680 also began a constitutional revolution: the king was formally freed from any obligation to govern subject to 'the advice of the Råd'. This ruling was the first of a series of declarations over the next thirteen years by which the parliament accepted Charles XI as an absolute monarch. The Riksdag's compliance enabled Charles to impose further reforms. The Ecclesiastical Law of 1686 placed Swedish Lutheranism strictly under royal control: the king could impose his own choice of bishop and even decide who should be pastor in a particular parish; no subject could enter into a marriage without basic knowledge and acceptance of the catechism; a year later provincial governors were ordered to ensure that proper order of worship was maintained. For the army, the king devised a system by which in peacetime officers and soldiers served as farmers or labourers on allocated land, from which they could be mustered for manoeuvres or if war loomed. A similar distributive system for the navy made seamen the responsibility of certain towns.

To assist him with administration Charles XI virtually created the Swedish civil service. It became a bureaucracy over which he presided in person, threshing out the details of any administrative proposal and insisting on reading every despatch to or from envoys to other lands. Yet, unlike many innovative monarchs, Charles XI must speedily have acquired some skill in delegating responsibility; for by the end of the reign the machine he oiled ran so smoothly that it functioned efficiently while his son and successor, Charles XII, was away from Swedish shores for fifteen years.

In retrospect, it is clear there were weaknesses in Charles XI's reforms. The distributive army proved slow to muster, and in the Baltic provinces the 'reduction' seemed to threaten the structure of Swedish colonialism. The largely German Livonian baronage sent a delegation to Stockholm to protest that the king was infringing rights he had already guaranteed. Charles showed some sympathy with the pleas advanced by their spokesman, Johann von Patkul, whose eloquent 'honesty' on behalf of his 'fatherland' he commended. But he was not prepared to drive the nobility of the homeland into revolt by concessions in the Baltic provinces. Soon Patkul was to show himself a greater menace than any territorial magnate in Sweden.

Had Charles XI lived longer he might have coaxed the Livonian barons into partnership. But, like so many Vasa kings, he died relatively young, on 5 April 1697, a widower of forty-one, the victim of stomach cancer. There followed a macabre episode that left a deep impression on contemporaries. While Charles XI's body was still at Stockholm's Castle of the Three Crowns awaiting burial, a disastrous fire swept through the building, leaving only one wing standing. The first public act of Sweden's new sovereign – who was not yet fifteen – was to lead to safety, calmly and with natural authority, his grandmother, two sisters and his father's coffin. The reign of Charles XII had begun, as it was so often to continue, with a drama larger than life.

On the day of Charles's accession his future enemy, Peter I of Russia, was on Swedish soil, travelling incognito across Livonia at the head of a long procession bound for Riga. For Peter had set out on his Great Embassy, an eighteen-month mission without precedent. Nominally he went in search of allies for Russia's chronic conflict with the Ottoman Turks. In practice he wished to observe the way the West worked and lived; craftsmen and engineers, seamen and soldiers must be encouraged to bring their skills to Russia. Privately he told his companions that he intended to learn how to build ships in Holland. Already he was obsessed by the sea and by seamanship.

Peter, the youngest son of Alexis, was ten years older than Charles XII. He acceded in 1672, sharing the throne at first with his half-brother Ivan but taking over the government in 1694. Soon his subjects saw the impact of his personality: the severed heads, knouted backs and mouths rendered tongueless that deterred plotters; nights carousing and (illegally) smoking tobacco in Moscow's German Quarter, full of contempt for Russian ways; journeys to the far north and into Arctic waters, taxing the endurance of companions; and the human cost of innovative concepts of war by land and sea. Lives were wasted, but they gained Peter his first victory, the capture in July 1696 of the Turkish fortress of Azov. Now, less than a year later, he was almost a thousand miles from the Sea of Azov, discovering the Baltic coast and the river ports that Ivan III, Ivan IV and Alexis coveted.

In Riga Peter made sketches of the new ramparts and citadel. Understandably, he fell foul of Governor General Dahlberg, a great military architect and engineer. The tsar's resentment at the alleged 'unpleasantness' of the people of Riga lingered and in 1700 was cited as a reason for making war on Sweden. From Windau he sailed down to Königsberg, in a ship supplied by the Duke of Courland. After seven weeks as a guest of the Great Elector he went on overland to Hanover, Zaandam and Amsterdam. By the time he reached ice-bound London, in January 1698, Peter Mikhailovich was a certified master-gunner of Prussia and a master-carpenter of Holland. During the four months he spent in England he was exhilarated by two days with the fleet in the Solent, where he watched a mock battle between towering ships-of-the-line. No earlier ruler in any land was ever so well primed in naval matters.

From Vienna he intended to go south to Venice, the greatest maritime republic in the world. Instead, he was forced to head back for Moscow, where four regiments had mutinied and his throne seemed at risk from an incipient revolt. But at Cracow came news that loyal troops had restored order and Peter was able to pause at Rawa, near Lemberg, for three days of heavy drinking and expansive talk with Augustus II the Strong, King of Poland and Elector of Saxony. He learnt with interest that his host was contemplating a joint venture with Denmark to oust the Swedes from their Baltic provinces. For Peter to join an offensive alliance of this character was impossible so long as Russia remained at war with Turkey and there were rebels to punish at home. But he was attracted by the prospect of a three-pronged assault on the young Charles XII's loosely knit empire of the North.

The alliance project was the grand design, not of Augustus, but of Johann von Patkul, who had fled his Livonian estate on learning the Swedes had sentenced him to death *in absentia* for treason and found refuge in Poland. Patkul visited Copenhagen where the newly acceded Frederick IV was young enough to hanker for a war of revenge on Sweden. Augustus the Strong welcomed Patkul's assurances that the Livonian nobility would willingly accept him as hereditary king provided they were freed from the Swedish yoke. And, on a secret visit to a monastery outside Moscow, Patkul found Tsar Peter attracted by the prospect of securing Karelia and Ingria and recovering the Baltic outlet that Ivan III once held. But Peter insisted he would not fight Sweden until he had made peace with the Turks: April 1700 was the earliest month he could contemplate a new war along Baltic shores.

Augustus sent 14,000 crack Saxon troops into Livonia in February 1700 and besieged Riga, without any declaration of war. They made no impression on Dahlberg's fortifications and the attack was soon repulsed. A month later Frederick IV of Denmark led his main army southwards from Jutland into the Duchy of Holstein-Gottorp, whose ruler was Charles XII's boon companion and brother-in-law; the Danes besieged Tönning, a town garrisoned by Swedes. This unprovoked resort to war angered the British and the Dutch, for it disrupted trade at a time when their navies awaited a new round of hostilities with France and were in urgent need of Baltic timber, hemp and tar. In 1658 the two countries sent fleets to the Øresund to support Denmark and prevent the Swedes challenging the status quo. Now, early in the summer of 1700, twenty-five Dutch and British ships-of-the-line entered the Kattegat to cover a Swedish landing on Zealand. London and Amsterdam were determined to encourage Charles XII to put an early stop to all this nonsense of a second northern war. Charles himself did not anticipate a long conflict when, on 13 April, he sailed from Stockholm for Blekinge and his baptism of fire in Zealand. He was wrong. Although he reigned for eighteen more years he never saw his capital again. When the fighting that began so casually was over, all that remained of Charles XII had lain in the vault of Stockholm's Riddarholmskyrkan for twenty months.

Sweden should have won the war within a year. The Zealand campaign lasted a mere fortnight, for the Danes were hopelessly outnumbered. Frederick IV hurried back from Tönning to find Copenhagen besieged, his navy rendered inactive, and no sign of relief from the allies Patkul had conjured up for him in the East. He sued for peace and received generous terms, for the British and Dutch insisted on virtual restoration of the status quo so that trade could soon flow freely again through the Øresund and Kattegat. Charles withdrew his troops to Karlskrona, determined that before ice closed the inner Baltic he would cross to Livonia and thrash the Saxons outside Riga. Augustus, however, abandoned his assault on the city and retired to winter quarters. A general peace seemed close. But in September news reached Karlskrona that the Russians and Turks had agreed on a thirty-year armistice. Tsar Peter could give his attention to Baltic affairs; within a fortnight he was at the head of an army invading Ingria, with the bastion of Narva as his first objective. Charles XII, with the Swedish vanguard, landed at Pernau on 6 October but over a month elapsed before successive convoys brought his army up to strength. On 13 November more than 10,000 well-trained troops began an exhausting 200 kilometre march northwards to save Narva. Remarkably they reached the historic fortress within six days.

On 16 November – the sixty-eighth anniversary of Lützen – the Swedes celebrated their first success: accurate fire from the horse artillery sent an advance Russian cavalry patrol reeling back to Narva. But the sight of the plateau Peter had selected as a field of battle sobered their elation. Facing them was an enemy army four times as large as their own, entrenched behind 6.5 kilometres of earthworks protected by a ring of cannon, resting at either end on the curving right bank of the Narva river. No experienced commander would risk an assault on such a position with a relatively small force of weary troops. There were only a few hours of daylight in late November and a constant threat of heavy rain, mud or swirling snow. So confident was Peter that the Swedes would pause, probe and await reinforcements that he left Narva and, with his foreign minister, set off for Novgorod and a round of diplomacy with an envoy from Augustus the Strong.

Charles, however, was not a textbook general; he was a teenage hothead, his ego flushed by easy victory in Zealand. He ordered the forty-five-year-old cavalry general Gustav Rehnsköld – who was in effect his chief-of-staff – to find a way to breach the Russian defensive line. At two o'clock in the afternoon of 20 November the well-disciplined Swedish infantry, some carrying fascines to cross trenches, concentrated at a point in the centre of the line. By chance, as they began to advance, lowering clouds broke and they went forward with sword or bayonet at the ready and a blizzard behind them blowing snow horizontally into the faces of the Russian defenders. Once the breach was made the Swedish infantry columns fanned out and the Russians fell back towards the river. There was no resolute commander to rally them. In panic the cavalry sought to escape by plunging into the water and heading for the old Russian fortress of Ivangorod on the left bank. Most were swept away and drowned in the fast-flowing icy current. Upstream a single bridge collapsed under the weight of an army in flight and hundreds more Russians perished in the river. On the right bank, protected by an improvised *gulaigorod*, two Guards regiments Peter had himself raised and trained, the Preobrazhensky and Semyonovosky, fought on defiantly until darkness fell and the hideous sounds of battle gradually died away.

By daylight next morning there could be no doubt Charles XII had gained a sensational victory at Narva. Meticulous Swedish mustering listed 677 dead and 1,205 wounded from an army of some 10,000; Russian casualties – including many hundreds taken prisoner – must have exceeded the total number of Swedes engaged in the battle. Peter also lost highly prized artillery and a large stock of cannonballs and powder. The Russians no longer threatened an advance on Reval and into Livonia. There seemed a danger than Charles might march on Moscow. Instead, he waited out the winter at Dorpat and, in the following summer, occupied Courland before turning his main army against Augustus and plunging into Polish-German affairs. So great was Charles's contempt for the Russians that he left a mere 6,000 men to hold the vital Narva-Dorpat line. Further north, no attempt was made to reinforce Swedish outposts in distant Karelia or the galleys and brigantines flying the blue-and-yellow ensign on the waters of Lake Ladoga.

For six years Charles was obsessed with Poland, giving free rein to a deep personal mistrust of his cousin Augustus. His political objective was to plant a Swedish puppet on the throne in Warsaw and give Swedish merchants, and the burghers of Riga, a stranglehold on Polish trade. At first he believed he could detach the *szlachta* from their Saxon ruler, for no Poles had participated in Augustus's abortive campaign to seize Riga. But inevitably Poland lapsed into a fractious civil war; the countryside was devastated by Swedish troops who ravaged and pillaged with the connivance of their commanders. Charles emerged as a shrewd tactician with instinctive perception of his enemy's weakness; victories at Kliszow in 1702, Pultusk a year later and Punitz and Wschowa in 1705 made him the scourge of the Saxon army. In January 1704 Charles and Cardinal-Archbishop Radziejowski induced a rump Sejm to depose Augustus and seek the election of a native Pole. The Saxons at once kidnapped the best candidate, Sobieski's son, but Stanislaw Leszczyński, a noble who was content to serve any puppet master, was elected and duly crowned. Sweden and the *Rzeczpospolita* made peace the following year. Poland avoided loss of territory but accepted trade restrictions: exports were to be diverted through Riga; merchants from

Stockholm and Gothenberg would receive concessions if they settled in Polish towns; there must be no transit trade with Russia, even were a general peace restored. The peace treaty pleased the English and Dutch merchants. They could now sail again to the ports of Livonia, Courland and Pomerania. For direct trade with Russia there remained in summer the long route to the White Sea; in August 1702 fifty-two Dutch merchant vessels and thirty-five British were moored in the river off Archangel.

The Russians were not inactive. In the summers of 1701 and 1702 General Sheremetev led successful forays into Livonia, and Tsar Peter supervised the building of some thirty small vessels, dependent on a single sail and oars, capable of harrying the Swedes on Lake Ladoga. So successful was this pioneer Baltic fleet that in the autumn of 1702 he mounted a combined operation of seamen, infantry and gunners against the Swedish fort of Noteborg, built at the point where Ladoga flows into the Neva. On 2 October 1702 the fort surrendered, after two weeks of siege. Significantly Peter re-named it Schlüsselburg ('key town' in German).

By the spring his fleet had expanded to sixty ships, and Sheremetev was at Schlüsselburg with an army of 20,000 men. Methodically the troops made their way through the forest along the Neva's north bank, while the ships sailed down 65 kilometres of muddy river to the head of the Gulf of Finland. A small Swedish settlement, with sawmills, was captured on 12 May 1703. Four days later, at a place the Finns called Hare Island, 8 kilometres downstream, legend relates that Peter cut the form of a cross in the ground with a soldier's musket and declared, 'Here there shall be a town'. The new foundation, he soon decided, should be named in honour of his patron saint.

St Petersburg was built with astonishing speed. By October the fortress of St Peter and St Paul covered Hare Island, though like all early buildings in the city it was made of timber. Houses on neighbouring Vassilevsky Island went up in the summer of 1704, to be followed within months by a ship-yard on the Neva's left bank, with a small central building that became the first Admiralty. A city that depended for expansion on piles being driven into a swamp and heavy balustrades giving (minimum) protection from flooding could only grow by careful planning and masterful direction and Peter appointed Domenico Trezzini, a Venetian architect who had practised in Copenhagen, to serve as Russia's Master of Building, Construction and Fortification. For ten years Trezzini sought to realize Peter's plans for the city. He designed not only forts, but a summer palace, and 'ideal homes' of varying size and character for the settlers whom the tsar cajoled into coming north as St Petersburg's earliest citizens. By 1708 Peter's kinsfolk and many of the noblest families in Moscow reluctantly obeyed orders to join him. Four years later St Petersburg became the seat of government. Other architects followed Trezzini. Most were of German origin, until in 1716 Peter appointed as Architect General Alexandre LeBlond, a Parisian with a fine eye for landscape, formal gardens and canals. But among the sculptors whom Peter encouraged to settle in St Petersburg was an Italian named Rastrelli, who travelled north with his young son Bartolommeo. By mid-century the architectural genius of the youngster had perfected the Russian Italianate Baroque classicism that determined the character of the city.

Other nations have created artificial well-planned capitals – Brasilia, Canberra and Washington among them. St Petersburg is unique in two respects: it was built on swampy ground by forced labour that cost the lives of at least 30,000 men, and probably more; and their work was undertaken in newly conquered territory at the height of a war in which the odds remained heavily stacked against their country. For, quite apart from the hovering menace of Sweden, Peter had to despatch armies to suppress local rebellions in the lower Don region, in Astrakhan and the middle Volga.

The first direct threat to St Petersburg came within two months of the legendary founding of the city. Peter defeated a Swedish force concentrated along the north bank of the Neva, while a Swedish naval squadron blockaded the mouth of the river throughout the summer. As soon as the earliest thin ice formed, in October 1703, the Swedes pulled back, enabling Peter to venture into Baltic waters and seize Kotlin island, where work immediately began on the fortifications that were to become the naval base of Kronstadt. Even more remarkably, despite the Swedish warships in the Gulf of Finland, merchantmen from the west moored in the Neva before the ice finally closed in; two ships were welcomed from the Netherlands, one from England.

Charles XII was so obsessed with his Polish politicking and his vendetta with Augustus that he long continued to ignore all signs of Russian revival. Peter renewed his thrust across Ingria and into Estonia. Both Dorpat and Narva were besieged in the summer of 1704 and fell to the Russians in July and August, at a time when Europe's attention was concentrated on Marlborough's march from the Netherlands up the Rhine to defeat the French at Blenheim. At last, in January 1706 Charles led some 20,000 men eastwards with great rapidity and for four hungry winter months besieged the fortress town of Grodno, on the upper Niemen. But when the thaw began, the Russians slipped away southwards, using the Pripet marshes as defensive cover. Charles recognized that an invasion of Russia needed long and careful planning.

From Pinsk, he turned back westwards and spent the late summer pursuing the Saxons into their homeland, meeting little resistance. By mid-September Swedish troops were in Leipzig and Dresden. A month later the Saxons signed the Treaty of Altranstädt (1706) by which Augustus II formally abdicated his Polish crown, recognizing Stanislaw Leszczyński as his successor. Saxony withdrew from the war. At Charles's demand, Augustus handed over 'the traitor Patkul', who after months of imprisonment suffered a slow and agonizing execution, by being broken and dissected on the wheel. Only with Augustus humbled and Patkul destroyed did Charles look decisively to the East.

The King despised the tsar and the troops whom his generals contemptuously dubbed 'bog Peters'. He still thought of them as the enemy who panicked at Narva. His most experienced commanders urged him to strike north-eastwards from the middle Vistula to clear the Russians from Livonia. Thus, they argued, he could recover Narva and Dorpat, benefit from sea communications on his left flank, and complete a pincer movement with the Swedish army in Finland. The blue and yellow flag would fly triumphantly above Kronstadt and the fortress of St Peter and St Paul; and Russia would again be excluded from the Baltic. This was the strategy that Peter anticipated and feared: he countered it in advance by ordering a ruthless scorched earth policy along the likely invasion route, so as to deprive the Swedes of shelter and food. A few months later, on the tsar's insistence, Dorpat was razed to the ground though there were no invaders within 160 kilometres of the town.

Charles XII did not head for the Baltic provinces. Instead, he made Moscow his main objective, looking ahead to a time when a puppet tsar would reign from the Kremlin. In January 1708 the king led his vanguard into Grodno and soon held the line of the Niemen and its tributaries as far north as Vilna. In this region – along what is now the borderland of Lithuania and Belarus – Charles established winter quarters, ready in the spring to make for the crossing of the river Dnieper at Mogilev. Once there, Charles would be within 160 kilometres of Smolensk and 500 of Moscow; but, crucially, 650 kilometres away from his Baltic supply base at Riga.

The going became harder. When the Swedes resumed their advance, the fire-scorched, barren fields and burned villages began to take a toll of the army. In early July 1708 Charles won his first victory of the campaign, at Golovchin, showing all his old courage and impetuosity by leading his men across a ford in which the waters swept up to his chest. Then, however, he paused at Mogilev for five weeks, urgently awaiting the arrival of a supply train, protected by a newly raised army of 12,500 men under the command of the Governor of Riga, Count Lewenhaupt. Wagons and carriages were loaded with winter clothing, medicine, cartridges and explosives, new cannon, and enough food to sustain the whole army for six weeks without foraging. But the wagons could never lumber along at more than 15 kilometres a day and in a wet and muddy July they managed on average slightly less than eight kilometres a day

Charles XII was not a patient man. In mid-August he made the first in a succession of strategic errors; the army would wait no longer for Lewenhaupt. He crossed the Dnieper and left Mogilev. At first he moved northwards, probing the Russian outposts, but on 15 September he decided to turn about and seek the unravaged wheatlands of the Ukraine, where the harvest was gathered in. The king was drawn southwards, not only by the prospect of fresh food supplies, but from reports that the Polish-educated Hetman Ivan Mazeppa would cut his links with the tsar and bring over to the Swedish side several thousand Cossack horsemen. At that moment he was 145 kilometres east of the supply train. Peter, whose scouts kept him well informed of the movement of his enemies, resolved to attack Lewenhaupt before the corridor narrowed. Had Charles remained in Mogilev and not crossed the Dnieper, Lewenhaupt's infantry and cavalry, together with the precious supplies from Riga, would by then have reached him.

On 28 September Peter intercepted the supply train at Lesnaya and in a fierce six-hour battle cut it to pieces. Half of the Swedish army and a third of their Russian assailants lay dead or gravely injured. On 8 October Lewenhaupt and 6,000 survivors finally reached King Charles's army. They brought with them not a single bag of supplies, no winter clothing and no artillery.

Snow had fallen in the last hour of the battle of Lesnaya, unseasonably early and giving warning of a grim winter ahead for all Europe. By Christmas there were ice-floes in the North Sea off the coast of Norfolk and Suffolk and horse carriages made their way across the frozen Øresund. On a comfortless scale of misery, the winter might be rated for Charles's army as 'terrible' rather than 'disastrous'. The Cossack rebellion was virtually crushed before Mazeppa could bring more than a few thousand horsemen to Charles's assistance, but the old Hetman was at least able to guide the Swedes to a fertile segment of the Ukraine, where there were stocks of food under shelter. Even so, to venture far from winter quarters either scouting or foraging was foolish; sentries froze to death on guard duty; and a survivor would later recall 'dragoons and cavalrymen sitting upon their horses stone-dead with their reins in their hands'. When spring came the army penetrated deeper into the Ukraine. The fortified town of Poltava, on a ridge above the river Vorskla, blocked its advance. On 1 May Charles ordered siege works to be constructed around the town, even though he was short of cannon. Like Napoleon in 1812 he had faith in his own destiny and thought little of the Russian soldiers' powers of resistance.

Once again King Charles awaited reinforcements, on this occasion Polish troops raised by King Stanislaw. They remained some 950 kilometres away, west of Lemberg. Instead, on the far side of the river, Tsar Peter arrived hot-foot from Azov on 4 June, with another 8,000 men to boost Russian numbers to more than 42,000, almost twice the size of Charles's army. The king might still have declined battle, withdrawn westwards, south of Kiev, and sought mediation and a negotiated peace. Pride precluded withdrawal; he preferred to wait for the right moment to launch a surprise attack on the Russian palisades.

Hubris fed Nemesis. While in the saddle on 17 June – his twenty-seventh birthday – Charles XII was hit on the heel by a musket ball that penetrated the length of his left foot. The wound festered and fever set in. For three days he seemed close to death. Within a week he was in command again, but only from a stretcher. Tactical decisions in the field would be taken by the ageing Field Marshal Rehnsköld. The battle began, 5 kilometres north-west of Poltava town, in the early dawn of a summer's morning, Monday 28 June 1709, by chance the tsar's name day. After fierce hand-to-hand fighting the Swedes broke through the outer ring, but the attackers were then left with almost 600 metres of open land before closing with the second line of Russian infantry. Massed cannons covered the open land maintaining, by eighteenth century battle standards, a withering fire. What the artillery began, the Russian infantry completed. By midday it was all over. Seven thousand Swedes died on the battlefield, 2,800 were taken prisoner, including Field Marshal Rehnsköld. Russian casualties were fewer than 1,500 killed and less than 3,000 wounded.

Some 15,000 Swedes and several thousand Cossacks retreated in good order. They followed the river Vorskla to its confluence with the Dnieper at Perevoluchna, 130 kilometres away. Among them, still on a stretcher though borne in a carriage, was the king. Neither the Vorskla nor the Dnieper was fordable at Perevoluchna and there were no bridges, only small ferries. Charles XII, his carriage, a 700-strong bodyguard and Cossack guides were ferried across the Dnieper in a painfully slow operation and set out for exiled sanctuary in Ottoman Bessarabia. The remainder of the Swedish survivors were trapped on a spit of land between the rivers. Morale was low: their apparently invincible leader had gone, wounded and

12

Imperial Russia in the Ascendant

Pᴏʟᴛᴀᴠᴀ ᴡᴀꜱ ꜱᴏ decisive a victory for Russia that it should have brought general peace to northern Europe. That was certainly Peter's expectation. With no Swedish armies in the field, it seemed as if he needed only to mop up the garrison towns of Karelia and the Baltic provinces to secure the expulsion of the Swedes from the Gulf of Finland and eventually from the whole southern shore of the sea. But Charles XII remained Sweden's autocratic master even while he was in Moldova. Couriers made the 2,000-kilometre journey, though it often took several months for messages to be exchanged between the sovereign and his council: the king consistently demanded that Sweden stay in the war. He envisaged a new coalition, in which freshly raised regiments would cross to Pomerania and into Poland while the Turks recovered the lands they had lost to Peter. Charles was even prepared to command a Turkish army in person to fight the common enemy, if the sultan wished. The Ottoman empire did, indeed, go to war with Russia and, in July 1711, inflicted a severe defeat on the tsar at Stanileski on the river Pruth; but the victory was achieved without Charles's participation. There was no Swedish-Ottoman alliance.

Eighteen months later Sultan Ahmed III, alarmed by the king's intrigues, had his guest taken into nominal custody at a castle close to the present Greco-Turkish frontier. Attempts to proclaim his sister Regent in Stockholm were thwarted and Charles retained his sovereignty: no peace could be made without his consent. In the autumn of 1714, and with Sultan Ahmed's encouragement, the king made his way back from the Balkans to the Baltic in an epic fourteen-day ride, travelling incognito either in a stage coach or, for more than 1,100 kilometres, up in the saddle. He made contact with the Swedish garrison at Stralsund in mid-November and so became once more an active fighter in the war that refused to end.

By then Stralsund was the last remaining fortress south of the Baltic to fly the blue and yellow flag, although Sweden still held the port of Wismar, farther west. Fortune had favoured Peter during the five years that Charles XII was sidelined. At first the Russians concentrated on expansion along both shores of the Gulf of Finland. Courland passed into Russian hands sooner and more easily than anticipated: Peter's niece, Anna Ivanova, became Duchess of Courland in 1710 when the young ruling Duke failed to recover from the prolonged drinking bouts with which he celebrated his marriage. Technically Courland remained a vassal duchy of the kingdom of Poland until 1795 when, with the third partition, it was absorbed in the Russian empire but it was virtually a Russian protectorate for most of the eighteenth century. Elsewhere more conventional ways of acquiring land were required. Riga in particular remained a hard nut to crack. A preliminary bombardment in the closing weeks of 1709 was followed by an eight-month siege in which more than 8,000 mortar bombs were lobbed over the walls and into the city. Riga fell in the second week of July 1710, a month after the Russians secured the Finnish bastion of Vyborg – 'the strong pillar of St Petersburg', as Peter explained in a letter to his wife, Catherine. Before the coming of winter, Reval too was in Russian hands.

Unlike his predecessors Peter envisaged the permanent annexation of the Baltic provinces. Ahead of the final assault on Riga he sought to win over the Livonian nobility and city burghers by assuring them of his respect for the Lutheran religion and their traditional privileges: lands confiscated by Charles XI's policy of 'reduction' would be restored, he promised; German, not Russian, would be the language of provincial administration; the peasantry would remain in virtual serfdom. Reval and Pernau were similarly wooed. A charter dated 16 August 1710 guaranteed 'benevolence . . . to the noble gentry . . . of the Principality of Estonia as well as to the noble city magistrates . . . of Reval' as soon as 'all this land, by God's dispensation, is completely subjected to our power'. All that Peter demanded in return was an oath of allegiance from nobility and merchants alike. To the largely Germanic gentry of the Baltic provinces the charters held out a prospect of greater liberties under a Russian tsar than a Swedish king.

Peter was personally respected in the Baltic provinces. In Reval he even enjoyed a certain popularity, for he had a single-storey cottage built for himself at the edge of the city and in 1718 he ordered Niccolo Michetti to begin work on a pink and white summer palace for Catherine, fringed by parterres, fountains and gardens. Kadriorg ('Catherine's Vale') survives in modern Tallinn, as the compact home of the Estonian Art Collection, with an elegant painted ceiling above the restored banqueting hall. It stands out as a small baroque jewel, set in parkland sloping down to the shore.

The war, however, dragged on, with the suffering intensified in these years by the worst onset of plague since the Black Death. The scourge travelled northwards from Constantinople and the Balkans. It crossed Poland in the winter of 1708–9 to reach the southern Baltic shore in the spring. Between a quarter and a third of the population in both Riga and Reval succumbed either to bubonic or pneumonic plague. Despite strict quarantine measures and the closing of frontiers in 1710 the pestilence ravaged Stockholm, where 40,000 people died. It then spread southwards to Lund and Malmö in the autumn. By the end of the year a third of Copenhagen's inhabitants had died and two-fifths of Helsingør's. A succession of poor harvests led to food shortages, thus weakening natural resistance to disease.

At this moment when peace seemed most desirable, Sweden's old enemies rekindled the glowing embers of past campaigns, seeking to benefit from Charles XII's absence. Frederick IV of Denmark made an unsuccessful bid to recover Skåne; and the Polish nobility acknowledged the shift of power in the East by deposing Stanislaw Leszczyński and restoring Augustus II of Saxony to their throne. The Russians had a free run of the Baltic hinterland, linking up with Danish troops in Holstein and joining Poles, Saxons and Prussians to besiege Stettin (which fell in September 1713), Stralsund, and Wismar. Hanover and Prussia, though mutually suspicious, were eager for easy gains from an embattled Sweden. For thirteen months Charles XII remained in Stralsund, beating off a succession of assaults by Saxons, Danes and Prussians. The Danish fleet gradually secured mastery of the sea lane to Sweden, leaving the defenders of Stralsund short of ammunition and supplies as well as of food. In the fourth week of December 1715 Charles XII escaped from the doomed fortress shortly before it fell, landing at Trelleborg on Christmas Eve and setting up his headquarters at Ystad, later at neighbouring Lund. He had been away from his homeland for fifteen and a quarter years.

As the siege of Stralsund reached a climax in the autumn of 1715, the Swedish defenders could see off Rügen a new naval presence, with deep significance for the coming years. Behind the familiar masts of the Danish squadron loomed the upper works of eight British ships-of-the-line: the Royal Navy had for the first time penetrated deeper into the Baltic than the Øresund. They came, however, not as belligerents. George I, who acceded as King in London on 1 August 1714, joined the anti-Swedish alliance in the following spring only as Elector of Hanover. Admiral Sir John Norris, commander of the British squadron, had orders to enter the Baltic solely to protect British merchantmen: he was not to fire on Swedish warships unless they fired first. But his squadron's presence off Stralsund signalled a major change of policy in London. In the next half-century British diplomacy, though often at variance with narrowly Hanoverian designs, accepted the need to maintain a balance of power in the North. By now the Board of Admiralty knew better than to treat the Baltic as a backwater.

Norris arrived off Stralsund at a time when the older maritime nations were beginning to recognize that Russia was now a sea power. There was incessant activity at Kronstadt, and Reval was developed as a naval harbour as soon as the Estonian coast passed into Russian hands. In 1710–11 Tsar Peter revised his assessment of naval needs. Ships-of-the-line, intended for a conventional battle fleet, continued to be launched from St Petersburg's yards or were purchased from England and Holland, but Peter also reverted to the type of craft that served him so well on Lake Ladoga and the Neva in the earliest phase of the war. He created a new fleet of sea-going galleys, vessels that were built rapidly and might be sailed or rowed into the shallows of the Finnish skerries. The bigger galleys carried up to 300 men and five small cannon. Oared frigates were added to the fleet in later years. On windless days, when enemy men-of-war lay becalmed off shore, the oar-powered galleys could move into positions to attack from all sides. The fighting longship was back in northern waters.

Peter enrolled Venetians and Greeks, well experienced in galley seamanship, to build up his fleet of small craft, much as he hired experienced Dutch and British naval officers for his larger vessels. He also sent Russians to Venice for training. In collaboration with the veteran land-commander, General Feodor Apraxin, he devised a strategy of amphibious warfare that led to the rapid conquest of the Finnish coast in 1713 from Helsingfors (Helsinki) round to Åbo (Turku). There was, however, always a risk that, in a running battle, the towering Swedish ships would smash the galleys with heavy shot from their cannons. At last, in August 1714, General Admiral Apraxin, assisted by 'Rear Admiral Peter Alexevich', trapped a squadron of Swedish frigates in an inlet off Cape Hangö on a day when no breath of wind filled their sails. Ten ships were captured and over a thousand officers or seamen killed or taken prisoner in this first Russian naval victory in the Baltic. Flushed with success, the Russians penetrated the Gulf of Bothnia, capturing Vaasa. Nine galleys crossed the Gulf at its narrowest point to raze the Norrland port of Umeå, in Sweden itself.

The Russian victories intrigued London. Admiral Norris made the first contact with the Elector of Hanover's ally when he escorted British merchantmen up to Reval in 1715 and was royally entertained by the tsar. He saw nothing of the galleys but Peter allowed him to inspect three sixty-gun ships from the St Petersburg yards. They were 'in every way equal to the best of that rank in our country and more handsomely furnished', the admiral reported to London. A year later Norris was back in the Baltic, with orders to give naval coverage should Peter decide to invade southern Sweden with Danish support; but the tsar abandoned the plan.

By now there was mounting unease in London over the potential Russian threat to British naval supplies. In October George I's principal minister, the Earl of Stanhope, pointed out to his colleague, Townsend, that 'It is our misfortune at this juncture, by the knavery of the Muscovites . . . to have our naval magazines so ill provided with stores, particularly with hemp, that if the fleet of merchantmen, now loading in the Baltic, should by any accident miscarry, it will be impossible for His Majesty to fit out any ships of war for the next year, by which means the whole navy of England will be rendered perfectly useless.' Hanoverian policy remained anti-Swedish, and the Royal Navy patrolled Baltic waters each summer, ensuring clear passage for British vessels to Riga, Reval and St Petersburg, but the mood of Norris's masters at the Admiralty grew increasingly hostile to Peter's pretensions.

In the summer of 1718 Charles XII seized the initiative. He seemed about to revive the war by invading Finland to end the Russian occupation. But, ever unpredictable, in August he ordered an invasion of Danish-held central Norway, with Trondheim as first objective; and in October he personally led his main army north-westwards towards Christiania. The war was unpopular. Within a few days, Norwegian resistance around the fortress town of Fredriksten checked the invasion, forcing the Swedes to resort to siege warfare. There, on 30 November, Charles XII went down into advance trenches at night to watch his sappers prepare a new assault against this 'petty fortress' on 'a barren strand'. Flares from the walls half lit the open ground, and there was sporadic shooting; a musket ball struck the king's left temple and passed through the head. Rumour hinted at assassination. More likely the king died as he had lived, courting danger recklessly.

With surprising speed, within a few days his sister Ulrika Eleonora was recognized as hereditary Queen by the Council of the Realm and immediately recalled both armies from Norway. But the Riksdag was too assertive to allow a change of ruler without extracting concessions. In the new year the Estates insisted on a formal ceremony in which Ulrika Eleonora received the crown only after a pledge to accept a constitution limiting royal authority. It is customary to refer to the new period of Swedish history as the Age of Liberty, with power apparently exercised by the Riksdag as a Diet of Four Estates, but the Age of Weak Kingship might be a truer description. Over the following quarter of a century two political groups emerged, to contest power: the protectionist 'Caps', who had some resemblance to the English Tories; and the more Whiggish 'Hats', who favoured trade and business. There was, however, as yet no sign of representative government in the Swedish constitution. The changes of 1719–20 merely made possible a choice of faction, within a broadened ruling oligarchy.

Now that one of the indomitable rivals was dead, King George I and his ministers mounted a diplomatic offensive to complete a reversal of alliances and force the other protagonist to accept peace. Admiral Norris's fleet – still non-belligerent – navigated the treacherous channels of the archipelago in July 1719 to be welcomed in Stockholm and give substance to George's proposed armed mediation. Queen Ulrika Eleonora dined aboard the flagship on 14 July and approved the king's initiative. Sweden signed treaties of peace with Hanover in November, Augustus of Saxony and Poland in December, Prussia in January 1720 and Denmark in July 1720, though an armistice had ended the conflict of Swedes, Danes and Norwegians as early as the previous October. Only Russia remained at war. The tsar was angered by the Anglo-Hanoverian intervention: he wished to dictate peace from a position of strength. A chance encounter in the Gulf of Bothnia in early June 1719 led to a conventional eight-hour running battle and the capture of three Swedish warships. Peter was elated, more than ever convinced that final victory lay close at hand.

While Norris was sailing towards Stockholm at high summer in 1719, Peter massed an invasion force of 32,000 men in the Ålands. Eight days after the queen dined aboard Norris's flagship, an observer stationed on the outer islet of Söderarm reported that he could see a fleet of galleys making good speed towards the narrows of the Stockholm archipelago. There were, in all, 132 large galleys and more than a hundred smaller oared vessels. For five weeks the Swedish coast from Gävle south to Norrköping was ravaged: some 20,000 families were left homeless. Seven coastal towns and many villages, manorial estates and isolated farms were burnt; ten of Sweden's largest iron foundries were destroyed and 300 new cannon intercepted and seized before delivery to the army. Raiders reached the approaches to Stockholm, but the Saltsjö was blocked by frigates and by the forts built in the previous century to protect the capital. At the end of August Peter decided the massive raid was over. His two fleets – of men-of-war and galleys – returned to the Gulf of Finland; and a Russian diplomat arrived in Stockholm with the tsar's peace terms: they included the surrender of Finland as well as of Livonia and the other Baltic provinces. These demands seemed preposterous and the talks foundered.

Ulrika Eleonora had no understanding of foreign affairs. In March 1720 she abdicated in favour of her husband, Frederick of Hesse, a king who passed rapidly from lingering adolescence to premature senility. The Swedish constitution was again revised, ensuring that Frederick I possessed even less power to shape policy than his predecessor, and from the spring of 1720 until Christmas 1738 General Arvid Horn – the prototype 'Cap' – controlled Swedish affairs as Lord President of the Council. His foreign policy relied in early years on support from Britain and Hanover and close co-operation with George I's young ambassador, Lord Carteret.

Two months after Frederick's accession Sir John Norris returned to Stockholm with a fleet of more than thirty ships and orders to induce the Russians to make peace with Sweden on reasonable terms. 'The scales of the North are in your hand,' Carteret told the admiral. 'If the Tsar refuses the King's mediation . . . I hope that you will by force of arms bring him to reason and destroy that fleet which will disturb the world.' With King Frederick's backing and eleven Swedish ships to augment his own fleet, the admiral set out for Reval, where he hoped to draw the Russians into battle. Apraxin outmanoeuvred him, however. As Norris headed eastwards, the galleys sailed for the west, hugging the Finnish shore, with its long line of rocky islands as protective cover. Soon, for the second year running, the Swedish coast was harried by raiders: some penetrated 50 kilometres inland. Norris was recalled, but too late to intercept the galleys. Four Swedish frigates chasing Apraxin's oarsmen into the skerries ran aground and were captured by the Russians. The campaign brought no battle honours to either the Swedish or British fleets. Yet a year later Norris was back in the Saltsjö with twenty-two ships, still unable to prevent Russian raids that again fired the largely wooden towns of Gävle and Sundsvall. During seven summers of cruising in Baltic waters Sir John Norris's ships never fired a shot in anger.

On 30 August 1721 peace was signed at last at Nystad (today the Finnish port of Uusikaupunki). Russia gained Livonia, Estonia, Ingria and eastern Karelia, including Vyborg. Sweden recovered the remaining occupied areas of Finland, together with pledges that Russia would abstain from interference in the kingdom's internal affairs, permit the free exercise of the Lutheran faith, allow grain to be purchased at a fixed rate and imported duty free from Riga and Reval, and pay compensation of two million thaler. Already, in 1720, Sweden had ceded Bremen and Verden to the Elector of Hanover for a million thaler. At the same time, Sweden ceded western Pomerania, including Usedom and Stettin, to Prussia for another million. No territory was surrendered to Denmark, but the Swedes agreed that they would resume paying Sound Dues on commerce shipped through the Øresund.

The Poles gained nothing from the Nystad peace settlement, despite their heavy involvement in the earlier stages of the war. For in November 1715 the *szlachta* had belatedly tried to free property-owners, great and small, from the burden of supporting the Saxon army that King Augustus II quartered on their estates. A threatened revolt brought a response from Russia. A settlement brokered by the tsar's envoys in Warsaw appeared to meet the *szlachta* demands. Augustus remained king, though his Saxon regiments were withdrawn; the Polish magnates kept control of the Vistulan basin, with almost autonomous Danzig as their outlet to the Baltic; and the Sejm retained its liberties, including the individual member's right of veto. But effectively the Warsaw agreement made the Commonwealth of the Two Nations a Russian protectorate. Militarily Poland was too weak to challenge Russian decisions. No spokesman for the *Rzeczpospolita* was even present at the Nystad peace talks.

Poland did at least retain its agreed frontiers. Inevitably the great loser was Sweden. All that remained of Charles XII's empire south of the Baltic after the signing of the Treaty of Nystad was western Pomerania (including Stralsund) and Wismar. By contrast, within eighteen years of founding St Petersburg Tsar Peter had acquired, not simply a window to the West, but a broad channel opening out into the Baltic and beyond. Small wonder that on 22 October the Senate and the Holy Synod honoured their sovereign by proclaiming new titles for the tsar. He became 'Father of the Fatherland, Emperor of All Russia, Peter the Great'. The ceremony was held in the cathedral church of the Holy Trinity (*Troitski)*, close to Peter's original house beside the Neva. Fire was to destroy the Troitski in 1913. Four years later the flames of revolution consumed the empire inaugurated within its walls.

Peter was not yet fifty when the Great Northern War ended, though he looked older and had less than four years to live. The Russian empire was not at peace – a war continued against Persia – but the fighting had at last moved away from the Baltic, and the tsar had the satisfaction of seeing the commercial value of his new port rising each year. Sixteen foreign merchantmen moored in the Neva in 1714; forty-three a year later; by the summer of 1724 the number had risen to one hundred and eighty. Administrative problems continued to absorb much of Peter's time. He changed the structure of the Orthodox Church, abolishing the patriarchate in favour of a Holy Synod, a team of management binding Church and State firmly together. A Table of Ranks defined status and salaries for fourteen levels of civil and military service, opening the door of promotion to men of humble origin. It was thus possible, by mid-century, for the son of a fisherman in Arctic waters, Mikhail Lomonosov, to use his gifts as a poet and scientist to climb up the table and become a State Secretary, remembered as the pioneer educationist who shaped literary Russian. But the outstanding legacy from the last years of the tsar's reign is architectural. Peterhof was built along the Baltic shore 30 kilometres east of the capital, an imperial summer residence clearly visible from ships entering or leaving the mouth of the Neva.

Work began on the palaces, pavilions and parkland in May 1714. The concept was the tsar's, conjured up from memories of visits to Versailles and Marly-le-Roi, but given form and shape by Alexandre LeBlond, who designed a two-storey palace above a sea-canal lined with statues and dominated by the Great Cascade. He also used Peter's own sketches to build the villa of Monplaisir which, with its Dutch-style interior, became the tsar's favourite home; Rastrelli's majestic grand palace is a later creation, built in the reign of Peter's daughter, Elizabeth, in the middle of the century. The seventy-five water-jets of the Great Cascade, and the sixteen acolyte fountains around it, played for the first time on 15 August 1723, the Festival of the Dormition. Yet the tsar's guests that day were celebrating, not an Orthodox Holy Day, but a cavalcade of victory, for the statuary at Peterhof uses biblical and classical allegory to portray the long struggle to humble Charles XII. On a granite rock in the lower pool of the cascade Samson forces open the jaws of Sweden's heraldic lion.

For Russia and for Sweden the titanic struggle was over. Foolishly in 1741 the Swedish 'Hats' made one last bid to recover Vyborg and Karelia, but the campaign ended in disaster; Sweden not only lost the fortress of Nyslott and further tracts of good forest in eastern Finland but also suffered the humiliation of having to maintain 12,000 Russian troops quartered in the homeland for two years. Yet this new and outwardly powerful tsarist autocracy remained soft at the centre. Peter thought little of hereditary right and looked with understandable scorn on the Polish device of elected monarchy. Accordingly, in 1722, he promulgated an edict declaring 'that the ruling sovereign shall always have the power to designate his successor'. It was a decision lacking in foresight that was to cause weakness and confusion until, at the end of the century, Tsar Paul restored primogeniture. Ironically the lack of a fixed succession made Russia seem at times not so much an autocracy as an oligarchy on the model of defeated Sweden, with power shared among a few aristocratic families.

When Peter the Great died, in the last week of January 1725, the throne passed to his widow Catherine Alexeievna, the one-time Lithuanian peasant

camp-follower Martha Skavronska, whom Peter had married in two ceremonies (1707 and 1712) and had crowned in the Kremlin eight months before
his death. Catherine I possessed qualities her husband lacked, notably com-
passion; she could act wisely and decisively, as when she refused to let a provocative voyage up the Gulf of Finland by Swedish warships rekindle doused
disputes; but she lived for little more than two years after her accession. Peter
II, the great tsar's grandson by his first wife, came to the throne aged twelve
and died from smallpox on his wedding day in January 1730, still only fifteen:
he was a wilful lad who sought deliberately to shut the window to the West,
even moving the capital away from the Baltic in 1728 and back to Moscow.
Empress Anne (reigned 1730–40), widowed Duchess of Courland and Peter
I's niece, had the good sense immediately to re-establish St Petersburg as the
capital. Yet, although Anne was a strong personality, she had little aptitude
for politics and was under the sway of her avaricious lover, Johannes Biron,
a Baltic German from Mitau – the first ruler of Russia to institute a police
terror machine, the feared *Bironschina*. On Anne's death, Biron became
regent for a four-month-old Romanov infant (Anne's great-nephew) who
was hailed as Ivan VI. This blatant attempt to perpetuate the Baltic German
oligarchy ended fourteen months later in a military coup that brought Peter
the Great's thirty-two-year-old daughter Elizabeth (reigned 1741–62) to the
throne.

Empress Elizabeth was a woman of intelligence but little learning. In
her first years on the throne she pursued pleasure for its own sake with
extravagant abandon and later she drank far too heavily, for she was after
all her father's daughter; but at least she showed a sense of responsibility
over settling the succession. As early as 1742 she designated her nephew,
Peter III, as the next tsar. It soon became evident that he was mentally
unstable and, being a Holsteiner born in Kiel, he grew to loathe Russia,
but Elizabeth did not waver in her intention. Instead, in 1745 she married
him to his sixteen-year-old first cousin, Catherine (Sophia-Augusta of
Anhalt-Zerbst by birth), hectored the ill-matched couple until a child
(Paul) was born, and remained convinced that Peter would soon lose the
throne and Catherine become Regent for the boy.

Here, however, Elizabeth underestimated her protégée's ambition and
the willingness of the Preobrazhensky Life Guards to give Catherine their
support. A military coup deposed Peter III in June 1762, within six months
of his accession. But there was to be no regency for the young Paul. The
wretched Peter was hustled off by the Guards to Ropsha, an estate 30 kilometres outside St Petersburg. There he was strangled or poisoned a week
later. Three months after Peter's death his consort – born in Lutheran

Stettin and, in a literal sense, a Baltic German – was crowned by the Metropolitan Archbishop of Novgorod in Moscow's Uspensky Cathedral. She became the most powerful woman in Europe, a ruler 'to be approached with all the dignity due to a divinity', an English diplomat commented apprehensively soon after his arrival in Russia. Yet it was Voltaire, not the Holy Synod and the Senate, who honoured her as Catherine the Great.

There were many Empress Catherines, for her character was full of contradiction: a ruthless schemer, heavily involved in the deaths of her husband and the long-imprisoned, almost forgotten Ivan VI; a business woman dutifully tied to routine administration; a devout believer who prostrated herself before Holy Russia's revered relics but advocated 'prudent toleration' of minority religions; a progressive who exchanged letters with the French rationalists and in her 'Instruction' of 1767 applied Montesquieu's rule of law to a basically despotic system; a doting grandmother who encouraged inoculation against smallpox and sent royal families in Stockholm and Berlin the pattern of a romper costume she designed for the future Alexander I. Among her most familiar roles was the Russian nationalist proud that through the generalship of her lover Potemkin she could fulfil Peter I's mission of securing mastery over the Crimea and the Black Sea's western littoral. Yet Catherine also paid homage to Peter's Baltic legacy. In August 1786 she unveiled Falconet's masterpiece, the *Bronze Horseman* statue in St Petersburg's Senate Square, a memorial rich in symbolism. The city's founder sits astride a horse that rears up proudly on a granite pedestal, with hoofs trampling a coiled snake: the tsar's outstretched arm points towards the Neva and the sea-lane to the West. Four words carved into the Finnish stone form a dedication of eloquent simplicity – *Petro primo Catharina secunda*. No doubt Catherine commissioned Falconet to honour Peter's creativity. Yet it is hard to escape a feeling that the incomer from Stettin was greeting Russia's first emperor as an equal. Grand Duke Paul, who was abroad on the day his mother unveiled the statue, had to wait until 1796 before he acceded. Is it surprising if at times he thought himself haunted by his great-grandfather, an apparition that seemed to stalk him through the capital murmuring, 'Paul, poor Paul'?

Under all three empresses – Anne, Elizabeth and great Catherine – Peter's city received and transmitted the culture of the West, as he had wished. From England came the concept of the landscape garden and even, in the 1770s, an exclusive English Club, a Baltic Athenaeum founded by an expatriate merchant and soon attracting the great names of high society. But the supreme intellectual influence of the Age of Reason was

French, and Parisian ideas and fashions determined the life and ways of any Russian family with social pretensions. The wealthiest sent their sons to be educated in Paris. Theatres were built and mounted foreign plays; a school of etiquette was established; ballet and opera arrived in the 1730s; architects designed sweeping colonnades and decorated porticoes, eagerly appropriating the neighbouring wasteland for their ventures. Anne began the practice of lavishing huge sums on lovers. Biron, whom she created Duke of Courland, had the good taste to engage Rastrelli to build two palaces for him far from St Petersburg: today the duke's official residence in Mitau (Jelgava) provides Latvia with a baroque national agricultural college, while 30 kilometres to the north-west is Rundale, a spacious rural palace with all the grandeur of Blenheim. Elizabeth had Rastrelli design the Anichkov Palace in the capital for her favourite Razumovsky, but she also showed a personal interest in the conversion of a villa built hastily in 1711–12 for her mother at Sarskaya myza (Farmstead Heights). The villa, 25 kilometres inland from St Petersburg, became the great Catherine Palace, with the place name changed to Tsarskoye Selo (Imperial Village). It was Elizabeth who, in 1755, commissioned Rastrelli to design the study that incorporated amber panels originally presented by the King of Prussia to her father. Characteristically Catherine invited the Scottish architect James Cameron to discipline the swaggeringly Baroque palace with a Graeco-Roman unity of form.

The two empresses complemented each other in cultural vision. Elizabeth allowed Rastrelli a free hand in building the Winter Palace, but it was Catherine who commissioned the three Hermitage annexes to it: Vallin de la Motte's pavilion in 1765; the Gallery, designed by a Russian, Yuri Velten, ten years later; and in 1780 a theatre added by the Italian, Giacomo Quarenghi. Elizabeth brightened grey northern skies with the blue domes of Smolny's Cathedral of the Resurrection, a convent for orphans on the site of her father's earliest summer palace; Catherine added the School for Noble Girls (200 pupils) to Elizabeth's foundation. She had the Marble Palace built for one favourite, Gregory Orlov, and the vast Tauride Palace for the most famous of them, Prince Potemkin. Other grandees emulated their sovereigns, embellishing the capital with mansions of classical dignity.

Although, as its founder intended, St Petersburg replaced Archangel as the empire's northern port and there was constant activity along the quays and in the shipyards, the city's principal industry long remained government. By the close of the century almost half the population were administrators, held lower bureaucratic posts or served at Court as functionaries or soldiers. A trade directory of 1794 reflects the veneer of elegance that distinguished the business enterprise of the Russian capital from the more naturally organic commercial life of Riga and the old Hanse ports or, indeed, of the Swedish and Danish capitals. Five factories pandered to luxury tastes: one made porcelain; another decorative wallpaper; a third printed playing cards; two rivals processed macaroni. The list includes fourteen manufacturers of lace, seven of silk and twelve hatters. Heavy industry – Charles Baird's iron foundry and engineering works – came from Scotland only at the turn of the century. Not surprisingly Baird's earliest task was to provide special machinery for the government's endless building operations.

No emperor or empress could remain simply a builder and decorator. The Treaty of Nystad confirmed Russia's status as a European Great Power, far behind France in authority and not yet up to the level of Austria or Britain but with a wider influence than the other newcomer, Prussia. Russia shared common interests with Austria in limiting the power of Turkey (already in decline) and curbing Prussian ambitions in Poland. There were strong economic ties with Britain: an Anglo-Russian commercial treaty safeguarding Baltic trade was signed in 1734; a revised commercial treaty in 1766 showed the extent to which George III's admirals still needed Russian hemp and flax. The British assumed that Russian policy would remain anti-French, partly because successive emissaries from Paris had supported Ottoman enterprises for two centuries, but also because French ministers tended to back Russia's ex-enemies, Sweden and Poland. There were, however, no basic issues dividing France and Russia, and during the Seven Years War (1756–63) Russia allied with Austria and France against Prussia and Britain.

Empress Elizabeth's foreign minister, Bestuzhev-Ryumen, had avoided entanglement in the War of the Austrian Succession, which began in 1740 with the newly acceded Frederick II of Prussia's seizure of the Austrian province of Silesia. The weight St Petersburg could apply to balance 'the scales of the North' was emphasized in 1747, when the imminence of London-subsidized Russian intervention in the conflict hastened French willingness to make peace. But eight years later the London subsidies were going to Berlin, and a war party in St Petersburg hoped to acquire East Prussia at a time when Frederick was distracted by campaigns in Saxony and Silesia.

During the last four years of Elizabeth's reign her armies fought on Prussian soil. It seemed as if they would deprive Frederick II of the territory won by his father and the Great Elector along the Baltic shores. The

Russians invaded East Prussia, defeating a Prussian army at Grossjägerndorf in August 1757, but this success was overshadowed by Frederick's two outstanding victories, against Austria at Rossbach on 5 November and against France at Leuthen a month later. Early in 1758, however, the Russian threat intensified. Königsberg struck an extraordinary bargain with the invaders, acknowledging the sovereign rights of Empress Elizabeth over the city in return for being spared the destruction of an assault.

By the summer of 1759 the Russians were ready to launch a full-scale invasion. General Saltykov marched a freshly raised army into eastern Brandenburg, with a detached Austrian corps in support. When Frederick learnt that the Russian vanguard was barely 80 kilometres from his capital, he concentrated 50,000 experienced troops around Frankfurt-an-der-Oder and gave battle at Kunersdorf. At first it seemed he would gain a third great battle honour, for Saltykov's left flank collapsed under the weight of the Prussian assault. Then, to Frederick's dismay, the Prussian cannons stuck fast in the sandy soil. While his gunners were floundering, Cossack horsemen bore down upon them, nearly capturing the king, whose snuff box was shattered in his pocket by a stray shot. Frederick lost 47,000 men that day – killed, captured or incapacitated. But Saltykov, too, had suffered heavy losses: 'Another victory as costly as Kunersdorf and I alone will bring news of it to St Petersburg,' the general wrote to Elizabeth. To Frederick's relief the Russians pulled back into Poland.

A year later the Russians did, indeed, briefly enter Berlin, and Frederick thought only a miracle could save him from disaster. He was rescued by Elizabeth's sudden death and by the accession of Peter III, who admired Frederick both as a soldier and a philosopher king. The new tsar ordered an immediate armistice and the restoration to Prussia of all occupied territories. He was negotiating an alliance with Prussia when in June 1762 he was overthrown and carried off to die at Ropsha. Catherine II had no wish to renew the war but she would not rush into new treaty commitments, though her first foreign minister, Count Repnin, was glad to work for better relations.

Frederick meanwhile punished Königsberg for its wavering loyalty by imposing heavy taxes on the townsfolk. Fortunately the city was by now so wealthy that it suffered little from the special levy; the money raised went to alleviate distress in war-ravaged Silesia. For the rest of his reign the 'philosopher king' held his second city in such contempt that he refused to visit it. Ironically, this was the period when the king of German philosophy was holding professorial court in Königsberg University; Kant propounded his 'Categorical Imperative' in 1785, the year before Frederick's death.

The old problem of the Polish succession soon drew Catherine and Frederick politically closer. When in August 1763 August III of Poland died, Catherine promoted the candidature of yet another former lover, Stanislaw Poniatowski, who was backed by kinsmen in the influential Czartoryski family. During 1764 the pace of events quickened: in April a treaty pledged Prussia and Russia to maintain the existing Polish constitution; in July a Russian army was invited by the Czatoryskis to safeguard order by occupying Poland; and in the first week of September a docile Sejm duly elected Poniatowski king, according him the title Stanislas II Augustus. By February 1768 the Russians and Poles concluded a treaty by which the Polish constitution was guaranteed for all time, provided that the overwhelmingly Catholic Sejm conferred full political and civil rights on Christian 'dissident believers', whether Lutheran or Orthodox. Catherine was exasperated when, a month later, the anti-Russian landowners came together in the 'Confederation of Bar' to defend the privileged position of the Catholic Church in the state. They convened a parliament of their own and rejected the treaty. For four years they hampered and harassed the Russian occupying forces in what was effectively a state of sporadic warfare.

The more far-sighted Poles had long feared that the constitutional anarchy of their monarchical commonwealth would end in partition. In the early 1770s Frederick the Great took the initiative. He persuaded Catherine that France was contemplating a general European war and that, in order to thwart French diplomacy, Austria should be wooed with the offer of territory in southern Poland. Russia would then regularize her position in the eastern and central part of the commonwealth, while Prussia would be content with the smallest of territorial gains in the north. There was, in reality, no threat from France, but Catherine swallowed the bait: she was anyhow glad to distract Austria from south-eastern Europe. On 5 April 1772 bilateral treaties signed in St Petersburg committed the three eastern autocracies to trimming the *Rzeczpospolita*. Austria would advance her frontier along the upper Vistula and the river San. Russia acquired most of present-day Belarus and a small strip of Livonia, gaining control of the headwaters of the river Dnieper, leading to the Black Sea, and of the river Dvina (Daugava) leading to the Baltic. But the prize-winner was undoubtedly Frederick II, for he scooped the lower Vistula and the long-coveted Baltic littoral of Polish 'Royal Prussia'. Although he was denied the Free City of Danzig itself, Prussia could exact tolls on Polish grain traders using the rivers to reach the Baltic ports. In September 1773 the Polish Sejm was bribed and cajoled into accepting the transfer of territories and the consequent loss of about a third of the population. The partition of Poland had begun.

The new boundaries remained intact for twenty-three years. Stanislas Augustus reigned benevolently; the University of Vilna shook off Jesuit influence and the general level of education was raised. The Polish Commonwealth at last secured the framework of a modern government, with a Russian-sponsored 'Permanent Council' in Warsaw co-ordinating the work of five ministries: war, foreign affairs, justice, finance and police. Catherine was content; she convinced herself that Russian control of the heart of Poland was not challenged. The garrisons policing the kingdom were gradually cut in numbers. In May 1789, at a time of mounting crisis, the empress took the calculated risk of accepting a request from the Permanent Council for their final withdrawal. She hoped that another gesture of her trust in Stanislas Augustus would thwart Prussian attempts to improve relations with Warsaw. But 1789 was a poor year in which to look to the future with confidence.

Prophets of gloom in Stockholm feared at mid-century that Sweden, too, was trapped in a Russian orbit. The dynastic bonds were thin, the great families fractious. Adolf Frederick of Holstein-Gottorp, who succeeded Frederick of Hesse as king in 1751, was a former favourite of Empress Elizabeth, with a distant claim to the Swedish throne through his mother's descent from Charles IX; the future Catherine the Great was the daughter of her sister. He ruled as a constitutional monarch, the first to take up residence in Tessin's newly completed Royal Palace. Politics held little interest for him and he was content for the most part to observe the cockfight of Caps and Hats from well above the parliamentary pit. Fortunately he was married to Frederick the Great's sister, Louisa Ulrika; not for her a Russian-dominated future. Like her brother the queen was happiest speaking and writing French, showed architectural good taste, and possessed an inquiring mind. Her eldest son, Gustav – born in 1746 – inherited her cultural Francophilia.

Never before had Swedish scholarship enjoyed such renown in Europe as under Adolf Frederick, even though the king may have lacked the intelligence to recognize its achievements. Emmanuel Swedenborg, scientist and mystic, had already produced mathematical treatises and pioneering studies of astronomy and navigation; he could write at great length and in the same work of both metallurgy and metaphysics. Like Leonardo da Vinci he has been credited with anticipating future inventions, including the aeroplane and machine-gun. In Adolf Frederick's reign Swedenborg completed nearly thirty volumes (in Latin) expounding his personal revelations on the spiritual structure of the universe; and he travelled to

Holland and England, dying in London. The great botanist, Linnaeus (Carl von Linné), also published his early work in the Netherlands, though it was to Uppsala University that he brought special distinction. The astronomer Andreas Celsius, who devised the centigrade thermometer, had been a luminary of Uppsala in the previous decade, conducting research into the Aurora Borealis as director of the observatory. But although Sweden's dominant academic links were with Protestant Holland and Britain, Crown Prince Gustav received his good education for the most part from French tutors or in Paris itself. By inclination he was homosexual and his marriage to Sophia Magdalena of Denmark was unhappy; two sons were born, though the younger lived for only seven months.

The young Gustav delighted in the literature and language of France. He loved the theatre and wrote several plays, but he was also interested in the history of war and diplomacy. At the age of twenty-five he travelled again to Paris, along with two of his brothers, in part to seek subsidies from Louis XV. The three princes were attending an opera at Versailles when, on 1 March 1771, they received grave news from Stockholm: a fortnight previously their father supped off oysters, sauerkraut, lobster, sticky buns and champagne; he was dead before morning. It was appropriate that Gustav III should learn of his accession in France and at a court theatre.

On his return home – perhaps even earlier – Gustav planned a royal *coup d'état*. He knew he could count on financial aid from Louis XV and the backing of senior officers. His natural gifts as a persuasive orator enabled him to exploit divisions in the Riksdag by denouncing the selfishness of the aristocracy. In August 1772 the Council was arrested collectively and royal prerogatives last exercised by Charles XII were reasserted. The Riksdag was retained, though with little opportunity to shape policy. Party labels, like Caps and Hats, were 'hated abominations' and were forbidden.

A decade of reform gave Sweden the benefits and restraints of enlightened despotism, as practised in St Petersburg, Potsdam and Vienna. Censorship and police spies functioned but the bureaucracy was purged, commerce and agriculture encouraged, and scientific research and the arts given patronage. The Swedish Academy was founded to protect and advance language and culture, on the model of Richelieu's Académie Française. Gustav gave Stockholm a Royal Opera House in 1782 and a Royal Dramatic Theatre six years later. Life became more tolerable. Torture was officially banned, the number of capital offences reduced, and freedom of Christian worship assured to newcomers from abroad. The Jew Regulations (*Judereglementet*) of 1782 allowed Jewish immigrants to live and trade in Sweden's three largest towns, Stockholm, Gothenburg and

Norrköping; although Aaron Isaac, the first Jew known to practise his faith in the capital, only seems to have settled there two years later. From King Louis XV Gustav received 300,000 livres for the Swedish exchequer, together with the Caribbean island of Saint-Barthélemy. The Swedish West Indies Company was founded, to trade with the new possessions. In exchange French merchants were granted special privileges at Gothenburg.

Like his first cousin in St Petersburg, Gustav basked in splendour and elegance. Almost certainly, no ceremony in Sweden ever matched the theatricality he contrived for his coronation. Drottningholm, where the Court resided from June to November, owes much of its magnificence to his mother, including the famous theatre, but it was Gustav who shaped social behaviour and etiquette on what he had seen at Versailles. After a further visit to France in 1784, he returned to Stockholm full of admiration for Louis XVI and Marie Antoinette. The exquisite delicacy of the Trianon must be transplanted to Stockholm's northern approaches, he decided. An 'English' park and palace were planned for Haga, beside the inlet of Brunnsviken. Only one pavilion – with a compact 'hall of mirrors' – was completed. It remains an attraction today, together with an Echo Temple in the park, a Chinese pagoda, and curious 'stables' that resemble royal battle tents from the era of the Crusades. Gustav also commissioned a theatre for the third floor of a tower at Gripsholm, an unexpectedly spacious miniature in gold and cream, with statues flanking the stage and a semi-circle of Ionic columns to screen the boxes. His taste was eclectic. Among British sovereigns only George IV matches Gustav III as a patron of fine building.

The king's critics complained that he over-dramatized day-to-day politics, tending to treat life as a protracted masquerade. Inevitably, over-expenditure and the increasing restraints on the political power of the nobility led to mounting opposition, compounded by bad harvests and a trade recession. To restore his popularity the king made a grave political error. He gambled on a short victorious war, to be fought in the first instance against the historic arch-enemy, Denmark.

Gustav had spent much money and ingenuity on defence. He followed Peter the Great's example by building up a two-fleet navy: the Battle Fleet of ships-of-the-line and large frigates was based at Karlskrona; and an Archipelago Fleet of large oared galleys and oared gun sloops was based at Stockholm and Sveaborg (off Helsinki). In 1783 Gustav met his cousin the Empress Catherine at Fredrikshamn (Hamina) to seek a pledge of non-belligerency if he attacked Russia's Danish ally by sea and by a land campaign aimed at securing Norway. But Catherine, heavily committed to expansion around the Black Sea, wanted no upheaval in the Baltic. Gustav postponed action.

When Turkey went to war with Russia in the winter of 1787–88 Gustav rashly decided to take advantage of Catherine's preoccupation with the South. Swedish soldiers wearing Russian uniforms attacked a Finnish outpost at Puumala in early June 1788, giving Gustav the *casus belli* he needed for a thrust aimed at St Petersburg itself. His Battle Fleet had already sailed from Karlskrona, commanded by the king's brother, Charles, Duke of Södermanland.

The war plan, in so far as it existed, called for the elimination of the Russian sailing fleet in battle or by close blockade in Kronstadt and Reval, a success to be followed by amphibious landings near the Russian capital. The fleets clashed in July off Hogland (Suursari), a mid-Gulf island some 70 kilometres east of Helsinki. The outcome was inconclusive, on paper a one-all draw. Duke Charles lost a ship-of-the-line and captured the Russian vessel, *Vladislav*. The Russians prevented the Swedes sailing farther eastwards, but suffered such damage that they had to break off the battle. Duke Charles ran short of ammunition, put into Finnish Sveaborg for replenishment, and was trapped there for four months by a Russian squadron. Ultimately the battle was a terrible disaster for Sweden: the captured *Vladislav* proved a talisman of death, for the ship and the Russian crew's clothing were infested with typhus-carrying lice. From Sveaborg the returning Swedish fleet carried the disease to Karlskrona, where 5,286 seamen died; and as the sailors dispersed to their homes so the typhus went with them, across Blekinge province and into many towns and villages of southern Sweden.

It was a strange war. On land, the main Swedish assault on Fredrikshamn was repulsed, and in the west Gustav almost lost Gothenburg. The Danes fulfilled their treaty obligations and assisted the Russians with an advance from the Norwegian frontier that exposed weaknesses in the defences of Sweden's second city. A threat of British and Prussian intervention, made by the British minister in Copenhagen, led to an early truce between Sweden and Denmark. Gustav was alarmed by evidence of major treachery and mutiny in the Swedish-Finnish army encamped east of Fredrikshamn. Over a hundred officers met at Anjala and declared the war 'illegal' while a group of junior officers who favoured Finnish independence were in touch with Imperial State Councillors in St Petersburg. There was little doubt that the war was unpopular. Even so, the army held out against Russian attacks through the winter months and the Battle Fleet bore down once more on Reval, though to little effect.

Unexpectedly in the summer of 1790 Gustav, whose military prowess was limited and experience of seamanship slight, took personal command of the Archipelago Fleet aboard his flagship, *Seraphimordern*. A bombardment of Fredrikshamn in support of the army failed through poor communication; and there was frightful confusion in the Gulf of Vyborg when a fireship, intended to cause havoc among the assembled Russian fleet, ignited several Swedish ships by mistake. On 7 July Gustav's luck changed: heavy seas held the Russians close together off Svenskund, and the oared gun sloops and larger galleys of the Archipelago Fleet closed in upon them like the claws of a crab. Throughout the short summer's night they maintained a steady cannonade. By dawn more than fifty Russian vessels were sunk or captured for the loss of only six Swedish ships. Rightly Svenskund could be celebrated in Stockholm as a royal naval victory. The ravaging of the Swedish coast by Peter the Great's galleys was avenged, after a lapse of seventy years.

Yet was the victory relevant to the present? By now both sovereigns accepted that they were engaged in a pointless conflict. While their fleets played a dangerous game of hide and seek in the Finnish skerries, other rulers were adjusting thoughts and policies to meet what was fast becoming the greatest challenge to European order since the Reformation. Five weeks after Gustav's victory at Svenskund a peace treaty that settled nothing was speedily drawn up and signed at Värälä. There were no territorial changes to dispute, no demands for compensation. The sole concession was a Russian undertaking to abstain from interference in Sweden-Finland's domestic affairs. Otherwise all was as it had been. Catherine the realist turned her attention to the Polish Question, fearing that Warsaw might import the latest and least desirable of Parisian fashions. Gustav III, having strengthened royal powers through an 'Act of Union and Security', called for a southern crusade, a joint monarchical venture to rescue his Bourbon friends. By temperament he was always more of a Quixote than a Vasa.

13

Thunder from the South

NEWS OF THE fall of the Bastille in July 1789 was greeted in the Baltic cities with surprise but no immediate concern: a riot in the capital had turned into a revolt against royal authority, but that still fell far short of a revolution. Rulers who had received subsidies from France were slow to realize that the Old Order faced political and economic bankruptcy, with a frightened and impoverished peasantry close to anarchy in many provinces. The unfolding drama at Versailles and Paris was followed with interest in Stockholm, Berlin and St Petersburg but there was little alarm before the following spring, when the first colourful reports arrived from émigrés who fled to the Rhineland. Yet war did not come to Europe until April 1792, when revolutionary France challenged the Habsburgs and invaded Belgium (the Austrian Netherlands); and even then, northern Europe stayed out of the conflict. The thunder of guns first broke the stillness of Baltic waters off Copenhagen in April 1801, and the tricolour flag did not fly over a Baltic port until the last day of October 1806, when the dashing cavalry general, Antoine Lasalle, tricked the defenders of Stettin into surrender.

One people followed events in Paris closely from the start. Across Poland patriots delighting in their rediscovered nationhood greeted the revolution with enthusiasm. In August 1789 the establishment of ministerial government in France and the debates on the Rights of Man were fully reported in Warsaw, where for the past year a revitalized Sejm had induced the king to tolerate a free press, untroubled by political censorship. Over the next eighteen months the moderate constitutionalism encouraged in Paris by Mirabeau set a pattern for Warsaw to follow. On 3 May 1791 the Polish progressives, now backed by the king, forced through the Sejm a new constitution, promising radical change: hereditary kingship would replace the elective monarchy; the *liberum veto* that had for so long prevented effective reform passing into law was abolished; and all landed proprietors and townsmen who paid 100 Polish crowns in tax were enfranchised. The constitution adopted the British concept of ministerial responsibility and borrowed from Montesquieu the separation of legislature, executive and judiciary, proposing the creation of central commissions to maintain a balance of powers, it was hoped. At heart the constitution was a statement of good intent rather than a precise charter of government. In London Edmund Burke, that confirmed enemy of the new France, warmly approved, though with a note of caution. The Poles, he declared, will be a 'happy people if they know how to proceed as they have begun'.

The opportunity was denied them. Alarm at the triumph of the progressives in Warsaw healed rifts between Russia and Prussia. In January 1792 the peace treaty of Jassy brought an end to Russia's five-year war with Turkey, confirming Catherine's sovereignty over the Black Sea coast from the mouth of the Dniester in the west to the mouth of the Kuban in the northern Caucasus. Three months later she encouraged a small group of Polish reactionaries, meeting in the village of Targowica, to set up a 'confederacy' pledged to restore the old system. The confederates were backed by 90,000 Russian troops, sent specifically 'to combat Jacobinism'; they speedily re-occupied Warsaw and other garrison towns. To Frederick William II in Berlin and the newly acceded Emperor Francis II in Vienna Catherine recommended that Prussia and Austria seek compensation in the West for their declining influence in the East, since by now it seemed clear their armies would soon be marching on Paris.

A surge of revolutionary patriotism defied the invaders of France, however. The Prussians were routed at Valmy on 20 September 1792 and forced to retreat only six weeks after crossing the French frontier. A fortnight later the Austrians were defeated at Jemappes but had to continue the campaign in order to protect their interests in Belgium. Frederick William sought to disengage. If he were denied 'compensation' in the West for putting an army in the field, he would seek it in Poland. In January 1793 the Russo-Prussian Treaty of St Petersburg partitioned Poland for the second time: Russia acquired most of eastern Lithuania, the province of Minsk and rich farming land southwards to the upper waters of the Dniester, in the province of Podolia. So great was the increase of Jews that Catherine sought to confine their residence to a Pale of Settlement in the empire's western provinces, although the restraints imposed on the Jewish communities were frequently flouted. Prussia at last gained Danzig, as well as 'Old Poland' – the historic heart of the kingdom around Posen and Gniezno and the Warta basin. Rump Poland was little more than a Russian province, still ruled by Stanislas Augustus although now deprived of its short-lived constitution.

On the last day of January 1793 news of King Louis XVI's execution reached St Petersburg, three weeks after the event. Empress Catherine was so distressed that she 'went to bed sick and mournful', a diarist at court noted. Her political reaction came nine days later, and was carefully calculated. The sin committed by the French 'monsters' in 'raising their hands against the Lord's anointed . . . and putting him to death' would be punished by ending all trade and contact between the two countries. Frenchmen who recognized the republican government were to be deported; 'newspapers, journals and other periodicals published in France' specifically banned from all lands under her authority. A month later the commander of the Russian army of occupation warned the Poles of 'unworthy' countrymen who were 'shamelessly inciting the godless rebels in the French kingdom and asking their assistance, so that they might unite with them involving Poland in a bloody civil war'. The Polish national cause was tarred with the evil of Jacobinism.

The patriots were not deterred. In March 1794 they rose in revolt. Their armed defiance of Russian and Prussian armies was led by Tadeusz Kosciuszko, veteran general and military engineer of the American War of Independence, where he had constructed defences at Philadelphia and West Point and besieged Charleston. At home in Poland he defended Warsaw so skilfully that the Prussians withdrew. He was handicapped by three disadvantages: relative inexperience in the open field; the problem of rallying the *szlachta* while promising peasant emancipation; and the inability of his friends in Jacobin Paris to offer any weightier support than fine rhetoric. After he was wounded and taken prisoner by the Russians at Maciejowice in October, the revolt soon collapsed.

Kosciuszko's services to Poland were far from over. Two years later he was freed by Tsar Paul. During many years spent living in Britain, America, France and Switzerland he made certain Poland's cause was not forgotten. He became the first of the legendary patriot exiles, a forerunner of crowd-pullers like Garibaldi and Kossuth. Coleridge wrote a sonnet in his honour, but it is Thomas Campbell's words that are remembered: 'Freedom shrieked when Kosciuszko fell,' the Scottish poet declaimed.

The revolt confirmed Catherine's fears that she could not hope to preserve a vestigial Poland, serving as a buffer to absorb future attacks on Russia from the West. Instead, she reverted to balance of power politics and sought alliance with Austria. Thugut, Emperor Francis's foreign minister, welcomed the Russian initiative. Prussia's half-hearted commitment to the campaigns against France intensified his mistrust of Frederick William II. Moreover, it was now Vienna's turn to seek 'compensation', for the French had by this time overrun the Austrian Netherlands. Militarily, however,

Fredrick William was in a strong position; his troops controlled both the upper and lower Vistula. There seemed only one answer to the Polish Question, a new definitive division of the occupied lands. In January 1795 Austria and Russia agreed on the Third Partition, accepting the need to assign a large segment of territory to Prussia in order to appease Frederick William. The final settlement was agreed a year later, after Stanislas Augustus had abdicated and Prussia withdrawn from the war against the French Republic. On 12 January 1796 a joint treaty concluded at St Petersburg settled the new boundaries. Russia's western frontier was advanced to the rivers Niemen and Bug; Austria absorbed Galicia, with Cracow; Prussia gained central Poland, including the capital. The treaty did not simply redraft a map. It recorded the determination of the three autocrats 'to abolish everything that recalls the memory of the existence of the Polish kingdom'. But signatures and seals at the foot of a decree cannot sweep away a pride in nationhood.

The Swedish response to France's revolution was different from that of any other power in Europe. Gustav III was the only Baltic sovereign with a deep sense of personal loyalty to the French Bourbons. He had received unconditional subsidies from Louis XV and, as recently as June 1784, was Louis XVI's guest of honour at Versailles in a visit celebrated by the last gala occasion of the *ancien regime*. 'Swedish gentlemen' mingled with more than a hundred guests at the Trianon that evening, enjoying opera and ballet, sixty-four dishes from which to eat, and the entrancement of a lake festooned with fairy lights around a Temple of Love. In Gustav's suite was Count Axel von Fersen, former commander of the *Royal-Suédois,* a regiment of mercenaries who had served France for many years in the Indies and North America. Fersen was on terms of personal friendship with Louis XVI and was even closer to Marie Antoinette. During the summer of 1791 Gustav and the Count planned to rescue the French royal family from the restraints imposed on them in the Tuileries. Gustav secretly travelled to Aachen, while Fersen prepared an escape route to the frontier. On the night of 20–21 June the Count personally took charge of the first stage of their flight by coach along the road to Montmédy. But after he left them at Bondy, matters went awry; they were recognized at Varennes and escorted back to Paris. Gustav returned to Stockholm. He never gave up hope of a dramatic rescue, vainly seeking foreign support for a collective royal crusade to save the doomed monarchy.

At the same time Gustav faced mounting opposition at home. The national debt was staggeringly high; royal expenditure reached levels unknown since Queen Christina's day; the nobility – as ever – resented lost privileges and sought a reversion to the old constitution. Although the king was warned of a lurking conspiracy he took no action. On 16 March 1792 he attended a masked ball at the Opera House; he was readily identifiable as he wore the insignia of the two highest orders of chivalry. It was easy for a disaffected junior officer, Captain Jacob Anckarström, to sidle up behind him and fire a shot into his back, above the left hip.

Had Gustav died instantly, Anckarström's fellow conspirators were ready to stage a *coup d'état*, but the king never lost consciousness. The conspiracy was soon unravelled and Anckarström arrested. Eventually he was publicly flogged on three successive days and beheaded. Gustav's wound turned to gangrene and he died thirteen days later. Sweden's Golden Age of culture ended with him.

For the fourth time in a century and a half the kingdom experienced regency rule. Gustav III's brother, Duke Charles of Södermanland, 'protected the realm' for his only surviving nephew, Gustav Adolf, thirteen when his father was murdered. Duke Charles, who was amiably idle by nature, entrusted government to Count Reuterholm, a critic of Gustav III's policies, though not a conspirator. He improved relations with Denmark and with France, according the republic recognition, but fear of incurring Catherine's displeasure made him act cautiously. In 1796 Gustav Adolf wrecked Reuterholm's attempt to win support from Russia. While on a visit to St Petersburg he refused to contemplate marriage to Catherine's granddaughter unless she abandoned the Orthodox faith. Gustav Adolf was a prig, too obstinate to compromise, too suspicious by nature to give ministers or generals his trust.

Ultimately the rebuff made little difference to the course of events; for soon afterwards – in November 1796 – Catherine the Great died and was succeeded by her unstable son, Paul. Almost simultaneously, Duke Charles's regency ended, with the coming of Gustav Adolf's eighteenth birthday. Tsar Paul, who (uncharacteristically) liked the young king when they met in St Petersburg, encouraged Russo-Swedish collaboration throughout the extraordinary vacillations in policy of his reign. It was a time of new beginnings. The King of Prussia died in December 1797, to be succeeded by his son, Frederick William III, a 'blockhead drill sergeant' (by Napoleon's reckoning), with the good fortune to have married Louise of Mecklenburg-Strelitz, an indefatigable German patriot of charm and character.

Briefly, during the years of neutrality, Danish, Swedish and Hanse merchants prospered from the general European war. The belligerents needed naval supplies and grain from the Baltic lands, where in contrast to England there was a succession of good harvests. In several ports along the north German coast, including Rostock, rioters attacked profiteers who loaded ships with corn for export while keeping grain prices artificially high at home. Well beyond Baltic shores, Swedish and Danish ships sailed the Caribbean and Mediterranean with relative impunity, the greatest danger coming from corsairs along the North African coast. Some cargoes even reached the Orient for, in both Stockholm and Copenhagen, East India Companies had been established with trading 'factories' as distant as the waterfront of Canton.

By the end of the decade this freedom of the seas was imperilled, for France and Britain both resorted to commercial warfare. French privateers intercepted 91 Danish or Norwegian vessels carrying British merchandise in the late winter and spring of 1798, seizing both ships and cargoes. The Royal Navy responded by making greater use of the 'right of search'. The Swedes and Danes instituted a system of convoys, with some Danish merchantmen protected as far south as the Cape of Good Hope. Clashes were inevitable: a Danish frigate fired on a British boarding party off Gibraltar shortly before Christmas in 1799 and the following July the 40-gun Danish frigate *Freja*, escorting six merchantmen in the southern North Sea, took similar action off Ostend, courageously engaging six British frigates. The *Freja* and her convoy were detained off Ramsgate while negotiations began in Copenhagen to resolve the rights of neutrals.

In December 1800 Tsar Paul, who had veered from alliance with Britain into open hostility, revived the League of Armed Neutrality, a combination of Baltic powers instituted by his mother twenty years previously to protect trade during the War of American Independence. On this occasion Paul ordered the seizure of British ships in Russian ports, imprisoned their crews and demanded the abandonment of the right of search. With some reluctance Denmark broke off all talks over neutral rights and joined Sweden, Prussia and Russia in closing the Baltic to British shipping. The Danes also occupied Hamburg, thus preventing English trade with north Germany.

In London – where Westminster was in crisis over proposals for Catholic emancipation – the outgoing Foreign Secretary, Grenville, pressed for a naval expedition to redress the balance in the Baltic and make certain that timber and hemp continued to reach the shipyards. On 12 March 1801 a formidable fleet, commanded by Admiral Sir Hyde Parker with Vice-Admiral Lord Nelson of the Nile as his deputy, sailed from Yarmouth. By 25 March some fifty warships were riding at anchor in the Kattegat, ready to give battle with the Danes and possibly the Swedes if it proved impossible to gain entry to the inland sea by 'amicable arrangement'. The ultimate objective was Reval, and the destruction of Russian naval power.

Nelson was familiar with the treacherous shoals of the Øresund. As captain of a frigate twenty years previously he had spent some weeks at Helsingør protecting more than fifty merchantmen trying to reach British ports, and made the mistake of underrating Danish naval skills. On 1 April Hyde Parker accepted his proposal that he should run the gauntlet of Danish defences and threaten Copenhagen from the south while Parker engaged the formidable Trekroner fortress with broadsides from his deep draught ships to the north.

The Vice-Admiral, flying his flag in HMS *Elephant*, led twenty-nine ships southwards at half-past nine next morning, Maundy Thursday. The guns of Kronberg opened up, but Nelson kept close to the Swedish coast and the shot fell short of its target. As the squadron closed on the line of Danish blockships and was forced closer to Copenhagen the exchange of fire intensified. Three of the twelve ships of the line and five smaller vessels ran aground. So fierce was the battle that Parker ordered the coded flag for breaking off the action to be flown from the yardarm. It was on this occasion that Nelson famously lifted a spyglass to his blind right eye and observed to the *Elephant*'s captain, 'I really do not see the signal.'

At last, in mid-afternoon, after four hours of cannonade, the Danish capital lay at the mercy of Nelson's remaining 954 guns. Only four years previously the worst fire in Copenhagen's history had made thousands homeless. Rather than expose the citizens to a prolonged bombardment Crown Prince Frederick recognized the need for a truce. Next day Nelson came ashore for talks at the Amalienborg Palace at which a general armistice was agreed. There would be no more fighting that Easter.

A thousand seamen had perished in what Nelson came to regard as the 'hardest' and most 'terrible' of his victories. Yet the battle need never have been fought; Tsar Paul, the champion of Armed Neutrality, was already dead, struck down by an apoplectic fit in the small hours of 24 March, or so his subjects were told. While the British and Danish ships were pounding each other off Copenhagen, hundreds of Petersburgers filed past the embalmed body of the ruler they had come to fear as it lay in state at the Mikhailovsky, the palace where Guards officers had choked him in a sordid scuffle by candlelight. The new emperor, his twenty-three-year-old son Grand Duke Alexander, knew of the conspiracy. He had shared the officers' alarm at Paul's increasingly non-sensible policies, but had naively accepted assurances from the Governor-General of St Petersburg that his father would be deposed, not killed or even harmed. The manner of his accession continued to trouble Alexander's conscience throughout the reign. Letters and journal entries bear witness to days of frustration, when the sin of parricide would darken his thoughts and his prayers.

Gustav IV Adolf observed the smoke and fury of the battle of Copenhagen from Helsingborg, on the Scanian shore. There was never any prospect of Swedish intervention. Sir Hyde Parker sailed through the Sound and led his fleet up to the approaches to Karlskrona, but there was no reason for a battle and the Swedes sensibly stayed in port until the intruder sailed back to the Øresund. Orders awaited Parker, recalling him to home waters and appointing Nelson to temporary command in the Baltic. Despite the news from St Petersburg Nelson pressed ahead with plans for a descent on Reval, though showing the flag as a gesture of goodwill rather than launching another assault. By his own reckoning he was well received, but a stern reproach arrived from St Petersburg: Alexander could not negotiate a settlement with Britain so long as the Royal Navy remained, uninvited, in Russian waters. Nelson sailed back to Copenhagen. A treaty abandoning Armed Neutrality and restoring commercial co-operation was signed on 17 June in St Petersburg. Two days later Nelson left the Øresund, landing at Yarmouth on 1 July. Britain's non-war in the Baltic was over.

Tsar Alexander was at first content to be a neutral observer. For a few weeks he was even flattered by First Consul Bonaparte into mistakenly believing he might be accepted as arbiter for Europe's quarrels. Baltic trade soon recovered its lost momentum, helped by the Peace of Amiens (1802–3), the fourteen months of non-belligerency between Britain and France. Denmark remained emphatically neutral, and as late as 1805 the Chamber of Commerce in Copenhagen could optimistically hail the year 'as one of the most propitious in the annals of Denmark's trade'. But by the spring of 1804 war clouds were gathering to the south. Alexander had become disillusioned with Bonaparte's government and mistrusted his ambitions. In March the seizure and subsequent execution of the Duc d'Enghien enraged him: Enghien was a member of the royal house of France and was abducted from Baden, whose ruler was father-in-law of both the tsar and Gustav IV Adolf. Dynastic pride was further incensed when, on 2 December 1804, the Corsican usurper crowned himself Emperor in the presence of the Pope at Notre Dame.

Alexander now sought to create a defensive league of Russia, Prussia, Austria and Sweden to counter French imperial expansion. Eventually, after months of tortuous diplomacy, common cause was made with William Pitt's government in London: in July 1805 an Anglo-Russian alliance treaty committed Britain to paying an annual subsidy of £1.5 million for every 100,000 men Russia put into the field against Napoleon. Austria subscribed to the treaty in August, soon followed by Sweden, whose king was also tempted by generous subsidies. Prussia, however, held back, thereby weakening this 'Third Coalition' from the start.

The war itself is best remembered for Nelson's victory and death at Trafalgar (21 October) and for Napoleon's great triumph at Austerlitz (2 December), the battle in which the armies of the emperors Alexander and Francis II were routed. The Austrians accepted a humiliating peace treaty, signed at Pressburg (Bratislava), which destroyed Habsburg authority in Italy and Germany, bringing the Holy Roman Empire to its grave. Russia remained at war, but the tsar withdrew his shattered regiments to Poland and returned to St Petersburg, sad at heart. The victorious Napoleon arrived back in Paris less than seventeen weeks after setting out from Saint-Cloud. He had reached his pinnacle of power.

While history was reshaped in the heart of Europe, there was – at least on paper – a Baltic Front, too. For on 31 October 1805 Gustav IV Adolf sailed from Ystad to take command of a 'Northern Army' of 12,000 Swedes and 19,000 Russians, based on Stralsund and intended to strike southwards through Hanover, to threaten Napoleon's communications. The king, with his ships unchallenged along the coast, was soon able to establish headquarters farther west, at Lauenburg on the approaches to Hamburg. Later he moved to Boitzenburg and Greifswald. It mattered little where precisely Gustav Adolf chose to strike martial attitudes for, so long as Prussia stayed out of the war, no enemy could be sighted. In the whole 'campaign' not a shot was fired. Yet there were still more than a thousand Swedish troops in Lauenburg a year later.

In the late autumn of 1806 the situation changed dramatically. Napoleon's Confederation of the Rhine alarmed Prussia by creating a French protectorate in the heart of Germany. Frederick William III demanded that French troops withdraw west of the Rhine. When Napoleon refused, the Prussians foolishly crossed the Saxon frontier without waiting to co-ordinate strategy with Russia. The French response was a rapid thrust into Saxony, heading directly for Berlin. For the first time the full strength of the *Grande Armée* was turned towards Europe's northern shores.

When Napoleon left Paris on 25 September 1806 he envisaged another short war, to be decided by the end of the year. The campaign began as successfully as in the previous year. Slow mobilization and lack of cohesive control on the part of the Prussians ensured a double victory for the French on the same day (14 October): Napoleon won at Jena, while Marshal Davout defeated Frederick William III at Auerstädt, 24 kilometres to the north. There could be no doubt that the redoubtable Prussian army was broken. The invaders fanned out across Brandenburg and Mecklenburg: Marshals Soult and Bernadotte pursued the already legendary veteran General Blücher northwards towards Rostock, his birthplace; Davout occupied Berlin for Napoleon; while Marshal Lannes and several detached cavalry brigades headed north-eastwards, to the mouth of the Oder. There, on 31 October, General Lassalle secured Stettin by bluffing the defenders into believing that he came with a full army corps under his command rather than a brigade of light horsemen.

But the first major Baltic prize fell to the one-time sergeant in Louis XVI's regiment of marines, Marshal Jean Baptiste Bernadotte, the Gascon from Pau whom Emperor Napoleon had created titular Prince of Ponte Corvo four months previously. On 5 November Blücher forced his way into the neutral 'free city' of Lübeck, hoping to use its walls and virtual encirclement by the river Trave as a refuge from his pursuers. Bernadotte, however, was hard on his heels, mounting an assault on the improvised defences while also holding in check his own troops, who had begun looting the rich city. He was successful on both counts. On 7 November Blücher surrendered to him, and the Council of Lübeck later presented the Marshal with six horses in gratitude for the restraint he imposed on his soldiery.

From Lübeck Bernadotte sent fifty captured standards to Napoleon. They included, unexpectedly, Swedish regimental colours. The last veterans of the phantom Northern Army had reached Lübeck from Lauenburg a few days ahead of Blücher, and the war finally caught up with them. Not that they had to fight in it: they were aboard ships in the Trave, with their arms stowed away, awaiting passage to Stralsund when the rival armies descended on the city; 'There was nothing for them to do but to keep their heads down,' the Swedish historian Pär Frohnert has pointed out. They survived, and received good treatment from their captor. Bernadotte ensured that they were well fed and speedily repatriated to their native province, Ostergotland, and he entertained their commander, Count Gustav Mörner, and other Swedish officers at his table. The Count's record of his conversations show the Marshal taking great interest in Swedish affairs: 'Was it not more natural for Norway to be joined to Sweden than to Denmark?', he asked one evening. His sympathetic and courteous treatment of the prisoners was to have unexpected consequences for Bernadotte four years later.

★

Napoleon had anticipated that, with Berlin and the central fortresses of the kingdom in French hands, Frederick William would sue for peace. Instead, Prussia chose to fight on, relying on Russian support and the difficulties facing any enemy seeking to advance across barren, waterlogged country in winter. Königsberg, Danzig and the Baltic coastal garrisons could defy the French until the coming of spring and the prospect of help from a newly raised Russian army.

Napoleon responded by occupying Poznania and the heartland of mediaeval Poland including Thorn and Warsaw. The first French troops – a brigade of Davout's cavalry – were welcomed into Posen by excited patriots on 4 November; Warsaw fell to Murat on 28 November, with three army corps in suppport. Napoleon made Posen his headquarters for the first half of December but then went forward to Warsaw, puzzled that the Hanoverian-born Russian general, Bennigsen, was massing an army to the east of the Vistula, apparently prepared to risk a set-piece winter battle.

At Pultusk on 26 December Bennigsen claimed victory in an indecisive encounter that served as a warning for the main clash of arms, fought at Eylau, 32 kilometres south of Königsberg, on 8 February 1807 after an overnight blizzard. So appalling were the losses on both sides that Napoleon, dictating the official bulletin after surveying the battlefield a day later, declared, 'Such a sight as this should inspire rulers with love of peace and hatred of war.' Although the Russians withdrew to Königsberg, he had come close to capture during the morning's fighting when, by chance, an enemy column stumbled across his headquarters during a blizzard.

There could be no question of returning to Paris at such a time. For much of the spring the French empire was governed from Finckenstein, a Prussian Polish fortress 80 kilometres inland from the Baltic that served as Napoleon's headquarters. Frederick William and Queen Louise clung tenaciously to Memel, the most easterly Prussian outpost, where they maintained a much diminished court. The Swedes were besieged in Stralsund, and Danzig was garrisoned by a Russo-Prussian force that resisted attacks by three army corps before capitulating at the end of May. Napoleon inspected the resources of Danzig in the first week of June.

By now both the French and British had turned again to commercial warfare. After Trafalgar, Napoleon lacked the naval strength to challenge merchant vessels on the high seas. He therefore instituted the Continental System, an attempt to impose a distant blockade by closing all ports on the continent to commerce with the British Isles. The Berlin Decree of November 1806 inaugurating the system was answered in London by the first of several Orders in Council that prohibited neutral shipping from trading between one French-held port and another. The return of embargoes and blockade to the Baltic threatened to impoverish communities that had so recently found the war profitable.

At the same time the French advance to the Vistula posed the Polish Question once more. Tsar Alexander had shown himself by no means unsympathetic to his Polish subjects; he was on terms of close personal friendship with Prince Adam Czartoryski, who served as Russia's assistant foreign minister from September 1802 until May 1806 and also brought new life and vigour to the Polish university at Vilna. But Napoleon could outbid offers to the Poles from the tsar. Two heroes of Kosciuszko's revolt, Henryk Dabrowski and Joseph Wybicki, raised Polish legions from prisoners captured in Bonaparte's Italian campaigns, and followed the French into Posen. Frederick William's Governor of Warsaw, Prince Joseph Poniatowski, nephew of Poland's last king, agreed to command a specifically Polish army in the *Grande Armée*. By early June, when the French and Russian armies were in contact along the steep banks of the river Alle, a Polish division and an artillery regiment was serving in Marshal Mortier's corps and Poniatowski could support Marshal Massena with 18,000 newly raised troops.

The decisive battle was fought at last on the Alle at Friedland (14 June 1807), only 26 kilometres from Eylau, in the region where Grand Master Kniprode had created his defensive line for the Teutonic Knights four and a half centuries back in time. The battle followed a familiar pattern, with initial success by the Russians countered by concentrated French artillery fire, and in the evening by converging flank attack by the cavalry. Russian casualties came to 20,000 dead or gravely wounded, more than twice as many as in the *Grande Armée*. Bennigsen's army was destroyed. Five days later envoys from the tsar sought a truce.

A rapid and far-ranging diplomatic revolution soon followed. Alexander was angered by the failure of the British to give him adequate support in his wars or to ensure that the promise of subsidies to him was scrupulously honoured. Napoleon, on reflection, favoured partnership rather than hostility with an empire so vast that it could threaten British India while, in Europe, keeping the balance between Austria and Prussia. From 28 June to 9 July Alexander and Napoleon held a series of meetings at Tilsit on the river Niemen, a small town now known as Sovietsk and in the Kaliningrad region of Russia. The first discussions were held in canvas pavilions on an improvised barge of state but subsequently the emperors met in Tilsit itself. They speedily settled their differences, although more easily over northern Europe than over central Germany or the Mediterranean. At the tsar's insistence Frederick William III, titular sovereign over Tilsit, was occasionally present, the king hastily summoning Queen Louise from Memel, in the conviction that her presence would strengthen the Prussian cause. It did.

Agreement was reached on four territorial changes: the creation of a Grand Duchy of Warsaw, under French protection and comprising all the lands taken by Prussia during the three Polish partitions, together with special status for Danzig; recognition of a kingdom of Westphalia; the survival of a Prussian kingdom, reduced to half its size; and the transference of Bialystok from Prussia. Defeated Russia lost no lands and was spared the payment of any indemnity. A secret treaty pledged the tsar to join the Continental System if Britain refused his offer to mediate a general peace; Alexander would also put pressure on Sweden and Denmark to collaborate in the System. Soon the two emperors were discussing the form of a close alliance, seeking to avoid disputes over the Eastern Question. Napoleon in effect gave Alexander a free hand in the Baltic, with encouragement to detach Finland from Sweden. All was settled within three weeks of the slaughter at Friedland. Napoleon presented Alexander with the Grand Cross of the Legion of Honour; the tsar awarded him the highest Russian order of chivalry, the Cross of St Andrew. Only later in the year, when Napoleon tightened the Continental System with decrees from Fontainebleau and Milan, did the Russians begin to recognize that the generous settlement imposed economic colonialism on their empire.

The greatest beneficiaries from Tilsit were the Poles, even if the creators of the Grand Duchy never used that historic emotive word, 'Poland'. Although King Frederick Augustus of Saxony became Grand Duke, the new pattern of government was French. The Poles received as a basic charter the Napoleonic Code which, with its emphasis on political equality under paternalistic authority, brought legal uniformity to the Grand Duchy for the first time. In December 1807 serfdom and all other feudal bonds were abolished by decree and attempts were made to give the Poles a Sejm on the French model. Equal civil rights were accorded to Jews and non-Jews, although the clericalist Senate in Warsaw began to discriminate against the Jews in 1809 and they were barred from purchasing land. In return, the Poles had to observe the trade restraints of the Continental System and supply Napoleon with good, hard-working soldiers; a division of Poles was even sent to fight for the empire in Spain.

Apart from Prussia, the immediate loser from Tilsit was neutral Denmark. The British were eager to keep open the entry to the Baltic, through both the Belts and, if possible, the Øresund. There was a fear in London that the combined pressure of France, Russia and Prussia would bring Denmark into their coalition and that Napoleon would seize the newly restored Danish fleet, eighteen ships-of-the-line and more than forty smaller vessels; at Hamburg a multi-national army was said to be massing, ready for an advance into Jutland. George Canning, the foreign secretary, acted as ruthlessly as Grenville six years previously. Copenhagen was threatened by a fleet of forty warships, commanded by Admiral Gambier, and by an expeditionary force of 18,000 men. The Danes rejected a British ultimatum to hand over their fleet for internment until the end of the war against France.

British troops, commanded by Lord Cathcart, landed on 16 August 1807 at Vedbaek, halfway between Helsingør and Copenhagen, and at Køge south of the capital, where Sir Arthur Wellesley, the future Duke of Wellington, commanded a brigade. For more than a fortnight Copenhagen was besieged, the Danes maintaining a proud defence. On 2 September Gambier's ships moved close inshore to begin a bombardment of Copenhagen but were driven off by coastal batteries and a gunboat squadron. The bombardment was therefore left to Cathcart's artillery. It lasted for three days and nights. Some 3,200 Danes were killed or gravely wounded, 300 homes were destroyed and another 1,500 houses or churches severely damaged. Never before had a European capital been subjected to systematic bombardment. When fires in the timber yards threatened to engulf the city, the Danes agreed to negotiate.

For six weeks the British occupied the citadel and dockyards, before sailing away with their prizes, thirty ships-of-the-line and frigates together with thirty smaller vessels. More reasonably, the British held on to two fortified Danish islands, Anholt in the centre of the Kattegat, and Heligoland in the North Sea, covering the German coast and the approaches to the Skagerrak. Their value was not only military. Small vessels from English ports unloaded goods at Heligoland that were then smuggled into the closed continent, most conveniently through Gothenburg or the fishing villages to the north. By November 1808 some 200 merchants lived on Heligoland, profiting from a lucrative trade in contraband. The garrison on Anholt fought off a Danish assault in March 1811; the island was handed back to Denmark three years later. Heligoland remained British until 1890, when it was ceded to Germany.

Inevitably Denmark joined the Continental System and a Franco-Danish treaty of alliance was signed three weeks after the British left Copenhagen. Napoleon was confident that Sweden, too, would join the Continental System. On the day Cathcart landed his troops north of Copenhagen,

Gustav IV Adolf was vainly seeking to rally the Stralsunders to save Sweden's last foothold in Pomerania from falling to the French; and on 6 September – the morning fire spread through Copenhagen's timber yards – the Swedish king finally left Rügen, having ordered his commander in the field to ask Marshal Brune for an armistice. It was therefore reasonable for Napoleon to assume that Gustav Adolf, like Frederick William III, would be glad of terms that left his personal position unchallenged. But, though Gustaf Adolf might be a poor soldier of limited intelligence, he was also a proud autocrat, disinclined to grovel. Napoleon's demands were contemptuously rejected. Instead, Sweden concluded a new treaty with Britain, with the prospect of naval backing and a promise of monthly sub-sidies, to be spent on re-equipping the Swedish army. In March 1808 Sir James Saumarez – aboard the most famous flagship of the Royal Navy, HMS *Victory* – led a fleet of thirteen ships-of-the-line into the Kattegat, with Vinga off Gothenburg as his main anchorage.

Like Admiral Norris eighty years previously, Saumarez returned to England each autumn as the ice threatened to close in, but he came back in four successive summers, giving support to Sweden, limiting Denmark's ability to help Napoleon and keeping trade flowing between British ports and Gothenburg, thus rendering the Continental System inoperable. Russia and Prussia were now technically at war with Britain and in July 1808 there was a running fight along the Gulf of Finland when HMS *Implacable* and HMS *Centaur* pursued the Russian *Sevolod* to the Estonian coast, where she blew up off Baltic Port (Paldiski). A close blockade was maintained on the Russian fleet in Baltic Port for the following ten weeks.

Gustav IV Adolf was also offered the services of 10,000 troops under General Sir John Moore. It was assumed in London they would either defend Sweden from invasion or intervene in Denmark should the French strike northwards to seal off the Baltic. But, with Napoleon's warm endorsement, on 21 February 1808 Russian troops had crossed Sweden's Finnish frontier, and the king proposed to employ Moore and the expedi-tionary force either to invade Norway or to serve under his personal com-mand in Finland. When Moore made it clear that this assignment ran contrary to his orders, Gustav Adolf lost his temper and placed him under house arrest. It appears that not even Admiral Saumarez's diplomatic skill could find a compromise, for less than seven weeks after landing, Moore and his men re-embarked for England – and eventually Corunna.

The Russo-Swedish war in Finland of 1808–9 was a strange conflict, marked by long strategic retreats, ceasefires of limited duration, apparent treachery by the commander of the key fortress of Sveaborg, and the folly of Gustav Adolf, who in September 1808 alienated the army by demoting prestigious Guards regiments for failing to achieve success in a madcap operation of his own devising. Less than three months after invasion began, the tsar had felt so certain of success that he proclaimed the incorporation of the 'Grand Duchy of Finland' into his empire and mounted a victory parade in St Petersburg. In reality the hardest fighting lay ahead, for though the Swedish commander General Klingspor was inept, officers of lesser rank showed initiative. In November 1808 the last Swedish regiments left Finland, but the Finnish people, and the Swedish-Finnish nobility living among them, improvised sub-Arctic guerrilla tactics that were to be perfected in later conflicts. The war created local heroes of fact and fiction and victories that passed into legend: a counter-attack at Lapua on 14 July 1808 makes *Quatorze Juillet* as much a day of celebration in central Ostrobothnia as in France. In the second winter of war the Russian generals Barclay de Tolly and Bagration took the risk of leading cavalry across the frozen waters of the Gulf of Bothnia, using the Åland Islands as stepping-stones to raid the mainland at Umeå while a second army invaded northern Sweden from Tornio. A further landing at Ratan in the summer was repulsed, but rather than endure a third winter the armies made peace at Fredrikshamn (Hamina) in September 1809. Sweden ceded Finland, thereby losing a third of the country and a quarter of the population. By a separate treaty with France, in January 1810, the Swedes undertook to enter the Continental System, in return for recovering Stralsund and Rügen. They were in no hurry to enforce the new restraints. Blockade running still flourished.

On the last day of February 1808 Denmark had declared war on Sweden as an ally of Russia. There was little fighting except for occasional forays along the borders of southern Norway. The Danes, however, experimented with a new weapon: an attempt was made to send balloons filled with explosive across the Øresund and into Scania, but without success. Instead, the balloons were loaded with leaflets urging the Swedish people to overthrow Gustav Adolf and join Denmark and Norway in a united Scandinavian kingdom. There was no apparent response to the 'leaflet raids' but their tone matched the mood of many Swedish officers and government officials at the time. The king – still aged only thirty-one, and much younger than his generals – suspected treason; the fate of both his father and Tsar Paul was in his mind. When, on 13 March 1809, General Adlercreutz and six senior officers burst into his room at the palace, he escaped down a secret passage, only to be arrested when he emerged. He was hustled into a closed carriage and taken to Gripsholm, convinced he was to be killed. His fears were groundless: it was a bloodless coup. He abdicated in favour of his uncle, the ex-regent, who on 6 June 1809 acceded as King Charles XIII. A new constitution was enacted on the same day, striking a careful balance between royal executive, elected legislature and independent judiciary. The deposed king, with his wife, son and three daughters, went into exile; he died twenty-five years later at St Gallen in Switzerland, where he was content to be known as 'Colonel Gustafsson'.

Charles XIII was childless. The Council of the Realm therefore resolved that the Riksdag should elect an outsider as Prince Royal and heir to the throne. The four Estates chose Christian August of Schleswig-Holstein, who rather curiously was commanding the Danish-Norwegian army poised to invade Sweden's western provinces. His status was recognized by Charles XIII in July 1809, and for ten months the Swedes accustomed themselves to accepting a Dane at court. But on 28 May 1810 Christian August suffered a heart attack while inspecting troops in Skåne and died half an hour later, apparently from natural causes.

Wild rumours of new conspiracies swept Stockholm, at a time when morale in the Guards regiments was low. The unrest culminated in an attack by a mob on the Marshal of the Realm's carriage during Christian August's funeral procession. The Marshal – the Count Fersen who sought to rescue the French royal family in 1791 – was seized and beaten to death, without the officers of the Guard ordering them to intervene. Charles XIII, shocked by the lawlessness in the capital, moved the sessions of the Riksdag convened to elect a second Prince Royal to Örebro Castle. The front-runner, dynastically, was Christian August's brother, though he had few personal qualities to commend him. Charles XIII wrote to Napoleon to seek his opinion, as the most powerful ruler in Europe. But Napoleon knew little of Scandinavian affairs and, intent on keeping the Baltic closed to British trade, he recommended his ally, King Frederick VI of Denmark. The thought of a Frenchman on the Swedish throne did not enter his mind.

Increasingly, however, a group of junior officers favoured an outsider, a soldier able to restore Sweden's authority in northern affairs and recover Finland. Traditional Francophiles looked to the Marshalate or to the emperor's family. The Swedish ambassador was consulted and envoys travelled, unofficially, to Paris. Napoleon approached his stepson Eugène de Beauharnais, Viceroy of Italy, who declined. There was talk of Murat or Berthier or Massena; but Bernadotte was the only marshal known to the Swedes. A nephew of Count Mörner visited Bernadotte in the Rue d'Anjou four weeks after Christian August's death and renewed the family link forged at Lübeck, surprising the marshal with news that he had strong support in Stockholm. Cautiously Bernadotte made his own enquiries, employing as his chief go-between Jean Fournier, for sixteen years a merchant living in Gothenburg. Napoleon was informed, and sought to interest the Swedes in another marshal, for his relations with the strong-headed Bernadotte were frequently strained. Fournier, a powerful advocate, reached Örebro two days before the twelve-man committee appointed by the Riksdag was due to make its final recommendation.

As Charles XIII was sinking into premature senility it was right for Sweden to seek a natural leader, with an understanding of a wider world. Napoleon sought to impose an undertaking that the Prince Royal would never take up arms against France, but Bernadotte insisted he should not be bound in vassalage and even won six months' grace in which to assess his new country's economic needs before rigidly committing Sweden to the Continental System: 'But then you must declare yourself – friend or foe!', the Emperor warned. In Stockholm Bernadotte's cause was supported by the influential General Wrede, the king's envoy to Paris for Napoleon's second marriage. Wrede spoke of the marshal's happy family life, of his wife, Desirée (*née* Clary, Napoleon's first love) and of their eleven-year-old son who bore the felicitously non-Catholic name of Oscar. Fournier, a good political campaign manager, emphasized Bernadotte's personal wealth, confirming that he was prepared to advance 8 million francs at 4 per cent and would settle claims by merchants or landowners for losses inflicted by the French in recent campaigns. On 21 August 1810 Charles XIII decided, as he later said, 'to gamble rashly'. Without waiting for a final decision from the committee, he declared Bernadotte his chosen successor. Ten weeks later the king presented him to the four Estates as Karl Johan (Charles John), Prince Royal, an affirmed Lutheran, his adopted son and heir to the hereditary kingdom. He was also commissioned as Supreme Commander of the armed forces. Charles XIII succumbed to the Gascon's charm, personality and vigour. Within hours of their first meeting he observed to his closest confidant that he thought the rash gamble won.

When Bernadotte arrived in Stockholm relations with France were under strain. In order to ensure there was no trade with the English ports, Napoleon required Sweden – like Russia – to declare war on Britain. Reluctantly on 18 November the Swedes complied. The state of war made little difference to daily life or the conduct of affairs. There were no clashes between British and Swedish warships in the Baltic or the North Sea. The commercial channel to Gothenburg was kept open by the simple expedient of employing ships that flew neutral flags. Enterprising captains used

Stralsund and the smaller ports of Swedish Pomerania to smuggle, not only British goods, but coffee and sugar into northern Germany, Poland and Russia. 'They are laughing at Sweden's declaration of war in London, and I even see a smile on Swedish faces in Stockholm,' the French ambassador reported to Paris. Without a good navy and enterprising commanders it was hard for France to wage commercial warfare. Across Europe the Continental System was crumbling at the edges.

Nor was the Tilsit alliance in better shape. At Erfurt in the autumn of 1808 Napoleon and Alexander met for the last time, in an empty show of solidarity, each critically assessing the other. In the following spring Napoleon again defeated Austria in a thirteen-week campaign, dictating peace later in the year from the Habsburg palace of Schönbrunn. Among other losses the Austrians had to cede western Galicia to the Grand Duchy of Warsaw. Russia was still France's nominal ally in 1809, even receiving Tarnopol and Czartow in eastern Galicia to 'compensate' for the enlargement of the Grand Duchy. It was the last carrot Napoleon would offer. By the close of the following year the tsar could write gloomily to his sister, 'It seems that blood must flow again.'

The artificiality of the Continental System was by now gravely weakening the economy of the southern Baltic shore. In September 1810 the collapse of the Rodda Bank in Lübeck sent a shock wave through other credit institutions that went beyond the Hanse cities and rocked banks in Paris itself. Petersburgers complained that while French perfumes and wines were readily available, more useful basic commodities from England's mills and factories were not. Chancellor Rumiantsev, the pro-French foreign minister, sought to reassure the senators in October 1810: the System stimulated Russian industry, he claimed, giving merchants an opportunity to find new markets. Few people were convinced, least of all the would-be exporters of cereal, hemp and flax. Alexander wavered, considering ways the landowners might export grain. Then dramatically on the last day of the old year he went further than seemed possible. A tariff decree imposed heavy duties on goods coming overland, lifted restrictions on imports by sea and promised almost total freedom to export.

The tsar's decision to break out of the Continental System was not entirely in response to economic needs, however. In December 1810 Napoleon incorporated the entire German Baltic coast in the French empire. Among the annexed territories was Oldenburg, a duchy on the left bank of the river Weser ruled by the Holstein-Gottorp dynasty, closely linked by marriage with the Romanovs. Alexander, who looked on Oldenburg as a distant fief of his empire, had upheld the sovereign rights of its ruler at Tilsit and Erfurt. The tsar was affronted by this latest instance of Napoleon going back on his word. He began to reshape policy, even contemplating a surprise attack across the borders of Poland while Napoleon was preoccupied with the mounting insurgency in Spain. Czartoryski was encouraged to sound out secretly Poniatowski in Warsaw, with the promise of raised status for the Poles – a kingdom of Poland to be created within the Russian empire. But, for the moment, the Poles were content; loyalty to France might win even more concessions, their leaders felt.

In Stockholm the new prince royal trod warily. He was prepared to collaborate with France if Napoleon chose to treat Sweden rather than Denmark as his favoured client in Scandinavia, provided the Swedes could acquire Norway. Until the late summer of 1811 Bernadotte passed on to Paris intelligence gathered by Swedish agents concerning the disposition of Russia's forces in the Gulf of Riga and Finland, although he dismissed invitations from Paris for Swedish volunteers to form a regiment in the French army or master the skills of ocean-going seamanship by serving with the fleet based on Brest. He grew concerned over the activities of his old rival, Marshal Davout, to whom Napoleon entrusted the governorship of Oldenburg and command over garrisons in the Hanse towns, including Danzig.

By November Davout had accumulated a formidable army along the coast. Its immediate purpose became clear in early January 1812, when he was ordered to occupy Swedish Pomerania. Swedish troops holding Stralsund and Rügen were interned; ships bound for Swedish ports were commandeered and their cargoes confiscated. The prince royal responded with a letter of pained reproof to Paris and, more significantly, by secretly sending personal envoys to St Petersburg and London.

By now there could be little doubt that war was looming between Russia and France. As early as early as 16 August 1811 Napoleon presided over a Council of State at which, after reviewing relations between the two empires since Tilsit, he ordered preparations be made over the winter months for a possible campaign in the East during the long daylight hours of summer. He would expect auxiliary troops from Prussia and Austria, as well as grateful Polish patriots, to support the *Grande Armée*. By Christmas Napoleon was ordering his librarian to find for him the 'most detailed account in French of Charles XII's campaign in Poland and Russia'. At the same time, Alexander prepared to resume the conflict halted so precipitately after Friedland: the arms factories at Tula and Alexandrovsk began to turn out weapons and munitions every day of the year, even on holy festivals; the defences of Riga and Dunaburg were strengthened with new heavy cannon; and moves were made to end the latest conflict with Turkey, releasing troops for the west.

Neither emperor had clearly defined objectives. Alexander wanted the French away from the Baltic, with their massed divisions out of northern Germany. Napoleon spoke grandly of making Russia turn towards Asia, of ending her 'baleful influence . . . on the affairs of Europe', but he also called on his soldiers to fight a 'second Polish war'. Yet as he pored over maps – assigning supply depots to the cities of Germany, conjuring up conscripts from twelve nations, planning how to bring the Army of Italy to the Vistula and the Guard from Portugal to Pomerania – it is hard to escape a feeling that his driving motive was a professional challenge, the ambition to crown his military career with a campaign more impressive than any past commander had achieved. He would not merely beat Alexander the Tsar: he would trump Alexander the Great.

The tsar was with his troops as soon as the roads were clear of the final thaw. He left St Petersburg on 21 April, officially 'to inspect his provinces'. Five days later he reached Vilna, 160 kilometres from the frontier with East Prussia though only 80 from the borders of the Grand Duchy. Under the *Rzeczpospolita* Vilna was eclipsed by Warsaw and Cracow. Now, for two months, it served as a capital for the empire. The minister of war, Barclay de Tolly, was already there. So was the minister of police, General Balashov. Other ministers followed, with members of the diplomatic corps and high-ranking officers. The population – 56,000 in normal times – almost doubled. Innkeepers and moneylenders chalked up good profits. High society, too, made the journey from St Petersburg, dismissive of any war cloud in the western sky. 'A storm was about to break over our heads and yet, feeling perfectly secure, none of us thought of anything but pleasure,' the young Countess Tieshausen recalled in 1828. 'We did not even know the French were crossing Germany, for no item of news was allowed to circulate in Lithuania.' On the evening of Wednesday, 24 June, a ball was in progress at Zakret, General Bennigsen's estate three kilometres outside Vilna, when Balashov quietly let Alexander know that a horseman had arrived from Kaunas: a huge army crossed the Niemen early that morning, with Napoleon at its head. The tsar slipped away to his residence in the governor-general's palace, and all the revelry was over.

Reports reaching Vilna indicated that Napoleon was employing a larger force than the Russians had thought possible. Half a million men were east of the Vistula, from the Prussians in Memel southwards to Schwarzenburg's Austrians in Lvov. Late on Thursday Alexander decided to make a last appeal for peace. Balashov was summoned to the palace and ordered to seek out Napoleon, hand him a letter and assure him that, as soon as the invaders crossed back across the frontier, he would be ready to discuss a settlement of differences.

Within an hour Balashov was following the road through Trakai to Kaunas. On the Friday morning he encountered the first French patrol, at the village of Rykonty. Napoleon was in no hurry to receive him. All was not going to plan; he had expected a decisive battle in Lithuania soon after crossing the Niemen. Instead, the Russians eluded him, Barclay de Tolly evacuating Vilna on Saturday, 29 June, before the armies made contact. Napoleon was soon in difficulties. Food convoys from the Prussian depots were delayed by cart track 'roads', and the weather was unexpectedly treacherous: blazing sunshine, raw nights and heavy thunderstorms. General Caulaincourt found that, even during these first days, 'many of the Young Guard perished along the road, from cold and hunger'; and a staff officer counted more than 1,200 dead horses beside 20 kilometres of the Vilna road. Napoleon gave orders that Balashov should not be allowed to see the *Grande Armée* in such plight; he must be brought back to Vilna by 'a different route'. When, on Monday afternoon, he consented to receive him, Balashov was ushered into the room from which the tsar sent him in search of Napoleon four days previously. Not surprisingly, the emperor was ill at ease, alternately patronizing or bullying, but he sent a lengthy reply. There could be no negotiations; Alexander was, however, assured that 'should fortune again favour my arms you will find me, as at Tilsit and Erfurt, full of friendship and esteem for your good and great qualities.'

Napoleon lingered at Vilna for two and a half weeks. The city became the key communications centre for his empire, with a courier system carrying letters to Paris in ten days. Maret, the foreign minister, remained there for four months, adding the administration of Lithuania to his responsibilities. Envoys from Vienna, Berlin, Copenhagen and Washington DC spent the summer and autumn in the city. But the war itself receded. The gruelling advance on Moscow, with a parched army pressing forward under a pitiless sun, took the line of battle away from the Baltic provinces to Vitebsk and Smolensk and to a climax in the battle of Borodino, 'field of bloodshot fame'. Little of this epic tragedy was known in Vilna. Yet between crossing the Niemen and entering Moscow eighty-two days later the *Grande Armée* shrank to a third of its strength in men, and lost thousands of horses. And the winter retreat was yet to come.

Rumours of pending disaster followed the first snow to fall on Vilna, at the end of October. A month later the army, by then east of the Berezina, turned back towards Lithuania. Ahead of it came a desperate plea to Maret, sent from Zembik on 29 November: 'The army is broken up in a terrifying manner,' Napoleon admitted, 'it needs fifteen days to reform . . . Food, food, food! Without it there are no horrors this undisciplined mass will not commit in Vilna . . . There must be no foreign envoys in Vilna; the army is today not a fine sight.' The truth was out at last. On 6 December emperor and foreign minister met outside Vilna as dawn was breaking. Napoleon had left the *Grande Armée* under the command of Murat and was hurrying back to Paris; he had no wish to be seen in the city that Sunday. By noon he was on his way.

There followed a week without precedent in Vilna's history. Isolated units reached the city twenty hours later. All remained orderly until the main body of troops arrived on Wednesday (9 December). The Dutch Governor, General van Hogendorp, was well prepared: monastic buildings were requisitioned and stocked with food, clothing and boots; outside the walls, posters directed each corps to the monastery to which it was assigned. But Napoleon had warned of an 'undisciplined mass', and he was right. The men broke through the gates in a rush for food and brandy. Three marshals, the grim-faced Davout among them, had to thrust their way through a drunken mob to seek refuge in the Governor's palace. No orders were obeyed. There was widespread looting; a remarkable drawing, sketched in the cathedral square that Wednesday, shows soldiers with rich liturgical vestments enveloping their tattered uniforms, giving them warmth. For twenty-four hours anarchy reigned. Then, as the Russians approached, Murat ordered evacuation. Those who were fit to resume the westward trek set out along the hilly road to Kaunas, with loose snow over a sheet of ice making the route impassable for guns or wagons. Three days later Marshal Ney shepherded the shattered remnant of the *Grande Armée* across the Niemen and into East Prussia.

Before daybreak on 23 December Tsar Alexander was welcomed back in Vilna. Next night a ball at the Governor's palace celebrated his thirty-fifth birthday. The revelry resumed. Yet within five square kilometres of the palace several thousand veterans of the retreat lay in freezing makeshift hospitals; most of the sick and wounded perished in the weeks ahead, short of medicine and finally of basic food. Excavation of mass graves in contemporary Vilnius has confirmed tales that some resorted to cannibalism at the end.

Marshal Macdonald, commanding 10th Corps in the *Grande Armée*, still had 30,000 men under arms in mid-December. Half were Prussians, under

General Yorck von Wartenburg, and there was also a Polish brigade. At the start of the campaign 10th Corps's objective was Riga, and through July and August Macdonald advanced steadily across Courland without any major clash of arms. He secured the left bank of the Dvina from the sea to Dünaburg (Daugavpils). Yorck held Mitau and enveloped Riga but Macdonald would not risk heavy losses by an assault on the city unless Napoleon ordered an advance on St Petersburg, 740 kilometres away. General Ivan Essen, the Baltic German defending Riga, lacked the resources for a counter-offensive. Off the coast of Courland Admiral Saumarez was again at sea with a British squadron, in contact with the Russians and denying 10th Corps supplies from the old Hanse ports.

Command of the sea assumed new importance after Bernadotte accepted an unexpected invitation from Alexander to meet him at the Finnish city of Äbo in the last week of August. The prince royal assured the tsar there would be no war of revenge to recover Finland, and undertook to co-operate with Russia against Napoleon provided Alexander supported troops operating south of the Baltic and would help Sweden obtain Norway from Denmark with an auxiliary corps of 35,000 men. He proposed a joint invasion from Skåne, followed by landings in Zealand and the seizure of Copenhagen. The Swedes assumed intervention on this scale would not be possible until the spring and would need financial and naval assistance from Britain.

As a first step, however, the tsar was able to withdraw troops from Finland. General Steingell's corps crossed the Gulf to land at Reval and march through Livonia to strengthen Essen's army holding Riga. On 29 September fighting flared up along the Dvina, but the Russian master-plan envisaged a pincer movement to cut off Napoleon's communications rather than isolated battles; Essen was ordered back into Riga, while Steingell's corps pressed southwards up the Dvina to join the Russian army threatening Vitebsk and Smolensk from the north.

In the first week of November Essen sent a letter to Yorck, letting him know that Napoleon was in full retreat and recommending Yorck should bring the Prussians over to the Russian side. The general took no action until the 10th Corps was ordered by Murat to fall back from Riga to the lower Niemen. He then made contact with Prussians already serving in the tsar's army – including Clausewitz, the great theorist of strategy – and defected. The Convention of Tauroggen (30 December 1812) recognized Yorck's Prussians as non-belligerents. The loss of Yorck's troops convinced Macdonald and Murat that it would be impossible to hold East Prussia against the Russians, and the French withdrew from Königsberg. Yorck and the tsar's Prussian political adviser, Baron Stein, occupied the region, and summoned the East Prussian Diet (Landtag) which mobilized all men aged between eighteen and forty-five into a *Landwehr* to protect the province. The hesitant King Frederick William III – by now a widower – left Berlin for the relative security of Breslau, concluded an alliance with the Russians (27 February 1813) and on 16 March declared war on Napoleon, calling on the German people (*Volk*) to wage a war of liberation.

By now the only French garrisons on the Baltic shores were at Danzig and Stettin, although Marshal Davout continued to hold Hamburg. Frederick VII of Denmark remained loyal to his ally, with his small army holding Holstein, including Kiel, and occupying Lübeck. In late March the first Swedish troops returned to Pomerania and *Te Deums* were sung in Stralsund's churches on 4 April to celebrate the restoration of sovereignty. But the prince royal was in no hurry to commit himself; he needed first to make sure of British subsidies and agreement among the allies on the transference of Norway; not until 18 May did he step ashore at Stralsund and even then it was well into August before he led his multi-national Army of the North southwards. Grossbeeren, on 23 August, was won by the Prussian contingent, without Swedish participation. On 6 September forty battalions of Swedes arrived at Dennewitz in time to swing the balance of battle towards the allies: the French lost 10,000 dead or wounded, the Prussians 7,000, the Swedes 20 wounded, none dead; it was a feat of arms Stockholm enjoyed celebrating. At Leipzig, 'the battle of the nations' (16–19 October), the prince royal – true to form – arrived late, but fought with great courage and bravado. A Swedish Lifeguard regiment joined in the assault on the city gate from the south-east, enabling the prince royal to reach the heart of the old city ahead of the three allied sovereigns (Russian, Prussian, Austrian). Casualties were again mercifully light: 54,000 men were killed or wounded during Napoleon's defeat on that day; only 170 of them were Swedish.

The Swedes took little further part in the war against France. At the end of November the prince royal divided the Army of the North, leaving the Prussians to advance through Westphalia and into France along with the Russian and Austrian armies, while the Swedes and some 6,000 Russians turned northwards against the Danes, whom they outnumbered by five to one. Swedish Hussars defeated Danish cavalry at Bornhöft (7 December) but there was no full-scale battle. After protracted negotiations a compromise settlement was reached at Charles John's headquarters in Kiel on 7 January 1814. By the terms of the treaty Denmark surrendered Norway to

14

Peaceful Change?

CASTLEREAGH, THE BRITISH Foreign Secretary, assumed that the basic spadework for rebuilding the European system could be done while the victorious sovereigns and their ministers were in the French capital. That was impossible: long years of campaigning deserved long nights of festivity. 'Paris is a bad place for business,' he gloomily told his cabinet colleagues at Westminster; it was too soon to begin waging peace. A treaty was indeed signed at Paris on 30 May, but it was concerned almost entirely with the restoration of the French frontiers of 1792, with the future of the Netherlands, Switzerland and Italy and with colonial issues. Article VI anticipated a 'federative bond' to bring the states of Germany closer together, including on the Baltic coast Prussia, Mecklenburg and Holstein. By an 'additional and secret article' France adhered to the Treaty of Kiel, thereby recognizing the union of the Swedish and Norwegian kingdoms and the cession by Denmark of Heligoland to Great Britain. There was otherwise no mention of northern Europe, and the future of Poland was ignored. The general settlement of Europe's affairs was postponed. Article XXXII of the Treaty of Paris provided for a congress to 'regulate a real and permanent Balance of Power in Europe' that would meet at Vienna in September and, it was confidently assumed, complete its work by the end of the year. Optimists – the tsar among them – thought all could be settled within six weeks.

One problem needed urgent attention, however. Many Norwegians resented being handed over from one sovereign to another as if they were royal chattels. The Viceroy of Norway – Prince Christian Frederick of Schleswig-Holstein-Sonderburg-Glücksburg, first cousin and heir of Frederick VI of Denmark – backed a Norwegian independence movement. More than a hundred delegates attended a national assembly at Eidsvold, a village 80 kilometres north of Christiania (Oslo), and on 17 May issued a liberal constitution providing for a parliament (*Storting*); Prince Christian Frederick was elected king of an independent Norway. Bernadotte could see his presence was needed in his adopted country. He left Paris for Sweden before the treaty was signed.

Among the Great Powers, Austria and Prussia were sympathetic to the Norwegians (as also was Frederick of Denmark) but Britain and Russia stood for strict observance of the Treaty of Kiel. Allied commissioners crossed to Christiania to talk sense to the newly elected king. They found him obdurate. Militarily he knew Norway stood little chance of defeating Sweden, though a long guerrilla war might be fought in the mountains. He thought, however, that with so many countries eager to restore normal commercial conditions in the Baltic the powers would not want to see trade through the Skagerrak hampered by a new conflict.

War came, nevertheless. On 26–27 July Swedish troops landed in the Hvaler Islands, an archipelago commanding the approaches to Oslofjord. By a well-planned pincer movement two army corps (led by the prince royal and by General Essen) engaged the line of Norwegian forts along the river Glamma and prepared to besiege Fredriksten, the fortress outside which, almost a century ago, Charles XIII had died. But the prince royal did not wish the union of the two kingdoms marred by a long and bloody conflict that would create lasting bitterness and resentment. When the small port of Fredrikstad fell on 3 August he induced a wealthy merchant to travel to Christiania with generous peace terms. Eleven days later a delegation from the Storting accepted armistice terms at Moss, the thriving port on the eastern shore of Oslofjord. By the Convention of Moss the prince royal recognized the Eidsvold Constitution as fundamental to the union, though Christian Frederick was obliged to abdicate and accept permanent exile from Norway.

The prince royal also sought to 'punish' King Frederick VI for his support of the separatist movement by withholding the transfer to Denmark of Swedish Pomerania promised under the terms of the Treaty of Kiel. Eventually, a settlement was reached at the Vienna Congress in June 1815, largely through the mediation of the Russian foreign minister, Nesselrode. Denmark received the small duchy of Lauenberg from Prussia, together with monetary compensation: and the Swedes sold Pomerania to Prussia. Thus, almost as a bargain under the counter, Sweden shed her last semi-colonial possession south of the Baltic. Henceforth a dual Scandinavian kingdom of Sweden and Norway consistently sought to avoid war and foreign commitment.

The future of Sweden's lost provinces in Finland had been settled already and caused no trouble to the peacemakers. Tsar Alexander I wooed the Finns by a series of gracious concessions. A deputation of eminent Finns, many of Swedish descent, was invited to St Petersburg as early as the autumn of 1808 and received assurances from Alexander that he would respect Finland's laws and institutions; the sole bond of union with Russia would be personal; he would never rule as Emperor in Finland but as Grand Duke. In March 1809 Alexander came to Porvoo – Borga to Swedes – and confirmed Finnish rights at a Diet of the four Estates, meeting in the Lutheran cathedral. Executive authority was exercised by appointed Governors General, the Finnish-Swedish soldier Göran Sprengtporten in 1809 but thereafter by a succession of Russians. The effective government was at first a hastily instituted council but by 1816 it had evolved into a nominated Imperial Senate of twenty Finnish members, mainly of Swedish descent. One group of senators formed a Supreme Court but others had departmental responsibilities – finance, health, education, police, industry, public works. In 1811–12, as a sign of his confidence in his Finnish subjects, Alexander restored all the Finnish territory annexed by Russia in 1721 and 1743 including the Karelian isthmus, districts in Karelia north and west of Lake Ladoga and the region around Vyborg (Viipuri). The border established between the Grand Duchy and the Russian empire remained the international frontier recognized by Soviet Russia until March 1940 and the end of the Winter War.

Despite the political upheaval, the language of government remained Swedish, the currency of Sweden was legal tender until 1840, and there was no change in the structure or teachings of the Swedish Lutheran church. But increasingly the Finns looked away from the West. By 1848 some 40 per cent of Finnish trade was with Russia and a mere 10 per cent with Sweden. New markets opened up in a vast empire and there were challenging opportunities for careers in the middle ranks of the imperial civil service or the army. Both peoples benefited from the growth of the Finnish merchant navy: Russia, with very few merchant ships in Baltic waters, gained valuable ports and shipyards from Kotka round to Oulu in the Gulf of Bothnia, as well as the seafaring skills and craftsmanship of the Åland islanders.

Gradually traditional links with Sweden were cut. Institutions moved away from Åbo (Turku), the old capital, to the much smaller port of Helsingfors (Helsinki), 160 kilometres nearer to St Petersburg and only 80 kilometres from the Estonian coast. Postal services were centred on Helsingfors in 1811; the public health authorities followed a year later. By August 1812, when Alexander travelled to Åbo for his meeting with Bernadotte, the decision had been taken to create a new capital at Helsingfors. This was a bold move, for it was a town of no more than 4,000 inhabitants, with little to commend it other than a fish market, a scattering of homes spared from a recent fire, and a magnificent natural harbour. Fortunately in Johannes Ehrenström the tsar found a town planner of vision, while in 1815 the Berlin-born architect Carl Ludwig Engel settled in Helsingfors, perfecting in the heart of the city a neo-classicism that also left a mark on St Petersburg and Tallinn. When in 1827 the Great Fire of Åbo devastated the old capital, Finland's national university moved to Engel's palatial building flanking Senate Square. The Finns were materially more prosperous and contented under Russian rule than Swedish. There was, after all, no longer a threat from the East.

In 1814 Alexander had hopes of settling Polish affairs just as amicably. His generals wanted the whole of Poland incorporated in the Russian empire, and there were moments when their emperor agreed with them, relishing his role as arbiter of Poland's future. But he sought a lasting solution of the Polish Question, not another improvised international bargain. He knew Poles far better than Finns; he thought he understood them and respected their intense patriotism; he even sent a Russian guard of honour to salute Kosciuszko in Paris. Although Adam Czartoryski had been out of favour for several years, he was at Alexander's side again in Paris in 1814 and during the tsar's subsequent brief visit to England. On his journey from St Petersburg to the congress that September Alexander spent several days on the Czartoryski estate at Pulawy, talking at length to members of the Polish aristocracy; he envisaged a Polish kingdom with some ten or eleven million subjects, independent of Russia's other provinces and, like Finland, bound only by bonds of personal allegiance to a joint sovereign. The tsar approved a statement of constitutional principles drawn up by Czartoryski, including the establishment of a bicameral parliament.

Alexander arrived at Vienna on 25 September 1814, clearer in his mind about Poland than any other question. He had, of course, to throw a tasty bone to satisfy Prussia's dogs of war, the rabid patriots proud of the *Landwehr*'s record in the War of Liberation. But Russian troops were in every Polish town and village and Saxony, too, was in their hands. The functions of the King of Saxony, ex-Grand Duke of Warsaw, were suspended in his own kingdom and it was a Russian general in Dresden, not Prussia's Central Administrative Council for Germany, who controlled public affairs across the Saxon lands. The tsar believed he could dictate from strength, not negotiate. 'I have conquered the Duchy [of Warsaw] and I have half a million men to keep it,' he reminded the British foreign secretary. 'I will give Prussia what is due to her, but not a single village to Austria.'

Metternich, the Austrian chancellor, and Talleyrand, the French foreign minister, rallied opposition from the many smaller German states alarmed by Russia's armed strength. Negotiations over the Polish Question dragged on for five months, during three of which Alexander declined even to speak to Metternich directly. By 3 January 1815 the rift between them over Poland ran so deep that Austria, Britain and France concluded a secret military alliance, providing for joint action if Russian and Prussian armies marched on Vienna. The alliance was a bluff to call a bluff. Nothing remained secret for long at the Congress: Alexander knew his 'half a million men' were in no condition to wage another war for the sake of Poland; nor were the armies of the three crypto-allies. Only the Prussian officer corps was prepared to risk a new winter campaign, but Frederick William III and the more hard-headed of his ministers and senior generals showed greater interest in the Rhineland than in acquisitions in the East. Moreover, both Prussia (directly) and Russia (indirectly) were concerned over the form of the proposed German Confederation and eager to curb Austrian dominance at Frankfurt, the Free City where the Diet was to assemble.

In the first six weeks of the new year these considerations – together with a mounting conviction of spiritual vocation and a nobler vision of general peace – induced Alexander to trim his Polish ambitions. By the final settlement, embodied in the Treaty of Vienna later in the year, Austria retained Galicia and received back from Russia the Tarnopol region, assigned to Alexander in 1809 by Napoleon; Prussia recovered Poznania, including Posen and Thorn; Cracow became a Free City; but the remainder of the Napoleonic Grand-Duchy, including Warsaw itself, was created a kingdom to be ruled in perpetuity by the Emperor of Russia. Czartoryski and his Pulawy associates were not entirely disappointed. The concept of Polish nationhood survived; Cracow, the earliest Polish cultural centre, enjoyed a tenuous freedom; 'Congress Poland', as Alexander's new kingdom was widely called, was to receive a Diet and could maintain a Polish standing army. Much would depend on the character, and even the passing whims, of Alexander and his successors. The track record of rational consistency among recent heads of the Romanov dynasty was not encouraging. The Poles were disappointed that Alexander appointed as his Viceroy General Joseph Zaionczek, a member of the lesser nobility who had served Napoleon; they would have preferred Czartoryski, who became president of the Senate. Real power rested with Grand Duke Constantine, to whom his brother entrusted command of the Polish army, and the Imperial Commissioner, Nicholas Novosiltsov, a close friend of the tsar. Yet, despite its shortcomings and

Berlin. Railways did not, however, reach the Baltic coast until the mid-Forties, first at Stettin and soon afterwards at Kiel.

The peacemakers at Vienna recognized the need for freer trade along Europe's rivers and canals. Unimpeded navigation, regular tariffs and uniformity of collection of dues were guaranteed along the Vistula, Oder, Elbe, Weser and their principal tributaries, as well as the Rhine, Scheldt and Moselle in the west. The vexatious question of the Sound Dues was also raised at Vienna, but it was not pursued. With forty or fifty ships sailing the Øresund each day and passing the customs control point at Kronborg Castle, the yield remained the largest single source of revenue for Denmark. As soon as war receded from the Baltic, the Danes reverted to traditional ways of levying dues and concluded a series of bilateral commercial agreements with the governments whose merchantmen made most use of the inland sea. There was a slight modification in 1816 when it was agreed that revenue from the tolls should go to the public treasury rather than be treated as a private patrimony of the ruling king.

Sound Dues remained highly unpopular. Commercial communities in ports like Stralsund, Danzig, Newcastle and Hull looked on them as inequitable and a hindrance to trade. Ships were delayed for twenty-four hours or more while the clerks in Kronborg Castle struggled with mounting paperwork. When, on 16 March 1841, the question of the Sound Dues was for the first time raised in the House of Commons William Hutt, MP for Hull, voiced his constituents' indignation that 'the King of Denmark (sic) . . . blocks up the road of communication between Hamburg and Lübeck and thus forces every article of commerce proceeding to the Baltic into his law trap at Elsinore.' Yet, despite protests from four countries and the Free Cities, it was not until after the Crimean War that an international conference in Copenhagen agreed on redemption of the transit dues. The British were shown to have had the greatest share of Baltic commerce (28.93 per cent) in the last 'undisturbed' years of seaborne trade (1843–47) and were therefore required to pay the largest redemption charge, £1,125,000 (all of which the Danish Government invested in Britain). The Russians (27.83 per cent of trade), the Prussians (12.62 per cent), and more than twenty other governments were assessed proportionately. Tolls on Baltic trade were levied for the last time on 31 March 1857, ending more than four centuries in which Denmark's rulers treated the Øresund as a river flowing through their lands.

Traditionally the years 1815 to 1848 form the 'Age of Metternich', a static period of reaction, dominated by the Austrian chancellor's fear of renewed revolution and by the tsar's repressive Holy Alliance. This, however, is an oversimplification, not least because Alexander genuinely believed the Holy Alliance was not an assertion of autocracy but a call on Europe's rulers to observe 'precepts of Justice, Christian Charity and Peace'. The first in the series of post-Vienna congresses, at Aix (Aachen) in 1818, was amicable and constructive; there was agreement on preserving Jewish rights in German cities and even on the protocol to be observed when foreign warships exchanged salutes at sea, a question that had once provided an excuse for war between Denmark and Sweden. As late as the Troppau Congress in 1820 the tsar supported, in principle, the 'dual freedoms' of 'national independence and political liberty'. But within Germany widespread hopes of liberal constitutions were dashed in September 1819 by the Frankfurt Diet's acceptance of the Carlsbad Decrees, measures advocated by Metternich to stamp out 'secret societies', tighten press censorship and restrict rights of political assembly. German universities along the Baltic coast – Rostock, Kiel, Greifswald, Königsberg – were placed under as close surveillance as students and teachers in the potentially more 'Jacobin' Rhineland.

At first Tsar Alexander refused to follow the example set by Prussia and Austria. He had shown his commitment to reform, not only in Finland and Poland, but also in the Baltic provinces where, between 1816 and 1819, a series of peasant laws abolished serfdom (except in Letgale whose peasants had to wait for personal freedom until 1861, and the famous act of imperial emancipation). In March 1818 Alexander told the Warsaw Diet that 'with the help of the Almighty' he hoped to establish 'free institutions' in 'all the regions entrusted by Providence' to his care. Work was in progress on a written constitution to give the Russian empire a federal structure, with bicameral consultative assemblies; and in 1819, while Prussia's students were under suspicion, Alexander almost defiantly raised the Pedagogic Institute in St Petersburg to the status of a university.

This imperial patronage of learning in the capital was Alexander's last 'progressive' gesture. For before he left Troppau news reached him of a mutiny in his personal Guard Regiment, the Semeonovsky. Although the root of the trouble was disgust at cruel punishments inflicted by a particular colonel, the tsar allowed himself to be convinced that 'incitement came from outside the army'. He warned General Arakcheev (in effect his security chief) that 'the secret societies' had infiltrated the most prestigious regiment in the army. Metternich, it seemed, was right after all.

Disastrously, from July 1820 to June 1821, Alexander was absent from St Petersburg, attending conferences or congresses concerned with the Eastern Question, Spain or Italy. 'Russia is governed from the seat of a post-chaise,' complained one of his grandmother's last surviving advisers. The day-to-day business of government was left to bumbling bureaucrats or to the martinets to whom Arakcheev entrusted authority. Discontent was never far below the surface. Secret societies became a reality, not a bogey. They proliferated, especially in St Petersburg, Kiev and Moscow. In Lithuania students at Vilna's university sought membership of either the Philomats ('lovers of learning') or the Philorets ('lovers of virtue'). The twenty-five-year-old Polish poet Adam Mickiewicz was among the Vilna virtuous, until a spy betrayed the society and he was banished to Odessa. So it was, too, for the intelligentsia across many provinces in these four years of Alexander's reign. By later standards of repression the regime was not harsh, but it had the power and the means to dampen down any smouldering undergrowth of radicalism.

The flame of liberty flared up beside the frozen Neva at the end of December 1825, amid the confusion that followed Alexander's death at Taganrog, three weeks previously. Was the new tsar the elder of Alexander's brothers, Constantine (reputedly liberal), or the much younger Nicholas (manically militarist)? In Warsaw Constantine, who in 1822 had written to Alexander renouncing his rights, proclaimed the accession of Nicholas I. In St Petersburg his brother, knowing nothing of the renunciation, proclaimed the accession of Constantine I and on 22 December presided over a solemn ceremony of oath-taking. Soon afterwards their youngest brother, Michael, arrived from Warsaw with loyal assurances from Constantine. Rumours swept the capital: was Nicholas, fearing that Constantine would give Russia a constitution, about to seize the throne? Police reports of conspiracy among the younger officers were handed over to the new tsar; the guard and garrison were ordered to parade in Senate Square, facing Falconet's *Bronze Horseman*, on 26 December, the morning he officially went into residence at the Winter Palace. A battalion of the Moscow Regiment, some companies of the Izmailovsky Guards and some marine guards refused to swear allegiance to Nicholas I. There were shouts of 'Constantine and the Constitution'; or perhaps, as Nicholas wrote to his mother, merely 'We're for Constantine'. Many regiments, including the Semeonovsky, remained steadfastly loyal to Nicholas. The Governor-General of St Petersburg, Count Miloradovitch, a popular and brave general, urged the mutineers to show sense and fell mortally wounded by the first shot to be fired; his assassin was a young civilian and not a soldier. A plea from the Metropolitan Seraphim, robed in full canonicals, went unheeded. A warning from the new tsar provoked more confusing cheers and shouts. He ordered three cannon loaded with grapeshot to fire on the troublemakers. No one knows how many perished that afternoon. 'This is a fine start to my reign,' Nicholas observed.

Worse was to follow; for it soon became clear that the mutineers in Senate Square had prematurely exploded a general conspiracy, with revolutionary cells in other cities, most actively in Kiev. Only five ringleaders were hanged but two hundred 'Decembrist' conspirators were exiled to Siberia, to labour under appalling conditions in the Urals. Some bore historic names – Obolensky, Muraviev and Orlov among them – and a few came from the Baltic baronage, notably the Estonian landowner, Andrei Rozen. The Senate Square drama determined the character of the reign, confirming Nicholas's prejudices. He became the 'Iron Autocrat', 'the gendarme of Europe', policing the continent to hunt down revolutionaries. All Russia was condemned to thirty years of political reaction wrapped in holy obscurantism.

Nicholas was known to detest everything Polish, but he was at first prepared to tolerate the structure of the kingdom Alexander created. He came to Warsaw to be crowned in May 1829 and was there again a year later to address the Polish Diet, when his brother Constantine assured him of the loyalty and efficiency of the Polish army he commanded. Yet only six months later – on 29 November 1830 – junior officers of the Fourth Polish Infantry Regiment, on guard duty in the capital, helped military cadets and university students break into the arsenal in northern Warsaw, and a revolutionary National Guard was established. Little planning had gone into the insurrection and prompt action should have stamped out the embers of rebellion. But Constantine, taken completely by surprise and by now doubting the loyalty of his army, hesitated and was lost. Within a week a provisional government of the Kingdom of Poland was proclaimed in Warsaw and General Chlopicki, a veteran of the *Grande Armée*, found himself appointed dictator by acclamation.

Astonishingly, this impromptu insurrection soon became a national rebellion. Polish garrisons across the Congress Kingdom rallied to support Chlopicki and so, too, did patriots in Lithuania. Climate helped the insurgents. In winter news took at least a week to travel from Warsaw to St Petersburg and the tsar needed another month to prepare an army to restore order. By the end of January, Chlopicki was forced out of office, the tsar-king formally deposed, and authority in the hands of a five-man council, under the presidency of Adam Czartoryski. The Russians threatened to overwhelm the Polish army at Grochow, outside Warsaw, in February but General Skrzynecki (another Napoleonic veteran) rallied the defenders, and turned defeat into a victory. In May he even launched a counter-offensive that cleared the north-eastern approaches to the city. The long-awaited Russian onslaught was delayed by the spread of the great cholera epidemic that swept so much of Europe during 1831–2: the Russian army commander, Marshal Diebitsch, fell victim to the disease and so, too, did Grand Duke Constantine. It was not until August that the main Russian army, under Marshal Paskevich, approached Warsaw. By then there were serious divisions within the ruling council; the aristocratic Czartoryski had little in common with urban rabble rousers. On 6 September Warsaw came under heavy bombardment. After forty-eight hours of defiance 33,000 Polish fighters were able to escape from the capital. Some made their way down the Vistula to Danzig or reached Posen; others sought a future in the West. By 1 October 1831 the rebellion was over.

Marshal Paskevich was created Prince of Warsaw and Viceroy, ruling Poland with an iron hand. Once again a long trail of prisoners headed for the Urals. An Organic Statute retained the Congress Kingdom as an entity but abolished the Diet. The University of Warsaw was closed and Polish educational funds were diverted to pay for a citadel, built on the banks of the Vistula, with guns trained on the heart of the city. A harsher vengeance was imposed on Poles who had supported the insurgents in Lithuania; inevitably all teaching in the University of Vilna was suspended. More than 5,000 estates of the 'traitor' nobility were confiscated. But 10,000 Poles reached sanctuary in France or Britain, some emigrating to the United States. The image of Nicholas I as a tyrant was implanted firmly in radical-liberal minds in Paris and London and such outward-looking cities as Glasgow and Newcastle, too. The government of Louis Philippe – King of the French by grace of the 'bourgeois revolution' of 1830 – granted pensions to more than 5,000 refugees. Until 1852 even the British exchequer set aside £10,000 a year for Polish exiles.

Fear that the revolutionary incubus would spread through Prussia's Grand Duchy of Posen and along the Baltic coast led Frederick William III to authorize a systematic policy of repression. Living standards were higher than in the Congress Kingdom, especially in the countryside where the peasants were virtually free from feudal obligations. Some of the great Polish landowners had worked to foster reconciliation, and the Polish language was in regular use in the schools. All this changed in the 1830s when Eduard Flottwell, as provincial resident, imposed restrictions on every aspect of Polish life and provoked such conflict between the Lutheran administration and the Roman Catholic episcopate that religious orders were suppressed and monastic estates confiscated. With the accession of Frederick William IV in 1840 Flottwell was dismissed and for six years a more tolerant atmosphere prevailed. But the Prussian police remained vigilant: links were discovered between liberals in Posen and the Polish Democratic Society, set up by the more radical exiles in Paris. When, in February 1846, Ludwik Mieroslawski arrived from Paris to prepare an insurrection across partitioned Poland, he was arrested together with his fellow conspirators in Posen. They were imprisoned in Berlin, receiving far milder treatment than Paskevich would have decreed across the frontier; but Flottwell's repressive measures were re-imposed. From St Petersburg Nicholas I approved his royal brother-in-law's belated endorsement of repression, while privately expressing alarm at his inconsistency.

Across the Baltic, Sweden stood splendidly aloof from such upheavals. For both Scandinavian kingdoms it was an era of peaceful change, shaped to a greater extent than is generally acknowledged by the willpower and wishes of the king. Charles XIV John – as Bernadotte became on his accession in February 1818 – ruled as a benevolent autocrat who respected the constitutional restraints of both Sweden and Norway. By the Swedish constitution of June 1809 a king retained executive power, exercised by a Council of State which he appointed himself. The council comprised a foreign minister, a justice minister, a court chancellor and six members without departmental posts. The councillors were responsible to parliament for the advice given to the king, though he need not take it. The king was obliged to summon a Riksdag parliament at least once every five years, with the Four Estates retaining the sole right to impose taxes. In practice the executive remained an aristocratic oligarchy throughout Charles John's twenty-six-year reign; not until 1827 was a commoner admitted to the council for the first time; and only after criticism in his final Riksdag did the king accept the notion that all councillors should have ministerial responsibilities.

Norway's Eidsvoll Constitution was more democratic: one of the measures to which (in 1821) the king, after some hesitancy, gave his approval was a decision by the Storting to abolish the nobility. Charles John did not always understand parliamentary niceties, such as the duties of an Opposition, but he never abruptly dissolved an assembly. He preferred to let tiresome deputies talk themselves into a series of compromises, even though on one occasion it took the Riksdag eighteen months to complete business. Towards the end of his reign, liberal deputies complained of the king's conservatism, protesting that he delayed social reform and the modernization of parliamentary procedure. Yet, despite his Gascon shortness of temper, he preserved the form of government at a time when constitutions south of the Baltic were being cast aside like last year's shoes.

His style of life was individualistic. Desirée's decision to return to Paris and remain in France 'for the sake of her health' throughout his regency and the first five years of the reign gave him the freedom of a general campaigning abroad. Routine business was transacted from his bed, as the king saw no need to get dressed before noon unless for a parade or public function; no Council of State was held before three in the afternoon. When possible he went into residence, not in the royal palace, but at Rosendal, a delightful villa on Djurgården island 3 kilometres from the city centre. There, like Napoleon and Josephine at Malmaison, he entertained guests to dinner in a room with woven curtains designed to create the illusion of a military commander's tent. He never acquired more than a smattering of Swedish; table talk, public speeches and exchanges with councillors or deputies were in French and generally required translation, with Oscar (who was fluent in Swedish and had a good grasp of Norwegian) often acting as his secretary.

Only once did the Swedish police sniff out a plot to kill Charles John (and Oscar), and that was as early as March 1817, before his accession. The details are obscure but a young cavalry officer, sympathetic to the exiled Vasas, was arrested and, soon afterwards, found hanged in his cell. The Bernadotte income freed the king from any need to raid the exchequer, as several of his Vasa predecessors had done. His subjects enjoyed their monarch's public spectacles. Charles John revelled in the theatricality of his coronations: at Stockholm on 11 May 1818 (the thirtieth anniversary of his promotion to Sergeant Major); and in Nidaros Cathedral at Trondheim four months later. There was a third coronation, in Stockholm in August 1829, when Desirée became Queen Desideria of the Swedes, Goths and Vandals. The family was growing rapidly. In 1825 Oscar married the Bavarian princess, Josephine, daughter of Napoleon's stepson Eugène Beauharnais and named after her grandmother, the empress. By 1830 Charles John had five grandchildren, including the future Charles XV and Oscar II. The dynasty seemed comfortably secure.

Complacent, too, perhaps? For Stockholm's newspapers, still liable for suppression if they attacked the sovereign, were becoming restless. In December 1830 the radical journalist Lars Hierta launched a satirical evening paper *Aftonbladet* that began by mocking the pretensions of the royal circle of French-speaking advisers. When Hierta became more daring and invented a 'King Long Nose', whose reign was lampooned, the law was invoked and *Aftonbladet* shut down. Undeterred, *Aftonbladet II* appeared, with the editor assuming a different name. The duel continued month after month. What Stockholm read in the evening, Uppsala read next morning and within a week Malmö and Gothenburg, too. By 1840 *Det tjugondeforsta Aftonbladet* (Evening Paper 21) enjoyed the biggest circulation in Sweden and the tsar's censors confiscated any copies in Finland. Hierta waged campaigns for cabinet government, a wider franchise, penal law reform, freedom of the press, and an end to chartered monopolies and the restrictive practices of guilds. Progress was made with all these reforms during the next decade, either under Charles John or Oscar I. In July 1838 there were demonstrations over the imprisonment of Magnus Crustenholpe for circulating a seditious pamphlet. The king was recuperating from a riding accident and decisions were taken by middle-ranking officers. Shots rang out: two protesters were killed. It was the only occasion in the reign when his troops fired on a political demonstration. In Sweden newspaper satire could achieve more than the barricades and bloodshed farther south.

Even though the king frequently clashed with the Storting, he enjoyed greater respect in Christiania and Trondheim than in Stockholm. His statue still stands in front of the royal palace of Oslo, looking down the city's principal shopping street, Karl Johans Gate, named in his honour. He achieved much for Norway, not least the first road to cut through the Scandinavian keel and link Trondheim with Gavle, Uppsala and Stockholm. Within Sweden, too, he was a road builder but his principal interest in civil engineering projects was the Göta Canal, the 100-kilometre waterway with fifty-eight locks linking Gothenburg and the Gulf of Bothnia through the central lakes and Söderköping. The building of the canal continued for the first fifteen years of his reign and he came frequently to inspect progress.

Steam power Charles John accepted for ships. There was a paddle steamer on Lake Mälaren by his accession; the earliest steam ferries were crossing from the Scanian shore to Copenhagen a few years later; the *George IV* made the first steamship voyage from the Thames to the Neva in 1827; and in the early 1830s the 80-horsepower, single funnel *Furst Menschikoff* ran regularly from St Petersburg to Helsingfors, Åbo, and Stockholm, though as the churning wheels could manage little more than 3 knots the voyage took five days. Railways were another matter. Tsar Nicholas, pleased with a 25-kilometre experiment that in 1837 brought Tsarskoye Selo and the capital together, allegedly laid his sword on a map and used it as a ruler to decide the route of the 650-kilometre straight line to Moscow. But Charles John could never act so imperiously. He had spent months encouraging intensive cultivation of the grain-yielding farmland of southern Sweden and he was not prepared to see the land wasted for an invention that would take away goods from the canal. He was totally opposed to railway engines: sparks would ignite the wooden homes of towns and villages, he maintained. His concern was understandable: he had personally supervised the making of firebreaks and the human chain of water carriers that saved the timbered alleys of Christiania in November 1814; and at the age of seventy-three he rode in from Rosendal at half-past three on a July morning in 1835 to command fire-fighters and troops battling flames fanned by a strong wind in the heart of Stockholm. Fire remained the scourge of northern capitals: shortly before Christmas two years later the Winter Palace at St Petersburg was nearly gutted, and in the last months of Oscar's reign Christiania's fifth major fire in two and a half centuries swept through the rapidly expanding city. This time there was no ex-marshal of France to check it.

Charles John was felled by a stroke on the morning of his eighty-first birthday but lingered for seven weeks, dying on 8 March 1844. In his later years Charles John's habitual political caution intensified. He mistrusted the new Scandinavianism, the growing friendship between young Swedes and young Danes that won qualified support from Oscar. He still wished to rule positively, but his proposal to remove the last remaining Jewish disabilities provoked such fierce anti-Semitic demonstrations in the autumn of 1838 that he accepted a weak compromise.

There was, too, one final testing issue in Baltic affairs: ought the king to back a project for creating a free port at Slite on the island of Gotland? The British wanted it, as a trading outlet well away from Prussia's *Zollverein* network. The shareholders of the Gota Canal were pleased by the prospect of trade coming to a new port barely eighteen hours' sailing time from Södorköping. But in foreign policy Charles John retained one simple conviction: never provoke Russia, and on this occasion there could be no doubt that St Petersburg feared the free port at Slite would strengthen British interests in the middle Baltic and encourage smuggling into Finland. So intense was Russian opposition that, to Charles John's consternation, the tsar himself descended on Stockholm uninvited to make his point. Peace and neutrality were Bernadotte's legacy to his adopted nation. Slite, he decided, was not worth a quarrel with Russia, especially one that brought the gendarme of Europe to Rosendal's parkland on a quiet Sunday in July.

15

Black, Red and Gold

'GENTLEMEN, SADDLE YOUR horses! France is a republic!' With this dramatic warning Tsar Nicholas I silenced a ball in the Winter Palace during the first week of March 1848. Ten days previously King Louis Philippe had fled Paris ahead of an angry mob marching on the Tuileries, after a Corsican sergeant shot dead a demonstrator demanding political reform. 'Europe finds herself today faced with a second 1793,' declared Metternich. The parallel was in the minds of rulers in Berlin, Turin, The Hague and Stockholm, too, while from London the young Victoria wrote to her royal uncle in Brussels, 'I fancy we have gone back into the *old* century'.

Worse was to come. On 17 March an uprising in Berlin forced Frederick William IV, the tsar's brother-in-law, to promise Prussia a constitution, and preparations went ahead for an all-German 'pre-parliament' to meet in Heidelberg at the end of the month in anticipation of a national assembly at Frankfurt; 'Prussia henceforth is merged into Germany,' Frederick William declared on 21 March. Other countries followed suit. In political frustration, or from social deprivation, radicals barricaded the streets of twenty cities from Seville to Lvov in Habsburg Galicia. By 19 April Metternich, Austria's foreign minister for thirty-nine years, was aboard a Rotterdam–London steam packet, seeking sanctuary in England. The long era that preserved external peace through internal repression seemed at an end. Of the architects of the Vienna Settlement only Russia's Count Nesselrode was, at sixty-eight, still in office.

Yet throughout this Year of Revolutions the Baltic lands remained relatively quiet. The tsar over-reacted; his gentlemen left their horses unsaddled. Nesselrode and his most trusted soldier-diplomat, Prince Andrei Orlov, persuaded him not to plunge the continent into war by sending 30,000 troops westwards into Prussian Poland. He contented himself with defensive measures. As early as 11 March all Russia's armies were put on a war footing. A sanitary cordon was thrown around Russia's borders when a 'reform banquet' in Stockholm led to the worst urban disturbance around

northern shores, a riot in which the soldiery shot dead eighteen demonstrators. Finland's frontier with Sweden was closed, Russia's postal links
with Stockholm cut, the reading matter of university students – foreign
books, newspapers or pamphlets – placed under close surveillance.
Incipient Finnish national sentiment at Helsingfors University was frowned
upon, even though it was as hostile to Swedish influences as to Russian.

From Warsaw Field Marshal Paskevich, the Viceroy of Congress Poland,
was reassuring. Over the past two years he had eased conditions for the peasantry, confirming security of tenure and encouraging landowners to commute labour dues into money rent. New textile factories brought peasants
into the towns, hoping for a rise in living standards. Communications, too,
were improving. Ironically, the spring that plunged Vienna into revolution
coincided with the first railway link joining Warsaw to the Austrian capital. To the tsar's relief, Congress Poland hardly stirred that year.

Beyond the Vistula and the upper Warta, Prussian Poland caused concern, however. Along the Baltic shore – in West Prussia (ex-Polish
Pomerania) and from Danzig up-river to Thorn – German speakers were
in the ascendant, particularly in the towns, and the Polish minority had
long been quiescent. But in Poznania – the Grand Duchy of Posen – the
Germans formed only a third of the population, except in the city of Posen
itself, where the national division was even. Soon after his accession in 1840
Frederick William IV made some attempt at reconciliation; he was on
terms of personal friendship with several Polish aristocratic families, the
Radziwills and Raczynskis in particular. There were concessions to Polish-
language speakers in the courts, administration and schooling though
restrictions were reimposed in 1846 after the discovery of Mieroslawski's
conspiracy. Around historic Gniezno, the cradle of the nation, the flame
of Polish patriotism had never been extinguished. Here, by the tsar's reckoning, lay the greatest threat to general peace. After Frederick William
agreed to give Prussia a constitution, Nicholas had no confidence in his
brother-in-law's resolve to meet the challenge.

For a few days, early in the spring of 1848, it did indeed seem as if Polish
patriots and Prussian radicals would join republican France in restraining
the Gendarme of Europe. Victimized Poland had long been a symbol of
enslaved oppression to liberal idealists in Paris; Lamartine, the foreign minister, expressed sympathy with the Polish cause, though he was soon to
prove reluctant to match words with deeds. In Berlin on 23 March,
Mieroslawski and his fellow conspirators were released from Moabit prison
and escorted through the streets by a cheering crowd: King Frederick
William greeted them at the Royal Palace. In the Grand Duchy itself a

Polish National Committee was set up at Posen, under Mieroslawski's presidency, with a Polophile staff officer, General Wilhelm von Willisen, authorized to raise a Polish army for a possible war against Russia. 'The German nation has spurned the alliance of its Princes with Asiatism and is ready to carry its flag of black-red-gold side by side with yours into the battle of light against darkness,' a leading German liberal assured the Poles on 22 March. And the euphoria was not confined to Prussia. At Heidelberg the all-German pre-parliament passed a resolution branding the partition of Poland 'a shameful crime' and declaring the restoration of a Polish state 'the sacred duty of the German nation'.

This goodwill soon evaporated. Poles and Germans living within the Grand Duchy found it hard to shed traditional habits and casts of mind. The peasants began attacking 'oppressive' German bureaucrats and 'greedy' German Jewish traders and money-lenders. Willisen's army, some 10,000 strong, was as ready to fight the Prussians in their midst as to march eastwards and free the Congress Kingdom. The Junker officer corps, fearing a descent into anarchy and attacks on their estates, showed more mettle than their sovereign and prepared to uphold the established order. A prospect of civil war loomed less than three weeks after Mieroslawski's release from prison.

In the event, it was the Prussians who fired first, attacking a Polish detachment that was taking up a strong position outside Trzemeszno on 10 April. Skirmishes between Prussian and Polish units continued, with the unfortunate General von Willisen disowned by his compatriots and forced to return to Berlin a fortnight after taking up his command. A series of pitched battles began on 19 April, fought over a region as large as Belgium. Twice the 'insurgents' defeated Prussian 'legitimists', but the outnumbered Poles were forced to surrender on 9 May; Mieroslawski made his way to Galicia and ultimately to Italy. When, in December 1848, Frederick William promulgated the Prussian constitution the Grand Duchy disappeared, to be replaced by the Province of Posen, with local administration headed by a Prussian Governor.

Polish affairs were not raised at the all-German Frankfurt Parliament until the fourth week in July. By then, collaboration between the two nationalities was out of the question. The parliament decided, by an overwhelming majority (342 to 31, with 188 abstentions), that Poznania was in character a German province. 'Our right [there] is that of the strongest, the right of conquest,' thundered Wilhelm Jordan, a delegate from Berlin who was by origin an East Prussian. The disavowal of Polish rights, first by the Prussian army and then by the parliament, had lasting consequences for towns and villages from the lower Oder across to the Niemen. Never again was there any prospect of a German solution to the Polish Question. Ninety years later Jordan's rhetoric in the Frankfurt Parliament was echoed by Nazi Gauleiters Germanizing the so-called Warthegau. But the immediate effect of the Frankfurt vote was to reassure Tsar Nicholas. Black, red and gold patriotism did not challenge the existing order. The threat of revolutionary liberators heading eastwards over the Vistula had gone.

Farther west, a political crisis was smouldering beside the Øresund even before the first barricades went up in Paris. The Treaty of Vienna had confirmed the centuries-old Danish suzerainty over Schleswig-Holstein, the Elbe Duchies, but it admitted Holstein, where the population was almost entirely German in speech and background, to membership of the German Confederation. By the 1840s the Holsteiners were benefiting economically from the success of the Prussian Zollverein, and the German minority in Schleswig, influential in the towns, wished to join the confederation. Strong Pan-German sentiment was backed by assertions that the duchies acknowledged the Salic Law of succession, whereas the Danes were free to allow the Crown to pass down through a female line. With the childless and dissolute Frederick VII succeeding his father, Charles VIII, on the throne in the first week of January 1848, this archaic dynastic problem threatened to become a live issue. The Germans in the duchies already had a royal figurehead to champion their cause; Christian, Duke of Augustenburg, could trace his descent back through Denmark's kings without finding a single instance of female succession blotting the line. His supporters in the Diets were, for the most part, aristocratic landowners and not the liberal burghers whose views prevailed at Frankfurt.

Charles VIII's last years had been marked by the rapid growth of a unified Danish liberal and peasant party (*Bondvennernes Selskab*) which campaigned for a democratic parliamentary constitution. To the alarm of Germans in the duchies, the *Bondvenners* sought a Danish kingdom that would extend as far south as the lower Elbe and Altona, at the gates of Hamburg. In late March 1848 King Frederick VII responded to liberal and radical unrest in Copenhagen by announcing that he would convene a Danish constituent assembly and was prepared to trim down his prerogative powers, to rule as a constitutional monarch. Already, however, spokesmen for the Germans in the duchies had met at the fortress town of Rendsburg, in southern Schleswig, and appealed for protection to the German Confederation. The Duke of Augustenburg visited Berlin and was well received by Frederick William IV. When, at the end of the month, the duke arrived back in Holstein he was surprised to discover that in their nominal leader's absence the Germans in the duchies had set up a provisional government at Kiel, the northern railhead of the newly constructed line to Hamburg and on to Berlin.

This unilateral declaration of independence prompted an armed response from the Danes, who defeated Augustenburg's hastily raised army in two small-scale battles. Inside Germany all good patriots were indignant; volunteers from across the confederation hurried to the Holstein battle-line and in mid-April Prussia intervened. The Prussian commander, General Wrangel, had the firepower to expel the Danes from the duchies, cross the internal border and threaten an advance into Jutland. It was Denmark's turn to seek help, militarily from Sweden and, in diplomacy, from the two powers most concerned with passage of the Øresund: Russia and Britain.

In Stockholm Oscar I showed a vacillating caution characteristic of the Bernadotte dynasty. It would be 'quixotic' to intervene, he told the State Council on the last Thursday of April: why risk bringing the tsar's wrath down on Sweden? Within a week he changed his mind, apparently after clarification of the Russian response: an expeditionary force of 15,000 men would help the Danes defend Funen and the approaches to the Sound.

From St Petersburg came reports of a ministerial council at which Nicholas I accepted that the duchies had lost their strategic importance: Russia's main trade artery now ran from the Black Sea through the Bosphorus and Dardanelles to the Mediterranean. The tsar did, however, protest to Frederick William IV at allowing a Prussian royal army to support a revolutionary 'national' cause against a brother sovereign. He hinted with a touch of menace that should the Danish royal house lose possession of the duchies, he might as head of the House of Romanov-Holstein-Gottorp feel obliged to intervene in the duchies, asserting rights he claimed to have inherited from his grandmother, Catherine. The bear's growl was effective: Wrangel's troops were pulled back from Jutland, though they remained in Schleswig. It was now Sweden's turn to put pressure on their neighbour. At a meeting in Malmö on 9 June the Danes were told that Oscar would not allow his troops in Funen to be deployed in any offensive against the Prussians. At a second meeting, late in August, Oscar took the initiative: Sweden would broker an armistice and join Russia and Britain in seeking means to resolve the dispute.

Both Nesselrode and Palmerston, the foreign secretary, favoured common sense: Holstein would become a German state and Schleswig partitioned along a clearly defined national boundary (a solution not unlike the settlement made after the First World War and still valid today). An international conference would meet in London under Palmerston's chair-manship to settle the matter. The Danes, however, were in no mood to compromise. There might be little prospect of military success on the Jutland peninsula itself, but they knew they enjoyed one advantage, denied to the Prussians – Denmark had a good, compact navy: Prussia no fleet at all. The longer the crisis dragged on, the greater the harm Danish ships inflicted on German maritime trade, in the Baltic and the North Sea.

Despite the shadow of war, throughout the late summer and the follow-ing winter Denmark's national constituent assembly was able to consider draft proposals completing the transition to constitutional monarchy. On 5 June 1849 King Frederick VII gave his assent to a Bill providing for a bicameral parliament (Rigsdag): an Upper House (Landsting), elected by indirect ballot and comprising men of property over forty; and a Lower House (Folketing), twice as large and elected by male householders over the age of thirty. These provisions were democratically more advanced than in any other Baltic country, though the secret ballot was not instituted until 1901, and even when universal adult suffrage was introduced in 1915 the voting age was only lowered by twelve months. Much time was spent clar-ifying the position of the Church: Article 3 of the Constitution granted freedom of worship; among office holders only the sovereign was required to be a Lutheran. Although the evangelical Danish Folk Church remained 'supported by the State', there would be no coronation for Frederick VII or any of his successors.

Attempts were made to reach a constitutional settlement with Augustenburg's supporters in the duchies, but tension remained high. The Malmö armistice was broken in April 1849: Prussian forts guarding the approaches to Kiel fired on two Danish warships in Eckernförde. After a day-long duel with the shore batteries both ships were disabled and forced to surrender; the larger vessel could not be saved, but the 46-gun *Gefion* became a prize of war. Skirmishes continued in Jutland until 10 July, when a truce was agreed. The government in Berlin took little interest in the campaign. Frederick William had long abandoned his championship of German nationalism. His main concern was to induce the Danes to relax their stranglehold on Baltic trade. A Danish-Prussian peace treaty was con-cluded at Berlin on 2 July 1850, though the Holsteiners were so obdurate that Frederick William's ministers threatened intervention on the side of Denmark unless they laid down their arms.

Two years later Palmerston's conference hacked out a settlement. It paid lip service to the bonds uniting Schleswig and Holstein while allowing the duchies some autonomy. They were separated territorially from Denmark but left under the personal sovereignty of the Danish King, who would rule as Grand Duke of Schleswig-Holstein. By the London Protocol of May 1852 Britain, Austria, Denmark, France, Prussia, Russia and Sweden accepted this arrangement. Holstein joined the reconstituted German Confederation. At the same time the powers persuaded Augustenburg to abandon his claims in return for a large sum of compensation. The Protocol designated Prince Christian of Glücksburg heir to all of Frederick VII's titles: through his mother he was a great-nephew of King Christian VII. It was hoped that, once revolutionary ardour died away, the intensity of nationalist feelings would cool and the duchies respond favourably to Danish pledges of reconciliation. But few people felt confident that the London Conference had solved the Duchies Question.

The prolonged crisis emphasized the continued importance of sea power in Baltic affairs. Prussia was a kingdom without a naval tradition. Although in the 1680s Frederick William, the Great Elector, fitted out armed merchantmen to protect the growing trade with West Africa, no Prussian king was sea-minded. The acquisition of Rügen from Sweden after the Napoleonic Wars brought with it six two-masted square-rigged sloops that were soon flying the Prussian flag, but no attempt was made to train seamen or set up a naval establishment. By 1840 Friedrich List, the economist who created the Zollverein and promoted railways, argued that Prussia needed a navy. Prince Adalbert, an independently minded cousin of King Frederick William, agreed with List. But Junker-dominated Prussia took no interest in naval matters before April 1848, when the Danes blockaded Kiel and threatened the Elbe estuary.

Indignation over the Danish move fired enthusiasm for a navy far beyond Prussia's borders. Demands for a fleet as a symbol of German unity puffed up every patriot orator at the Frankfurt Parliament; voluntary subscriptions for the purchase of ships came from across Germany, although the actual money − the equivalent of a million pounds sterling − was advanced by the parliamentary deputies from funds set aside by the German Confederation in earlier years for common defence. The deputies established a German Naval Committee headed by Prince Adalbert. He drew up plans for a German fleet of twenty ships-of-the-line and thirty frigates and smaller vessels, with officers and ratings recruited from laid-off naval personnel in Britain, the Netherlands, France and the United States. Two vessels laid up at Hamburg were hastily commissioned and flew the black-red-gold ensign of national liberal Germany at moorings in the Norder Elbe; one, the *Barbarossa*, became the first flagship of a German navy. The ex-Danish *Gefion* was taken into service and re-named *Eckernförde* after the fjord where she had fallen into German hands. Some smaller ships were purchased while, optimistically, vessels were commissioned from navy yards overseas, including Brooklyn. Palmerston declared that the Royal Navy would treat black-red-gold as a pirate flag. He need not have worried. The warships lacked crews to take them to sea.

By the winter of 1850–51 the national liberal Frankfurt Parliament had long since dispersed and a new Frankfurt Diet was about to revive the loose federalism of 'pre-March' Greater Germany. When the black, red and gold flags were furled, most of the improvised navy went to the breakers. Yet the strategic argument for having a Prussian fleet to counter any future challenge from Denmark – or indeed from Sweden or Russia – remained valid. The *Barbarossa* and *Eckernförde* became a nucleus for the Royal Prussian Navy, at first a neglected toy of the War Ministry, but in 1853 given independent status under Prince Adalbert. A proposal to promote him Fleet Admiral was dropped when Frederick William protested 'We have no fleet.' Instead, in March 1854, the prince became Admiral of the Prussian Coasts, an interesting designation reminding Europe that Prussia now looked both to the North Sea and to the Baltic.

16

Bombarding Bomarsund

———◈◈◈———

BY MARCH IN 1854 ships of war were again riding at anchor off Kiel Bay. Now, however, they flew the White Ensign and, confusingly, they were in northern waters because of the Eastern Question. For, once order was restored in the Baltic, Tsar Nicholas had turned his pursuit of Europe's natural rebels across frontiers. The Hungarian struggle for independence from Austria, led by Lajos Kossuth, attracted radical support from beyond the borders of the Habsburg Empire. Many Poles, including the veteran generals Jozef Bem and Henryk Dembinsky, fought for Kossuth, feeding the tsar's political paranoia: 'The symptoms of a general plot against everything sacred, and especially against Russia, are clearly visible in the Hungarian rebellion,' he wrote to Paskevich in Warsaw on 7 May 1849. 'At the head of the rebellion are our eternal foes, the Poles.' On his orders, Paskevich left the Vistula, to take command of two Russian armies invading Hungary from the north and the east; three months later Paskevich accepted Hungary's capitulation. When Bem and Dembinsky (like Kossuth) escaped to Turkey, Nicholas demanded the Ottoman authorities should surrender the two generals and 800 other Poles who had crossed the frontier. Palmerston's diplomatic support, and the presence of a British naval squadron off the Dardanelles, toughened the sultan's response; the Turks refused to hand over Bem, Dembinsky or any other refugee, whether Polish or Hungarian. In anger the tsar recalled his ambassador.

The episode heightened mistrust of 'Europe's gendarme' in the West, especially in Britain. When eventually Kossuth visited England he was widely fêted: 'Do not give a charter to the Tsar to dispose of the World,' he told a mass open-air rally in Islington. Over the following years almost every political group in Britain voiced indignation at Russia's affairs. St Petersburg, liberal idealists maintained, housed the executants of a cumbersome despotism. Business houses complained of threats to their Asian markets. Scaremongers, their fantasy fired by muddled tales of Viking raiders, conjured up a Russian bogey: a phantom fleet that would slip out of the Baltic unobserved, to materialize mysteriously off the coast of Norfolk.

It is not surprising that, although Nicholas I had genuine hopes of an Anglo-Russian understanding over the future of Turkey, his proposals stirred suspicion in London. There seemed a contrast between his apparent moderation and the arrogance with which his ambassador to the sultan asserted Russia's right to protect Orthodox Christians across all the Ottoman lands. A series of misunderstandings and a conflict of personalities in Constantinople itself deepened the crisis. Unexpectedly, shared interests in the Levant brought the statesmen of London and Paris closer together, even though the nephew of the great Bonaparte had ruled France since 1848, becoming – in December 1852 – Emperor Napoleon III. By the following summer London and Paris were collaborating to forestall a Russian assault on the Bosphorus. When in December 1853 news came that a Russian squadron had sunk the Turkish fleet at anchor in Sinope, there was little doubt Britain and France would soon be fighting Russia to restore the existing order in the Black Sea and curb the tsar's dominance over Europe's affairs.

No one as yet thought of the coming conflict as a 'Crimean War'. Until the summer of 1855 it remained 'our war against Russia'. Even before the fighting began, there was a strong feeling that the allies should strike also at Russian mastery of the Baltic, 1,600 kilometres from Sinope. As early as the first week in October 1853 Lord John Russell urged the prime minister to ensure 'England and France . . . employ their mighty resources in the Baltic and at every point where Russia can be resisted and attacked'. Two days before Christmas *The Times* reported that 'an expedition to the Baltic in the early spring' was under consideration. A few days later the paper was suggesting the ideal commander for Baltic naval operations: Sir Charles Napier, the sixty-seven-year-old Vice Admiral 'with the Nelson touch'.

In fifty-two years at sea Black Charlie – Mad Charlie to some – had chased privateers off the West Indies, commanded frigates in the Mediterranean, helped Portuguese liberals secure Lisbon, and fought his way up Chesapeake Bay to attack Baltimore. Only the waters of northern Europe were unfamiliar to him. Napier's appointment to command a Baltic fleet was made public on 15 February 1854 and it unleashed a fortnight of extraordinary public adulation. When on 11 March the admiral was piped aboard HMS *Duke of Wellington* at Portsmouth, 'the water was thronged with craft of all kinds' and 'as far as the eye could reach, the shores were covered with spectators'. Perhaps intentionally, the scene recalled Nelson's departure for Trafalgar almost fifty years back in time, when (in Southey's words) 'the people would not be debarred from gazing upon the hero – the darling hero – of England'. Queen Victoria and her consort were in the royal yacht *Fairy* off Spithead, to see 'our noble fleet passing us close by and giving us three hearty cheers'. The fleet, so readers of *The Times* were assured, was only the first of 'the terrible squadrons' that were going 'to swamp the Baltic'. Never before had the fate of the northern inland sea aroused such interest across Britain.

Napier sailed through the Great and Little Belts before the ice had finally broken up in the Sound. By the end of March, when Britain and France at last joined Turkey in the war against Russia, a fleet of forty-four ships carrying 2,200 guns was strung out between Kiel Bay and Gotland. 'We have Napier in the right place at the right time,' the First Lord of the Admiralty, Sir James Graham, wrote to the Foreign Secretary. 'More decisive results may be obtained in the Baltic and with greater ease than in the Black Sea.' Although Graham accepted the need to capture Sebastopol ('The eye-tooth of the bear must be drawn') he favoured a northern maritime alliance of Britain, France, Denmark, Prussia and Sweden that would 'press the Czar much nearer home'. 'My hopes rest on Sweden,' Graham wrote in another note. So, too, at that time did the hopes of Palmerston and Napoleon III. It was felt in London and in Paris that the Swedes would welcome an opportunity to recover Finland.

King Oscar I hesitated; and with good reason. Popular sentiment over the last two decades had promoted a new 'Scandinavianism' that emphasized linguistic and cultural bonds drawing Denmark, Norway and Sweden together. Did Finns qualify for membership of the group? Apart from their Lutheran faith, were they a Scandinavian people? Would retrocession condemn Sweden to constant vigilance in the East and rekindle disputes that had led to ten wars with Russia in the past three centuries? The sentiment of 'Scandinavianism' mattered in that spring. The prevailing mood encouraged the Danish and Swedish governments to issue a joint proclamation affirming a neutrality that came close to co-belligerency. Britain and France could count on the provision of moorings and naval stores at Danish Kiel, at Vinga in the Gothenburg archipelago and in the old pirate lair of Gotland.

To commit ground troops to a war in Finland was another matter. Oscar – who was virtually his own foreign minister – made it clear Sweden would only intervene if guaranteed a subsidy, strategic territorial gains, and the likely prospect of Austrian entry into the war, so as to open up another land front against Russia, in Poland. And as a first step, Sweden wanted proof that Napier could inflict a crushing defeat on the enemy. In the Black Sea only nine ships had been needed to destroy Odessa by bombardment on St George's Day: surely the firepower of Britain's 'noble fleet' could strike at Kronstadt and win a rapid victory at the heart of the tsar's empire?

★

All began well. A close blockade closed Russia's trading outlets to the West, and in May Napier trailed the flag up the Gulf of Finland. But, to his chagrin, the Russian admiral failed to oblige by putting to sea and giving him a northern Trafalgar. The shallowness of the inshore waters worried Napier; he feared his ships might run aground within range of the guns of Kronstadt or of Sveaborg (now Suomenlinna), the fortress that rambled over seven islands off Helsingfors. The low draught steam frigates *Hecla* and *Arrogant* exchanged fire with shore batteries at Ekenäs on the Hanko peninsula and seized a large merchant ship as a prize. Raiding parties attacked less well-defended harbours along the Gulf of Finland. Ironically random shelling started fires in forests that supplied timber for British shipyards. By the end of May Napier's reconnaissance was over and his flagship back in Swedish waters.

Off Gotland, Napier welcomed the arrival of Admiral Deschenes, with fourteen modern French vessels. The two admirals led a combined squadron of sixteen British and six French warships eastwards on 21 June, taking full advantage of the 'white nights' to navigate treacherous waters. Five days later, members of the tsar's family watched from Peterhof as the allied squadron took up position beyond the range of Kronstadt's guns: 'The entire enemy fleet was clearly visible for several days,' Grand Duke Alexander wrote to his aunt, Queen Anna Pavlovna, in the Netherlands. St Petersburg high society came out by carriage to see the spectacle. Not a shot was fired; on 4 July the elated onlookers watched the enemy turn away again. An assault 'appears to me, with our means, perfectly impossible', Napier reported to London.

The Admiralty gave serious thought to proposals for a secret weapon that would enable sulphurous fumes to overcome the defenders of Kronstadt. A gas cloud, borne 25 kilometres eastward by prevailing winds, might then cause panic in the streets of the enemy capital. But the opinion of experts, including the great Michael Faraday, was sceptical. An Admiralty committee turned down the idea: the fumes could kill 'our men', it argued; moreover, the project was fundamentally 'inhumane'. St Petersburg was spared an early initiation in chemical warfare.

It was spared, too, any more visits from Black Charlie. 'We must expect to see the enemy fleet reappearing one of these mornings,' Tsar Nicholas wrote to his sister. He was wrong. Kotka, where the wharves were stacked with timber awaiting export to England, was bombarded and set on fire; and an attempt was made to penetrate the heavily defended sea approaches to Vyborg. But Napier's attention turned more and more to the Gulf of Bothnia. While the combined fleet was heading eastwards on 21 June

Captain Hall in HMS *Hecla* had exchanged fire with Bomarsund, the modern fortress on East Åland, the largest island in the archipelago that straddled the entrance to the Gulf, only a few hours' sailing from Stockholm. When a fused shell landed on the deck of the *Hecla*, it was seized by Lt Charles Lucas and hurled overboard before it could explode. Lucas's valour is the earliest exploit for which a Victoria Cross was awarded. For Captain Hall, however, the immediate reaction was a rebuke from Napier. The admiral was angry that he should have dared to throw 'away all his shot and shell against stone walls'.

Raids along the Bothnian coast went as far north as Oulu and Raahe. Sometimes they were indisciplined affairs that came close to looting. A mismanaged assault was made on Kokkala, one of the main harbours for exporting tar, an essential commodity for wooden shipbuilding. The *Hecla* and the *Arrogant* sent landing parties ashore in nine boats, but attempts to fire the town were frustrated by militia from Vaasa. Nine seamen or marines were killed and twenty-two captured; so, too, were a cannon and one of the boats (which, 150 years later, is still on display in Kokkala's central park). Attacks on other ports, including Nystad and Pori, caused widespread distress. 'One shriek of woe sounds all through Finland', *The Times* reported from Stockholm; and on 29 June a Radical MP from Manchester protested in the Commons at these activities. But what else could the Royal Navy do if the Russians refused to come out and fight? Sir James Graham responded, a little too glibly.

A month later a French expeditionary force, 9,000 strong, reached northern waters and Napier was stung into action. On 9 August the combined fleet returned to Bomarsund, ready to invade the Ålands. Landings were made by French infantry and by British marines to the north and south of the fortress. The garrison was cut off from the larger town of Kastelholm and its much smaller castle. For a week the 'stone walls' of Bomarsund defied assault, bombardment and the explosive ingenuity of sappers. As so often in the Crimea itself, there were touches of surrealism to the fighting. In the wake of the warships sailed an eight-ton yacht, *The Pet*, with the Revd Edward Hughes of Magdalene College, Cambridge, aboard to jot down in his notebook all he could hear and see. And as the sound of the bombardment echoed round the islands, excursion steamers arrived with onlookers from the Swedish coast.

There was plenty for them to observe, for the battle raged on twice as long as Cathcart's amphibious attack in 1807 on Copenhagen. Bomarsund was still under construction but its defences were carefully sited, taking advantage of the slopes of a hill. At last, early on Wednesday, 16 August,

Napier was forced to turn the 10-inch guns of seven warships on the centre of the fortress, with orders to 'Give them a shot and shell every five minutes.' In the afternoon, 2,000 of the tsar's soldiers passed into captivity. Almost all were Finns and were allowed to remain in the islands but 180 Russian prisoners-of-war were shipped to England, some with their wives and children. Lewes prison in Sussex awaited them.

News of Bomarsund's fall reached London and Paris in good time for Saturday's newspapers, thanks to the new telegraph service from Danzig. There was widespread rejoicing. It was the first victory of the war, coming a month before the landing in the Crimea. Unknown Bomarsund was featured in London's newspapers as the 'Gibraltar of the North'. Its fall plunged a 'mortal thrust' into the tsar's empire, one weekly claimed. Even better tidings would follow, *The Times* confidently predicted.

But the bombardment of Bomarsund proved a weekend wonder. The British and French army commanders pressed for an immediate sweep up the Gulf of Finland and an assault on Sveaborg. Napier hesitated, and pondered: if it took a week to secure Bomarsund, how long would it take to invest a larger fortress, with its defences strengthened by warships protected by a primitive minefield? A council of war, convened on 12 September aboard the admiral's flagship, decided it was too late in the year for any operation against Sveaborg, still less Kronstadt. The blockade continued, and the Russians retained 200,000 men to protect the capital and the northern shores who might otherwise have fought in the Crimea; but the main allied fleet was ready to leave the Baltic for home. No hero's welcome greeted Napier, however. By the time his flagship berthed at Portsmouth all the talk was of Inkerman and Balaclava. Compared with the drama played out in the Black Sea, the Baltic had become a sideshow.

Yet next spring a new Baltic fleet made ready for action. It left Spithead in the first week of April 1855, with Rear-Admiral James Dundas in command, and it was joined by a French squadron, under Admiral Charles Pénaud. Tsar Nicholas I had died from pneumonia a month earlier. *The Times* warned his successor, Alexander II, that Dundas's 'force is stronger and the duty more terrible than last year'. During the summer the Anglo-French fleet ravaged the southern Baltic coast, bombarding Reval and Narva, sailing into the Gulf of Riga, and raiding the coast of Courland. Finland was not spared: HMS *Arrogant* put a landing party ashore on Svartholm island, razing the fort that protected Loviisa.

At last, on 9 August 1855 – seventeen months into the Baltic naval campaign, and a year to the day after the bombardment of Bomarsund – came the long heralded assault on Sveaborg. Meticulous pounding of the seven islands continued throughout that Thursday, with the occasional roar as powder magazines within the main citadel exploded. But the captains of several of the largest warships were concerned at the wear and tear on their gun mountings and laid offshore through Friday and Saturday, leaving smaller mortar vessels to continue the attack. Parties of marines were put ashore on Drusö and Sandhamn (in the nineteenth century large islands east and west of Sveaborg, but now suburbs linked by bridges to Helsinki). On neither island could the landing parties establish a foothold, and they were soon re-embarked. The centre of Helsingfors was left undamaged. By Friday morning the townsfolk felt it was safe to gather along the granite quays of the harbour and the Salutorg market place and watch the flash and fury of battle across the bay. All went quiet on Sunday, though the spectral rigging and funnels of allied ships could be seen from Helsingfors for four more days. On Thursday, 15 August, they headed back to the shelter of Vinga and Kiel Bay.

The Sveaborg operations aroused little interest in the West. The London press was full of Queen Victoria's State Visit to France, the first by a British sovereign to Paris (18–27 August). Her return home was followed by news of the massive final assault on Sebastopol. With the fall of the city, a fortnight later the main objective of the Black Sea campaign was accomplished. But the war was far from over. Alexander II left St Petersburg and set out for the Crimea in defiant mood: 'Two years after the burning of Moscow our troops marched in the streets of Paris,' he reminded his peoples in a proclamation that invoked the spirit of 1812. 'We remain the same Russians, and God is still with us.'

In London Palmerston (who succeeded Aberdeen as prime minister in February 1855) advised the Archbishop of Canterbury that, unlike Waterloo, Sebastopol's fall did not merit a Day of Thanksgiving; he preferred prayers each Sunday for the war against Russia to be carried through to final victory. Napoleon III's approach was pragmatic: the grand strategy for 1856 must look well beyond the Black Sea, he told his foreign minister. He envisaged 'a long line of circumvallation to confine the further extension of Russia'. While support should be sought from Vienna and Berlin, the northern hinge of the line lay in Sweden; and early in November General Canrobert, newly returned from command of the army in front of Sebastopol, was sent to Stockholm on a special mission. He was to convince King Oscar that next year's war would be fought in and around the Baltic and that Sweden could not afford to remain neutral.

Canrobert was a social success in Stockholm, not least with Oscar's mother, the widowed Queen Desideria, long experienced in greeting

French generals back from the wars. Her son welcomed Canrobert as a soldier whose ideas he could understand. After four days of talks, on 21 November Oscar I signed a defensive treaty with France and Britain, ensuring western support for Sweden should the kingdom be attacked by any other power. The treaty was to remain valid throughout the coming years of tension and into the twentieth century. The immediate consequence was an understanding that, should Russia continue to dispute reindeer grazing land in Lapland or send warships into Sweden's waters, the French and British would help the king uphold his peoples' rights. Canrobert would become generalissimo of an army of 165,000 men – French, British, Swedes, Norwegians and, it was hoped, Danes – that would eject the Russians from Finland, raze the fortress of Kronstadt and march on St Petersburg itself. Landings south of the Gulf were to threaten Riga and Reval, while the Austrians and Prussians would be encouraged to intervene in Poland. By 30 November Canrobert was at Kiel, planning operations on both shores of the Gulf in eight hours of talk with the British and French admirals aboard Dundas's flagship.

But was this Baltic grand design a plan for war or a key to peace? On 8 December *The Times* carried reports of the Canrobert mission, based upon leaks to a paper in Brussels. The details were not entirely accurate: thus, the Kiel conference was set aboard the French flagship rather than the British, and more emphasis was laid on a campaign in the Baltic provinces than in Finland; but the inference was clear. The tsar and his ministers (who reputedly scanned *The Times* for intelligence) were left in no doubt of the mounting threat of a northern war – especially after the Swedish minister let Nesselrode know of the defensive alliance with Russia's enemies. Despite Alexander II's fine patriotic phrases, common sense suggested a negotiated settlement. There was a flurry of family diplomacy over Christmas, with supporting roles for Napoleon III's half-brother, for Napoleon I's illegitimate son and for Nesselrode's two eminently respectable daughters. In January two imperial conferences in St Petersburg considered the threat of revolts in Finland, Poland and the Baltic provinces and the near certainty that Austria was about to enter the war as an ally of France and Britain. Alexander II found that almost everyone present at the two conferences favoured an early peace.

At the same time Napoleon III, in Paris, was presiding over daily sessions of a Grand Council of War, summoned allegedly to decide where best to strike next at Russia. In practice, the much-publicized council was too large to function well. Even Napoleon I's surviving brother, Jerome, who had (ineffectually) commanded the Third Army in July 1812, was present. Admiral Dundas assessed the naval prospects, though few were familiar with the place names he mentioned. The newly promoted Marshal Canrobert sought to explain plans for taking St Petersburg, only to break off apologetically when he decided they were impracticable. Fortunately the confusion mattered little, for the Grand Council was about to reach a peak of anticlimax. On the eighth day of discussion, news came from Vienna that the Russians were ready to conclude an armistice. There was no need for the war to spread northwards after all.

Within six weeks Napoleon III was host to a Congress of Peace in Paris. But Baltic issues were rarely raised around the conference table. Once the fighting ended, the emperor lost all interest in Sweden, Finland or any region north of Warsaw. In vain King Oscar, having brushed aside an invitation to occupy the Åland islands after Bomarsund, sought to present a belated claim and pressed for demilitarization of the Finnish coast west of Sveaborg. No spokesmen for non-belligerent Sweden or Denmark were present; and the congress had been in session for three weeks before an invitation was sent to Berlin, and then only on Austrian insistence. It is hardly surprising that there is no mention of the Baltic in the final Treaty of Paris. But Lord Clarendon, head of the British delegation, had not forgotten Bomarsund or the potential menace of 'a northern Gibraltar'. On 30 March 1856 – the day the definitive treaty was signed – Britain, France and Russia concluded a separate Convention settling the future of the Ålands. The archipelago was to remain under tsarist rule but without forts, military establishments or naval facilities.

Oscar I was almost satisfied: demilitarization of the Ålands strengthened the safety of Stockholm. More drastic changes were imposed in the Black Sea which, in theory, became as peaceful as a Swiss lake, with not a warship on its waters nor a fort along its shores. But the settlement in the south humiliated Alexander II, and Russia shook off the Treaty's Black Sea fetters at the first opportunity. The demilitarization of Sebastopol lasted a mere fifteen years. The Gulf of Bothnia fared better than that: demilitarization of the Ålands survived for fifty years and was reimposed in 1921 by decision of the League of Nations. East Åland remains idyllically peaceful today: a Swedish-speaking people enjoy autonomy within Finland, driving their cars or riding their bicycles along post-roads the Russians built a century and a half ago.

17

Finns, Poles and Danes

———— ⧈ ————

Less than six months after the signing of the Treaty of Paris, the thirty-eight-year-old Tsar Alexander II was crowned with great splendour in the Uspenski Cathedral within the Kremlin. The traditional Coronation Manifesto, issued a few days later, held out a prospect of liberal reform and modernization across his empire. Many political prisoners, who had fallen foul of Nicholas's 'Iron Autocracy', benefited from an amnesty. The tax burden on the tsar's poorest subjects was eased, with total exemption for war-ravaged regions, including the Finnish coastal districts attacked by the allied fleet. Supplementary taxes imposed on Jews were abolished. So, too, were restraints limiting the activities of the Polish nobility and Catholic priests in both Poland and Lithuania. Alexander was known to favour the abolition of serfdom in provinces untouched by earlier reforms, including Lithuania and the Latgale region of modern Latvia. Preliminary discussions on emancipation were held in Moscow after the coronation, but problems over compensation and the amount of land held by the peasants delayed promulgation of the statute ending serfdom until March 1861, the sixth anniversary of Alexander's accession.

Other matters discussed at Moscow brought speedier results, notably railway plans. An imperial decree in January 1857 provided for a network of four main lines, including one to the ice-free port of Libau to promote industrial growth and the export of grain in the Baltic provinces. A minor reform with major consequences was the abolition of Nicholas I's prohibitively high passport fee: easier access to Sweden or Prussia opened wider the window to Western ideas.

Alexander II already enjoyed popular respect in southern Finland, after several visits to Helsingfors as chancellor of the university before his accession. The tsarevich had seen the need for a public works programme within the Grand Duchy. He encouraged construction of the Saimaa Canal, a water-route linking the seaport of Vyborg to the extensive Päijänne lake system that was completed within eighteen months of his accession. Like Sweden's Gota Canal a quarter of a century earlier, the waterway opened up for development inaccessible regions of the interior, lakeside forests thick with fir and pine. Potentially the canal was of even greater economic value than its Swedish forerunner for, though the waterway had twenty-eight locks, it was broad enough to allow the passage of small sea-going vessels. The steamer *Suomi* began plying the waters of Lake Päijänne in the summer of 1856, pioneering a regular 400-kilometre service from Kuopio to Vyborg. By the end of the reign there were ironworks, papermills and sawmills along the wooded arms of the lakes.

The tsar returned to Helsingfors during a ten-day visit to the Grand Duchy, soon after the war ended. In his accession speech to the Senate he praised the Finns for their courage; he urged them not to hanker for the Swedish past but to see themselves as one of many nations within a great empire. There was, at the time, little pro-Swedish or separatist sentiment in the Grand Duchy, not least because of resentment over Oscar I's devious policy during the war. The Finnish Diet had not deliberated since 1809 and there were hopes that Alexander would soon summon a meeting. The tsar, however, was cautious: if he convened an elected assembly, what would be the reaction elsewhere in the empire, especially in Warsaw? When the Rector of Helsingfors University delivered a lecture on the constitutional significance of the Diet, he received a stern reprimand from his chancellor. But the rector was not suspended: the Senate was invited to elect two members to serve on a Committee on Finnish Affairs, established in St Petersburg with the Diet Question having priority in its discussions.

Progress was, however, slow: a nationalistic demonstration by radical students led to a tightening of the censorship; public life in St Petersburg was dominated by the long discussions on serf emancipation and there was mounting concern over events in Poland. The committee did not complete its work until the summer of 1862. Elections for a traditional Four Estates Diet were held a year later and were won by moderate liberal Finns rather than by radicals.

On 15 September 1863 Alexander opened the Diet at Helsingfors in person: 'In the hands of a wise nation,' he declared, 'liberal institutions are not dangerous but guarantee order and well-being.' By the Diet Act of 1869 he recognized that the assembly should be summoned at least every five years (though, in reality, the Diet met far more frequently). Laws were passed setting up a national system of education, backing the development of railways, safeguarding local self-government in the villages, establishing a specifically Finnish coinage and (in 1879) modernizing the electoral procedure and broadening the franchise. Most importantly, the Language Decree of August 1863 ruled that within twenty years Finnish was to have equal status with Swedish in public business. A second decree, two years later, stipulated that transactions in the state bank, the customs service, post offices and the forestry service should be in Finnish if requested.

Yet the Governors-General of the Grand Duchy remained Russian-speaking outsiders, not Finns by birth. Even Johann Snellman, the dedicated promoter of Finnish philology and language from the 1840s to the late 1890s, spoke and wrote in Swedish. A Baltic German general, Count Theodor Berg, was governor-general for the first five years of the reign. He was succeeded by Platon Rokossovsky, a soldier of Polish origin, who presided over the Diet once the tsar had returned to his capital. Families of Swedish descent, with close connections across the Gulf of Bothnia, held high posts in the administration. Alexander Armfelt, state-secretary for Finland at St Petersburg, was a Finno-Swedish grandee, from a family eminent at the Stockholm Court in the last century; he encouraged and strongly supported the work of the Committee on Finnish Affairs. Fabian Langenskiöld, a Swede from Åbo, became Finland's minister of finance in 1857, and served as Berg's chief assistant in giving the Finnish economy firm foundations.

Much was achieved. Work began in 1858 on a railway running inland from Helsingfors to Hämeenlinna; it took four years to complete the 108 kilometres of track, which was eventually extended northwards to the textile centre of Tampere and westwards to Åbo. Not until 1870 were the Finnish and Russian capitals linked by rail: a line from Vyborg met the northern route at Riihimäkki, midway between Helsingfors and Hämeenlinna. Even before the Diet was convened, Langenskiöld had founded a credit bank for agriculture (1860) and a Finnish private bank to encourage industry (1861). He also eased fiscal restraints on mill construction, secured the lowering of Russian tariffs on goods from the Grand Duchy, and established a Forestry Service. The Diet gave formal approval to his proposals, modifying them and at subsequent sessions extending the original programme. So rapid was the growth of Finland's timber and textile industry that the tariffs had to be raised again in 1885 to protect Russian manufacturers from competition.

Despite rebuffs in the later years of the reign, never before – and never again – did the Finns give such loyal support to the Romanov dynasty as under Alexander II. When, in February 1880, anarchists sought to kill the tsar by blowing up the Winter Palace in St Petersburg, his Finnish Guards Regiment took the brunt of the explosion: at least twelve guardsmen perished. Thirteen months later another assassin succeeded in killing Alexander II close to the palace: the Finns mourned a liberal grand duke. A bronze statue, paid by public subscription and erected thirteen years after his death, still presides over Helsinki's Senate Square. Around the plinth figures dedicated to Enlightenment, Law, Work and Peace record the nation's debt to the ruler who, more than any other, carried Finland into the modern age.

For the first six years of Alexander's reign there was a parallel thaw in the Kingdom of Poland. As in Finland, he visited the capital when the war ended. A speech to Polish notables at Warsaw in May 1856 was conciliatory in tone; they should, however, be politically realistic. There could be no return to autonomy, he warned: *'Point de rêveries, Messieurs'* ('No empty dreams, gentlemen'); and with backing from his brother Constantine, he tried to appeal to the moderates by a series of reforms. But the Polish temperament, and Poland's past, differed from the Finnish. The Poles seized every opportunity to demonstrate their patriotism: Russia's conservatives, particularly in the army command, responded with stern repression, often foolishly. At Warsaw – on Tuesday, 11 November 1861 – Russian soldiers broke into churches and arrested thousands of worshippers attending Requiem Mass for the forty-fourth anniversary of Kosciuszko's death. In protest at such desecration the city's religious authorities – whether Catholic, Protestant or Jewish – closed all places of worship, an act that again focused the attention of France, Britain and Austria on the enormities of tsardom. Attempts to conscript young Poles into the army, and so fetter their radicalism with military discipline, provoked revolt. On 22 January 1863 a Provisional National Government proclaimed a war to liberate and unite the Polish lands lost to Russia in the past ninety years. At one stroke a rebellion nurtured in the heart of the old kingdom was carried to Minsk, Vilnius and the Lithuanian coast.

It was an uneven contest, in which there were no pitched battles. With 100,000 troops stationed inside the Polish kingdom and as many again in Lithuania and present day Belarus, the Russian soldiery outnumbered the rebels four to one. At best the Poles could only muster 50,000 men, lacking weapons and, for the most part, military experience. In April the provisional government, hoping for support from Napoleon III's France, rejected an offer from the tsar of a ceasefire and an amnesty. This was a mistake: Napoleon was faced with too many problems nearer home to risk a quixotic crusade for Polish liberties. The only aid he could offer the insurgents was diplomatic: he urged the tsar to solve the Polish Question by creating a unified autonomous kingdom that would include Lithuania and the adjoining provinces. Similar appeals came from London and even from Vienna, despite Austria's continued possession of Galicia and Cracow.

They had little chance of success. Alexander may have been more liberal by inclination than his father (or his son) but he was still styled 'Autocrat of All the Russias': he could never appear to appease nationalist rebels. And though Austria might be wavering, the third partitioner of Poland offered the tsar practical assistance. Any refugee found to have crossed the western frontier was handed back and Russian officers were allowed to hunt down revolutionaries on Prussian soil.

Guerrilla warfare dragged on for fifteen months, in a campaign of murder, intimidation and terror. When General Berg, brought from Helsingfors to command the army in Warsaw, narrowly escaped assassination, he ordered grim reprisals; and in Lithuania Governor-General Michael Muraviev gained a lasting notoriety as the Butcher of Vilnius. By the summer of 1864 the rebellion was over. On 5 August the last insurgent leader was hanged at the Gate of Executions in Warsaw's newly-built citadel. No less than 80,000 Poles were exiled to the wastes of Siberia. It was the largest single instance of enforced transportation under the tsars.

Sweeping changes followed the defeat of the rebellion. Even before the end of the year 1864 the property of the Roman Catholic Church was confiscated and most of the monasteries closed. Church administration was supervised by a department of the Ministry of the Interior in St Petersburg, from whom the bishops and clergy received their salaries. In 1865 the Congress Kingdom ceased to exist: a year later Poland became the Vistula Region, split into ten provinces and under a Russian governor-general, not a viceroy. Schoolchildren were taught exclusively in Russian; a law of 1885 confirmed that Polish could only be taught as a foreign language, though instruction in the Catholic religion might be given in the native tongue. From 1869 the University of Warsaw was wholly Russianized.

In an attempt to weaken the hold of the Polish nobility over the peasantry, the Russians carried through land reforms, enabling almost 750,000 families to become freeholders and, it was assumed, pillars of order and stability. Patriotic Poles of all classes did, indeed, abandon political defiance, turning instead to what they regarded as 'organic work'. Specifically Polish business and commercial enterprises were supported and, so far as possible, Polish culture was protectively cherished in anticipation of an eventual withering away of Russian autocracy.

Conditions were far better for Prussia's Polish subjects. William I (Regent of Prussia from 1858 until 1861, when he succeeded his brother, Frederick William IV) relaxed many restraints imposed after the 1848 revolutions. By 1864 twenty-six Polish deputies sat in the Prussian parliament and there were no disturbances in sympathy with the rebels of the Congress

Kingdom. Archbishop Ledochowski of Gniezno encouraged loyal obedience to Berlin, banning the anthem 'God Bless Poland' from being sung in
any Catholic church. More than 20,000 immigrants arrived from Russian
Poland. Although many travelled farther westwards into exile, some settled
with their compatriots, increasing the proportion of Polish-speakers to
Germans. The migration also created for the first time Jewish communities
within Poznania, though the number of Jews in the province remained
lower than elsewhere in historic Poland. Life for Polish Catholics became
difficult after 1871 during the *Kulturkampf*, Bismarck's conflict with ultra-
montanes in the Church. The Primate, Ledochowski, was imprisoned in
1874 and, on his release two years later, expelled from Germany.
Reconciliation with the Church under the pontificate of Leo XIII ensured
that by the late 1880s parochial clergy served as bulwarks against the rising
tide of allegedly atheistic socialism.

Positive Germanization began only in 1886 with formation of a
Colonization Commission to encourage German peasants from the west
to settle in the borderlands. More aggressive was the Eastern Marches
Union for Strengthening Germanism (*Ostmark Verein*), which included
many schoolteachers and local bureaucrats. The standard of education was
high in Poznania, but irksome regulations limited the use of the Polish language, not only in schools, but in any public meeting. In the first years of
the new century schoolboys and schoolgirls offered courageous resistance
to linguistic Germanism by persistent strikes, in which they received backing from their mothers and fathers. The movement was only stamped out
in 1906 by mass canings and parental fines.

At the time of the Polish Rebellion there were still few manifestations of
national sentiment along the Gulf of Finland's southern shore. A Latvian-
language satirical weekly was published at St Petersburg in 1862 and survived for some 200 issues before it fell foul of the censor for mocking
officialdom. In both Reval and Riga trade flourished but was controlled
either by Baltic Germans or by Estonians and Latvians who thought of
themselves as German. The first Estonian-language newspaper was
founded by Johann Jannsen in 1857 in the comparatively small port of
Pernau (Pärnu, to Jannsen). When, in 1864, he sought a wider readership
Jannsen moved, not to Reval, but to Dorpat (Tartu), where contacts with
the Finnish intelligentsia were stimulating an Estonian national awareness
at the German-speaking university. The movement did not become political until the last years of Alexander's reign: it remained loyal to the tsar but
hostile to all German influences. When the first Latvian-language news-

papers circulated in Riga in the early 1870s they, too, backed friendship with St Petersburg and Moscow and railed against 'Germanism'. The hostility was not limited to the towns. For at least four centuries the ruling landowners across the Baltic provinces had been German, and the peasants wanted more substantial holdings in the great estates than the emancipation reforms of 1811, 1819 and 1861 offered. Resentment at the status and feudal mentality of the Baltic Germans intensified among educated Estonians, Latvians and many Orthodox Russians in the late 1860s after Bismarck's success in 'putting Prussia in the saddle' of German nationalism. For Otto von Bismarck was a Junker landowner. His ancestral home was Schönhausen, in the Altmark west of Berlin, but he managed a family estate at Kniephof in Pomerania, less than 50 kilometres from the sea. There was a close affinity between the Junkers and the Baltic German barons. The Bismarcks were among many families with traditional links in Courland: Otto's great-grandmother had founded 'a home for indigent gentlewomen' in Mittau.

'Schleswig-Holstein – that is the diplomatic campaign of which I am most proud,' Bismarck reminisced one winter's evening at the peak of his career. As an arch-conservative in the Prussian Landtag of 1848 he had despised the national liberal enthusiasm of the Frankfurt Parliament, its support of the German cause in the Elbe Duchies, and the ambitions of the Augustenburg family. He was more interested in Polish affairs and the need for joint action with Russia than in what was happening north of the Elbe. But in March 1863, six months after he became chief minister of Prussia, a rash move by Frederick VII of Denmark focused his attention on the Jutland peninsula. Under pressure from 'Greater Denmark' National Liberal politicians in Copenhagen, the king proposed a new constitution. Its unitary character would curtail the autonomous rights of the Germans within the duchies, a breach of Denmark's obligations in the London Protocol. There was anger in Berlin, Frankfurt, Hanover, Dresden, and even at a meeting of the civic authorities in Vienna. Bismarck could not ignore what German patriots saw as a question of national honour. After simmering for eleven years, the Schleswig-Holstein Question was back on the boil.

In July the Diet of the German Confederation threatened military intervention in Holstein unless the proposed constitution was withdrawn. As in 1848, Frederick VII hoped for support from Sweden where, four years previously, Charles XV had succeeded his father, Oscar I, on the throne. Charles crossed to Zealand at the end of the month for talks with Frederick and his ministers at Skodsborg. Exactly what was settled at the meeting remains in dispute: the Swedes appear to have offered 20,000 men to defend Schleswig, but not Holstein. On 13 November the Danish Council of State approved the unitary constitution amid scenes of great political excitement in Copenhagen. But constitutions were fast becoming a health hazard for Denmark's kings: Christian VIII had not survived the heady days of January 1848; his son died at Glücksburg two days after the council's decision, with the constitution still awaiting promulgation. Christian IX, the successor designated by the London Protocol, duly ascended the throne. But ought he to approve the constitution? The turmoil in Germany made him hesitate. Delay might well provoke a revolution at home, his prime minister warned him. On 29 November 1863 the constitution finally received royal assent. In theory it was to become effective on New Year's Day.

Meanwhile the Holsteiners, and much of liberal national Germany with them, were backing a Young Pretender. The thirty-four-year-old Duke Frederick of Augustenburg revived the claims his father had renounced. In the last week of the old year Saxon and Hanoverian troops entered Holstein and advanced to the border with Schleswig. The Danes fell back without resistance. The Young Pretender followed the Saxons into Kiel, where he was warmly welcomed. But neither the Prussian government nor the Austrians supported Augustenburg. To Bismarck he was a representative of the smaller, liberal German states; to Emperor Francis Joseph and his ministers he seemed a demagogic nationalist, almost a revolutionary. Although Austria had no direct interest in Denmark or the Baltic, the emperor would rather ally with Bismarck than allow an increasingly powerful Prussia to act alone in German affairs. The German railway system made it possible for Austrian troops to be deployed alongside a Prussian army on the banks of the lower Elbe. Austria's main contribution to the alliance was, however, naval: Admiral Tegetthof led a squadron of modern armourclad warships from the Adriatic to northern waters so as to neutralize the Danish fleet. The Prussian navy remained small and outdated; the first Prussian non-sailing ironclad was not launched until August 1864, and even then the vessel was built at Blackwall, London, rather than in a German shipyard.

On 1 February 1864 Prussian and Austrian troops advanced into Schleswig. They made slow progress. It took two and a half weeks for the Prussians to capture the strategically important town of Kolding, though nobody had even bothered to rebuild the 600-year-old fortress destroyed in the Napoleonic Wars. There was heavy fighting around Sonderborg, spanning the narrow Sound between Als island and eastern Jutland, where the fortress of Düppel (Dybbøl to the Danes) defied Prussian assaults and bombardment for more than two months. Material comforts such as woollen socks came across from Sweden but no military help, and in the second week of May King Christian sought an armistice. As in 1848, Palmerston convened a conference in London, hoping he could induce the Prussians and Austrians to withdraw their troops and the Copenhagen government to compromise. But nobody would concede a point. Fighting flared up again in June and July. When Copenhagen itself seemed in danger, the Danes belatedly recognized their cause was hopeless. Christian IX dismissed his National Liberal government and on 11 July called on the Conservative spokesman, Christian Bluhme, to form a new ministry and negotiate directly with the invaders. By a final peace treaty, signed at Vienna on 30 October, Denmark handed over the duchies to joint Austro-Prussian military government. With this act Christian IX surrendered a third of his kingdom.

The Danes had lost. But the fate of Schleswig-Holstein was not yet settled. A combination of bluff, threats of war and apparent concessions let Bismarck out-manoeuvre his Austrian ally. By an agreement signed at Gastein in July 1865 Prussia was to administer Schleswig and Austria administer Holstein; it was agreed that the Prussians were to develop a naval base at Kiel and ultimately construct a ship canal linking the Baltic and the North Sea. Francis Joseph sold the small duchy of Lauenburg to King William, Prussia's first extension of territory in half a century.

Briefly Bismarck hoped the Austrians might sell Holstein, too. But when Francis Joseph seemed determined to retain his distant footing beside the Baltic, Bismarck resumed his diplomatic offensive. His objective was to destroy Habsburg leadership of Germany, sweep away the ineffectual thirty-nine-state German Confederation and lift the authority and stature of Hohenzollern Prussia. A series of provocative acts hampering the administration of Holstein led the Austrians to raise the Schleswig Question at the Federal Diet and seek federal punishment of Prussia for fostering subversion in the duchies: every German state backed Austria and condemned Prussia. A new and even greater conflict was inevitable.

Bismarck struck before the Diet could act. Prussian armies marched on Hesse, Hanover and Saxony on 15 June 1866. Against the expectations of all Europe they defeated the main Austrian army on 3 July at the great battle of Sadowa (Königgrätz) in Bohemia. But, although the duchies provided an ostensible reason for the war, there were no operations on Baltic shores. The Austrian governor in Holstein pulled his troops back across the Elbe before the fighting began. At the start of the campaign the Prussian navy exchanged fire with Hanoverian forts along the rivers Elbe and Weser. But the Seven Weeks War was, above all, a triumph for the Prussian army, revived only a few years earlier by King William I, modernized by General von Roon, and strategically directed by General von Moltke.

The Peace Treaty of Prague (23 August 1866) confirmed Prussian annexation of Schleswig, Holstein and Lauenburg, as well as of Hanover and Hesse. Other states north of the river Main joined the new Prussia in a North German Confederation, centred on Berlin and allied to the king-doms of southern Germany. Lübeck, along with Bremen and Hamburg, remained a Free City, proud of its Hanse heritage, although now a member of the Zollverein. Four years later the Roon–Moltke partnership achieved even greater success. Napoleon III was defeated and taken prisoner at Sedan. On 18 January 1871, beneath the long mirrors of Louis XIV's Versailles, Bismarck proclaimed a unified Germany. At the age of seventy-three, King William I of Prussia was hailed as the first specifically German Emperor. Across northern Europe there were no further adjustments of frontier, but the political outlook of the great Baltic towns was significantly changed. For the latest imperial capital was not in the centre of the conti-nent nor facing westwards towards the Atlantic. Victory over Austria in 1866 and France in 1870 had raised Berlin's status. Neither Vienna nor Paris could serve any longer as a pivotal point of Europe's diplomacy. That role now passed to a city less than 150 kilometres from the Baltic coast.

18

Towards Democracy

ORDINARY FAMILIES AROUND the northern shores faced more basic day-to-day problems than the machinations of statesmen and generals. For Finns and Swedes the decade that saw Austria and France humbled is remembered as the Hungry Sixties. Too many people had come to depend on too few resources of food. A wet summer or harsh winter – and, more rarely, the impact of land reforms or the disruption of trade by political upheaval – could tip the balance between sufficiency and deprivation. In 1862 a shortage of grain in Finland plunged the Grand Duchy into the worst famine for 165 years, especially intense in Ostrobothnia. Poor harvests in 1867 and 1868 led to an even more disastrous famine over a wider area. The Russians allowed the formation of the Riga Latvian Association as a charity to help famine victims; it survived as an influential but overtly non-political national society. But it was along both shores of the Gulf of Bothnia that the famine was at its worst, with the greatest scourge running through rural Sweden. Bread baked with ground bark to supplement a thin ration of flour became a staple diet in two hard winters.

Since the middle of the century there had been a steadily rising flow of emigrants taking ship from Gothenburg for the United States, transplanting Swedish ways to Nebraska, Minnesota and Kansas. In the famine year 1869 the figure leapt dramatically: as many as 40,000 Swedes left for the New World, one per cent of the total population. Two years earlier the historian Zachris Topelius, lecturing to his students at Helsingfors University, observed, 'Nature seems to cry out to our people "Emigrate or die!"' Thousands of Finnish families chose nature's more adventurous option. Like the Swedes, they headed for America's Mid-West or for Canada.

During the Hungry Sixties three in every four Swedish families relied on agriculture for a livelihood. Eighty-seven per cent lived in villages or farms rather than in towns, with about half of them peasant farmers owning their own land; the remainder were tenant farmers or labourers. In Finland and in Denmark an even higher proportion lived directly off the land and continued to do so until the end of the century. In Sweden, however, conditions began to change in the course of the decade. A decision of parliament in 1854 to authorize the construction of a railway network held out the prospect of tighter economic unity, with a freer movement of labour from the land into the towns.

Even so, Sweden did not get its first railway until 1859 and ten years elapsed between parliament's vote and Charles XV's grand state opening of the southern line out of the capital. Completion of the railway route drastically cut travel time between Stockholm, Malmö and Copenhagen, and trains were soon challenging the canal trade that had completed Gothenburg's economic recovery after the Napoleonic upheaval. The railways brought other industries closer together. Gustaf Pasch's invention of the safety match created a factory complex in Jönköping, at the southern end of Lake Vättern, while neighbouring Huskvarna turned out sewing machines. Norrköping, like Tampere in Finland, was the centre of a textile industry that became modernized with the advent of steam-power. By 1910 Norrköping employed over 6,000 factory workers; the only other town with more than 5,000 factory workers within Sweden was the metallurgical centre of Eskilstuna, south of Lake Mälaren. Timber-processing remained an essentially rural industry. The Norrland Inland Railway, planned to develop forests and natural resources across the Arctic Circle, was not begun until 1907 and took thirty years to complete. Long before then – as early as 1888 – an iron-ore rush to Kåkstan trumpeted the return of the North's most profitable industry. When mining was revived at Kiruna the shortest route to the outside world was the railway opened in 1898 across the Scandinavian keel, linking Luleå, Gällivare and the ice-free port of Narvik. It was to acquire a strategic importance greater than any other line in the northern Baltic.

In Sweden, heavy industry benefited from the growing sophistication of the banking system. New financial institutions, like Wallenberg's Stockholms Enskilda Bank, attracted foreign investment. There was a boom in steel production in the last decades of the century, backed by the ingenuity of Swedish scientists like Alfred Nobel, who returned to his native Stockholm from America in 1859 and built up an industrial empire based on his discovery of dynamite seven years later. Housing conditions for the artisans were poor and they were bullied and harassed at work; from 1858 onwards employers could no longer thrash adult workers, though they could still inflict corporal punishment on minors. Tuberculosis was rife in the towns and industrialized villages; alcoholism kept life expectancy low. Fire remained a great hazard: in 1878 the huge Eldkvarn Mill was gutted, at the heart of Stockholm's waterfront industrial zone (the

City Hall is on the site today); and in 1888 the sawmills and timber ware-houses of Sundsvall – the centre of Sweden's first workers' strike nine years earlier – were burnt to the ground, together with the wooden houses around them.

There were cycles of rural unemployment in some provinces, especially in the south. In hard years a regular summer migration from Skåne across to the compact and orderly Danish island of Bornholm ensured a certainty of basic food, even though working conditions were harsh. But Swedish middle-class families, settled in the rapidly expanding capital or a small town, enjoyed as cosy an existence as the climate and the gloomy tenets of an increasingly puritanical church permitted. The restraints of urban life at the turn of the century are sharply evoked in Ingmar Bergman's classic film *Fanny and Alexander;* fifty years back in time they had been even more oppressive. Not until 1873 were Swedes who worshipped in the Lutheran Church given the freedom to join other denominations. Fifteen years earlier there had been protests abroad when six women were forced into exile for converting to Roman Catholicism. Frederika Bremer's novel *Hertha* (1856) encouraged a movement for women's rights in State and Society. In 1868 the obligation of an unmarried woman to have a male legal guardian was ended. But Swedish society remained male dominated. Even though, in the early 1880s, Strindberg shocked his contemporaries by the sex-awareness of his novels and plays, much of his later work – including *Miss Julie* (1888) – reflected the prevailing social misogyny. Strindberg, unlike Ibsen, loathed women of intelligence and emancipated ambition.

Yet there was no uniform pattern of slum drabness in Sweden, as there was across such a large swathe of Victorian Britain. A unique feature of the kingdom's industrial revolution was the integration of surviving seven-teenth century *bruks* with the banking and credit system of large-scale cap-italism. The *bruks* were, in effect, factory estates serving industries like copper-mining or glass-blowing. They were specially built villages, often deep in forest clearings, managed by an owner with a sense of social responsibility; he lived with some style in a manor house, while the work-ers' families were decently housed in cottages along the village street. In Uppland, ironwork *bruks* were operating well into the twentieth century. At Lövstabruk and the overgrown village of Österbybruk the owners' mansions still radiated an elegant self-assurance in the 1970s, and no doubt continue to do so today. Each house gave an impression of being, not so much the home of a mining boss, as the country seat of a paternalistic squire of industry.

★

Throughout Oscar I's last years Swedish politicians lamented the kingdom's archaic constitutional structure. The Riksdag of four Estates seemed far behind the 'people's constitution' Frederick VII had given Denmark. Oscar's son and successor, Charles XV, was by nature opposed to modernization. By temperament, however, he was so indolent that he was disinclined to cling on to royal power if faced by firm opposition. Louis de Geer, his minister of justice and senior councillor of state, secured passage of a series of domestic reforms, long overdue: reform of the penal code; the spread of elementary education; and in 1862 changes in local government. In December 1865, after a long and remarkably peaceful agitation for constitutional reform, a bicameral parliament replaced the four-estates Riksdag. The upper house would be indirectly elected on a franchise that limited representation to men of wealth and property; the lower house was directly elected by men over the age of twenty-one. Less than 22 per cent of men had voting rights. The franchise depended on a taxable income of at least 800 kronor a year, a level well above the earnings of labourers and industrial workers. Sweden was not yet a democracy. The upper chamber still shaped the law in the elegant House of Nobility (Riddarhuset); the elected deputies conducted sonorous debates in neighbouring Fleming House. The two chambers constantly clashed. Louis de Geer remained Sweden's outstanding statesman from 1858 to 1880, and in 1876 was recognized as the first Prime Minister, but ironically he achieved more reforms under the old system than the new. Only in 1885 did Oscar II accept a constitutional amendment that effectively transferred the conduct of foreign affairs from the king's nominated councillor to a member of the cabinet. Not until 1909 were all men over the age of twenty-four given the vote. The autumn general election in 1911 was the first decided by universal suffrage and proportional representation.

In Denmark, too, the advance of democracy faltered. Defeat in 1864 led to conservative complaints that the irresponsible demagogy of the National Liberals had promoted the idea of a unitary constitution and rushed the kingdom into war. In July 1866 the 'people's constitution' was modified, with the king given extensive rights of nomination to the upper house. Fear of a reversion to autocracy rallied the rural voters, ensuring that Venstre Free Traders formed the largest group in the lower house (Folketing) throughout the last three decades of the century. There was a hard core of traditional Liberalism in Venstre, but a total lack of party cohesion; feuds and factions weakened the movement. For most of his reign King Christian IX turned to the upper house with its built-in conservative majority for a government and put his trust in Johannes Estrup, an independent man of the Right, who from 1875 to 1894 combined the offices of prime minister and finance minister. As in Sweden, there was a continuous struggle between the two chambers, mainly over the levying of taxes. When the Folketing consistently rejected Estrup's budgets, the conservatives argued that the king had a constitutional right to impose taxes by approving a provisional budget that did not need parliamentary sanction. A compromise was reached after Estrup's long-delayed resignation, and an overwhelming Venstre victory in the 1901 election – the first conducted through secret ballot – led the king to accept the need for a Liberal government. Social Democrats had won and held seats in Copenhagen from 1884 onwards and in 1910, four years after Christian IX's death, their party became the second largest in the Folketing.

Both in Sweden and Denmark the main cause of conflict between the chambers was expenditure on defence, with the two lower houses preferring to see money spent on social reforms, including the provision of smallholdings for peasants. There were long debates in Copenhagen over the merits of modernizing the navy or of protecting the capital by new defences on land and islands in the Sound. The Swedish parliament passed a succession of laws on conscription between 1885 and 1901 increasing the length of training from a basic seven weeks to 240 days in the army and 300 days in the navy. The Swedish Admiralty remained on Stockholm's Skeppsholmen island, but the outer defences of Vaxholm, Karlskrona and Gothenburg were restored and extended. After Prussia's resort to three wars in six years it is small wonder the Baltic kingdoms remained vigilant.

19

National Pride

———————

FOR THE FIRST nineteen years of the German empire, policy in Berlin continued to be determined by a landowner steeped in Lutheran Junker traditions east of the Elbe. Bismarck was not a professional soldier; his military service as a junior officer had been limited to a few wintry months of Baltic guard duty on a sandy promontory at Greifswald. Before entering politics he was a scientific farmer who, in nine years, raised the value of his estate at Kniephof by a third, despite an agricultural depression. As chancellor, it was natural for him to uphold the interests of Germany's eastern squirearchy. Concern at a sudden doubling of grain imports from Russia in 1877 finally decided him to protect agriculture, and in July 1879 moderate tariffs were imposed on wheat, oats, barley, maize as well as on livestock and timber. But the surest guarantee of continued prosperity for the great estates was an era of peace, and after 1871 Bismarck sought to avoid further conflict. War would destroy the delicate balance of Prussian interests he had secured inside and outside Germany.

Bismarck's ideal was a conservative Europe, in which he could manipulate a system of largely secret alliances to keep France isolated and unable to launch a war of revenge. His basic Austro-German defensive partnership of 1879 became the Triple Alliance in 1882 with the adhesion of Italy. At the same time, links were maintained with Russia, first in collaboration with Austria-Hungary, but from 1887 until his resignation in 1890 through the secret so-called Reinsurance Treaty. Only after his downfall did Europe divide into two mutually suspicious armed camps, with the Franco-Russian dual alliance forming a potential challenge to the central powers. Britain remained outside the European alliance system until after the outbreak of the First World War. Colonial differences with France were settled in April 1904 by a treaty that established an *Entente Cordiale* between the two nations. The *Entente* stopped short of being a formal alliance. It was an 'understanding' rather than a committed 'marriage' – and perhaps for that reason all the more binding.

In later years Bismarck claimed to have learnt the conduct of diplomacy from trading in the horse fairs of Pomerania. It was his style rather than the content of his treaties that kept the Baltic kingdoms on the alert. From 1875 onwards the chancellor used newspaper contacts to engineer crises in foreign affairs as a distraction from internal problems. He rallied support from a younger generation eager to flaunt a pride in national self-recognition and, soon afterwards, to see Germany join the scramble for Africa. Between 1884 and 1886 South-West Africa, Togoland, the Cameroons and 'German East' were acquired. No other government with ports on the Baltic took part in the new colonialism. Sweden's last Caribbean colony, Saint Bathélemy, was sold to France in 1878. Denmark retained three islands in the West Indies until 1917, when they were purchased by the United States. Sweden and Denmark had no African ambitions.

Nor did Russia, apart from the Orthodox Church's passing interest in Ethiopia. Russian empire builders and adventurers concentrated on opening up farthest Asia. In 1891 work began on a Trans-Siberian Railway, long advocated by Sergei Witte, the Baltic German who served Alexander III and Nicholas II as Minister of Communications (and from 1892 to 1903, Minister of Finance too). At the end of the decade the Russians, and their French bankers, were investing heavily in railway projects in China. By 1903 the maps showed 8,850 kilometres of continuous railroad linking the Baltic (St Petersburg) and Pacific (Vladivostok) by way of Chelyabinsk, where it joined the line from Moscow and crossed Siberia by a single track.

Colonies required fleets to defend them. So too did Russia's distant outposts in the Far East. Naval expenditure soared, although not so dramatically as at the turn of the century. The Admiralty in London and the Ministry of Marine in Paris were long accustomed to viewing each other's activities with deep suspicion; neither as yet perceived any threat from Germany, where in July 1888 only twenty-four warships, including the smallest of vessels, assembled at Kiel for the first naval review of William II's reign. Successive First Lords of the Admiralty were as anxious as Bismarck to keep France isolated and, in particular, to prevent a Franco-Russian alliance. There was genuine alarm in London in the winter of 1888–89 when news of French loans to St Petersburg coincided with a leap in Russian naval expenditure. The Admiralty resolved to maintain a fleet 'at least equal to the naval strength of any two other countries'. This Two Power Standard shaped British naval policy for the next twenty years. In practice the Admiralty regarded it as an absolute minimum to ensure continued command of the seas.

London's fears were heightened in the last week of July 1891 when a French naval squadron sailed up the Gulf of Finland and entered the road-stead of Kronstadt. Officers and men were fêted for a fortnight and Alexander III visited the flagship. The Autocrat of All the Russias was seen to stand at attention, bare-headed and massively erect, as a band thundered out the *Marseillaise*, the historic anthem of revolution. The significance of the tsar's gesture was not lost on foreign observers, though the nature of the Russo-French partnership remained a matter of speculation. A secret military convention drafted in August 1892 was not, in fact, finally agreed for eighteen more months; but by October 1893, when the Baltic fleet was welcomed at Toulon, no public figure in London or Berlin doubted that Imperial Russia and the French Republic were allies. They remained so until the Bolshevik revolution.

The Russian Bogey, dormant for twenty years, again raised fantasies in London. The popular novelist William le Queux rushed out a best-seller, *The Great War in England in 1897*, which envisaged a Franco-Russian inva-sion, with the Baltic fleet emerging from the mists of the North Sea while the French came across the Channel. The Admiralty had its own phantom: a class of cruisers on the stocks of St Petersburg's shipyards, allegedly faster than any cruiser in the Royal Navy, with greater fire-power and enough coal aboard to steam halfway round the world. The 11,100 tonne *Rurik* was launched in November 1892; work began on the 12,730 tonne *Rossia* four months later; others were to follow. Rear-Admiral Fisher, the Third Sea Lord (responsible for 'equipping' the fleet), feared the Russians would have ten *Ruriks*. He wasted no time on assessing reports of sea-trials. Two 14,400 tonne cruisers, HMS *Powerful* and HMS *Terrible,* were laid down to coun-ter the menace from Baltic waters. Even their names breathed defiance.

In June 1895 a British squadron was invited to Kiel Bay for the opening of the Kaiser Wilhelm Canal, on which work had begun eight years pre-viously. The canal, 105 kilometres long, cut across the neck of Schleswig-Holstein, enabling German warships to move from their base at Kiel to the naval station of Wilhelmshaven overnight. The British, however, were less interested in the canal or in Germany's warships than in the other visiting squadrons, especially the Russian. At last naval officers and journalists could go aboard the *Rurik*. They were not impressed; the cruiser had very little protective armour, especially for guns' crews. Neither officers nor men showed the efficiency or seamanship of their French allies. The *Rurik* scare proved a false alarm. That summer the Russians had only one first-class battleship in the Baltic, though seven were under construction. The British had pondered the possibility of maintaining a Baltic presence, presumably at anchorages leased from Sweden. After the Kiel experience they settled for a general strategy of wait and see, ready either to establish a distant blockade or to enter the Kattegat should war come.

Colonialism and naval rivalry were, in part, manifestations of the pride in nationhood that swept through so much of Europe in the late nineteenth century. Great powers trumpeted an imperialism that soon receded. Smaller powers did little to curb a mounting protectionist xenophobia: thus 'Sweden for the Swedes' was a slogan in the 1887 elections across the central Bergslagen industrial region. Subject peoples, more modestly, were content to encourage the revival or invention of folk traditions in literature and music: Estonia's first song festival was celebrated at Tartu in 1869, though with only two lyrics in the national tongue; and at midsummer 1873 a similar event in Riga's Imperial Garden attracted thousands of Latvians. Thereafter song festivals with patriotic undertones continued to stimulate local nationalism so long as tsarist Russia remained in being. But against them was arrayed an ideological imperialism that received spiritual endorsement from an established Church. In 1880 Konstantin Pobedonostsev, the arch-conservative layman who tutored both Alexander III and Nicholas II in constitutional law, became Procurator of the Holy Synod, a ministerial post that enabled him for twenty-five years to control the day-to-day running of the Russian Orthodox Church.

Pobedonostsev was a man of strong principles, rabidly anti-Semitic and equally hostile to Catholicism, Islam and to any form of representative government ('Parliaments are the great lie of our times,' he wrote in 1896). More positively, he believed in the Providential mission of Great Russian nationalism and in the divine sanction of authority exercised by an All-Russian Emperor as Supreme Autocrat. Jewish believers, both inside and outside the Pale of Settlement, suffered more grievously than any other community from his prejudices. Anti-Semitic journalists, encouraged by the Holy Synod, blamed the assassination of Alexander II in March 1881 on Jewish anarchists. Two months later mob violence against Jewish families and property in the Ukraine introduced the grisly noun 'pogrom' to Europe's vocabularies. Although the most serious attacks did not reach the Baltic region until 1905, the wave of anti-Semitism made sweeping demographic changes in the mainly Lithuanian provinces of Kovno, Vilna and Suwalki. The 'Temporary Orders concerning the Jews' (May 1882) were savage restrictions that hampered Jewish business dealings and deprived families of land and property. Half a million Jews, living in rural areas within the Pale, were ordered to move into the towns, and over the following nine years 700,000 Jews from outside the Pale were uprooted and forced into the settlement. Among them were 20,000 Jews expelled from Moscow and 2,000 from St Petersburg, some transported westwards in chain gangs like criminals.

The hardening attitude of the Russian authorities caused a mass exodus of those families who could afford to emigrate. Most refugees crossed into Austrian Galicia. Some, however, made their way to Gothenburg or Hamburg and took ship to New York. In the eighteen years after the Temporary Orders were issued, New York's Jewish population increased fourfold (though of course not all new arrivals came from Russia). A tide of impoverished immigrants swept into Harwich and Hull as early as July and August 1882, some using England as a stepping-stone to the New World. By 1889 a weekly steamship service was running between Libau and London.

For poorer Jews the principal refuge within the Pale was Vilna, a sanctuary for more than 500 years. By the turn of the century the city housed 150,000 Jews, of whom at least a quarter had to rely for food and fuel on the charity of their wealthier co-religionists. Yiddish newspapers were avidly read. So, too, were primers of revolutionary socialism. It was at Vilna that in 1897 the General Union of Jewish Workers in Russia and Poland (the *Bund*) was set up. But there was also at Vilna a strong movement in favour of 'auto-emancipation', the ideas of Leon Pinksner, from which Theodor Herzl developed modern Zionism. In 1903 Herzl, a Hungarian by birth, visited Vilna. Some enthusiasts hailed a 'king' to be. He was a hope for the future, lighting a dark present.

In effect, Pobedonostsev directed the only Northern Crusade in the history of the Orthodox Church, a political and cultural drive to purge the Baltic borderland of corrupting beliefs and proclaim faith in the protective power of autocracy. 'The key to the so-called Baltic Question' lay in the conversion of the 'local peoples' to Orthodoxy, he maintained. Already Russification was falling with a heavy hand on young Poles. In Warsaw in 1877 a clever ten-year-old, Marie Sklodowska, was humiliated by a school inspector for being unable to recite the Lord's Prayer in Russian or recall from memory the names of the imperial family. A nobler pursuit of knowledge soon challenged her mind: as Marie Curie, in academically free Paris, she discovered the elements radium and polonium (named to honour her homeland) and received the first of her Nobel prizes before Pobedonostsev went out of office.

In the 1880s and 1890s the Procurator imposed this stultifying system of Russification across European Russia. Church schools – where the teaching stressed the interdependence of Orthodoxy, Autocracy and National Unity – multiplied rapidly. Between 1887 and 1890 all schools in the Baltic provinces, whether Church administered or privately owned French style *lycée,* were compelled to teach in Russian. Even the Baltic Germans, so long pillars of tsardom, were not spared vexation. In 1893 Estonia's prestigious German-speaking university at Dorpat was closed and replaced by the all-Russian University of Yuriev, soon the seventh largest in the empire. Only in Yuriev's small Lutheran theological faculty were lectures given in German. By 1890 all juridical and legal business in the Baltic provinces had to be conducted in Russian, a reform that infuriated lawyers in Estland (Estonia), Livonia and Courland, most of whom had German as a first language and French or the local vernacular as their second.

A fund was set up, under Pobedonostsev's auspices, on which provincial governors might draw for the building or restoration of Orthodox churches in the borderlands. Riga's cathedral could only be completed in 1884 after the funding became available; the seminary in the city was extended at the same time. More controversially, work began in 1894 on cathedrals dedicated to Alexander Nevsky at the heart of Catholic Warsaw and on the heights above Lutheran Reval. Kaunas, where there had been a Catholic cathedral since the fifteenth century, gained a neo-Byzantine Orthodox basilica in 1895; on the collapse of the godless Soviet regime it was to re-open under the authority of Rome. Smaller towns in the Baltic provinces where new churches were planted included Lutheran Windau and Mitau in Courland and Catholic Šiauliai in Lithuania. In May 1883 laws prohibited the building of Protestant or Catholic places of worship without special permission. Two years later the Holy Synod forbade mixed marriages, unless a pledge was given that any children would be raised in the Orthodox faith

Pobedonostsev's crusade was a failure. It alienated Estonians and Latvians who had remained passively obedient earlier in the century and rekindled resentment within Lithuania. Instead of furthering the ideal of a unified empire, Russification stimulated the Baltic peoples' national pride. Even so, political sentiment across the Estonian and Latvian provinces favoured autonomy rather than full independence. Jaan Tönisson's Estonian-language newspaper *Postimees* ('The Courier', published in Tartu at the end of the century) advocated comprehensive liberalism, with recognition of national rights for all the Baltic peoples within the Russian empire. As so often in modern times, Finland stood out as the role model for Estonia's moderate spokesmen.

★

But by 1894 – the year the Tsar Liberator's statue was unveiled in Helsinki's Senate Square – the Grand Duchy's special status was becoming less secure. Finnish literature and music flourished in the last decade of the century, with Sibelius's *The Swan of Tuonela* performed at Helsinki in 1895 and the tone poem *Finlandia* composed four years later. At first the authorities tolerated such outpourings of reflective patriotic Romanticism: Alexander III enjoyed Finnish folk music during his family's many holiday visits; and as late as 1897 Governor-General Heiden approved a grant from public funds to support Sibelius. Within Finland Russification was economic in origin rather than cultural-religious. The rapid growth of timber and textile enterprises outpaced developments across the border, and the tariff which favoured the Grand Duchy was revised in 1885 in order to protect Russian industry. Political restraint soon followed, however. Alexander III annulled reforms of the criminal code passed by the Diet and incorporated Finland's postal institutions in the less efficient Russian system; and Nicholas II, who acceded on his father's death in November 1894, was even less sympathetic to the Finns. In 1898 the moderate Heiden was succeeded as Governor-General by Nikolai Bobrikov, a soldier prepared to treat Finland as a mere province of the tsar's empire. A plan to impose five years' military service on Finnish conscripts was followed in February 1899 by a Manifesto giving Russian imperial law precedence over measures passed by the Finnish Diet.

This assault on the Grand Duchy's autonomy was a grave blunder. The Finns were well-educated and politically conscious: in the capital that year the public had a choice of seven newspapers in Finnish and twelve in Swedish. A petition seeking withdrawal of the Manifesto collected 522,931 signatures in two weeks, backing from a fifth of the population. Nicholas II refused to accept the petition, which was brought to St Petersburg by a deputation of 500 Finns. He also rejected an appeal signed by 1,000 eminent foreigners – Zola, Ibsen and Florence Nightingale among them.

Some 'Old Finn' senators favoured compliance in the new order, hoping by their co-operation to win an eventual compromise. The 'Young Finns' and Swedish-speaking Liberals became Constitutionalists and urged a campaign of civil disobedience. More than half the conscripts of the year 1902 failed to report for training; many slipped across the border, to find sanctuary in Sweden. Of 870 conscripts due to muster in Helsinki on 17 April, only 38 reported for inspection, of whom 31 were promptly declared unfit for military service. Next day the passively defiant mood in the capital so riled the commanding general that he sent mounted Cossacks into Senate Square, lashing out with whips indiscriminately at protesters. Some sought shelter up the granite steps of the Lutheran cathedral. A barrage of stone-throwing checked the Cossacks, who were recalled to barracks before they could perpetrate an even greater outrage. Senate Square was spared the bloodshed that tragically marred the Palace Square protest in St Petersburg three years later.

A small faction of Activists continued to encourage strikes and armed resistance (although they did not become organized as a political party until 1904). General Bobrikov responded to the mounting unrest by bringing in Russians to run government services, including the railways. On 9 April 1903 Nicholas II authorized Bobrikov to suspend the constitution and assume dictatorial powers. As in the Baltic provinces, all the administration was now to be conducted in the Russian language. The Finns seemed about to lose every concession Alexander I had granted at Porvoo. On 16 June 1904 a young Activist lawyer and son of a senator, Eugen Schaumann, shot and fatally wounded General Bobrikov, before turning the gun on himself. 'Finland! Ah, here it is wonderful to live. No-one throwing bombs, no bandits,' Alexander III once remarked on holiday near Kotka. Now Russian folly had driven even the most passive of peoples to the politics of murder.

In St Petersburg – a city more accustomed than Helsinki to assassination – terrorism struck again four weeks after the killing of Bobrikov: a Socialist Revolutionary hurled a bomb that blew to pieces the minister of the interior, Viacheslav Pleve. 'Russia has been made by bayonets, not by diplomacy,' Pleve told the Imperial Council in May 1903 at which he recommended 'a little victorious war' as a means of smothering political unrest with patriotic euphoria. By the time of his death, Russia was indeed at war: trade rivalry with Japan in Manchuria and Korea had culminated in a surprise Japanese attack on the Russian fleet at Port Arthur on the night of 8/9 February 1904. But the war brought the Russian people no victories to celebrate, only humiliation.

Over the following four months further losses at sea and a costly campaign in Manchuria induced the Russian Admiralty to prepare the Baltic fleet for a voyage to the war zone, to recover the initiative. Assembling the fleet was a slow process, but by early October Admiral Rozdhestvensky was in command of seven battleships, five relatively modern cruisers, ten destroyers and some twenty other ageing vessels. Tsar Nicholas visited the ships at Reval and, as he later told the British ambassador, was impressed by Rozdhestvensky's resolve 'to carry out the work entrusted to him'. The admiral suspected the Japanese would attempt 'a secret attack' before the fleet left European waters. He would, he assured the tsar, fire on any 'vessels that approached too near and . . . entertained hostile designs'.

The epic, and ultimately disastrous, voyage focused world attention on the Baltic fleet for the first time since its creation by Peter the Great. The Admiralty in London, having exaggerated the strength of the fleet a decade ago, now despised it. In any sortie from Baltic waters no more than 'three battleships and a few cruisers' were likely to reach the North Sea, the Director of Navy Intelligence (Prince Louis of Battenberg) had reported the previous spring. This assessment magnified Russian deficiencies, but the fleet that steamed slowly southwards from Libau for the Øresund in the third week of October was far from being an awesome armada. The crews lacked training in tactical exercises, and Rozdhestvensky's captains shared his fears of a surprise attack. Why had the Japanese naval attaché in Berlin travelled recently to Copenhagen? Were fast Japanese torpedo boats lurking in Norway's fjords? As a precaution, guns were trained on low-lying Danish and Swedish merchantmen in the Sound. Fortunately Russian diplomats had secured the services of Denmark's most skilful pilots, men who knew local shipping as well as they did local waters, and the fleet left the Baltic without a shot being fired.

The North Sea was regarded as a high risk area, not least because Britain was on good terms with Japan. Around midnight on 21 October the fleet approached a group of some fifty Hull fishing-boats on the Dogger Bank. The first Russian division, including Rozdhestvensky's flagship, sailed on without incident, but a lookout in the second division reported seeing two small and fast-moving vessels. They were probably carriers, used to convey the daily catch back to Hull speedily, but the nervous Russian officers suspected they were Japanese torpedo-boats. Searchlight beams scoured the waves, and the cruisers *Aurora* and *Dmitri Donskoy* seem to have sent up starshell independently, their logbooks suggesting that each believed an enemy was firing on them. In some three or four minutes of general confusion at least two Russian warships turned their guns on nine of the fishing smacks, sinking the trawler *Crane*, seriously damaging three others, and leaving two fishermen dead and many injured. The Baltic fleet then headed southwards to the Nore and the Channel, without lowering boats to help the victims of the attack.

'A most dastardly outrage,' noted King Edward VII on the first telegram from Hull with news of the attack. The Admiralty at once alerted the Home, Channel and Mediterranean fleets. By 26 October, when Rozhdestvensky put into the Spanish port of Vigo, there was a grave risk of war between Britain and Russia over the incident. Fortunately the Baltic Fleet had ignored trawlers from Fleetwood and Milford Haven at fishing grounds off the Portuguese and Spanish coasts. One battleship squadron sailed on to Tangier, closely shadowed by the Royal Navy. For four days the British warships kept their shells fused and their decks cleared for action. The skill of French diplomats proved the value of the new *Entente Cordiale*: they induced their Russian ally to put ashore the responsible officers at Vigo and accept an enquiry conducted by an International Commission of Admirals. Eventually the Russians admitted their grave error and paid compensation.

A hundred years later it is hard to appreciate the sustained anger of the British public in that autumn of 1904. Ironic black-edged cards, 'In disgraceful memory of the Russian Navy, the world's stumbling block to civilization', went on sale in London; thousands were bought in a few days. The men of the Baltic fleet were '20th century savages', the card declared. When next summer the Admiralty announced that the Channel fleet would for the first time conduct exercises in the Baltic, some in Britain welcomed the innovation as a response to Russia's 'barbarism', even though it was in reality prompted by the growing naval power of Germany.

By then the Baltic fleet had virtually ceased to exist. On 27 May 1905 Admiral Togo surprised Rozhdestvensky off Tsushima island, in the Straits between Japan and Korea. In a running battle that continued from early afternoon until the small hours of the following day the Japanese sank twenty-two Russian vessels, including eight battleships, and captured six others, including the flagship. Like Admiral Villeneuve after Trafalgar, Rozhdestvensky – who during the long voyage had shown courage and enterprise – surrendered his sword and became a prisoner-of-war. Not a single Japanese warship was lost. Only one Russian cruiser and two torpedo boats reached Vladivostok; six Russian ships made for neutral ports. The *Aurora* found refuge in American-administered Manila, eventually returning to the Baltic and to a legendary role in the Bolshevik Revolution. After innumerable refits, the *Aurora* survives in the Neva today, a historic relic, the only warship of Nicholas II's fleet still afloat.

The war ended four months after Tsushima, with a treaty signed at Portsmouth, New Hampshire. Witte, who led the Russian peace delegation in America, secured remarkably lenient terms, frustrating Japanese efforts to impose an indemnity that would have required more taxation. Although the fighting took place thousands of kilometres from Baltic shores the effects of the war were felt in European Russia, even as far west as Poland. The transference of a largely conscript army across the Eurasian land mass disrupted trade and communications, caused hardship in many families and reduced industrial output. Anti-war agitation increased the

20

The Last Years of the Long Peace

IN ST PETERSBURG the year 1905 opened disastrously. On Sunday, 22 January – 9 January in the Russian calendar – Father Gapon, a radical priest from an industrialized suburb, led a peaceful workers' deputation to the Winter Palace, seeking to present a petition to the tsar for political reform and improved working conditions. Gapon had told the authorities of his intentions, but he seems not to have known that Nicholas II would be with his family at Tsarskoye Selo that Sunday. On the preceding Friday the Orthodox Church had celebrated Christmas: some of the hundreds of men, women and children who slowly crossed the Neva bridges carried holy banners; many had ikons and sang Christmas anthems. The procession was met by Cossacks, who at first used their whips. As the crowd pressed forward into the great Palace Square, the Cossacks fired blank shot, but when reinforcements arrived an order was given for live volleys. At least 130 demonstrators were killed, several hundred wounded. 'A painful day,' Nicholas began his diary entry that night.

Anger over Bloody Sunday brought simmering discontent to the boil across European Russia. During the following eleven months the fate of the incipient revolution was determined in the capital. In February the tsar was prepared to consider proposals for a consultative assembly, though he would not necessarily accept them. Widespread strikes continued; and tension mounted with the worsening news from the war zone in the Far East.

The tsar's proposals for an elected consultative assembly were not published until August. Both liberals and the rapidly growing socialist movement treated them with derision, criticizing the narrow franchise and the refusal to concede legislative power. A general strike was called as winter approached. In early October industry and communications were paralysed. At the same time, menacingly, a Soviet of Workers' Deputies met in St Petersburg, its deliberations dominated by the fiery eloquence of Leon Trotsky. At last on 30 October the stubborn tsar accepted the need for drastic change. He agreed to form an executive council of ministers and to summon a legislative parliament, though he reserved his autocratic authority over matters of foreign policy and defence. In December the drama of the revolution was played out in Moscow, where there was ten days of fighting between the regular army and Social Revolutionaries manning barricades and loyal to a Moscow Soviet.

By mid-January 1906 the tsarist authorities had re-established order. It was proposed that the upper chamber of parliament, known as the Council of State, should comprise imperial nominees and members 'elected' by the Church, the nobility, the universities, local government assemblies and business organisations. The 486 members of the lower chamber, the State Duma, were to be elected on a limited franchise. When the voting was completed in late March, the constitutional democrats (Kadets) emerged as the largest party, with land reform and greater religious liberties prominent in their programme. The opportunities for launching reforms were limited by a series of decrees further safeguarding imperial autocracy. In exasperation the experienced Witte, appointed prime minister in October 1905, angrily resigned in April 1906, a fortnight before Nicholas ceremonially opened the first Duma at the Tauride Palace, the prize Catherine II bestowed on Potemkin. Despite the grandeur of their chamber, the prospects for genuine parliamentary government looked bleak

Among the Duma deputies were forty-four spokesmen for the nationalities, including Poles, Lithuanians and Estonians. The revolutionary unrest of 1905 had deep social and political consequences throughout Russia's western borderlands. Militant Social Democrats preached a class war, especially in the Latvian provinces. In the immediate aftermath of Bloody Sunday, there were violent clashes in Riga, where as many as seventy workers may have died. Mass demonstrations in Vilna brought Jews and non-Jews together in protests over government repression, while in Kaunas the trams did not run for several weeks and factories and shops closed. In Poland students boycotted lectures and classes given in Russian, and industrial workers around Warsaw went on strike for more than a month. The tsarist authorities made concessions in April: the Catholic church had many restrictions lifted and permission was given for founding, or re-founding, privately funded schools in which all teaching would be in Polish.

With the return of troops from the Far East the situation in the countryside deteriorated. A peasant *jacquerie* swept along the Baltic littoral, marked by attacks on the estates and homes of Baltic German landowners. In what is today the Letgale region of Latvia 72 manor houses went up in flames during the summer and autumn and another 111 estates were ravaged, while in Courland 42 manors were torched and 187 estates ruined.

Some 70 manors are estimated to have burnt to the ground in Estonia. The violence in the countryside led to the organization of baronial protection squads (*Selbstschutzen*), ruthless in their pursuit of vengeance. On 16 October 1905 Russian soldiers opened fire on a mass demonstration in Reval itself, leaving 150 Estonians dead or seriously wounded. Briefly in November more moderate counsels prevailed: 1,000 Latvian local government officials met in Riga to seek unified autonomy for all the Latvian provinces; while at Tartu Jaan Tõnisson convened a national congress which sought an autonomous, unified Estonia and major land reform. The political thaw did not last. By the end of the year, with all the Baltic provinces placed under martial law, the protection squads could count on support from regular troops. Repression was again rampant.

Finland received different treatment. As early as March 1905 Nicholas II withdrew the hated conscription decree and restored freedom to the Finnish judiciary. A powerful radical socialist strike committee in Tampere called for the setting up of a provisional government. But in Helsinki the Finns were slow to respond to the autumn strike call. As late as 28 October packed trains were carrying Petersburgers fleeing chaos in the capital the 30 kilometres to Valkeasaari, the Grand Duchy's border post. Three weeks later the tsar's November Manifesto rescinded the remaining decrees of the Bobrikov era and 'authorized the Senate to prepare a proposal for a new Parliament Act embodying reform of the Finnish people's assembly fitting for the times'. The senate worked with astonishing speed. Within six months the Finnish Diet had approved the creation of a unicameral parliament (Eduskunta) to be elected by universal male and female suffrage. Perhaps the least anticipated consequence of the Russian revolutionary movement was that it enabled European women to vote for the first time – on 15–16 March 1907 in the earliest elections for Finland's Eduskunta.

While the eastern Baltic lands were shaken by the revolutions of 1905, within Scandinavia the ninety-year dynastic union of Sweden and Norway ended peacefully, though only after a threat of war between the two nations. The Norwegian people had taken little interest in Baltic affairs since Bergen ceased to be a Hanse port. They saw themselves as heirs to the Viking tradition, and looked westward to Atlantic waters and beyond for their livelihood. Their parliament, the Storting, loyally upheld the basic Einsvoll Constitution of 1814 until, in the later years of Charles XV's reign, resentment grew over the king's reluctance to accept the principle of ministerial responsibility. This grievance Oscar II righted in 1884, when for the first time the leader of the majority party received official status as prime minister. Almost immediately, however, tension mounted over Swedish ministerial conduct of foreign affairs. Norway's mercantile fleet grew rapidly in the last years of the century and the Storting wanted the ships to sail under a specifically Norwegian flag, while trade would be protected by a consular service. In 1898 the Storting resolved the flag question unilaterally. When in May 1905 Oscar II forced the government to resign by rejecting a Storting Bill establishing a separate consular service, the Norwegians declared royal power in abeyance and in early June dissolved the union. The Norwegian militia manned defensive posts along the four main routes into the country from the east and the Swedish high command responded across the border.

Fortunately the ailing King Oscar and Crown Prince Gustav, showing more sense than hot-headed politicians and generals, sought reconciliation. After a plebiscite in which almost every voter in Norway opted for independence, talks were held in a small town beside Lake Vänern and reached an early settlement. Nothing could save the union, but at least the separation was amicable. The Karlstad Convention of 26 September 1905 provided for the dismantling of border fortresses and set up a 15 kilometre demilitarized zone down the long frontier between the two nations. Oscar II abdicated as ruler of Norway in October and, after his younger son declined the crown, Prince Charles of Denmark – a serving naval officer – accepted the Storting's invitation to the Norwegian throne. He acceded as Haakon VII, bolstered by a plebiscite in which 80 per cent of his subjects gave him their support. By Christmas the king, who had married Princess Maud of Wales, was in residence at the Royal Palace in Christiania. King Haakon was crowned in a simple, dignified service at Trondheim Cathedral in June 1906. Europe's first democratically elected monarch remained popular and deeply respected until his death, fifty-two years later.

The reordering of Scandinavia, the political uncertainty within Russia and her naval humiliations provided William II with an opportunity to assert his influence and authority in Baltic affairs. In the immediate aftermath of the Dogger Bank crisis he sought improved relations with Russia, even having Heinrich von Tschirschky of the foreign ministry draft a possible treaty of alliance, but once the tsar insisted on the need to consult France, in the hope of bringing Russia's ally into the combination, the matter was dropped. The draft treaty was filed, ready for use when 'Nicky' next sought German support.

That moment came sooner than he anticipated. In November 1904 the tsar still clung to a hope that the Baltic fleet would restore Russian primacy in the Far East. Tsushima shattered this already fading illusion. By June 1905 the Russians needed strong backing to avoid relegation from the Great Power league. The Kaiser suggested to the tsar that during his customary summer cruise in the imperial steam yacht *Hohenzollern* the two emperors might meet. While he was cruising off the Swedish coast he received an invitation to turn eastwards for a rendezvous with the tsar's *Polar Star* in the Gulf of Finland. At William's request the aborted alliance treaty was telegraphed to him from Berlin. He made a fair copy, adding the qualifying words 'in Europe' to the original draft.

On 23 July the *Hohenzollern* nudged cautiously through reedy shallows off Björkö island, 40 kilometres south of Vyborg. 'Grey sky, grey water, no human habitation as far as the eye could reach,' a member of the Kaiser's suite noted. The shining white steam yacht, her gold-plated rails glistening around the promenade deck, moored 'a few cable-lengths' away from the more compact *Polar Star*. Boats were lowered; social visits exchanged; cousinly small talk roundly abused Edward VII, the 'mischief-maker' of politics. No ministers or serving ambassadors were present. The Kaiser included Tschirschky from the foreign ministry among his suite; a spare admiral was in attendance on the tsar. Next morning, after more exchanges of confidence aboard *Polar Star*, William encouraged Nicholas to study the treaty he 'happened to have' in his pocket. 'If one of the two empires is attacked by a European Power, its ally will aid it in Europe with all its forces on land and sea,' the tsar read. A later article obliged him to 'initiate France into the accord' once the treaty became operative so that 'she will associate herself with it as an ally'.

'"That is quite excellent. I fully agree", the Tsar said. My heart beat so loudly that I could hear it,' the Kaiser wrote next day to Bülow, his chancellor. 'I pulled myself together and remarked casually, "Would you like to sign it? It would be a very nice souvenir of our meeting." He glanced over the paper again. Then he said, "Yes, I will."' William ended his rapturous account to Bülow on a high note: 'By the grace of God, the morning of 24 July 1905 at Björkö is a turning-point in the history of Europe and a great relief for my beloved Fatherland, which will now at last be free from the Gallo-Russian strangler's grip.'

William was deceiving himself. On returning to Berlin he found his chancellor coldly polite. Bülow emphasized the folly of the Kaiser's last-minute addition: by limiting 'aid' to Europe, he ruled out a possible diversion in Central Asia. In reality Bülow was grieved at the Kaiser's independent initiative, the autocratic stroke that reduced the chancellor and his ministers to mere administrative clerks. He threatened to resign but decided to wait upon events, suspecting that Russia's Council of Ministers, too, would rule out dynastic diplomacy as anachronistic.

He was right: the tsar disentangled himself from the reeds of Björkö only to be held tight by bonds of finance. Six weeks went by before he mustered sufficient confidence to show the 'nice souvenir' to his foreign minister, Count Lamsdorff, who was privately appalled. But three more weeks passed before the count, together with Witte and Grand Duke Nicholas, travelled out to Peterhof to persuade their sovereign to disown the treaty. Why reconcile France and Germany? they asked. More pertinently, why risk offending France when Russia needed loans and investment to stave off revolution and recover the authority of a Great Power? The objections that pigeon-holed the original draft treaty remained valid. Eleven weeks after that impetuous morning aboard the *Polar Star*, the Kaiser learnt from Nicholas that his Björkö goal was unattainable: the French obstinately failed to perceive the turning point William saw so clearly defined. For the rest of his life he looked back on Björkö as the greatest of missed opportunities.

Yet if the tsar's hands were bound by the Paris Bourse, the Kaiser was a captive of his own rhetoric, those all too frequent public utterances when he revelled in *Weltmacht*. He might cruise in Baltic waters but his vision ranged to wider oceans. Admiral von Tirpitz, State Secretary of the Navy Office since 1897, was building up the battle fleet his imperial master demanded to safeguard Germany's 'place in the sun'. By 1905 there were fourteen modern battleships at sea and eight on the stocks. Tirpitz had served for a year (in 1891) as naval chief of staff in the Baltic, but though the Navy Academy, the torpedo school and the main naval base remained at Kiel, the admiral took little interest in Baltic affairs. He looked upon the fleet as a deterrent to 'England' on the high seas. It would, he wrote soon after taking office, 'reveal its greatest military potential between Heligoland and the Thames'.

In London the government responded more quickly to the new threat than senior serving naval officers. Agitation in the press and a cabinet memorandum in October 1902 alerted the prime minister (Balfour), who in March 1903 told the Commons that a North Sea naval base would be constructed at Rosyth, in the Firth of Forth. The public mood in Britain changed, too. By 1905 the novelist William le Queux, whose *The Great War in England of 1897* had sold well during the *Rurik* scare of 1894, was writing *The Invasion of 1910*, in which the enemy was Germany. It sold even better. A reader in Berlin ordered his Navy Office to study the book closely.

Another echo of the *Rurik* alarm rang with far greater resonance. Admiral Sir John Fisher, who as Third Sea Lord in 1894 commissioned the building of two modern cruisers to counter the apparent menace in the Baltic, was by 1905 First Sea Lord, effectively the senior executive officer in the Royal Navy. Fisher now carried through a revolution in naval shipbuilding: Britain would have an all-big-gun turbine powered battleship, able to deliver shells at a greater range and to sail faster than any warship afloat. Work began on HMS *Dreadnought* on 2 October 1905; she was launched on 10 February 1906 and began her sea trials on 3 October 1906 – a revolutionary warship of over 18,200 tonnes displacement completed in 366 days.

Other navies were known to be planning similar vessels. None, however, could be developed with the speed or resources shown by the British shipyards. The first German dreadnought, *Nassau*, was not launched until March 1908 and only joined the fleet two years later, together with a sister ship, the *Westfalen*. Both battleships possessed better protective armour than their British equivalents but they had slightly lighter firepower and were slower, as they were not propelled by turbines. Soon all pre-dreadnought battleships, including the eight in German shipyards in 1905, were considered obsolete (though two survived to serve Hitler in the Baltic).

An expensive naval arms race was soon under way, with America and Japan among the competitors. By 1911 Russia, France, Italy and Austria-Hungary were building dreadnoughts. There had been so many improvements to the original model that journalists were by then writing of 'super-dreadnoughts'. The German Naval Estimates peaked at £22.4 million in 1914, a threefold increase since the start of the century, though less than half British naval expenditure (£47.4 million in 1914). There was full employment in the shipyards of Kiel, Danzig and Stettin, as well as at Hamburg and Bremen. All German warships had their sea trials in the Baltic. In case of war it was essential for them to reach the High Seas Fleet at Wilhelmshaven or Heligoland safely and speedily. Tirpitz eased the passage of dreadnoughts and heavy cruisers to the North Sea by having the Kiel Canal broadened and deepened. But the work dragged on for nearly six years – and added yet another £12.5 million to Germany's naval budget.

At Björkö Nicholas II and William II had deplored Edward VII's 'mischievous intrigues', his alleged attempts to fix agreements with other countries: 'I can only say that he will not get one from me,' the tsar affirmed. Two years later – on 31 August 1907 – an Anglo-Russian convention was signed in St Petersburg defining spheres of influence in Persia and regulating the relations of the two governments with Tibet and Afghanistan. Like the

1904 settlement with France, the convention was a settlement of old disputes in distant places; it made no reference to Europe. But Sir Edward Grey, the foreign secretary from December 1905 to December 1916, saw agreement with Russia as essential: 'An entente between Russia, France and ourselves would be absolutely secure,' he noted in a cabinet memorandum nine weeks after taking office. 'If it is necessary to check Germany it could then be done.' On 9 June 1908 Tsar Nicholas was aboard the imperial yacht *Standart* off Reval to welcome the 'mischievous intriguer' on the first British State Visit to Russia.

'The meeting of the monarchs at Reval is a feast of peace,' the newspaper *Novoe Vremya* commented, with satisfaction. Yet it was a curious State Visit for, though by now all was quiet in Estonia, Reval was thought too dangerous for King Edward to step ashore. All that the visitors saw of Nicholas's empire was the delightful view of the bay from the decks of the royal yacht *Victoria and Albert* or the attendant Russian ships. But the Reval meeting was more gregarious than Björkö. Queen Alexandra and her ladies accompanied the king; Nicholas had with him the empress and his five children and in the *Polar Star* his mother, who was the queen's sister. There were banquets, luncheons, balls and much champagne, a family reunion amid the fashionable finery of a protracted Royal Ascot. Briefly, the tsar's subjects even intruded, for on one evening a steam launch of Estonian singers and musicians serenaded the visitors. Yet the visit was not all truffles and triviality. Serious conversations took place: both the Russian prime minister (Stolypin) and the foreign minister (Izvolsky) were present; and so too were the British ambassador (Nicolson), the Permanent Under-Secretary at the Foreign Office (Hardinge), the First Sea Lord (Sir John Fisher) and the Inspector-General of the Army (Sir John French). Secret military staff talks had already begun between the British, French and Belgians. Nothing so positive was agreed at Reval and no specific undertakings were made, but the burgeoning entente held promise of collaboration between the two governments for the first time in eighty years. With an impromptu gesture King Edward created the tsar an Admiral of the Fleet: 'The Emperor is simply like a child in his delight,' Admiral Fisher noted.

Edward had wished to discuss the Jewish Question, but he stopped short of raising Russia's internal problems with his host. On the king's behalf, however, Hardinge held private talks with Stolypin, who sought to reassure him: conditions would improve for the Jews once peace and order returned to the countryside, he declared. Yet it was clear to the visitors that political life in semi-constitutional Russia remained far from normal: would they not otherwise have been welcomed in St Petersburg itself? The tsar never reconciled himself to the Duma system thrust upon him by the 1905 revolution. The First Duma survived for only ten weeks before it was dissolved and Nicholas reverted to autocracy, in July 1906 appointing Peter Stolypin as his prime minister. But Stolypin's past record made him both hated and feared by the extremists, for he had proved himself ruthlessly efficient as a provincial governor and, more recently, as minister of the interior. A month after taking office he narrowly escaped death, when three Social Revolutionary suicide bombers broke into his St Petersburg home, causing an explosion that killed twenty-five people and seriously injured his two children.

To counter terrorism Stolypin instituted a system of summary courts-martial: more than a thousand executions were carried out over the next seven months. Unlike Pobedonostsev, he did not promote anti-Semitism. But, despite his disavowals to Hardinge, he did little to restrain mob violence against the Jews. He remained a prime target for assassins, and in September 1911 was eventually shot and fatally wounded by a Jewish revolutionary, in the presence of the tsar and two of his daughters at the Kiev opera house.

Rather surprisingly, in retrospect Ambassador Nicolson adjudged Stolypin 'the most notable figure in Europe' of his time. He left statecraft to the successive foreign ministers, Izvolsky until September 1910 and thereafter Sazonov. Yet in some respects Stolypin seemed a would-be Bismarck, a retro-progressive reformer who harnessed Great Russian nationalism to offset liberalism and was ready to promote social insurance and a limited peasant ownership of land if he could retain the conservative structure of society. The tsar was persuaded to accept a Second Duma (March–June 1907) and, when that body proved too radical, even a Third Duma, which ran its full five-year term, though it was less representative than its predecessors as it had been elected on a much reduced franchise. A Fourth Duma, similar to its immediate predecessor, was elected a year after Stolypin's murder. The deputies were highly critical of defence expenditure in 1913–14 and the Duma was prorogued on the outbreak of war. In each of these Dumas non-Russian national groups continued to be represented, the best organized being the Poles, with eleven members in the Third Duma. Arguably, however, the most spectacularly successful was a Muslim group, for they changed the skyline silhouette on the right bank of the Neva. A large mosque with two minarets – the first in the Baltic – was completed in 1912, a kilometre north of the slim gilded spire above the burial cathedral of the tsars.

Stolypin treated the Duma with patronizing contempt. He exploited a constitutional loophole that allowed the sovereign to rule by legislative decree. The subject nationalities suffered accordingly. Concessions made to the Poles in 1905 were rescinded. In the Estonian and Latvian provinces, the Baltic Germans were reinstated as guardians of order. Some private German-language schools were allowed to function again, but the university at Dorpat/Yuriev remained specifically Russian. The Baltic Germans were left in no doubt that they survived as a privileged élite only on sufferance.

The abandonment of Russification in Finland particularly dismayed Stolypin. 'You, gentlemen, as representatives of the Russian people, cannot repudiate the heritage of Peter in the Gulf of Finland,' he told the Duma in May 1908, only fourteen months after the first elections to Finland's parliament. A Russo-Finnish Commission was set up to define the topics of an 'all-imperial' nature that could not be considered by the Eduskunta. Finland's parliamentarians sustained a passive rearguard action to thwart a succession of unenlightened governors-general. Twice the speaker of the Eduskunta, Pehr Svinhufvud, criticized the policy of the Duma in St Petersburg. On each occasion the Finnish parliament was dissolved and new elections returned an even more radical assembly. When, after the third election, the Duma imposed an agenda on the Eduskunta, Speaker Svinhufvud very properly protested to Finland's Grand Duke. In anger, the governor-general resorted to rule by decree. By the time of Stolypin's murder the restraints on political life in the Grand Duchy were almost as severe as in the Bobrikov era. Right-wing deputies in the Duma were demanding the transfer of the Vyborg area and much of Karelia from the Grand Duchy to Russia itself. In 1914 Svinhufvud was exiled to Siberia.

Renewed Russification in Finland angered the Swedes. So, too, did attempts by Izvolsky to win international approval to revise the Treaty of Paris so as to permit the re-fortification of the Ålands. Pressure from France and Britain led him to modify his policy. He sponsored a treaty agreed in April 1908 by which Russia, Germany, Sweden and Denmark guaranteed the Baltic *status quo*: a supplementary protocol avoided any mention of neutralization, ambiguously recognizing Russia's 'full sovereignty' over the islands. The French were uneasy, believing that Izvolsky sought a Russo-German understanding

The Swedes continued to be deeply suspicious of Russia, anxiously watching developments in the Grand Duchy. Their sympathies were, for the most part, with the Finns. At the fifth modern Olympiad, held at Stockholm in July 1912, the crowd applauded the Finnish runner Hannes Kolehmainen who took the gold medal in the 10,000 and 5,000 metres (though cheers were muted when he won the cross-country, forcing

Swedes into second and third place). Briefly Scandinavianism seemed again in the ascendant, with Finland on this occasion welcomed to the side of the trolls.

Reports of Russian military activity in the Ålands revived the long-running disputes in Stockholm over government expenditure. Should the budget give priority to pensions and social reform, as the ruling Liberal–Social Democrat coalition wished, or to battleships and new artillery? In the first week of February 1914 a widespread agrarian-conservative movement urging greater expenditure on defence culminated in a rally of 30,000 peasant farmers and a petition to Gustav V.

Astonishingly, the fifty-five-year-old monarch – who as crown prince and king had more than thirty years' experience of politics – publicly backed the rally. In full military uniform he delivered a speech to the farmers in the inner courtyard of his Stockholm palace, attacking his ministers for failing to give Sweden the modern army and navy the kingdom required. The government at once resigned; elections, held in April, cost the Liberals over a third of their seats but also increased Social Democratic representation, leaving the conservative groups in a minority. Gustav V, unable to find a political leader to whom he could give his trust, turned instead to a widely experienced civil servant and provincial governor, Hjalmar Hammarskjöld, who formed a non-party administration. Throughout the spring and summer of 1914 Sweden was in the grip of a constitutional crisis. It was by no means certain that parliamentary government would survive. Like the Irish Problem in the United Kingdom, the coming of war in Europe led to a political truce between the parties. In seeking neutrality abroad, king and politicians postponed the confrontation at home.

21

Emperors at War, 1914–1917

O N MIDSUMMER DAY in 1914 Kaiser William II reopened the newly broadened Kiel Canal. For northern Europe it was a moment of great strategic significance. When the first ships made their way through the original canal in June 1895, Germany was one of the lesser naval powers. By 1914 the Imperial Navy had become second in strength in European waters only to the Royal Navy of Great Britain. The largest German warships could now move between North Sea and Baltic overnight; gone was the need for a long voyage through the Skagerrak, Kattegat and Danish coastal waters. With understandable satisfaction, the Germans invited other navies to join their celebrations, including ships from the fleet they envied and feared. Perhaps wryly, the Royal Navy accepted the invitation. Four super-dreadnoughts and three cruisers rode at anchor in Kiel Bay on that Wednesday. Diplomatic tact ensured a naval squadron was at the eastern end of the Baltic, too, and Tsar Nicholas and his family were entertained aboard HMS *Queen Mary* one evening that week, during the 'white nights' festivities.

At Kiel the squadron stayed for several days after the ceremonial reopening and took part in the annual regatta: 'Great cordiality' on both sides, a British diplomat later recalled, though one German admiral detected 'a certain coldness in the air'. William II dined aboard the flagship named in honour of 'my cousin George' on 26 June wearing, for the last time, the uniform of a British Admiral of the Fleet. During Sunday afternoon's races a telegram arrived from the consul at Sarajevo reporting the assassination that morning of the heir to the Austro-Hungarian thrones, Archduke Franz Ferdinand, and his wife. A fortnight previously they had entertained William in Bohemia and he was deeply affected by their murder: the yacht racing was cancelled. He left Kiel next morning by train for Berlin. A few hours later HMS *King George V* led the squadron out of German waters. The sympathies of officers in both fleets were with Austria, the target of a Serb militarist conspiracy executed by young Bosnian fanatics. Kiel's flags fluttered at half-mast, but there was no sense of impending disaster for

Europe as a whole. The Baltic world, at peace for sixty years, and the constantly troubled world of the Balkan peoples seemed a continent apart.

So it remained for four more weeks, while tension mounted in the chancelleries. Outwardly the Kaiser blustered aggressively. 'The Serbs must be disposed of, and *that right soon*,' he scribbled in the margin of a report from Vienna three days after his return to Berlin. In conversation, however, he made it clear that he was thinking of a strictly localized conflict: Russian sentiment might back Serbia, but anyone could see the Russian army was 'not ready for war'; and 'the tsar would not put himself on the side of the regicides'. Nicholas II received news of the Sarajevo murders aboard the *Standart* while enjoying a family holiday off the Finnish skerries; he had seen no need to hurry back to St Petersburg and spent several more days messing around in canoes with his two elder daughters. Kaiser William approved: he did not want the crisis inflated by alarming movements of troops or warships. Eight days after the murders William returned to Kiel, embarking in the *Hohenzollern* for his annual cruise up the Sognefjord, with a light cruiser and a pinnace as escort. For twenty of the thirty-five days between the Sarajevo murders and Germany's entry into the war, the Kaiser was at sea in the Norwegian fjords or the Baltic.

He was not the only head of state in northern waters that fateful month. On 15 July President Poincaré and his premier, René Viviani (who was also France's foreign minister), left Cherbourg in the battleship *France* for a state visit to St Petersburg. The president's mission, planned long before the archduke's murder, was intended to bolster the Franco-Russian Alliance. He wished in particular to make certain that, if war came with Germany, the Russians would begin an invasion of East Prussia within sixteen days, in order to tie down German troops otherwise sent west to march on Paris. The state visit kept the international crisis from coming to the boil. For Poincaré's activities were carefully analysed by the policymakers in Vienna and Berlin. The Austrians feared that if their demands on Serbia became known while he was at St Petersburg, the news would strengthen Russo-French solidarity and military collaboration. They therefore delayed presentation of their ultimatum in Belgrade until 25 July, the day *France* and her escorting cruisers began the homeward voyage down the Gulf of Finland.

When news of the ultimatum broke, the president was about to call at Stockholm, seeking to improve relations between Sweden and Russia, France's ally and Sweden's historic enemy. Proposed visits to Copenhagen and Christiania were cancelled and *France* at once headed for Cherbourg.

But for four critical days the French republic had an absentee president, prime minister and foreign minister. Not until the afternoon of 29 July did they reach Paris. By then Austria-Hungary and Serbia were at war. On the previous evening the tsar had approved proclamation of a Preparatory War Period, a form of partial mobilization requiring reservists to report for duty in the military districts of Kazan, Kiev, Moscow and Odessa. Even so, there was no call-up in the Baltic provinces or down the long frontier with Germany, inviolate for a hundred years. The crisis was still primarily an Austro-Slav affair.

The Kaiser knew of Vienna's intentions as early as 11 July and he approved the 'pretty strong note' to Belgrade. But Russia's initial reaction to the tough terms took him by surprise: would Tsar Nicholas support Serbia after all? For the first time he contemplated action in the Baltic: on 25 July Admiral Ingenohl, commander of the High Seas fleet, was told he must be ready to destroy the facilities of Reval and Libau, the newest Russian naval base, in Latvian Courland. The admiral was uneasy. To send heavy ships close inshore in the Baltic's shallow waters was to risk disaster. Moreover he knew that the *Admiralstab* assumed the fleet would seek battle in Heligoland Bight and stand on the defensive in the Baltic. Ingenohl chose not to argue with his sovereign. It was better to listen – and ignore his wishes completely.

That attitude prevailed among army and navy chiefs in Berlin. They clung to existing war plans with rigid inflexibility. The Kaiser arrived home after noon on 27 July and busied himself with conferences and councils of war. He still hoped to avoid a general conflict. As late as the evening of 29 July he was urging the tsar 'to remain a spectator' rather than 'involve Europe in the most horrible war she has ever known'. Conciliatory 'Willy–Nicky' telegrams were exchanged between Potsdam and Peterhof up to – and even beyond – the outbreak of hostilities. They achieved nothing. The unfolding drama was shaped, not by the emperors, but by the rival General Staffs in Berlin, St Petersburg and, to a lesser extent, in Vienna and Paris.

The Preparatory War Period, authorized by Tsar Nicholas on 28 July, satisfied neither his war minister nor his chief of staff. They sought an early order for total mobilization because they feared Germany would invade before the slow-moving Russian army was on a war footing. In the afternoon of 30 July, reluctantly and under great pressure, the tsar approved general mobilization as a precautionary measure. When the news reached Berlin (at 10.30 in the morning of 31 July) Moltke, the chief of the Great General Staff, convinced the Kaiser and his chancellor that, once the Russians had completed their mobilization, they would have overwhelming numerical superiority in the East. Late in the afternoon of 31 July telegrams were sent from Berlin to St Petersburg and Paris: 'every war measure against Austria and ourselves' must be suspended 'within twelve hours': if Russia failed to comply, Germany would mobilize. There followed the chain reaction everyone feared. At seven in the evening of 1 August the German ambassador handed over a declaration of war in St Petersburg; the campaign against France began on 3 August with the invasion of Belgium; Britain went to war with Germany a day later, ostensibly in support of 'brave little Belgium'.

By then, the first action in northern Europe had already come, at sea. Gunfire reverberated across Baltic waters less than twelve hours after the declaration of war on Russia, and at a point mentioned by the Kaiser in his conversation with Ingenohl eight days previously. For soon after daybreak on 2 August the cruiser *Magdeburg* shelled Libau, while other vessels laid mines off the approaches, to keep the enemy in port and save the East Prussian and Pomeranian coasts from bombardment. The German initiative – undertaken by the Baltic squadron, not the High Seas fleet – brought little reward. No Russian warships were at Libau. They had sailed eastwards to support a protective barrier of ageing battleships guarding the Gulf of Finland. Before the end of the month Admiral Ingenohl's earlier doubts were confirmed: the *Magdeburg* was never able to shell Reval, for the cruiser was lost on rocks as she approached the Estonian island of Osmussaar. An escorting destroyer saved most of her crew – but vital naval code books, with ciphers, were salvaged by the Russians, who passed on one copy to the Royal Navy, an invaluable asset for the fledgling Intelligence Room at the Admiralty. The war in the Baltic Sea had begun badly for the Germans.

They had greater success in the Baltic hinterland, however. On 17 August the Russian First Army, commanded by General Rennenkampf, invaded East Prussia, but the advance on Königsberg from the Vilnius–Kaunas railway was checked soon after the frontier by a flank attack, leading to the capture of some 3,000 prisoners. This first minor victory made the Germans over-confident, and on 20 August they were surprised when Rennenkampf's artillery inflicted heavy casualties on three Grenadier regiments of the Eighth Army at Gumbinnen (Gusev) and withstood a counter-attack by the German XVII Corps, including the élite 'Death's Head' Hussars. That same day, some 95 kilometres to the south, the Russian Second Army, under General Samsonov, moved forward around the forested lakes of Masuria. The Germans were alarmed. The modified

Schlieffen Plan, on which grand strategy was based, provided for concentration in the West in order to defeat France before the slow-moving Russians could mount an invasion – unlikely, it was assumed, before the fortieth day of war. To their consternation, two Russian armies now threatened the historic heartland of the Junker officer corps as early as Day 19. General von Prittwitz, the Eighth Army commander, even warned Moltke at Imperial Headquarters that he might not be able to keep the Russians from crossing the Vistula 'because of the low level of water in the river'.

Headquarters reacted vigorously. Prittwitz lost his command. He was replaced by General Paul von Beneckendorf und Hindenburg, a veteran of Bismarck's wars, six weeks short of his sixty-seventh birthday. General Erich Ludendorff, whose initiative had recently made possible the capture of Liège, was appointed Hindenburg's chief of staff. But before the newcomers reached East Prussia a gifted staff officer, Colonel Max Hoffmann, devised a plan which when adopted by Hindenburg and Ludendorff gave the Germans their first great victory of the war.

Basically the plan sought to deflect the threatened Russian envelopment and substitute for it a German pincer movement that would clear the enemy from East Prussia. Hoffmann, aware of a personal vendetta between the two Russian generals, proposed concentrating the field army on the southern front against Samsonov: he was confident that if Rennenkampf thought the Germans were falling back on the Baltic coast he would commit the First Army to securing the prestigious prize of Königsberg, rather than swing his troops southwards to support the Second Army. Rennenkampf fell for the bait: a captured army order, found on a dead Russian officer, revealed that he would halt his advance at the approaches to Königsberg on 26 August and await the arrival of heavy artillery before launching an attack on the heavily fortified city. The information completed Hindenburg's resolve to back Hoffmann's plan to the hilt. German feint withdrawals divided Samsonov's invading force: the left wing almost reached the Vistula but was caught by a German counterattack on 27 August which separated it from the centre, forcing the Russians to pull back in panic. Next day the XVII Corps, striking southwards from Gumbinnen, dented Samsonov's right wing while the Russian centre, approaching the village of Tannenberg, came under heavy attack to the south-west of Lake Mühlen. Before noon on 29 August German troops from north and south met in the town of Willenberg: Samsonov's army was encircled. No less than 92,000 Russians passed into German captivity over the next two days and at least 50,000 are thought to have perished on the battlefield. So great was the disaster that, in his despair, Samsonov shot himself.

Ludendorff drafted a message to the Kaiser reporting the victory from his advanced headquarters in the village of Frögenau; and by that unfamiliar name the battle might have gone down in history. But a deeper sense of the past prevailed. A Beneckendorf and a Hindenburg were slain at Tannenberg in 1410 when the Teutonic Knights suffered defeat at the hands of Jagiello's Polish-Lithuanian warriors: so were the ancestors of many other Prussian Junkers. Now, more than 500 years later, the humiliation of 1410 was avenged by a victory of Teuton over Slav in the same sandy, forested lakeland. From the cluster of villages in the area, Hindenburg chose Tannenberg rather than Frögenau as the name of the battle. His victory passed into legend, sustaining German morale through the vicissitudes of thirty years, until the Red Army overran the East Prussian border in January 1945 and old place-names disappeared from the map. Today's Polish villages of Stębark and Sudwa prefer to forget that in the 1920s and the 1930s their fields and hillocks were hallowed ground for German patriots.

Tannenberg gave Germany a historic victory but not a decisive triumph. The Russian First Army remained in the field, at the outer approaches to Königsberg. Hindenburg, strengthened by two army corps brought speedily by railway from the Western Front, sought to encircle Rennenkampf's First Army in the battle of the Masurian lakes (7–14 September), one of the strangest engagements of the First World War. In unseasonably hot weather the Germans thrust northwards along the three main routes winding between fifteen lakes and yet, except in the centre at Lötzen, they never totally cut off any Russian units. Rennenkampf threw two divisions into a counter-attack on 10 September, allowing the main body of his First Army to fall back to the pre-war frontier; the weary infantry had to march 30 kilometres a day under a scorching sun down roads clogged by the guns, wagons and trucks that were to have besieged Königsberg. Either from exhaustion or momentary indecision, the Germans failed to press home their advantage and the battle ended in unexpected deliverance of an apparently doomed army.

Rennenkampf lost more than a quarter of his men and more than 200 pieces of artillery in the month-long campaign. Even so, with the survivors bolstered by reinforcements, he was able to launch a surprise counter-offensive on 25 September that recovered a small segment of territory south of Gumbinnen. Not until the third week of February 1915 were the Russians finally evicted from East Prussia, after the 'winter battle of

Masuria', fought mainly in fog or blizzard within the dense, ice-encrusted Augustów forest. Another 12,000 Russians passed into captivity.

By the spring of 1915 the Eastern Front ran from Memel on the Baltic coast to Czernowitz (Chernovtsy), some 800 kilometres away, in the eastern Carpathians. Hindenburg and Ludendorff favoured a scythe-like sweep through the Baltic provinces so as to envelop the tsar's main armies. They were overruled: High Command (OHL) was more interested in plans for a breakthrough in central Poland or Galicia. But strategic advances were made in the north in order to keep in step with movements farther south: Libau was taken on 8 May, with support from a powerful naval force including four cruisers and four old battleships; and two months later the navy gave similar backing to the capture of Windau. Zeppelins from a base near Königsberg bombed distant railway junctions. But the brunt of the fighting was borne by highly trained specialist troops. Inland, Kaunas was bombarded into surrender by 1,360 heavy guns on 18 August; Vilnius fell a month later, and for a few days three cavalry divisions roamed the boundless undulating plain to the east. They penetrated 150 kilometres into Belorussia without being able to hold any town, village or railway junction long enough for the infantry to consolidate their gains. There were no trophies of victory. Villages, farmsteads, granaries and factories were fired by the retreating Russians so as to deny the enemy any resources of value.

The German offensive petered out, with the prize of Riga still in Russian hands and a defensive line of some 225 kilometres established from the sandhills and marshland of the coast upstream along the river Dvina to Dvinsk. An advanced Zeppelin base was constructed at Vainode, near Libau, with five hangars; elaborate plans were made to raid Petrograd (as St Petersburg was renamed in a burst of patriotic anti-Germanism early in the war). But icy conditions over the northern sea fouled engines and made the airships over-heavy, ruling out long-range flights and any terror bombardment of Russia's capital from the air. Thereafter the Front changed little for the next two years. German preoccupation with Verdun and the Somme and the need to support Austria-Hungary in Galicia and Romania prevented any initiative along the Baltic seaboard: 'We must do without Riga – unless the Russians abandon it to us. We are too weak up there,' Hoffmann wrote in his diary late in August 1915. The general's assessment remained valid a year later.

From the earliest days of the war, the clash of rival empires posed questions of loyalty and commitment for all the Baltic peoples. Wisely the tsar never attempted to conscript his Finnish subjects, though a special war defence tax was levied in the Grand Duchy. A Finnish volunteer corps fought courageously beside the Russians in the harsh winter conditions of March 1915 along the slopes of the Carpathians, and Baron Gustaf Mannerheim, a Finn of Swedish descent from Askainen who was commissioned in a prestigious cavalry regiment, rose to the rank of major general. His personal loyalty to Tsar Nicholas II was never in question; even as late as 1939 a signed portrait of 'my emperor' was prominently displayed in the sitting room of Mannerheim's home in Helsinki.

Other Finnish patriots thought their cause could best be advanced under German patronage and a meeting was held on 26 January 1915 at the War Ministry in Berlin to consider how best to employ them. It was agreed that Finnish sympathizers should travel secretly across Sweden to the Lockstädt 'instruction camp' near Altona, where they would receive basic military training. They would then return to Sweden, ready to assist the Germans if the High Command decided to invade Finland or to respond to an anti-Russian uprising. But the number of Finns making the journey to Altona was much greater than the Germans had anticipated. Rather than keep them in reserve, as what would later be called a Fifth Column, the Kaiser authorized the formation of a Finnish light infantry battalion within the Prussian army, assigned in 1916 to the Daugava sector of the Eastern Front.

The persistent social democratic tradition in Courland and Livonia, so active in 1905, raised doubts in Petrograd over the loyalty of the tsar's Latvian subjects. But local volunteers helped regular Russian troops defend Jelgava, the old capital of Courland, in August 1915 and showed such courage and initiative that, with the tsar's sanction, eight specifically Latvian battalions were raised to strengthen resistance to the German invader. The Latvian Riflemen Regiments (as they soon became known) were to fight with great tenacity in defence of Riga. Most of the riflemen later supported the Bolsheviks, but some transferred their loyalty to the movement for total independence when the Red Army sought to impose a Soviet system on their country.

Two social groups (who were, in fact, mutually antagonistic) aroused much mistrust in Petrograd. The loyalty of the Baltic Germans was suspect, especially families who had arrived in Courland and Livonia during the past hundred years: many had kinsmen among the great Junker landowners, with whom they were commonly believed to be in contact. At the same time, tsardom's institutional anti-Semitism bore heavily down on the Jews of inner Lithuania: they were considered 'Germanized' because they spoke Yiddish, a language regarded by the Russians as a dialect of German. On 3 May 1915 all Jews living west of a line from Kaunas to Bauska were given forty-eight hours to collect their belongings and board trains that carried them eastwards for resettlement in Poltava and Ekaterinoslav, the two easternmost provinces within the Pale. There were, in reality, deep social and political divisions among Jewish communities in the Baltic provinces. A more subtle government would have sought to exploit these differences rather than resort to heavy-handed repression.

The Poles remained an enigma. In the 1830s Adam Mickiewicz had urged his compatriots to 'pray for the universal war for the freedom of nations': only from a general conflagration would a phoenix Poland re-emerge, he believed. But how? Eighty years later the dilemma puzzled and divided his successors. As so often in earlier years, the Russians hoped to win support from the Poles for 'the common fight against Germany'. In the first days of the war, before Tannenberg brought an end to the advance on the lower Vistula, Grand Duke Nicholas, the supreme commander of Russia's armies in the field, published a manifesto in which he declared that 'under the sceptre of Russia, Poland should be born again, free in religion, in language and in self-government'. Tsar Nicholas II repeated the pledge in November and December 1916, but past experience left the Poles mistrustful of any offer from Petrograd.

The Poles showed no greater enthusiasm for German-Austrian proposals for a kingdom of Poland militarily dependent on Berlin and Vienna. Josef Pilsudski, who was born in the outskirts of Vilnius and had been a rebel against tsarist autocracy for some twenty years, commanded a Polish brigade in the Austro-Hungarian army. He was allowed to set up a Supreme National Council in Cracow. After the fall of Warsaw in August 1915 he was even prepared to accept office as minister of war in a puppet Polish administration. The Germans, however, distrusted Pilsudski and in July 1917 he was ousted and imprisoned at Magdeburg.

Yet as the war dragged on into a fourth year, a German solution looked less and less attractive and a Russian solution impossible. It was natural for the Poles to turn for support to their traditional patrons, the French. In Paris Roman Dmowski, who had led the Polish group in the Third Duma, presided over a Polish National Committee which claimed the status of a government-in-exile. At the same time, the concert pianist Ignace Paderewski became a skilled spokesman for the Polish cause in the United States, where so many emigrants from Eastern Europe were settled in flourishing communities and President Wilson, elected for a second term in 1916, was increasingly respected as the prophet of a new world order based upon the right of subject peoples to determine the future of their nation.

By contrast, Wilhelmine Germany wasted little sympathy on the aspirations of Europe's submerged peoples. Both the High Command and Chancellor Bethmann Hollweg sought territorial expansion along the Baltic coast. Proposals to include the annexation of Lithuania and Courland among the list of German war aims were put forward in the aftermath of Tannenberg and revived two years later, when Ludendorff and other generals began to encourage the 'colonization' of the occupied territories by families from East Prussia and the Altmark. The Foreign Ministry also backed emigrant groups – particularly any associated with Russia's Baltic Germans – and in April 1915 welcomed the establishment of a League of Foreign Peoples of Russia (*Fremdvölker Russlands*). Satellite administrations were subsequently set up in occupied Lithuania and Courland.

A totally different set of problems faced the countries controlling entry to the Baltic. On 1 August 1914 the church bells of Sweden had rung out as a mobilization call for all army reservists; but within a few days Denmark, Norway and Sweden all declared their neutrality and in December their kings met at Malmö to emphasize Scandinavian unity. Before work had begun on broadening the Kiel Canal, the German Admiralty (*Admiralstab*) had urged the army to give the occupation of Denmark, and possibly Norway, high priority in their war plans, a proposal roundly rejected by the great Schlieffen as diverting men and material from the main initial objectives of German strategy. In 1914 the small Danish army stood guard along a land frontier by now held for half a century. At sea the Danes laid minefields in the Belts and in the Sound, providing pilots to guide merchant ships through safe channels. They also completed five years of work on the island fortress of Middelgrund, to strengthen Copenhagen's defences against any latter-day Nelson.

The Swedes were reluctant to encumber their territorial waters with mines and it was not until July 1916 that they laid a protective field on their side of the Kogrund Channel, at the southern end of the Sound. Yet Sweden rather than Denmark was the kingdom most at risk from a preemptive strike. On the outbreak of war the Swedish navy – ten old battleships, one modern cruiser, a destroyer flotilla and some fifty torpedo boats – concentrated off Faro and northern Gotland. The commander of Russia's Baltic fleet, Admiral Essen, was convinced the Swedes would enter the war on the German side and land an army on Finland's southern coast. In collaboration with his chief of operations, Commander Kolchak (the future anti-Bolshevik leader), Essen planned a surprise descent on Faro, where an ultimatum would be delivered to the Swedish admiral warning him that the Russians would open fire unless he agreed to return to

Karlskrona under escort and remain there until the war ended. On 9 August 1914, on his own initiative, Essen sailed from Helsinki for Faro with five battleships, ten cruisers, destroyers and torpedo boats. Fortunately news of his sortie reached St Petersburg in time for a peremptory wireless message to be sent ordering him back to port. Had the encounter taken place it is hard to see how Sweden could have avoided entering the war as Germany's ally.

The General Staff in Berlin would have welcomed a working partnership. On the opening day of the war, General von Moltke told the foreign minister: 'We should strive to get Sweden to mobilize her entire armed forces immediately. Sweden's undertakings should be so guided that her measures would inspire and maintain in Russia the fear of an attack by her on Finland.' Any of 'Sweden's desires' must be met, 'so long as they are compatible with German interests'. As soon as the Swedes agreed to enter a joint war, Denmark and Norway would be requested to follow Stockholm's example: 'the Scandinavian nations' should unite 'with Germany to oppose Russia's unappeasable hunger for territory'. But the Foreign Ministry preferred a benevolent neutrality from Germany's northern neighbours, especially Sweden: it was better for trade, and Swedish contact with the Finns provided opportunities to promote revolution among the tsar's disaffected subjects.

Within Sweden public opinion was traditionally anti-Russian, and became increasingly anti-British when London imposed a blockade of Germany. As early as 7 August 1914 the British ambassador warned Sir Edward Grey that Sweden might join the enemy camp; and in May 1916 Grey commented to Lloyd George on Germany's 'desperate efforts to bring Sweden into the war'. 'She may succeed in doing so,' he added. But Sweden's prime minister, Hjalmar Hammerskjöld, was too canny to fall into line beside the German generals; and although King Gustav V never concealed his dislike of everything Russian, he was no more inclined than his grandfather in 1854 to see his army bogged down in Finland.

The blockade inevitably led to social hardship. A rationing system was introduced in the winter of 1916–17, with the government belatedly trying to check food hoarding and unscrupulous profiteering. 'Hunger-skjöld', the prime minister was now called by satirical journalists. His resignation in April 1917 uncorked the political crisis left unresolved when war enveloped Europe. It was followed by four months of political uncertainty, with violent demonstrations in the heart of Stockholm on 5 June – Sweden's national day – and demands for genuinely democratic government. After a general election in September 1917 a coalition of Liberals and

Social Democrats, led by Nils Eden, kept Sweden at peace during the last turbulent year of the Great War and completed preparations for the introduction in 1921 of universal suffrage for both sexes.

Sweden's neutrality was not unprofitable. The gold reserves increased by £10 million between 1914 and 1919, almost entirely through trade with Germany. Despite the food shortage in many homes and the high price of basic commodities, some working-class families benefited from the war, with steady employment in the heavy industries and mining in particular. By early summer 1915 Swedish iron ore from the mines around Gällivare, essential to German steel production, was shipped from Luleå in convoy down the Gulf of Bothnia, escorted by Swedish naval vessels as far as the island of Öland and then by torpedo boats to the north German coast. From October to April, when ice kept Luleå closed, the railway in the far north brought the iron ore to the ice-free Norwegian port of Narvik, whence it was carried southward by ship through the Innereled (Inner Leads), Norwegian territorial waters lying inside the string of coastal islands and free of minefields until the last winter of the war.

The iron-ore trade put relations between London and Stockholm under strain. Even so, in the early stages of the war Sweden kept her neutrality fairly balanced. The Swedish navy facilitated the return to home ports of twenty-nine British ships trapped in the Baltic by the declaration of war, interposing torpedo boats to prevent attacks on the merchantmen by German warships within their territorial waters.

For the western allies the Baltic remained a closed arena for most of the war. On 1 May 1914 the foreign secretary had notified Britain's ambassador in Paris that 'It would not be considered safe in time of war for the British fleet to enter the Baltic, lest the fleet should be caught in a trap and find its communications cut off'. Yet fourteen weeks later – on 19 August – Winston Churchill, as First Lord of the Admiralty, was ready to propose joint naval and military action in Baltic waters to Grand Duke Nicholas, the Russian commander-in-chief. A powerful British fleet, preceded by minesweepers and escorting ships able to accommodate large numbers of troops, would sail down the Kattegat, brush aside resistance from Germany's Baltic Squadron, embark a Russian expeditionary force in the Gulf of Riga, and sail back westwards to land the troops on Germany's Pomeranian coast 'only 90 miles [145 km] in the direct line' from Berlin. It was the earliest Churchillian flight of imaginative strategy. Grand Duke Nicholas, replying on the eve of Tannenberg, tactfully welcomed the proposal 'should the general military situation lend itself to its application' but the project courted disaster and was, fortunately, abandoned. As a gesture of support, however, three submarines were sent to the Baltic in mid-October: one was forced to return home, but *E.1* and *E.9* duly made their way through the Sound and were eventually based on Lapvik in south-western Finland, remaining under Russian operational command until the Bolshevik Revolution.

At times there seem to have been echoes from sixty years back, when Napier's 'terrible squadrons' were expected to 'swamp the Baltic'. For Churchill was not the only champion of Baltic initiatives at the Admiralty. On 29 October Admiral of the Fleet Lord Fisher became in effect the professional executive commander of a Royal Navy at war. At the age of seventy-three, he was reappointed First Sea Lord, the post he held from 1904 to 1910, years in which on several occasions he had sent the fleet into the Baltic for summer manoeuvres. As a midshipman Fisher served in northern waters at the end of the Crimean War, an experience he never forgot. Like Churchill, he thought Germany's Baltic coast vulnerable. His printed correspondence shows that even when out of office Fisher was obsessed with landing an army under the heavy guns of the fleet '90 miles from Berlin on that 14 miles of sandy beach'. Where the beach was located he did not make clear. Is it possible the admiral placed too much faith in the infallibility of Baedeker? On page 165 of the 1913 edition of *Northern Germany* the nearest beaches, at Warnemünde, are shown as 82 miles (132 km) by rail from Berlin, whereas the real distance was close to 140 miles (225 km). Stettin was indeed about 90 miles (145 km) from the capital, but more than 40 miles (65 km) upriver from any stretch of sandy beach.

As soon as Fisher was back as First Sea Lord he called for the rapid building of two fast cruisers, with four 15-inch guns and low draught, designed specifically for operations in the Baltic. Churchill's earlier proposal of employing Russian troops was replaced by a succession of plans for landing a British invasion force, either by using a captured German North Sea island as a stepping-stone or in collaboration with Denmark, which would be tempted into the war with promises of recovering Schleswig-Holstein. So enthusiastic was Churchill that he told the War Council late in January 1915 that 'the ultimate object of the Navy was to obtain access to the Baltic'. He was still prepared to advocate this strategy in northern waters two months later, at a time when he was primarily concerned with the attempt to force the Dardanelles and enter Europe's innermost protected sea.

Failure at the Dardanelles and the tragic mishandling of the Gallipoli campaign discouraged speculative enterprise elsewhere in Europe. Fisher, increasingly critical of Churchill, resigned in a huff on 15 May 1915, and when Churchill himself left the Admiralty ten days later the prospect of British surface ships operating in Baltic waters receded. A raid by destroyers and light cruisers was mooted in the autumn of 1915 and a Russian request for a 'weighty and prolonged' diversion when the ice melted considered in February 1916. Both proposals were rejected: they would have wasted ships and men's lives, it was argued; and they were more likely to offend neutral Denmark and Sweden than assist the allied cause. But the Royal Navy gave the Russians increased support in the submarine war: three more E-class submarines made the dangerous voyage through the Sound and reached Reval in September 1915. Twelve months later two smaller C-class vessels arrived at Kronstadt, having been shipped to Archangel and carried slowly by barges down 1,450 kilometres of northern Russia's rivers and canals.

Although Russia's smaller warships engaged in skirmishes on several occasions and attacked German convoys between the Åland Islands and Gotland, there was no major battle at sea in the Baltic. 'We do not want a second Tsushima,' Tsar Nicholas insisted, gloomily. The vital need was to protect Petrograd. Minefields, coastal batteries and anti-submarine nets covering the 80-kilometre channel between Helsinki and Reval were backed up by a screen of battleships and heavy cruisers, while a second defensive squadron – including two old battleships – remained in the vicinity of the Åland Islands in case Germany or Sweden sought to cross the Gulf of Bothnia and land troops on the Finnish coast. Admiral Essen chafed at the restraints imposed upon him, especially when intercepted signals gave a clear idea of German dispositions. Essen, however, died suddenly in May 1915 and was succeeded as commander of the Baltic fleet by a cautious mine-laying specialist, Vice Admiral Kanin, who was content to stay on the defensive. The *Rurik* and her sister ship *Rossiya*, the cruisers that caused such alarm in London when they were launched twenty years previously, were among the heavy ships limited to mine-laying tasks.

In September 1916 the more enterprising Admiral Nepenin, a former head of naval intelligence, took command. He had an immediate stroke of good fortune when a German flotilla, bombarding positions along the Estonian coast, ran into one of Kanin's minefields and lost seven destroyers in a single night (9–10 November). The Baltic fleet acquired three newly built dreadnoughts that autumn, but there was no time for Nepenin to complete sea trials before the ice closed in. Throughout the winter the capital ships remained inactive off Helsinki, with their crews short of food. The men were bored, demoralized and receptive to insidious anti-war propaganda. So, too, were sailors in the Russian capital.

On 8 March a demonstration in Petrograd by industrial workers in favour of 'Bread and Peace' was supported by many conscripts in the army. Bloodshed soon followed. On 13 March the captain of the twenty-year-old cruiser *Aurora*, refitting in Petrograd, was murdered by some of his crew; forty officers and petty officers at Kronstadt suffered a similar fate that same day. Revolution had come to Russia. Nicholas II abdicated on 15 March. Members of the Duma formed a Provisional Government, although its authority was challenged by a rival Soviet of Workers' Soldiers' and Peasants' Deputies. Chaos prevailed across the capital, with more than a hundred factories on strike. A tide of wild rumour spread to other cities and to the troops at the Front. When news of events in Petrograd reached the disaffected seamen at Helsinki, they too rose in revolt and on 17 March murdered several officers, including the admiral in command of the Second Battleship squadron. Discipline in the big ships of the fleet had completely broken down.

At first the Germans remained passive observers of the revolutionary chaos: an offensive on land, or by sea in the Gulf of Finland, might rally their enemy in defence of the homeland. Instead, they preferred to stoke the flames of revolt by helping exiled extremists return to Russia. Over the previous eighteen months Count von Brockdorff-Rantzau, the German Minister in Stockholm, had built up a network of agents in contact with Russian exiles in Switzerland, including the leader of the Bolshevik faction, Lenin. On the fall of the tsar, Brockdorff-Rantzau urged the authorities in Berlin to use the radical socialists 'to create the greatest possible chaos in Russia', a policy welcomed not only by Chancellor Bethmann Hollweg but also by Ludendorff, who from August 1916 was the principal architect of German strategy. On his initiative a train was provided on 9 April to take Lenin and some thirty companions back from Berne to Sassnitz, on the Baltic coast. It was agreed that, during the journey, the Russians would have no contact with any German. A Swiss Social Democrat travelled with them as a neutral intermediary.

The 'sealed train', trundling thirty sticks of human dynamite 1,200 kilometres across one autocracy to blow up another, figures prominently in the mythology of the Russian Revolution. Yet the lesser-known second part of the journey, from Sassnitz to Petrograd, makes a more interesting tale, a commentary on Baltic uncertainties in this fateful spring. From Sassnitz the whole party took the regular ferry service across to Trelleborg, south of Malmö, and went on by train to Stockholm. Lenin was briefly feted at the

Hotel Regina; he met Swedish socialist parliamentarians and Russian exiles but took care to avoid all contact with Germans or known agents of Brockdorff-Rantzau. The newspaper *Politiken* carried his photograph, describing him as the leader of Russia's revolution. After such publicity, he decided against crossing by ferry to Turku, where he might be arrested as soon as he stepped ashore. Instead, he obtained a travel permit from the Consul General and set out on another – far longer – train journey around the Gulf of Bothnia to the Finnish western provincial city of Oulu and into Karelia. To Lenin's consternation it looked as if British soldiers were augmenting the Russian guards at Tornio, the first station in Finland, but after he completed the necessary form – 'Vladimir Ulyanov . . . journalist of Russian nationality and Orthodox religion . . . political refugee, not intending to stop in Finland' – he was allowed to continue his journey.

On 16 April he arrived, famously, at Petrograd's Finland Station, where hundreds of workers had been waiting for several hours to greet him. Lieutenant Maximov with a volunteer guard of honour from the Baltic fleet saluted the Bolshevik leader. A band, as yet unfamiliar with the *Internationale*, played the *Marseillaise*, the anthem that had rung out for President Poincaré a thousand days earlier. Lenin was escorted to the tsar's waiting room and on to Bolshevik headquarters in Mathilde Kshesinskaia's mansion, 'the satin nest of a court ballerina' (in Trotsky's characteristic phrase). 'The war that is now waging is not our war,' Lenin emphasized each time he addressed the faithful; peace must come soon.

Yet Russia was still technically a belligerent partner of Britain and France, and the depth of their ally's war-weariness was not recognized in London or Paris. Six days after Nicholas II's abdication the French commander-in-chief sent a telegram to Russian field headquarters asking for an offensive to be launched against the Germans within a month so as to prevent the enemy from transferring troops to the Western Front. It was an absurdly unrealistic request: throughout April the desertion rate in the Russian army consistently stood higher than a thousand a day, and the arms and munitions factories around Petrograd remained on strike. Along the Latvian and Estonian coast Russian minelayers were active, but the larger vessels stayed at their moorings.

Russia was also still nominally a monarchy, and Prince Lvov's Provisional Government hesitated over the fate of the Romanovs. Might a British warship be allowed by the Germans to cross the Baltic and take Tsar Nicholas and his family into exile? Four days after the tsar's abdication Paul Milyukov, Lvov's foreign minister, suggested to the British ambassador that the imperial family might go to Britain, and sanctuary was formally offered in a reply from London on 22 March. Kaiser William subsequently asserted that he had forbidden German surface or submarine attacks on any ship with the family aboard. Nothing came of the proposal: some members of the Provisional Government were alarmed by rumours that Nicholas would go no farther than Denmark, his mother's homeland; and King George V, increasingly aware of the unpopularity of 'Nicky and Alicky' in England and worried over the stability of his own throne, changed his mind. Kerensky, who became minister of war on 15 May and prime minister on 25 July, at last proclaimed Russia a republic. In the third week of August 1917 the tsar and his family were removed from the turbulent Baltic hinterland to Tobolsk in Siberia, allegedly for their personal safety. They were killed by the Bolsheviks at Ekaterinburg eleven months later

The Eastern Front flared up again in midsummer 1917. Allied threats to cut off all supplies to the Provisional Government induced Kerensky to risk launching an offensive on 30 June in Galicia. For two days reports from the Front led him to believe all was going well, but in reality the Russians were suffering heavy casualties and their second-line reserves lacked the courage of the first wave of assault troops. There were mass desertions and, in the rear, anarchy. In the third week of July a German and Austro-Hungarian counter-offensive swept away all resistance. Similar disasters in the French Revolution advanced the career of General Bonaparte, and momentarily it seemed as if Kerensky had found a Russian Napoleon: at this grave hour he appointed as commander-in-chief Lavre Kornilov, a soldier of the people and a Cossack. He expected General Kornilov to use cavalry and his own, personally loyal, troops from the mountains of the Caucasus to rid Petrograd of the Soviet before rallying patriotic support against the German enemy at the gates. But Kornilov lacked the Bonaparte touch. Although Lenin left the city and went into hiding in Finland, Kornilov failed to disarm or disperse the Red Guards. And when Kornilov turned on his patron and attempted a coup d'état, Kerensky outwitted him.

The victory in Galicia, and the chronic chaos in Petrograd, persuaded the Germans to resume the advance in the Baltic provinces, where the front line had changed little since the capture of Windau in July 1915. Ludendorff ordered a surprise attack on Riga in late August, preceded by a short but heavy artillery barrage to cut a pathway through the city's defences. The tactic was successful, and on 3 September Riga, the finest Russian port in the Baltic, finally fell. The wharves and docks could not, however, be used as an advance base for a march on Petrograd: nor, indeed, could the facilities of Dünamünde, the smaller port at the mouth of the Daugava. For the Russian navy still controlled entry to the Gulf of Riga, with shore batteries on Ösel – now the Estonian island of Saaremaa – covering both minefields and the main coastal roads. The Baltic fleet had a protected anchorage off Kuivastu on Moon island (Muhu), where two battleships, three cruisers and more than thirty smaller craft, together with three submarines of the Royal Navy, kept watch on the Gulf. Apart from the crew of one minelayer, discipline and morale at Kuivastu was better than along the Finnish shore; the ships had remained on vigilant patrol, rather than swinging round buoys waiting for nothing to happen, like the squadron at Helsinki.

The threat of mutiny hung over other navies, too, including Germany's High Seas fleet. There was serious trouble at Wilhelmshaven on several occasions, mainly over the poor quality of food. Ominously, on the very day German newspapers were celebrating the capture of Riga, a stoker and a seaman from two of the dreadnoughts faced a firing squad for 'treasonable incitement to rebellion'. As a senior naval officer told Tirpitz, it was imperative to 'bring a fresh breath of air into the fleet'. Accordingly, within a fortnight of the fall of Riga, Kaiser William personally approved a joint operation (codename 'Albion') to capture the islands of Ösel and Moon. The German armada comprised some 300 vessels, supported by more than 100 aircraft and six airships, with an assault force of 24,000 infantry (including a brigade of cyclists). Eleven capital ships – as many as the first line of allied battleships in the thrust up the Dardanelles – were detached from the High Seas fleet and sent through the Kiel Canal to the Baltic's shallow waters. Five cruisers, three flotillas of destroyers, torpedo boats and minesweepers followed the dreadnoughts to supplement the fleet at Kiel. Admiral Hipper had led a squadron of High Seas battleships eastwards to support the army's advance along the Latvian coast two years previously, but the planners envisaged 'Albion' as a far grander operation. Never before in Baltic history had such firepower been unleashed on such limited objectives.

The landings were successful: the assault troops sustained less than 400 casualties and took 20,000 Russian prisoners. But it was still impossible to open up the channel to Dünamünde and Riga. Behind their minefields, the heavy guns of the Russian ships fought back for a whole week (12–19 October 1917). The Germans lost a destroyer, three torpedo boats and eight minesweepers. More significantly, three dreadnoughts were among several warships mined before the bombardment began: the *Bayern* was damaged so severely that she was still limping back to Kiel at the end of the month. The Russians lost a modern destroyer and a twenty-eight-year-old battleship. Yet when their remaining vessels at last steamed up the coast to Reval, three blockships, a netted boom and a new minefield kept the channel out of Riga closed. The almost forgotten battle of Moon Island was a last act of defiance by the fleet Tsar Peter had founded.

The coming of a fourth winter of war intensified the suffering and chaos in Petrograd. On 29 October Lenin returned secretly from Finland, to learn from Trotsky that the Bolsheviks could count on 20,000 committed Red Guards in the capital, together with many thousands of regular troops and the backing of the fleet at Kronstadt. It was, however, Kerensky who decided to take the initiative, and for two days there were clashes with demonstrators in the streets of the capital until, on the evening of 7 November, the cruiser *Aurora* sailed up the Neva. At a range of 2.5 kilometres, she trained her 6-inch guns on the Winter Palace, home of the Provisional Government. A blank shot was fired at twenty minutes to ten, the first of a volley.

Red Guards broke into the palace. The government ministers fled or were held captive. The Bolsheviks, 'the Party of Bread and Peace', had triumphed. Executive power passed to the Soviets. Lenin called for a ceasefire and on 15 December a three month armistice was concluded at Brest-Litovsk pending peace talks. After 1,232 days of conflict Russia went out of the 'imperialist war'.

22

Revolution and Independence

THE DRAMA OF events in Petrograd in the spring and summer of 1917 alternately elated and alarmed the Baltic peoples of the fallen empire. None of their leaders anticipated the sudden and complete disappearance of the Russian monarchy, nor had they mapped out possible paths towards independence. Each nationality was at a different stage of development. The Finns had the advantages of a long tradition of self-government, experienced parliamentarians, and widely acknowledged national boundaries. The Estonians were newcomers, administratively and socially; the Latvian-speaking provinces were not even unified and increasingly under German control; Lithuania was totally occupied, its future uncertain. As in 1905, most politicians in Finland and the Baltic provinces still thought in terms of national autonomy within a reconstituted liberal Russia.

So, it would appear, did the Provisional Government in Petrograd. For as early as the second week of April 1917 Finland's full constitutional rights were restored and the repressive restraints of a quarter of a century lifted. At the same time a Law of Estonian Autonomy authorized the creation of an elected assembly (Maapäev), to weld together the administration of a unified province within Estonia's 'natural boundaries'. Jaan Poska, the liberal mayor of Tallinn, was appointed Government Commissioner. On 21 April he began raising a local militia, an embryonic Estonian army, and in May and June there were elections to the Maapäev even in remote rural areas. Only one communist candidate was successful. Estonia's path to independence seemed promisingly uncluttered. But in October 1917 Bolsheviks seized power in Tallinn, forcing the Maapäev to delegate authority to an underground committee.

Jaan Tõnisson, the Estonian National Liberal spokesman in Petrograd, had urged the Provisional Government to make comparable concessions in neighbouring Latvia. His advice was ignored. So, too, were pleas for national political recognition put forward in May by 300 delegates to a Lithuanian proto-Diet, convened in the Russian capital by refugees from their occupied homeland. Prince Lvov's ministers, abandoning their initial liberal stance, began to argue that imperial rights of sovereignty were not dissolved by the fall of the tsar but were transferred to his successors in authority. Claims to complete independence advanced by the Social Democrats in Finland and Estonia were rejected. As for Latvia, the Provisional Government insisted that the peoples of southern Livonia, Courland and Latgale had nothing in common; they were not yet ready to form a unified and indivisible political entity.

Briefly the Latvians seemed likely to gain more from the Petrograd Soviet than from the Provisional Government. For in early April 1917 the Bolsheviks affirmed that all the nationalities in Russia had a right of 'free separation' and a right to form 'free and independent states'. By the end of the month Riga, the most industrialized non-Russian port of the old empire, was effectively controlled by a local Soviet. In the Latvian countryside, too, the peasants welcomed promises of land redistribution. A simplistic agrarian communism had taken root among them, not yet blighted by the doctrinaire Marxism that imposed state control on all confiscated estates.

With the emergence of Kerensky as the dominant figure in the Provisional Government the Russians adopted a more constructive approach. On 5 July a decree authorized an autonomous administration for Latvia, with elections promised in two months' time. Even so, Kerensky again emphasized that neither the Baltic nationalities nor Finland might anticipate full independence until a National Constituent Assembly could convene in Petrograd and express the collective will of Russia's peoples on their future.

Kerensky's speeches sounded impressive, but he was whistling in the wind. The onset of the German offensive that led to Riga's fall on 3 September intervened. On the day proposed for the Latvian elections Kaiser William himself was in Riga, taking the salute at a victory parade on the boulevard in front of the Orthodox cathedral. The leaders of the Riga Soviet escaped capture. It was left to a 'national council' of refugees, meeting at Valka on the Estonian border in late November, to proclaim an autonomous Latvia, a new state that in theory would bind together Courland, Latgale and southern Livonia.

The Provisional Government's intentions were of little importance to the Baltic peoples. Even before Lenin took Russia out of the war it had become clear that recognition of nationality in any of the western provinces depended on the grace and favour of the government in Berlin. Lithuania had been under German occupation for two and a half years and now most of Latvia suffered a similar fate. Policy in the region was increasingly determined by General Ludendorff, the principal arbiter of German strategy in the third and fourth years of the war. Briefly, and misleadingly, Ludendorff seemed not unsympathetic to nascent Lithuanian nationalism, but he could never have favoured genuine independence: he was committed heart and Prussian soul to German expansionism in the *Land Oberost*, the territories overrun by the army in the east.

His war memoirs reveal the convictions that shaped Ludendorff's policy. He recounts, for instance, his reactions on seeing Kaunas for the first time, after its capture by his troops in 1915.

> On the further bank of the Niemen there stands the tower of an old German castle of the Teutonic Knights, a symbol of German civilization in the East ... My mind was flooded with overwhelming historical memories: I determined to renew in the occupied territories that work of civilization at which the Germans had laboured in these lands for many centuries.

By Ludendorff's reckoning the free development of any of the peoples in the region was out of the question, on economic and strategic grounds: they would inevitably slip back into Russia's orbit unless bolstered by the Reich. Lithuania was the best suited of the Baltic provinces for colonization: its people seemed malleable, it was good farming land and, before the war, it had close commercial links with East Prussia. And, ever a realist, Ludendorff calculated that a compliant Lithuania could become a valuable counterweight for Germany should a resurrected Polish kingdom threaten to become over-mighty.

With Ludendorff's backing a Diet met at Vilnius in September 1917 and elected a National Council (Taryba), which called for recognition of a fully independent, democratic state. The Taryba resolutions were endorsed by Lithuanian émigrés in Berne and eventually by the Diet in Petrograd, too. But the Taryba's twenty members were not free agents. A curt message from Headquarters in the East reminded them that, unless they specifically sought support from the Reich, the new German frontier would run along a line from Kaunas to Daugapils, denying the Lithuanians access to the Baltic and leaving them dependent for seaborne trade on Polish goodwill. On 11 December 1917 the Taryba duly proclaimed Lithuania an independent state, with Vilnius as capital, but the proclamation emphasized close links with the Reich, accepting the need for a military alliance and currency and customs unions. A further declaration nine weeks later was more wisely phrased. It avoided any reference to German patronage and established 16 February 1918 as Independence Day.

★

By the end of the year 1917 German military authority south of the Baltic was at its zenith. Lenin had followed the Bolshevik seizure of power in Petrograd with a Decree of Peace, and on 17 December an armistice became effective 'on the land front between the Black Sea and the Baltic Sea'. Three days later delegations from Imperial Germany, Austria-Hungary, Bulgaria, the Ottoman Empire and Soviet Russia converged on Brest-Litovsk for the strangest of peace conferences. Prince Leopold of Bavaria, son-in-law of Emperor Franz Joseph and commander-in-chief of Germany's armies on the Eastern Front, presided at the conference table although he left all decisions to his chief of staff, General Hoffmann. The Soviet delegation was led at first by Adolf Joffe, an archetypal revolutionary intellectual, but he was succeeded by Leon Trotsky in the second week of January. Hoffmann sought an early peace in order to release experienced troops for service on the Western Front. His intentions were frustrated by Trotsky, who skilfully combined procedural wrangling with legalistic digression in the hope that the fuse of revolution would fire Berlin and Vienna before the treaty was drafted. He had moments of optimism; 1918 opened with strikes in both Austria and Germany, Tallinn's Bolsheviks tightened their hold on Estonia, and in Finland the revolutionary faction dominated the Social Democratic Party. But no uprising was reported from the two 'imperialist' capitals, nor did Trotsky's leaflet barrage of anti-war propaganda weaken German front-line discipline.

As a final delaying tactic Trotsky announced on 10 February that Russia would neither accept peace terms which denied the principle of self-determination nor make war. He led the Soviet delegation back to Petrograd, convinced that the Germans were so anxious to concentrate on the coming battle in France that they would not crank up the war machine in the east for a fourth winter campaign. He miscalculated. General Hoffmann lost patience: the Russians must be given 'another taste of the whip', he decided. On 18 February 1918 German troops resumed their advance. In the northern sector they crossed Livonia and penetrated deeply into Estonia, meeting little resistance.

'The most comical war I have ever known,' Hoffmann wrote in his diary: the infantry used captured rolling stock on local railways to cover 250 kilometres in five days, despite the snow and ice. Yet one scene of historical significance intruded on Hoffmann's comedy. The people of Tallinn found themselves with a single day – Sunday, 24 February – between the flight of local Bolsheviks and the coming of the field-grey invaders. The Maapäev's underground Salvation Committee seized the opportunity:

Konstantin Päts, its leader, declared Estonia independent, six days behind Lithuania; 24 February is still celebrated as Independence Day.

On that Sunday Hoffmann received from Petrograd a frantic appeal for a second armistice. Trotsky recognized his ploy had failed: there could be no lasting condition of 'neither war nor peace'; a new delegation was ready to leave for Brest-Litovsk. But Hoffmann was determined to go on cracking his whip until the peace envoys crossed the lines. By Tuesday the Germans were in Narva, 150 kilometres from Petrograd. On the following afternoon Lenin was left in no doubt of their proximity: a German plane flew over the city and bombs fell along the embankment beside the Fontanka canal. Never before had a foreign enemy struck at the heart of Peter the Great's chosen capital.

The delegation reached Brest-Litovsk next day. This time round there would be no parleying at a conference table. The terms presented were harsh, but on 3 March a Peace Treaty was signed, though final details were only settled at Berlin in August. As well as losing huge areas around the Black Sea, the Soviet government renounced Russian sovereignty over all Polish and Lithuanian lands, Courland, Livonia, and Estonia. By the time the ice thawed in eastern waters, Russia was left with only the narrowest of footholds on the Baltic, 150 kilometres of shoreline on either side of the Neva delta. It is small wonder that in early March Lenin moved Russia's capital away from the Baltic and back to Moscow.

While the advancing German infantry were herding their prisoners into trucks along the railways of Estonia, a bitter civil war was being waged on the northern shore of the Gulf. At first it seemed as if Finland would cut free from Russia through negotiation with the Soviet authorities. After nation-wide elections the Eduskunta, Finland's parliament, voted in favour of independence on 6 December 1917. Pehr Svinhufvud, who as speaker of the Diet in 1909 had offended the tsar by his protests at the policy of Russification, had returned from exile in Siberia to head a non-socialist coalition government. He at once sought recognition of independence from France, Great Britain, the United States, Denmark, Norway and Sweden. At the same time the influential committee of expatriates in Berlin sounded out the German government. The allies and America prevaricated, unsure of what was happening in Russia itself: Sweden and Germany insisted they would only recognize Finland's independence if the Soviet regime was prepared to do so, too. Svinhufvud duly took the train to Petrograd on 30 December for discussion with the Bolshevik leaders. He found them surprisingly accommodating, and on New Year's Eve received a signed declaration that 'the Soviet of People's Commissars, in accordance with the principle of national self-determination, has decided to present the Executive Central Committee with the proposal to recognize the political independence of the Finnish republic.'

A Finnish diplomat noted in his diary that as 'both heads of government cordially shook hands, Lenin asked jocularly "Are you satisfied now?", to which Svinhufvud mumbled his thanks.' His expression of gratitude may well have lacked conviction, for at fifty-seven Svinhufvud was too versed in politics to harbour illusions over Soviet intentions. Finnish trade had suffered from wartime conditions; a chronic shortage of food in the towns was exacerbated by a poor harvest and the dislocation of grain supplies from Russia. Trotsky was known to have expressed surprise that the numerically strong Social Democratic Party did not exploit the social grievances in the centres of industry, and in September 1917 the Finnish socialists began to organize Red Guards on the Petrograd model.

By mid-January 1918 a Finnish civil war seemed imminent. Even before the meeting with Lenin, landowners were raising White Guards to protect their property and themselves from the Reds. On 26 January Svinhufvud legitimized the White Guards, enrolling them as an embryonic army of the nation. The socialists contended that the new force was a spearhead of counter-revolution. Reports that the Whites were clamping down on workers' rights in the Tampere region led the Reds to seize power in Helsinki on 27–28 January. Within a fortnight Otto Kuusinen, already a veteran of Eduskunta politics and the most articulate member of the People's Commissariat, was claiming socialist control over all southern Finland.

Svinhufvud and his ministers had anticipated the coup. They left the capital before they could be arrested and found refuge at Vaasa on the Gulf of Bothnia, where they re-established the government. Significantly, General Mannerheim had been appointed commander of the White Guards as early as 16 January and was at Vaasa training the force he preferred to call the Finnish Peasant Army a week before the Reds' coup in Helsinki. He was confident that unless the Russians intervened on a large scale he could lead his peasants to victory. Svinhufvud, however, was less sanguine and, against Mannerheim's wishes, sought military aid from Berlin.

The Germans welcomed an opportunity to extend their sphere of influence to the Baltic's northern shore. Both the High Command and the Admiralty Staff had been considering such operations for several months and their contingency planning took advantage of the Finns who, intermittently during the past two years, had received Prussian army training at Altona. The battalion fighting in Latvia was immediately released for service under Mannerheim and a German expeditionary force was ready to sail within four weeks of the Helsinki coup. On 28 February two dreadnoughts and three cruisers escorted troop transports to the Åland islands, where their arrival surprised a Swedish force protecting Eckerö, the most westerly ferry port, from any incursion by the Reds. Over the following month General Rüdiger von der Goltz concentrated some 9,000 men at a base near Mariehamn and on 5 April his 'Baltic Division' landed at Hangö, in south-western Finland, covered by German warships.

By then, however, Mannerheim had broken the back of the Red Guards. His 'peasant army' stormed their defensive positions at Tampere in three days of intensive fighting and could have entered Helsinki without Goltz's support. The Germans poured in even more troops, the navy transporting a full brigade from Tallinn to the Kotka area, 130 kilometres east of the Finnish capital. Soviet aid to the Red insurgents was limited to consignments of arms, though Russian military units still in Finland fought back in the many instances when they were attacked by the Whites. The Russian ships in harbour at Helsinki took no part in the struggle; some were so neglected that they could not even raise steam. Icebreakers towed vessels up the Gulf to avoid capture by the Germans, but several warships took more than a week to reach Kronstadt, normally a voyage of between ten and twelve hours.

The fighting was over in three and a half months. On 15 May 1918 Mannerheim rode into Helsinki at the head of a victory parade. Yet though Finland's civil war was brief it was, like most internal conflicts, intensely cruel. More than 10,000 Finns died in the actual fighting. Half a century later a dispassionate examination of evidence by a Finnish historian estimated that 1,649 lives were lost in the Red Terror while, in response, the Whites killed 8,380 workers or their families. This is a higher figure than earlier assessments: it is known that 2,000 Red prisoners were summarily shot during the Civil War and 125 executed after later treason trials. In addition to these killings, some 90,000 alleged Reds and their families were held in prison camps, often under ghastly conditions; more than one prisoner in ten died in the camps, notably in the historic island fortress of Suomenlinna, off Helsinki.

By the middle of May the surviving Red Guards had fled across the border and, apart from the families held in detention, all Finland was 'White'. Inevitably, however, the whole country was under German patronage and closely integrated in German economic and strategic plans for the future of the Baltic. It was all too much for Mannerheim who, as early as 5 March, telegraphed to Ludendorff asking, in vain, that German troops be placed under his command while serving on Finnish soil. On 30 May Mannerheim resigned, dismayed by the powers that Regent Svinhufvud was handing over to the enemy whom he had so recently fought in Galicia. The general, always independently minded, held patriotic ambitions of his own devising. They included an advance beyond the historic boundaries of the Grand Duchy so as to bring East Karelia within the new frontiers. To this ambitious programme he returned on several occasions in the following years.

Strategically, Germany's Finnish Expedition was a self-indulgent sideshow squandering manpower and material. It coincided with 'the Kaiser's Battle' on the Western Front, the decisive thrust of March 1918 intended by Ludendorff to break the allied line before the trickle of American reinforcements reaching Europe became a flood. Germany urgently needed battle-hardened veterans of the struggle against the Russians to fight in France. Already, troop trains had transported many regiments and weapons westwards, particularly artillery, but they were not enough to tip the balance. On the day Goltz's Baltic Division landed at Hangö, Ludendorff admitted privately that, after more than a fortnight's heavy fighting in Picardy, the resistance of the allies 'is beyond our strength'. Yet even in these critical weeks in the West the old dream of expansion in the East continued to fascinate him. He found time to turn his thoughts away from the battle and encourage Kaiser William's fantasy kingdom-building. William himself added Duke of Courland to his titles in March. His sister's husband, Prince Friedrich Karl of Hesse, was proposed as king of Finland and, with German thoroughness, started to learn the language of his future subjects. A Württemberg prince, Duke Wilhelm of Urach, awaited the call to be crowned King Mindaugas II of Lithuania, a throne to which he was duly 'elected' in July.

The duke was still waiting on 2 November, when the changing fortunes of the war in the west induced the Taryba to nullify his election. Nine days later the Armistice was signed in the Forest of Compiègne and the Kaiser began his long exile in Holland. The kingdoms of Finland and Lithuania were stillborn and so, it seemed, were all the grandiose schemes of colonization in the east. The Great War was over. Article 12 of the Armistice agreement insisted that 'all German troops . . . in territories which before the war formed part of Russia shall . . . withdraw within the German frontiers . . . as soon as the Allies shall consider this desirable'; and Article 15 provided for the annulment of the Treaty of Brest-Litovsk. Two days later, a decree of the Soviet Central Executive Committee also declared 'the dictated peace of Brest-Litovsk' null and void.

★

With reports reaching Moscow of red flags flying over a mutinous Kiel and Hamburg and Bremen controlled by Workers' and Soldiers' Councils, the Soviet authorities were jubilant. Lenin's prophecies of imminent world revolution seemed close to fulfilment. In Latvia a provisional government hurriedly formed by the peasant leader, Karlis Ulmanis, on 18 November was forced to seek refuge at Liepāja, when a Soviet regime was re-established in Riga. Trotsky's newly raised Red Army at once began a two-pronged advance into the lost Baltic provinces, from Petrograd and from Pskov. Many German units, demoralized and verging on mutiny, were only interested in getting home to the Fatherland as soon as possible. They left arms and equipment for the Reds to seize, or they simply threw them into the sea. The Baltic fleet, seaworthy again after a summer of repairs, emerged from Kronstadt and shelled Narva, which was soon overrun by the Seventh Red Army, commanded by Jakums Vācietis, an ex-colonel in the Latvian Rifles.

Farther west, it remained unclear who ruled Lithuania: communists, socialists, liberal nationalists and Polish federalists struggled ineffectually for power in Vilnius. Their quarrels enabled the Red Army to advance from Minsk and gain control of the city by the second week of January, forcing the Lithuanian government – like the Latvian – to move, in this instance to Kaunas. Political life across all the Baltic provinces was too anarchic to predict the immediate future. On 25 December the Moscow newspaper *Izvestia* confidently declared 'The Baltic Sea is now become the Sea of Social Revolution.'

This claim was banner-waving hyperbole. Little had changed on western Baltic shores. Danish political life remained unaffected by what happened in the Gulf of Finland, apart from efforts at Copenhagen to safeguard securities invested in Russian banks. Within Sweden a group of militant socialists favoured a general strike as the first step towards a soviet-style republic, but trade unionists rejected the call and the Social Democrat Party settled innocuously for the gentler path of franchise reform instead. German revolutionary ardour – at its most intense on the eve of Christmas – cooled down after the Spartacist rising of January 1919 failed to destroy the moderate socialist government of Ebert and Noske. Moreover no German regime, however radical its ideology, would have risked the loss of food supplies in that hungry winter by imposing social changes on the great estates of Pomerania and East Prussia. In Finland, too, there was little prospect of renewed Red revolt. The Whites' hold on the country had not been loosened by the fall of the kingmaker Kaiser: a pro-German regent, Svinhufvud, simply made way for a pro-allied regent, Mannerheim, with a presidential election promised once parliament had approved a revised constitutional law. Although social democracy remained influential in many Finnish towns, the very bourgeois republic of 1919 was unlikely to be swamped by any 'sea of social revolution'. Only in the Zemgale region of Latvia was there, at first, some popular backing for a Soviet regime. Support came from 'exploited' workers in Riga's many factories and, outside the towns, from landless peasants still hopefully anticipating the break-up of the Baltic German estates.

Even before *Izvestia*'s challenging assertion appeared in print, the Bolsheviks were in trouble. General Johan Laidoner – like Vācietis a former tsarist colonel – virtually created an Estonian army and, with backing from both the militia and Baltic Germans, checked the incursion of Vācietis's Reds. Moreover for the first time the western allies seemed prepared to intervene. Caution prevented them from giving official recognition to the national movements, but nine days after the Armistice, the War Cabinet in London did at least agree to send a fleet into the Baltic. Rear-Admiral Alexander-Sinclair was given command of a squadron that was to include four cruisers, nine destroyers and seven minesweepers. No one seems to have been quite sure of the squadron's purpose, not least because the cabinet was divided over the extent of British involvement in Russia's Civil War. Were the warships to enforce the continued blockade of Germany or institute a blockade of Red Petrograd? At the Admiralty a mood of splendid detachment prevailed and Alexander-Sinclair's orders were patriotically laconic. 'Show the British flag and support British policy as circumstances dictate,' he was told.

The venture began badly: the light cruiser HMS *Cassandra* struck a mine in the approaches to the Gulf of Riga and sank within half an hour. Although ten lives were lost, 400 of her crew were saved. Yet, despite the mines, Sinclair's squadron reached Tallinn within three weeks of the cabinet decision to intervene. The admiral refused to put a landing-party ashore to protect the city, but he obliged General Laidoner by shelling the coastal road near Narva. He also made certain that no Russian ships hampered the passage of 3,000 Finnish volunteers from Helsinki, sent to bolster Laidoner's army. When, at Christmas, the Soviet destroyer *Spartacus* unexpectedly emerged from the mists of Tallinn Bay and began shelling the dockyard the British sailed in pursuit and forced her to surrender; a second Russian destroyer was taken soon afterwards. Admiral Sinclair covered an Estonian landing behind the Russian lines and then took his vessels down to ice-free Liepāja to encourage Latvia's anti-Bolsheviks. In mid-February 1919 Laidoner's motley army cleared the last Reds from northern Estonia and, in uneasy alliance with General Yudenich's Russian Whites, threatened Petrograd.

By then, however, Sinclair's vessels were back in England. The more formidable 6th Light Cruiser squadron had sailed into Liepāja on 17 January with Rear-Admiral Sir Walter Cowan, a pugnacious martinet, flying his flag in HMS *Delhi*. 'Cowan's Force', later augmented by the arrival of several French warships, was to rule the waves in the Baltic throughout the year. At one time Cowan had 200 vessels under his command.

These distant events coincided with the opening on 18 January 1919 of the Paris Peace Conference, which was to culminate in the Treaty of Versailles, signed on 28 June. Few delegates paid more than lip-service to President Wilson's conviction 'that all nations have a right to self-determination', though some shared his hope that imperfections in the settlement could be rectified by a League of Nations that would revolutionize international relations. Baltic affairs seemed incomprehensible, understandably perhaps. Even the French diplomatic service – the most professional in the world – had its moment of weakness, the Quai d'Orsay preparing a credit note for Riga or Liepāja in *yen*, in the belief that Latvia must be one of the Russian islands off Japan: 'Courland' and 'Livonia' were familiar names, but there was no 'Latvia' in even the best atlases. The French were more at ease with Vistulan geography, ready to back Polish claims against both Germany and Lithuania, while wistfully hoping that a restored White Russia might honour the loans and investments which had bolstered the pre-war Russian alliance for more than twenty years. French policy reflected – and occasionally determined – the vicissitudes of Russia's Civil War.

'Intervention' was in British minds, too. Balfour, the foreign secretary, was clearly more interested in Petrograd than in Tallinn: he received a delegation of Estonians on 12 June and told them that 'no satisfactory or final settlement of the status of the Baltic States could be secured without the consent of the Russian Government, whenever a government was set up in Russia which could be recognized by the Allied Powers'. It was still assumed the Soviet regime would be short-lived, for Admiral Kolchak controlled much of Siberia and Generals Denikin, from southern Russia, and Yudenich, at the head of the Baltic, were threatening Moscow and Petrograd. Any successor government would need cosseting by the West, and it was becoming clear that none of these White leaders was likely to accept the loss of the Baltic provinces. The Grand Duchy of Finland had a different past: no one in Paris questioned Finnish assertions of nationhood, and on 3 May the Council of Foreign Ministers at the Peace Conference recognized the country's independence.

'Finland is the key to Petrograd, and Petrograd is the key to Moscow,' *The Times* had told its readers a fortnight earlier. But Yudenich and Denikin were unwilling to become indebted to Mannerheim. Even over the independence of Finland the White Russian contenders for power remained obdurate. They had learned nothing, and forgotten a great deal.

At Paris, the victorious allies regarded Germany as a defeated, broken enemy. Most of the High Seas Fleet, including surface vessels from the Baltic squadron, was interned at Scapa Flow, where on 21 June 1919 fifty-one warships were scuttled by their crews. Allied armies of occupation kept a 'watch on the Rhine'. They did not, however, keep watch on the Elbe or the Oder, and OHL remained in being until the Treaty of Versailles was signed: Ludendorff, dismissed by his Kaiser a fortnight before the Armistice, was no longer First Quartermaster-General, but until 25 June 1919 Hindenburg remained in command as General Field Marshal. Even if the frontier in the west was lost, it seemed essential to OHL to protect the frontier in the east. There was so much to repel: the incursions of Poles or Lithuanians; the menace of Bolshevism and the threat of a 'social revolution' destroying the Junker estates, the nursery of Prussian militarism. Headquarters were established at Kolberg, on the Baltic coast, 200 kilometres west of Danzig. From there, in late January 1919, the General Field Marshal issued a proclamation calling on 'old comrades who fought with me at Tannenberg and the Masurian Lakes' to 'come quickly' to the defence of the eastern Marchlands.

Marshal Foch, the allied generalissimo, viewed OHL's activities with suspicion. A peremptory warning that to order an advance in the east would be a breach of the Armistice terms silenced the rallying call. It did not, however, end German military activity in the fledgling Baltic states, for Hindenburg appointed the independently minded Major-General von der Goltz to overall command of all German units still in former Russian territory. Most of the troops were in Latvia. They included remnants of the regular army stranded in the east, *Freikorps* volunteer brigades unwilling to accept the realities of a lost war, and the *Baltische Landswehr*, a militia raised by Baltic Germans to safeguard their family estates. OHL claimed that Goltz's duties were consistent with Article 12 of the Armistice, for he would maintain discipline in an army that, as yet, the allies had not ordered back to the Fatherland. Goltz himself had no intention of bringing the troops home so long as their presence in the east allowed him to play high politics on an anti-Bolshevik stage. At Kolberg nobody was inclined to probe too deeply into the motives behind the general's sense of commitment.

Goltz reached Liepāja on 2 February 1919. By the end of the month there were 25,000 men under his command, the core of a well-equipped Iron Division, ready to march on Riga, 210 kilometres away. He launched an offensive on 3 March, advancing to the cathedral city of Jelgava, formerly Mitau and the ducal capital of Courland. When Jelgava was captured, on 18 March, Goltz's troops found that the retreating Reds had massacred entire families held as hostages in the citadel: the general had difficulty in restraining the *Freikorps* brigades from an undisciplined and potentially disastrous 45-kilometre dash on Latvia's heavily fortified Red capital. Even had he so wished, he could not prevent his troops from avenging the Jelgava killings on any Bolsheviks who fell into their hands. No prisoners were taken.

Throughout February and March Admiral Cowan and most of his squadron were farther west, keeping well clear of the frozen sea. When he returned to Liepāja on 4 April the port was virtually in the hands of his ex-enemies. As he stepped ashore a German sentry on the quay asked for his pass: the admiral expostulated. Tension remained high, with German confidence encouraged by rumours of friction between the Big Four peacemakers in Paris. British and American journalists predicted that the Peace Conference would soon break up in disarray. The crisis deepened on 16 April, when a *Freikorps* brigade staged a coup in Liepāja, of which Goltz (in Jelgava) ingenuously denied prior knowledge. All the officers of Latvia's embryonic general staff were taken into custody while Prime Minister Ulmanis, who had been forced out of Riga by the Reds a few months back, sought sanctuary aboard a British warship. The situation was highly confused, for there were now three would-be heads of government: Peteris Stucka, chairing the discredited Latvian Soviet in Riga; a Lutheran pastor, Andrievs Niedra, puppet of the *Freikorps* in downtown Liepāja; and Karlis Ulmanis heading an offshore government aboard a British cruiser. London offered little guidance. 'The work of British naval officers in the Baltic would be much facilitated if they could be informed of the policy which they are required to support,' a senior officer at the Admiralty complained icily to the Foreign Office. Cowan was left to shape his own course of action.

The admiral had no intention of becoming involved in Latvia's internal affairs: a newly arrived military mission could attend to them. His principal task was to enforce the blockade of Petrograd and prevent the capital ships in the Baltic fleet emerging from Kronstadt. He therefore left a cruiser squadron in Latvian waters, crossed to the Finnish shore, and improvised a base and protected anchorage in Björkö Sound, where in 1905 the Kaiser and the tsar had sought to reshape Europe's alliance system aboard the *Polar Star*. On 18 August 1919 the smallest vessels in Cowan's Force gained a striking, decisive and largely forgotten victory. For from Björkö eight coastal motor torpedo boats (CMBs), capable of reaching a speed of 40 knots, set out for Kronstadt, some 80 kilometres to the east. They received navigational advice from patriotic Finnish smugglers, who knew the waters well. The flotilla outflanked the forts which had deterred Napier in 1854 by taking advantage of the CMBs' low draught to enter Kronstadt's shallow, and defensively neglected, North Channel. Under cover of an air raid by Sopwith Camel biplanes the CMBs then torpedoed and sank at anchor a submarine depot ship and the two most formidable warships of the Baltic fleet, the dreadnought *Petropavlosk* and the fifteen-year-old battleship *Andrei Pervozanni*. Three CMBs failed to return to Björkö and six officers and nine ratings perished during the attack. All the survivors were awarded decorations for bravery, two officers – Commander C. Dobson and Lieutenant G. Steele – receiving the Victoria Cross. Although during the summer more than a dozen allied warships were sunk by mines or submarine torpedoes, the Kronstadt raid consolidated the power of the Royal Navy in the eastern Baltic. It ensured that throughout the last phase of the emerging republics' struggle for independence the heavy guns of the Soviet Baltic fleet remained silent.

Meanwhile General von der Goltz plunged into Latvian affairs with single-minded purpose. His immediate aim was to ensure a continued German presence in the lands where the Sword Brothers had vanquished the heathen, 700 years back in time. On 22 May 1919 the Iron Division made a surprise assault on the Bolshevik positions defending Riga; crack assault troops stormed the citadel, though too late to prevent a massacre of prisoners. By next evening the city was in Goltz's hands, with German officers again in control of the municipality. The patriotic press in Germany reported the storming of Riga with pride. Conversely the peacemakers in Paris were alarmed: on 13 June they at last demanded the evacuation by the Germans of all pre-war Russian territory. But Goltz – and OHL at Kolberg – temporized: did the allies *really* want the Reds back in Riga?

Nemesis awaited Goltz, however. After securing Riga he began an advance north-eastwards into the region now known as Vidzeme. Here, along the forested slopes of the Gauja valley, the *Freikorps* and the *Landswehr* were forced to move more slowly than in the spacious plains of Courland and the Daugava basin. They met mounting resistance from Latvians loyal to the Ulmanis government and marshalled in an embryonic army by General Balodis. At the same time Estonian troops anxious to prevent the Baltic Germans recovering their ascendancy in the pre-war Russian provinces crossed the border into Vidzeme and headed southwards, under General Ernst Põdder's command. On 23 June the Estonians and Latvians defeated the Germans after a four-day battle at the head of the valley around Cēsis, once the Hanse town of Wenden and dominated by a thirteenth-century castle. Ironically it was this bastion of the Teutonic Knights that checked the incursion of the German *Freikorps*. Estonians still celebrate 23 June as Victory Day, honouring Cēsis as a symbolic triumph over historic oppressors.

To Goltz's consternation, the Latvian Bolsheviks were also once again active, mounting a counter-attack down the river Daugava that threatened the overstretched defences east of Riga. Hurriedly Goltz sought talks with Estonia's General Põdder at Strasdenhof and, swallowing his pride, accepted British mediation. On 3 July Colonel Stephen Tallents, assisted by Colonel the Hon. Harold Alexander, imposed an armistice: Goltz would leave Riga, though not southern Courland; Põdder withdrew his troops from active campaigning; the Ulmanis government was reinstated in the Latvian capital, protected by an Inter-Allied Commission, headed by a French officer.

But, despite the Strasdenhof armistice, the Latvian imbroglio became even more tightly entangled. For, while Goltz retired to Jelgava, most of his *Freikorps* – almost 50,000 men – remained under arms, led by a former tsarist staff officer, Colonel Bermondt-Avalov, an ambitious intriguer who wished to use them to support the offensive against Petrograd. At the same time the (often strained) link binding the *Baltische Landswehr* to the *Freikorps* was severed. The 6,000 militia were now organized as a separate unit, committed to resisting the Latvian Bolsheviks. And, in this strangest of conflicts, on 25 July the twenty-eight-year-old Colonel Alexander was seconded to command the *Landswehr*, a post he held for seven months.

The colonel, who had fought in the Irish Guards with distinction in France and was to win fame and a field marshal's baton in the Mediterranean in the Second World War, admired the fighting qualities of the German militia. He led them in a three-week winter offensive which by early February 1920 had thrust the Reds back 150 kilometres across Latgale. 'It was an honour to command a force consisting of nothing but gentlemen,' he wrote home to his family. Briefly the young colonel wondered if he might resign his commission, buy an estate in Latvia and farm, hunt and paint in rural tranquillity once peace was secured.

That idyll still seemed far away. The *Freikorps* continued to defy the allies and the German government. In August 1919 a renewed order for the Iron Division to leave Courland and return to the Fatherland was rejected by its commander, Major Bischoff. He informed Berlin he would bring his men home only if 30 per cent of them were enrolled in the treaty-pruned German army (*Reichswehr*), with guaranteed postings along the borders of East Prussia. His freebooters also had a grievance against Ulmanis who, they maintained, had promised them free land in return for their help in the first days of the struggle against the Reds. With Bermondt-Avalov's acquiescence, the *Freikorps* broke the Strasdenhof armistice and made two attempts to recover Riga, which was strongly defended by the Latvian army. On 15 October British and French ships in Cowan's fleet supported the Latvians by shelling the *Freikorps* positions, forcing the Germans to pull back once more to Jelgava.

By now the struggle resembled the baronial conflicts that plunged so much of Europe into anarchy during the High Middle Ages. Each *Freikorps* cherished its particular traditions and created its own insignia, several adopting forms of the swastika, hitherto unseen on German uniforms or helmets. But, unlike the mediaeval bands of brothers, there was no bond of chivalry to lift their companionship. They had become military adventurers, field-grey condottieri. Villages were fired, their inhabitants shot down, their crops destroyed. From Jelgava an Iron Division column marched on Liepāja, which was saved from capture only by repeated salvoes from the heavy guns of HMS *Hercules*, sailing close inshore. Other towns, away from the sea, were less fortunate. Yet, though Latvians of all political persuasions looked on the *Freikorps* with revulsion, many Germans in the Fatherland were proud of their achievements in lands so redolent of the Teutonic past. When early in November the Latvian army surrounded Jelgava and cut off all supplies, the Iron Division avoided defeat, for – like US Marines in a Hollywood melodrama – a new force of eager *Freikorps* volunteers from East Prussia arrived in the nick of time to lift the siege.

The *Freikorps* phenomenon made allied observers uneasy. It was reported that Ludendorff had emerged from nominal retirement to visit the Iron Division at Jelgava: was he again dabbling in Baltic 'colonization' projects? General Turner of the British military mission thought not. Ludendorff was more concerned with plans for a nationalist coup in Berlin, he maintained; and he was right. On 21 November the Iron Division headed south, finally abandoning Jelgava. Although skirmishes with the local soldiery continued for several days, by the end of the month the last *Freikorps* had left Latvian soil. They were soon heavily involved in the turbulent politics of post-war Germany, taking part in the abortive Kapp Putsch of 13 March 1920 and the subsequent suppression of Red subversion in Münster and the Ruhr. A year later *Freikorps* brigades disputed possession of Upper Silesia with the Poles, ahead of a plebiscite that kept the greater part of the province inside Germany. But, though many veterans settled in East Prussia, the Baltic states were at last rid of the incubus.

Estonia and Latvia were also anxious to avoid deeper entanglement in Russia's civil war. The presence of Cowan's fleet in the Baltic gave Britain considerable influence on both governments, and during the spring and summer of 1919 arms and equipment continued to reach Tallinn for Yudenich's much-heralded advance on Petrograd. But despite the intense anti-Bolshevism of the war minister (Churchill), British support for Yudenich and other White leaders elsewhere in Russia soon began to waver. Lloyd George, the prime minister, was disturbed by reports of mounting labour unrest at home and by estimates of the size of any expeditionary force needed for effective intervention; and the Foreign Office, speculating on the prospects for British trade in the region, deplored the persistent refusal of the Whites to accept the loss to Russia of Finland and the Baltic provinces. There were also clear signs of anti-war feeling within Russia's nearest Baltic neighbours: in Finland the interventionist General Mannerheim lost the presidential election of July 1919 to the liberal Kaarlo Ståhlberg; and in Estonia a centre-left coalition sought peace with the Soviets at the earliest opportunity, despite General Laidoner's past collaboration with Yudenich's White army. Lenin exploited all this uncertainty. In mid-September Chicherin, his foreign commissar, sent telegrams to Helsinki, Tallinn, Riga and Kaunas proposing peace talks.

A week later (24 September 1919) Lloyd George persuaded his cabinet to end Britain's shipment to the Baltic of arms for the Russian Whites. Ironically this decisive rejection of intervention coincided with the arrival of Yudenich's troops at the approaches to Petrograd, a development that postponed any Baltic peace talks. For four weeks the Whites continued to thrust forward, but they were never strong enough to storm the city street by street nor besiege it without Finnish backing. The stalemate induced Estonia to act unilaterally and begin secret talks with Chicherin. On 23 October Trotsky committed the Red Army to a counter-offensive that forced the Whites back to the Estonian border. By 14 November when they were at Narva, Estonia and the Soviets had reached a preliminary agreement, and the White army was disarmed and interned, pending disbandment. For some eight weeks talks between Estonia and Soviet Russia continued at Tartu – the university city then still known as Dorpat – where a peace treaty was signed on 2 February 1920. So eager were Lenin and Chicherin to seek contact with the West that the Soviets not only recognized Estonian independence but ceded Ivangorod and Petseri, two ethnically Russian districts held by Estonian troops when the peace talks started. Both governments agreed not to allow foreign armies or navies to establish bases nor foreign political groups to operate within their territories. By now Cowan and his fleet had left Baltic waters.

The Estonians hoped their neighbours would follow their example, seek agreements with Chicherin, and finally put a seal of international recognition on Baltic independence. Latvian envoys began talks in Moscow early in February, after the last Bolshevik troops had been cleared from Latgale, with help from Poland. A final peace treaty was signed in Riga on 1 August 1920 conceding almost all the Latvian demands, including the whole of Latgale. A hurried treaty with Lithuania was concluded in Moscow three weeks earlier (12 July 1920): the Soviet government accorded recognition to a large Lithuanian state which specifically included Vilnius, even though the city had been under Polish occupation since Easter.

These generous concessions in the peace treaties reflected Russia's need to keep the Baltic republics well disposed towards them during the fluctuating campaigns of 1920 over Poland's eastern frontier. The Lithuanians went beyond strict neutrality. They gave the Soviets transit rights through the Vilnius region, which the Red Army crossed between 17 and 20 July in General Tukachevsky's 950-kilometre enveloping movement on Warsaw. Unexpectedly, the resistance of the Poles stiffened on 15 August, under Pilsudski's inspirational influence. Through 'the miracle of the Vistula' they saved their capital and, in a great counter-offensive, the whole Polish state, too. Two months later the exhausted armies agreed on an armistice: the Poles were left in occupation of lands far to the east of the frontier recommended by the Paris peacemakers, the so-called Curzon Line running from Grodno through Brest-Litovsk to Przemyśl and the Carpathians.

Lithuania paid dearly for the rights accorded to Tukachevsky's army. Vilnius, the birthplace of Mickiewicz and of Pilsudski himself, was regarded in Warsaw as a Polish city, despite its historical role as the heart of the Lithuanian Grand Duchy. On 10 October 1920 a Polish general, Lucijan Zeligowski, seized the city and the province around it on his own initiative, although with Pilsudski's compliance. For eighteen months Zeligowski administered a nominally independent state, Central Lithuania, but on 22 March 1922 all pretence was dropped and Vilnius incorporated in Poland. Thereafter, throughout the inter-war period, the Polish flag flew from the tower high on Vilnius's Gedimino Hill, to the chagrin of every patriotic Lithuanian. In Kaunas the government refused to accept the loss of Vilnius. The Latvians settled their frontier with Estonia in March 1920 after the British mediator, Colonel Tallents, resolved a dispute over the town that was shown on pre-war maps as Walk by drawing a line through the centre. Even today the Tallents Ruling holds good: Valga, with a railway station on the main Riga–Tartu line, is in Estonia, while Valka remains 'on the wrong side of the track', in Latvia. It took the Latvians another year to reach agreement with Lithuania, for in this instance, too, relatively minor differences over the border called for international arbitration. But Britain and France formally recognized Latvia and Estonia as independent republics on 26 January 1921 and the three Baltic republics were admitted to the League of Nations eight months later.

Lithuania, however, remained a problem for the West. The Vilnius dispute caused chronic tension with Poland, and the government in Kaunas urgently needed to secure a trade outlet to the sea. The old Teutonic Order town of Memel was a natural port for the Lithuanians (to whom Memel was, and is, known as Klaipéda). In 1914 the population of the town itself was more than 90 per cent German, though more evenly balanced in the surrounding countryside. With scant regard for the ideal of self-determination, Article 99 of the Treaty of Versailles compelled Germany to surrender the port and its hinterland as far as the river Niemen, a segment of territory as large as the Grand Duchy of Luxembourg. An interim administration was set up, French troops were assigned to police the area, but a final decision over the port's future was shelved, first by the peacemakers and later by the League of Nations. In exasperation, on 10 January 1923 armed volunteers from Kaunas and Palanga seized Memel and proclaimed the union of the whole district with Lithuania. The League acquiesced: a Statute of Autonomy, effective from August 1925, upheld the rights of the German community. Lithuania's status as the largest of the three new Baltic republics was at last formally recognized. But, ominously, Lithuania remained on bad terms with occupied Poland over lost Vilnius and with Germany over Memel.

Down the eastern periphery of the Baltic lands, the Finns were left to make their own final settlement with Soviet Russia. Britain's abandonment of intervention frustrated Mannerheim's earlier hopes of absorbing eastern Karelia within the Finnish republic. A provisional administration for the region, set up in February 1919 at Uhtua, collapsed in the spring of 1920, its members seeking refuge with their kinsfolk across the old Finnish border. The Finns thereupon belatedly responded to Chicherin's peace overture and sent a delegation to Tartu, headed by the sagacious Juho Paasikivi, a fifty-year-old former senator who had acquitted himself well in conference with Kerensky before the Bolsheviks seized power. When the peace talks began on 12 June 1920, Paasikivi found the Russians prepared to allow Finland an outlet to the White Sea through the ice-free port of Petsamo (never included in the Grand Duchy) and the Russians were also willing to accept demilitarization of the islands in the Gulf of Finland. But over east Karelia they remained unyielding, refusing Paasikivi's request for a plebiscite and insisting that Finnish troops be withdrawn from two communes they had occupied to the east of the old Grand Duchy. The sole concession he could obtain was a promise of autonomy, and in 1923 Karelia did indeed become a Socialist Soviet Republic. When the peace treaty was eventually signed at Tartu on 14 October 1920 Paasikivi's political enemies complained that he was abandoning their kinsfolk, and east Karelia remained an emotive issue to right-wing Finns for the next twenty years. Yet Paasikivi secured not unfavourable borders for the new Finland and a binding commitment to 'peaceful and good neighbourly relations'. Along a frontier extending to within 30 kilometres of Russia's second city that pledge was not to be taken lightly.

One Baltic non-belligerent benefited from the final peace settlement. Denmark had maintained scrupulous neutrality, despite concern for the Danish families under Prussian rule since the first of Bismarck's wars. But in 1919 the Wilsonian ideal of national self-determination, together with France's less high-minded policy of seeking to weaken Germany at every point of the compass, revived the Schleswig-Holstein Question, dormant for half a century. There was even talk at Copenhagen and at Paris of drawing Germany's frontier along a demilitarized Kiel Canal, a proposal that would have made a mockery of self-determination. The more moderate politicians were content to recover the region where there was undoubtedly a Danish majority, and in a plebiscite held on 10 February 1920 the people of northern Schleswig voted three-to-one in favour of Denmark. In a second plebiscite five weeks later in central Schleswig (including the very German town of Flensburg) the vote went four-to-one for Germany. Acceptance of the plebiscites in Denmark was delayed by a political crisis in Copenhagen at Easter when radicals and socialists complained that the king was ruling through an unelected camarilla, but early in May agreement was reached. On 10 July 1920 the injustice imposed by Bismarck in 1864–5 was finally righted: King Christian X led his army into North

Schleswig, renamed *Sønderjylland* (South Jutland). The settlement gave
Denmark a German minority of 35,000 and left 25,000 Danes living and
working in German Schleswig. The new frontier ran more than 50 kilometres north of the Kiel Canal. It is unchanged today.

Germany's other frontier on the Baltic had been settled much earlier.
When President Wilson outlined his peace programme to Congress in
January 1918 the thirteenth of his Fourteen Points promised a resurrected
and independent Poland with frontiers to include 'all territories inhabited
by indisputably Polish populations' and enjoying 'free and secure access to
the sea'. His Entente allies warmly supported Wilson, although showing as
little understanding as the president himself of the ethnic complexities in
the region: Polish independence was speedily accorded.

All the peacemakers were agreed that the natural outlet for Poland's
commerce lay at the mouth of the Vistula. Before the partitions, Danzig
had flourished as a Free City for three and a half centuries under Polish
suzerainty. It was no longer a great centre of commerce: during the last
year of peace twelve other ports in the Baltic had handled more ships and
greater tonnage. But Danzig provided a direct railway route to Warsaw and
to the Polish coalfields. To outsiders, studying maps in distant Paris, there
seemed no reason why new boundaries should not help the Hanseatic city
recover that lost prosperity.

Differences arose, however, over the precise status of Danzig and the size
of the proposed 'Corridor' that, by giving Poland access to the Baltic, would
separate German Pomerania from German East Prussia. The French and the
Poles assumed that the port must become a sovereign part of Poland, even
though – as at Memel – the townsfolk were overwhelmingly German. But
when the Commission on Polish Affairs submitted a report that recommended acceptance of nearly all Poland's claims, the British prime minister
was uneasy. He deplored proposals that, in Poland as a whole, would place
two million Germans under foreign rule. As Margaret MacMillan has
shown in her definitive study of the Paris Peace Conference, Lloyd George
was afraid of 'creating fresh Alsace-Lorraines and the seeds of future wars'.
On 27 March 1919 he warned his colleagues in the Council of Four: 'We
must not create a Poland alienated from the time of its birth by an unforgettable quarrel from its most civilized neighbour.'

With American backing, Lloyd George secured a compromise. Poland's
'access to the sea' was limited to 32 kilometres of coast around the mouths
of the Vistula. Danzig itself would be neither in Germany nor in Poland:
it became a Free City under the protection of the League of Nations and

with a neutral Commissioner who, it was assumed, would resolve problems between the German and Polish communities. The Free City was to have an elected Senate and be linked to Poland by a customs union. The Poles would have the right to maintain a token military presence on the Westerplatte isthmus, overlooking the deep-water harbour at the northern mouth of the Vistula, and they might use the port's facilities for their embryonic navy. The creation of the Free City seemed a distantly academic solution to a perplexing problem, eminently reasonable if the two nationalities were prepared to seek to understand and trust each other. But was either of these two proudly patriotic peoples likely to forgo the past in order to safeguard the future?

Lloyd George secured a further compromise, beyond the territorial limits of the Free City. Despite protests from the Warsaw government it was agreed to seek and respect the wishes of local inhabitants in two East Prussian districts, Allenstein and Marienwerder, originally placed within the Polish Corridor. When plebiscites were eventually held, in July 1920, the voters overwhelmingly chose to remain in Germany: only 3.5 per cent preferred Polish rule. The Corridor was duly reduced in size, though it remained pear-shaped, barely 19 kilometres wide at the Free City apex but broadening to 95 kilometres in the south. It included much of the lower Vistula and one of two railway routes running from Warsaw to the sea. The towns were German in character and there remained a vociferous German minority, but most of the people who lived in the Corridor were Polish by origin, though observers reported that their dialect included many German elements.

The main provisions of the Versailles settlement became effective on Tuesday, 20 January 1920, six months ahead of the Allenstein–Marienwerder plebiscites. In Warsaw many members of the re-constituted parliament were disappointed by the treaty: they had hoped for a longer stretch of coast, to be held in full sovereignty; and they feared that the artificial Corridor would prove indefensible. But in Danzig Bay their compatriots were, for the moment, content. Early on that icy Tuesday morning they welcomed the treaty with open arms, literally; they waded out chest-deep into the sea to greet incoming Baltic waves breaking once more on a Polish shore. After a century and a quarter of partition the realm of the Jagiellons, once the largest state on the continent, was firmly stamped on the new map of Europe.

23

Nine Nations and a Free City

IN 1914 TWO empires and two kingdoms bordered the Baltic. Seven years later, when the last peace treaties had been signed, both kingdoms still survived, but to the east and south of them were seven new republics, and a Free City administered by a League of Nations Commissioner. Never before had the political map of northern Europe changed so drastically in such a brief span of time. Only Sweden retained her pre-war boundaries. Autocracy was gone. Apart from Soviet Russia, every country around the Baltic was by now a representative democracy. But for how long?

Some were accustomed to a deep-rooted concept of popular sovereignty. In Denmark four kings had ruled as constitutional monarchs since the basic charter of June 1849, scrupulously maintaining a balance between parliamentary rights and their limited prerogatives. It was therefore natural that when, in June 1915, Christian X approved a revised charter extending the franchise and broadening the class structure of the Upper House, he remained president of the executive Council of State. Similar changes in Sweden were accepted by the conservatively-minded Gustaf V in 1921, though with some reluctance: the vote was given to men and women over the age of twenty-three; and the king, well aware of widespread republican sentiment in the country, finally conceded to his ministers even greater responsibility than in Denmark. Finland, too, already had firm foundations of democratic government in its Eduskunta, a unicameral parliament chosen by direct, proportional election with universal suffrage similar to that of Sweden. The only innovation in 1919 was an elected head of state, a president who appointed the ministerial cabinet but could not hold office if he lost the confidence of parliament.

The most striking constitutional changes came in Germany which, though deprived of an eighth of its pre-war lands, remained a major Baltic power, with fifteen ports along the coast. The constitution agreed at Weimar in July 1919 was a charter of popular sovereignty: it guaranteed universal suffrage for men and women over the age of twenty, a directly elected president serving a term of seven years, and a bicameral parliament with laws initiated in a Reichstag chosen by proportional representation; provision was made for referenda and plebiscites. The political structure contained weaknesses, notably the president's right to govern by emergency decree; but the flaws went unnoticed at the time. The democratic Weimar blueprint provided a model for Germany's neighbours in the east.

The Polish constitution of March 1921 established a powerful lower chamber (Sejm) chosen by proportional representation, and a presidency for which election would be held every seven years. The Baltic states experimented with unicameral parliaments, universal suffrage and proportional representation. Referenda gave a sense of participation in government. There were constitutional variations: thus Latvia and Lithuania had a president chosen by parliament while in Estonia the prime minister presided over ceremonial functions as State Trustee. All three republics suffered from a lack of parliamentarians with understanding of practical politics, even at local level. By contrast, many Sejm members were experienced in government administration, though from three fallen empires with differing habits and traditions.

Proportional representation encouraged a multiplicity of parties. The Polish Sejm of 1922–3 comprised 444 members: five were independents; the remaining 439 came from fifteen separate parties. In 1923 fourteen parties contested the Estonian election, and between 1922 and 1934 thirty-nine sent members to the Latvian parliament. Except in 1919–20 when the Labour-Socialist groups championed land reform, governments tended to be coalitions of the moderate Right intent on keeping out the suspect Left. Most governments were short-lived. Between January 1920 and December 1926 Poland had 13, Estonia 9, Latvia 7, Lithuania 6 governments.

It is easy to mock these years of experiment as 'party time in the Baltic', a game of ministerial musical chairs. Yet much of value was achieved. Latvia's parliamentarians drafted an average of 204 laws a year throughout the 1920s and early 1930s; their neighbours were not far behind them. Latvia won respect for its social insurance schemes and – like Estonia – gained favourable reports from the International Labour Organization for enlightened factory laws: no child labour; a basic eight-hour working day; good opportunities for advanced education. Liberals and social democrats in the West optimistically hailed the Baltic newcomers as 'model democracies'.

Much parliamentary business concerned minor matters, but at an early stage issues fundamental to the structure of the new states were raised and thrashed out. Notable among them were the future of land ownership and the protection of national and religious minorities. The Baltic republics were primarily agricultural (Lithuania 77 per cent; Latvia 66 per cent;

Estonia 60 per cent). So, too, was much of Poland. Land reform was there-fore a social priority for all four nations. In Estonia some 1,000 estates were broken up by the Expropriation Law of October 1919, a process that more than doubled the number of smallholders in the country. There was a sim-ilar measure in Latvia, with the redistribution of 1,300 estates, although in this instance landowners could keep up to 16 hectares, twice the average size of the new holdings. In both Estonia and Latvia the greatest losers were the Baltic German families. The Lithuanian Land Law (March 1922) was less radical, partly because of the influence of the Roman Catholic Church, much of whose income came, directly or indirectly, from the estates. Existing owners might retain up to 150 hectares and (if they were not Russians) they could be sure of receiving compensation for the loss of larger areas. The Church's power also delayed land reform in Poland where, in 1921, 64 per cent of the total population derived an income from agri-culture, despite concentrations of heavy industry and mining at the heart of the country. The redistribution of land was accepted by the Sejm in 1920 as a principle but not implemented until 1926 – and then on a smaller scale than the original draft proposed.

The peacemakers of 1919–20 sought to protect national minorities by treaty pledges given by applicants to the League of Nations as a condition of membership. Each state in east-central Europe (except Soviet Russia and Germany) guaranteed its minorities equality before the law, religious free-dom and linguistic and cultural rights. Some Baltic countries needed no prompting. Denmark treated the 25,000 Germans of southern Jutland with scrupulous regard, though inevitably there were instances of local preju-dice. The Finnish constitution anticipated the pledges of the Minority Treaties by guaranteeing the rights of the Swedes, almost 11 per cent of the total population. The League, however, was called on to settle the status of the Åland islands: in 1921 a treaty, backed by ten nations, confirmed that the islands should remain under Finnish sovereignty but should be demil-itarized and accorded semi-autonomy.

Farther south, the Baltic republics began with good intentions. Estonia's constitution guaranteed rights to the minorities: Russians (8.5 per cent), Germans (1.7 per cent) and Swedes (0.7 per cent) were promised school-ing in the mother tongue and control over cultural life. In 1925 a Law for Cultural Autonomy for National Minorities, sponsored by a Baltic German parliamentary deputy, went even further: any minority of more than 3,000 people could become a legal corporation and administer cultu-ral, educational and charitable affairs, and raise a 'culture tax', receiving funds from both central and local government. Latvia and Lithuania also accepted constitutional obligations, though neither carried through such radical measures as in Estonia. Germans within Latvia – 3.6 per cent of the population – won concessions over schooling and the maintenance of theatres and educational institutes; their status was better in the towns than in the countryside, where the land reforms had undermined their privileged position. Lithuania's early governments included ministers responsible for minority affairs, but a nationalistic bitterness engendered by the Vilnius dispute soon led to discrimination against the Polish community (3.2 per cent). By the late 1920s official attitudes towards minorities were hardening in all three Baltic republics; even in Tallinn there was friction between a 'nationalizing' government and the authorities of both the German and Russian cathedrals.

The Jewish communities of tsarist Russia's former border territories posed special problems, except in Finland and Estonia (where in 1921 fewer than 4,500 Jews were settled). In Latvia they constituted about 5 per cent of the population and in Lithuania 7.6 per cent; many were Orthodox by faith and Yiddish-speaking, unassimilated and mistrusting cultural initiatives by outsiders, including their more liberal co-religionists. Latvia's Jews were so divided that they formed three distinct parliamentary parties. The anti-Semitism endemic to many Russian cities was never far below the surface and by the mid-1920s Jews could rightly complain of discrimination in Latvia, and to an even greater extent in Lithuania. Neighbouring Poland had a larger Jewish community than any other country in the world, apart from the United States. Successive democratic governments in Warsaw barely observed rights guaranteed by the Minority Treaties, which had assumed that the crude discriminatory legislation of Russian officialdom lost all validity with the fall of the empire. Not until 1931, under an authoritarian regime headed by Pilsudski, were tsarist restraints finally ended and the religious and educational rights of Jews protected by law. Even then, prejudice persisted in the civil service and the universities. No serious attempt was made to assimilate Polish Jewry before the onset of a more hideous tyranny at the end of the decade.

There was little overt anti-Semitism in the two Baltic kingdoms: Jews formed 0.16 per cent of the population in Sweden and 0.17 per cent in Denmark. In both countries the main concern of liberal progressives and social democrats was to ensure that the gradual transition from small-town agrarian life to industrialized urban society continued smoothly. Hjalmar Branting, the founding father of Sweden's labour movement, entered the liberal-dominated coalition in October 1917 and after the election of April

1920 was prime minister of a short-lived coalition government. He headed two more minority governments before his death in 1925, piloting through parliament basic social reforms, including an eight-hour working day; he was helped by the improbable coincidence that he had been at school with his obstinately conservative king. After Branting's death, rising unemployment led to labour unrest and the need to curb defence expenditure caused tension at Court.

In the autumn of 1928 a right-wing government came to power in Stockholm. There were savage wage cuts and violence on picket lines, and in 1931 five protesters were shot dead by the army at Ådalen. But Sweden's tradition of political restraint prevailed. Per Albin Hansson, who had succeeded Branting as party leader, skilfully brought trade union and agrarian interests together in the progressive camp. When financial scandal discredited the Liberals in 1932 the whiter-than-pink respectability of Hansson's *Socialdemokratiska Arbeiderparti* made the movement acceptable to the king. Hansson became prime minister in September 1932: apart from fifteen weeks in 1936, the Social Democrats remained in office until 1976, though in partnership with the Agrarians in 1936–39 and 1951–57, and forming the leading group in a broader coalition during the Second World War.

Denmark's prosperity was still dependent on agriculture, either directly through arable farming, pig-breeding and livestock or from dairy products and related industries. Foreign competition led to falling prices in the early 1920s and to a Social Democratic government, headed by Thorvald Stauning. But the radical wing of the labour movement was at variance with the centre and Stauning's proposed state intervention was on such a small scale that he could not keep his government together. Elections were held in 1926 at a time when one in every five of Denmark's workers was unemployed, but internal feuding lost Stauning many seats and he resigned. A Liberal minority government economized by slashing civil servants' earnings, cutting unemployment relief and closing two-thirds of the kingdom's labour exchanges. Not surprisingly, by the end of 1929 Stauning was back in office. He weathered the economic blizzard of the next three years, in part because he enjoyed Christian X's confidence. By May 1933 Stauning was able to co-ordinate existing legislation on pauperism and pensions in a four-point charter of public assistance and public care that became the cornerstone of Denmark's broadening structure of social welfare.

Farther east, foreign observers were surprised at the apparent ease with which Russia's successor states adapted economic life to the new conditions. The wealthy families of Swedish descent who held such a high position in

Finnish society ensured that the currency of the Grand Duchy, the *markka*, remained on the gold standard. There was social dislocation among lower middle class families in southern Finland: perhaps as many as 100,000 Finns employed in St Petersburg in administrative posts, domestic service, commerce or teaching found themselves forced back jobless among their kinsfolk; and favourite summer resorts like Perkjarvi and Lappeenranta spa lost their clientele (as also did Pärnu and Haapsalu in Estonia). But foreign trade figures confounded the pessimists. When revolutionary chaos cut exports from Russia, Finland met overseas demands by a rapid increase of trade in timber and other forestry products, notably sawn and planed softwoods. Latvia and Lithuania similarly exported timber, while also capturing new markets in Britain and Germany for flax and dairy produce. German exporters and German banks proved quicker off the mark than their British and French competitors and gained a key hold on commerce along the Baltic's southern shores, including the Free City of Danzig. So steady was the trade balance in Latvia and Lithuania that, by the autumn of 1922, their currencies were stabilized.

Riga's resilience was especially remarkable. Before 1910 200,000 people – two-thirds of the population – were dependent on heavy industry, with 350 factories in or around the city. They included the Provodnik rubber complex, chemical plants, works turning out ship's boilers and a variety of metal tools, and straggling establishments that gave Russian towns tramcars, railway rolling stock and their first native motor cars. Surprisingly, most factories remained in being after the upheaval of 1917–18, although they functioned on a smaller scale and were backed by German rather than Russian or French capital. The Rigans are an enterprising people. Between 1924 and 1930 the five Zeppelin hangars erected at Vainode for the proposed bombing of Petrograd were dismantled, transported 200 kilometres, and re-erected to give Riga a huge covered central market (which flourishes today). The city's character – a curious blending of St Petersburg, Hamburg and Vienna – survived all the changes. Inter-war Riga flaunted an Art Nouveau façade above a substructure of émigré reminiscence and conspiracy. In the city's streets and cafes secret agents, real or fake, proliferated.

Estonia had more difficulty than the other Baltic states in coming to terms with changed conditions. As late as 1922 a quarter of foreign trade was still with Russia, but the monopolistic state capitalism favoured by Lenin and Trotsky in that year finally brought the barrier down. A shadow of industrial unemployment enveloped northern Estonia, where the factories were barely six railway hours from the old imperial capital. The mills on the island of Kreenholm, upriver from Narva, had been as big as any cotton works in the world, but their fabrics sold almost entirely within the tsar's empire and their geographical location made it difficult to impinge on other, new markets. At Tallinn, the Baltic shipyards lay idle and the recently built naval base empty; few orders were placed at the Dvigately works, which had once specialized in carriages for Russia's longer railways. A bad harvest in 1923 pushed up food prices and heightened discontent. The Estonian government, worried by Bolshevik propaganda among dock workers, sacrificed democratic correctness and sought to enforce a ban on the communists who as the Estonian Working People's United Front had received almost 10 per cent of the vote in the recent general election. In the autumn of 1924 several trade union leaders were put on trial and on 15 November one was executed, for treasonable conspiracy.

Anger at the trade unionist's death sparked off an abortive communist coup in Tallinn on 1 December 1924 in which the railway station was seized and the minister of transport killed in an exchange of fire: the army restored order within a few hours, though at the cost of another twenty lives. This 'Red Threat', magnified by newspaper reports of emissaries from Moscow slipping across the border, caused consternation abroad. The League of Nations bolstered the economy by providing financial aid: a banking and currency reform loan in 1927 duly stabilized the currency. Estonia remained a democracy, but the 'railway station putsch' raised doubts over the easy-going character of the constitution. From 1925 onwards there was persistent right-wing agitation for a stronger executive. Fortunately for Tallinn the city found in Anton Uesson an exceptional mayor who improved social welfare, employment protection and education in the rapidly expanding capital.

The first challenge to parliamentary democracy did indeed come from the radical Right rather than the communist Left – but in Poland, not the Baltic states. In drafting their constitution, Warsaw's parliamentarians were acutely aware that the nation's soldier hero might make himself dictator. They insisted that their head of state should have no more than ceremonial duties: they knew that Pilsudski – made a marshal by popular acclaim in March 1920 – would never agree to become a mere figurehead shackled by parliamentary restraint. After a few months as chief of the General Staff, in April 1923 he left Warsaw and settled on his estate at Sulejowek, sourly watching the Sejm seek credible recognition.

It was not an edifying spectacle. Even before Pilsudski retired to Sulejowek his friend Gabriel Narutowicz was assassinated by a political opponent, two days after becoming president. With so much fractious fighting among members of the Sejm genuine parliamentary government became impossible. By the winter of 1925–6 the republic was in financial crisis, losing a tariff war with Germany that lessened the value of Danzig as a port, while the Bank of Poland was unable to protect the *zloty* from the pressure of German institutions. On 11 May 1926 Marshal Pilsudski, whose sympathies were with the workers rather than capitalists, published a blistering attack on the self-seeking politicians in the Sejm. The army turned to Pilsudski as custodian of the national will to exist and the railway unions backed him as an ex-socialist visionary. On 12 May there was fighting outside Warsaw between loyalist troops and 'patriot' insurgent regiments supporting the marshal. Resistance was stronger than anticipated. In sixty hours of civil war 500 Polish lives were lost, but by the morning of 15 May all power was in Pilsudski's hands.

He still refused to become president, even though a new, compliant parliament amended the constitution to create a strong executive, with powers to govern through emergency decree. Trade unions and Opposition newspapers were tolerated so long as their activities were not deemed subversive; the judiciary retained independence; but the marshal's personal friends were nominated to the presidency and ministerial office. He was himself prime minister from October 1926 to March 1928, and again briefly two years later; and as Inspector General of the army, he was given the powers of a commander-in-chief. His authority emanated, however, not from any titular post but from a masterful personality that, at times, treated opponents with humiliating brutality.

Pilsudski's trusted economic adviser, Kasmierz Bartel, a professor of mathematics and an old friend, checked inflation by means of government austerity, by curbing state railway expenditure and by boosting exports through the fast-growing port of Gdynia where the first cargoes had been unloaded as recently as August 1923. Bartel took advantage of the British miners' strike of 1926 which gave Poland the opportunity to meet the needs of the Baltic states and Scandinavia for coal – and to provide it at a lower cost. But Bartel could achieve nothing without Pilsudski's sanction. The marshal's views prevailed over every issue of domestic and foreign policy until his death in 1935, on the ninth anniversary of the coup that brought him to power.

Ironically, it was estranged Lithuania that followed Poland's example. In three successive elections the Lithuanian Nationalist Party, led by two veterans of the independence struggle, Antanas Smetona and Augustinas Voldemaras, had failed to attract voters, who preferred either the Catholic parties or differing brands of social democracy. But in 1925 clerical influence on the electorate was weakened by Vatican acknowledgment of Polish sovereignty over Vilnius. A few months later the moderate socialist coalition caused offence by opening diplomatic relations with Russia and concluding a non-aggression pact. Not even Moscow's recognition of Lithuania's claim to Vilnius could reconcile the military to this supping with the Soviet devil. The army lost patience with parliament and a week before Christmas in 1926 backed a Nationalist coup in Kaunas. Smetona became president, with Voldemaras as prime minister. Soon afterwards parliament was dissolved. For Lithuania the party political game was at an end.

Predictably the two nationalist governments in Kaunas and in Warsaw almost stumbled into war over Vilnius. Voldemaras closed forty-eight Polish schools in Lithuania and Pilsudski responded by shutting many Lithuanian educational establishments around Vilnius. The League intervened: the rival leaders travelled to Geneva and in December 1927 angrily confronted each other in the League Assembly. There were talks in Geneva itself and at Königsberg. The crisis eased, but tension lingered and frontier barriers remained firmly in place between the two countries. A letter posted in Vilnius for Kaunas, barely 130 kilometres down the river Neris, had to cross and re-cross Latvia's border in a journey of some 550 kilometres.

The dispute also reduced the commercial value of Lithuania's seizure of Klaipėda. Before 1914 logs from the forests of Russian Poland were floated down the Niemen and prepared for export in Memel's factories. Now the closed frontier left the city's sawmills dependent on more limited resources from Lithuania's own forests: Polish timber went by rail to Riga or Danzig and increasingly to Gdynia. Yet commercially, Klaipėda flourished, handling most of Lithuania's mounting exports of dairy produce and meat. But, significantly, twenty-seven of the twenty-nine members of the district's semi-autonomous council were Germans.

The Vilnius dispute frustrated any attempt of the Baltic peoples to work together. As early as September 1917 the Estonian liberal Progressive Jaan Tõnisson had spoken of the need to create a Scandinavian-Baltic bloc, 'a union of thirty million people' which would check the emergence of a dominant Great Power and give northern Europe an era of stability. The need for Pan-Baltic co-operation became stronger once France began to impose an alliance system intended as a barrier to isolate Bolshevik Russia and contain defeated Germany. But Tõnisson was a visionary statesman ahead of his time. Neither Norway nor Denmark could envisage a Scandinavia tied to the East rather than looking out to the Atlantic world, and although a pressure group in Stockholm briefly advocated a more positive Baltic policy, the Swedes saw no reason to abandon their well-tried, profitable neutrality.

It was left to Finland's foreign minister, Rudolf Holsti, to take up Tõnisson's proposal and promote collaboration between the Russian successor states. In January 1920 he presided over a conference in Helsinki attended by representatives from Estonia, Latvia, Lithuania and Poland; a second meeting in August drafted plans for co-ordinating defence and adopting a common policy towards outside powers. But these two gatherings marked the high point of Baltic collaboration. In October 1920 Zeligowski seized Vilnius and created his Polish satrapy in central Lithuania. Thereafter, though all five states collectively discussed economic problems in August 1930, they never again came together for a specifically political conference.

Holsti himself was reluctant to turn away from the southern shores of the Gulf and in 1922 even travelled to Warsaw for talks with the foreign ministers of Poland, Estonia and Latvia. But Finns and Poles had few interests in common. When Holsti returned to Helsinki he found his colleagues advocating Swedish-style neutrality. It was the end of Finland's championship of wide-ranging Baltic projects. Estonia and Latvia were content to conclude a treaty for common defence in November 1923 and shape their policies to come gradually closer to Lithuania.

Behind the improvised diplomacy of these years lay uncertainty over the fate of the wounded bear in the East. 'I cannot forecast to you the action of Russia. It is a riddle wrapped in a mystery inside an enigma,' Winston Churchill famously told a radio audience four weeks into the Second World War: the observation might well have been made at any moment during the preceding twenty years. Even when the Civil War and Intervention were over and a shaky peace returned to Petrograd, it was still not clear if Leninism would survive. After three years of 'war communism' factories were closed for lack of raw materials, food and fuel in short supply and Party leaders out of touch with the people. At the end of February 1921, in the misery of a bitterly cold and hungry winter, the sailors of Kronstadt sought once more to fire 'the will of the workers and peasants'. The crews of the battleships *Sevastopol* and *Petropavlovsk* (refloated and repaired) called a mass meeting at which resolutions were carried demanding the basic freedoms and elections for an 'honest and just' Soviet. Had the sailors marched on Petrograd next day, they might have roused the discontented workers and spread rebellion across the countryside. Instead, as in 1917, they remained in their island fortress waiting for news of acts of defiance by others and a call to intervene.

It never came. In Petrograd the Cheka secret police were omnipresent, ready to round up dissident suspects. On Lenin's orders, Tukachevsky concentrated crack infantry, clad in white capes, along the snow-covered northern shore of the Gulf. For six days in mid-March 1921 the Kronstadt sailors repulsed wave after wave of assault troops sent forward across the frozen sea. Eventually fewer than a hundred seamen escaped to Finland. The remaining 15,000 men either died in the fighting or were summarily executed in its aftermath. As many as 20,000 of the Red Army's assault troops may have perished in battle or beneath the shell-cracked icy wastes around Kotlin island.

The rebellion was followed by changes in the Soviet structure. Lenin's New Economic Policy of state capitalism mixed centralized industry with small-scale peasant agriculture and, by allowing some freedom of internal trade, improved food distribution. But the policy was adopted too late to avert the great famine and wave of disease that in the following winter brought Western relief workers to Russia to save the people from disaster. Political change came too, though not the free elections and devolved authority the Kronstadt seamen had sought. On 30 December 1922 the Congress of Soviets in Moscow formally agreed to bind together one-sixth of the land surface of the globe in the Union of Soviet Socialist Republics. Yet with Lenin incapacitated by a series of strokes, his economic policy still on trial, and the Party already weakened by a power struggle between Trotsky and Stalin, it was hard to see any immediate threat in this new communist colossus. Even the activities of the Comintern – the movement established in March 1919 to promote revolutionary Marxism abroad – seemed inept, as the bungled coup in Tallinn was soon to confirm. When Lenin died in January 1924, Petrograd (so recently St Petersburg) became Leningrad. Few thought the newest name would last any longer than its predecessor.

There remained, however, one potential challenge to the stability of the region – an alliance of the two displaced Great Powers. By the Treaty of Rapallo (April 1922) Soviet Russia and post-Versailles Germany undertook to 'co-operate in a spirit of mutual goodwill to meet the economic needs of both countries'; a further commitment four years later referred to the need for 'understanding on all political questions'. Secretly the Soviet authorities allowed Germany to evade many of the military restrictions in the peace treaty. Junkers aircraft were built at a German-financed factory at Fili, outside Moscow; a chemical plant in Samara produced poison gas; and near Kazan tanks were manufactured, with German specialists in armoured warfare training junior officers of the Red Army, including Zhukov, the future conqueror of Berlin. But outwardly Soviet policy remained peaceful, accommodating and, towards the three Baltic republics, even solicitously protective.

When, in 1927, the Soviet envoy to Poland was assassinated in Warsaw by a counter-revolutionary émigré, neither government sought to stir up a war crisis over the incident. Litvinov, who succeeded the ailing Chicherin as foreign commissar later that year, followed up the earlier non-aggression pact with Lithuania by promoting the so-called Litvinov Protocol of February 1929 by which the Soviet Union, Poland, Latvia and Estonia (together with Romania) renounced aggressive acts across Soviet frontiers. At the same time trade agreements marked Russia's reappearance on the world market. Railway wagons began to bring more and more timber to the quayside at Tallinn, Riga and Memel.

Not surprisingly, in the summer of 1928 there was a sudden slump in the world price of timber. The Finns were particularly hard hit: out of a forestry work force of 20,000 in northern Finland, 13,000 were jobless by the following spring. Production was drastically reduced in Sweden, too. Not only the timber trade was thrown into disarray. Protective barriers went up across northern Europe when it became clear that too many countries were exporting eggs, bacon and dairy produce. Indirect taxation subsidized Swedish butter and Estonian bacon. But the Depression deepened. Over-cultivation and mechanized production of grain and cereal in the USA and Canada sent the price of wheat cascading downwards. A fever of speculation in America led, in the first instance, to the withdrawal of funds from Europe and, after the Wall Street panic of October 1929, to a slump in investment and banking. The ending of French short-term credit to Austrian banks caused the dramatic crash of Vienna's Credit Anstalt in March 1931, sending shock waves through Germanic financial institutions in the old Hanse cities. Hardly less damaging to economies within Scandinavia was the suicide of the Swedish 'match king', Ivar Krueger, who shot himself in Paris on 12 March 1932, leaving liabilities of some £50 million and precipitating the collapse of Sweden's Liberal government.

The threat of mounting unemployment prompted far more state initiative in the northern democracies in the early 1930s than during the previous decade. There were tighter exchange controls, quotas on imports, unprecedented consultation between farmers' representatives, trade unionists and manufacturers, and ambitious public works programmes, notably in Sweden and (to a lesser extent) Denmark. Britain's decision to abandon the gold standard (September 1931) and protect the empire as a self-contained trading unit outdated existing commercial relations in Europe. Under new agreements London accepted limited imports of dairy produce but stipulated that the Baltic countries must make purchases from Britain in return. In the United Kingdom the chief beneficiaries were heavy industry and coalmining. Much of the market lost to Poland in 1926 was wrested back eight years later. By 1935, 78 per cent of the coal imported by Estonia, Latvia and Lithuania and 80 per cent of Denmark's coal and coke came from British mines.

Politically the Depression led to local protest movements and the rapid growth of authoritarian ideologies. The most notorious consequences were in Germany where between late 1929 and late 1932 industrial production was halved, unemployment trebled and membership of Hitler's National Socialist Workers' Party doubled. The Nazis' earliest successes had come in southern Germany, but the voting patterns of 1930 and 1932 reflected the party's growing appeal not so much to the unemployed in the cities as to the small businessmen, frustrated farmers and skilled workers of the north, particularly the young.

In the Reichstag elections of July 1932 more than half of the traditionally pastoral God-fearing Lutheran voters in Schleswig-Holstein backed the Nazis. A few days later Sir Horace Rumbold, British ambassador in Berlin, reported a wave of terror at Königsberg, the capital of East Prussia: Nazi thugs attacked suspected socialists and communists in their homes and smashed the windows of Jewish shops, which were then looted. Kiel, like Hamburg, stood out against Hitler, but from Lübeck eastwards towns and villages allegedly threatened by Polish minorities welcomed the coming of a 'dynamic' National Socialism. In the first round of the presidential election of April 1932 the appeal of the Austrian-born corporal was even strong enough to deny Hindenburg a majority of votes in the region around Tannenberg and the Masurian Lakes, the birthplace of the field marshal's personal legend. When, eleven months later, the last free elections were held, voters along the Baltic hinterland confirmed their faith in Hitler's advocacy of narrowly Germanic interests and gave the Nazi and Nationalist parties together a majority of sixteen seats in the Reichstag.

The Depression also brought the curtain down on parliamentary democracy in the Baltic republics. In Lithuania acquisition of an authoritarian ideology strengthened the pragmatic dictatorship imposed in 1926: President Smetona upstaged Voldemaras, replacing him as head of government in 1929 with his own brother-in-law, Jonas Tubelis. When, in June 1934, Voldemaras planned a putsch with the aid of the para-military Iron Wolf movement, the president struck first and imprisoned his rival in a Kaunas fort for four years before sending him to exile in France.

At the same time Smetona harnessed the right-wing radicalism of 'Iron

Wolf' to inspire his Nationalist Party with idealized reverence for Greater Lithuania's past. There were strong echoes of Nazi political technique: Smetona was hailed as Leader of the Nation with the up-stretched arm salute. A youth movement, recruited from the high schools, bore 'Lithuania for the Lithuanians' on its banners; and anti-Semitism became fashionable, though without the cruel persecution so blatantly practised across the East Prussian border. When trade improved again there was a momentary prospect of returning to parliamentary democracy and in the spring of 1935 a general election was called. Shortly before the poll, however, it was ruled that only candidates approved by the government might stand for election. Few bothered to vote: forty-six Nationalist Party members and three Germans from Klaipėda-Memel were returned to an assembly that rubber-stamped Smetona's decrees.

Democratic Estonia suffered a similar fate. A League of Veterans of the War of Liberation grew rapidly between 1929 and 1933, under the leadership of a young demagogue, Artur Sirk, who transformed the movement into a para-military body that staged mass rallies and paraded in shiny uniforms. The Veterans League won nationwide backing in October 1933 for a referendum on constitutional reform, including a reduction in the powers of parliament and the setting up of an authoritarian executive presidency.

Three months later the new constitution became effective and Estonia was plunged into the unfamiliar excitement of a presidential steeplechase, with rival generals leading the field. Would voters back the former supreme commander, General Laidoner, who was good at clearing political fences? Or would they go for the Veterans' candidate, his one-time deputy General Larka, whose reins were in the skilful hands of Artur Sirk? Also in the race were the veteran Farmers' Party leader and incumbent prime minister, Konstantin Päts, and a socialist, August Rei, of whom little was known except that he was an anti-communist. Pre-election lists of pledged support gave Larka and the Veterans a clear lead (51 per cent), followed by Laidoner (30 per cent), Päts (15 per cent) and Rei (4 per cent).

But the presidential runners never got under starters' orders. On 12 March 1934, five weeks before polling was due, Päts summoned a cabinet meeting, to which he invited General Laidoner. The prime minister told his colleagues that Laidoner had discovered the Veterans were about to seize power. To frustrate their knavish tricks, Päts declared a political emergency, postponed the elections indefinitely, dissolved parliament, and appointed Laidoner Head of Security and Supreme Army Commander. All public meetings were banned and every leading member of the

Veterans League arrested, except General Larka. It was a smooth and bloodless political coup.

For the next six years Päts remained dictator of a militaristic state, in which Laidoner commanded the army and ultimately determined foreign policy. When the Veterans planned a counter-putsch on 8 December 1935 Laidoner acted decisively; the conspirators were arrested on the evening before they were due to strike. Päts saw to it that the Veterans League was proscribed: General Larka remained in detention for two years; Sirk fled into exile. In August 1937 he was found dead under the open window of a hotel at Echternach in Luxembourg. Officially he was said to have killed himself, but suspicion fell on Laidoner's secret service agents. A 'not proven' verdict would seem in order.

Päts was held in high regard. In one respect he was untypical of Estonians, for he remained Russian Orthodox in a country overwhelmingly Lutheran in faith and culture. But he never doubted the republic's national identity. He had headed the first provisional government in 1918 and was prime minister four times before becoming dictator. It was not hard to channel the Veterans' hot-air patriotism into a Fatherland League, anti-communist and loyal to the government. Yet another constitution – the third in eighteen years – bolstered the authoritarian regime by providing 'guided democracy' through a bicameral parliament, with an elected Lower House and a nominated State Council. The Estonian people were sceptical; press censorship was retained and the old political parties banned. Elections were held on the last weekend of February 1938 and a fifth of the seats were won by opposition groups, but the Päts–Laidoner partnership remained in control and was by no means unpopular. The economy revived. Tariffs, and government subsidies, cosseted the farmers. Corporate bodies marshalled state guidance of business enterprise, as in fascist Italy. The chemical industries of the north-east provided phosphate for Germany's vast IG Farben combine and the oil-shale of Sillamäe fuelled Hitler's new diesel navy.

The founding father of the Latvian Republic, Karlis Ulmanis, having headed five democratic governments, soon followed Päts's example and chose dictatorship. On 15 May 1934 he declared a state of emergency and induced the titular president to suspend parliament. Two years later Ulmanis himself became head of state, backed (like Päts) by Latvia's symbolic hero of the war of independence, General Balodis. Ulmanis did not bother with constitutional reform nor submit his personal government to election. Economic corporatism was encouraged, as in Estonia, and the balance of exports over imports looked more and more healthy: five times as much foreign trade left Riga in 1938–39 as in the early years of full independence. It was not a harsh dictatorship, and there is no doubt Ulmanis and Balodis defended the republic from the xenophobic anti-Semitism of a fascist 'Thunder Cross' movement as well as from communism. But they did nothing to check the spread of a primarily anti-German linguistic nationalism. Sadly the spirit of cultural tolerance that held such promise in Latvia during the previous decade evaporated.

Enduring model democracies could not be created at the stroke of a pen. The fate of the Baltic republics showed that to survive the frustration of economic recession their institutions had needed deeper roots in popular sovereignty. The Finnish experience was significantly different. In November 1929 a rash attempt by young communists to stage a mass demonstration in the staunchly White market town of Lapua provoked a populist reaction – the Lapua Movement – which soon became a nation-wide anti-Red crusade: the Depression, it was claimed, was a Soviet plot to overthrow world capitalism by using slave labour to cause the timber crisis – which was to many Finns the root of all evil. The Finnish government resigned and the veteran Pehr Svinhufvud formed an interim administration pending a general election in October 1930 to gain approval for anti-communist measures. Svinhufvud was sympathetic to many of the Lapua Movement's ideals. But Lapua followed too closely the pattern of street brawling associated with the crisis in Weimar Germany to win popular backing: more than 200 alleged communists were beaten up or kidnapped by Lapua thugs. They included the respected ex-president, Kaarlo Stahlberg, and his wife.

Svinhufvud received enough electoral support to outlaw the Communist Party, and in 1931 he became president. Yet he was too shrewd a political manipulator to be trapped by Lapua. Finnish democracy was never seriously in danger. An embryonic putsch by Lapua army officers at Mäntsälä in February 1932 was nipped in the bud. Svinhufvud went ahead with elections in 1933 and 1936 that confirmed voters' confidence in parliamentary ways. Even though sixteen radical Right deputies were returned to parliament, in 1937 Social Democrats served once more in the ruling coalition.

The Mäntsälä officers wrongly assumed that General Mannerheim would be Finland's Pilsudski. He remained, however, a professional soldier, his services to the nation acknowledged in 1933 when he received a marshal's baton. Unlike Laidoner and Balodis, Mannerheim stood well above politics, though there was no doubt of his deep hostility to communism.

Technically he lived in retirement. In practice, he was heavily engaged in the planning and construction of the defensive line named after him. A cluster of 2,000 fortified posts, many sunk in concrete, was to run for 135 kilometres across the Karelian isthmus, confronting any Soviet thrust westwards from Leningrad. In Helsinki a new parliament house was completed in 1930, with a façade of fourteen granite columns topping more than thirty steps. It was – and remains – an impressive building, confidently permanent in character. Twenty years after gaining independence the Finns were ready to offer a robust defence of their frontier and, within their republic, to uphold the democratic heritage they cherished.

24

Hitler's Challenge

HITLER BECAME GERMAN Chancellor on 30 January 1933. Seven weeks later he stood beside President Hindenburg in Potsdam Garrison Church at a ceremony that (in Hitler's own words) 'celebrated the union between the symbols of old greatness and new strength'. Few experienced politicians inside or outside Germany took him seriously: a wild demagogue who would be tamed by office or soon stumble to personal disaster. The Germanophile King Gustav V of Sweden visited Berlin in the spring, met both president and chancellor and claimed to have 'taken Hitler by one ear' and persuaded him to modify his anti-Semitism. But in Poland Marshal Pilsudski reacted more sharply to what he perceived as a mounting challenge. He was so enraged by the clamour of pro-Hitler demonstrations in Danzig that he ordered his small garrison at Westerplatte to be strengthened. In March, and again in April, he approached his French ally with proposals for preventive action: Poland would use the Danzig demonstrations as a pretext to occupy the Free City and enter East Prussia, provided that France moved troops into the Ruhr. The twin occupations would continue until Hitler was replaced by a chancellor who would give assurances to uphold the Versailles settlement. But France, with mounting domestic disquiet, could never accept the risks of such a policy and there were doubts in Paris whether the marshal was in earnest. The year 1933 passed without a crisis over Danzig. The League reprimanded Poland for reinforcing Westerplatte, and the extra troops were withdrawn.

Hitler was at first prepared to be conciliatory. The Gauleiter of Danzig, Albert Forster, was called to order. His Nazis began to show more discipline in the streets and in elections in May won a majority of seats on the Free City's assembly, the Volkstag. Soon, however, Gauleiter Forster was introducing laws to curb political opposition. But the impact of Nazification was reduced by moves in Berlin to improve German–Polish relations in general. As early as 2 May Hitler told the Polish envoy that he favoured a dispassionate review of problems confronting the two countries. In August an agreement was signed in Danzig between Poland and the Volkstag's executive safeguarding the rights of the Polish minority within the Free City. A month later Goebbels, the Nazi propaganda chief, held talks with Pilsudski's protégé, Colonel Beck, who had become foreign minister in November 1932; he was to be a key figure in the unfolding crises of the next seven years.

Joseph Beck was vain, a dabbler in diplomacy posing as a master of statecraft, a Francophobe who deplored his country's close political links with Paris. He believed that Poland's position astride the Vistula made her the fulcrum of power in central Europe and the southern Baltic. His influence increased rapidly in the autumn of 1934 when Pilsudski's health began to fail and he made his first objective the attainment of freedom of manoeuvre. He sought to create a Beck System, a 'Third Europe' that would keep the Russians – whom he loathed – at bay while enabling him to bargain with Germany. Despite his contempt for the Bolsheviks, he had welcomed proposals from Litvinov of a non-aggression pact (agreed soon after Beck came to office) and in 1933 he responded to the overtures from Berlin in the hope that a similar pact would ease tensions in the Corridor and raise Poland's status in Europe as a whole. On 26 January 1934 Germany and Poland concluded a non-aggression pact, valid for ten years: mutual problems would be resolved by direct talks, not by force.

Beck took pride in becoming the first foreign minister to settle differences with Hitler. On the other hand Danzigers, Memellanders and many Prussians were puzzled and disappointed. Despite Goebbels's constant anti-Versailles propaganda it looked as if Hitler was giving priority to the Austrian Question rather than to righting Germany's wrongs in the lost marchlands of the Teutonic Knights. The Soviet reaction was significant. Within nine weeks of the German–Polish Pact Litvinov proposed to the German ambassador in Moscow a joint guarantee of the Baltic lands that 'had formed part of the former tsarist empire' (a formula no doubt chosen to exclude Memel). When Hitler showed no interest in such an undertaking, Litvinov turned to Paris and backed the initiative by the French foreign minister, Barthou, for a Treaty of Regional Assistance. Nothing came of so unwieldy a project, though indirectly it brought the Soviet Union into membership of the League of Nations later in the year.

The Baltic states particularly mistrusted the Barthou Plan, for it would have permitted the Red Army to enter their lands to render 'assistance'. They remained uneasy, and in September 1934 agreed on limited military co-operation, creating the so-called Baltic Entente. But Latvia and Estonia specified that they would not help Lithuania in any war over Vilnius or Klaipėda/Memel, and the Lithuanians hurriedly distanced themselves from

Estonian approaches to Finland over modernizing shore batteries on either side of the Gulf.

The Finns welcomed refortification as a way of complementing the Mannerheim Line defences against Russia, but shunned the Baltic Entente or any other commitment beyond the southern shore. There was an influential pro-German lobby in Helsinki: 'In an emergency there is only one power that can quickly render aid to Finland, and that is Germany,' President Svinhufvud was to remark in February 1937 to the German Minister in Helsinki. But as early as December 1935 Finland officially proclaimed a 'Scandinavian orientation'. Finnish presidents joined the Scandinavian kings in 'Nordic meetings' each autumn and staff talks with Swedish officers emphasized that the Finns now looked to the West.

In a different sense, the West as a whole increasingly turned to the Baltic. Never before had there been such contact between ordinary folk from Britain or America and the peoples of the inland sea. Mass tourism did not come until far later in the century, but by the early 1930s favourable rates of exchange were opening up resorts long patronized by German holiday-makers: the beaches of Travemünde and Peenemünde or the bays and lakes of Rügen, for example. Some yachtsmen sailed farther east, though the authorities eyed long, lingering voyages with suspicion, for the region was, understandably, spy sensitive. Cheap ferries and coastal steamers made island hopping attractive and, away from the coasts, newly surfaced roads tempted cyclists to push ahead across the plains to towns rich with the unfamiliar history of a Hanse past. For a reasonable price you could take Baltic cruises from the Thames to Copenhagen, Danzig and Stockholm, occasionally to Helsinki or Riga, too. Conversely, spectator sports made athletes from the Baltic known abroad, with Finland's middle-distance runners outstanding. By contrast, Lithuania's folk heroes were two pioneer airmen who in July 1933 set out to fly non-stop home from New York. Sadly, after thirty-seven hours in the air, Steponas Darius and Stasys Girenas were killed when their plane crashed among the trees of a German forest 750 kilometres short of Kaunas, where one in six of the population had gathered at the aerodrome to greet them. The tragedy caught the attention of the world press. By 1936 the Baltic nations were far from being distant peoples of whom the West knew nothing.

British officialdom eyed the region with characteristic uncertainty, however. City banks and chambers of commerce followed developments with interest; Chatham House – London's 'think tank' for international affairs – commissioned a concise study of the Baltic's recent past and economic potential; departmental heads at the Foreign Office circulated paternalistic memoranda commending the Baltic republics' achievements. But successive governments remained reluctant to make military commitments or even to raise the level of diplomatic missions in an age when the symbolism of status still mattered. In Berlin, Warsaw and Moscow ambassadors represented their sovereign and presided over impressive embassies, but in the remaining Baltic capitals the accredited envoy was officially termed a 'minister', the spokesman of one government to another, and lived and worked in an unpretentious legation: the British reckoned that the needs of all three Baltic republics could be satisfied by a single minister, resident in Riga. Although foreign ministers met at the League Assembly in Geneva they had little acquaintance with each other's homeland. The thirty-five-year-old Anthony Eden – in the government as Lord Privy Seal, but not yet in the cabinet – went to Oslo, Stockholm and Copenhagen in October 1934 and a few months later Berlin, Warsaw and Moscow: he did not visit Helsinki, Tallinn, Riga, Kaunas or Danzig. 'The interest of His Majesty's Government in the Baltic States is not like their interest in Belgium,' Eden explained to Litvinov, though he hastily added, 'They are, of course, interested from the point of view of general security in Europe.'

In principle all British governments believed in upholding the collective authority of the League of Nations. But over naval policy they continued to show independence, preferring to seek a balance of power in home waters by direct negotiation, with little reference to allies or associates. After 1919, Weimar Germany had maintained the Reichsmarine, a relatively small coastal defence force. Between 1925 and 1935 three light cruisers and three fast, diesel-fuelled and heavily armoured 'pocket battleships' were built: all conformed to the limitations imposed by the Treaty of Versailles, at least on the drawing-board. Hitler personally had little interest in maritime affairs: he had seen the sea for the first time only in October 1918 when recuperating at a military hospital near Stettin, and he was always a poor sailor. But to Nazi Germany it was humiliating for a despised treaty to deny the nation a modern fleet and, at the start of his third year in office, Hitler began to please the navalists. The Reichsmarine was renamed Kriegsmarine; and in a speech on 21 May 1935 he offered the British a guarantee limiting the size of the new navy. Early in June his foreign policy adviser, Ribbentrop, flew to London with powers to sign an agreement.

Within a few days Ribbentrop was back in Berlin, preening himself on a personal triumph. The Anglo-German Naval Treaty provided for a Kriegsmarine with a surface fleet 35 per cent the size of the Royal Navy's and a submarine fleet rising to 45 per cent, or even higher should Germany decide on a lower total tonnage for surface warships. The pact did not worry the Admiralty: improved underwater sound-ranging equipment would, they believed, make detection and destruction of U-boats far easier than in 1917–18; and they were convinced that post-war capital ships like the battle-cruiser HMS *Hood* and the battleships *Nelson* and *Rodney* could outpace and outgun German surface vessels. But to Europe in general the pact was a matter of grave concern. It confirmed Britain's willingness to appease Nazi Germany and turn a blind eye to Hitler's abrogation of the Versailles Treaty.

Ensigns of war were rarely seen in northern waters after the departure of Cowan's force in 1920. At both Tallinn and Riga there long lingered an assumption that, in time of crisis, the Royal Navy would again come to the rescue. In November 1921 the Baltic Sea was considered of so little importance in maritime warfare that no country in the region was represented at the conference on naval disarmament which opened in Washington that month. By 1935 the Danish and Finnish navies possessed no ships larger than coastal defence ironclads, of less than 4,500 tonnes displacement. Poland had only four destroyers and five submarines. In July 1933 Estonia sold her two remaining warships to Peru. Sweden maintained Charles XI's historic naval base at Karlskrona, but the biggest ships in the Swedish navy were three ironclads of 7,110 tonnes built in 1916–17; the first modern cruiser, the 4,850 tonne *Gotland*, was only launched in 1933. Soviet Russia still relied on the three old dreadnoughts, refitted in Leningrad and now known as *Oktiabrskaia-Revolutsia* (ex-*Gangut*), *Pariskaia-Kommuna* (ex-*Sevastopol*) and *Marat* (ex-*Petropavlosk*); they were of questionable seaworthiness. More than once, Soviet diplomats put out feelers suggesting the Baltic Sea be neutralized, a project first mooted as early as October 1920 in the Russo-Finnish peace treaty. The idea had a few champions outside Russia but, like so many projects emanating from Moscow, it aroused widespread suspicion too. No progress was made.

The creation of the Kriegsmarine and news of the Anglo-German agreement finally destroyed any hope of a neutralized sea in the North. Germany, it seemed, would soon rule the Baltic waves, with little threat of any challenge from Britannia. The Swedes at once began modernizing their fleet, concentrating on destroyers, minesweepers and submarines but also providing for the eventual building of two more coastal defence ships and a cruiser. By 1940 Sweden, so long a model social welfare state, was allocating more of the annual budget to the navy than to pensions; forty-seven warships were in commission and as many again under construction.

The most dramatic change in naval planning was in the Soviet Union. Work began on widening the main canals of Russia so that warships could pass from the White Sea into the Gulf of Finland and ultimately down to the Black Sea, too. To bolster morale the ships based on Kronstadt were renamed Red Banner Baltic Fleet, honouring the sailors' role in the Bolshevik Revolution. Three dockyards in Leningrad began a major build-ing programme, with the first modern cruiser launched in the autumn of 1936 and a second a few months later. In 1940 a 35,500 tonne battleship and two aircraft carriers were on the stocks. None was ready before the invasion of Russia a year later, but many smaller vessels were completed on time. By 1941 the Baltic fleet included nineteen destroyers, sixty-five sub-marines and a shore-based naval air arm. The enemy, it was always assumed, would be Nazi Germany.

Hitler, for his part, never doubted the inevitability of war with Russia. The destruction of 'Jewish Bolshevism' and the attainment of living space (*Lebensraum*) in the East had been pillars of the National Socialist ideology since the earliest years of the movement. Until the spring of 1939 he counted on Polish backing in the crusade against Bolshevism, for he remained convinced that differences with Warsaw could be settled peace-fully. This was a reasonable assumption. From 1935 onwards Polish policy was shaped by a triumvirate of Pilsudski's nominees: President Ignacy Mościcki, a relative lightweight; Marshal Smigly-Rydz, the new Inspector General of the army, who had long shared his predecessor's hostility to Russia; and Colonel Beck as foreign minister. Hitler's southward expan-sionism, well away from the Baltic, suited Beck's pattern of diplomacy.

On 17 March 1938, four days after the *Anschluss* incorporating Austria in Greater Germany, an ultimatum from Warsaw was presented in Kaunas: on 11 March a Lithuanian guard had fired on a patrol across the closed fron-tier and killed a Polish infantryman; and the ultimatum demanded a resumption of normal diplomatic relations and, implicitly, Lithuania's rec-ognition of Polish sovereignty over Vilnius. German troops in East Prussia were put on alert next day, ready to join the Poles in dismembering Lithuania should President Smetona reject the ultimatum. Despite his patriotic fervour, the Leader of the Nation had no real choice. After eight-een years of defiance Kaunas ended the state of war with Poland. The fron-tier was re-opened.

In contrast to events in Vienna, Poland's show of strength went almost unnoticed in Europe as a whole. Even along Baltic shores it caused hardly a ripple of interest. Hitler made no move. For the moment, he was con-tent for the good Germans of Memel to remain outside the Reich.

The German–Polish partnership continued throughout the year. When, after the Munich agreement of 29 September 1938, Germany detached the Sudetenland from Czechoslovakia, the Poles pressed their own demands on the government in Prague. On 2–3 October Polish troops occupied the southern sector of the former Duchy of Teschen, which in July 1920 had been divided by the peacemakers in Paris between Poland and Czechoslovakia. But within a fortnight there were signs of renewed German interest in the Baltic. On 21 October Germany's military and naval leaders were secretly ordered 'to be prepared at all times' for an immediate seizure of Memel; and on 24 October Ribbentrop – foreign minister since February – told the Polish ambassador in Berlin the time had come for a 'general settlement' of Polish–German relations. Danzig, Ribbentrop stated, must return to the Reich; the Poles would give Germany extra-territorial rights in the Corridor; and Poland would accede to the Anti-Comintern Pact, the alliance against Bolshevism sponsored by Germany and Japan in 1936. In return, Poland was offered trade concessions in Danzig itself, a lengthy extension of the Non-Aggression Pact, and a guarantee of frontiers.

The government in Warsaw refused to countenance any loosening of Polish control over the mouths of the Vistula. But Hitler was not, as yet, contemplating war with Poland: a General Staff directive of 24 November 1938 ordered preparations 'for the surprise occupation of Danzig . . . in a lightning seizure'; it made no provision for an extended campaign in Poland itself. To German observers in Warsaw, Colonel Beck seemed less obdurate than his colleagues in government and over the next three months they sought to win him over. On one occasion Ribbentrop even reminded him that 'the Black Sea is a sea, too', stirring memories of the mighty Jagiellonian realm and tempting him with the prospect of a future Polish port on the coast of the Ukraine. Beck was invited to meet the Führer at Berchtesgaden in the first week of January 1939 and Ribbentrop was courteously received in Warsaw later in the month. In the notorious speech Hitler delivered in the Reichstag on 30 January threatening 'annihilation' for Europe's Jews, he was prepared to praise, calmly and rationally, the lasting value of German–Polish friendship. As late as the third week in March, when Prague was occupied and Czechoslovakia replaced by a German protectorate over Bohemia-Moravia and a puppet Slovak republic, the Poles still hoped for compensation in central Europe.

Two events on 23 March 1939 shattered Beck's illusions. On that Thursday Germany signed a treaty with Slovakia, putting the armed forces of the new puppet republic under Hitler's control; and on the same day Germany at last struck in the north, occupying Memel and a strip of land extending 150 kilometres along the right bank of the river Niemen. From the outer balcony of the city's neo-classical theatre Hitler personally proclaimed 'the Memel territory reunited with the German Reich'. Suddenly Poland was gripped in an armed vice: German troops were deployed along the western and southern frontiers, while in the north motorized divisions were now within six or seven driving hours of Vilnius.

For the Baltic nations 'Memel' was more ominous than the two better-known pre-war crises, 'Munich' and 'Prague'. A swift operation by the German army and air force had deprived Lithuania of her only sizeable port and a third of her industrial capacity. Moreover Hitler arrived at Memel on that Thursday afternoon aboard the pocket-battleship *Deutschland*, which had sailed from Swinemünde the previous evening. The significance of the naval presence in the redeemed Hanse port was duly noted. As Lipski, Poland's ambassador in Berlin, commented six months later, 'the entry of German troops into Memel and the Chancellor's demonstrative voyage along our coast was as great a surprise to Polish public opinion as the German entry into Slovakia had been.' The Poles responded by mobilizing four divisions and a cavalry brigade to strengthen their western frontier.

The British, too, were surprised. Neville Chamberlain, prime minister since May 1937, had convinced himself that beneath the menacing tone of Nazi Germany lay some legitimate grievances. In partnership with Lord Halifax, who succeeded Eden as foreign secretary in February 1938, he sought to propitiate Hitler by concessions over matters that threatened war. This 'policy of appeasement' reached a climax at Munich in September 1938, where the heads of government of Britain, Germany, France and Italy imposed frontier changes on Czechoslovakia without inviting any envoy from Prague (or from Moscow, even though the Russians had alliances with both the Czechs and the French). Chamberlain flew triumphantly back from Munich with a guarantee of rump Czechoslovakia and a pledge signed by Hitler and himself that Britain and Germany would 'never go to war with one another again'. He was hailed as the saviour of peace. Disillusionment came six months later. With the German entry into Prague on 15 March 1939 and the creation of the Slovak state, Chamberlain saw he had been duped.

There followed three weeks of flurried diplomacy, much of which puzzled the Baltic capitals. On 17 March, in a speech at Birmingham on the eve of his seventieth birthday, Chamberlain cautiously indicated a major shift in policy. Over the next few days attempts were made to promote a

British–French–Russian–Polish declaration of joint action should the independence 'of any European State' be threatened. Colonel Beck, suspicious of Russia, suggested as an alternative a bilateral Anglo-Polish agreement 'in the spirit of the declaration'. By chance, his proposal reached the Foreign Office at the same time as news of Hitler's latest unexpected move, the seizure of Memel. Lord Halifax, who favoured a positive statement guaranteeing Poland's frontiers, strengthened the prime minister's resolve. On 31 March Chamberlain told the Commons that if 'Polish independence' were threatened 'His Majesty's government would feel bound to lend the Polish Government all support in their power'. Never since the First World War had Britain contemplated a security commitment in the Baltic, or indeed in Eastern Europe as a whole. Appeasement was at an end. 'The House cheered,' one MP wrote in his diary that night: 'Cheers from every side,' noted another.

Four days later Beck came to London, taking up an invitation originally broached in February. A twelve-year-old schoolboy happened to be in Downing Street as the Polish statesman's car turned into the Foreign Office that morning: the contented superiority of Beck's cold smile remains etched in memory even today. The colonel's ego was flattered by the red carpet treatment offered by his hosts; a special train took him to Portsmouth to see for himself the size and firepower of the Royal Navy. On 8 April, as the visit came to an end, Chamberlain announced that Britain and Poland had agreed to sign a mutual assistance pact, complementing the Franco-Polish alliance treaty of 1921. Soon, assurances of support were also offered to Romania and to Greece. The policy of appeasement gave way to the policy of guarantees, although the ultimate commitment of a definitive Anglo-Polish alliance treaty was not signed for almost five months.

Hitler was infuriated by the news of Chamberlain's guarantee. While he was aboard the *Deutschland*, he had been confident Ribbentrop would entice Beck to make another journey to Berlin. Instead came reports of Poland's partial mobilization and of the visit to London. The Führer, so Ribbentrop warned ambassador Lipski, was losing patience with the Poles. Secretly, on 11 April, he issued a directive to the heads of the armed forces for 'Case White' (*Fall Weisse*), the invasion of Poland: all operational plans should be completed so as to allow implementation of Case White by 1 September – a date that fell between the garnering of the harvest and the onset of the autumn rains. Publicly, in a speech on 28 April, Hitler renounced both the German–Polish Non-Aggression Pact and the limited restraints on sea power agreed in the Anglo-German Naval Treaty. For once, his speech said nothing about Russia or the Bolshevik threat in the East. The omission went unnoticed at the time.

Chamberlain now faced a dilemma familiar to any British government contemplating action in the Baltic. To offer a paper guarantee was a declaration of good intent: but what practical help could the United Kingdom give to a country threatened by the strongest military power around the inland sea? The best hope for Poland lay in partnership with London, Paris and Moscow, a variant of Litvinov's consistent advocacy of a triple alliance of Great Powers to deter a German attack. In mid-April French diplomats began softening up the rabidly anti-Soviet military leaders of Poland, while the British cautiously opened discussions with the Russians.

There were, however, three grave obstacles to progress: Chamberlain's ideological antipathy to a military or naval convention with the Soviet Union; the fear among Russia's Baltic neighbours that Moscow's embrace was a stranglehold as deadly as Berlin's enmity; and, most immediately, Stalin's mistrust of the capitalist West after the apparent betrayal of Czechoslovakia. On 3 May Litvinov was dismissed, axed like a failed football manager; and Molotov, Stalin's prime minister since 1930, assumed responsibility for foreign affairs as well. Litvinov was Jewish, his wife was English, and he was accustomed to negotiating with British and French envoys who, like him, sought some form of collective security. By contrast, Molotov had little knowledge or experience of any country outside Russia. At the end of May his first speech as foreign minister to the Supreme Soviet showed impatience with the British and French; and he spoke favourably of commercial links with Germany.

Despite the ominous shift of emphasis in Moscow, exchanges between Britain, France and the Soviet Union continued for three months. Molotov sought not merely a pledge of joint action if Germany launched an unprovoked attack on Russia's border states (including Finland), but a collective guarantee to counter 'indirect aggression'. This phrase was seen as a Soviet attempt to gain backing in the West for military moves into the Baltic countries in anticipation of a German attack and, as such, it was unacceptable to the British. Stalin and Molotov doubted Britain's sincerity, and not without good reason. Influential figures in London privately questioned Russia's military value. The Stalinist purges of 1937–38 seemed to leave the Red Army leaderless: three of Russia's five marshals had been executed, including Tukachevsky, the best-known Soviet commander in the West. Reports suggested that more than 200 generals and 400 colonels were liquidated (figures confirmed half a century later in the Gorbachev era). Senior officers in the fleet and the air defence system had also disappeared. Why make concessions to placate a headless Hydra? London wondered.

The Russians wanted a member of Chamberlain's government to travel to Moscow to discuss differences. London thought the talks warranted no more than a departmental head from within the Foreign Office and in mid-June sent William Strang, a rising star of forty-five who served in the Moscow embassy for three years at the start of the decade. By now friction between German officials and Polish customs officers was creating tension in the Free City that was exploited by the Nazi propaganda machine. Goebbels himself visited Danzig to make three fiery speeches. But there was no sense of urgency at the Foreign Office in London; messages from Warsaw reiterated Beck's hostility to Russian military moves and his suspicion of any British initiative.

In late July Chamberlain and Halifax relented: if the Russians wanted a military mission, they should have one. But not led by the Chief of the Imperial General Staff as Marshal Voroshilov expected. Admiral the Honourable Sir Reginald Plunkett-Ernle-Erle-Drax, one of Beatty's captains at Jutland, would take with him a team of more than forty assistants, including a major-general, an air marshal and a French delegation led by General Doumenc. They were to travel, not by air nor aboard a speedy cruiser, but in the *City of Exeter*, an elegant ship chartered from the Ellerman Line, able at best to steam at 13 knots.

'Go very slowly,' the Foreign Office told the military mission, seeking time for diplomacy to dissolve the crisis. The *City of Exeter* obliged: the voyage took five days. On 10 August, when she berthed at Leningrad, it was too late to catch the night train to Moscow. At last – on Monday, 14 August – serious talks began. Not unreasonably, Marshal Voroshilov sought a right of passage across northern Poland 'to fight the common enemy' and was exasperated by the lack of response from Warsaw. Voroshilov also proposed that the western powers should seek bases from Finland and the Baltic republics, to be subsequently used by Soviet forces. No progress was made in four days of discussion. On Thursday the Russians cited the imminence of a Soviet holiday as good reason to adjourn until the following Monday (21 August). Though Plunkett and his team did not realize it, the talking was over: Molotov had an alternative policy on hand.

Throughout the summer 'the slow motion negotiations' (as the *New York Times* dubbed the Moscow talks) received unusually wide press coverage in Britain, France and the eastern seaboard of the United States. *The Times* of London did not specifically mention the problem of 'indirect aggression' until 6 July, but rumours of Soviet proposals had alarmed Helsinki, Riga and Tallinn a month earlier. In the first week of June Lord Halifax received the Estonian envoy to London, Augustus Schmidt, who presented a joint protest complaining that the three powers proposed to guarantee Finland, Latvia and Estonia against German aggression without their backing.

Berlin exploited these concerns. On 7 June Estonia and Latvia concluded non-aggression pacts with Germany; and at the other end of the Baltic a similar agreement was accepted by Denmark. The new heavy cruiser *Admiral Hipper* protectively flew the swastika naval ensign in the Gulf of Riga and up the Estonian coast. On 19 June the British were warned by a senior Estonian officer that rather than accept Soviet assistance, 'every Estonian would fight on the side of Germany'. A week later Colonel-General Halder, chief of the German Army's General Staff, was welcomed to Tallinn by General Laidoner. Significantly Admiral Canaris, head of the German Intelligence Service (*Abwehr*), soon afterwards came to Estonia and met Laidoner and his intelligence assessor, Colonel Maasing.

By the time Admiral Canaris reached Tallinn, Halder was across the Gulf, seeing for himself the Mannerheim Line forts and conferring with the Finnish General Staff. Here he was following a trail set a few days earlier by Britain's Director-General of the Territorial Army. As reported in *The Times* of 20 June, Sir Walter Kirke made a 'playful' speech in Helsinki: Finland, he suggested, was 'a pretty girl with many suitors, although . . . not eager to get a partner for the next dance'. Nobody in Britain wanted 'to disturb her maidenly modesty', the general assured the Finns.

Halder wasted no words on such patronizing pleasantries. He had a mission to complete. Twice in fifteen months the Finns had received clear warnings of the Soviet intention to acquire bases on their south-west coast, most probably on the Hangö peninsula. Such a move would have placed the Swedish ore traffic essential to German industry under threat. Halder's visit affirmed Germany's continued interest in the region. Mannerheim hardly needed reminding that, in 1917, Goltz's expeditionary force had landed at Hangö.

These were months of assessment and preparation. No British general was on hand to speak playfully at Tallinn or Riga, but in mid-July the Chief of the Imperial General Staff, Sir Edmund Ironside, travelled to Poland to judge for himself the military capability of Britain's prospective ally. He rated the army's fighting quality highly, watched a divisional exercise under a live barrage and admired the cavalry brigades but he suspected (rightly) that modern equipment was thinly spread. In Warsaw he had talks on the Danzig problem with Marshal Smigly-Rydz and Colonel Beck: the Poles were ready to fulfil international obligations but did not think war imminent; they favoured joint three-power talks in Berlin to meet the demands of Gauleiter Forster and the local Nazis. Mistrust of Soviet Russia remained widespread, after Ironside's return to London. On 19 August Colonel Beck informed the French ambassador, with an air of finality, that Poland had no wish for any military agreement with the Soviet Union and would not allow foreign troops 'to use any part of our territory'.

By that Saturday, however, Beck's diplomacy no longer enjoyed the freedom of manoeuvre for which he had striven. Despite their deep ideological divide, Nazi Germany and Soviet Russia were fast moving towards a pragmatic partnership. A commercial agreement, based on interdependence of raw materials and manufactured goods, was ready for signature. Talks on trade and payment had begun in December 1938 but proceeded secretly, intermittently and at the customary Moscow snail's pace until late July, when it became clear to the Germans that Molotov was showing genuine interest. Thereupon Hitler, who in April realized the British guarantee to Poland was militarily worthless without Soviet backing, gave Ribbentrop a free hand. The scope of discussion suddenly widened. On 3 August – while the *City of Exeter* was being made ready for the military mission – Molotov had an 'unusually open' political exchange of views with the German ambassador, hinting at a possible partition of Poland. There was further, well-concealed, diplomatic sparring in Moscow and Berlin while Admiral Plunkett and his team were in session with Voroshilov during the following week: the Russians were particularly anxious to safeguard their ascendancy over Finland and the Baltic States, where General Halder and Admiral Canaris had so recently been active.

At last, on the evening of 19 August, the German ambassador telephoned Ribbentrop to confirm receipt of a Soviet draft for a non-aggression pact; Molotov was willing to receive him in Moscow to settle details of a supplementary protocol defining spheres of influence, especially 'in the Baltic area'. After Hitler took the unprecedented step of writing personally to Stalin, it was agreed that Ribbentrop should arrive in Moscow on Wednesday, 23 August. The Germans announced the forthcoming visit before midnight on 21 August, in time for British listeners to hear the startling news on the BBC's late radio bulletin.

Next morning banner headlines informed a Europe largely on holiday that a Russo-German Pact was imminent. In England Beaverbrook's *Daily Express* no longer carried the optimistic assertion 'There will be no war this year' at the head of its front page. Even before the Pact was signed,

Chamberlain's cabinet decided to recall parliament, summoning MPs back from their summer recess. The tightening crisis seemed so threatening that the West Indies cricket team, who drew the Oval Test Match with England on that Tuesday, at once cancelled the last seven games of their tour and sought an early passage home. So, too, did the chastened Anglo-French military mission in Moscow.

Early on Wednesday afternoon Ribbentrop arrived at the Kremlin and was surprised to be received by Stalin as well as by Molotov. The text of the Non-Aggression Pact, which was to be made public, caused little difficulty. Stalin cut claims of enduring friendship inserted into the preamble by the Germans; public opinion in Russia and Germany would scoff at them, he thought. The secret protocol caused more difficulty: Poland would be partitioned between Germany and the Soviet Union, with the rivers Vistula, Bug, San and Narev forming a demarcation line; the Germans would also recognize Finland and Estonia as falling within the Soviet sphere of influence. Hitler had intended Germany to have a free hand in Lithuania and also in western Latvia – the old Courland.

By now, however, the Führer was in a hurry: local Nazis were encouraging incidents to discredit the Poles; the hand-picked Danzig Senate was ready to proclaim Gauleiter Forster executive head of state in the Free City; the German surface fleet and U-boats had received sailing orders; and precisely while Ribbentrop was at the Kremlin Hitler confirmed to his generals that the attack on Poland would be launched on the coming Saturday. When the Russians made it clear that they needed the Latvian ports of Ventspils and Liepāja in the Soviet sphere, Hitler authorized Ribbentrop to let Stalin have his concession rather than disrupt the timetable of events. It was assumed that the Kaunas government would receive Vilnius when Poland was overrun and that, since Lithuania and the Soviet Union had no common frontier, the enlarged republic would remain within the German sphere. Some questions were left for further consideration, notably whether Germany might tolerate a residual Polish protectorate around Warsaw. Whatever the final settlement, it was certain Poland would lose her outlet to the Baltic. The treaty and secret protocols over spheres of influence were signed in the small hours of 24 August, though they bore the previous day's date.

Some forty hours later – in the early evening of Friday, 25 August – the Anglo-Polish alliance treaty was at last signed in London. Uncertainty over Beck's attitude to the Anglo–French–Soviet negotiations in Moscow had delayed affirmation of the pledge given by Chamberlain in April. Even now this treaty, too, had secret protocols which, among other details, limited the agreement to an act of aggression by Germany; Britain never guaranteed Poland's frontier with the Soviet Union. But the treaty was intended as a direct response to Ribbentrop's Pact, and the main commitments were made public that same evening. In August 1914 the Kaiser had doubted if Britain would go to war for the sake of Belgium. Twenty-five years later the Führer could be certain of the British response if he invaded Poland.

Or could he? For was appeasement really dead? Within an hour of learning of the Anglo-Polish treaty, Hitler countermanded orders for the German attack, timed to begin at dawn next morning. There were other reasons for the delay, among them uncertainty over the position of Germany's nominal ally, Italy, logistical problems in the mobilization of two million men, and a hitch in preparations for action in the Baltic, with the cruiser *Königsberg* hampered by engine trouble. But the main cause was Hitler's desire for a quick, localized victory rather than a general European war. Through the British ambassador and the willingness of Birger Dahlerus, a Swedish civil engineer and friend of Göring, to fly secretly between London and Berlin, the Germans made attempts to resuscitate appeasement and put the Poles in the wrong. 'We demand Danzig, a corridor through the Corridor and a plebiscite,' General Halder jotted down in a note on the afternoon of Monday, 28 August, adding that 'England will perhaps accept, Poland not'; it should prove possible to drive a 'wedge between them'. And in his diary next day Halder referred again to Hitler's hopes of 'driving a wedge between British and French and Poles'.

In London Halifax, a man of peace, wavered: he urged the Poles to avoid provocation and to send an envoy for talks about Danzig in Berlin. Beck persuaded his colleagues to delay plastering the streets with mobilization notices but maintained that it was too late for further talks with Ribbentrop and Hitler. The British, well aware that public opinion was in no mood for another Munich, respected Beck's decision. The wedge on which Hitler counted could not be inserted.

On Thursday, 31 August, a German warship steamed into Danzig Bay on a 'goodwill mission' to congratulate Gauleiter Forster and, it was widely assumed, complete the union of the Free City and the Reich. In the absence of the cruiser *Königsberg*, Admiral Raeder had reluctantly sent the training battleship *Schleswig-Holstein*. She had been launched in 1905, was considered too antiquated for surrender at the end of the First World War and was now manned by naval cadets. Improbably, at 4.40 a.m. on 1 September the 11-inch guns of this floating museum piece fired the first salvo of the Second World War. Shells fell on Westerplatte, the fort where some 180 Poles guarded the approach to Danzig's deep-water harbour.

Soon afterwards Luftwaffe bombers took off from airfields in East Prussia and Pomerania to attack Polish towns and railway routes near the frontier. Invasion followed an hour later. On that Friday afternoon forty-one German planes bombed Warsaw.

Great Britain supported her newest ally by going to war with Germany at 11 a.m. on Sunday, 3 September. France followed suit, with some hesitancy, six hours later. Although on this occasion a European war had sprung from a Baltic issue, the remaining countries around the inland sea chose for the moment to watch and to wait. Only the Russians flexed their muscles, ready a fortnight later to go forward and complete the Fourth Partition of Poland.

25

Nazi–Soviet Partnership

THE POLISH CAMPAIGN was soon over, for the Germans proved far stronger than their opponents. Poland had to defend borders from East Prussia across to Silesia and round to the Carpathians, while a token force kept watch on the Russian frontier. The Polish army, divided into seven Groups, had a peacetime strength of 30 infantry divisions, with 13 cavalry brigades, two of which were mechanized. When completed, the mobilization of reservists would allow the formation of another 15 divisions. The air force had some 400 front-line aircraft, a quarter of them good medium-range bombers (Elks), but most of the remainder obsolescent. By contrast, Germany was able to mass 60 divisions for the invasion, five of them armoured, with nearly 900 bombers and more than 400 fighters in support. Stuka dive-bombers strafed roads, railways and airfields, cutting communications, destroying Elks on the ground, and leaving the thinly-spread Polish defenders isolated.

By midday on 3 September the German Fourth Army, advancing eastwards from Pomerania, had met the German Third Army advancing westwards from East Prussia, cutting the Corridor at its base and trapping a sixth of the Polish forces on the third day of war. The two armies then formed the northern arm of a pincer movement heading up the Vistula, to meet General von Rundstedt's Army Group South and encircle Warsaw.

The Poles offered brave resistance. On 9 September the Poznań Army Group checked the Germans with a flank attack from behind the river Bzura at Kutno that forced it to retreat some 16 kilometres. But, though the advance on Warsaw was delayed for several days, Rundstedt had enough reserves to prevent a breakthrough and by 14 September was again pressing forward. At Wola, a Warsaw suburb, the German vanguard suffered another setback, losing tanks and field guns. It made little difference. The capital was soon encircled.

Throughout the campaign, individual Polish units fought with great courage. For fourteen hours on 1 September some fifty workers in Danzig's main Post Office defied German attempts to seize the strategically important building; the heroic survivors were put on trial as *francs tireurs* and executed five weeks later. The 180 defenders of Westerplatte, the target of the *Schleswig-Holstein's* opening salvoes, defied German landings for seven days; and at Hela, the peninsula 20 kilometres from Westerplatte that curves like a crooked finger around the Bay of Danzig, resistance continued until 2 October. In the first days of the fighting an attempt by local Nazis to seize the town of Bydgoszcz, at the foot of the Corridor, was frustrated by Polish troops, whose commander executed captured Fifth Columnists. When the Germans eventually took Bydgoszcz several hundred Poles from the city were shot as a reprisal. The war began, as it was to continue, with ruthless brutality. Six million Polish citizens, half of them Jewish, were to die during the German occupation of their homeland.

Warsaw held out until 27 September, the government escaping to Romania, where President Mościcki and the commander-in-chief, General Smigly-Rydz, were interned; so, too, were many ministers, including Beck (who died in internment in June 1944). After heavy air raids and a fortnight of artillery bombardment little remained of the Polish capital but Hitler, who had been rapturously received in Danzig on 19 September, came to Warsaw on 5 October to take the salute at a triumphant parade beside the Vistula. Three weeks later Stefan Starzynski, the mayor whose proud defiance had inspired the people of Warsaw, was seized by the Gestapo and subsequently executed.

Stalin did not wait for the fall of Warsaw before claiming the territories promised in the secret clauses of the Nazi–Soviet Pact. The Red Army crossed the Polish frontier from Belorussia and the Ukraine on 17 September, encountering only token resistance. Four days later German and Russian officers met cordially in the citadel at Brest-Litovsk, where Lenin's emissaries had signed the humiliating peace treaty twenty-one years previously. Now Brest-Litovsk stood at the centre of a demarcation line running from Grodno to the south of the Pripet marshes and then swinging west to the river San and the Slovak border in the Carpathians. But the Russians moved more slowly than Stalin anticipated. At some points the Germans had advanced farther east than the secret protocols stipulated, taking the city of Lvov and the Sambor-Drohobycz oilfields, the most-developed in Poland. There was disquiet in the Kremlin. On 20 September Molotov informed the German ambassador that it was time to settle 'the structure of the Polish area'.

Final details of the Fourth Partition of Poland were agreed a week later, when Ribbentrop made a second visit to Moscow. More land went to Russia than Germany, though only a third of Poland's pre-war population.

The Germans withdrew from Lvov and from the oilfields, Stalin having undertaken to supply Germany with 300,000 tons of oil a year from the wells in exchange for coal and steel tubes. Hitler annexed Poland's western provinces and Greater Danzig; they joined the Reich as the Warthegau and were speedily Germanized. The remaining territory occupied by the Germans – including Warsaw, Cracow and Lublin – was organized as the General Government and became a labour colony for the Reich administered by the élite protective guard of the Party, the SS (*Schutz Staffeln*), accustomed to acting outside the law. Under the General Government, as in the Warthegau, Polish citizens were denied basic human rights. As many as 16,000 Poles were summarily executed in the first eight weeks of German occupation. The Nazi creed of Aryan racial superiority sought to wipe out any manifestation of Polish culture.

The three million Polish Jews now under Nazi rule faced a terrible future; few survived the war. Their fate was decided in the earliest days of conflict. After being deported from the smaller towns and villages and confined within newly created ghettos in the major cities, they were to be systematically slaughtered. The first concentration camp on Polish soil was set up on 2 September. It was sited at Stutthof (Sztutowo) on the Baltic coast 6 kilometres east of Danzig, with the sea to the north, the Vistula to the west and treacherous fenland to the east. Escape was almost impossible. The camp never became so notorious as Chelmno and Auschwitz, deeper into Poland, but by 1943 Stutthof had a gas chamber and a crematorium. Before the war ended more than 70,000 prisoners had met their deaths in the camp beside the Baltic.

Soviet repression of the Poles was scarcely less harsh. The secret police (NKVD) rounded up likely 'enemies of the state' in the newly annexed western lands. More than three dozen categories were proscribed: among them were writers, priests, teachers, bank managers, lawyers, civil servants and police officials. In many instances, the SS and the NKVD worked closely together. Over the following eighteen months at least a million Poles were transported to the wastes of the Soviet Arctic or central Siberia; and in March 1940 Stalin authorized the execution of thousands of Polish reserve officers held as prisoners-of-war. The most notorious massacre occurred in the woods of Katyn two or three months later, not far from the prisoner-of-war camp at Kozielsk, near Smolensk: 5,000 Polish officers were shot in the back of the neck beneath the trees of Katyn. Their remains were discovered in April 1943 by Russia's German invaders. The fate of a further 10,000 Polish officers, held captive in Russia, is unknown. There were mass killings at other sites besides Katyn.

In the autumn of 1939 Hitler's henchmen had no interest in Stalin's treatment of the Poles. Officially, the agreement signed at the Kremlin on 29 September was a treaty of 'friendship' delineating the German–Soviet boundary. A new partnership was forged. Bonhomie prevailed: Ribbentrop was taken to the Bolshoi to see Ulanova dance in *Swan Lake*, a memory he was to recall in his Nuremberg prison cell seven years later. The Russian partners were assured of a free hand, not only in Estonia and Latvia, but across most of Lithuania, too. An exchange of populations was agreed: the Germans in the Soviet sphere would move west, while Ukrainians and Belorussians from Germany's acquisitions were to be sent to the east. This principle of racial resettlement extended to the German Baltic communities of Estonia and Latvia, among them families settled in the region for six or seven centuries. By Christmas 1939 66,000 Germans had been encouraged to leave the Baltic states and find new homes in the Warthegau.

So close was Nazi–Soviet 'friendship' that the two governments agreed to strengthen economic links and consult together if the British and French persisted in continuing with the war. In December Hitler sent Stalin a congratulatory telegram on his sixtieth birthday. Yet both dictators were realists: 'Hitler knows his business,' Stalin dryly commented during his talks with Ribbentrop. Less than thirty hours after the Friendship Treaty was signed, a Führer Directive ordered the new German–Soviet frontier to 'be constantly strengthened and built up as a line of military security against the East'.

The Polish tradition of challenging foreign rule, dormant for a quarter of a century, soon reasserted itself and the earliest resistance groups came together even before the defenders of the Hela peninsula laid down their arms. By February 1940 surviving members of the main interwar political parties were collaborating in an embryonic political council which became so extensive and active that many Poles refer to it today as the Underground State. A secret army, known originally as the Armed Struggle Union (SZP), was created, maintaining close contact with prominent Poles in exile, and expanding in 1942 into a Home Army (AK) of skilled saboteurs. Polish Jews, herded into ghettos, also resisted courageously whenever they could acquire arms, establishing their own secret Fighting Organisation (ZOB) in Warsaw. During April and May 1943 the Jews of the Warsaw Ghetto valiantly fought a pitched battle against their Nazi SS oppressors, killing some 400 of them. But in the fighting and its aftermath 14,000 Jews perished.

Poles abroad continued the fight against Germany in every way open to them. From his place of internment in Romania President Mościcki nominated Wladyslaw Raczkiewicz as his successor and General Sikorski was appointed prime minister of a government in exile. By the following summer more than 24,000 Polish troops were training in Scotland and England, Polish airmen bombed German ships, and fighter squadrons were engaged in the Battle of Britain.

Some Polish warships had survived the fall of their country. When the Germans took Gdynia, three destroyers and a submarine were at sea and reached British ports; the destroyer *Blyskawica* was to cover both the Dunkirk evacuation and the Normandy landings four years later. A second submarine, the *Orzel*, was on patrol in the Baltic. On 15 September she put into Tallinn to land her captain, who was ill. Neutral Estonia, very properly, interned the *Orzel*: guards boarded her, rendered her guns useless and removed her charts. Nothing daunted, the crew surreptitiously prepared to sail. They overpowered the guard and on 18 September slipped out into Tallinn Bay under cover of darkness. Somehow, without charts, *Orzel* evaded Russian and German patrols and minefields and made her way unseen through the Øresund, the Kattegat and the Skagerrak. After a four-week epic cruise she was met in the North Sea by a British destroyer and escorted into port, to serve with the Royal Navy.

The *Orzel*'s escape triggered a diplomatic incident, however. She had put to sea from Tallinn a few hours after the Red Army entered Poland, and Molotov used her crew's defiance of internment as an excuse to put pressure on Estonia. On 24 September the Estonian foreign minister, who had come to Moscow expecting to sign a trade agreement, was confronted with a virtual ultimatum: Molotov insisted that the *Orzel* affair proved Estonia could not be trusted to keep war away from the Gulf of Finland; a Soviet ship was reported to have been torpedoed in these waters by an unidentified submarine (though it was more likely she struck a mine). To protect Leningrad it was essential for the Soviet Union to have naval, military and air bases within Estonia. Under threat of invasion, the Estonians signed a so-called Treaty of Mutual Assistance. The Russian naval authorities would use facilities on the islands of Saaremaa and Hiiumaa for ships and aircraft and would restore the base at Paldiski, an ice-free harbour 55 kilometres west of Tallinn, once known as Baltiski (Baltic Port). While Paldiski was under construction the Baltic fleet would be permitted to use Tallinn. The treaty limited the number of troops stationed in Estonia to 25,000 and gave pledges of non-interference in the republic's economic system or political structure. For eight months these pledges were observed. Estonia survived as a sovereign state, with President Päts broadening the basis of government to emphasize national unity.

A week later a similar treaty was imposed on Latvia. Molotov again emphasized the need to protect the approaches to the Gulf of Finland: Liepāja, like Paldiski an ice-free port, would once again become a Russian naval and air base, and so too would Ventspils. There would be no Soviet presence in Riga itself and never more than 30,000 troops stationed at the agreed bases. They would be withdrawn as soon as the war in Europe ended. Meanwhile the Latvians could count on a trebling of trade with the Soviet Union and no change in the republic's economic or political character.

Lithuania was treated differently. In early September President Smetona had considered ordering the army to march into Poland and recover Vilnius. But before the Kaunas government could agree on a policy, the Soviet Union intervened: on 18 September the Red Army entered Vilnius. Lithuania's Treaty of Mutual Assistance, signed on 10 October after a week of consultation, gave the Russians the right to maintain 20,000 men in Lithuania, without specifying where they should be stationed. To offset this ominous commitment, the Russians pulled out of Vilnius city and on 28 October Lithuanian troops marched back into the cherished goal of so much political rhetoric in the past twenty years. Although the Soviet authorities retained Svietcany and some other districts seized by the Poles in 1919, over the following months Russian seamen and soldiers could count on a friendlier reception in Lithuania than in Latvia or Estonia. Once again there was to be no interference with the republic's internal affairs.

As yet neither of the western allies could intervene in Baltic affairs. The RAF raided Wilhelmshaven and Brunsbüttel, at the North Sea exit of the Kiel Canal, on 4 September but Kiel itself and the Baltic coast were, at that time, beyond the range of aircraft with heavy bomb loads. With tragic irony, the first civilian casualty in western Europe was a woman killed by a British bomb dropped in error on Esbjerg in neutral Denmark. A fortnight later the Scandinavian foreign ministers met in Copenhagen to affirm the neutrality of their countries. As in 1914, Denmark laid mines in the Belts and in the Kogrund Channel to protect the capital, while providing pilots to guide merchant vessels through the minefields. Sweden took similar preventive measures.

The Norwegians, however, refused to place any barriers to navigation within the Inner Leads, the waters between their outer islands and the mainland, which in the winter of 1917–18 they had mined – under British pressure – to hamper shipment of Swedish iron ore from the Norwegian ice-free port of Narvik to Germany. Hitler's steelworks were even more heavily dependent on Swedish ore than their predecessors in the earlier war, when the industry could draw on other resources, notably in Lorraine.

In 1939 Germany sought to import 20,320,000 tonnes of iron ore from the mines around Gällivare, shipping it from Narvik in the winter and from Swedish Luleå once the ice had melted. To the British it became essential to find ways of blocking these shipments.

Habits of thought recollected through a quarter of a century's passage in time shaped many attitudes during this first winter of the war. This is hardly surprising: in Stockholm, Oslo and Copenhagen the same three kings reigned as at the start of 'the Kaiser's War'; and in London Churchill, First Lord of the Admiralty in 1914, returned to his former office on the evening of 3 September 1939. Within four days Churchill asked his naval staff to prepare a plan to enter the Baltic, reviving projects mooted twenty-five years previously. On 12 September he completed a five-page memorandum giving details of his proposals. As Churchill explains in *The Second World War*, the operation was named 'after Catherine the Great, because Russia lay in the background of my thought'. A second memorandum a week later shows that in the foreground of his thought was a need to block the May-to-September ore shipments from Luleå down the Gulf of Bothnia and across to Germany.

Operation Catherine was envisaged as a major naval offensive to give the allies control over the Baltic. Churchill proposed to fit out two or three old battleships with protective armour and send them through the Belts, together with an aircraft carrier, five cruisers, two flotillas of destroyers, a dozen converted minesweepers, and tankers with three months' supply of oil. Once clear of Danish waters, the task force would be in a position to sever Germany's trade links with Sweden, plunging the steel industry of the Reich into grave difficulty. Churchill argued that naval mastery in the Baltic would bring the Scandinavian states and possibly Russia into a grand coalition against Nazism. The fleet would make use of a Swedish base in the Gulf of Bothnia – Gävle or Harnösand were later suggested – and strike at Germany from the north. Before the end of September Churchill found an enthusiastic commander for the operation in Admiral of the Fleet the Earl of Cork and Orrery, a veteran a few months older than himself. If he could count on receiving two more carriers and nine cruisers, Lord Cork believed he could assemble the fleet by mid-January 1940 and sail for the Baltic a month later. The spectre of Napier seemed again to stalk the Admiralty.

Sir Dudley Pound, the First Sea Lord, did not initially oppose Churchill's proposals. He preferred to assemble arguments of sound common sense against so dangerous an enterprise gradually: the fleet's vulnerability to air attack; the need for '*active* co-operation' of the Swedes (who showed no inclination to abandon their traditional neutrality); the risk of having so many warships locked up in an inland sea. Churchill, however, was tenacious: 'The entry of the Baltic . . . would soon bring measureless relief,' he minuted on a report by the First Sea Lord on 3 December; a month later, he asserted more remarkably that 'Russia might veer towards the Allied side at any moment.' Pound persisted: 'The sending of capital ships into the Baltic is courting disaster,' he warned the First Lord on New Year's Eve. The matter was settled by a report from Lord Cork in the second week of January 1940: heavy commitments in the dockyards and the demands of the fleet at sea had delayed modification of the necessary ships; no protective armour had as yet been fitted to strengthen the larger vessels. Reluctantly Churchill accepted defeat: Operation Catherine 'will not be practicable this year', he told Pound on 15 January. But the Baltic, and especially the iron-ore shipments, remained firmly within his strategic sights.

There was, indeed, far more action around the Baltic than along the Franco-German border in that first winter of war. On 5 October 1939 Molotov formally invited the Finnish foreign minister to Moscow to discuss recent political changes in the Baltic region. The Finns, however, wanted a more experienced diplomat and, to the Russians' irritation, sent the veteran sixty-nine-year-old negotiator Juho Paasikivi. Stalin himself was principal spokesman for the Soviet government in three rounds of talks. The Russians sought to advance their frontier in the Karelian isthmus by some 40 kilometres, acquire a cluster of strategic islands in the Gulf, and lease Hangö as a military and naval base for thirty years: 'We must be able to bar the entrance to the Gulf of Finland,' Stalin told Paasikivi at their second meeting on 14 October, 'for once it is entered, Leningrad cannot be defended.' He also sought cession of the Rybach'ye Peninsula, controlling the approaches to Murmansk. In return Paasikivi was offered a generous frontier readjustment in central Finland.

The Finns, however, were not impressed; they would have made concessions over the islands, but a Russian garrison as far west as Hangö threatened to undermine their own system of defence. Finland's president and his foreign minister went to Stockholm for the annual Nordic heads of state summit meeting, but they found their neighbours unwilling to offer them armed support against Russia. From Berlin came advice to seek an amicable agreement with Moscow. In London, the Chamberlain government was sympathetic but unhelpful; and at the Admiralty Churchill observed to the First Sea Lord that it was better for Soviet forces to hold bases in the Gulf than see them pass under German control.

There need have been no war between Russia and Finland. Stalin wanted territorial readjustment, not a winter campaign, and he was prepared to negotiate a compromise. So was Paasikivi, who was backed by Marshal Mannerheim. But for neither the first time nor the last in Finland's history, the parliamentarians in Helsinki remained obstinately unyielding. The Moscow talks dragged on for three and a half weeks with no sign of agreement. On 13 November the Finnish delegation returned home, and for a fortnight it seemed as if the crisis had evaporated. Yet tension remained high along the frontier, with Soviet planes making frequent sweeps westward. In mid-afternoon on Sunday, 26 November, four Russians were killed by shellfire at Mainila, on the frontier. Molotov complained that the shells came from Finnish guns; the Finns, who were short of heavy artillery, not unnaturally blamed the Russians. Whatever the truth, the incident provided the Soviet Union with a pretext for action. At dawn on Thursday (30 November) the Red Army crossed the border. Like Warsaw twelve weeks before, Helsinki was bombed soon afterwards, without any declaration of war. The Red Banner Baltic Fleet bombarded the Finnish coast and sought to cut links with Sweden.

The Finnish army seemed hopelessly outnumbered: 10 divisions defended a 950-kilometre frontier against 26 divisions. But, unlike Poland, Finland had secured eight weeks of negotiation in which to mobilize and to evacuate civilians from the frontier region. In Marshal Mannerheim the Finns possessed an experienced commander-in-chief who had trained his small army for mobile war in Europe's strangest arena of battle, straddling the Arctic Circle. By contrast Stalin's purge had robbed the Soviet High Command of many of its best brains. The Red Army massed 1,500 tanks and twice as many aircraft, but was without skis or effective snow camouflage. The Finns had, in the south, the Mannerheim Line of field works and concrete bunkers (though promised mortars and anti-aircraft guns had not yet arrived). In the forests and frozen terrain of the north they could count on the finest long-distance ski troops in the world. Although the Soviet Fourteenth Army advanced from Murmansk to take the Arctic port of Petsamo and reach the frontier with Norway, it could make no headway southwards through the icy wilderness of Lapland. The winter of 1939–40 was intensely cold, with the antagonists waging war at temperatures as low as -40°C.

As soon as the campaign began, an alternative Finnish People's Government was set up at Terijoki, the first small town across the southern border. At its head the Russians installed Otto Kuusinen, a survivor from the People's Commissariat of the Finnish civil war. But Kuusinen was no more successful in winning support from 'Middle Finland' than in 1918. He wooed socialists and trade unionists: they ignored him. His political misjudgement was surpassed by strategic errors. General Meretskov, commanding the Seventh Army's assault on the Mannerheim Line, had not allowed for the shortness of daylight hours. He could not count on tactical support from his aircraft nor hold his tanks in massed formation. When isolated in the prevailing darkness the tanks became easy targets for infantry patrols armed with the new improvised 'Molotov cocktails', bottles filled with petrol and turned into explosive devices by rags serving as fuses.

By Christmas there was stalemate along the whole front, with the Finns claiming a striking victory on Christmas Eve at Tolvajärvi, where two Russian divisions were destroyed. A second victory twelve days later at Suomussalmi in central Finland eliminated another two divisions. The harsh winter favoured the Finns. As in 1918 the Soviet authorities dumped Kuusinen. Through their envoy in Stockholm they made contact with the legitimate government in Helsinki, now headed by Risto Ryti. By the end of January 1940 a negotiated peace seemed in sight.

It was now the Finns' turn to miscalculate. They began to count on foreign intervention. Diplomatic backing from the West had secured the expulsion of the USSR from the League of Nations on 14 December, and a call by the League Council that members should assist Finland raised Ryti's hopes of armed support from abroad. Five days later the (Anglo-French) Supreme War Council discussed the possibility of sending troops to Finland: the French approved; the British did not. By mid-January, however, the two allies agreed to accept the idea of intervention, in principle; two British divisions were held in reserve in the United Kingdom instead of crossing to France. Foreign volunteers reached Finland in large numbers: some 8,000 Swedes, 725 Norwegians and groups of Danes and Americans of Finnish descent. In Britain 2,000 soldiers sought leave to enlist. It was known that more volunteers would soon be on their way from Hungary, Denmark and the United States. Reports that, on 5 February, the allies had decided to send an expedition by way of Norway and Sweden lifted Finnish morale at a time when the Red Army was mounting a fresh offensive in Karelia. A week later Väinö Tanner, the foreign minister, in a public statement defiantly insisted that Finland would never accept peace terms dictated in Moscow.

But Ryti and Tanner should have seen the warning signals. The Scandinavian states had either abstained from voting at the League Assembly or made scrupulous reservations. Per Albin Hansson, Sweden's prime minister, broadened his government in December so as to include conservatives and liberals; but the newcomers to the unified coalition remained as convinced as their socialist colleagues that intervention in Finland was inconsistent with Sweden's historic commitment to a general policy of neutrality. Denmark and Norway followed suit. Unofficial aid was tolerated, but neither the Swedes nor the Norwegians would give transit rights to allied troops. Even if there were a change of heart in Stockholm and Oslo, it was unlikely an allied expeditionary force could reach northern Finland before the coming of spring.

The war turned decisively against Finland once the hours of daylight and twilight lengthened and the Red Army could co-ordinate the use of tanks and aircraft. The Soviet Thirteenth Army (nine divisions and an armoured brigade) reinforced the Seventh Army in the Karelian isthmus. General Timoshenko, who succeeded Meretskov early in the New Year, at last broke the Mannerheim Line at Summa on 11 February. By the end of the month his troops confronted the Finns' final defensive positions along the route to Helsinki, running through Viipuri, Karelia's historic capital. On 3 March Timoshenko attacked Viipuri itself while sending a task force across the frozen inshore waters of the Gulf to secure a footing west of the city; the ice was sufficiently solid to support light tanks. Six days later Mannerheim advised Ryti to seek an immediate peace. The government made a last bid for Swedish intervention. When this attempt failed, peace delegates flew to Moscow, at Russian insistence.

The Peace Treaty of Moscow, signed on 12 March 1940, deprived the Finnish Republic of a tenth of its lands, including Viipuri and all the Karelian isthmus, together with the northern shore of Lake Ladoga and the Hangö peninsula; Petsamo was returned to the Finns but the Russians held on to the Rybach'ye Peninsula. Three members of the Finnish parliament – among them the future president, Urho Kekkonen – voted to reject the Peace of Moscow and to continue the fight, but other parliamentarians feared that renewed war would lead eventually to Soviet occupation of the whole country. The war formally ended on 13 March, 100 days after it began. Some 25,000 Finns were dead and 55,000 wounded. The Soviet authorities gave no final figure of casualties; Mannerheim believed they were eight times as high. But proportionately Finland suffered far more grievously; Finland's population was less than five million; the Soviet Union's was more than 170 million.

Within four weeks the Winter War was followed by the Spring Surprise. The German conflict flared up along the Baltic's western flank, in Norway and through Denmark. Although Operation Catherine had been shelved in mid-January, Churchill still pressed for action against iron-ore imports, particularly shipments through Norway's territorial waters. Plans were drawn up, and postponed, for landings at the Norwegian ports of Narvik, Namsos and Trondheim and an advance up the railway and across the Swedish frontier to Gällivare, where it would be possible to seize the iron mines at Malmberget and isolate the larger deposits at Kiruna. Allied hopes of tempting Stockholm and Oslo into co-belligerency aroused fierce opposition in both capitals; the Norwegians were also incensed by naval activity in the Inner Leads and the threat of mines in their territorial waters. By the third week of February German Intelligence suspected that the Allies wished to carry the war to Norway and into Sweden.

German naval strategists had long coveted Norwegian fjords as anchorages from which attacks could be launched on British shipping far out in the Atlantic. In the previous October Grand-Admiral Raeder, commander-in-chief of the German navy, had pressed Hitler to secure bases in Norway for submarines and surface vessels. Planning for an invasion of Denmark and Norway began on 27 January. A month later Hitler entrusted operational command to General von Falkenhorst, who in 1918 served on Goltz's staff in Finland. Plans for the joint-services project (Exercise-Weser) were completed by 10 March. Six divisions, including 2,000 initial assault troops trained for mountain warfare, would be concentrated around Hamburg, Bremen, Danzig and Stettin, supported by 800 bombers and fighters, more than 300 transport planes and some half a million tonnage of shipping. It was agreed that the invasion could start as soon as the western Baltic was free of ice. Here, however, the planners ran into an unexpected problem. Like Finland, southern Scandinavia was experiencing an unusually cold winter. As late as 31 March, ice-floes were reported in the Belts, Denmark's inland sea. But over the next days the temperature rose. Within a week all was ready for Exercise-Weser to begin.

Falkenhorst had the advantage of surprise. From 26 March onwards reports from Stockholm, Copenhagen and even from an agent in Berlin, supplemented by aerial reconnaissance, should have alerted London to the danger of a German naval expedition, but the information was never collated. On Thursday, 4 April the Danish government learnt from the military attaché in Berlin that invasion was imminent and yet, inexplicably, not until the following Monday (8 April) were the defences of Copenhagen and southern Jutland strengthened. By then the main German fleet was at sea. At three o'clock on the Sunday morning the battle-cruisers *Scharnhorst* and *Gneisenau*, the heavy cruiser *Admiral Hipper* and fourteen destroyers packed with assault troops had steamed out into the North Sea from the Schilling Roads, off the estuaries of the Weser and Elbe. By daylight the fleet was sailing parallel to the Jutland peninsula. Later that morning the new heavy cruiser *Blücher* left Kiel with a destroyer escort, met transports from Danzig and Stettin, and passed through the Belts before midnight.

Norway's minister in Copenhagen warned Oslo of the fleet movements. But the Norwegian government refused to believe their kingdom was under threat. Confirmation came on Monday evening when Oslo learnt that 100 shipwrecked soldiers in field-grey uniforms had come ashore at Kristiansand, Norway's closest port to Denmark. They explained that their ship, the *Rio de Janeiro*, had sunk in the Skagerrak while carrying them to Bergen to help Norwegians 'defend the port against England'; although the survivors did not know it, the *Rio de Janeiro* had been sunk by the Polish submarine *Orzel*, back in familiar waters. Some of Norway's coastal forts were then put on alert.

Next morning (Tuesday, 8 April) the battery of three seventy-year-old guns at Oscarsborg fired on the *Blücher* as she made her way through the Narrows of Oslofjord towards the capital. A shell exploded inside the magazine. The cruiser sank, and 1,000 seamen, soldiers and administrators perished. But the loss of the *Blücher* could not save Oslo. Parachutists seized airfields close to the capital, allowing two battalions of troops aboard Junkers-52 transport planes to land safely. Before the end of the day the swastika flag flew over Oslo – and Kristiansand, Bergen and distant Narvik too.

Copenhagen was already in German hands. At 4.15 that Tuesday morning the frontier was crossed and, for more than an hour, the Danes offered strong resistance in south Jutland. But in the capital a German collier, with troops hidden below decks, was allowed to berth not far from the Kastellet and soon airborne troops secured the airfields. The leading members of the government conferred with King Christian X at 5 a.m. and, with his consent, ordered a ceasefire an hour later. Denmark accepted a German military presence in return for an assurance that the occupying authorities would not interfere in the kingdom's internal affairs. The parliamentary system was allowed to survive, at least until August 1943: a new coalition government imposed censorship on newspapers and the radio and banned political demonstrations.

In the early years of occupation King Christian continued his pre-war practice of riding on most days through the streets of Copenhagen, emphasizing to his subjects that their sovereign was still among them. Unfortunately Christian X's show of passive defiance was brought to an end on 19 October 1942 when his horse shied and he was thrown to the ground, seriously injuring his head and his left leg. The king was confined to a wheelchair for the last five years of his life.

With Denmark's capitulation German troops stood guard over some 1,500 kilometres of Baltic shore, from the northern tip of Skagen eastwards to Memel. They also held the historic fortified islands of Bornholm and Christiansø, 150 kilometres from the Danish coast. Denmark, however, was merely a stepping-stone to the greater strategic prize to the north. Initially Germany seemed to gain both of Hitler's objectives: a 1,300-kilometre Atlantic waterfront for Raeder to outflank the Royal Navy; and protection of the iron-ore traffic from Sweden. But land and sea operations in Norway continued for two months after the surprise invasion. There was some hope of ejecting the Germans from Narvik and holding an allied bridgehead in northern Norway, from Trondheim and Namsos up to the Arctic frontier with Swedish Lapland and Finland. In all some 36,000 troops – Norwegians, the French Foreign Legion and *Chasseurs Alpins*, three Polish brigades, a British Guards brigade and territorials – engaged Falkenhorst's army, soon reinforced by a seventh division. Intrepid destroyer flotillas of the Royal Navy, supported by cruisers and capital ships from the Home Fleet, covered landings from the sea in central Norway and, most effectively, around West Fjord, the waterway to Narvik. The aircraft carriers *Furious* and *Glorious* brought two fighter squadrons from the Royal Air Force to give air cover from improvised landing strips for the multinational force closing in on German-held Narvik.

Severance of the iron-ore route from Sweden remained the main allied objective. The slim prospect of Swedish military aid was dashed when a courteous exchange of telegrams between Hitler and King Gustav V was followed, on 19 April, by the transit through Sweden of 355 tonnes of provisions (but not munitions) for the Germans in Narvik. Allied pressure intensified in the second week of May, with the British and Poles checking a German relief force in difficult terrain. When, on 28 May, Norwegian troops – backed by the French – at last re-entered the port of Narvik they found the quays and ore-loading facilities already wrecked by shellfire.

Churchill, who became prime minister on 10 May 1940, had envisaged a long campaign in northern Norway, with Gällivare itself in allied hands before the autumn, either with or without Sweden's concurrence. But that fateful 10 May also saw the opening of Germany's *blitzkrieg* in the West. Events in Belgium and France made it impossible to sustain the allied force in Norway, for entry into Narvik coincided with the second day of evacuation from Dunkirk of the whole Allied Northern Army Group on the

Western Front. Within a week preparations were well advanced for pulling out of northern Norway, too. King Haakon and his government left Tromsø on 7 June aboard the cruiser HMS *Devonshire*. After destroying as much as possible of the railway track, 25,000 allied troops safely returned to the United Kingdom over the following three days. Tragically, on the afternoon of 8 June HMS *Glorious*, her hangar deck packed with eighteen RAF fighters in addition to her own aircraft, was intercepted by the *Scharnhorst* and sunk, as too were her escorting destroyers, HMS *Acasta* and HMS *Ardent*. Some 1,500 officers and other ranks of the Navy and the RAF went down with these three warships, more than a third of the total British casualties in the campaign. One of *Acasta*'s torpedoes badly damaged *Scharnhorst*.

Victory in Norway enabled the Germans to consolidate their mastery over the western Baltic. There was no need for Sweden to be occupied. Ten days after the last allied force left Narvik the Swedish government agreed to German demands for troop transit rights, phrased menacingly by the insufferably arrogant Ribbentrop: the Swedes had to permit munitions, arms and supplies to be transported along Swedish railways for Falkenhorst's army in Norway and to allow leave parties of soldiers to use the Swedish rail network to travel down as far as Helsingborg. Christian Gunther, the Swedish foreign minister, later claimed that he finally recommended acceptance of these demands because of reports emanating from within the Foreign Office in London that Britain would soon seek 'common sense' peace terms. Few in Stockholm believed that Britain would fight on alone, after the collapse of France.

Some members of the Swedish royal family were sympathetic to the allied cause but the octogenarian king remained well-disposed towards the Germans; as late as December 1941 Hitler could send a message of 'thanks for the very comforting personal attitude of Your Majesty'. By contrast, in late July 1940 Gustav V's conduct deeply offended King Haakon, to whom he thereafter became, quite simply, 'the old rogue': the crown princess of Norway, who found refuge in Stockholm when Oslo fell, telegraphed her husband in England warning him of an alleged palace intrigue by which Gustav V would accept a German plan to depose Haakon, exclude the Norwegian crown prince from the succession and set up a Quisling-chosen regency for Haakon's three-year-old grandson Prince Harald. This project, if it really existed, never reached maturity, and the crown princess and her children were able to exchange royal Stockholm for a safer wartime exile in Washington DC. But Gustav V remained suspect to the British Foreign

Office, especially when in early August 1940 he put out peace feelers directly to King George VI in London.

The Swedish government's conduct in 1940–41 was cautiously pragmatic. Efforts were dutifully made to curb anti-Nazi comments in the liberal Swedish newspapers, as Ribbentrop and Hitler repeatedly required, but there was no vigorous attempt to discipline editors. At the same time the Swedes stepped up their rearmament programme. The air force was equipped with modern bombers and fighters and doubled in size. Cavalry regiments, unmotorized as late as 1937, found themselves with more than 700 tanks seven years later; and in the Bofors light automatic anti-aircraft gun the Swedes perfected a weapon against low-flying aircraft which both sides of combatants sought to purchase. After the terms of the Peace Treaty of Moscow were implemented, Sweden helped the Finns construct new coastal fortifications. In their desire to prevent further Soviet encroachment, the Swedes even gave the Finnish military authorities financial assistance.

As in the First World War, Sweden's neutrality proved commercially profitable. Despite the courageous efforts of the allied forces to cut off supplies of iron ore, substantial yields from the mines of Kiruna and Malmberget continued to reach Germany with little interruption. Railway and port facilities at Narvik were soon repaired, with help from the Swedish Grängesberg Company. Imports of iron ore from Sweden in 1940 were barely 16 per cent lower than in the last year of peace, and over the years 1941–44 only 9.9 per cent lower.

Yet not every gain from industrialized Sweden was Hitler's. An Anglo-Swedish trade agreement, concluded in October 1939 and providing for steel tubes, ball-bearings and other war essentials, had not been fulfilled before 'Exercise-Weser' effectively sealed off the Baltic. But in the last week of January 1941 five Norwegian ships, stranded at Gothenburg in the previous April, slipped unseen into the Skagerrak on a dark night, crewed by Norwegians, Englishmen and Scots and by Swedish volunteers. The five ships brought 25,500 tonnes of the purchases promised in the trade agreement safely to Britain. At Gothenburg anti-Nazi Swedes in sympathy with the Norwegians enabled several more 'blockade busters' to bring similar cargoes across the North Sea during the later years of the war. And it would appear to have been from the cruiser *Gotland*, patrolling off Gothenburg, that on 20 May 1941 the British naval attaché received the first reports enabling the Admiralty to deduce that the new German battleship *Bismarck* was at sea.

★

Outwardly the Russians approved of their German partner's victories of 1940 in Norway and France. In April, once Ambassador Schulenburg had given assurances that no action would be taken in Sweden or Finland, Molotov 'wished Germany complete success in her defensive measures'. Two months later, as the defeated French prepared to seek an armistice, Molotov stood beside Schulenburg again, ready to offer 'warmest congratulations on the splendid success of the German Armed Forces'. But the bland friendship was wearing paper thin; there could be no lasting accommodation between Bolshevism and Nazism. Stalin wanted a buffer zone, an extensive *glacis* to put the towns and industrial enterprises of the pre-war Soviet Union well distant from German military might. By the early months of 1940 the Kremlin was re-assessing policy towards all three Baltic republics.

The first move was an attempt to encourage intellectuals and surviving veteran communists in Latvia to overthrow President Ulmanis and form a Popular Front government closely dependent on Moscow. The Latvian secret police – with an agent planted in the Soviet Legation – nipped this conspiracy in the bud, throwing left-wing activists into prison. The tone of the Soviet press ominously hardened: the Baltic republics were showing too much sympathy for Norway and the bourgeois allies of the West. Wisely, in the third week of May Ulmanis authorized the Latvian envoy in London, Karlis Zarinš, to speak on behalf of the Latvian government if circumstances should prevent it from acting independently. At the same time he arranged for the republic's gold reserves to be transferred to the United States.

At the end of May Moscow concentrated on the most distant of the republics, Lithuania. It was alleged that several Russian soldiers had been kidnapped and one of them killed. Lithuania's prime minister was summoned to the Kremlin and, on 11 June, accused by Molotov of encouraging military talks with senior Estonian and Latvian officers. That evening the Lithuanian envoy in Berlin sought support for his country from Ernst Woermann, deputy State Secretary at the Foreign Ministry: Woermann took note of the Soviet demands but could offer the envoy no grounds for hope. Three days later – the Friday on which the German army entered Paris – the Lithuanians received an ultimatum demanding an immediate change of government and the arrest of the head of the Security Police, who was said to be in German pay (and probably was). Soviet tanks sped across Lithuania on the Saturday and Sunday (15–16 June). Smetona, having failed to persuade his ministers to order armed resistance, advised Lithuanian troops to seek refuge in Germany; he followed them across the frontier a few hours later. Moscow sent deputy Foreign Commissar

Vladimir Dekanozov to guide the Lithuanians in choosing an amenable government. A left-wing writer became president and a professor of Slavonic literature, Vincas Krėvė-Mickevičius, formed an administration in which there was not a single communist. Dekanozov was well satisfied.

Within a week events in Latvia and Estonia followed a similar pattern. Both governments were alleged to have encouraged contact between the General Staffs of the Baltic republics during the Winter War against Finland. Tallinn and Riga were given six hours to purge their governments and bring to power administrations well disposed towards the Soviet Union. Warships of the Red Banner Baltic fleet waited off Tallinn and sailed up the Daugava river to Riga. Andrei Vyshinsky 'advised' the Latvians; Andrei Zhdanov, the Party boss of Leningrad, was on hand in Tallinn. By 21 June a left-wing poet headed the Estonian government, an eminent bacteriologist the Latvian. Once again no communists served in the new puppet administrations.

On 22 June 1940 – the day the Franco-German Armistice was signed in the West – Moscow's official Tass Agency confirmed that eighteen divisions of the Red Army were already stationed in the Baltic republics and that two more divisions might soon supplement them. In theory Estonia, Latvia and Lithuania retained independence for another three weeks. In practice it was already lost. On 14–15 July elections were held in each republic: voters were given the choice to support or reject a single list of candidates sponsored by 'The Union of Toiling Peoples'; many were communists although some had never shown any party allegiance. Over 90 per cent of the voters in each republic registered their approval of the lists. A week later parliaments met in Tallinn, Riga and Kaunas. Resolutions were passed adopting the Soviet economic system (though not collective farming) and endorsing applications to be admitted to the Soviet Union. On 1 August 1940 Lithuania became the fourteenth Soviet Socialist Republic; Latvia followed on 5 August; Estonia on 8 August.

By early August the former political and military leaders of the independent republics were in Soviet prisons or on their way to labour camps. Even today the final fate of most of them remains unknown. President Ulmanis of Latvia was imprisoned first in Moscow and later at Stavropol, where in 1942 he died; President Päts of Estonia endured sixteen years of detention before finally succumbing in 1956, held in a Soviet 'psychiatric centre'. No one is certain what happened to General Laidoner or to that visionary champion of Baltic-Scandinavian collaboration, Jaan Tõnisson, once they were taken into Soviet custody. Anton Uesson, mayor of Tallinn through most of the years of independence, died in 1942 at Sverdlovsk in the Urals. General Balodis, arrested in Riga, was allowed to return to Latvia in 1956. Among Lithuanians, Voldemaras (having rashly returned from exile before the débâcle) is believed to have perished in a labour camp. His rival, President Smetona, made good his escape, but in 1944 died in a fire in the United States. Many public figures of lower rank also disappeared at this time. But the cruellest and most extensive wave of mass deportation did not come until the following summer.

German diplomatic missions received a circular telegram from Berlin in late June insisting that what was happening in the Baltic states should be regarded as a purely Russian concern; the friendly relations between the Reich and the Soviet Union were 'unaltered', they were assured. But in reality the partnership was under strain. More than 70 per cent of exports from the Baltic republics had gone to Germany in the previous six months: wheat, timber, butter, eggs, and chemical products. There was no guarantee Berlin could continue to rely on this valuable, efficiently-run and blockade-free source now the three states were absorbed in the Soviet Union. Strategically, too, Germany was at a disadvantage. Stalin had completely ignored Hitler's often professed interest in Lithuania, especially the Suwalki salient on the frontier. Eight days after Lithuania became a Soviet Republic, a German military directive ordered logistical planning for a campaign in the East and the preparation of field army headquarters in East Prussia. At the same time General Thomas, head of the General Staff's armaments section, was told by Göring that, from the spring of 1941 onwards, there was no need to plan for the punctual delivery of arms promised and purchased by the Soviet Union.

There was also a suspicion in Berlin that Russia had not yet finished with Finland. As soon as the Winter War ended, Germany began to restore and expand commercial links with Helsinki, showing particular interest in exploiting the nickel ore deposits around Petsamo, Finland's only port outside the Baltic. At the same time many Finns, despairing of the West after the confused diplomacy of recent months and the failure of allied arms in Norway, turned again to Germany for support. An enthusiastically pro-German organization called (significantly) 'The Resurrection of Finland' was founded in the autumn of 1940, attracting recruits from all the old parties except the social democrats. Marshal Mannerheim secretly met an envoy from Göring on 17 August and succeeded in persuading the government to follow the example of Sweden by granting transit facilities for German troops in Norway on leave as well as the use of Finland's railways for transporting supplies and munitions to the men garrisoning Arctic

Norway. The first uniformed German soldiers were seen disembarking in Finland at the Bothnian port of Vaasa on 21 September, ready to take a special train northwards. Contacts between the High Commands of Finland and Germany were maintained over the following months, culminating in a visit to Berlin in the following May by Mannerheim's chief-of-staff. Arms purchases, held inside Greater Germany during the Winter War, were released and formed a welcome replenishment for the Finnish army.

The Russians sombrely took note of the latest twist in Hitler's Baltic policy. Molotov – still titular head of the Soviet government as well as foreign minister – was invited to Berlin for a three-day visit in mid-November, ostensibly to consider a closer partnership. In the event, he submitted his hosts to sharp questioning. As well as discussing differences over south-eastern Europe, Molotov asked why the Germans were active in Finland, which fell within the Soviet sphere of influence. He was told by the Führer in person that Germany had no political interest in Finland: 'At no price do we wish to have a new war in the Baltic,' Hitler assured him.

Yet while Molotov was in the Wilhelmstrasse, 29 kilometres away at Zossen the General Staff was well advanced in planning the next campaign. 'Irrespective of the results of these discussions [with Russia] all preparations for the East which have been verbally ordered will be continued,' Hitler insisted. Five weeks later, on 18 December, he issued his famous General Directive, No. 21, Operation Barbarossa: 'The German Armed Forces must be prepared to crush Soviet Russia in a quick campaign even before the conclusion of the war against England . . . Preparations are to be completed by 15 May 1941.' The main initial blow would be delivered in the north, between the Pripet marshes and the Baltic coast, with Leningrad as the immediate objective rather than Moscow. After the Red Army's cumbersome operations earlier in the year, prolonged resistance was not anticipated. The war would be all over before the snows returned. There was no need to prepare for a winter campaign. Germany would be supported by the Finnish army from Petsamo down to the Karelian isthmus and by unrestricted use of Sweden's roads and railways, most probably even earlier than the opening of hostilities. Preparations should be concealed for as long as possible. The mutual trade agreements with Moscow must be honoured, for Germany gained food, petroleum products, copper, nickel and tin from within Soviet Russia along railways that could not be blockaded or bombed by the British. So gullible were the Russians at this time that early in January 1941 a new economic agreement was concluded, boosting the amount of raw materials to be sent week after week from the Soviet Union.

★

From its inception Barbarossa was regarded as an ideological crusade, and political preparations went ahead side by side with the military build-up. Several rival figures in the Party were eager to serve as viceroy of the new German empire in the east. Heinrich Himmler, as head of the SS, already had experience of Germanization in Poland. Gauleiter Lohse, from Schleswig-Hostein, was grimly efficient and eventually achieved administrative control of the three Baltic states. But in the winter of 1940–41 the leading contender was Alfred Rosenberg, a would-be philosopher of pretentious Aryan supremacist theories, who had been born in Tallinn of German parentage and spent some of his youth at Moscow studying architecture. As head of APA, the Nazi Party's foreign affairs department from 1933 onwards, Rosenberg maintained contact with sympathizers in the Baltic states. He was prepared to claim that the Estonians were already Germanized, not only culturally and intellectually, but also 'in blood'; Latvians he considered less reliable and Lithuanians 'racially inferior' though – like Ludendorff before him – Rosenberg thought Lithuania ripe for German colonization. In April 1941 Hitler, who rated Rosenberg more highly than did the other leading Nazis, made him responsible for planning protectorates in the 'occupied East'. Rosenberg's first directive to his future colleagues in what became known as the *Ostministerium* was not especially original: 'suitable elements' in Estonia, Latvia and Lithuania should be 'assimilated' and 'undesirable elements exterminated'. But the overall intention of policy could not be more clearly stated: 'The Baltic Sea must become an inland German lake, under the protection of Greater Germany,' Rosenberg declared.

Stalin's reaction to the mounting evidence of Hitler's aggressive intentions remains a matter of dispute. The future Marshal Zhukov, Chief of the General Staff in 1941, says in his memoirs that as early as 20 March Stalin received and read a Soviet intelligence assessment predicting a German attack in late May or mid-June but chose to ignore it, preferring to believe he could himself strike a bargain with Hitler over the delivery of oil and other essential materials. It has been argued, not too convincingly, that by the spring of 1941 Stalin was preparing a pre-emptive strike: for that reason on 6 May he became head of the government (retaining Molotov as foreign minister), called up reservists, authorized the construction of nearly 200 airfields in the newly acquired western territories from the Baltic to the Black Sea, and proposed drastic changes in the Red Army's putative armoured divisions. But none of these reforms could become effective for many months ahead. Meanwhile the Bolshevik–Nazi partnership of convenience must continue. Ironically, the Kremlin had become the last home of Appeasement. Stalin assumed time was on his side: Hitler would not risk a two-Front war while Britain remained defiant across the Channel; tales of German troop movements along the Soviet Union's western frontiers were fabrications emanating from British intelligence sources.

The internal Soviet security services remained ruthlessly alert. It is probable that the NKVD knew of Rosenberg's plans. Throughout the winter the routine arrest of alleged dissidents continued in Vilnius, Kaunas, Riga, Tallinn, and Tartu; then suddenly, in early summer, systematic large-scale deportations were ordered in all three Baltic Soviet Republics. As in the Polish lands in 1939, the new arrests were taken from names on lists of professional categories, with particular emphasis on teachers, lawyers and groups with contacts abroad. On the night of 13–14 June 1941 trains made up of 490 cattle trucks filled with 15,000 people headed eastwards out of Latvia; one-third of the deportees were Jewish. An unknown number of similar sinister trains left Lithuania at the same time. A second railway exodus was planned for the following weekend.

Estonia, too, fared badly, with the great deportation beginning twenty-four hours later than in Latvia. Anna Reid in her fascinating historical study of Siberia, *The Shaman's Coat* (2002), describes how, far north of Tomsk, she met Kalyu Kallismaa, a lawyer's son who had been deported from his native Narva at the age of seventeen, some sixty years previously. He recalled that at two in the morning of Saturday, 14 June the family were woken by an NKVD lieutenant, given an hour to pack and taken to the railway station, where that evening they were herded into cattle trucks to begin a five-week journey of some 2,700 kilometres by train and river-barge, with no food except what they had brought with them. Those who survived the ordeal eventually reached a fishing camp beside a tributary of the Ob where they had to clear the forest and build a collective farm. Within a year Kalyu lost his parents and two brothers. Kalyu stayed on and took pride in the *kolkhoz*. Although some hardy survivors went back to Estonia in 1991–2 when independence was regained, Kalyu was too settled in his life and ways to return. It was, as Anna Reid observes, 'a family tragedy . . . repeated millions of times in Stalin's Siberia'.

While Kalyu's cattle-truck train was waiting to leave Narva station on that fateful Saturday evening, at the Kremlin the effective heads of the armed forces were conferring with Stalin and Molotov. Both Marshal Timoshenko (defence commissar) and General Zhukov emphasized the significance of the latest troop concentrations across the frontier and urged Stalin to order mobilization. He refused: 'That means war!' he exclaimed angrily. The naval commander-in-chief, Admiral Kuznetsov (who has left an account of the meeting), reported German fleet movements in the Baltic, where forty-eight small warships had sailed into Finnish waters, possibly to lay minefields. He also said that German merchantmen were hurriedly leaving Tallinn, Riga and other Soviet ports with their loading incomplete. Neither Stalin nor Molotov was impressed: 'Only a fool would attack us,' Molotov said.

Exactly a week later, on the evening of 21 June, Timoshenko and Zhukov were again in the Kremlin. Deserters had said that the attack would begin next morning, they reported. After much persuasion Stalin authorized a low-key border alert, provided the Soviet troops avoided any act of provocation, and preparations could begin to black out Soviet cities and likely targets from the air. There was still no sense of urgency at the Kremlin. That night – the shortest of the year – the Moscow–Berlin Express ran in both directions as usual, the carriages passing each other close to the border at Brest-Litovsk. On Hitler's orders, a long freight train full of the regular quota of Soviet supplies to the Reich was allowed to trundle across the bridge into German Poland about one o'clock in the morning of Sunday, 22 June.

Three and a quarter hours later Operation Barbarossa began. More than 3,000,000 German soldiers moved forward to invade the Soviet Union along a 1,450-kilometre front from the Baltic to the Black Sea. Kaunas and Liepāja were among the towns bombed before dawn. Technically Finland remained neutral until 26 June, but on that same Sunday a Finnish task force occupied the Åland Islands. Two of the largest Soviet warships, already cruising in the vicinity, ignored the Finnish action and headed back towards Kronstadt, strictly observing the Kremlin directive not to provoke an incident. But it was with Stalin's approval that at 7.15 a.m. on the Sunday, General Zhukov ordered the Red Army 'to attack and destroy' enemy forces wherever they had crossed the frontier.

26

Nazi–Soviet War

IN 1812 NAPOLEON had begun his invasion of Russia by crossing the Niemen on the morning of 24 June, occupying Kaunas before nightfall and Vilnius within four days. Hitler's massive attack started two days earlier in the year and along the Baltic shores gained comparable successes. Kaunas fell within twenty-four hours, Vilnius within sixty. An armoured column entered Daugavpils on 26 June, another was at Riga by the last night of the month. A few hours later in Estonia, the university city of Tartu rose in revolt against the Soviet authorities and the rebels held out until the Germans arrived on 6 July. By the middle of August the German 18th Army was across the pre-1940 frontier at Narva. On 21 August Field Marshal von Leeb's Army Group North cut the Moscow railway route at Chudovo, 145 kilometres south-east of Leningrad.

In some strongholds the Russians offered stubborn resistance. The isolated garrison of Brest-Litovsk held out until 30 July and Soviet forces in the naval base of Hangö frustrated Finnish attempts to recover the lost peninsula from 29 June until 3 December. Across the Gulf, Tallinn was still in Soviet hands in the last week of August, though encircled on land. Admiral Vladimir Tributs, commander of the Red Banner Baltic fleet, tried to rescue soldiers, naval personnel and civilian officials trapped in the Estonian capital. At night on 27 August and through the following day, he evacuated more than 20,000 Russians in 29 troop transports and 160 smaller craft, seeking the protection of Kronstadt, 240 kilometres away.

The long voyage eastwards was fraught with danger. German warships based on Helsinki had laid a vast minefield off Cape Juminda even before the war began. Although Tributs knew of the mining operations he seems to have under-estimated their extent: five destroyers and ten minesweepers or torpedo boats were lost, as well as forty-two merchant ships. As at Dunkirk, many small vessels reached safety, running the gauntlet of hostile artillery on both shores of the Gulf as well as the mines and attacks from the air. But the troop transports were bigger targets; only four of the twenty-nine completed the voyage and at least 5,000 of the evacuees from Tallinn perished at sea.

The Red Banner Fleet kept the Germans guessing. Hitler thought Tributs might break out into the western Baltic before the Gulf froze over and accept internment in Sweden rather than face capture at Kronstadt; he could even seek a rendezvous with British ships off the Norwegian coast. A German Baltic fleet, including the new battleship *Tirpitz*, was therefore improvised in the autumn, but it saw no action and was soon dispersed. For two and a half years Tributs kept his surface fleet at Kronstadt, employing the warships' guns to strengthen Leningrad's defences. Patrolling Soviet submarines risked the minefields during 1942, sinking twenty-eight ships, five of them Swedish neutrals. But ten submarines were lost and the patrols ceased when, in the autumn of 1942, the German Navy completed a defensive boom across the Gulf from Porkkala in Finland to the Estonian coast at Keila-Joa.

In the Baltic republics the departure of Soviet troops raised hopes of a return to independence. Lithuanian nationalists took control of the radio station at Kaunas shortly before noon on 23 June, called on their compatriots to rise 'against the Red Russia occupation' and announced the formation of a Lithuanian government headed by the career diplomat Kazys Škirpa (who was in Berlin) with General Raštikis (who was in Königsberg) as defence minister. Half an hour later Škirpa reported to the German Foreign Ministry, handing over a letter to the Führer which thanked 'the victorious German Army . . . for saving Lithuania from the Bolshevist occupation'.

That afternoon the former Latvian minister in Berlin followed Škirpa to the ministry, seeking the establishment of a similar government in Riga. But Hitler did not intend to set up puppet regimes in the East, though Lithuania's provisional government was not dissolved until six weeks after the invasion. Neither Škirpa nor his Latvian colleague received encouragement from Ribbentrop. On 26 June Rosenberg reminded the High Command and the Foreign Ministry that in April he was given responsibility for the Ostland; everything relating to these territories must be referred to him.

When the Germans finally entered Riga five days later a Committee for Liberated Latvia and a Latvian State Council awaited them. Rosenberg did not entirely quash Latvian hopes. Before the end of July a local administration was in being, permitted to supervise agriculture, education, internal transport and social welfare and headed by a Latvian, General Oskars Dankers. This 'Self Government' (*Pašpārvalde*) maintained a fiction of autonomy throughout the occupation, although major decisions were taken by Rosenberg and his chief executant, Heinrich Lohse. By the early autumn a force of Auxiliary Security Police (*Schutzmannschaft*), recruited from former Latvian soldiers and police, took over some guard duties from the German army. Ominously, the auxiliaries were also ready to assist the SS with 'special operations'.

Estonian hopes of recognition were raised by Tartu's defiant rebellion. But when on 11 August Jüri Uluots, the last prime minister, suggested the formation of an Estonian government and army to the occupying authorities his proposal was automatically passed back to Rosenberg and his *Ostministerium* and no action was taken: Berlin remained undecided over Estonia's future status. Rosenberg and Himmler wished to assess the value of an Estonian National Socialist movement set up, in the preceding months, by exiles in Helsinki. Eventually, on 9 December, Hitler authorized the formation of a 'Self Government' in Estonia on the Latvian model. It was headed by Hjalmar Mäe, once Sirk's deputy in the Veterans League and more recently active among Helsinki exiles (where he had grown a Hitler moustache). By the warped standards of Nazism, Estonia soon merited praise in Berlin, for in January 1942 Mäe could assure Rosenberg that their common country of birth was *Judenfrei*, a region 'free of Jews'.

There had never been many Jews in Estonia, probably no more than a thousand when the German 18th Army arrived. Tragically, within four months, all within this small community were dead, executed by the SS Special Task Force, supported by local fanatics. In Latvia and Lithuania, where Jewish families formed some 5 per cent and 8.5 per cent of the pre-war population, the toll of executions was horrific. A German report, circulated a fortnight after the invasion, noted that before the army entered Kaunas 2,500 of the city's 35,000 Jews were killed by Lithuanians incensed by alleged Jewish support for the 'Sovietization' of the republic over the previous twelve months. The SS continued the terrible 'Special Task' in Kaunas: 463 Jews executed on 4 July; more than 2,500 on 6 July. The Ninth Fort, a key bastion built in Alexander III's reign to protect Russia's western frontier, became Kaunas's principal place of execution. Over the next three years 80,000 Jews and hundreds of Soviet prisoners of war perished within the confines of the Ninth Fort. It is a chilling place to visit today.

The Jewish community in the Latvian capital suffered similarly, the atrocities beginning at almost the same time as in Kaunas. On 4 July 1941 some 300 of Riga's Jews were locked into a synagogue that was then set on fire, while grenades were thrown into the interior. Before the coming of winter thousands of Jews were executed in neighbouring forests. Andrievs Ezergailis, a scholarly recent historian of this grim period of his country's history, cites a contemporary German report that in the first three months of occupation 30,025 Latvian Jews were killed. Dr Ezergailis himself calculates that by the end of the year the figure was twice as high.

Genocide enveloped all the occupied ex-Soviet regions: eastern Poland, Belarus, Ukraine and Russia itself. But no city suffered so terribly as Vilnius, with its Jewish community dating back 600 years. In 1941 there were as many as 100 synagogues or houses of Hebraic prayer within Vilnius, with refugees from German-occupied Poland raising the Jewish population to at least 80,000. On 17 July 700 Jews were taken to a popular picnic clearing in the forest of Paneriai (Ponary), 13 kilometres southwest of the city: there they were shot by the SS. Over the following seven weeks an estimated 35,000 Jews perished at Paneriai. There was then a pause in the killings while a Small Ghetto was sealed off around the Great Synagogue and a Large Ghetto created farther to the south-west. But in the third and fourth weeks of October the Small Ghetto was destroyed and another 11,000 Jews murdered in the forest. On 24 October 3,700 Jews were rounded up in what remained of the Small Ghetto and the adjoining Large Ghetto and either shot in the streets or taken along the tragic route to Paneriai, where their bodies could be thrown dead or half-alive into pits in the sandy soil. Among those killed that Friday were 885 children. These atrocities were committed three months ahead of the infamous Wannsee Conference (20 January 1942), with its recommendation of a 'Final Solution of the Jewish Question', by annihilation.

The Large Ghetto of Vilnius remained in being for two more years. It was a source of slave labour for the Nazis, as also were the ghettos established in Kaunas and Šiauliai in central Lithuania. The slaughter continued, with whole families seized and shot in the forest as reprisals for gestures of defiance or sabotage. By July 1944, when the Red Army returned to Vilnius, 70,000 Jews and 10,000 non-Jews had been executed in the killing woods of Paneriai. Tragically the Soviet authorities maintained the sequence of mass murder outside Vilnius, with more than 700 Lithuanians executed in neighbouring Tuskelenai Park during the first three years of 'liberation'.

In the autumn of 1941, however, with the Soviet killings at Katyn as yet unsuspected in the West, the honour of the Red Army remained untarnished and the indomitable resistance shown by the Russian people heartened their allies. Most admired of all epics of endurance was the siege of Leningrad and the courage of civilians and soldiery in defending the city their kinsfolk had created for Tsar Peter ten generations back in time, with an equal suffering and loss of life.

The first long-range shells fell on the old imperial capital on Sunday, 1 September, ten weeks after the start of the invasion. By the following Sunday the Russians still held an isolated strip of coast 19 kilometres long and 32 kilometres deep around Oranienbaum and some of the south-eastern and south-western shores of Lake Ladoga, but the city itself was encircled. The Germans were in Schlüsselburg, the fortress Peter the Great built on the historic site commanding the point where Lake Ladoga's waters flow into the Neva, and Finnish troops stood along the 1939 frontier in the Karelian isthmus. Farther east, the Finns were poised to cut the Leningrad–Murmansk railway. The longest siege in the history of modern Europe had begun. It was to continue for 880 days, by official reckoning, and cost at least 640,000 Russians their lives.

Leningrad was ill-prepared for the rigours of blockade. Some 100,000 refugees had raised the number of mouths to feed to 2.6 million, but disruption of the railways in the wake of the invasion, together with sheer bureaucratic bumbling, limited food stocks to eight weeks, at best. Heavy air raids on 8 September and 10 September destroyed food warehouses and a refrigeration plant. Until the second week in November some supplies trickled through from the railhead at Tikhvin, by the use of barges across the southern waters of Ladoga and a light railway from Osinovets into the north of the city. But the German capture of Tikhvin on 8 November, and the freezing of the lake waters soon afterwards, blocked the route. Not until the frost hardened did it become possible to create a perilous ice road across Ladoga. Although Tikhvin was retaken a month later and a narrow and circuitous Lifeline Road cut through the forests east of Lake Ladoga, the closing weeks of the year formed the grimmest period of the siege. On 25 December 1941, while housewives in Britain were improvising their third Christmas dinner on wartime rations, no fewer than 3,700 Leningraders died from starvation.

Hitler expected Leningrad would soon be starved and shelled into surrender. As early as the third week of September he ordered seven armoured divisions to be transferred from General von Leeb's army in front of Leningrad to the Moscow front, where he was gambling on victory before the coming of snow and ice. He had hopes of increased Finnish support for Army Group North: two years previously the Finns had proved themselves masters of winter warfare. Yet it soon became doubtful if Finland could ever serve Germany as a reliable ally. Risto Ryti, who was elected president in December 1940, saw the operations which began at the end of June 1941 as the Continuation War, Round 4 of a Soviet–Finnish contest in which blows had first been exchanged a third of a century back in time. German co-operation, so Ryti assured Hitler on 1 July, 'finally guarantees a successful conclusion of Finland's long fight for independence'. But two months later, with the Red Army pulling back from Finnish soil and the first shells falling on Leningrad, the Germans had doubts over the Finnish army's whole-hearted commitment. President Ryti had to deny rumours that Helsinki was seeking a separate peace: Bolshevism, he told Hitler's envoy, must be destroyed and Leningrad cease to be a metropolis.

Politically Ryti was devious; he continued to avoid close ties with Berlin. Like Estonia, Finland never had a large Jewish community and the Eduskunta was unlikely to pass anti-Semitic legislation. At one point, however, Himmler and Ribbentrop exerted such pressure on Helsinki that fifteen Jewish refugees were handed over to Germany. So great was the indignation in Finland when it became known they had been executed that the cabinet insisted to Ryti that any further demand for deportation must be rejected; Finland's remaining 2,000 Jews survived the war.

Finnish elation at recovering towns lost in the Winter War died away once the old frontier was reached at Terioki and Mainila at the end of August. On 4 September General Jodl, Hitler's chief of staff, flew to Finnish headquarters to confer all three classes of the Iron Cross on Mannerheim and urge him to send his troops forward into northern Leningrad. The field marshal was prepared to order an advance into East Karelia, in a vain attempt to link up with Army Group North on the river Swir, and a thrust into Lapland that cut the main railway to Murmansk; but nothing would induce him to cross the traditional Finnish–Russian border in the Karelian isthmus. Casualties had been heavy, food stocks were low, and the army was not trained for warfare in a huge, sprawling city like Leningrad. In the second week of September, Hitler's envoy in Helsinki reported that the Finnish army, 400,000 strong when Barbarossa began, needed to be reduced to 140,000 or 150,000 men 'as soon as the military situation permitted', in order to revive the economy. Thereafter the Northern Front – 950 kilometres from the Gulf of Finland to the Barents Sea – remained important to Germany strategically, for the Finns posed a potential threat Stalin could not ignore; but the High Command recognized that as an active fighting force the Finns carried little weight.

In November 1941 a crisis in food supplies and the prospect of a declaration of war from London revived talk of a separate peace in Helsinki. Germany immediately sent 70,000 tons of grain across the Baltic, with the promise of more to follow, and the peace talk died away. Reluctantly, on 5 December, Britain went to war with Finland (and with Hungary and

Romania, who were also Germany's co-belligerents against the Soviet Union). The United States – against whom Hitler rashly declared war three days after the Japanese attack on Pearl Harbor – did not break with Finland; there were many second or third generation Americans in the Midwest who, though loyal to the land of their birth, remained proud of their Finnish family links.

Public sentiment in Britain sympathized with the Finns, whose courage and ingenuity in the Winter War remained fresh in the memory. There was never any clash of arms between British and Finnish forces, although two squadrons of RAF Hurricane fighters operating from Vaenga airfield near Murmansk flew over tracts of the Fisherman's Peninsula (Kalastajasaareto), close to Petsamo, and on one occasion a few bombs fell on the key supply port of Turku. Until the Normandy Landings opened the Second Front in 1944 Churchill could offer Stalin little direct diversionary assistance, although the Arctic convoys from Scapa Flow to Murmansk or Archangel brought aircraft, tanks, trucks and other equipment from August 1941 onwards, at great cost in ships sunk and lives lost. By the beginning of 1942 the convoys were also carrying American Lend-Lease aid. Most supplies went to the Moscow Front; not until October was it possible to get tanks and artillery to the Volkhov sector and relieve the pressure on Leningrad.

As yet, the British had made few forays into the Baltic: in 1940 the RAF dropped bombs on Kiel and anti-Hitler propaganda leaflets fell harmlessly and ineffectually on Lübeck and Travemünde. But in the early spring of 1942 Sir Arthur Harris, who had become head of Bomber Command on 22 February, brought a terrible form of warfare to the Baltic coast, precursor of the firestorms that would ravage Hamburg, Dresden and other German cities later in the war. A week before Harris assumed command, a directive from the Air Staff implementing decisions of the War Cabinet outlined a new strategy of 'area bombing', intended to offer support to the Russians and break German civilian morale. Harris found awaiting him at Bomber Command's headquarters in the Chilterns a list of some twenty possible targets. Among them was Lübeck. The city was described in Baedeker as 'a busy commercial industrial place' that 'still contains reminiscences of its mediaeval greatness in its lofty towers, its ancient gabled houses . . . and its venerable Rathaus'.

Early on 29 March, with Lübeck's fourteen historic churches ready to celebrate Palm Sunday a few hours later, almost 200 heavy bombers struck at the city. The first wave dropped incendiary bombs; the second wave followed half an hour later with high explosives. 'Lübeck was an exceptional town, built more like a firelighter than a human habitation,' writes Air

Commodore Henry Probert in *Bomber Harris*, his judiciously fair biography of a controversial warrior. That night 2,000 buildings were destroyed. More than 300 civilians were killed and as many as 15,000 left homeless. Twelve aircraft were lost, in a long flight that called for courage and persistence from the aircrews.

The docks and factories of Lübeck were legitimate targets. U-boat parts were manufactured outside the town and there was a naval training establishment for underwater operations. Iron ore from Sweden was unloaded in Lübeck and supplies shipped from the port to the army besieging Leningrad. But post-war justification of the raid makes uneasy reading: 'The main object of the attack was to learn to what extent a first wave of aircraft could guide a second wave to the aiming point by starting a conflagration,' Air Chief Marshal Harris wrote with characteristic honesty in *Bomber Offensive*. He added candidly, 'Lübeck was not a vital target, but it seemed to me better to destroy an industrial town of moderate importance than to toil to destroy a large industrial city.' Harris's experimental lesson left four-fifths of the Hanse old town razed by fire.

On 24 April Bomber Command made a similar attack on Rostock, the former capital of Mecklenburg and the oldest university city in the Baltic lands. The Heinkel aircraft works were badly damaged; but so too, inevitably, was the heart of the town. Almost three-quarters of the historic buildings were destroyed. Over the next three years the fires of modern war increasingly consumed the Hanse past. Nor was it only the cultural heritage of Germany that went up in smoke. On the night the RAF raided Rostock, the Luftwaffe struck at Exeter and Bath to avenge the devastation of Lübeck. Norwich and York suffered similar 'Baedeker raids' a few nights later.

Farther east the historic treasures of imperial St Petersburg were also under threat. In their advance on Leningrad the Germans had taken Gatchina, Tsar Paul's castle-palace, on 30 August 1941 and the complex of palaces and parks around Pavlovsk and Tsarskoye Selo on 16 September. By the end of that week they were in Peterhof on the shore of the Gulf. But the Russians offered fierce resistance. The 11-inch guns of the old dreadnoughts at Kronstadt shelled Gatchina for two days; the bombardment caused heavy German casualties but also destroyed the Marble Hall of the palace, the Throne Room and much of the Crimson Drawing Room. Both Peterhof and Tsarskoye Selo remained in the front line of the German perimeter around Leningrad for twenty-seven months and suffered grievously. The first Russian infantry to force their way back into the forecourt of the

Catherine Palace at Tsarskoye Selo on 15 January 1944 found facing them, not the faded turquoise of Rasterelli's long facade but a gaunt, windowless skeletal shell from which the Nazis appear to have 'retrieved' as loot the exquisite amber panels Frederick William I presented to Peter the Great. At Peterhof broken statuary littered the waterfall stairways of the Great Cascade. Oranienbaum, 11 kilometres to the west, was never occupied by the invaders but the Chinese Palace that Rinaldi had built for Catherine the Great was caught in the crossfire between German artillery and the protective guns of Kronstadt and was severely damaged.

Throughout the first three months of 1942 an average of 233 high explosive shells a day fell on inner Leningrad, although it was as late as 24 July 1943 that the city suffered its heaviest bombardment. None of the architectural gems was totally destroyed in the war and the artistic treasures of the Hermitage, together with many statues, were sent eastwards to Sverdlovsk in two special trains before the siege began, but no historic building in Leningrad was left unscathed. Yet, remarkably, even at the height of the fighting, inspectors for the Protection of Monuments were sent by the City Board of Architecture and Planning to conserve fragments of material in damaged rooms, take architectural measurements and look confidently ahead to post-war reconstruction. At the Yusupov Palace in December 1941 a shell crashed through the roof of the private theatre, lodged between fire-protection barriers and failed to explode. It remained there for five and a half years, while around it artists and craftsmen were at work, restoring the palace oblivious to danger. Eventually, in 1947, three junior officers and a private in the Engineers volunteered to extricate the shell manually and it was detonated harmlessly in open gardens; the spirit of beleaguered Leningrad survived the war.

With the coming of spring in 1942 morale rose among the besieged, although there were more and more burials when frozen corpses were discovered as the snow and ice began to melt. On 15 April, for the first time in nine months, a tram clattered down Nevsky Prospekt; it was garlanded with paper streamers and carried Party officials as passengers. Repairs to pumping stations ensured a limited supply of fresh water for the Leningraders. A labour force was conscripted to clear the streets of snow and rubble. Prefabricated iron barges were constructed to serve in the supply convoys on Ladoga that ran the gauntlet of German E-boats and Italian midget submarines operating from Schlüsselburg. In September both the Russians and their enemies mounted offensives around the outer perimeter, but the opposing armies were so well balanced that at the end of the month the fighting died away inconclusively.

The city was better able to sustain a blockade than at the start of the previous winter. Some civilians had been evacuated across the lake during the summer; their departure, together with conscription into locally raised regiments and the grim death toll, left the city council with no more than 750,000 mouths to fill, less than a quarter of the population figure given in the 1939 census. Spirits were raised by good news from other fronts: the invading armies checked west of Moscow; their thrust into the Caucasus halted with the oil derricks of Grozny visible on the horizon. In the third week of November it became clear that the vaunted German Sixth Army was caught in a trap at Stalingrad, surrounded by two heavily armoured Soviet armies.

For the people of Leningrad the best news of all during that winter came on 18 January 1943, the day the swastika flag was lowered at Schlüsselburg. After a week's heavy fighting on the ice of the Neva or in perilously snow-covered boggy forest, the Germans were forced to abandon their fixed defences or risk encirclement. Their withdrawal cleared Ladoga's southern shore and allowed the Russians to begin opening up a railway route through the narrow liberated corridor. Red Army sappers laid 29 kilometres of track with astonishing speed, despite the threat of bombardment from the new German positions. Remarkably, as early as 7 February 1943 the first train reached Leningrad, bringing coal to boost factory output and increase electrical power. Another year would pass before the blockade was finally ended, but by now it was clear to besiegers and besieged alike that Leningrad would never fall.

Five days previously the last German troops had surrendered in Stalingrad, shattering the illusion of *Wehrmacht* invincibility. Across Europe neutral governments and resistance movements in occupied lands took stock and adjusted their policies or changed their objectives. At Stockholm King Gustav V and his ministers faced a dilemma. They had always been anti-Soviet: in June 1941 a press release confirmed that the government had allowed the Germans to transport 15,000 men in the Engelbrekt division by rail from Norway across Sweden to support the Finns in their war with Russia, though 'in a way safeguarding Swedish sovereignty'. Although the king's views hardly changed, the Hansson government became less accommodating to Hitler, and Sweden refused to allow an Alpine division to make a similar journey. Nevertheless throughout 1941 and 1942 trains carrying supplies to the garrisons in Norway and taking German servicemen on leave ran regularly down to Helsingborg and on at least one occasion a captured British officer was taken through Sweden to a German prisoner-of-war camp.

By 1943 the mood in Sweden as a whole was growing increasingly hostile to Germany, largely from mounting evidence of Nazi oppression in Norway and Denmark. The Hansson government sought closer links with the Western allies and in August 1943 cancelled the railway transit agreement of June 1940, concluded under pressure from Berlin. Five months previously the Swedes had given sanctuary to a Norwegian saboteur, fully armed and in uniform, who arrived at the frontier on skis after assisting nine of his compatriots to blow up the heavy water plant at Vermork, essential to the German quest to produce an atomic bomb. Even if Kiruna's iron ore continued to boost the industries of the Ruhr, there was by now no doubt where Swedish sympathies lay.

The Swedes also allowed refugees from Norway to organize 'police troops', in effect a light infantry reserve that attracted more than 1,200 recruits in two years. Most strikingly, when it became clear that the SS were about to round up Denmark's Jewish population, the Swedish government backed an operation by the Danish Resistance that, on 1 October 1943, enabled fishermen to smuggle more than 5,000 Jews across the Øresund to safety at Helsingborg.

Tenuous links kept the Swedes in touch with the West. A week after the rescue of the Danish Jews Harold Nicolson, a fifty-seven-year-old British MP and man of letters, landed at an airfield near Stockholm, having flown from Scotland wedged in the bomb compartment of an RAF Mosquito. His mission was to assess the mood of the country and promote the British cause in Sweden. Food he found plentiful, but he was surprised that a shortage of petrol forced the Swedes to 'run their cars on gas generated from charcoal'. His month-long visit was a propaganda success. 'The Swedes of course fear the Russians, and are anxious lest we shall be too late to share the Russian victories in Europe,' Nicolson wrote to his sons. 'They are almost unanimously on our side.' He saw for himself the Jewish refugees at Helsingborg. There he also met Danish officers who had escaped across the Sound: '"Can you take us to England?", they said, "We wish to fight those devils", pointing to where the hills of Denmark glimmered in the sun.'

The 'devils', having treated Denmark with relative leniency for three years, became exasperated by the growth in acts of allegedly communist sabotage during the summer of 1943: on 29 August Germany imposed martial law on the kingdom. A fortnight later Danish patriots responded by secretly setting up a Freedom Council (Frihedsradet) to co-ordinate resistance and keep in touch with London through SOE, the Special Operations Executive agents dropped by parachute into Denmark over the preceding two years. An intelligence network was created and the council organized the printing and circulation of clandestine newspapers. In June 1944 there were acts of collective defiance in Copenhagen, a general strike and rioting. The famous Tivoli pleasure gardens were burnt to the ground, fired by the occupying authorities as a punishment, Danish patriots declared.

One of the leaders of the Resistance on the southern Danish island of Lolland was the London-born aristocrat Monica de Wichfeld. She was arrested by the Gestapo and condemned to death by a military court. Fear of creating a martyr heroine comparable to Edith Cavell led the Germans to commute Monica de Wichfeld's sentence to penal servitude. She died, aged fifty, in a prison hospital in Saxony eight weeks before Denmark was liberated.

The Frihedsradet had many contacts in Sweden, where the government did nothing to check the formation of a 'Danish Brigade' from among the refugees. Like the Norwegian 'police troops', the Danish Brigade was ready to give support to the western allies should they invade German-occupied Scandinavia. For the Swedes the great merit of these phantom armies was their freedom from communist control. Already the political leaders of the Scandinavian lands were looking ahead to the post-war world, determined to frustrate Soviet designs to succeed the Nazis as supreme masters of the Baltic.

As yet, however, the Third Reich was far from collapse. Politically Hitler counted on a culturally superior revulsion among the 'Germanic races' – now, by his reckoning, including Scandinavians and the Baltic peoples – against the barbarian invaders once again sweeping westwards 'out of the steppe'. The self-governing dependencies in Latvia and Estonia were encouraged to recruit 'volunteers' to serve in the Waffen-SS, the military arm of the stormtroopers, a force remaining technically independent of the German army. Two attempts by Mäe to rally Estonians to the cause during 1943 proved a failure. The Nazis had more success in neighbouring Latvia, where between February 1943 and July 1944 some 146,000 anti-Bolshevik volunteers were mobilized in three divisions of the Waffen-SS, serving initially in the Leningrad sector. One Latvian battalion was still fighting fanatically amid the burning buildings of Berlin in the last days of the war. The Latvian Legion swore an oath of loyalty to the Führer personally and came under German command, but wore the armband 'Latvija'; a former Latvian general was appointed their Inspector-General. In Norway some two thousand of Quisling's followers formed the nucleus of a Scandinavian Waffen-SS division that included some Danes, but it never reached full strength. Ideologically the Nazi International was an unconvincing after-thought to the Führer's teachings.

Militarily Hitler placed his faith in the 'secret weapons' with which he first threatened his enemies in a speech delivered a fortnight after the outbreak of war. As early as the summer of 1936 the German army had set aside a remote stretch of Baltic coast at the mouth of a small river on the island of Usedom for developing and testing long-range artillery rockets propelled by liquid fuel. The site at Peenemünde, about 80 kilometres from Stettin, was first reported to British Intelligence in December 1939 and attracted the attention of the RAF Photographic Reconnaissance Unit in May 1942, though it was not until the following January that Spitfires fitted with cameras began a series of regular flights. Allied experts were at first puzzled: were the secret weapons ballistic rockets, pilotless aircraft or long-range 'torpedo' shells? Intelligence reports indicated that they were intended for use against London and other cities in southern England from sites under construction in northern France.

Churchill took the Peenemünde threat very seriously: a sustained bombardment of southern England would hamper preparations for D-Day, the Normandy landings. On the night of 17–18 August 1943, 600 British aircraft attacked Peenemünde in the heaviest precision raid on any military target in the Baltic. It was carried out in bright moonlight and at low level, a totally different operation from the terror area bombing of Hanse cities in the previous year. The site was heavily defended, and the RAF lost more than forty planes and aircrew, but the raid was a success: the programmes for both the pilotless-aircraft 'flying bomb' (V-1) and the rocket (V-2) were put back several months, thereby postponing the assault on England until after D-Day. Even so, within five days of the raid an experimental rocket with a dummy warhead was fired from Peenemünde. Perhaps for propaganda purposes, the firing was ordered too soon for an efficient launch: the rocket overshot its sea target and landed on Bornholm, where it was photographed by a Danish naval officer, Hasager Christiansen. Despite being caught by the Gestapo, he was able to send to London the invaluable snapshot and some drawings of the weapon he hurriedly sketched. His enterprise was typical of the individualistic spirit of small-scale defiance that kept the challenge to Nazism active in the western Baltic that year. With help from the Danish Resistance, Commander Christiansen escaped from Bornholm to neutral Sweden.

In the East a huge-scale conflict continued to be waged across vast distances. By the second anniversary of Hitler's invasion the Red Army comprised 6,000,000 front-line troops, while factories deep in the Soviet Union were turning out far more tanks and aircraft than Germany could hope to produce. To the south-west, along the river Don from Voronezh to Rostov, the Germans had increasingly to rely on the armies of their reluctant allies, Hungary and Romania, together with ten well-equipped Italian divisions. The decisive battle of the war in the East – a clash of 4,000,000 men and 13,000 armoured vehicles – was fought in July and August 1943 in the Kursk salient, some 1,200 kilometres south of the Baltic coast: a German counter-offensive ended in a phased withdrawal that was to carry Soviet armies into the Ukraine by the autumn.

By now half the territory overrun in 1941 and 1942 was clear of the invaders, but on either side of the Gulf of Finland and around Leningrad little had changed in two years, apart from the recovery of Schlüsselburg and Ladoga's southern shore. In October 1943, however, Army Group North – now commanded by Field Marshal von Küchler – decided not to wait for a Soviet attack: a defensive line 175 kilometres long was prepared from Narva southwards, to take advantage of the natural obstacles of the Narva river and Lakes Peipus and Pskov. To reach this line Küchler needed to fall back 110 kilometres but Hitler, who had authorized construction of this East Wall, changed his mind and refused to permit any strategic retreat. Küchler's troops were still in their old positions outside Leningrad when in mid-January 1944 Generals Govorov and Meretskov launched the first major Soviet counter-offensive in the Baltic region.

Operation *Iskra* (Spark), as the counter-offensive was codenamed, took Küchler by surprise. His staff officers knew there had been intensive activity in the Oranienbaum area since the second week of November, with motorized barges, coastal steamers, tugs, minesweepers and (later) ice-breakers making regular voyages under cover of darkness from the mouth of the Neva to Kronstadt and across to the bridgehead. They assumed that the Baltic fleet was evacuating men and material from the bridgehead to reinforce other sectors. In reality, the fleet's warships and air arm were ferrying 44,000 troops, together with 600 guns and other equipment, *into* the Oranienbaum salient. When, on 14 January, the Spark ignited the Baltic region, the combined assault from the bridgehead and from the main defenders of Leningrad around the Pulkovo Heights forced Army Group North to pull hurriedly back to the East Wall along the Narva river. With this retreat the battle line receded some 110 kilometres westwards and the trunk railway between Russia's two greatest cities was finally cleared. On the evening of 27 January 1944 the people of Leningrad could at last celebrate the end of their blockade.

Stavka (the General Headquarters of the Soviet Supreme Command) urged Govorov to press forward, take Narva before the end of February and head for Tartu, isolating and enveloping Tallinn. But a Soviet amphibious landing at the mouth of the Narva river on 1 February proved abortive and, like Tsar Peter in 1700, the Russians were checked by the nature of the terrain. A fortress stood on either bank at Narva. Upstream the river was at some points 650 metres wide, with high steep banks and, behind them, almost impassable swamps and woods stretching down to Lake Peipus. The advance came to a halt. Ironically, what was once Russia's historic defensive moat now became Estonia's longest and deepest anti-tank ditch.

To the south of the Narva river, the imminence of invasion rallied resistance. The Estonians had thwarted Mäe's earlier attempts at mobilization. But with the approach of the Red Army interwar political survivors like Uluots, who deplored Nazism, saw the struggle as a fight for survival, a second war of independence. Uluots and others like him gave their backing to Mäe. In early February 38,000 men responded to Mäe's call to arms, twice as many as he had anticipated. The Germans, however, were uneasy at the prospect of an embryonic Estonian national army. Irrespective of their ideological beliefs, all the Estonian recruits were enlisted in the Waffen-SS.

The combination of geographical obstacles and determined resistance forced Stavka to revise its grand strategy and the structure of its front-line force. Armies, generally comprising two or three corps, each with three or four divisions, were to be grouped together as 'Fronts', taking their names from the area where they began their offensive. The main thrust in the Baltic region would now come south of Pskov, crossing Letgale (the region of Latvia around Daugavpils) and present-day Belarus and entering Lithuania, with Vilnius and Kaunas as objectives. The Baltic Front armies would eventually reach the Gulf of Riga from the south-east, thus isolating German Army Group North and cutting it off from East Prussia. When pontoon bridges, rafts and heavy artillery could be assembled outside Narva, Govorov's Leningrad Front army was to head for the northern shore of the Gulf of Riga. But there was no prospect of implementing these plans until the summer.

Meanwhile, despite the end of the siege of Leningrad, Finnish troops remained within 32 kilometres of the city centre and still controlled the strip of land between Lakes Ladoga and Onega. Yet there had been little activity in this sector for two years and the Russians knew the Finns had no heart for the war. In Stockholm the Soviet ambassador, Alexandra

Kollantai, held tentative peace talks with that veteran go-between, Juho Paasikivi, and in February the Eduskunta pressed President Ryti to seek terms 'that would permit us to withdraw from the war'. When Ryti failed to respond, the Russians began a series of night air raids on Helsinki, Viipuri, Poorvoo and Turku.

Early in March the Soviet bomber offensive shifted south of the Gulf, to the port with the closest Finnish links. On the night of 9 March 1944 a Harris-style Soviet air raid was made on Tallinn: fierce fires swept through the lower town; but the second wave of aircraft was confused by the smoke and by flames reflected on the surface of Lake Ülemiste. Many high-explosive bombs intended to destroy historic Toompea fell harmlessly into the waters of the lake. The raid hardened rather than weakened Estonian resistance: it alerted the people of Tallinn to the mounting danger of a return to the brutality of Soviet rule.

The Finns were apprehensive, fearing that they, too, would soon face total Soviet occupation. Ryti learnt, however, from Swedish intermediaries that if Finland went out of the war Stalin would respect the nation's independence, and Paasikivi was sent to Moscow by air to discuss an armistice. He returned on 1 April; it was a fitting date, for he felt fooled; the peace terms were harsher than anticipated. On 18 April the Eduskunta rejected them; but through Swedish contacts the Finns let it be known that they were willing to continue peace talks. By now the Germans were well aware of their ally's initiative. Indirect pressure was applied: arms supplies cut to a minimum, grain deliveries totally suspended. Finland remained in the war, though as Germany's sleeping partner, it seemed.

The long lull gave the Finns time to prepare defence in depth, restoring many pill-boxes, gun emplacements and block-houses that once formed the Mannerheim Line. They needed them in the second week of June, when the Russians lost patience and heavy artillery pounded the Finnish positions in the Karelian isthmus. On 9 June the rolling thunder of 240 guns was audible in Helsinki, 250 kilometres to the west. Warships from the Baltic fleet joined the bombardment and at dawn next morning General Govorov sent his infantry forward on a 15-kilometre front, with close support from 1,000 aircraft. The sheer weight of the attack overwhelmed the Finns. Within five days the Red Army smashed its way through the first two lines of defence and began the assault on the third line, covering Viipuri. Finland no longer had any troops in reserve and Mannerheim urgently sought German support. He was promised reinforcements of infantry and guns but, before they could arrive, on the evening of 20 June Viipuri fell. Next morning General Meretskov began a second Soviet offensive between Lakes Ladoga and

Onega. The Finnish troops fought bravely but were gradually forced back to the pre-war frontier.

German aid came with strings attached by Ribbentrop, who on 25 June flew in to Helsinki. President Ryti accepted the German demand for a signed undertaking that Finland would not make a separate peace; he did not, however, seek parliamentary approval of the agreement. While he was in Finland, Ribbentrop discussed with Wippart von Blücher, the German Minister, the prospects for a military coup. Could an administration led by a pro-Nazi Finn be set up? Blücher dismissed the possibility: Germany no longer had the manpower to establish and police a puppet regime. Ribbentrop concurred.

Over the following weeks the president became convinced that in these weeks of crisis only Mannerheim could hold the country together. On 28 July Ryti travelled out to field headquarters at Mikkeli, told the marshal he intended to resign office, and begged him to serve as his successor. Four days later Mannerheim duly became president, with parliament's backing and every intention of seeking an early peace. Not even a visit from Field Marshal Keitel with the Führer's congratulations and Oak Leaves to upgrade his Iron Cross could flatter him into collaboration. By his reckoning the Ribbentrop–Ryti agreement was a private undertaking, not binding constitutionally, as it was never submitted to the Eduskunta. On 25 August, a week after Keitel's departure, Finland formally sought armistice terms from the USSR and Britain. Diplomatic relations with Germany were cut on 4 September; the guns fell silent next day; and a fortnight later the Eduskunta approved conditions of peace dictated by Molotov. On 19 September 1944 Finland went out of the war.

Although Finland avoided Soviet occupation, the armistice terms were severe. The 1940 frontier was restored, except in the north where the Finns now also lost the Petsamo region; Finland retained Hanko, but the Soviet Union acquired a fifty-year lease on the naval base of Porkkala, a peninsula 40 kilometres west of Helsinki. The Finns were to pay the Russians $300,000,000 reparations in specified goods delivered at agreed dates over the following six years. All German troops were to be expelled from the country or interned. On 15 September a German force tried to seize the strategic island of Suursari, midway between the Finnish and Estonian coasts, but the attack was repulsed by Soviet and Finnish forces, fighting together.

By now the war map of Europe was changing significantly day by day. American, British and Canadian troops landed in Normandy on 6 June (D-Day), beginning the liberation of Europe from the west. Little more than a fortnight later, on the third anniversary of Hitler's invasion of Russia, Marshal Vasilevsky launched Operation Bagration, the advance into Belarus and Lithuania that Stavka had been preparing for three months. Along 300 kilometres west of Smolensk and east of Vitebsk no less than 1,700,000 troops went forward, with the support of more than 2,700 tanks and armoured vehicles, 28,000 guns and rockets, and 6,000 aircraft. The impetus of the advance swept the Red Army into the outskirts of Vilnius on 9 July but the troops then met determined resistance along the forested banks of the river. The Russians were helped by units of the Polish Home Army, eager to reassert Polish political claims to the city. Even with aid from the Home Army, it took the Russians four days to clear the centre of Vilnius. Another eighteen days elapsed before they entered Kaunas, 100 kilometres away, partly because of conflict with the Poles. The Soviet 'hero' was General Bagramyan, whose 1st Baltic Front advanced 480 kilo- metres in five weeks. He reached the coast near Jūrmala, west of Riga, on the last day of July, though German counter-attacks a fortnight later forced him on the defensive.

Operation Bagration was followed by the long-delayed assault on Germany's East Wall. Early on 25 July two Russian divisions crossed the Narva river aboard rafts and amphibious craft, supported by a heavy barrage and air attacks. The city of Narva fell at last on 28 July, but Tartu held out for another four weeks and desperate German-Estonian resistance kept Russian tanks from entering Tallinn until 21–22 September. For the first time in the war Germany risked large warships in the eastern Baltic's shal- low waters: the pocket battleships *Lützow* (ex-*Deutschland*) and *Admiral Scheer*, together with the heavy cruiser *Prinz Eugen*, served as floating artil- lery in support of the army. Smaller vessels evacuated Nazi officials and troops from Tallinn and on 17 September from Pärnu, in the north-eastern corner of the Gulf of Riga. What remained of Pärnu's Hanseatic Old Town was wrecked in the fighting.

As in earlier wars, Riga became the prize objective. By 23 September four Soviet commanders were converging on the city across lands fought over many times in the past eight centuries. Fedyuniniskii's 2nd Shock Army, having cleared Tallinn and Pärnu, was across the Latvian border in the north but had less weight of firepower than the Baltic Fronts. Bagramyan's troops (1st Baltic) were only 16 kilometres south of the city's outskirts, along the route from Jelgava, where the Iron Division had first flaunted the swastika a quarter of a century earlier. Maslennikov's 3rd Baltic Front, advancing from the north-east, was fighting its way from the swamps around Valka to the forested hills of Sigulda, difficult terrain first contested by rival knightly Orders during the northern crusades. Yeremenko, with 2nd Baltic Front, was 65 kilometres east of Riga, but held up by formidable resistance on the right bank of the Daugava river.

Next day Marshal Vasilevsky made a decisive change of strategy. Bagramyan was ordered to break off the drive on Riga, redeploy his armoured columns to face north-westwards, and head for the Lithuanian coast, in order to cut land links between Germany's Army Group North and its East Prussian homeland. There were more than 1,300 tanks in 1st Baltic, and on 1 October Bagramyan took by surprise the five German divisions on his flank. Army Group North pulled back to the Courland peninsula, building defences around the ports it knew as Windau and Libau. Within nine days 1st Baltic entered the Lithuanian port of Palanga and cut off another four German divisions holding Klaipėda (Memel to its fanatical defenders). By the end of the month a corridor 160 kilometres wide separated Army Group North from the main German central army, defending East Prussia.

On the Tuesday that Palanga fell – 10 October – forward troops of 3rd Baltic twice tried to storm Riga's outer defences, but the German line held. Next day Yeremenko's 2nd Baltic joined the assault and again met fierce resistance, not only from regular German troops but from Latvian infantry, too. At last on Thursday morning the lines of defence began to crumble. By Friday evening the metropolis of Riga was in Russian hands. Within hours, fireworks brightened the night sky above the Kremlin, as Moscow celebrated the 'liberation' of all three Baltic Soviet Republics. In one sense the celebration was premature, for Army Group North continued to hold out in the Courland peninsula, using Ventspils and Liepāja as supply ports until the end of the war. But the Russians had good reason for self-congratulation. Their sixteen-week offensive destroyed thirty German divisions and cost Hitler half a million men, killed or seriously wounded or taken prisoner.

As early as 4 January 1944 the Russian vanguard crossed the old inter-war frontier between the Soviet Union and Poland near the railway junction of Sarny, beyond the Pripet marshes and some 500 kilometres south of the Baltic. At once problems left unresolved in the earliest years of the war threatened the future of Poland and the unity of the allied Great Powers. To Polish exiles Stalin remained as much a despoiler of their homeland as Hitler. When, in April 1943, the Germans announced the discovery in Katyn forest of the remains of thousands of Polish officers killed three years previously by the Russians, all co-operation between the Soviet authorities and General Sikorski's government in London came to an end. Three months later, Sikorski was killed in a plane crash at Gibraltar. He was succeeded as prime minister by Stanislaw Mikolajczýk, leader of the Peasant Party, a shrewd parliamentarian but inexperienced in statecraft and lacking his predecessor's military prestige. The Russians raised a Kosciuszko Division, led by General Zygmunt Berling, to fight on the Eastern Front; and in November 1943 a Polish Workers' Party was set up in Moscow, under the chairmanship of Boleslaw Bierut, with Wladyslaw Gomulka as secretary-general. By February 1944 Bierut headed a National Council of Poland that challenged the right of the Mikolajczýk government to speak for the nation. The military power of the advancing Soviet army gave the unrepresentative council political authority in the liberated territories. It also enabled Stalin to propose to Churchill and Roosevelt that the Soviet Union should restore the frontier of 1939–41, while 'the home of the Polish state and nation' should be extended westwards to the line of the Oder and include all of East Prussia.

The Home Army, which kept in close touch with London during Sikorsi's leadership, increasingly acted independently. By the summer of 1944 it could count on support from some 36,000 men and women, armed with machine guns, rifles and revolvers. Its commander, General Tadeusz Komorowski (code-named 'Bor'), was an aristocrat from a crack cavalry regiment; politically he had little in common with Mikolajczýk. Bor planned a rising in Warsaw, true to the tradition of 1794 and 1830. If it succeeded, spokesmen for the old order would be in a strong position to bargain with the Red Army and with the Polish communists in its baggage-train. On 26 July Mikolajczýk authorized Bor to call for a rising by the Home Army when, and if, he thought local conditions were favourable. On that evening Mikolajczýk, with Churchill's warm backing, left London to fly to Moscow via Cairo hoping to persuade Molotov and Stalin to accept a genuinely unified Polish provisional government.

The 1st Belorussian Front, heading for the Polish capital, was commanded by Marshal Rokossovsky, the son of a Polish stonemason. By 27 July the rumble of Rokossovsky's guns could be heard in Warsaw and Bor resolved to strike. He hoped to secure the city within ten days and then negotiate its surrender to the Russians who, he assumed, would by then have cleared the east bank of the Vistula. Strategically this was a miscalculation. Four German armoured divisions were deployed between the 1st Belorussian Front and the Polish capital. Rokossovsky needed to regroup before attempting to cross the Vistula. His supply line was already 500 kilometres long, his men were close to exhaustion. A direct assault on the

Polish capital was not part of his plans. He was counting on an outflanking movement through the Bialowieza forest to force the Germans to pull back, ahead of the attack on Warsaw.

The rising began on 1 August 1944, as dusk fell. Within three days, two-thirds of the city was in the hands of the Home Army, although no strategic centres were seized. The Germans, who had suspected a rising was being planned, brought up SS reinforcements and isolated the insurgents. By the third week of August they could communicate with each other only through the labyrinth of sewers. Bor appealed for outside help as soon as the rising began, but there had been no prior consultation with the Russians and Warsaw lay beyond the range of troop-carrying aircraft from the west. From Italy, heavy bombers of the RAF and the USAAF brought food and supplies to be dropped by parachute: about half fell into German hands. Rokossovsky sympathized with his compatriots but told Stavka that news of the rising 'put us in a great state of alarm'. He went forward to an observation post in a factory chimney and studied the city carefully through field-glasses but could see no immediate way of giving assistance. Stalin was suspicious of the rising's political implications. On only one occasion did he allow American planes to land and refuel at a Soviet airfield. Eventually, in the third week of September, Berling's Kosciuszko Division entered the suburb of Praga and crossed to the west bank of the Vistula, but they were unable to secure their bridgehead. Shortage of food and ammunition forced Bor to surrender to the Germans on 3 October. During the Uprising some 15,000 fighters of the Home Army were killed and more than 200,000 civilians perished, almost a quarter of Warsaw's inhabitants. On Hitler's orders, demolition squads began the systematic destruction of the Polish capital. By the time the Red Army entered Warsaw, on 17 January 1945, four-fifths of the city lay razed to the ground. It was by then 379 days since the Russians first crossed Poland's 1939 frontier.

The Warsaw Uprising was a courageous disaster. It destroyed the last resistance army in east-central Europe. Henceforth Stalin could exercise a map-shaping mastery of power similar to the authority enjoyed by Alexander I in 1814. Over the following months the nominated members of Bierut's council, established in the town of Lublin, became Poland's *de facto* rulers. When eventually a National Unity Government returned to Warsaw, it comprised sixteen 'Lublin Poles' and three 'London Poles' (among them Mikolajczýk). They accepted the great westward movement of frontiers decreed by Stalin and reluctantly acknowledged by Churchill and Roosevelt at the Yalta Conference of early February 1945.

The boundaries of the new Poland were set far deeper into Europe and included more than 300 kilometres of Baltic coast.

These lands, however, had still to be conquered. On Friday, 12 January 1945 the greatest Soviet offensive of the war began, with the wall maps at Stavka showing twenty-five arrow-heads pointing westward and northward. The main parallel thrusts by Marshal Zhukov's 1st Belorussian Front concentrated on leaping from the middle Vistula to the Oder. By 1 February bridgeheads had been established in woods beside the frozen marshes north of Kustrin, barely 65 kilometres from the centre of Berlin: a sudden thaw hampered further progress in this sector. Stalin decided to delay the final attack on Berlin, partly to ensure his southern armies had cleared Austria and central Europe before the German surrender, and it was not until 21 April that Zhukov's vanguard made contact with the outer defences of Berlin. Four days later the city was encircled.

To the north the Russians had made a similar rapid advance towards the Baltic coast during the second half of January. The Kaiser's eldest grandson, Prince Louis Ferdinand, spent Christmas and the New Year as usual with his family at Cadinen, the Hohenzollerns' seaside villa on the Frische Haff, 24 kilometres from Elbing. On the thirteenth day of the offensive all the communities around the Haff were startled by news of a tank battle within Elbing itself. Sleighs were harnessed for a rapid departure. The prince 'drove over the Haff on 25th January 1945 – it was bitter cold but there was radiant sunshine,' he recalls in his memoirs. 'I was one of the last to depart. The Bolsheviks reached the Haff half an hour later.' Among the alleged 'Bolsheviks' were enthusiastically patriotic volunteers in the First Polish Army, a successor to Berling's Kosciuszko Division, commanded by General Poplawski. But the main drive of the First Polish Army – which now numbered 78,000 men – concentrated on Western Pomerania. In the first week of March the Poles reached the Baltic at Kolberg, the old Hanse fortress port they knew as Koł obrzeg.

Rokossovsky's 1st Belorussian Front and Chernyakovsky's 3rd Belorussian Front were assigned similar tasks to the armies of Rennenkampf and Samsonov that entered the East Prussian heartland in the opening weeks of the First World War. The two Soviet Fronts were stronger and more mobile but they faced familiar geographical obstacles, though the forested lakes and sandy soil were transformed by the wintry conditions. The terrible novelty in 1945, both in the towns of East Prussia and in the advance to the Oder and on to Berlin, was the unbridled rapacity of the invaders. This demonic partnership between a conscious urge for collective vengeance and sheer animal lust has been judiciously assessed from newly opened archives by Antony

Beevor in his *Berlin*, a graphic study of the last weeks of the Third Reich.

Many place names evoked memories of earlier campaigns. On 21 January the Russians advanced victoriously across the frozen fields of Grünwald and Tannenberg, blowing up the massive Hindenburg mausoleum Hitler erected on the site ten years previously. The field marshal's coffin had hurriedly been disinterred and was by then somewhere among the line of vehicles heading westwards. A few days later the Soviet invaders sped past the pine forest of Rastenburg and the village of Gierloz, home of the 'Wolf's Lair', Hitler's bunker command post for all operations in the East from 1941 until 20 November 1944, only eleven weeks back in time. A far older military sanctuary offered formidable resistance. Marienburg, the massive citadel of the Teutonic Knights, which for seven weeks defied siege by Jagiello in 1410, delayed the Soviet advance on Elbing and Danzig for five weeks in 1945, with its east wall shattered by a steady bombardment. Remarkably the defenders of Marienburg were supported by a long range counter-bombardment from the eight 8-inch guns of the heavy cruiser *Prinz Eugen*, firing across the Frische Haff from out to sea.

The retreat of Army Group North into the Courland peninsula and the isolation of garrisons in Königsberg and Memel increased German dependence on the navy. Refugee families and wounded troops congregating in Pillau were crammed aboard small coastal ferries and brought to Danzig in the last week of January. Grand Admiral Dönitz, commander-in-chief of the Kriegsmarine, at once sought to bring order out of chaos by mounting Operation Hannibal, a large-scale evacuation in escorted vessels to the relative safety of Schleswig-Holstein. On 30 January the *Wilhelm Gustoff* – a 25,400 tonne liner launched in 1937 to reward 2,000 good Nazi workers with a 'Strength through Joy' holiday cruise – left Gdynia, dangerously overcrowded. Some estimates put the number of civilians and servicemen aboard as high as 8,000, though a figure between 6,500 and 6,800 seems more realistic. The ship steamed slowly westwards with a single motor torpedo boat as escort. Next evening she was hit by three torpedoes from a Soviet submarine. Within an hour she sank. The escort and the cruiser *Admiral Hipper* rescued 1,300 survivors from the *Wilhelm Gustoff*'s boats but at least 5,500 perished in the icy waters, more than three times as many as in the *Titanic* disaster. No previous sinking – from war, accident or natural causes – cost so many lives.

The mass evacuation continued, nevertheless. Not all 'passengers' were refugees or service personnel. Russian prisoners-of-war and several thousand victims of concentration camp brutality were herded aboard merchant vessels; few survived the rigours of their voyage; some perished when RAF bombers attacked shipping in the river Trave at Lübeck. An improvised hospital-ship – not, apparently, carrying Red Cross markings – was sunk off Pillau on 12 February, with the loss of another 2,000 lives; and six days of basic supplies for Danzig went down into the Baltic when a ship returning from Kiel struck a mine. There was no conventional battle at sea but constant naval activity, with guns firing at waves of bombers, destroyers on patrol against submarines, crews sent in to commandeer any seaworthy vessels. Although some 15,000 lives were lost, during the last three months of the war the Kriegsmarine evacuated about 1,000,000 soldiers and seamen from the endangered Baltic ports, and perhaps as many as 1,500,000 civilian refugees. There is no larger sea migration of peoples during so short a span of time in recorded history.

In March, as the ground assault on Danzig and Gdynia intensified, the pocket battleships *Admiral Scheer* and *Lützow* joined the *Prinz Eugen* and the cruiser *Leipzig* in pounding the ever-shifting Russian positions. So, too, did the two pre-dreadnought museum pieces, the *Schleswig-Holstein* and *Schlesien*. On 21 March the *Schleswig-Holstein*, loosening her salvoes close to the point where she fired the first shells of the war in September 1939, took evasive action during a bombing raid and ran aground in the shallows of Danzig Bay. There she was scuttled. A fortnight later the *Schlesien* struck a mine dropped from an aircraft of the RAF's Coastal Command and sank off Swinemünde. Halifax bombers of Coastal Command caught the *Lützow* in the same waters on 16 April; the pocket battleship was damaged and ran aground but was refloated. The most serious RAF attack on the German fleet came on the night of 9–10 April at Kiel: the *Admiral Scheer* was sunk, capsizing in the inner basin, and the cruisers *Emden* and *Leipzig* badly damaged.

Farther east the Russians remained the chief enemy, not the British. Despite the lurking submarines and attacks by the land-based air arm of the Baltic fleet, the Kriegsmarine kept in contact with the Courland peninsula, where 200,000 veterans of Army Group North defied repeated assaults of the Soviet Baltic Front armies. Hitler personally refused to countenance evacuation or surrender, arguing that the enclave tied up Soviet troops who would otherwise engage in the drive on Berlin. The warships did not begin taking off wounded and exhausted men until Hitler's death was reported. Over the following week they evacuated 18,000 men but when the fighting officially ended more than ten times as many passed into Russian captivity. Among them were no fewer than forty-two generals.

Berlin surrendered to Marshal Zhukov on 2 May, some forty-eight hours after Hitler shot himself in the bunker of the Reich Chancellery. One hundred kilometres west of Berlin there was in these apocalyptic days another, less publicized, suicide. It was deeply symbolic: the eighty-one-year-old Countess Sybille von Bismarck, a favourite niece and daughter-in-law of the Iron Chancellor, shot herself at Schönhausen, as the German Twelfth Army was preparing a last desperate stand on the estate beside the river Elbe. Within hours of their arrival, the Russians torched the mansion. When the guns fell silent, the ancestral home of the Bismarcks was an empty shell, like so much of the old Prussian kingdom that the family had served.

The war in Europe formally ended half an hour before midnight on 8 May 1945, when an instrument of unconditional surrender signed at Rheims on the previous morning was ratified at Marshal Zhukov's headquarters in Berlin. British troops were by then back on the Baltic, holding a strategically important stretch of coast and safeguarding Denmark from Soviet invasion. On Wednesday, 2 May, the 11th Armoured Division entered Lübeck, after forcing a crossing of the Elbe at Lauenburg on the previous Sunday and heading at speed along the 65-kilometre route to the sea. Churchill was concerned that the Russians might thrust forward into Jutland and gain control over the Baltic approaches. As early as 18 April he ordered Field Marshal Montgomery to head for Lübeck rather than Berlin in order to secure 'the land-gate of Denmark'. Briefly Montgomery's 21st Army Group also held Wismar, 50 kilometres farther east. To the dismay of the Mecklenburgers the British subsequently pulled back to the agreed demarcation line along the river Trave and the Russians moved in.

West and north of the Trave Montgomery's authority went unchallenged. On a trestle table outside a tent on Lüneburg Heath in the early evening of 4 May a delegation headed by Admiral von Friedeburg, the senior serving officer of the Kriegsmarine, surrendered to him as commander-in-chief of the 21st Army Group all the German forces in Holland, north-west Germany, Heligoland, the Friesian Islands, Schleswig-Holstein, Denmark, 'and all the other islands'. The Instrument of Surrender also stipulated that warships in the area should be handed over. By now, however, there were few naval prizes up for grabs. The *Hipper* was scuttled at Kiel on 3 May; she was joined on the seabed by the *Lützow* only a few hours before the ceremony on the trestle table. In Copenhagen the Royal Navy took possession of the *Prinz Eugen* and the cruiser *Nürnberg* and what remained of the *Leipzig*. Anything in the captured shipyards of Danzig and Gdynia – including the much damaged *Gneisenau* – went to Russia.

Field Marshal Montgomery was welcomed in Denmark as a liberator and received by the ailing King Christian. Yet, even while the Danish people were celebrating VE-Day, a shadow drifted in ominously from the western Baltic. The island of Bornholm, with its five small towns and the round churches that doubled as anti-piracy forts, had seen little of the war over the past five years, but it housed a German garrison, responsible to the commanding general of occupation forces in Denmark itself. The commandant on Bornholm believed that the island was covered by the Lüneburg Heath capitulation and that the garrison should become prisoners of the British, even though the Russians held the Pomeranian coast, barely 100 kilometres to the south. When, on 7 May, he rejected Soviet demands to haul down his flag, bombers from the Baltic fleet's air arm attacked the towns of Rønne and Neks. They returned the following morning, VE-Day itself. Fortunately, few people were killed, but the damage was considerable. Next day Soviet warships appeared off Rønne: rather than risk bombardment from the sea, the German commandant surrendered; he and his small garrison joined the hundreds and thousands of Hitler's soldiers held captive by the Russians. The island, its farmers and its fisher folk spent the next twelve months under Soviet occupation.

Soon, the greater dramas of a climactic year pushed the Bornholm Incident to the back of people's minds. Yet doubts anxiously posed that day lingered. Were the bombs that fell on Rønne harbour the last blasts of war in the Baltic or the first warning of worse to come? It was a question to which only at the close of the century was it possible to offer a hopeful answer.

27

Tragedy of Victory

———

TEN WEEKS AFTER the German surrender the victorious allied leaders
met for the last summit conference of the war, at Potsdam. The prospect ahead for Europe was grim. Russia dominated the Baltic lands and
overshadowed Scandinavia. The Red Army stood, for the first time, on the
Arctic frontier of Norway and at the outer fringe of Lübeck, a mere two-
hour drive from Danish Jutland. Peoples were on the move across huge
areas of the southern Baltic hinterland. Russians and native-born communists flocked into Estonia, Latvia and Lithuania. Poles, forced westwards by
the Soviet return to the 1941 frontier, found compensation in the former
German lands east of the Oder and the western Neisse. 'Displaced persons'
reached out for safety to Lübeck and British-occupied Holstein. Before the
surviving 130,000 Lübeckers could find food and shelter for 80,000 refugees from East Prussia and Pomerania in their ruined city a second wave
swept in from neighbouring Mecklenburg, making their way through the
sandy woods east of the Trave ahead of the barbed wire and watch towers
that would soon mark the demarcation line along the river. Tragically, victory over Hitler was bringing Europe not unity, but division.

At Potsdam the allied leaders were concerned with global issues and in
particular with ways to end the war in the Far East. But they also sought
to resolve problems around them, including the military administration of
Germany and the Soviet *fait accompli* in annexing the northern region of
East Prussia and handing over to Polish control the areas up to the Oder–
Neisse line. The joint 'Potsdam Declaration' expressed a hope that all
expulsions would be 'orderly and humane', but that was not the experience of Germans ejected from such historic towns as Königsberg (renamed
Kaliningrad), Insterburg (Chernyakhovsk) and Tilsit (Sovetsk). It was
announced that the Council of Foreign Ministers would gather in London
in September to begin a series of meetings 'to do the necessary preparatory work for a peace settlement'.

No comprehensive settlement was ever reached. Soon new phrases
passed into general usage, acknowledging a divided continent. The Polish

occupation of Szczecin, less than 160 kilometres from Potsdam, was in Churchill's mind when he spoke at Fulton, Missouri, in March 1946: 'From Stettin in the Baltic to Trieste in the Adriatic an iron curtain has descended across the continent,' he declared. Seven weeks later Churchill's friend Bernard Baruch addressed the state legislature of South Carolina: 'Let us not be deceived – we are today in the midst of a cold war,' he warned. Yet, despite the descent into fresh confrontation, some unfinished business was cleared up. In February 1947 treaties were signed at Paris between the nations that had fought 'Hitlerite Germany' and five of his former allies, each of whom had concluded a separate peace and made war on the Nazis before the final surrender. In northern Europe only Finland fell into that category, and the peace treaty closely followed the armistice terms agreed in September 1944; Finland accepted the loss of Petsamo as well as of the swathe of land taken by the Soviet Union in 1940, including the historic city of Viipuri (Vyborg to the Russians); and Finland also undertook not to conclude any alliance aimed against the Soviet Union, a pledge the Russians reciprocated. Some 300,000 Finns and Sami left the lost lands to settle in the south and west.

The treaty was followed in September 1947 by the departure from Helsinki of the Soviet-dominated Allied Control Commission, although units of the Baltic Fleet remained at Porkkala, the peninsula west of Helsinki, leased to the Soviet Union for up to fifty years. Seven thousand Finns living on the peninsula had received a mere ten days' notice to leave their homes and settle elsewhere. Many returned after 1955, when the Russians cut short their lease.

Although Finland was spared Soviet occupation, members of the Eduskunta were left in no doubt that they must tread warily. Before leaving Helsinki the senior military Control Commissioner, General Savonenkov, warned the prime minister that Moscow would regard as an unfriendly act any Finnish participation in the US-sponsored Marshall Plan to aid Europe's economic recovery. Six months later Savonenkov came back to the capital as Soviet ambassador, with an invitation from Stalin for the Finnish president to go to Moscow for talks on a mutual assistance pact.

The Finns were fortunate that since March 1946 the presidency had been held by the experienced Juho Paasikivi, who had in his time negotiated with Nicholas II, Kerensky and Chicherin as well as with Stalin and Molotov. In the past, hotheads in the Eduskunta often frustrated his diplomacy, but in 1948 his authority as president in succession to Mannerheim enabled Paasikivi to carry parliament with him. The Treaty of Friendship, Cooperation and Mutual Assistance concluded with the Soviet Union in

April 1948 – known in Helsinki as the YYA Treaty, from its Finnish initials – was the cornerstone around which Paasikivi built Finland's unique form of impartial non-alignment, a more positive neutrality than neighbouring Sweden professed. The YYA Treaty was a succinct document of eight Articles, with a preamble that emphasized Finland's 'desire to remain outside the conflicting interests of the Great Powers'. Finland and the Soviet Union undertook to resist jointly 'an armed attack by Germany or any state allied with the latter' through Finnish territory and to 'confer with each other' if such an attack was considered imminent. The two governments respected each other's sovereignty and 'the principle of non-interference in internal affairs'.

The statecraft of Paasikivi and his successor, Urho Kekkonen (President, 1956–81), ensured that, as Cold War attitudes hardened, Finland was able to serve as a strategic safety valve for the Baltic and beyond. Eventually, in 1973, President Kekkonen took the initiative in encouraging a series of discussions to ease tension. After two years of talks at Helsinki and Geneva, he was host of the thirty-five–nation Helsinki Conference on Security and Co-operation in Europe (31 July and 1 August 1975) that reaffirmed respect for human rights and stimulated a revival of diplomacy to douse potential flashpoints of war. In retrospect it seems extraordinary that neither Paasikivi nor Kekkonen received a Nobel Peace Prize.

In 1948, however, the enduring value of the YYA Treaty was far from apparent. There were rumours of a possible 'red coup', as in 1918, but Finland's communists were unsure of their standing with Moscow and the social democrats better organized than in the republic's earliest years. Other countries failed to recognize the maturity thirty years of troubled independence had brought to Finnish politics. The Swedes in particular were alarmed, both by the treaty and the alleged weakness of the Helsinki government, suspecting that their neighbour, like Hungary and Czechoslovakia, was being drawn into the Soviet bloc. A month after the conclusion of the YYA Treaty, Östen Undén, Sweden's foreign minister from 1945 to 1962, took the lead in seeking a Nordic defence union, ensuring that Denmark, Sweden and Norway would act together, independent of any larger coalition. Talks on military collaboration were held intermittently over the next twelve months, but Norway was more interested in Atlantic affairs and Denmark felt unable to raise the level of the armed services without help from Britain and the United States. Undén's initiative came to nothing. In April 1949 Norway, Denmark and Iceland were among the eleven original signatories of the North Atlantic Treaty, concluded in Washington at a time when Soviet occupation forces were blockading partitioned Berlin, leaving the western zones of the city dependent for food and fuel on an improvised Anglo-American air lift.

An international commitment of this nature was too great a breach of Sweden's traditional neutrality for Undén to accept. The Swedes were relieved that Norway and Denmark only agreed to join NATO on the understanding that no foreign bases would be established in either kingdom. Sweden's defence budget remained high for the next quarter of a century and there was at times secret collaboration and exchange of information over military and naval matters with Britain and other NATO members.

Sweden's armed neutrality was never isolationist. Count Folke Bernadotte, nephew of King Gustav V, became an early martyr for the United Nations when, in September 1948, he was murdered by Jewish terrorists while seeking a truce in Palestine. Dag Hammarskjöld, an economics professor from Stockholm University and in 1951 deputy to Östen Undén at the foreign ministry, became the UN's second Secretary-General in April 1953, succeeding a fellow Scandinavian socialist, Trygve Lie of Norway. Hammarsksjöld was re-elected four years later but in 1961 perished in an air crash on the Zambian border while on a peace mission to the Congo. His impartiality and ineffable aura of dignified authority, especially over Suez and Hungary in 1956, raised the stature of the UN secretariat to a level never attained by its forerunner at Geneva. For fifty years detachments from the Swedish army have served the UN as peacekeepers in three continents.

Regional collaboration, advocated by social democrats in Scandinavia at the end of the war, came closer in March 1952 with the establishment in Copenhagen of the Nordic Council, an advisory body of parliamentarians from Denmark, Norway, Sweden and Iceland concerned with economic and social affairs. The Finns had taken part in the original discussions, but were inhibited by protests from Moscow early in 1952 at a time when preparations were being completed for the Olympic Games at Helsinki in August; the Russians even suspected that new coastal roads built for the Olympics had a military purpose. Only after Kekkonen became president in 1956 could Finland join the Nordic Council, taking a lead in developing it into a two-tier organization with a general forum of delegates meeting once a year and a permanent praesidium of ministers and secretariat based in Copenhagen.

Sweden enjoyed the highest standard of living in any Baltic nation during the quarter of a century after the Second World War, partly because its industries were not scarred by battle or by bombs. The reign of social democracy, begun in 1932, was resumed in 1945 with the disintegration of

Hansson's national coalition. It continued throughout the premiership of Tage Erlander (1946–69) and then until 1976 under Olof Palme. These were years of social reform and, as a corollary, increasingly high taxation: generous child allowances came in 1948, a (highly contentious) retirement pensions scheme in 1959, a national health service less ambitious than the original British model, and well-planned housing projects, as in the south-western Stockholm suburb of Välingby. Daily life was drastically – and expensively – changed in 1967, when Sweden at last abandoned driving on the left and conformed to the road habits of her neighbours (and all Europe apart from Ireland and the United Kingdom). With high employment assured so long as the car industry flourished, the Swedes encouraged immigration, initially providing asylum to skilled 'displaced persons' and their families. Among earliest arrivals (while the war was still in progress) were several thousand fishermen and farmers of Swedish descent from the Estonian islands, Saaremaa (Ösel) and Muhu.

During the 1950s, more than a quarter of a million Finns headed west-wards into Sweden to benefit from the industrial boom. By the mid-1960s, however, the Finnish economy was in good shape, thanks largely to trade agreements with Russia and the recovery of the timber-processing indus-tries. There was no need for Finns to look abroad for employment. Between 1962 and 1966 two centre-right coalition governments began the transition to a welfare state, loosely modelled on Sweden, with a social insurance scheme and retirement pensions.

Swedish Liberals and the more doctrinaire socialists mooted fresh ways to advance democracy, and under Olof Palme the kingdom absorbed a new concept of sovereignty. The bicameral parliament gave way in 1970 to a single chamber of 350 members, elected every three years (changed to four years in 1994); and in 1973 a general election approved a revised constitution based upon the principle that 'all power emanates from the people'. A king – the newly acceded Carl XVI Gustav – remained head of state but without any executive powers. In 1979 a supplementary Act of Succession decreed that the Crown should pass to the ruler's eldest offspring, whether male or female. The two-year-old Crown Princess Victoria therefore became heir apparent in that year rather than her recently-born brother Charles.

Denmark already had a unicameral parliament (Folkething), and in 1953 a revised constitution accepted female succession to the throne; Margrethe II acceded in 1972 as Denmark's first ruling queen since 'Margrethe Valdermarsdotter', almost 600 years back in time. Like Sweden, Denmark became a welfare state shaped, at least from 1953 to 1967, by social demo-crats dependent on coalitions with radicals or smaller parties. There were differences of emphasis from Sweden, a more regimented unitary educational structure, for example. Moreover the Danish economy had been slow to pick up again after the war. Denmark experienced more wildcat strikes and the government was forced into an early devaluation. By the late 1950s conditions were changing. Foreign loans allowed banks to encourage the spread of light industry, reducing the kingdom's dependence on dairy produce for export and boosting employment in the smaller towns rather than in affluent Copenhagen. No Danish town had a single basic industry, comparable to Gothenburg's reliance on Volvo, even though Copenhagen continued to be associated with the beer trade. Exports could now include, not only well crafted porcelain and silverware, but the functional furniture made fashionable in the aftermath of austerity by the designer Hans Wegner. Membership of EFTA – the European Free Trade Association founded in Stockholm in November 1969 – opened up new markets for, though EFTA contained familiar trading partners like Sweden, Norway and Britain, the association also included Austria, Switzerland and Portugal. In 1961 Finland, still scrupulously loyal to her YYA Treaty pledge of friendship with Soviet Russia, cautiously became an associate member.

In many respects post-war Denmark seemed self-consciously Viking, a Nordic rather than a Baltic power. Constitutional ties perpetuated traditions of Atlantic seamanship, linking the eighteen Faeroe Islands and Greenland with Copenhagen. The Faeroes gained home rule in 1948; Greenland was formally integrated with Denmark in 1953 and began a transition to autonomy in 1979; but both the Faeroes and Greenland returned elected members to the Folkething. Denmark also maintained close relations with Iceland, whose people had acknowledged Christian X as king from 1918 until 1944, when the island became an independent republic; and in 1970 Icelanders joined Danes in EFTA. Successive governments in Copenhagen tended to look across the North Sea for reassurance over the rapid recovery of West Germany, both politically and economically. Denmark kept in step with Britain in moving from EFTA to the EEC common market in January 1973 and subsequently shared much of the United Kingdom's doubt and hesitancy over transition to a full European Union.

The relative affluence of the western Baltic peoples, grumbling at tax demands or tinkering with outmoded constitutions, was in striking contrast to the stagnation Soviet rule imposed on the peoples of the eastern Baltic. Even before the war ended, the Supreme Soviet 'adjusted' the borders of the Estonian SSR and the Latvian SSR, incorporating in the RSFSR not only ethnically Russian areas east of the Narva river but also most of the Setu inhabited lands around Pechory and the Latvian town and district of Pytalovo (Abrene), immediately to its south. Few Setu communities survived. The renewal of deportation to labour camps in Siberia struck at the three principal nationalities. Worst hit, in each instance, were the small farmers. Soviet policy aimed at imposing collectivization on an agricultural system for which the size and character of the farms were ill-suited. By 1952 some 120,000 'kulaks' had been carried off from Estonia, two-thirds of them in 1949, with the regular despatch of transportation trains from all three republics reaching a peak in the last week of March that year. Reliable estimates suggest that, between 1944 and 1952, at least 136,000 were deported from Latvia and 245,000 from Lithuania. When attempts were made to build up heavy industry in north-eastern Estonia and around Riga, thousands of dutiful Russian workers and their families were encouraged to move westwards from other parts of the Union. There was also an influx of well-trained Soviet party leaders, administrative officials and managers, especially in Latvia. The ethnic population balance in the Baltic republics permanently changed. By 1959 the native proportion of the population in Estonia was some 20 per cent down on the pre-war figure. In Latvia it had fallen by 13 per cent.

Fewer Russian migrants settled in Lithuania than in the two smaller republics. There are four reasons for the difference: more births in Lithuanian Catholic families than Lutheran Estonian and Latvian; an influx of ethnic Lithuanians from within the old borders of Poland; persuasive bargaining with his Moscow masters by Antanas Sniečkus, the native-born First Secretary of the Lithuanian Communist Party from 1936 until his death in 1974; and, above all, the dangers confronting any Russian family seeking to settle amid the Baltic people who maintained the bloodiest resistance to Soviet occupation.

It was in Estonia that sabotage and sporadic attacks on Russian occupation forces began in late 1944, and the last partisan 'terrorist' was an Estonian, seventy-year-old August Sabe, who was either drowned or shot in 1978 seeking to avoid KGB capture in the southern forests by swimming a lake. During Stalin's final years there were many acts of courage and patriotic resolve in Latvia, especially by groups operating in the wooded uplands of central Vidzeme. But Lithuania has the thickest and deepest forests of the three republics; to approach Vilnius by plane today is to look down on a seemingly endless green carpet of oak and beech, birch and pine, broken by a few lakes and receding slightly to give the main highways a narrow cleared edge. From hideouts in this northern tree jungle the 'Forest Brothers' waged guerrilla war for more than nine years. At first they were in action against regular troops in the Red Army, but by 1947 their main enemy was the NKVD Soviet auxiliaries.

It is tempting to romanticize the Forest Brothers as an update of Robin Hood's legendary Merry Men, defying harsh laws in a Sherwood Forest of sacred oaks and silvery birch. In retrospect some Lithuanians do indeed see these acts of defiance as a struggle to save traditional ways from the onset of a red urban juggernaut. The Brothers lacked a charismatic leader but there was, it would seem, a certain comradeship, with lairs in which it was possible to print clandestine newspapers, plan operations through a General Staff and train new recruits, many of them dodging Soviet call-up papers. Yet there was nothing 'merry' about the Forest Brothers. Like the partisan war of 1941–45 in Yugoslavia, this was a very bitter struggle, ruthlessly fought, with both sides lapsing into brutality. Ideologically the Brothers had more in common with the chetniks of Mihailović than with Tito's partisans; like chetniks, some even let their hair trail down to their shoulders and grew beards, vowing not to shave until Lithuania was free. They believed that if a land war broke out and armoured divisions pierced the Iron Curtain, they would have a patriotic role to play: who else could resurrect the real Lithuania from the ruins?

Yet their cause was hopeless. The possibility of liberation by NATO was remote. Little aid from the West reached any resistance groups; in Latvia agents put ashore on secluded beaches by 'spy ships' were so quickly rounded up that the KGB must have received prior information of their coming. After the death of Stalin in March 1953 some Brothers took advantage of an amnesty. Most of the remaining bands dispersed during the false dawn of the Khrushchev era, when many surviving kulak deportees were allowed home from Siberia; but as late as 1965 at least one guerrilla action was fought out in the Lithuanian woods.

'The most long-lived and heroic guerrilla struggle in postwar Europe', its earliest historian, Andres Küng, calls the forest war. Estimates of casualties vary considerably. A Russian source gives 20,000 dead on each side, which may well be right, though the Lithuanians also executed alleged 'collaborators', and the KGB and NKVD tortured and killed hundreds of 'traitors' to the Soviet Fatherland. Today many liberal-minded Lithuanians prefer to blot out memories of a conflict in which both sides put farms and homes to the torch and, in the passion of battle, killed the innocent wantonly. Yet in some villages off the A12 route from Šiauliai through the Joniškis region and on towards Riga, memorials recall heroic actions in a war of which the world knew little while it was fought, and less once it was over.

Materially the three Baltic republics, though not the indigenous Baltic peoples, benefited from the reimposition of Soviet rule. Textile production at Narva revived, while the new towns in north-eastern Estonia that housed Russian immigrant families boosted the yield from oil-shale mining. In Latvia, heavy industry returned to Riga and brought huge factories to Daugavpils, a town that was soon turning out more bicycles than any other in the Soviet Union. Two pipelines, long projected but not completed until 1979, linked the Latvian port of Ventspils, a Lithuanian oil refinery at Mažeikiai and Polotsk, now in Belarus. In general, Russian industrialization was slower in Lithuania than in Latvia and Estonia, possibly because of the long resistance struggle, but Soviet economic planning determined that Lithuania should ultimately provide electrical power for the whole region from the Gulf of Riga to Kaliningrad. At the height of the Khrushchev era the largest conventional power station in the USSR was completed at Vievis.

Nuclear power posed fresh problems. In 1975 a new town, originally named in memory of Sniečkus but now called Visaginas, was established in the Ignalina region of Lithuania, 130 kilometres north-east of Vilnius, near the Latvian border with Belorussia (Belarus). By 1984 the first graphite moderated reactor of this 'Ignalina Nuclear Power Station' was generating sufficient electricity to meet half of Lithuania's needs. But in April 1986 came the Chernobyl disaster, when a similar reactor in the Ukraine exploded, releasing fallout ninety times as radioactive as at Hiroshima. In Ignalina a second reactor began operating in 1987 and work was well advanced on a third. But after local and international protests, construction work stopped at Visaginas and safety precautions, supervised by international monitors, were undertaken. Not everyone was satisfied. The 'Ignalina Threat' outlasted the USSR itself, to trouble Lithuania's negotiators when they sought to join the European Union ten years later.

There was nothing Green about Red rule. Pollution of the sea, the shores and the land became the worst legacy of Soviet Russia's cumbersome technological advancement. There were gains, however – notably at university level, where Soviet funding of scientific projects looked to the future: as early as 1960 the Estonian Academy of Science set up a Cybernetics Institute. And unexpectedly in 1980 Estonia received the fittings and equipment of an Olympic Sailing Centre, when Pirita in Tallinn Bay hosted the yachting events for the twenty-second Olympiad at Moscow, more than 650 kilometres away. Despite the menacing rigours of a police state, by 1953 the standard of urban life in the Baltic cities was higher than in other autonomous republics. Tallinn and Turnu, in particular, benefited from the close relationship that the YYA Treaty brought to Finno-Soviet relations during Kekkonen's presidency, rekindling the familiar Finnish–Estonian empathy.

Yet a tyranny over the mind persisted in all three republics. The delights of being able to hum and ha over what to read, or see in the cinema, or hear on the radio were denied to peoples who, before 1939, enjoyed freedom of thought, if not always of political expression. Occasionally, however, students dared to protest in the streets, most notably at Vilnius in 1956, at the time of the Hungarian National Rising. The need to enforce conformity of belief prompted new 'anti-God' campaigns by the communist authorities. Attacks were made on both Jewish faith and Jewish culture, increasing in intensity in Lithuania in the late 1970s, when in Riga the many dissidents who were Jews vigorously championed the human rights declaration agreed at the Helsinki Conference. In Estonia many Lutheran churches had long closed, though not necessarily under government pressure: an Estonian seems, by temperament, agnostic; moreover, the Lutheran Church was associated with Baltic German supremacy. In Riga the red-brick Lutheran *Dom* served as a concert hall from 1958 to 1988 and the Orthodox cathedral as a cinema, with a café where holy ikons are now on sale. Ominously in Kaunas a Soviet psychiatric clinic was established in a Catholic monastery, while as late as the 1960s the Jesuit baroque church of St Casimir in Vilnius opened as a Museum of Atheism. The cathedral in Vilnius was already an art gallery. Not all the conflict was with Christians and Jews. A movement to revive pagan worship and ritual came into being in the Kaunas region in 1967, only to be banned four years later, not least because it appealed to a specifically Lithuanian folk culture. But it was also at Kaunas, in May 1972, that the nineteen-year-old Catholic Romas Kalanta ended his life in flames in the Miesto Sodas Gardens as a protest at the persecution of his country and his church. Rioting students made certain that the world's media knew of Kalanta's self-immolation and the cause for which he chose to suffer so agonizing a death.

Patriotic pride and a religious faith actively shared by four-fifths of the nation sustained Lithuania's southern neighbour. In 1945 the new Poland was a devastated wasteland. Warsaw had suffered from bombardment and from Hitler's orders to have the nation's capital razed to the ground; Gdańsk – as Danzig was now officially called – had been bombed by the RAF, shelled by opposing armies and finally set ablaze by its liberators after valuable pre-war German machinery was sent eastwards to serve as reparations. The Workers' Party was better organized in Poland than the Communist Front in any other country liberated by the Red Army, but it is small wonder that along the Baltic coast and down the Vistula anti-Russian sentiment ran high.

By January 1946 the Peasant Party, led by the returned leader of the London Poles Mikolajczýk, claimed to have 600,000 registered members. The Government of National Unity postponed a promised general election for a year, allegedly because of the internal migration caused by the new frontiers. During the interlude many large estates were expropriated for redistribution among the peasants, a resumption of the inter-war reforms, though for the moment leaving Church lands intact. An electoral law, promulgated in September 1946, gave proportionately higher representation in the Sejm to the ex-German areas in the west. Peasant Party members were discredited and put on trial, either as Nazi collaborationists or, more often, as contacts with British or American Intelligence. In his memoirs Mikolajczýk claims that 100,000 party members were imprisoned during the election campaign. When the votes were finally cast, at the end of January 1947, a combined communist–socialist bloc won 394 seats, small pro-government parties 22 seats, and the Peasant Party Opposition a mere twenty-eight. Josef Cyrankiewicz, a pre-war socialist student leader who survived the concentration camps of Auschwitz and Mauthausen, became prime minister in February, securing the immediate passage of a Soviet-style constitution. Mikolajczýk fled the country later in the year to escape a state trial.

In December 1948 Poland's socialists and communists combined to form a United Workers' Party. From its ranks all governments were formed for the next forty years. Eleven months later, under pressure from Stalin, Marshal Rokossovsky was appointed Poland's minister of defence. The new Poland was as much under Russian control as in 1831, when Nicholas I made Marshal Paskievich Prince of Warsaw and Viceroy.

Rokossovsky had been born in Warsaw, but his name was anathema to many Poles for his halt on the Vistula in 1944 and his failure to support the uprising in the capital. For Stalin his continued command over the postwar Soviet and Polish armies was a strategic necessity. Communications had to be safeguarded with the annexed Königsberg region and with Soviet bases in Germany. The formation in May 1949 of the Federal Republic of Germany, with its capital at Bonn, evoked a Soviet response in October 1949, when the former German provinces of Brandenburg, Mecklenburg, Saxony, Saxony-Anhalt and Thuringia were unified to create the German Democratic Republic (DDR), a socialist satrapy with its political centre in the Berlin suburb of Pankow. A few months after Stalin's death, heavy-handed collectivization of agriculture in the DDR, together with harsh labour conditions, culminated in serious rioting in Berlin (June 1953), with several hundred demonstrators arrested and executed. Order was restored only after the DDR security chiefs called on Soviet tanks for assistance.

During this crisis Rokossovsky ensured that Poland's military machine was well oiled. A month after the Berlin riots he took the salute at an impressive parade in Katowice to let the world see the strength of the new army. In 1955 the marshal stage-managed the conclusion of the Warsaw Pact, a treaty whose signatories – Bulgaria, Czechoslovakia, the DDR, Hungary, Romania, Poland and the USSR (and briefly Albania) – agreed to help each other if attacked and accepted the need for a unified army command in Moscow.

There was already a clash of wills between the Polish government and the Roman Catholic hierarchy. The secularization of education and newspaper attacks on Catholic social teaching were followed by the arrest of priests, by a law giving the state the right to make all major ecclesiastical appointments, and by the imprisonment in September 1953 of the Bishop of Kielce. Cardinal Wyszynski, the Primate of Poland, who had spoken out courageously against state interference, was himself arrested at the end of the month. In October there were demonstrations in cities from Gdańsk down to Cracow. Resistance in Poland was not as bloody as in Lithuania's forests but its methods attracted more attention in the West. Twice in 1953 defecting Polish pilots broke the peace of Danish Bornholm when they landed new MiG fighters on the island. In the same year the captain of the liner *Batory* dramatically chose freedom in England as he sailed the 'pride of the Polish merchant fleet' from Gdynia to Bombay.

The mounting discontent in Poland finally exploded on 28 June 1956 when engineering workers at Poznań went on strike against their low wages. Other strikers joined them in a march through the city. The army was sent in and fifty-three strikers were killed. A high level delegation, including Marshal Zhukov, arrived from Moscow to urge the Polish government to take a strong line with the rioters, but prime minister Cyrankiewicz and the party boss, Edward Ochab, insisted that the Poznań troublemakers had a just grievance: only light sentences were passed on hundreds arrested, and the wages were duly raised. August 25–26 1956 saw the tercentenary of Poland's dedication to the protection of the Virgin Mary, and half a million Poles gathered at Częstochowa to affirm a massive witness of loyalty to nation and faith. Among the priests at Częstochowa that weekend was Karol Wojtyla, at thirty-six newly appointed Professor of Ethics at Lublin. Twenty-two years later he was to become the first non-Italian pope for eight centuries.

In October, at the very time when a national uprising was brewing in Hungary, Polish nationalism won a modest but significant victory. In 1948 Wladyslaw Gomulka, the minister responsible for the newly 'recovered territories' in the East, had been dismissed, having offended Stalin by a speech that praised the 'historical traditions of the Polish labour movement'. As a political outcast, however, Gomulka attracted a wide following and, with the dead Stalin's reputation reassessed critically by Khrushchev at the Twentieth Party Congress in Moscow (February 1956), many Poles felt his hour had come. His conviction that Federal Germany was a dangerous revisionist power eager to restore the 1939 frontiers was shared by many of his compatriots: better Russians in Kaliningrad than Prussians in Königsberg. In mid-October 1956, after personally assuring Khrushchev that he would be loyal to the Warsaw Pact and keep open the Soviet communication line to Berlin, Gomulka was accepted as first secretary of the United Workers' Party. A veteran Polish guerrilla leader, General Spychalski, replaced Rokossovsky as minister of war.

The Gomulka era (1956–70) did not see all the hopes of his followers fulfilled: Poland remained a one-party state dependent on the Soviet Union. But doctrinaire agricultural collectivization was stopped, police powers curbed, and for the first four years the Catholic Church was allowed free pastoral activity in the schools and even the army. By 1965, however, Gomulka was in full retreat; the simultaneous impact of a population bulge and contraction of the economy lifted unemployment figures to a quarter of a million and, as so often in Poland's history, anti-Semitism re-surfaced. Gomulka preferred to blame the priests: 'insidious teachings', he complained, were blocking 'the Polish road to socialism'.

On the eve of yet another religious anniversary the Church was in trouble again, this time for advocating 'the slave philosophy of forgiving your enemies'. The Polish hierarchy – including Archbishop Wojtyla of Cracow – had invited bishops from West Germany to the millenary celebrations in May 1966 of the coming of Christianity to Piast Poland; and the letter called for mutual forgiveness for all that happened in the war. Gomulka forbade the issue of visas to any foreigner wishing to attend the celebrations. Several hundred thousand Poles duly observed the anniversary, though not so many as at Częstochowa ten years previously; and this time the Party organized counter-demonstrations.

Theoretically all the Poles along the Baltic coast had good reason to be grateful to Gomulka. His government took particular care to stimulate new industries in the 'recovered territories' of north-west Pomerania. More housing blocks went up in Szczecin and the Gdańsk triangle (Gdynia,

Sopot and the city itself) than in any other region except Warsaw. After an amnesty in 1956 repatriated internees from Soviet camps and prisons were settled in the three towns, bringing with them a challenging mood of sceptical suspicion. The bogey of a war of revenge receded early in 1970 when Federal Germany formally recognized the Oder–Neisse frontier. But by then corrupt administration and trade rivalry – not least with Rostock, the DDR's one subsidized port – had brought unemployment to the northwest, and in the cold of the Baltic winter there were riots and strikes over the rising cost of food. The disturbances of December 1970 were centred on the three ports of Szczecin, Gdynia and Gdańsk, where, among the younger and less conspicuous protesters an electrical mechanic in the shipyards called Wałęsa was in trouble for criticizing the management.

Gomulka could not weather the Baltic storm. He was succeeded as first secretary of the ruling eight-man Party Secretariat by Edward Gierek, the Party boss of industrialized Silesia. The pattern of government hardly changed. Gierek lifted living standards slightly, through the dangerous tactic of borrowing from Western banks to pay for producing more consumer goods, but by 1975 the hard currency had run out. With the return of food rationing there was renewed rioting in several towns during the following summer. The economy sank even more into the red.

The Seventies proved an uneasy decade for all the Baltic nations, capitalist and communist alike. In October 1973 the Yom Kippur War between Israel and her neighbours closed the Suez Canal for twenty months. The Arab oil-producing states put pressure on other governments by cutting supplies of petroleum products in protest at Israel's expansion beyond the ceasefire lines agreed after earlier conflicts. The Arab action forced up the price of oil, with severe repercussions to Western economies. As the world slipped into the first major recession in forty years, Danish industry was especially hard hit and Sweden's balance of trade totally changed, although there was no rush on the banks or financial panic. Both Denmark and Sweden at first lost markets abroad, but the recession eased in Scandinavia once its effects began to strike the less sophisticated economies of more distant low-wage trading rivals. Environmental issues were already making voters reassess traditional loyalties; there was strong opposition to the construction of new hydro-electric power stations and demonstrations against nuclear energy were widespread, even before the Chernobyl disaster. The Finns suffered far less: 90 per cent of the oil they needed came from the Soviet Union at a relatively cheap rate in return for the export of heavy goods from the rapidly expanding steel industry as well as cheap clothes and shoes. Poland and the DDR became increasingly dependent on Russian goodwill. The Soviet economy itself was, however, near to collapse, with excessive spending on defence and on the prestigious space programme. Yet until his death in November 1982 Brezhnev kept as firm a hold on Party and State as Stalin. The USSR emanated the authority of a Super Power and the polarized menace of a third world war still cast deep shadows over Baltic waters.

By 1979 the Soviet navy was the second largest in the world, with 250 submarines, more than eighty of them nuclear powered. The principal strategic naval ports were near Murmansk or at Vladivostok, but the Baltic Fleet still operated from Kronstadt, Tallinn Bay, Liepāja and particularly from Kaliningrad. There were occasional moments of tension, notably in September 1981 when an 'invasion force' of more than 250,000 men was landed at various points on the shores of Latvia and Lithuania in a realistic naval exercise. Soon afterwards, at the end of October, a Whisky class Soviet submarine, engaged in 'intelligence operations', ran on to the rocks in the approaches to Karlskrona and was boarded and detained for a week by the Swedish navy, who remained on the alert for further encroachments over the months ahead.

Sweden's general election of September 1982 brought Olof Palme and the Social Democrats back to office after a six-year interlude of centre-liberal coalition government. Palme was an internationalist in the Hammarskjöld tradition, but far more outspoken. He was unpopular in the United States because of his sympathy for the Vietnamese struggle for independence and he was also critical of Israeli policy, especially over the Lebanon. During his six years out of office he undertook missions for the United Nations and served as chairman of the UN Commission on Security and Disarmament. In April 1983 he warned the Soviet Union that any naval vessel that entered Swedish waters illegally would be sunk. But his great concern was to avoid any errors or accidents that might precipitate war. Accordingly in January 1984 Palme convened a thirty-five-nation conference in Stockholm to ease tension between the NATO and Warsaw Pact powers. After ten sessions the conference concluded the Stockholm Accord, a treaty that pledged NATO and Warsaw Pact members to give advance notice of troop movements, naval exercises and army manoeuvres so as to reduce the risk of accidental conflict. The Accord was signed on 21 September 1986.

By then Palme was dead. Shortly before midnight on 28 February an unknown gunman shot him in a side street off Sveavägen, in central Stockholm, as he walked home with his wife from a cinema. It was Sweden's first assassination since 1792, when Gustav III was stabbed at the masked ball. The police could find no motive for the murder, nor could they officially assign responsibility to any organization. There was talk of the CIA, the KGB, Israel's Mossad, Swedish right-wing extremists, even of fanatical environmentalists opposed to nuclear power stations; rumour inevitably fed wild conspiracy theories. Despite losing their leader, the Social Democrats remained in power for five more years, with Ingvar Carlsson as prime minister.

Palme's murder briefly concentrated media attention on Stockholm, but interest soon switched back across the Baltic to Poland. By the late 1970s Gierek was faced by mounting unrest among workers in the Baltic ports and coalminers in the Katowice region of Upper Silesia. The election of Cardinal Wojtyla as Pope John Paul II in 1978 and the ecstatic reception he received on a 'religious pilgrimage' to his homeland in the following summer brought fresh, supranational power to the opposition. In 1979–80 Lech Wałęsa set up an inter-factory strike committee in the Gdańsk ship-yards to work together for civil rights and higher wages. Soaring food prices and an honest admission by Gierek that the economy was under bad management gave Wałęsa the opportunity to join forces with strikers in Szczecin and Katowice and in August 1980 he established Poland's first independent trade union, Solidarity (*Solidarność*), based upon the Lenin shipyard at Gdańsk. Gierek conceded relaxation of censorship and reduc-tion of the working week and promised a better supply of food and access to the media, even the broadcasting each Sunday of a Catholic Mass. Cardinal Wyszynski, still Poland's Primate, personally received the Solidarity leaders and assured them of the Church's backing.

At this point – 5 September 1980 – Gierek suffered a heart attack; he was rushed to hospital, though he lived on for fourteen years. His unfor-tunate successor, Stanislaw Kania, was confronted by a bad harvest, muddy roads that made food distribution difficult, and fuming army leaders impa-tient to take counter-measures. Outside observers feared a Soviet military move, for Brezhnev was known to believe that socialist states had a duty to intervene in any other socialist state in which socialism itself was thought to be in danger. In the hope of forestalling action by Moscow, Kania made his defence minister, General Jaruzelski, prime minister in February 1981. For Kania personally, this was an injudicious appointment: the general ousted him as party secretary six months later. Overnight on 13–14 December 1981 the fifty-eight-year-old Jaruzelski carried through the first military coup in the Warsaw Pact. Martial law was imposed, and for twelve months Poland was governed by a 'Military Council of National

Salvation'. Solidarity leaders including Wałęsa were arrested and interned. The movement itself was outlawed for the next seven years.

The Jaruzelski regime was characterized by a stop-go policy of repression and hesitant reform. Restrictions were relaxed in May 1982, only to be reimposed after new demonstrations in June. A visit by Pope John Paul to Częstochowa in August 1982 was postponed, but was permitted nine months later while martial law was still in force. It was on this occasion that Lech Wałęsa – who was awarded the Nobel Peace Prize that year – was allowed to meet the pope for forty minutes of private discussion. But the Church had brutal enemies within the State machine. In October 1984 Polish Catholics were shocked – and Jaruzelski dismayed – by the discovery in a river of the tortured body of Jerzy Popieluszko, a young and popular priest with Solidarity connections, who had been abducted earlier in the month. Appeals by the pope, the bishops and Wałęsa prevented irresponsible acts of revenge by Solidarity members, and in the following year four police agents were sentenced to long terms of imprisonment for Father Popieluszko's murder.

In the autumn of 1985 Jaruzelski became head of state, a few months after Mikhail Gorbachev – who was eight years his junior – was accepted as general secretary of the Soviet Party. From early in 1986 the United Workers in Warsaw kept their Party antennae tuned to Moscow to catch the latest refinement of Kremlin teaching, Gorbachev's advocacy of *glasnost* and *perestroika*. It was hard to judge how much 'openness' and 'restructuring' Catholic Poland could absorb without consigning socialism to an unmarked grave. Cautiously Jaruzelski set up a Consultative Council that included Catholic laymen and a civil rights lawyer; state enterprises were promised wider autonomy. When inflation again forced up food prices in 1988 and Solidarity banners once more draped the shipyards Jaruzelski turned to Wałęsa, and in the following February the general from Lublin and the electrician from Gdańsk met and took the lead in a series of round table conferences in an effort to resolve the nation's problems.

Wojciech Jaruzelski, the son of devout Catholics transported to the Soviet Union when he was sixteen, remains an enigmatic figure. Was he the Pilsudski of the People's Republic, dextrously balancing security forces, the Church and Solidarity to protect national independence? Or did he simply bumble from one improvisation to the next, until the communist state withered away under the weight of its own incompetence? Like Pilsudski, his personal record is stained with Polish blood: rifle fire, as well as tear gas, was turned on the Katowice miners, and after his retirement he was accused of having caused forty-four deaths in 1970 by ordering his troops to fire on demonstrators when he was minister of defence. Yet almost certainly in 1981 his wary statesmanship saved Poland from Soviet invasion; and, perhaps fortuitously, he rendered Poland one final service.

For, after the Round Table talks of February 1989, Jaruzelski agreed to lift the ban on Solidarity in April and allow its members to stand for the Sejm in a partial election held on 4 June. They swept the board. A Solidarity nominee, Tadeusz Mazowiecki, headed a coalition government. Jaruzelski retired into private life in December 1990, and Wałęsa became Poland's first democratically elected President for more than half a century. After a long struggle, Baltic Gdańsk had imposed the workers' will on Warsaw.

28

Baltic Way

POLAND, A NATION long buffeted by the changing fortunes of history, shook off the shackles of communism through the courage and persistence of trade union activists backed by the moral authority of an extra-territorial Church. The people of the Baltic republics followed a slightly different path to recover independence. They won back freedom by their proud burnishing of folk traditions and willingness to risk direct confrontation and by the gradual grafting of multi-party assemblies on to Soviet institutions. But, though the final form of the new eastern Baltic was shaped locally, the timing and course of what happened in all four countries was determined by events elsewhere, especially in Moscow. At the same time, movements for change along the Baltic influenced, and were influenced by, the mounting challenge to the established order in neighbouring Warsaw Pact countries, notably Hungary, East Germany and Czechoslovakia. The winter of 1989–90, like the apocalyptic year 1848, proved to be a springtime of revolution for subject nations across much of central and eastern Europe.

By the close of 1982 respect for the Communist Party in the USSR was dwindling away rapidly, though fear remained a deterrent to action. Morale in the Red Army was low after Brezhnev's invasion of Afghanistan in December 1979 ended in a phased withdrawal of troops nine years later. There were food shortages, and housing remained poor. Widespread corruption was rife; party officials at all levels formed a much resented 'new class' of privileged élite. Brezhnev's successors, Andropov and Chernenko, made some attempt to curb corruption and combat inefficiency, but both were ailing men of seventy or more; their combined span of office was no more than twenty-eight months. When Gorbachev came to power in March 1985 it was too late to restructure the system without financial aid from the West. At midsummer in 1988 he told a specially convened party conference in Moscow that he sought 'a new image of socialism' through 'democratizing our government'. By then both the Estonians in early April and the Lithuanians on 3 June had created Popular Front combinations of reformers. But more striking than the postures of politicians to thousands at the Baltika Song Festival that midsummer was the sight of the three national flags flying together for the first time under Soviet rule. What was popularly termed 'the Singing Revolution' had, in its modest way, begun on key.

Song had long been a powerful weapon of passive resistance. During the last half century of tsarist rule the Estonian and Latvian song festivals served as a means for two subject peoples to assert their nationhood in huge assemblies without breaking the law. The festivals continued through the inter-war period, with Lithuania hosting one for the first time in 1924. They became more self-consciously nationalistic under the semi-fascist regimes, with traditional peasant costume as normal wear. After the Soviet occupation Riga was allowed to stage a Latvian Song Festival in 1948, though the programme included choral tributes to Stalin and the Soviet Motherland. When in 1950 Tallinn sought to revert to the passive defiance of tsarist times, the secret police struck and the conductors of three Estonian choirs received long prison sentences. The 1988 festival was proof that police surveillance was at last relaxed. A few weeks later – on 23 August – thousands of demonstrators attended rallies in all three republics to denounce the Nazi–Soviet Pact, seen as the source of the evil that destroyed their countries. The observance of fateful days from past calendars made good propaganda. A year later, on the fiftieth anniversary of the pact, two million people joined hands to form the 'Baltic Way', a 600-kilometre human chain that linked Tallinn, Riga and Vilnius in a call for independence. Europe and America took note.

The Popular Front in Lithuania had already made an impressive beginning. *Sajūdis*, as the Front was called, opened its first Congress at Vilnius on Sunday, 23 October 1988, in the first instance concentrating on change within the existing republic. But, even before the congress adjourned, Monday morning's *Independent* in London commented on the speakers' 'torrents of pent-up nationalism', in a report that was headed 'The Rebirth of a Proud Nation'. The congress elected as chairman the bespectacled fifty-six-year-old musicologist Vytautus Landsbergis, a member of a family of academics associated with the national movement since the turn of the century. Though lacking populist charisma, he proved an effective leader over the following three years, much respected in the West, especially during 1991 after he showed resolute courage in the most dangerous hours of conflict.

Sajūdis also attracted genuinely dissentient communists (as well as a few KGB informers), for since the Sniečkus era the Lithuanian Party had preserved a certain independence of spirit. Four days before the congress opened, an able economist, Algirdas Brazauskas, became first secretary of the Party. He sympathized with the reformists and one of his first acts as secretary was to hand back Vilnius Cathedral to the Church, but he remained critical of *Sajūdis* and particularly of Landsbergis. Brazauskas was a popular figure in many parts of Lithuania, especially after his decision in December 1989 to cut the ties binding the Lithuanian Party to the Soviet Party. As leader of the renamed Lithuanian Democratic Labour Party (LDDP) and head of the opposition to Landsbergis, his political career flourished and in February 1993 he was elected president of Lithuania for a five-year term of office. In July 2001, by now heading the Social Democrats, he became prime minister. At seventy-two Algirdas Brazauskas was still the head of government when, in May 2004, Lithuania joined the European Union.

In Tallinn Arnold Rüütel, the chairman of the Estonian Soviet since 1983, took pains to ensure continuity of government and, like Brazauskas, despite his communist associations he won support from the peasantry. The Estonian Soviet approved a declaration of national sovereignty in November 1988, asserting its right to veto federal laws decreed by Moscow. Two months later it passed a law making Estonian the language of state. With a third of the population non-Estonian, it is hardly surprising that the minorities denounced this action as being discriminatory. At the end of March 1989 'Interfront', a movement in favour of preserving the existing relationship with the Soviet Union, was founded in Estonia. Conservative communists in Latvia and Lithuania followed suit, and in the summer the loyalists called a general strike in Estonia, protesting at the discrimination shown towards local Russians.

As yet, the three republics stopped short of openly declaring their independence, and Gorbachev avoided any speech or gesture condemning their actions. He still had hopes of restructuring the Soviet Union from within. 'To live anywhere between Bonn and Moscow in 1989 was to be witness to a year-long political fantasy,' David Remnick recalls in his vividly perceptive *Lenin's Tomb*. At the end of March 1989 the first Union-wide election took place in which candidates not sponsored by the communists were allowed to stand. The final count showed that barely 20 per cent of the 2,250 elected deputies for the new People's Congress were independents and Gorbachev was assured of a five-year term as president of the Soviet Union. Yet the results were hardly encouraging for him. Not all the 1,820 card-carrying communists were docile party members. Even in Moscow, in one constituency, 89 per cent of electors voted for the ex-Politburo dissentient Boris Yeltsin, who was still technically within the Party. So, too, were most delegates returned in the Baltic Republics. They were not necessarily hostile to Gorbachev's programme of immediate reform, although independence remained their ultimate objective. Optimistically, Gorbachev persevered. Only after the Baltic Way linking of hands, on the fiftieth anniversary of the Nazi–Soviet Pact, did the bear at last growl. Brazaukas was told by telephone on 28 August that mass demonstrations of this character were unacceptable; and in a tetchy television address next day Gorbachev specifically warned 'the Baltic peoples' of the dangers of 'nationalist excesses'.

It was not, however, the 'Baltic peoples' who set the pace of change that year. In the second week of January the Hungarian parliament in Budapest had passed a law permitting the formation of political parties. The first test came in a series of Easter by-elections at the end of March. They were won by the Hungarian Democratic Forum, whose programme included democratic government, 'the preservation of Hungarian values' and integration into Europe. As a first step towards this ideal, in early May work began on dismantling the security fence that linked the watch-towers to form a not-quite-iron curtain down Hungary's western border. It could be argued that this event, virtually ignored by Western media at the time, was of greater significance for Europe as a whole than the dramatic breach of the Berlin Wall six months later. For to East Germans, eager to lift their standard of life, the levelling of the barriers provided a circuitous escape route to the West. They could already travel easily through Czechoslovakia and Hungary. Over the four summer months as many as 150,000 East Germans were now able to cross from Hungary into Austria and on into West Germany. The economy of the DDR descended into chaos. Czechs and Slovaks, already restless and demanding reform, were stirred into action. Across Hungary's eastern border, in the Ukraine, the people of Lviv – Polish during the inter-war years – marked the fiftieth anniversary of the Soviet occupation of eastern Poland with a candle-lit vigil through the centre of the city. The example of the Baltic Way was spreading rapidly. The vindication of Solidarity in Poland and the formation of the non-communist coalition in September allowed Warsaw to follow the example of Budapest and open its western frontier to German refugees, some of whom then headed for Szczecin and Gdańsk and the ferries to freedom. But was their journey necessary? On 9 November the East German authorities announced the removal of all border crossing restrictions, including the Berlin checkpoints.

Gorbachev continued to woo the Baltic leaders. On 13 September he had summoned them to Moscow and put forward his ideas for a genuinely federal Soviet Union in which the republics would enjoy a high level of economic autonomy with equal treatment and status assured to every nationality. In Latvia – where Russians, Ukrainians and Belorussians formed 42 per cent of the population – there was some support for the federal project, and the Estonian Soviet had originated the proposal for economic autonomy in the first place. But there was no holding back the Lithuanians. In October the Soviet in Vilnius asserted that the Russians were illegally occupying the country, a verdict endorsed for Estonia a month later. Then, on 19 December, came the momentous decision that the Lithuanian Communist Party should formally disassociate itself from the All-Russian Communist Party. Early in the New Year Gorbachev flew into Vilnius for talks with Brazauskas and Landsbergis in an attempt to check the rush towards independence. All threats and blandishments failed, though the Russian leader acknowledged the possibility of 'a divorce'. On 11 March 1990 the Lithuanian Supreme Soviet voted by 124 votes to none in favour of the republic's independence, with Landsbergis as *de facto* head of state. A week later Kazimira Prunskienė, an expert on rural economy and a founding woman member of *Sajūdis*, became prime minister.

The Russian mood hardened. On Sunday, 25 March, a column of tanks swept into Vilnius from a northern suburb and rumbled menacingly down the Gedimino Prospektas, the main avenue from the cathedral to the parliament house beside the river; it had still been named after Lenin a fortnight earlier. The tanks lingered for some hours, occasionally going up and down the avenue like a pacing sentry on guard duty. Always they turned back to positions covering parliament. Not a shot was fired and by late afternoon the tank crews were back in barracks, but the warning was clear. On Tuesday military police patrols began rounding up alleged deserters in the woods around Vilnius. Over the next fortnight the army seized several buildings that had housed Communist Party offices or apartments. Finally on 18 April Gorbachev fulfilled his threat to impose an economic blockade. All supplies of oil to Lithuania were cut off. Was this the counter-revolution that the West had assumed the humane Soviet president would never condone? Anxiously President Mitterrand and Chancellor Helmut Kohl urged Landsbergis to delay implementing the decree of independence and hold further talks with Gorbachev.

Uncertainty prevailed throughout the summer of 1990, with both Latvia and Estonia asserting their independence in early May, but agreeing there should be a transition period before full independence was declared. On 29 June Lithuania fell into line and postponed any further gestures of statehood. The Russian economic blockade was immediately suspended.

Gorbachev's international standing as an enlightened statesman, one who was able to conclude treaties with the Americans defusing the threat of nuclear war, remained unimpaired. Yet at the May Day parade in Red Square, there was an unprecedented demonstration. Unauthorized marchers joined the traditional procession waving Estonian and Lithuanian flags; others carried placards with anti-communist slogans. After half an hour Gorbachev stepped down from the reviewing stand of the Lenin Mausoleum, impassively dignified in moral defeat. Later that year he became the first Soviet politician awarded the Nobel Peace Prize. Inevitably he was also the last.

The April crisis of 1990 had one lasting consequence. On 12 May a Baltic summit conference was held at Tallinn: the three acting presidents revived the Baltic Entente of 1934, the sole project of co-operation in the region between the wars. On this occasion, however, the treaty was given teeth. Arnold Rüütel of Estonia encouraged the establishment of a Baltic Council of presidents and senior government figures who would meet to discuss common problems on a regular basis. The first meeting of the council was held at Riga little more than a month later and coincided with Latvia's Baltika Song Festival, a celebration that in this summer attracted thousands of participants, singing with greater jubilation. The council agreed to establish a secretariat, originally with headquarters at Vilnius but later at Riga. In November 1991 co-operation extended still further, with the setting up of the Baltic Assembly, a body of sixty nominated parliamentarians who would meet twice a year at each capital in turn and also join the presidents and ministers for a full annual Baltic Council meeting. It has become, in many respects, a parallel organization to the Nordic Council.

During the autumn of 1990 opposition to the independence movement mounted within the three republics themselves. In industrialized north-eastern Estonia, where more than 90 per cent of workers were Russian-speakers, attempts were made to set up an alternative government or a co-ordinating committee linking the factories with Moscow and Leningrad. In Latvia hardline anti-reformers in the security services defected from the increasingly liberal Interior Ministry to form a para-military police force, the OMON or, more simply, the Black Berets. At the turn of the year a similar force took shape in Vilnius. National Salvation Committees, pledged to restore the Soviet system of the Brezhnev era, came into being in each Baltic republic.

As the new year of 1991 opened, a political crisis erupted in Lithuania. On Sunday, 6 January, Prime Minister Prunskienė was forced to resign when the Vilnius parliament refused to back the higher prices she recommended. Russian paratroops were flown in to strengthen the army of occupation on Tuesday, while on Wednesday army helicopters flew over the main cities of all three republics, dropping leaflets encouraging the townsfolk to come out into the streets and demonstrate against their bumbling governments; few responded. On Thursday crack troops from a motorized rifle brigade stormed into the Vilnius Press Centre, firing shots into the air as a last warning. Barbed wire barricades and concrete 'dragon's teeth' obstacles were erected around parliament, where the tanks had made their show of strength ten months previously. On Friday night the newly appointed prime minister and his family disappeared, and he could not be contacted until he re-emerged on Monday.

Meanwhile at midnight on Saturday (12 January) the long awaited counter-revolution began, preceded by a proclamation from the Lithuanian National Salvation Committee that it was assuming power. The government had expected the main assault to fall on the parliament house, from where Landsbergis co-ordinated resistance with Churchillian rhetoric and defiance. Instead, the Black Berets and paratroopers attacked the television and radio centre to the east of Vingis Park and the television transmission tower, 3 kilometres away from it. Outside the centre a human shield courageously blocked the progress of armoured personnel carriers, supported by tanks. Thirteen Lithuanians were killed and more than two hundred injured. The immediate military objective was attained: Vilnius's television broadcasts ceased (though the studios and transmitter at Kaunas remained on the air). But the local commander, and ultimately President Gorbachev himself, faced a dilemma: there was no doubt that the defenders of the parliament house and other government buildings could be swept aside, but only through a brutal action, comparable to the Chinese massacre of 3,000 protesters in Tiananmen Square eighteen months previously. This would be morally indefensible and politically a disaster; an outraged world would never give the president the loans he needed to complete the transformation of the Soviet economy.

A week of nervous tension in Vilnius was accompanied by the first of a series of Black Beret attacks on the newly established frontier posts that were to culminate on 31 July in the killing of seven Lithuanian guards at Medininkai, on the border of Belarus. In Riga on Sunday, 20 January – while the world's media watched the opening phases of the Gulf War – the Black Berets unleashed their fury on a pro-independence rally in Raina Bulvaris, the elegant road in which the Ministry of the Interior stood (as does the American embassy today). Five Latvians were killed, including two highly respected members of a film crew. Like Lithuania, Latvia now had martyrs it continues to honour.

The Soviet action in Vilnius and Riga strengthened the resolve of the Baltic peoples. Four weeks after the attack on the television centre 90 per cent of the Lithuanian electorate confirmed independence in a national referendum; the Estonians followed suit a month later, though 23 per cent still wished to remain in the Soviet Union. Even Russia itself – the core of the USSR – achieved democratic independence of a sort: on 12 June Boris Yeltsin, who had roundly condemned the use of force in Lithuania and Latvia, was elected to a newly created executive presidency over a non-communist Russian Federation that included Kaliningrad in the west and Vladivostok in the east, an eighth of the globe's land surface. Incongruously Gorbachev remained technically a world statesman. In late July he received President George Bush for talks in Moscow.

Belatedly the last diehard Brezhnevians planned a military coup, seizing power in Moscow on 19 August while Gorbachev was on holiday in the Crimea. It was a bungled affair that left Yeltsin able to rally support and, with personal courage and popular backing, regain control of the capital within three days. On northern shores 200,000 people in Leningrad took to the streets in protest at the attempt to re-impose communist good order. Briefly naval commanders sympathetic to the coup sought to blockade Tallinn, where students and townsfolk blocked the road to the Upper Town by rolling into position cemented stone obstacles hewn from the granite of Toompea. At Riga there was a clash with the Black Berets outside the Latvian parliament and in Vilnius a Lithuanian was killed in renewed fighting with OMON auxiliaries.

Back in Moscow, Gorbachev resigned from his Communist Party post on 23 August, though clinging to the presidency until 25 December, the day before the Soviet Union formally dissolved. Throughout the last four months of 1991 real power rested with President Yeltsin of Russia, seen in Moscow and abroad as the hero who defeated a military putsch. Yeltsin, sympathetic to the liberals in the other republics, acknowledged Estonia's full independence on 24 August and Latvia's and Lithuania's soon afterwards. By mid-October 1991 all three republics were recognized by foreign governments and had become members of the United Nations. The Baltic way of winning independence had triumphed, though not without assistance from the folly of the military putschists and the skill of the Russian leader who frustrated them.

Finland anxiously watched the unfolding drama across the Gulf. She was concerned for her own security should Russian nationalists sweep into power, as well as for the economic consequences of lost trade with

Leningrad and the Soviet market, and for investments in Estonia. A basically conservative government was formed in April 1990, headed by Esko Aho of the Centre Party. For the first time in a quarter of a century the ruling coalition did not include a party of the Left. Finland had no inclination to come into the NATO fold; neutrality remained good business, it was felt; but for the first time serious thought was given to seeking membership of the European Community. There was closer political interdependence than in earlier years between Helsinki and Stockholm, despite occasional friction over trade rivalry; and the Swedes seemed already to have changed their minds over EEC membership. The Danes were (almost) good Europeans from 1973 onwards (though in 1985 autonomous Greenland withdrew) and the Norwegians were considering a second application for membership. If Finland had to look to the south and west for trade rather than to the east, how long could she afford to stay out of the club and in the Nordic cold?

Sweden applied for membership of the European Community on 1 July 1991 and Finland soon afterwards. But, under the Moderate Centre coalition that came into office in Stockholm that autumn, the Swedish economy again sank into recession. There was a run on the krona in 1992, followed by devaluation. The growth of the pharmaceutical industry and mastery of the mysteries of cyberspace technology encouraged a boom later in the decade but, at first, uncertainty over the economy slowed progress towards EU membership; and the Finns held their referendum first. On 16 October 1994 57 per cent of Finnish voters approved membership. The Swedish referendum came a month later, a delay caused partly by the need for another general election that was to bring the Social Democrats back into office, again under Ingvar Carlsson. When the votes of the referendum were counted, the 'Yes' majority was lower than in Finland. The Norwegian electorate, at the second time of asking, emphatically said 'No' to membership.

On 1 January 1995 Sweden and Finland accordingly joined the European Union, as the Community had been renamed in November 1994, when the Maastricht Treaty came into force. Both countries retained doubts over problems of international sovereignty, looking more for trade co-operation – the 'common market' concept – than political union. Yet Finland was willing to promote economic and monetary union and accepted a single currency, while Sweden – like Denmark and Britain – did not. The Swedes retained the krona after 1 January 2002, when euro notes and coins were introduced in Finland and ten other member states. By the following year, however, Stockholm and Gothenburg and most other centres of trade and industry sought a currency referendum. The Swedish foreign minister, forty-six-year-old Anna Lindh, was campaigning vigorously in favour of the euro when, on 10 September 2003, she was stabbed while shopping in a Stockholm department store, dying later that day. As after Palme's murder, there was widespread shock and sorrow, but on this occasion no suggestion of political assassination. The referendum went ahead as planned, on 14 September, when the Swedish electorate overwhelmingly rejected the single currency.

On that Sunday the people of Estonia, too, were voting in a referendum, giving their approval for the country to join the European Union in the following May. For all three Baltic republics the twelve years since recovery of independence had formed a period of great difficulty. The last Russian troops left Lithuania in 1993 and Estonia and Latvia in the late summer of 1994. The replacement of the Soviet Union by a fledgling Commonwealth of Independent States, with Russia, Ukraine and Belarus as founder members, created almost as many economic problems as did the fall of empires after the First World War. Some problems were familiar: new frontier posts, cutting off towns and markets, for example. More fundamental was the transition from an artificially managed economy bordering on bankruptcy to free-market privatized capitalism. In Estonia, ruthless competitiveness out-Thatchered Thatcherism: there would be no helping handout of subsidies to inefficient factories or agriculture, despite the difficulty of reverting from ineffectual Soviet collective farms to smallholdings. Finnish investment bolstered Tallinn and its port but, with St Petersburg so close, the economy was too dependent on a Russian economy that needed shots in the arm from the International Monetary Fund to stave off disaster. When Russia devalued the rouble in 1998 the Estonian economy faltered but it began to recover with the spread of tourism. Latvia had already been financially shaken in 1995 when a leading commercial bank in Riga collapsed and she now suffered severely from the fall of the rouble; many small companies were ruined. At the same time the Lithuanians lost a fifth of their export market. All three republics and Poland, too, had applied for membership of the EU in 1995. After the scare of 1998 there was good reason to push ahead rapidly, so far as the commissioners in Brussels would permit.

Because of their financial plight Latvia and Lithuania were at first tentatively offered only partnership, while full negotiations began in March 1998 with Estonia and with Poland. By 2000 Latvia and Lithuania could meet the required standards in democratic stability, rule of law and a free market economy. At the Copenhagen EU summit of December 2002 the

Baltic republics and Poland were among the ten applicants invited to join. On 20 September 2003 Latvia was the last to complete her referendum when, in a remarkable turnout of 72.5 per cent of the electorate, slightly more than two-thirds voted for accession. The ten newcomers were formally admitted on 1 May 2004, raising EU membership to twenty-five.

The Estonian president, leading the celebrations in Tallinn at seventy-five, was Arnold Rüütel, chairman of the Estonian Supreme Soviet for the last nine years of its existence, a genuine early convert to independence, far from sympathetic to the Russians who stayed on in the republic. His wife, Ingrid, was the daughter of a leading Estonian communist who in 1941 was captured and executed by the Nazis. Among the ten newcomers to the EU, Latvia was the only republic to have a woman president. At the age of seven Vaira Vike-Freiberga escaped with her parents from Riga and Soviet rule. From the comfortless safety of a 'displaced persons' refugee camp in Germany she eventually crossed to Morocco and a French education. She studied in Canada, became a professor of psychology, returning to her native Riga in 1998 at the age of sixty-one. There her qualities of non-partisan leadership were so impressive that in the following June she was elected president, winning a second term of office four years later. Post-independence politics in all three republics drew on a wide range of experience.

'East European awkward squad could wreck EU,' Anthony Browne warned readers of The Times on 6 April 2004. There was certainly much to feed Euroscepticism: mistrust of agricultural policy among farmers; suspicion of incompetence and/or corruption at a high level in Poland, doubts over the integrity of a Latvian minister, and, on that particular Tuesday, President Paksas of Lithuania was impeached over a cash scandal involving a Russian businessman, said to be linked to organized crime. No mass political parties offered 'a solid basis of popular support' in any of the republics. Governments were short-lived: eleven in ten years in Lithuania, ten in Latvia, seven in Estonia, six in Poland, Browne calculated; Finland scored five in his league table. Low support at home, he argued, would hamper decision-making at Brussels.

The parliamentary scene was reminiscent of the early 1920s, when in a mere six years Poland had thirteen governments, Estonia nine, Latvia seven and Lithuania six. Those years remain the most constructive under democratic rule in the region. Four generations later, the talk was once more of political instability though springing, it would seem, from seedy corruption rather than the woolly-minded idealism that took the blame of old. In 1996 a Lithuanian prime minister was forced to resign after it was discovered that he had removed his savings from a bank shortly before it was mysteriously forced to close. Now eight years later Rolandas Paksas, a young and popular ex-stunt pilot and former mayor of Vilnius, was embroiled in a scandal that hit the headlines for six of his fifteen months as president. He was duly removed from office on 6 April 2004, and on 12 July the Kaunas-born Valdas Adamkus, a civil engineer who had spent more than thirty years of his life in Chicago, was sworn in to succeed him. 'Now we can heave a sigh of relief, think about the future and address current problems,' the veteran Brazaukas told *The Times*.

By the end of the year Lithuania was climbing well out of recession, with steadily rising exports to Britain – manufactured commodities rather than the traditional yield of the fields and forests. Though unemployment remained high and Kaunas lagged behind Vilnius and Klaipėda in outward prosperity, the future for the EU's Baltic newcomers looked bright. The European Parliament had approved their three commissioners. There was no sign of the 'turmoil' that earlier in the year had been predicted when 'the Balts' came to Brussels and Strasbourg. Confidence in the Baltic way of conducting affairs was shown by the readiness with which the General Secretariat of the EU turned to the experienced Polish and Lithuanian leaders for counsel during the critical week in 2004 that followed November's Ukrainian presidential election.

Yet too often in the decades after independence past history has seemed to haunt present politics. Tension over the status of Vilnius long hampered Polish–Lithuanian relations; some Poles still resented the loss of the city they knew as Wilno; Lithuanian nationalists wanted a formal apology from Warsaw for Zeligowski's coup. The terrible fate of the Jews justified days of contrition and acts of apology. Access to Soviet archives has raised doubt over the probity of some patriot heroes of the inter-war struggle for survival. In Estonia (where 35 per cent of the population are Russian by origin) and in Latvia (30 per cent) ex-Soviet citizens complain of discrimination and accusations of covert membership of the KGB. As early as November 1991 there were foreign protests over a reunion of Estonian war veterans, many of them SS men.

Monuments provoke the greatest local controversy. In all three republics the governments seek to prevent honouring the dead from harming the living. When in June 1997 the Latvian nationalist Perkonkrusts movement damaged the Soviet Victory Memorial in Riga, the authorities sought donations towards its repair. In eight weeks they received $400 from some of the city's poorer Russian-speakers, and the memorial was duly restored.

Five years later, in July 2002, feelings ran high in Pärnu, Estonia's 'summer capital'. A new memorial showed an Estonian Waffen-SS soldier with gun pointing towards St Petersburg and the inscription, 'To all Estonian soldiers who fell in the Second War to liberate their homeland and to free Europe in 1940–45'. When the authorities removed the 'inappropriate' statue, flowers and a lighted candle appeared on the concrete base where it had stood. Who were liberators and who oppressors? The volunteers who helped Laidoner repulse the Reds in 1918 are remembered with pride in Pärnu, as in other Estonian cities. Is it all, as Talleyrand would cynically have said, 'a matter of dates'? But it is not hard to empathize with survivors passionately stirred by memory of the darkest of days. Once more the mind's eye focuses on fading images of SS guards herding the innocent, their swastikas side by side with Estonian or Latvian or Lithuanian insignia; and one wonders. Moral judgements, unlike photographs, should rarely come in black and white

Along Pärnu's carefully cleansed golden sand or down 100 kilometres of thin grained dunes on Lithuania's Curonian spit the future seems bright and assured. In Pärnu, as in the central squares of Tallinn and Riga, pop music flourishes. The singing revolution attained a new level in 2001 and 2002 with successive wins for Estonia and Latvia at the Eurovision Song Contest, a much ridiculed entertainment credited with boosting tourism; in 1974, when the contest was young and prestigious, it gave Abba the chance to make *Waterloo* a Swedish victory. Outdoor sport, on both sides of the inland sea, is arguably less successful than during the interwar years: eight Baltic states won only ten gold medals between them at the Athens Olympics. But the range of sport is increasing: rugby posts could be seen in the Tallinn Hippodrome in 2002, for example; *Wisden Cricketers' Almanack*, which has long brought news from Denmark, carried reports from Estonia in 2001 and 2002, and has given summaries of club cricket in Finland, where there is also a women's league. Even in cricket there seem close links between Helsinki and Tallinn.

Despite the relaxed atmosphere of enjoyment so prevalent in recent years, apprehension remained. In all three Baltic republics teachers and students in private conversation showed a greater eagerness to enter NATO than to join the European Union. Poland came into NATO in 1999, together with Hungary and the Czech Republic. Estonia, Latvia and Lithuania accepted membership in March 2003 and, after giving reassurances to Russia, officially entered NATO in March 2004, a month ahead of their entry into the European Union. There had already been collaboration with some NATO members under the Partnership for Peace programme, which the Lithuanians joined in 1994, only a year after the last

Soviet troops left the republic. By 2004 NATO planes could use modern airfields constructed in Lithuania by Soviet forces for the Warsaw Pact. But still the Russians hold on to Kaliningrad. It is both an outpost in the West and testimony to imperial endeavour; for *oblast* Kaliningrad is Russia's sole prize from Hitler's pre-war Reich, 14,350 square kilometres of marsh, dunes, woodland, ruined towns, and, perhaps, the ghosts of a city that was for half a millennium German.

Great questions remain, rooted deep in history and yet unanswerable. Have the Baltic republics the wisdom and patience to absorb and integrate their Russian and Ukrainian minorities? What future has the Baltic if a Russian nationalist comes to power in Moscow? Is the bear tamed or merely sleeping? Yet it is reasonable, if unfashionable, to be optimistic. In today's Baltic, confrontation has given way to collaboration. Never before have so many international councils and agencies sought to preserve and promote co-operation across the inland sea. To the East another 'Baltic Way' is slowly taking shape, a route by road along the southern Finnish coast, around St Petersburg and on to Riga, Vilnius and, perhaps, Gdańsk. In the West two magnificent bridges – the 1997 road and rail link over the Belts that joins Zealand and Fyn, and the Øresundforbindelsen with its tunnel bringing Copenhagen and Malmö together – at last provide Adam of Bremen's girdle with a clasp. A Baltic that is at peace with itself holds out for Europe the prospect of unity and understanding.

Royal Chronology

Some Baltic rulers, with brief reference to any outstanding event in their reigns

DENMARK

Gorm the Old dies *c.* 940
Harald Bluetooth *c.* 958–87; coming of Christianity
Sven Forkbeard 986–1014
Harald II 1014–18
Canute the Great 1018–35; joint rule over England
Hardicanute 1035–42
Magnus the Good 1042–7
Sven II 1047–74
Harald III 1074–80
Canute II 1080–6; murdered at Odense and canonized
Olav I 1086–95
Eric the Good Hearted 1095–1103
Niels I 1104–34
Eric II the Memorable 1134–7
Eric III 1137–46
Canute III 1146–57
Valdemar I the Great 1157–82; creates strong monarchy
Canute IV 1182–1202
Valdemar II the Victorious 1202–42; expansion eastward to Estonia
Eric IV Ploughpenny 1242–50
Abel 1250–2
Christopher I 1252–9
Eric V Klipping 1259–86
Eric VI Menved 1286–1319
Christopher II 1320–6; 1330–2
Valdemar IV Atterdag 1340–75; seizes Gotland; expansionism checked by Hanse
Olav III 1376–87
Margaret I 1387–97 (Margrete Valdemarsdotter, *d.* 1412); Union of Kalmar
Eric VI of Pomerania 1397–1439; imposes first Øresund dues
Christopher III of Bavaria 1440–8; Copenhagen becomes capital city
Christian I 1448–81
Hans (aka John) 1481–1513

Christian II of Oldenburg 1513–23; end of Kalmar Union; deposed by nobility
Frederick I 1523–33
Christian III 1534–59; the Reformation
Frederick II 1559–88; Seven Years Northern War
Christian IV 1588–1648; Thirty Years War; architectural golden age
Frederick III 1648–70; royal absolutism established
Christian V 1670–99; loss of Lund, Malmö to Sweden
Frederick IV 1699–1730; Great Northern War
Christian VI 1730–46
Frederick V 1746–66
Christian VII 1766–1808; British attacks on Copenhagen
Frederick VI (regent 1784–1806) 1808–39; Norway lost
Christian VIII 1839–48
Frederick VII 1848–63; first constitution; end of Øresund dues
Christian IX, 1863–1906; Glucksburg dynasty; Schleswig-Holstein lost to Germany
Frederick VIII 1906–12
Christian X 1912–47; votes for women; south Jutland recovered; two world wars
Frederick IX 1947–72; membership of NATO and EFTA
Margaret II 1972– ; membership of EU; Øresund land link with Sweden

POLAND (continuous only from 1306)

Mieszko I Piast *c.* 965–91
Boleslaw the Brave 992–1025; conquers Pomerania
Mieszko II 1025–37
Casimir I the Restorer 1038–58
Boleslaw II the Bold 1058–79
Wladislaw Herman 1079–1102
Boleslaw III the Wry Mouthed 1102–38
Wladislaw the Exile 1138–46
Boleslaw IV the Curly Haired 1146–77
Casimir II the Just 1177–94
Wladislaw I the Elbow High 1306–33
Casimir III the Great 1333–70; legal codes; towns built; Cracow university
Louis of Anjou, K. of Hungary 1370–82
Jadwiga 1384–6, co-monarch 1386–99 with her husband
Wladislaw Jagiello of Lithuania 1386–1434; first battle of Tannenberg
Wladislaw III 1434–44
Casimir IV Jagiello 1444–92
John Albert 1492–1501
Alexander 1501–6
Sigismund I 1506–48; period of prosperity
Sigismund II Augustus 1548–72; Union of Lublin extends from Baltic to Black Sea

LITHUANIA

Mindaugas 1236–63; baptized in 1251; crowned king in 1253
Traidenis 1269–82; first ruler to be styled Grand Duke
Vytenis 1295–1315
Gediminas 1315–41; establishes Vilnius as a capital city
Jaunutis 1341–5
Algirdas 1345–77; Grand Duke in eastern Lithuania
Kęstutis 1345–77; Grand Duke in western Lithuania
Jogaila 1377–92; son of Algirdas; King of Poland (as Jagiello) 1386–1434
Vytautas the Great 1392–1450; son of Kęstutis; Grand Duchy of Lithuania extends
    from the Baltic to the Black Sea
Švitrigaila 1430–2
Žygimantas 1432–40; last Grand Duke (thereafter see Polish–Lithuanian
    Commonwealth – below)

POLISH-LITHUANIAN COMMONWEALTH, ELECTED KINGS

Henry of Valois 1573–4
Stefan Batory of Transylvania 1576–86
Sigismund III Vasa of Sweden 1587–1632; failed personal royal union with Sweden
Wladislaw IV Vasa 1632–48
John Casimir 1648–68; Swedish 'deluge' invasion checked at Częstochowa
Michael Wisniowiecki 1669–73
John Sobieski 1674–96; leads Polish army to relief of Vienna
Augustus the Strong of Saxony 1697–1704; 1709–33
Stanislas Leszczynski 1704–9 (1733–6 rival king)
Augustus III of Saxony 1733–63
Stanislas Augustus Poniatowski 1764–95; last Polish king

PRUSSIAN RULERS 1640–1918

Frederick William, the Great Elector of Brandenburg, 1640–88
Frederick I 1688–1713; became King in 1701
Frederick William I 1713–40
Frederick II the Great 1740–86; 'enlightened despotism'; Potsdam
Frederick William II 1786–97
Frederick William III 1797–1840
Frederick William IV 1840–61
William I 1861–88 (regent 1858–61); became German Emperor 1871
Frederick III German Emperor 1888

William II German Emperor 1888–1918; naval rivalry; First World War; deposed

RUSSIA

Some early rulers

Rurik in Novgorod *c.* 862–79
Oleg, Prince of Kiev 880–912; raids on Constantinople
Igor 912–45
St Olga 945–*c.* 957
Sviatoslav of Kiev, *c.* 957–*c.* 980
Yaroslav the Wise, 1019–54
Alexander Nevsky of Novgorod and Vladimir 1240–63; Teutonic Knights defeated
Dmitri Donskoy of Moscow 1350–89; Kremlin built

Tsars of Moscow and all Russia

Ivan III the Great 1462–1505; became Tsar 1473
Vasily III 1505–33
Ivan IV the Terrible (Awesome) 1533–84
Feodor I 1584–98
Boris Godunov 1598–1605; followed by 'Time of Troubles'
Michael Romanov 1613–45
Alexis Mikhailovich 1645–76
Feodor Alexeyevich 1676–82
Ivan V 1682–92 joint ruler with
Peter I the Great 1682–1725; first Emperor 1721; St Petersburg founded; Poltava
Catherine I 1725–7; ex-peasant, Peter's widow
Peter II 1727–30
Anne 1730–40
Ivan VI 1740–1
Elizabeth 1741–62; embellishment of St Petersburg
Peter III 1762; deposed and killed in favour of his wife
Catherine II the Great 1762–96; enlightened despot, partitioner of Poland
Paul 1796–1801; deposed and killed
Alexander I 1801–25; Napoleonic wars; Congress of Vienna
Nicholas I 1825–55; 'Gendarme of Europe'; Crimean War
Alexander II 1855–81; liberal in Finland; repressive in Poland; assassinated
Alexander III 1881–94; extreme Russian nationalism; anti-Semitism
Nicholas II 1894–1917; war and revolution; deposed; killed 1918

SWEDEN (from 1250)

Birger Jarl 1250–66; royal guardian
Valdemar Birgersson 1266–75; Stockholm founded
Magnus Barnlock 1275–90; first monarch buried in Riddarholmen church
Birger Magnusson 1290–1318
Magnus Eriksson 1319–64; national code of laws; St Birgitta
Albert of Mecklenburg 1364–89; real power exercised by Bo Jonsson Grip
Margaret I 1389–97 (d. 1412); Union of Kalmar
Eric of Pomerania 1397–1439; Union King, deposed
Karl Knutsson, Protector of Realm, 1438–40
Christopher of Bavaria, 1441–8; Union King
Charles VIII Knutsson, 1448–57; 1464–5; 1467–70
Christian I 1457–64; Union King
Sten Sture the Elder, Protector 1470–97; 1501–03; victory at Brunkeberg
Hans (aka John) 1497–1501; Union King; paid to stay away from Sweden
Svante Sture, Protector 1504–11
Sten Sture the Younger, Protector 1511–20
Christian II 1520–1; last Union King; Stockholm Bloodbath
Gustav Vasa, Protector 1521–3; King Gustav I, 1523–60; Reformation
Eric XIV 1560–8; deposed after mental breakdown
John III 1568–92; religious traditionalist, crypto-Catholic
Sigismund 1592–9; also Polish king; deposed
Charles IX 1599–1611
Gustavus II Adolphus 1611–32; Thirty Years War; the 'Vasa' ship
Christina 1632–54; under regency to 1644; cultured age
Charles X Gustav of the Palatinate 1654–60; gains Skane and Livonia
Charles XI 1660–97; under regency to 1672; absolute monarch; the Reduction
Charles XII 1697–1718; wins Narva; loses Poltava
Ulrika Eleonor 1719–20; constitution limits royal powers; succeeded by husband
Frederick I of Hesse 1720–51; the 'Age of Freedom'
Adolf Frederick 1751–71
Gustav III 1771–92; restores absolutism; assassinated at masked ball
Gustav IV Adolf 1792–1809; under regency to 1796; loses Finland; deposed
Charles XIII 1809–18; 'adopts' Marshal Bernadotte who becomes
Charles XIV John 1818–44; Sweden–Norway Union
Oscar I 1844–59
Charles XV 1859–72; liberal reforms
Oscar II 1872–1907; end of union with Norway
Gustav V 1907–50; two world wars; growth of social democracy
Gustav VI Adolf 1950–73
Carl XVI Gustaf 1973– ; new constitution leaves king with few powers

Notes and Select Bibliography

Publication details are given only after the first reference to a book or periodical.

Chapter 1: Sentinels Above the Sound

Fynes Moryson's account of his Baltic journey is in his *Itinerary*, (reprint, Glasgow) Vol. 1, pp. 120–31, with Kronborg on p. 122. All extracts from Tacitus, *Germania* are from chapters 41–44. On amber in classical times see Cunliffe (ed.), *Oxford Illustrated Prehistory of Europe* (Oxford, 1994), p. 54. The 'French geographer' is André Caillaux in Deffontaines (ed.), *Larousse Encyclopaedia of Geography, Europe* (New York, 1961), p. 54. Anthony Cross, *Russia under Western Eyes, 1517–1825* (London, 1971) includes Algarotti's letter to Hervey, pp. 183–8 and Robert Lee on the Neva flood, pp. 371–4. Anna Pavlovna on the flood: S. Jackman, *Romanov Relations* (London, 1969), pp. 103–4. For other impressions of St Petersburg see A. Palmer, *Russia in War and Peace* (London, 1972), pp. 72–8. 'Desecrated pomp': T. Karsavina, *Theatre Street* (London, 1931), p. 268. Berlin as a backwater: Veit Valentin, *1848, Chapters in German History* (London, 1940), p. 127. On Vilnius: M. Gilbert, *Jewish History Atlas* (London, 1968), pp. 68–9; for the inter-war period see the memoirs of C. Milosz, *Native Realm* (London, 1981), pp. 54–107. Peter Unwin, *Baltic Approaches* (Norwich, 1996) is a reflective, historically informative account of a journey through the region soon after the collapse of the Soviet Union.

Chapter 2: Peoples on the Move

For accounts of the archaeological discoveries in Sweden see E. C. Elstob, *Sweden, A Traveller's History* (Woodbridge, 1979), pp. 1–10 (who also considers the early importance of iron ore, p. 16) and L. O. Lagerqvist, *History of Sweden* (Stockholm, 2001), pp. 7–15 with illustrations of the Bäckaskog skeleton, p. 8 and the Vendel discoveries, p. 14. Finnish origins are discussed in F. Singleton, *Short History of Finland* (revised edition, Cambridge, 1998), pp. 10–15 with reference to Matti Klinge's theory on p. 13. On Latvian origins and Courland: A. Plakans, *The Latvians* (Stanford, 1995), pp. 3–13.

Chapter 3: The Viking East

Principal books used are: Magnus Magnusson, *The Vikings* (revised edition, Stroud, 2000), especially Chapter 4; G. Jones, *History of the Vikings* (Oxford, 1968); and J. Haywood's excellent *Penguin Historical Atlas of the Vikings* (London, 1995) which is so much more than a collection of maps. On Lindisfarne: Magnusson, pp. 23–5, with Alcuin's comment, p. 26. Extracts from the Russian Primary Chronicle in G. Vernadsky (ed.), *Source Book for Russian History from Early Times to 1917* (London, 1972), Vol. 1; Rurik and Novgorod, pp. 15–16; Photius, p. 11; Oleg at Kiev, p. 19; Oleg at Byzantium, pp. 19–20, including 'brocade sails'. But compare D. Obolensky, *The Byzantine Commonwealth, Eastern Europe, 500–1453* (London, 1971), pp. 184–8. On the Varangian Guard and Harald Hardrada, ibid., pp. 232–6; Magnusson, pp. 202–6; Haywood, p. 124; and N. Ascherson, *Black Sea* (London, 1995), pp. 271–3. Magnusson has illustrations of the marble lion (p. 61) and the inscription at St Sophia; in colour in Haywood, p. 105. Kyrksstigen runic inscription: Elstob, p. 14. Birka: ibid., pp. 12 and 16; Lagerqvist, with illustration, p. 16. Haywood considers Birka (pp. 13, 17, 27, 32, 42, 45), Kaupang (p. 39) and Hedeby (pp. 38, 42 including Cordoba merchant's account, p. 45); also Magnusson, pp. 52–4 and 207. The ODNB (*Oxford Dictionary of National Biography*, 2004) includes a judicious reassessment of Canute by M. K. Lawson. For Gotland I have profited from a report of the Council of Europe Teachers' Seminar at Visby in 1993 and kindly given to me by Sean Lang, the Rapporteur General.

Chapter 4: Pagans and Piasts

Eric Christiansen's *The Northern Crusades* (London, 1997), pp. 20–43 provides a fine general survey, with an analysis of Wendish paganism on p. 33. B. and P. Sawyer, *Mediaeval Scandinavia* (Minneapolis, 1993) is invaluable on Denmark and Sweden in this period. Rimbert's life of Anskar was critically edited by the German scholar Waitz in the 1880s and translated by C. H. Robinson (London, 1921). Lagerqvist's *History*, pp. 18–22, succinctly surveys 'old and new religions'. For the Jelling rune stones, with illustrations: Magnusson, pp. 66–7, with a report on twentieth century archaeological discoveries on the site. The most recent general survey covering Novgorod and Kiev is G. Hosking, *Russia and the Russians, A History* (London, 2001), pp. 31–65. Early settlement at Tallinn: R. Pullat, *Brief History of Tallinn* (Tallinn, 1998), p. 11. On Poland: N. Davies, *God's Playground, A History of Poland* (Oxford, 1981), Vol. 1, early chapters; A. Zamoyski, *The Polish Way* (London, 1987); W. F. Reddaway (ed.), *Cambridge History of Poland* (Cambridge, 1941), Vol. 1. For Casimir the Great and his background: P. W. Knoll, *The Rise of the Polish Monarchy: Piast Poland in East Central Europe 1320–70* (Chicago, 1972).

Chapter 5: Holy Warriors and Hanse Merchants

This chapter owes much to Christiansen's *Northern Crusades* and P. Dollinger, translated and edited by D. S. Ault and S. H. Steinberg, *The German Hansa* (London, 1970). For the mediaeval papacy J. N. D. Kelly, *Oxford Dictionary of Popes* (Oxford, 1988) is invaluable. On Nyklot: Christiansen, pp. 33–5, 53–6, 65–6, with the bishop's scathing comment at Stettin, p. 56. Helmond's account of Lübeck's founding: Dollinger, pp. 379–80. For Visby see his second chapter; for founding of Riga, p. 28, supplemented by Christiansen on the Sword Brothers, pp. 79–82, 99–103 (on Saulė, p. 102) and Plankans, *Latvia*, pp. 19–21. Valdemar II at Reval: Christiansen, pp. 111–112 and Pullat, pp. 21–2. On the Teutonic Order, the second and third chapters of Christiansen may be supplemented by J. Smith and W. Urban, *Livonian Rhymed Chronicle* (Bloomington, 1977), a scholarly edited translation of a contemporary source. See also A. Forey, *The Military Orders* (London, 1992); Vernadsky's *Source Book*, Vol. 1, p. 64 for the Novgorod chronicle on Alexander Nevsky; Singleton, pp. 20–22 for the Swedish-Finnish ventures. For Lithuania: two articles in *Oxford Slavonic Papers* by M. Giedroyc on the arrival of Christianity, Vol. 18 (1967), pp. 1–30, and on the early conflicts, Vol. 19 (1968), pp. 34–57.

Chapter 6: The Rise and Fall of Marienburg

On the Hanse and the Teutonic Order: Dollinger, pp. 33–5, 73–8, 149–50, 198–9, 399. Kniprode's grand mastership: Christiansen pp. 162–3. For English connections and Bolingbroke's crusading activities: K. B. McFarlane, *Lancastrian Kings and Lollard Knights* (Oxford, 1972), pp. 38–9; F. du Boulay and C. Barron, *The Reign of Richard II* (London, 1971), pp. 153–71. For the Polish-Lithuanian union and the treaty of Krevo: N. Davies, *God's Playground*, Vol. 1, pp. 115–55; text of treaty is in Vernadsky, *Source Book*, Vol. 1, p. 91. Conquest of Samogitia: Christiansen, pp. 166–7. First battle of Tannenberg: ibid., pp. 227–9, with later decline of the Order, pp. 231–8. For parallel treatment see Dollinger, pp. 291–3 (including consideration of the treaties of Thorn). G. C. Evans, *Tannenberg 1410:1914* (London, 1970) compares the two battles and the myths surrounding them.

Chapter 7: Ships, Pirates and Adventurers

Dollinger on Hansa ships, ship-building and seamanship: pp. 141–55, including warships on p. 143. My estimate of falling import of wax during the English Reformation is based on his trade statistics, p. 436. On Paul Beneke in 1473 see the extract from Weinreich's Danzig chronicle, ibid., p. 393; see also C. Field, 'Paul Beneke and the German naval campaign against England in the 15th century', *Journal of the United Royal Services Institute* (London, May 1915), an article that echoes pre-Jutland jingoism. For a full treatment of Anglo-Hanseatic trade: E. F. Jacob, *The Thirteenth Century* (Oxford, 1961), pp. 69–71, 356–60, 554. For the early days of the Merchant Adventurers: ibid., pp. 350–2. For an English merchant on the sack of Bergen: Dollinger, p. 391. The Vitalien pirates: ibid., pp. 79–81. Fynes Moryson on Elbing mud, *Itinerary*, Vol. 1, p. 129. Increase in Dutch trade and late fifteenth century changes in the region: D. Kirby, *Northern Europe in the Early Modern Period, The Baltic World 1492–1772* (London, 1970), pp. 8–14. Pullat's *History of Tallinn*, though confusingly compressed, has details on the Hanse and eastern Baltic trading in general.

Chapter 8: The Chimera of Kalmar

Basic to Danish history: S. P. Oakley, *The Story of Denmark* (London, 1971). On Atterdag and Magnus II, F. D. Scott, *Sweden: The Nation's History* (Minneapolis, 1978), pp. 69–79. For St Bridget as a critic of society, C. Bergendorff in J. Cate and E. Anderson (eds), *Mediaeval and Historical Essays in Honour of James Westfall Thompson* (Chicago, 1938), pp. 3–18. For the Black Death in Sweden: Lagerqvist, pp. 31, 55; Elstob, p. 35. Atterdag's attack on Visby: Elstob, pp. 38–9; and from Hanse standpoint, Dollinger, pp. 67–9. Peace of Stralsund and heyday of the Hanse: ibid., pp. 70–71. Queen Margaret and Albert of Saxony: Elstob, pp. 39–41. Letter of Union creating Union of Kalmar: ibid., p. 42 and Lagerqvist, p. 34. For the introduction of tolls on shipping in the Sound: C. E. Hill, *The Danish Sound Dues and the Command of the Baltic* (Durham, N.C., 1926), pp. 11–15. The age of Engelbrektsson, Karl Knutsson and Sten Sture the Elder is considered in Elstob, pp. 44–52 and Lagerqvist, pp. 35–9; both books illustrate Bernt Notke's St George and the Dragon. Michael Roberts' definitive histories of Sweden begin with the Stockholm bloodbath, *The Early Vasas* (Cambridge, 1968), pp. 16–18, and consider the career and early reign of Gustav Vasa, pp. 20–84. Elstob, Lagerqvist and Scott also fully cover this period.

Chapter 9: Muscovy and Wittenberg

J. Fennell, *Ivan the Great of Moscow* (London, 1961) is more than a biography. There is a German language biography of Plettenberg by M. Hellman; otherwise see Christiansen, pp. 254–7. Diarmaid MacCulloch's *Reformation, Europe's House Divided 1490–1700* (London, 2003) outstrips all earlier works: Luther personally, pp. 115–62; Peasants' Revolt, pp. 160–1; printing, pp. 152, 191 (but Kirby, p. 80, notes shortage of presses in Sweden); iconoclasm at Riga and Dorpat, pp. 155–6, and at Tallinn, Pullat, *History of Tallinn*, p. 30. For Albert of Brandenburg and for the 'dirty deal' admission: Christiansen, pp. 246–8. On Poland and 'Royal Prussia', Davies, *God's Playground*, Vol. 1, pp. 142–3; Prussia as 'first evangelical state church', MacCulloch, pp. 162–3. Gustav Vasa and Lutheranism, ibid., pp. 189–90, with Olaus Petri and his brother, pp. 335–6. On the Swedish Reformation in general, Elstob, pp. 83–5. Estonia becomes Swedish: Pullat, pp. 30, 64, 65, 77–9. On Ivan IV's Baltic Wars, Hosking, *Russia*, pp. 119–22. For the Kettler dynasty, Platans,

Latvians, p. 70. For the Livonian Wars: Kirby, pp. 107–23. On the making of the Polish-Lithuanian Commonwealth: N. Davies, *God's Playground*, Vol. 1, pp. 350–70; Kirby, pp. 103–4. For Eric XIV, Roberts, *Early Vasas*, pp. 235–42. For John III and Sigismund: Elstob, pp. 87–93; Lagerqvist, pp. 50–3; MacCulloch, pp. 361–66. For Charles IX: Elstob, pp. 91–4; Lagerqvist, pp. 54–5. On Pedar Oxe: Hill, *Danish Sound Dues*, pp. 17, 18. For the Danish kings, Oakley, *Story of Denmark*, pp. 203–12.

Chapter 10: Lion of the North

Michael Roberts has written extensively on the king, notably in *Gustavus Adolphus: A History of Sweden 1611–1632* (London, Vol. 1 1953, Vol. 2 1958), more concisely in *Gustavus Adolphus and the Rise of Sweden* (London, 1973), *The Swedish Imperial Experience 1560–1718* (Cambridge, 1979), and in two *Essays in Swedish History* (London, 1967). Oxenstierna is clearly delineated in C. V. Wedgwood, *Thirty Years War* (London, 1938), especially pp. 273–4. For Knäred treaty and Älvsborg ransom, Elstob, pp. 100–01; Lagerqvist, pp. 60–61. Gustavus Adolphus's tactics, strategy and military system: Roberts, *Essays*, pp. 64–75. The 'military revolution' attributed by Roberts to Gustavus Adolphus, ibid., pp. 195–225, aroused much academic controversy, ably summarized by Christopher Bellamy in R. Holmes (ed.), *Oxford Companion to Military History* (Oxford, 2001), pp. 586–88. See Wedgwood for Christian IV's campaigns (pp. 203–12, 233–8), Ulvendal meeting (pp. 250–1), Peenemünde landing (pp. 270–1), Salvius (p. 276), Barwalde Treaty (pp. 278–9), Breitenfeld (pp. 297–303), Lützen (pp. 324–7). Geoffrey Parker, *The Thirty Years War* (London, 1984) is stimulating. On Gustavus Adolphus's German plans: Roberts, *Essays*, pp. 82–102. For English attitudes to the war: Christopher Hill, *Puritanism and Revolution* (London, 1958/1968), pp. 131, 133. Disputes over Sound Dues: C. E. Hill, pp. 93–136. Veronica Buckley's excellent *Christina, Queen of Sweden* (London, 2004) was published after this chapter was completed: otherwise, see Roberts, *Essays*, pp. 111–31; Lagerqvist, pp. 67–9; and Elstob, pp. 115–17, 123, who also has an interesting survey of burgher mansion development in this period, pp. 119–20.

Chapter 11: Nemesis at Poltava

For intrusion of Cossacks: Hosking, pp. 163–5. Charles X in Poland: Kirby, pp. 184–87. Frederick William the Great Elector, ibid., pp. 186–91, supplementing F. L. Carsten, *The Origins of Prussia* (Oxford, 1954), and on Częstochowa, Davies, *God's Playground*, with foreign reaction Roberts, *Essays*, pp. 166–71. Mountagu, Pepys and Copenhagen: Richard Ollard, *Pepys* (London, 1974), p. 49. Treaty of Oliva: Kirby, p. 119. Jacob Kettler in Courland: ibid., p. 244 and Plakans, pp. 51–2. For Frederick III and Danish developments: Oakley and E. Eckman, 'The Danish Royal Law of 1665', *Journal of Modern History* (Chicago, 1959), no. 31. Revised

(Princeton, 1968). Frederick the Great: a short biography by A. Palmer (London, 1974) but the major works are G. Ritter, *Frederick the Great* (London, 1968); P. Paret (ed.), *Frederick the Great, a Profile* (London, 1972); C. Duffy, *Frederick the Great: A Military Life* (London, 1985) and D. Showalter, *The Wars of Frederick the Great* (Harlow, 1985). International politics between 1763 and 1848 are studied in detail in Paul W. Schroeder, *The Transformation of European Politics* (Oxford, 1994; abbreviated below as PWS), with first partition of Poland, pp. 10–19. For Gustav III: H. A. Barton, *Scandinavia in the Revolutionary Era* (Minneapolis, 1986), pp. 133–7; Lagerqvist, pp. 99–112; Elstob, pp. 149–56, 171–3, 180–1. See also Ralph Edenheim on palaces in Marita Jonnson, *The Soul of Stockholm* (Stockholm, 1999), pp. 87–126, with delightful photographs by Ingalill Snitt. For the Swedish navy under Gustav III: L. O. Berg in F. Sandstedt (ed.), *Between the Imperial Eagles* (Stockholm, 2000), pp. 77–107, with the spread of typhus traced on p. 82.

Chapter 13: Thunder from the South

Influence of French Revolution: PWS, pp. 67–74. Poland: see the early sections of Davies, *God's Playground*, Vol. 2; R. H. Lord, *The Second Partition of Poland* (Cambridge, Mass., 1915). Vernadsky, *Source Book*, Vol. 2, pp. 422–3 has Catherine's reaction to news of execution of Louis XVI and the manifesto on the second partition. For Fersen see H. A. Barton, *Count Hans Axel von Fersen* (Boston, 1975). On Gustav III's last days, Scott, *Sweden, The Nation's History*, Chapter 10. O. Feldbaek, *Denmark and the Armed Neutrality, 1800–1801* (Copenhagen, 1980) puts Nelson's conduct in context: see also Sandstedt, *Eagles*, pp. 203–04 and Christopher Hibbert, *Nelson: A Personal History* (London, 2000). For Paul's later years and murder: A. Palmer, *Alexander I, Tsar of War and Peace* (London, 1974), pp. 39–46; Russian foreign policy 1801–05, pp. 62–67, 78–90, but more extensively in P. K. Grimsted, *The Foreign Ministers of Alexander I* (Berkeley and Los Angeles, 1969), pp. 3–193; see also PWS, pp. 232–75. On the Swedish campaign in Pomerania 1805–1807, see P. Frohnert in Sandstedt, pp. 256–70. For Lübeck and Swedish prisoners: A. Palmer, *Bernadotte: Napoleon's Marshal, Sweden's King* (London, 1990), pp. 135–7. For Napoleon's winter campaign and his revulsion at Eylau: Chandler, *Campaigns of Napoleon* (London, 1966), pp. 509–51; for Friedland, pp. 572–85. Berlin Decrees and Orders in Council: PWS, pp. 307–10. Tilsit: Palmer, *Alexander I*, pp. 132–46; PWS, pp. 320–8. British amphibious attack on Copenhagen: E. Longford, *Wellington, Years of the Sword* (London, 1964), pp. 134–6; Sandstedt, *Eagles*, pp. 204–7; see also Ryan, 'The causes of the British attack on Copenhagen', *English Historical Review* (London, 1958), Vol. 68, pp. 37–55. The publication of Saumarez's Baltic papers has upgraded his reputation: see A. B. Sainsbury in ODNB for a modern assessment; cf. Oliver Warner, *The Sea and the Sword* (London, 1965), pp. 116–28. On the downfall of Gustav IV Adolf: Lagerqvist, pp. 124–6; Elstob, pp. 159–61. For the Russo-Finnish War, Sandstedt, pp. 287–319, 348–71 and Scott, *Sweden*, pp. 292–300. D. Kirby (ed.),

Finland and Russia, 1808–1920 (London, 1975), pp. 12–24 includes all the basic documents on Alexander's Finnish policy. For the lynching of Fersen see Lagerqvist, pp. 129–30 and the last chapter of Barton's biography. Jan Dahlstrom's contribution on 'Schnapps, freedom and wenches' in Sandstedt, pp. 388–419 examines the mood of the soldiery at the time of the lynching. For Bernadotte's candidature and election see Gabriel Girod de l'Ain, *Bernadotte Chef de Guerre et Chef d'État* (Paris, 1968), pp. 297–319. Palmer's biography (pp. 164–76) covers his arrival in Stockholm, as well as Napoleon's reactions, and is based on French and Swedish sources. For the causes and course of the 1812 campaign: PWS, pp. 416–30, 445–50; Palmer's *Napoleon in Russia* (London, 1967; rev. ed. 2004) and *Alexander I*; Adam Zamoyski, *1812: Napoleon's Fatal March on Moscow* (London, 2004), with rare Polish and post-Soviet Russian sources as well as the sketch of the army's loot from Vilnius's cathedral. The Tiessenhausen account of life in Vilna: Comtesse de Choiseul-Goufier, *Historical Memoirs* (London, 1904), pp. 90–93, 131–44. On Prussian vacillations and York's conduct see G. A. Craig, *The Politics of the Prussian Army*, pp. 52–63; PWS, pp. 450–59. For Sweden's role in the 1813–14 campaigns: Palmer, *Bernadotte*, Chapter 12. Treaty of Kiel: F. D. Scott, pp. 144–8; PWS, pp. 487–8.

Chapter 14: Peaceful Change?

Peacemaking in Paris and Vienna: H. Nicolson, *Congress of Vienna* (London, 1946); A. Palmer, *The Chancelleries of Europe* (London, 1983), pp. 7–24. Sweden at war with Norway: T. K. Derry, *History of Modern Norway* (London, 1957), pp. 5–16; Scott, *Sweden, Nation's History*, pp. 312–13; Lars Ericsson in Sandstedt, pp. 438–74. On Finland: Singleton, pp. 26–8. For Czartoryski: M. Kukiel, *Czartoryski and European Unity 1770–1861* (Princeton, 1955); Grimsted, *The Foreign Ministers of Alexander*, pp. 122–3; and W. Zawadzki, *A Man of Honour* (Oxford, 1993). For extracts from the Vienna Congress Treaty see Michael Hurst (ed.), *Key Treaties for the Great Powers 1814–1914* (Newton Abbot, 1972), pp. 41–96. On Germany and the Vienna Settlement: PWS, pp. 538–47; E. E. Kraeke, *Metternich's German Policy, 1814–1815* (Princeton, 1985). For the *Zollverein* and the German economy in general: J. H. Clapham, *Economic Development of France and Germany, 1815–1914* (Cambridge, 1945), pp. 85–101, 107–113. On the Sound Dues 1814–56: C. E. Hill, pp. 222–266, supplemented by the ODNB for William Hutt MP. The fullest study of the Decembrists is M. Raeff (ed.), *The Decembrist Movement* (Englewood Cliffs, 1966); see also N. V. Riasanovsky, *History of Russia* (Oxford, 1984), pp. 320–3; and the background in Vilnius, as portrayed in N. Ascherson, *Black Sea*, pp. 145–7. R. F. Leslie, *Polish Politics and the Revolution of November 1830* (London, 1956) provides background and foreground. J. H. Gleason, *The Genesis of Russophobia in Great Britain* (Harvard, 1950) stresses the importance of Polish affairs in moulding British opinion. The fullest account of Charles XIV John's reign is in Swedish, the third volume of Tson Höjer, *Carl XIV Johann Konungstiden* (Stockholm, 1960, completing a project of which earlier volumes appeared in 1939 and 1943). The three volumes were translated into French and in 1970 published in a two volume edition in Paris. See the biographies of Bernadotte by Girod and by Palmer. For Queen Desideria: G. Girod de l'Ain, *Désirée Clary* (Paris, 1959). Industrial development in Sweden: Scott, *Sweden History*, pp. 444–7: on Gota Canal and railways see also Elstob, pp. 183–4 and Palmer, *Bernadotte*, pp. 238–9. For the *Fürst Menschikoff* paddle steamer: Matz, *Sea Lanes*, p. 81. On Hierta and the *Aftonbladet*: Palmer, pp. 242–3 and Lagerqvist, pp. 140–146. For the tsar's visit and the Slite Question: D. Kirby, *The Baltic World 1772–1993* (London, 1995) and Palmer's biography, p. 245.

Chapter 15: Black, Red and Gold

For the tsar's reaction to the 1848 revolutions: W. Bruce Lincoln, *Nicholas I* (London, 1978), pp. 278–80. On the revolutions in northern Europe: Kirby, pp. 107–9, 111–13; L. Steefel, *The Schleswig-Holstein Question* (Cambridge, Mass., 1932). For central Europe: A. Palmer, *Metternich* (London, 1972), pp. 204–9 and (including Russian response) *Chancelleries of Europe*, pp. 81–95; V. Valentin (cited Ch. 1, above); L. B. Namier, *1848: The Revolution of the Intellectuals* in *Proceedings of the British Academy for 1944* (London, 1948), Vol. 30, pp. 1–124. See also Namier, *Vanished Supremacies* (London, 1958). For Nesselrode's policy and proposals: *Lettres et Papiers du Chancelier Comte de Nesselrode* (Paris, 1912), Vol. 9, pp. 92–95, and W. E. Mosse, *The European Powers and the German Question* (Cambridge, 1958), pp. 19–20. For the embryonic German navy see Holger Hervig, '*Luxury Fleet*', *The Imperial German Navy 1888–1918* (London, 1980), pp. 9–12; E. Gröner, *German Warships 1815–1945* (Annapolis, 1990), Vol. 1.

Chapter 16: Bombarding Bomarsund

For Kossuth's speeches, see the anonymous *Louis Kossuth, His Speeches in England* (London, 1851). In this chapter I have drawn heavily on my *The Chancelleries of Europe* and *The Banner of Battle: the Story of the Crimean War* (London, 1987), for which I had access to Foreign Secretary Clarendon's papers in the Bodleian Library, Oxford. Lord Dundonald's chemical warfare project, and Faraday's comments, are in the Martin Papers, as British Library Add. Mss. 41370. See also B. Greenhill and A. Giffard, *The British Assault on Finland 1854–55* (London, 1988). For the diplomatic context of the naval campaign: P. W. Schroeder, *Austria, Great Britain and the Crimean War* (Ithaca, NY, 1972) and, for the later phases and peace settlement, W. E. Mosse, *The Rise and Fall of the Crimean System, 1855–1871* (London, 1963). The Revd Edgar Hughes, *Two Summer Cruises with the Baltic Fleet* (London, 1855) recounts his odyssey aboard *The Pet*. The Tsarevich's letters to Queen Anna Pavlovna are in Jackman, *Romanov Relations*, pp. 341, 344, 345. Hurst, *Key Treaties*, Vol. 1, includes the treaty of Stockholm of 21 November 1855 on pp. 315–16, the peace treaty of Paris (pp. 317–28) and the Åland Islands Convention of 1856 on pp.

332–4.

Chapter 17: Finns, Poles and Danes

Hugh Seton-Watson, *The Russian Empire 1801–1917* (Oxford, 1967) for Finland, pp. 328, 415–16 and Poland, pp. 370–8; see also W. E. Mosse, *Alexander II and the Modernisation of Russia* (London, 1958), pp. 107–25. Kirby's *Finland and Russia* includes Alexander II's speech to the Diet in 1863 and other relevant extracts, pp. 50–55. On Estonian language revival: Seton-Watson, p. 414 and Kirby, *Baltic World*, pp. 128–30. R. F. Leslie, *Reform and Insurrection in Russian Poland 1856–1865* (London, 1963) is excellent. R. W. Tims, *Germanizing the Prussian Poles* (New York, 1941) deals mainly with events after 1894 but is useful for the earlier period, too. Steefel, *Schleswig-Holstein Question* may be supplemented by A. Palmer, *Bismarck* (London, 1976), Chapter 7. Lothar Gall, *Bismarck, der Weisse Revolutionar* (Frankfurt, 1980), pp. 293–313, is a detailed, revisionist study of the Duchies Question, with pp. 340–65 on the links between the wars of 1864 and 1866. The best account of the power struggle in the 1860s remains A. J. P. Taylor, *The Struggle for Mastery in Europe* (Oxford, 1954), pp. 142–206.

Chapter 18: Towards Democracy

Hungry Sixties and emigration: Elstob, p. 187; Lagerqvist, pp. 142, 148; Kirby, *Baltic World*, pp. 141–2, 224–5; Singleton, *Finland*, pp. 86, 88 (with the context of Topelius's advice, 'Emigrate or die', explained on p. 86). A. W. Hoglund, *Finnish Immigrants in America* (Madison, 1960) is primarily concerned with the period after 1880. Dr Kirby's analysis of mid-century social life in the Baltic lands (pp. 144–68) is interesting reading. For Swedish industrialism and railways: Lagerqvist, p. 145; Elstob, pp. 186–8. D. Verney, *Parliamentary Reform in Sweden, 1866–1921* (Oxford, 1957) amplifies the general histories.

Chapter 19: National Pride

For Russian fleet modernization, the *Rurik* alarm and the British response see A. J. Marder, *British Naval Policy 1880–1905, The Anatomy of British Sea Power* (New York, 1940; London, n.d.), pp. 162–4. T. Ropp, *The Development of a Modern Navy* was originally a doctoral thesis on the French marine 1871–1904 but was published in book form, edited by S. S. Roberts (Annapolis, 1987) and is useful for Franco-Russian naval policy. On Estonian and Latvian folk festivals: Kirby, *Baltic World*, pp. 129–30. For Pobedonostsev, see his *Reflections of a Russian Statesman* (London, 1898); for his policies in action see Seton-Watson, pp. 461–87, and for their consequences, J. S. Curtiss, *Church and State in Russia, 1900–1917* (New York, 1940). E. Thaden (ed.), *Russification in the Baltic Provinces and Finland* (Bloomington, 1981) has some useful contributions, especially by Andrejs Plakans (see also his *The*

Latvians, pp. 100–101). For Russian Jews at the turn of the century: Seton-Watson, pp. 493–6; for anti-Semitism in the 1890s see particularly L. Greenberg, *The Jews in Russia: The Struggle for Emancipation* (New York, 1976), Vol. 2, pp. 30–47. On Finland: Singleton, pp. 96–99; Kirby, *Finland and Russia*, pp. 68–97, including on pp. 92–3 contemporary reports on the 1902 call-up riots and the Cossack attack in Senate Square. Dr Kirby also considers Finland in his *Baltic World*, pp. 181–4. J. Paasivirta, *Imperial Borderland* (London, 1995) is a detailed study of Finnish russification in the Bobrikov era. For Alexander III's 'no bombs, no bandits' remark see the entertaining article by Coryne Hall in *Royalty Digest* (Ticehurst, 2003), Vol. 12, no. 11, May 2003, pp. 329–33, the first of two articles based on J. and P. Tuomi-Nikula's illustrated *Kejsaren I Skärgarden* (Helsinki, 2003). On the fleet's voyage to the Far East, the Dogger Bank crisis and its consequences: Marder, pp. 428, 439–41, 476, 513, 530–33 (with card 'in disgraceful memory of the Russian navy' reproduced on p. 439). G. P. Gooch and H. W. V. Temperley, *British Documents on the Origins of the War, 1898–1914*, Vol. 4 (London, 1929) prints 26 documents on the Dogger Bank incident; they include Edward VII's indignant comment (p. 6) and an account of the ambassador's audience with the tsar, reporting Nicholas's visit to the fleet at Reval (pp. 25–8).

Chapter 20: The Last Years of the Long Peace

For Russia in general in this period: Seton-Watson, pp. 598–649. The most detailed treatment of events in the capital is in G. Surh, *1905 in St Petersburg* (Stanford, 1989), but for Gapon's background and the petition see W. Sablinsky, *The Road to Bloody Sunday* (Princeton, 1976). Kirby, *Baltic World*, pp. 227–235 covers events in the Baltic provinces but see also Plakans, pp. 104–7 and T. Raun, *Estonia and the Estonians* (Stanford, rev. ed. 1991), pp. 72–88. Kirby, *Finland and Russia* includes material on the strike week, pp. 105–17. R. Lindgren, *Norway-Sweden: Union, Disunion and Scandinavian Integration* (Princeton, 1969) is comprehensive; concise treatment in Lagerqvist, pp. 157–8 and Kirby, *Baltic World*, pp. 185–9. For the tsar and Kaiser meeting at Björkö: A. Palmer, *The Kaiser* (London, 1978), pp. 113–16 and William's retrospective comment on p. 220. A. J. P. Taylor's *Struggle for Mastery* offers a wise assessment of Björkö (pp. 432–4). Robert Massie, *Dreadnought* (London, 1992) is a readable account of British policy 1898–1914 with an emphasis on naval rivalry, but the basic source remains A. J. Marder, *From the Dreadnought to Scapa Flow* (London, 1961–68), Vols 1–3. Seven of 31 articles in F. H. Hinsley (ed.), *British Foreign Policy under Sir Edward Grey* (Cambridge, 1977) are relevant; the book is abbreviated below as BFP. On the Anglo-Russian Entente: R. P. Churchill, *The Anglo-Russian Convention of 1907* (Cedar Rapids, 1939); R. T. Sweet and R. T. B. Langhorne, 'Great Britain and Russia, 1907–1914', BFP, pp. 236–55. See also H. Nicolson, *Lord Carnock* (London, 1930), pp. 232–57. For the Reval meeting: BFP, pp. 244–45; P. Magnus, *King Edward VII* (London, 1964), pp. 404–5 and 407–9. On Stolypin: Seton-Watson, Chapter 18; Nicolson, pp. 225–8;

Kirby, *Finland and Russia*, pp. 123–28. On the Åland islands: F. A. Lindberg, *Scandinavia in Great Power Politics, 1905–1908* (Stockholm, 1958) and D. W. Sweet, 'The Baltic in British Diplomacy before the First World War', *Historical Journal*, Vol. 13 (Cambridge, 1970). J. van der Kiste, *Northern Crowns* (Stroud, 1996) is sympathetic to Scandinavian monarchism. For Gustav V and the farmers' protest: Kirby, *Baltic World*, pp. 240–1, 251–2, 272.

Chapter 21: Emperors at War, 1914–1917

For this chapter and its successor I profited from M. Gilbert, *First World War* (London, 1994) and J. Keegan, *The First World War* (London, 1998), and the specialist articles in the Purnell compendium edited by B. Pitt and P. Young, *History of the First World War* (London, 1969–71), 8 vols (cited below as Purnell). For Kiel regatta 1914: M. Gilbert, *Sir Horace Rumbold* (London, 1973), p. 105; W. Görlitz (ed.), *The Kaiser and his Court* (journal of Admiral von Müller, London, 1961), p. 2. The best brief collection of documents on the coming of war is I. Geiss (ed.), *July 1914* (London and New York, 1967); the Kaiser's 'right soon' comment is on a despatch from the German ambassador to the Chancellor from Vienna on 30 June. J. Joll, *1914: The Unspoken Assumptions* (London, 1984) stands out among many studies on the war crisis, but see also F. Fischer, *War of Illusions* (London, 1975), pp. 470–515. For the first phase of the Baltic naval war: P. G. Halpern, *A Naval History of World War I* (Annapolis and London, 1974). For the land fighting: J. W. Wheeler-Bennett, *Hindenburg, The Wooden Titan* (London, 1936); D. Goodspeed, *Ludendorff* (London, 1966); D. Showalter, *Tannenberg* (Hampden, 1991); N. Stone, *The Eastern Front, 1914–1917* (London, 1975); M. Hoffmann, *War Diaries and Other Papers* (London, 1929). For Finland: Singleton, pp. 103–6. For Latvia, Plakans, pp. 113–16. T. Komarnicki, *The Rebirth of the Polish Republic* (London, 1957) covers the war years and the peace settlement; P. Latawski, *The Reconstruction of Poland 1914–1923* (London, 1992). For German policy on Poland: F. Fischer, *Germany's Aims in the First World War* (London, 1967), pp. 138–44; for League of Foreign Peoples of Russia, ibid., pp. 125, 145–6. For Sweden, see in general, S. Koblik, *Sweden the Neutral Victor* (Stockholm, 1972) and for Norway's relations with the belligerents, O. Riste, *The Neutral Ally* (London, 1965). For Churchill, Fisher and northern waters: Halpern, pp. 101–05; Marder, *Dreadnought to Scapa Flow*, Vol. 2, pp. 178–90; M. Gilbert, *Winston S. Churchill* (London, 1971), Vol. 3, pp. 52–3, 225–6, 259, 265, 272 ('access' ultimate object), 324, 348. M. Wilson, *Baltic Assignment: British Submariners in Russia, 1914–1919* (London, 1985) is comprehensive. Nicholas II and need to avoid a second Tsushima, Halpern, p. 184; on Nepenin and demoralization, ibid., pp. 211–13; fullest treatment is in E. Mawdsley, *The Russian Revolution and the Baltic Fleet* (London, 1978). For German support for Lenin and his return to Petrograd: Fischer, *Germany's Aims*, pp. 365–9; R. Payne, *The Life and Death of Lenin* (New York, 1964), pp. 278, 285–319; L. Trotsky, *History of the Russian Revolution* (London, 1934), pp. 307–12 and the article by Harry Hanak in Purnell,

(London, 1974) is comprehensive. So too is Ezra Mendelsohn, *The Jews of East Central Europe between the World Wars* (Bloomington, 1983). For Sweden, Denmark and Finland see the national histories cited above and Kirby, *Baltic World*, pp. 303–16. Andres Kasekamp, *The Radical Right in Interwar Estonia* (London and New York, 2000) is an excellent study, wider in scope than the title suggests and including much of interest on Finland. The R.I.I.A. survey, *The Baltic States* (London, 1938) remains a quarry of information. Israel Getzler, *Kronstadt 1917–1921; the Fate of a Soviet Democracy* (Cambridge, 1984) is a pioneer study, as also is J. Hiden, *The Baltic States and Weimar Ostpolitik* (Cambridge, 1987). The most judicious assessment of Soviet Russia between the wars is in Hosking, pp. 427–92. On the Depression and its consequences, Macartney and Palmer, pp. 272–300, updated by Kirby, *Baltic World*, pp. 311–16. The clearest narrative account of German affairs 1930–33 is G. Craig, *Germany 1866–1945* (Oxford, 1978), pp. 534–68. For the Lapua movement see Kasekamp, pp. 71–2, 142–52 and Kirby, pp. 321–2.

Chapter 24: Hitler's Challenge

The ceremony at the Potsdam Garrison Church: A. Bullock, *Hitler* (London, 1954), pp. 242–4. Pilsudski's reactions are a matter of dispute: Macartney and Palmer, p. 305; Hans Roth, *Polen und Europa* (Tubingen, 1957), pp. 65–7, 75–7. On Danzig: C. Kimmich, *The Free City* (London, 1968) for the years 1919–34 and H. Levine, *Hitler's Free City* (London, 1973) for the Danzig Nazis, 1925–39. Beck's memoirs *Dernier Rapport* (Neuchatel, 1951) convey both his personality and his policy. He is much criticized in the French ambassador's memoirs: L. Noël, *L'Agression allemande contre la Pologne* (Paris, 1946). See Eden's impressions of him in Lord Avon, *Facing the Dictators* (London, 1962), pp. 466–7. Eden comment to Litvinov on British interests, ibid., p. 149. On the Anglo-German naval treaty: Ian Kershaw, *Hitler, 1889–1936* (London, 1998), pp. 556–8 and Michael Bloch, *Ribbentrop* (London, 1994), pp. 69–73. For German naval policy, J. Dülffer, *Weimar, Hitler und die Marine, 1920–1939* (Düsseldorf, 1973). The best survey of the immediate origins of the Second World War is D. C. Watt, *How War Came* (London, 1989). The English translations of *Documents on German Foreign Policy* (henceforth DGFP) are in 6 volumes for Series C (years 1933–36) and 13 volumes for Series D (1936–41); the directive for action against Memel is D, Vol. 4, pp. 99–100. For recovery of Memel, Watt, pp. 156–8. Lipski's comments on significance of Memel are cited from his 'final report' in L. B. Namier, *Diplomatic Prelude 1938–39* (London, 1948), p. 88. Andrew Roberts, *The Holy Fox* (London, 1991) is both a fascinating biography of Halifax and a refreshingly revisionist assessment of British policy, particularly good on the Polish problem (pp. 147–50) and Chamberlain's attitude to Russia (pp. 154, 156, 158, 160). The diarists who noted backing for a Polish guarantee were Harold Nicolson, *Diaries and Letters, 1930–39* (London, 1966), p. 394 and Channon in R. Rhodes James (ed.), *Chips* (London, 1967), p. 190. The directive for the attack on Poland is DGFP, Series D, Vol. 6, pp. 224–5.

Beck, p. 186, mentions Ribbentrop's comment on Poland and the Black Sea. Some libraries list Admiral Plunket's *Mission to Moscow* (Wareham, 1966), with the author's name as Drax. For the Baltic republics and their neighbours: D. M. Crowe, *The Baltic States and the Great Powers; Foreign Relations 1938–1940* (Oxford, 1992); and with great clarity in Hiden and Salmon, who cite the warning on Estonians fighting on the German side, p. 103. The making of the Nazi–Soviet Pact is treated at length in Ian Kershaw, *Hitler 1936–45* (London, 2000), pp. 224 ff. and A. Bullock, *Hitler and Stalin* (London, 1991), pp. 679–83. For the last weeks of peace: Robert's *Holy Fox* and Watt.

Chapter 25: Nazi–Soviet Partnership

Basic to this chapter are: M. Gilbert, *The Second World War* (London, 1989); the R.I.I.A. survey, *The Initial Triumph of the Axis* (London, 1958); C. Barnett, *Engage the Enemy More Closely* (London, 1991; Penguin edition, 2001), pp. 93–139 for the Royal Navy; W. Carlgren, *Swedish Foreign Policy during the Second World War* (London, 1977), supplemented by Roberts, *Holy Fox*, pp. 231–5 for misunderstanding over Swedish mediation in 1940; and the works by Crowe and Bloch cited above. On Poland: R. M. Kennedy, *The German Campaign in Poland* (Washington DC, 1956); J. Garlinski, *Poland in the Second World War* (London, 1985). Avraham Tory's Kaunas ghetto diary, *Surviving the Holocaust* (Cambridge, Mass., 1990) is deeply moving; it is strongly hostile to Lithuanians. Sir Martin Gilbert's *Atlas of the Holocaust* (London, 1982) is more graphically tragic than his authoritative *The Holocaust* (London, 1986). Paul Allen's *Katyn* (New York, 1991), 'the untold story of Stalin's Polish massacre', seems definitive. For Ribbentrop in Moscow: A. Bullock (ed.), *The Ribbentrop Memoirs* (London, 1954), p. 130. For the Soviet move against the Baltic states: R. J. Misiunas and R. Taagepara, *The Baltic States, Years of Dependence, 1940–1990* (London, 1993); Plakans, *Latvians*, pp. 142–3; and Hiden and Salmon, pp. 110–12. Churchill, *The Second World War* (London, 1948), p. 364 for the inception of Operation Catherine, with basic Minute in Appendix G. A. J. Marder, 'Winston is Back', *English Historical Review* (London, 1972), supplement 5, considers the project at length; see also Gilbert, *Winston S. Churchill* (London, 1983), Vol. 6, *Finest Hour*, pp. 26–7, 37–8, 100–1, 103–4, 194–5. Finland: W. R. Trotter, *The Winter War* (London, 2003); A. Upton, *Finland 1939–1940* (London, 1974); M. Jakobsen, *The Diplomacy of the Winter War* (Cambridge, Mass., 1961). For Scandinavia in 1940: R. Petrow, *The Invasion and Occupation of Denmark and Norway* (London, 1974); T. K. Derry, *The Campaign in Norway* (London, 1952) and C. Barnett, pp. 97–139. Gallivare as an objective: Churchill, Vol. 1, pp. 443, 481, 485, 499. Sovietization of the Baltic republics: Misiunas and Taagepara, cited above; Plakans, pp. 143–5; Katyu's tale is in Anna Reid, *The Shaman's Coat* (London, 2002), pp. 54–7. German preparations for Barbarossa can be followed in Kershaw, pp. 381–9. Bullock, *Hitler and Stalin*, pp. 794–7 cites the memoirs of Zhukov and Kuznetsov to assess the mood in the Kremlin on the eve of the invasion. So, too, does Gilbert, *Second World War*, noting on p. 196 the passage of trains across the demarcation line four hours before the invasion.

Chapter 26: Nazi–Soviet War

John Erickson's *The Road to Stalingrad* (London, 1975) and *The Road to Berlin* (London, 1983) remain masterly narratives; Alexander Werth, *Russia at War* (London, 1964) is a fine account from an eye-witness. Gilbert's *Second World War* provides a good survey, especially informative on Polish affairs and the terrible fate of the Jews. For the occupation of the Baltic republics: Misiunas and Taagepara in general; Kasekamp, pp. 134–6 on Estonia; Plakans, pp. 148–52 on Latvia. DGFP Series D, Vol. 13 is a revealing source: document nos. 3, 6, 18, 39 for Lithuania; nos. 4 and 39 for Latvia; nos. 39 and 223 for Estonia. Jewish persecution: works cited above, together with Gilbert, *Atlas*, map 87, p. 77 on deaths in Lithuania. The siege of Leningrad is covered at length by H. E. Salisbury (London, 1969) and more concisely by Alan Wykes (London, 1968). For Finland's continuation war: A. Upton, *Finland in Crisis, 1940–1941* (London, 1964) and Singleton, pp. 130–33. DGFP Series D, Vol. 13 includes: exchanges between Berlin and President Ryti, nos. 52, 301 and 436; a report of talks between General Keitel and Mannerheim, no. 228. For Arctic convoys: C. Barnett, pp. 693–752. On the bombing of Lübeck: Harris, *Bomber Offensive* (London, 1947), p. 106; Henry Probert, *Bomber Harris, His Life and Times* (London, 2001), p. 223 for 'built more like a firelighter than human habitation' comment. For Swedish reactions in 1941–43 see Carlgren, cited above, and the *Revue d'histoire de la deuxième guerre mondiale* (Paris, January 1978), no. 108, which is entirely devoted to Sweden during the war. See also DGFP Series D, Vol. 13, document nos. 8, 17, 172 (transit rights); nos. 16, 430, 574 (King Gustav's pro-German sentiments); no. 181 for the English prisoner-of-war found on a transit train; and no. 364 for threats from Ribbentrop. Gilbert's *Atlas*, maps 213–214 on pp. 166–7 for Jewish refugees in Sweden. Harold Nicolson's visit to Sweden: Nicolson, *Letters and Diaries* (London, 1967), pp. 325–8. For Denmark in 1943 see H. Nissen (ed.), *Scandinavia in the Second World War* (Minneapolis, 1983), pp. 220–38; and, for resistance outside Copenhagen, Christine Sutherland, *Monica* (New York, 1990), pp. 113–220. On Peenemünde see F. H. Hinsley (ed.), *British Intelligence in the Second World War* (London, 1984), Vol. 3, pt. 1, pp. 337–443, *passim*. For Lt-Commander Christiansen, Gilbert, p. 453. For Finland's separate peace see, in addition to works cited above, Mannerheim, *Memoirs* (London, 1954). For military aspects of the Warsaw Rising, Erickson, *Road to Berlin*, pp. 329–88; background politics, S. Mikolajczyk, *The Pattern of Soviet Domination* (London, 1948). For the campaign in Germany Erickson can be supplemented by Antony Beevor, *Berlin* (London, 2002). Escape from Cadinen, Louis Ferdinand of Prussia, *Rebel Prince* (Toronto, 1952), p. 202. Fate of Schönhausen: Palmer, *Bismarck*, p. 269.

Chapter 27: Tragedy of Victory

Arnold and Veronica Toynbee (eds), *The Realignment of Europe* (London, 1955) has a valuable chapter by S. Lowery on the peace settlement of 1947. E. Wiskemann's *Germany's Eastern Neighbours* (Oxford, 1956) is partly concerned with the Oder–Neisse Line. D. Kirby, *Baltic World*, pp. 377–408 considers the affluence of the Nordic welfare states after the war. On Sweden from 1945 to 2000 see Lagerqvist, pp. 182–95. R. Allison, *Finland's Relations with the Soviet Union 1944–1984* (London, 1985) is a basic study. M. Laar, *War in the Woods* (Washington DC, 1992) is an account of Estonian resistance from 1946 to 1956. A. Lieven, *The Baltic Revolution* (London, 1993) is a mine of information, with detailed knowledge of the region. Andres Küng, *A Dream of Freedom* (Cardiff, 1980) includes the first serious study of the Forest Brothers but covers events in all three Baltic republics. For Latvia see also Plakans, pp. 167–94. For Poland: N. Ascherson, *The Struggle for Poland* (London, 1987) and N. Davies, *Heart of Europe* (Oxford, 1984) place events in a historical context. N. Bethell's *Gomulka, his Poland and his communism* (London, 1969) survives as an interesting period piece. M. Craig, *The Crystal Spirit* (London, 1986) is mainly a tribute to Wałęsa but is also enlightening on Jaruselski.

Chapter 28: Baltic Way

For much of this chapter I am again indebted to Lieven's *Baltic Revolution*, especially for the Song Festivals and the events of which he was an eyewitness. D. Remick, *Lenin's Tomb* (London, 1993) also records personal impressions, notably in Vilnius and Riga. A. Senn, *Lithuania Awakening* (Berkeley, 1990) concentrates on the years 1988 to 1990. Clare Thomson, *The Singing Revolution* (London, 1992) recounts a 'political journey' through the Baltic republics. R. Sakva, *Gorbachev and his Reforms* (London, 1990) looks at their effect on the Baltic republics. B. Arkadic and M. Karlsson, *Economic Survey of the Baltic States* (London, 1992) was, significantly, sponsored by the Swedish Foreign Ministry. Hiden and Salmon's revised edition continues as far as March 1994. For more recent events I have relied on *Keesing's Contemporary Archives* and on good journalism, especially in *The Times* and *The Independent*. On occasions I have read with interest the weekly *Baltic Times*: no. 318, for the first week of August 2002, reported the dispute over the war memorial in Pärnu, a city I visited soon afterwards. While travelling in the Baltic republics I consulted Lonely Planet's *Estonia, Latvia, Lithuania* (Footscray, Victoria, 2000), chief editor Nicola Williams, and found it informative, entertaining and totally reliable.

Index

Åbo, Finland, 185–6
Absalon, Archbishop of Lund, 40, 68
Adalbert, Prince of Prussia, 204–5
Adalbert, St, 36
Adam of Bremen, 3
Adamkus, Valdas, 404
Adolf II, Count of Holstein, 38, 40–1
Adolf Frederick, King of Sweden, 152
Aesti (people), 18
Aftonbladet (Swedish newspaper), 195–6
Ahmed III, Ottoman Sultan, 137
Aho, Esko, 401
Aix-la-Chapelle, Congress of (1818), 190
Åland archipelago: position, 8; Vikings in, 22;
  Peter I assembles invasion force in, 142; skills,
  185; attacked in Crimean War, 210–11;
  demilitarization agreement (1856), 214, 250;
  Russian attempts to refortify, 250–1; German
  troops reach (1918), 277; remains under
  Finnish sovereignty, 295; Finnish task force
  occupies (1941), 348
Albert of Mecklenburg, King of Sweden, 68–70
Albert von Buxhoevden, Bishop of Uxhüll,
  43–4
Albert von Hohenzollern, 80–2, 87
Albrecht, Bishop of Stettin, 39
Alcuin of York, 21
Aldercreutz, General Carl Johan, Count, 172
Alexander I, Tsar: confers privileges on Finland,
  9; Catherine II designs baby clothes for, 147;
  accession, 163–4; in Napoleonic wars,
  164–5, 168, 175; negotiates Treaty of Tilsit,
  168–9; lifts trade restrictions, 175; resumes
  war against Napoleon, 176–7; and
  Napoleon's invasion of Russia, 177–9; policy
  in Finland, 184–5; and Polish question,
  186–7; progressive reforms, 190; death, 191
Alexander II, Tsar (*earlier* Grand Duke), 209,
  211–14, 215, 217–20, 233
Alexander III, Tsar, 232–3, 236–7
Alexander IV, Pope, 49
Alexander VI, Pope, 78
Alexander, Colonel Harold (*later* Field Marshal
  Earl), 285
Alexander Nevsky, Prince of Novgorod, 48–9

Alexander-Sinclair, Rear-Admiral Sir Edwyn,
  280–1
Alexandra Feodorovna, Empress of Nicholas II
  of Russia, 268
Alexandra, Queen of Edward VII, 248
Alexis Romanov, Tsar, 116–17, 121
Algarotti, Count Francesco, 10, 12
Allenstein, 292
Altmark, Treaty of (1629), 99, 104
Älvsborg, Sweden, 86, 88–9, 95, 97
amber, 4–5
Amiens, Peace of (1802–3), 164
Anckarström, Captain Jacob, 161
Ancylus, Lake, 3–4, 6
Andrew II, King of Hungary, 46
Andropov, Yuri, 393
Andrusevo, Truce of (1667), 121
Angantyr, ruler of Jutland, 19
Anholt, 170
Anklam, Germany, 13
Anna Pavlovna, Grand Duchess, 11
Anna, Princess of Kiev (Vladimir's wife), 34
Anne, Tsarina (*earlier* Duchess of Courland),
  138, 146
Anschluss (Austria), 315
Anskar, Archbishop of Hamburg, 31–2
Anti-Comintern Pact, 316
anti-Semitism *see* Jews
Anund Jakob, Swedish king, 32
Apraxin, General Feodor, 140, 143
Arakcheev, Count Nikolai, 190–1
Arboga, Diet of (1435), 72
Archangel, 88
Arctic convoys (Second World War), 355
Armed Neutrality, League of, 162–4
Armfelt, Alexander, 217
Askold, Viking earl, 22–3
Atterdag *see* Valdemar IV, King of Denmark
Augustenburg family, 221
Augustine, St, Archbishop of Canterbury, 30–1
Augustus II (the Strong), King of Poland-
  Lithuania, 123, 127–8, 130, 132–3, 144
Augustus III, King of Poland, 151
Aurora (Russian cruiser), 238, 239, 266, 270
Austerlitz, battle of (1805), 165

Austria: frontiers advanced, 151; revolutionary wars with France, 158; in anti-Napoleon alliance, 164–5, 175; and Treaty of Vienna, 187; and Schleswig-Holstein Question (1863), 222–3; Prussians defeat (1866), 223–4; and outbreak of 1914–18 war, 252–5; strikes (1918), 274; *Anschluss* (1938), 315
Austrian Succession, War of (1740–7), 49
Azov, 127

Baedeker, Carl: *Northern Germany*, 264
'Baedeker raids' (Second World War), 356
Baghdad: Vikings threaten, 24
Bagramyan, General I. K., 366–7
Bagration, General Piotr, 172
Baird, Charles, 149
Balashov, General Alexander D., 177–8
Balfour, Arthur James, 246, 281
Balk, Provincial Master of Teutonic Knights, 47
Balodis, General Janis, 285, 307–8, 344
Baltic Assembly, 398
Baltic Council, 398
Baltic Germans, 220–1, 235, 242, 250, 259, 261, 282, 285
Baltic Sea, the: icing, 2, 4; names, 3; form and geography, 5–10; early settlement, 15–16, 35, 38; Royal Navy in, 139–40, 142, 170–1; closed to British shipping in French revolutionary wars, 162; naval and military activities in Crimean War, 207–13; treaty guarantees *status quo* (1908), 250; in First World War, 255–66, 269; British naval force in (1918–19), 280–1, 283–4, 286–7; co-operative bloc proposed, 301–2; as tourist region, 312; in Second World War, 332–3, 350
Baltic Way (1989), 394, 396
Baltika Song Festival, 394, 398
Baltische Landswehr, 282, 285
Baner, Johan, 110
Bar, Confederation of, 151
Barbarossa, Operation (1941), 345–6, 348
Barclay de Tolly, General Mikhail Bogdanovich, Prince, 172, 177–8
Bartel, Kasmierz, 300
Barthou, Jean Louis, 311
Baruch, Bernard, 376
Barwalde, Treaty of (1631), 107
Basiliscus, Emperor, 19
Beauharnais, Eugène de, 173
Beck, David, 114
Beck, Colonel Joseph, 311, 315–16, 318, 321–2, 324, 327
beer: trade in, 60
Beevor, Antony: *Berlin*, 371
Belgium: in French revolutionary wars, 157–8
Belts, the, 3–4
Bem, Jozef, 206
Beneke, Paul, 61

Bennigsen, General Leonty (Levin) von, 167–8, 177
Berestechko, battle of (1651), 118
Berg, Count Theodor, 217
Bergen, Norway, 62
Bergman, Ingmar, 227
Berlin: described, 12; dominance, 224; Soviet army attacks and captures, 370, 373; Soviet blockade (1949), 378; rioting (1953), 386
Berling, General Zygmunt, 368–70
Bermondt-Avalov, Colonel P. M., 285–6
Bernadotte, Count Folke, 378
Bernadotte, Marshal *see* Charles XIV Johann, King of Sweden
Bernard of Saxe-Weimar, 110
Bestushev-Ryumin, Field Marshal A., 149
Bethmann Hollweg, Theobald von, 261, 266
Bible, Holy: Scandinavian translations, 82
Bierut, Boleslaw, 368–9
Birger Jarl Magnusson, 49
Birgitta, St (Birgitta Gudmarsson), 66–7
Birka, Sweden, 27, 29
Biron, Johannes, Duke of Courland, 146, 148
Bischoff, Major Josef, 286
Bismarck (German battleship), 4, 341
Bismarck, Prince Otto von, 221–3, 230–1, 290
Bismarck, Countess Sybille von, 373
Björkö agreement (1905), 245–7, 284
Bjorn, King of Svealand, 31
Black Death, 67
Blanche of Namur, Queen of Sweden, 66
Blücher (German heavy cruiser), 338
Blücher, Marshal Gebhard Leberecht von, 166
Blücher, Wippart von, 365
Bluhme, Christian, 223
Bobrikov, General Nikolai, 236–7
Bogislav, Duke of Pomerania, 106
Boleslaw I (the Brave), King of Poland, 36–7
Boleslaw II (the Bold), King of Poland, 36–7
Boleslaw V (the Bashful), King of Poland, 37
Bolsheviks: win power in Russia, 270, 272
Bomarsund, East Åland, 9, 210–11, 214
Bona Sforza, Queen of Sigismund I of Poland, 81
Bonaparte, Jerome, 213
Boniface VIII, Pope, 52
Bor-Komorowski *see* Komorowski, General Tadeusz
Bornhöft, battle of (1813), 181
Bornholm (island): position, 7; seized by pirates, 62; Swedish seasonal workers in, 227; German garrison surrenders to Russia, 374
Bornhöved, battle of (1227), 41, 65
Bothnia, Gulf of: extent, 7
Brandenburg-Prussia, 116–17
Brannkyrka, battle of (1517), 74
Branting, Hjalmar, 296–7
Brazauskas, Algirdas, 395, 397
Breitenfeld, battles of: (1631), 107; (1642), 110

Bremen: supplies beer, 60
Bremer, Frederika: *Hertha*, 227
Brest-Litovsk, Treaty of (1917), 270, 274–5, 278
Brezhnev, Leonid, 389, 393
Briesmann, Johann, 80
Britain: economic ties with Russia, 149; in anti-Napoleon alliance, 164–5; trade sanctions against Napoleon, 167–8; bombards Copenhagen (1807), 170; Sweden declares war on (1810), 174–5; Baltic commerce, 189; Baltic actions in Crimean War, 207–10; and *Entente Cordiale*, 230, 239, 248; naval development, 231; and German naval threat, 246–7; convention with Russia (1907), 247–8; enters First World War (1914), 255; proposed Baltic strategy in First World War, 264–5; intervention in Russian Civil War, 280–7; abandons gold standard, 304; diplomatic representation in Baltic republics, 313; naval treaty with Germany, 313–14, 318; mutual assistance pact with Poland (1938), 318, 323; declares war on Germany (1939), 325; declares war on Finland (1941), 354–5; bombing campaign against Germany, 355; troops advance to Baltic, 373; *see also* England
Brockdorff-Rantzau, Ulrich, Count von, 266–7
Brömsebo, Peace of (1634), 111
Browne, Anthony, 403
Brune, Marshal Guillaume Marie Anne, 171
Brunkeberg, battle of (1471), 73–4
bubonic plague: in Baltic ports (1625), 100
Bugenhagen, Johann, 83
Bülow, Prince Bernhard Karl von, 245
Bund (General Union of Jewish Workers), 234
Burgundians (people), 16
Burke, Edmund, 158
Byzantium, 18, 23, 25–6

Campbell, Thomas, 159
Canaris, Admiral Wilhelm, 321–2
Canning, George, 170
Canrobert, Marshal François, 212–14
Canute II, St, King of Denmark, 33
Canute VI, King of Denmark, 40
Canute I (the Great), King of the English, Danes and Norwegians, 29, 33
Carlsbad Decrees, 190
Carlsson, Ingvar, 390, 401
carracks (ships), 58
Carteret, John, 2nd Baron (*later* Earl Granville), 143
Casimir I, King of Poland, 36–7
Caspian Sea: Vikings in, 24–5
Cassandra, HMS, 280
Castlereagh, Robert Stewart, Viscount, 183
Cathcart, General William Schaw, 10th Baron, 170, 210

Catherine II (the Great), Empress of Russia: amber room, 5; accession and reign, 146–8, 150–2; meets Gustav III of Sweden, 154; and Polish Question, 156; peace settlement with Turkey, 158; and execution of Louis XVI, 159; death, 161; relations with Sweden, 161
Catherine, Queen of John III of Sweden, 91–2
Catherine (*née* Martha Skavronska; wife of Peter the Great; *later* Empress), 138, 145–6
Catholicism: in Lithuania, 13–14; in Poland, 36–7; in Thirty Years War, 101, 105
Caulaincourt, General Armand-Augustin-Louis, Marquis de, 178
Celsius, Andreas, 153
Cêsis, battle of (1919), 285
Chamberlain, Neville, 317–20, 323, 333
Chancellor, Richard, 88
Charles VIII, King of Denmark, 201
Charles I, King of England, 106
Charles II, King of England, 120
Charles IX, King of France, 90
Charles V, Holy Roman Emperor, 81–2, 85
Charles I Knutsson, King of Sweden, 72–3
Charles IX, King of Sweden (*earlier* Duke of Södermanland), 92–3, 95
Charles X Gustav, King of Sweden (*earlier* Charles Gustav of the Palatinate), 112–13, 116–20
Charles XI, King of Sweden: qualities, 124; regency, 124; war with Denmark, 124–5; reforms, 125–6; reign, 125
Charles XII, King of Sweden: absence abroad, 126, 128; accession, 126–7; and war with Denmark (1700), 128–9; Narva victory (1700), 129–30; Polish policy, 130–2; campaign against Russia, 132–4, 145; Poltava defeat and exile, 135, 137; reaches Stralsund from exile, 137; rules Sweden from exile in Moldova, 137; returns to Sweden (1715–16), 139; death in Norway, 141; Napoleon studies, 176
Charles XIII, King of Sweden, 173–4
Charles XIV Johann, King of Sweden (*formerly* Marshal Bernadotte): in Napoleonic wars, 166; adopted as Swedish king, 173–4; and Russian threat to Napoleon, 176; meets Tsar Alexander, 180, 185; supports Russians against Napoleon, 181; and Swedish sovereignty in Norway, 182–4; travels to Belgium, 182; rule, 194–7; assassination plot against, 195; lifestyle, 195; death, 197
Charles XV, King of Sweden, 221, 226, 228, 243
Charles, Duke of Södermanland, 155, 161
Chatham House, London (Royal Institute of International Affairs), 312
Chaucer, Geoffrey: *The Canterbury Tales*, 53
Chelmno *see* Kulm
Chernenko, Konstantin, 393
Chernyakovsky, General Ivan, 370

Chicherin, Georgi, 287–8, 290, 304
Chlopicki, General Joseph, 192
Christian I, King of Denmark, 72–3
Christian II, King of Denmark, 74–6, 82, 85
Christian III, King of Denmark, 83
Christian IV, King of Denmark, 94–5, 97, 101–2, 104–6, 110–11, 118, 120
Christian VIII, King of Denmark, 222
Christian IX, King of Denmark, 222–3, 228–9
Christian X, King of Denmark, 290, 293, 297, 338–9, 374, 380
Christian, Duke of Augustenburg, 201–3
Christian, Prince of Glücksburg, 204
Christian August, Prince of Schleswig-Holstein, 173
Christian Frederick, Prince of Schleswig-Holstein, 183
Christiania, Norway: built, 94; Charles XIV John and, 196–7; fires, 197
Christianity: introduced to North, 30–4, 39–40, 43–7, 54
Christiansen, Commander Hasager, 361
Christiansø, 8
Christina, Queen of Sweden: and Oxenstierna's regency, 96, 109–10; birth, 108; accession and reign, 112–13; qualities and interests, 112; abdication, conversion and exile, 113–14; influence, 114
Christopher, Count of Oldenburg, 85
Christopher (of Bavaria), King of Three Kingdoms, 72
Churchill, (Sir) Winston: First World War Baltic strategy, 263–5; and British intervention in Russian Civil War, 287; on Soviet Russia, 302; Baltic proposals in Second World War, 332–3, 337; and Norway campaign, 339; limited support for Stalin, 355; and German 'secret weapons', 361; and Polish frontiers, 368–9; fear of Soviet advance into Denmark, 373; on 'iron curtain', 376
Clarendon, George William Frederick Villiers, 4th Earl of, 214
Clausewitz, Karl Marie von, 180
cogs (ships), 58
coinage, Viking, 26–7
Coleridge, Samuel Taylor, 159
Comintern, 303
Confederation of the Rhine, 165
Constantine I, Grand Duke of Russia, 191–3, 218
Constantine I (the Great), Roman Emperor, 19
Constantine, Grand Duke of Warsaw, 187
Constantinople (Mikligadur): Vikings attack, 23, 25
Continental System (Napoleonic), 167, 169–72, 174–5
Copenhagen: name, 14; founded, 40; captured by Hanse-Dutch force (1639), 68; surrenders in Count's War (1534), 83; resists Swedish

attack (1658), 120; Kastellet built, 123; plague deaths, 139; Nelson attacks (1801), 157, 163–4; Gambier bombards (1807), 170; Germans occupy (1940), 338
Copenhagen, Treaty of (1660), 121
Cork and Orrery, Admiral William Henry Dudley Boyle, 12th Earl of, 332–3
Cossacks, 115, 121, 134
Count's War (Denmark, 1533–4), 83, 85
Courland (Kurzeme; Kurland), Duchy of: origins, 17; settled, 35; Sweden suppresses, 122; Russians occupy, 138; revolutionary unrest in, 242; in First World War, 259, 261
Cours (Curonians; people), 17
Cowan, Rear-Admiral Sir Walter, 281, 283–4, 287, 314
Cracow, 37, 90, 187
cricket: and 1939 crisis, 323; in Estonia and Finland, 405
Crimean War (1854–5), 207–12; ends, 213–14
Cromwell, Oliver, 109
Crusades: against Muslims, 38, 51; in North, 39–40, 43–9, 51
Crustenholpe, Magnus, 196
Curie, Marie (née Sklodowska), 234
Curzon Line (Poland), 288
Cyrankiewicz, Josef, 385, 386
Czartoryski, Prince Adam, 168, 176, 186–7, 192–3
Czechoslovakia: Nazi German actions in, 316–17

Dabrowski, Henryk, 168
Dahlberg, Governor General of Riga, 127–8
Dahlerus, Birger, 324
Dalarna (Dalecarlia), Sweden, 69, 71, 74–5, 122
Danish East India Company, 162
Dankers, General Oskars, 350
Danzig (Gdańsk): founded, 36; as Free City, 56, 64, 291–2; Hanse merchants lose from Teutonic Knights' defeat, 56; shipbuilding, 58; foreign ships and merchants in, 63–4; privileges, 90; treaty with Oxenstierna, 100; Prussia claims, 158; in Napoleonic wars, 167; Frederick William III's rights to, 188; status redefined by Paris Peace Conference, 291–2; pro-Hitler demonstrations in, 310; Nazi Germany threatens, 316, 320, 324; defies German attack, 326–7; Solidarity movement in, 390; see also Poland
Darius, Steponas, 312
Davout, General Louis Nicolas, 166, 176, 179, 181
Decembrists (Russia), 192
Dekanozov, Vladimir, 343
Dembinsky, Henryk, 206
Denikin, General Anton I., 281–2
Denmark: Bronze Age, 15; Crown and Church unite, 32–4; national flag, 45; supports

Christianization of Estonia, 45; rule in Middle Ages, 65–6; Black Death in, 67; wars with Sweden, 67–8, 73–4, 88–9, 95, 97, 111, 118–20, 124–5, 128, 139, 181; and Scandinavian disunity, 70; imposes tolls and taxes on neighbours, 71; religion in, 82–3; peasant rebellion, 83, 85; alliance with Sweden (1534), 85; late sixteenth-century prosperity, 94; in Thirty Years War, 101–2, 104; loses primacy in north, 111; Swedes attack (1644), 111; concessions to Sweden at Peace of Roskilde, 119–20; Frederick III's constitutional reforms, 123; and Peace of Nystad, 143; supports Russia in war against Sweden (1788), 155; neutrality in Napoleonic wars, 162, 164, 169–70; and Treaty of Tilsit, 169; joins Continental System, 170; uses balloons in war with Sweden, 172; surrenders Norway to Sweden, 181–2; settlement at Vienna Congress (1815), 184; gives up Sound Dues, 189; reform movement and constituional changes (1849), 201, 203; peace treaty with Prussia (1850), 203; and Scandinavianism, 208; and Schleswig-Holstein crises: (1848), 201–4; (1863), 221–3; rural population, 225; democratic reforms in, 228–9; new constitution (1863), 221–2, 228; revised (1866), 228; West Indian colonies, 231; neutrality in First World War, 261–2; and Soviet threat, 275; and Russian revolution, 279; and post-First World War peace settlement, 290; constitutional monarchy in, 293; German population, 295; Jews in, 296; social welfare, 297, 379–80; declines participation in Baltic bloc, 301; state economy in, 304; naval weakness, 314; non-aggression pact with Germany, 321; declares neutrality in Second World War, 331; Germans invade and occupy (1940), 337–9; Germans impose martial law in (1943), 359; Jews smuggled to Sweden in Second World War, 359; resistance movement in, 359–60; British troops protect from Soviet army, 373–4; joins NATO, 377–8; constitutional reforms (1953), 379; Atlantic links, 380; post-war economic development, 380, 388; EU (EEC) membership, 401

Derby, Henry, Earl of see Henry IV, King of England
Descartes, René, 112
Deschenes, Admiral, 209
Désirée (Desideria), Queen of Charles XIV Johann of Sweden, 174, 195, 212
Deutschland (German pocket battleship; later Lützow), 366, 372, 373
Diebitsch, General Johann Karl, 193
Dir, Viking earl, 22–3
Dirschau, battle of (1627), 99
Dmowski, Roman, 260

Dobrava, wife of Mieszko I of Poland, 36
Dobson, Commander C., VC, 284
Dogger Bank incident (1904), 238
Dönitz, Grand Admiral Karl, 371
Dorpat see Tartu
Doumenc, General, 320
Dreadnought, HMS, 247
Drottningholm, Sweden, 154
Dünamünde, 269
Dundas, Rear-Admiral James, 211, 214
Dunkirk evacuation (1940), 339
Dutch, the: ships in Baltic, 63–4; support Hanse in capture of Copenhagen, 68; in Thirty Years War, 102; resent Danish Dues at Sound, 110; ally with Swedes against Denmark, 111; oppose Swedish expansion in Baltic, 116; fleet relieves Copenhagen, 120; mediate between Denmark and Sweden, 121; war with Sweden (1676), 124; support Denmark against Sweden (1700), 128; see also Netherlands

Eastern Question, 206
Eastland Company, 63–4
Ebert, Friedrich, 279
Eden, Anthony, 313, 317
Eden, Nils, 263
Edward II, King of England, 66
Edward III, King of England, 53, 63
Edward VII, King of Great Britain, 238, 245, 247–8
Edward of Woodstock, Prince (the Black Prince), 53
Ehrenström, Johannes, 186
Eisenstein, Sergi, 48–9
Ekaterinburg, 268
Elbe Duchies, 221
Elbing: restrictions on foreigners, 63–4
Elizabeth, Empress of Russia, 146–50, 152
Engel, Carl Ludwig, 186
Engelbrektsson, Engelbrekt, 71–2
England: Viking raids on, 21; ships in Baltic, 63; acquires timber in Baltic, 100; supports Danes against Charles X Gustav, 120; Peter the Great visits, 127; supports Denmark against Sweden (1700), 128; Baltic naval presence and policy, 139–43; joins anti-Swedish alliance (1715), 139–41; see also Britain
Entente Cordiale (Britain-France), 230, 239, 248
Erfurt, 175–6
Eric II, King of Denmark, 33
Eric VI, King of Denmark, 65
Eric VIII, King of Denmark (earlier Boleslaw of Pomerania), 70–2
Eric XIV, King of Sweden, 84, 87–8, 91–2
Ertholmene archipelago, 8
Eskil, Archbishop of Lund, 40
Essen, Admiral N., 261–2, 265

Essen, General Ivan, 180, 184

Estonia: Christian missions in, 45–6; purchased from Danes (1346), 52–3, 66; Danish colony in, 65; sixteenth-century wars, 87; as Swedish possession, 92; nationalism, 220, 233; Russian language in, 235; universities, 235; revolutionary unrest in, 243; autocracy resumed, 250; and Bolshevik revolution, 271–2, 274; declares independence (1918), 274–5; defeats German invasion army (1919), 285; avoids Russian Civil War, 287–8; frontiers agreed, 289; recognized, 289; democratic government in, 294; agricultural economy, 295; land redistributed, 295; minority rights, 295; economic conditions, 298–9; inter-war economy, 305; anti-democratic coup in, 306–7; non-aggression pact with Nazi Germany, 321; racial resettlement, 329; Treaty of Mutual Assistance with Soviet Russia, 330; becomes Soviet Republic (1940), 343, 380; Soviet Russia hardens policy on, 343; Soviet deportations from, 347; supports Germany against Russia, 349; Germans occupy in Second World War, 351; German recruitment in, 360, 363; borders changed, 380; under Soviet control, 380–4; relations with Finland, 384, 405; Popular Front reforms, 393–4; moves to independence from Soviet Union, 395, 397, 400, 402; EU membership, 402–3; market economy, 402; ethnic tensions in, 404–5; membership of NATO, 405

Estrup, Johannes, 228–9

Eugenius III, Pope, 38–9

European Free Trade Association (EFTA), 380

European Union (EU; *earlier* EEC), 380, 401–5

Eurovision Song Contests, 405

Eylau, battle of (1807), 167

Ezergailis, Andrievs, 351

Faeroe Islands, 380

Falconet, Etienne, 147, 191

Falkenhorst, General Nikolaus von, 337, 339

Falster, Denmark, 6

Falun, Sweden, 59, 93, 97

Fanny and Alexander (Bergman film), 227

Faraday, Michael, 209

Faro, 261–2

Fehrbellin, battle of (1675), 124

Ferdinand I, Holy Roman Emperor, 87

Ferdinand II, Holy Roman Emperor, 101–2, 106

Ferdinand III, Holy Roman Emperor, 110, 118

Fersen, Count Axel von, 160, 173

Finland: lakes, 7; early settlement, 16; and Muscovite threat, 78; Peter I's conquests in, 140; Peter I demands surrender from Sweden, 142; Swedish rule in, 143; Russo-Swedish

war in (1808–9), 171–2; Sweden cedes to Russia, 172; Russian rule and policy in, 184–6, 236–7, 250; merchant navy develops, 185; nationalism, 199, 216, 235–7, 250; and Scandinavianism, 208; and Crimean War, 209–12; and peace congress (1856), 214; Alexander II's popularity in, 215–17; waterway and railway development, 215–17; Diet and franchise reform, 216; emigration from, 225; food shortages (1860s), 225; and Estonian nationalism, 235; popular protests in, 236–7; parliamentary reforms (1905–7), 243, 250; women first granted vote in, 243; position in First World War, 259; constitutional rights restored (April 1917), 271; and Russian revolution, 271; demands independence, 272, 275; civil war (1918), 276–7; German intervention in (1918), 277–8; republic established, 280; independence recognized, 281–2; territorial settlement with Russia (1920), 289–90; democratic government, 293; Swedish minority in, 295; economic conditions, 298; considers Baltic collaboration, 302; timber trade decline, 304, 308; Social-Democratic government in, 308; defensive measures against USSR (Mannerheim Line), 309, 312, 321, 334–5; pro-German faction in, 312; proclaims Scandinavian orientation, 312; naval weakness, 314; Soviet threat to, 321–2; rejects Soviet demands for military concessions, 333; Winter War with Russia (1939–40), 334–6; foreign support for, 335–6; Soviet peace treaty (1940), 336; Swedish military and financial support for, 341; Germany restores relations with, 344–5; and German invasion of Russia, 348–9; relations with Germany in Second World War, 353–4; Britain declares war on (1941), 354–5; position of Jews in, 354; withdrawal from war and armistice terms, 363–5; Soviet assaults on (1944), 364–5; peace treaty (1947), 376; Treaty of Friendship with Soviet Union (YYA Treaty, 1948), 376–7, 380, 384; joins Nordic Council, 378; economic prosperity, 379, 388; associate membership of EFTA, 380; relations with Estonia, 384, 405; imports oil from Soviet Union, 388; and Baltic republics' move to independence, 400–1; membership of EU (EEC), 401

Finnish language, 16, 216–17

Finno-Ugrians, 15–17

First World War (1914–18): outbreak, 253–5; conduct in north and east, 256–60; ends, 278

Fisher, Admiral Sir John Arbuthnot (*later* 1st Baron), 232, 246, 248, 264

Fleming, Klas, the Younger, 101

Flottwell, Eduard, 193–4

Foch, Marshal Ferdinand, 282

Forest Brothers (Lithuania), 382
Forster, Albert, 310, 322–4
Fournier, Jean, 174
France: subsidizes Sweden in Thirty Years War, 107; mediates in peace negotiations for Sweden, 121; Charles XI secures subsidies for Sweden, 124; wars with Habsburgs, 157; and Napoleonic wars, 164–8; revolution of 1848, 198; and Crimean War against Russia, 207–9; Prussians defeat (1870), 224; alliance with Russia, 230–2; and *Entente Cordiale*, 230, 239, 248; naval development, 231–2; and outbreak of First World War, 253–4; Pilsudski proposes joint action with, 310; and Nazi German threat, 319; surrenders to Germany (1940), 343
Francis II, Holy Roman Emperor, 158, 165
Francis Joseph, Emperor of Austria-Hungary, 222–3
Frankfurt Parliament, 200–1, 205, 221
Franks (people), 16
Franz Ferdinand, Archduke of Austria, 252
Franzen, Anders, 104
Frederick I, King of Denmark, 75
Frederick II, King of Denmark, 87, 94
Frederick III, King of Denmark, 118–20, 122–3
Frederick IV, King of Denmark, 128, 139
Frederick VI, King of Denmark, 173, 181, 184
Frederick VII, King of Denmark, 123, 201, 202, 221, 228
Frederick II, Holy Roman Emperor, 41, 46
Frederick II (the Great), King of Prussia, 149–51
Frederick I, King of Sweden, 142–3
Frederick Augustus, King of Saxony and Grand Duke of Poland, 169, 186
Frederick, Crown Prince of Denmark, 163
Frederick, Duke of Augustenburg, 222
Frederick William II, King of Prussia, 158–61
Frederick William III, King of Prussia, 161, 166–8, 181, 182, 188, 193
Frederick William IV, King of Prussia, 194, 198–205
Frederick William (the Great Elector), 116–18, 120, 124
Frederiksborg, Denmark, 94
Freikorps, 282, 285–7
Freja (Danish frigate), 162
French, Sir John, 248
French Revolution, 157, 159
Frey (god), 30
Friedeburg, Admiral von, 373
Friedland, battle of (1807), 168–9
Friedrich Karl, Prince of Hesse, 278
Frohnert, Pär, 166
fur trade, 35, 59

galleys, 58, 142, 143, 154, 156
Gambier, Admiral James, 1st Baron, 170

Gapon, Father Georgiy, 241
Gardie, Jacob de la, 94, 98
Gardie, Count Magnus Gabriel de la, 114, 124–5
Gardie, Pontus de la, 91
Gatchina, 356
Gaunt, John of, 54
Gdańsk *see* Danzig
Gediminas, Grand Prince of Lithuania, 50
Geer, Louis de, 96–7, 101, 114, 228
George I, King of Great Britain, 139, 142
George III, King of Great Britain, 149
George V, King of Great Britain, 268
George VI, King of Great Britain, 341
George William, Elector of Brandenburg, 106
German Confederation, 187–8, 201, 221
German Democratic Republic (East Germany), 385–6, 389, 396
German Federal Republic (West Germany), 385
Germany: Christian missions, 32, 34; colonizes west Baltic, 38; federalism, 205, 220; under Bismarck's chancellorship, 230; African colonies, 231; naval development, 231, 246–7, 252; and outbreak of First World War, 254–5; conflict with Russia in First World War, 255–8, 268; naval action in Baltic, 269–70; First World War policy in Baltic states, 273–4, 278; strikes (1918), 274; Finnish expedition (1918), 276–8; post-First World War revolutions, 279, 287; and Treaty of Versailles, 281–2; High Seas fleet scuttled (1919), 282; military action in eastern marches after 1918 armistice, 282–6; frontiers redrawn in 1919 Versailles Treaty, 290–1; constitutional reform (1919), 293–4; co-operation with USSR, 303, 311, 329, 345; economic depression, 305; inter-war rearmament and naval development, 313; naval treaty with Britain (1935), 313–14, 318; as threat to Poland, 315; occupies Memel, 316–17; pact with Soviet Russia (1939), 322–4, 394, 396; invades and conquers Poland (1939), 325–8; invades and occupies Denmark and Norway (1940), 337–9; advances in west (1940), 339; restores relations with Finland (1940), 344–5; invades Russia, 345–6, 348, 349; policy on Baltic states, 350–1; campaign in Soviet Russia, 356–7, 361; wartime 'secret weapons', 361; and Finnish withdrawal from war, 365; evacuations from Baltic ports, 371–2; Montgomery accepts surrender, 373
Gibbon, Edward: *The Decline and Fall of the Roman Empire*, 25
Gierek, Edward, 388, 390
Girenas, Stasys, 312
Gniezno, 35–6
Godfred, Danish King, 28
Goebbels, Joseph, 311

Golovchin, battle of (1708), 133
Goltz, General Rüdiger von der, 277, 278, 282–3, 284–5, 321
Gomulka, Wladyslaw, 387–8
Gorbachev, Mikhail, 391, 393, 395–400
Göring, Hermann, 324, 344
Gorm the Old, king in north Jutland, 33
Göta canal, Sweden, 196–7, 215
Götars (people), 19
Gothenburg, Sweden, 97–8, 122
Gotland: described, 8; ship graves, 15; as Viking base, 22, 27; independence, 32; Christianity in, 34–5; trading, 41–2; as Hanse cenre, 42; Denmark seizes, 43; Valdemar IV Atterdag attacks, 67–8; Eric VIII seizes, 72; Sweden regains (1634), 111
Govorov, General Leonid, 362–4
Graham, Sir James, 208, 210
Great Belt (Store Bælt), 3
Great Depression (1920s), 304–5
Greenland, 380
Gregory I (the Great), Pope, 31
Gregory VII, Pope, 36
Gregory IX, Pope, 44, 46–8
Grenville, William Wyndham, Baron, 162
Grey, Sir Edward, 262
Grip, Bo Johansson, 69, 73
Gripsholm, Sweden, 86, 154
Grodno, 132
Grotius, Hugo, 112
Gunther, Christian, 340
Gustav I (Eriksson), King of Sweden, 74–6, 83–6
Gustav II Adolph (Gustavus II Adolphus), King of Sweden: power, 75, 97; accession, 95; character and qualities, 96; military prowess, 96–8, 107, 109; campaigns against Russia, 98; reforms army, 98–9; war with Poland, 99; in Thirty Years War, 101, 103–8; and warship Vasa, 104; death at Lützen, 109; invades Semigallia, 122
Gustav III, King of Sweden: birth, 152; accession, 153; education and interests, 153–4; war plans, 154–6; aids Louis XVI of France, 160; assassinated, 161, 389
Gustav IV Adolf, King of Sweden, 161, 164–5, 171–3
Gustav V Adolf, King of Sweden, 244, 251, 262, 293, 310, 339–40, 358

Haakon VI, King of Norway, 68–9
Haakon VII, King of Norway (earlier Prince Charles of Denmark), 244, 340
Haakon Longlegs, King of Norway, 66
Hadrian IV, Pope (Nicholas Breakspear), 34
Halder, Colonel-General Franz, 321–2, 324
Halfdan (Viking), 26
Halifax, Edward Frederick Lindley Wood, 1st Earl of, 317, 320–1, 324

Hall, Captain (of HMS Hecla), 210
Hamburg: sacked by Vikings (845), 31; beer trade, 60; overland route to Lübeck, 62
Hammarskjöld, Dag, 378
Hammarskjöld, Hjalmar, 251, 262
Hammerstein, battle of (1627), 99
Hanse (Hanseatic League): amber trade, 5; as commercial federation, 29, 42–3, 69; Teutonic Order's dominance in, 51–2; shipping, 58; trading practices and cargoes, 59, 63; rivalry and conflicts, 60–1, 63; subdues Denmark (1370), 68–9; resists Danish tolls, 71; in Novgorod, 77–8; power declines, 85
Hansson, Per Albin, 297, 335, 359, 379
Harald Bluetooth, King of Denmark, 33
Harald Hardrada, 25–9
Harald Klak, King of Denmark, 31
Hardinge, Charles, 1st Baron, 248–9
Harris, Air Chief Marshal Sir Arthur, 355–6
Hedeby (now Haithabu, Schleswig), 28–9, 41
Heiden, Feodor, Count, 236
Heilbronn, League of (1633), 109–10
Helgö, Sweden, 27, 29
Heligoland, 170
Helmond (Holstein priest), 41
Helsingborg: Denmark and Sweden contest, 66
Helsingør, Denmark: anglicized as Elsinore, 1
Helsinki (Helsingfors): described, 9–10; founded, 86–7; as capital city, 185–6; popular protests in, 236–7; Olympic Games (1952), 378
Helsinki Conference on Security and Co-operation in Europe (1975), 377, 384
Henry III, King of France: elected king of Poland-Lithuania, 90
Henry IV, King of England (earlier Earl of Derby), 54, 63
Henry VIII, King of England, 59, 84
Henry the Lion, Duke of Saxony, 38–42
Hercules, HMS, 286
Hermann Keep, 7
Hermann of Salza, Prince of Holy Roman Empire, 46, 51
herring trade, 60
Herzl, Theodor, 234
Hierta, Lars, 195–6
Himmler, Heinrich, 346, 351, 354
Hindenburg, Field Marshal Paul von Beneckendorff und, 256–8, 282, 310, 371
Hipper, Admiral Franz von, 269
Hitler, Adolf: rise to power, 305, 310; and Poland, 311; and naval development, 313; renounces Versailles Treaty, 314; foresees war with Russia, 315; meets Colonel Beck, 316; threatens annihilation of Jews, 316; occupies Memel, 317–18; and Anglo-Polish mutual

assistance pact, 318; and invasion of Poland, 318, 323–4; dismisses British guarantees to Poland, 322; relations with Stalin, 322, 329; and pact with Soviet Russia (1939), 323; in captured Warsaw, 327; annexes partitioned Poland, 328; sanctions invasion of Denmark and Norway, 337; disavows interest in Finland, 345; and invasion of Russia, 345, 348–9; declares war on USA, 355; exalts Germanic races, 360–1; forbids strategic retreats, 362; orders destruction of Warsaw, 369; refuses evacuation of troops in Courland, 372; suicide, 373

Hoffmann, Colonel (*later* General) Max, 256, 274–5

Hogendorp, General Dirk van, 179

Holstein: in German Confederation, 188; and 1863 crisis, 222–3; *see also* Schleswig-Holstein

Holsti, Rudolf, 301

Holy Roman Empire: ends, 165

Honorius III, Pope, 43, 46

Horn, General Arvid, 143

Horn, General Gustav, 110

Horn, Admiral Klas, 89

Hughes, Revd Edward, 210

hulks (ships), 58

Hungary, 206, 393, 396

Huns, 18

Hutt, William, 189

Ibsen, Henrik, 227

Iceland, 380

Ignalina (Lithuania): nuclear reactor, 383

Ignatius, Patriarch, 34

Ingenohl, Admiral Friedrich von, 254–5

Innocent III, Pope, 40, 43

Insterburg (Chernyakhovsk), 375

'iron curtain', 376

iron ore: in Sweden, 19, 331–2, 337, 339, 341

Iron Wolf movement (Lithuania), 305–6

Ironside, General Sir Edmund, 321–2

Isaac, Aaron, 154

Islam: spreads in Mediterranean area, 19, 20

Ivan III (the Great), Tsar (Great Prince of Moscow and Vladimir), 74, 77–8

Ivan IV (the Terrible), Tsar: builds Ivangorod Castle, 7; invades Livonia, 87–9; and war against Turks, 89; truce with Poland, 90; defeated at Wenden (1578), 91

Ivan VI, Tsar, 146–7

Ivangorod, 78; Castle, 7

Izvestia (Russian newspaper), 279–80

Izvolsky, Alexander, 248–50

Jadwiga, 'King' of Poland, 37, 54

Jagiello, Wladyslaw II, co-King of Poland (*earlier* Grand Duke Jogaila), 54–6, 257

James I, King of England (James VI of Scotland), 95

Janssen, Johann, 220

Japan: war with Russia (1904–5), 237–40; naval development, 247

Jaruzelski, General Wojciech, 390–2

Jasna Góra monastery (Poland), 117

Jassy, Treaty of (1792), 158

Jelgava *see* Mitau

Jemappes, battle of (1792), 158

Jesuits: in Sweden, 92

Jews: in Sweden, 153–4, 197, 296; Catherine the Great restricts, 158; in Poland, 169, 220, 387, 404; Russian taxes relaxed, 215; blamed for assassination of Alexander II, 233; persecuted, 233–4, 248–9; in First World War, 259–60; status, 296; Nazi persecution of, 316, 352; exterminated in Poland, 328; deported from Baltic states, 347; exterminated in Baltic states, 351–2; smuggled from Denmark to Sweden, 359; in Baltic republics, 384

Jodl, General Alfred, 354

John II Casimir, King of Poland, 116–18, 121–3

John II (Hans), King of Sweden, 74

John III, King of Sweden, 91–2

John George, Elector of Saxony, 106–7

John Paul II, Pope (Karol Wojtyla), 386–7, 390–1

John Sobieski, King of Poland-Lithuania, 13, 123

John Sverkersson, King of Sweden, 45

Johnson, Robert, 12

Jordan, Wilhelm, 200–1

Josephine, Queen of Oscar I of Sweden, 195

Juel, Admiral Niels, 124

Jungingen, Conrad von, 54–5, 62

Jungingen, Ulrich von, 55

Junkers, 221, 259, 282

Jutland: arable land, 6

Kadets (Russian party), 242

Kalanta, Romas, 384

Kalevala (Finnish epic), 16

Kalevipoeg (Estonian epic), 16

Kalinin, Mikhail, 47

Kaliningrad *see* Köningsberg

Kallismaa, Kalyu, 347

Kalmar, Union of (1397), 70–1, 74, 77

Kalmar, War of (1611–13), 97, 101

Kania, Stanislaw, 390

Kant, Immanuel, 150

Kapp Putsch (1920), 287

Kardis, Treaty of (1661), 121

Karelia, 49–50, 289–90; Sweden acquires, 98

Karin Mansdotter, Queen of Eric XIV of Sweden, 92

Karlskrona: founded, 125; as naval base, 314

Karlstad Convention (1905), 244

Kärnan, Sweden, 1
Karsavina, Tamara: *Theatre Street*, 12
Kashubs (people), 17
Kastelholm Castle, Åland, 8
Katherine of Sachsen-Lauenburg, Queen of
 Gustav I of Sweden, 84
Kattegat, 1
Katyn forest massacre (1940), 328, 352, 367
Kaupang, Norway, 27
Keitel, Marshal Wilhelm, 365
Kekkonen, Urho, 336, 377, 378, 384
Keppler, Gotthard, Duke of Courland, 87
Kerensky, Alexander, 268, 270, 272, 290
Kettler, Jacob, Duke of Courland, 122
Kexholm, Finland, 91
Khakan (Khazar ruler), 24–5
Khazars, 22–5
Khmelnitsky, Hetman Bohdan, 115–16
Khrushchev, Nikita S., 387
Kiel: Treaty of (1814), 181, 183–4; in Schleswig-
 Holstein crisis, 201, 204; canal to North Sea,
 223, 232, 247, 252, 261
Kiev, 22–4, 26; Christianity in, 34–5
Kirke, General Sir Walter, 321
Kirkholm, battle of (1605), 94
Klaipėda see Memel
Klinge, Matti, 16
Klingspor, General Mauritz, 172
Knäred, Treaty of (1613), 97
Knights of Dobrin, 46–7
Kniprode, Winrich von, Teutonic Grand Master,
 53–4, 68
knorrs (or knarrs; ships), 21, 27, 58
Knutsson, Karl see Charles I Knutsson, King of
 Sweden
Kohl, Helmut, 397
Kolbberger Heide, battle of (1644), 111
Kolchak, Admiral Alexander V., 261, 281
Kolehmainen, Hannes, 250
Kollontai, Alexandra, 364
Komorowski, General Tadeusz ('Bor'), 368–9
Königsberg (Kaliningrad): founded, 47;
 Teutonic Knights retain, 56; and
 Lutheranism, 81; acknowledges Empress
 Elizabeth of Russia, 150; in First World War,
 255–7; Germans ejected (1945), 375; as Soviet
 naval base, 389; Russian Federation retains,
 406
Konrad, Duke of Masovia, 46
Kornilov, General Lavre, 268
Kosciuszko, Tadeusz, 159, 186
Kosice, Privilege of (1374), 37, 54
Kossuth, Lajos, 206
Kramar Recess (1484), 73
Kreutz, Philip von, 81
Krėvė-Mickevičius, Vincas, 343
Kristiansand, Norway, 94
Kristianstad, Sweden, 94
Kronan (Swedish warship), 124–5

Kronborg, Denmark, 1, 94, 120, 189
Kronstadt: described, 10; fortified, 132;
 develops as naval base, 140; British threaten
 in Crimean War, 208–9, 211; French naval
 squadron visits, 232; British blockade (1919),
 283; British motor torpedo boats attack, 284;
 mutiny suppressed (1921), 302–3; in Second
 World War, 349, 356
Krueger, Ivar, 304
Kshesinskaia, Mathilde, 267
Küchler, Field Marshal Georg von, 362
Kulm (Chelmno), battle of (1222), 46
Kunersdorf, battle of (1759), 150
Küng, Andreas, 382
Kursk, battle of (1943), 362
Kuusinen, Otto, 276, 335
Kuznetsov, Admiral Nikolai, 348

Ladislav IV, King of Poland, 109, 115
Ladoga, Lake, 11, 22, 48–9, 131
La Gardie see Gardie
Laidoner, General Johan, 280, 287, 306–7, 321,
 343, 405
Lamartine, Alphonse de, 199
Landsbergis, Vytautas, 394–5, 397–9
Landskrona, 49
Langenskiöld, Fabian, 217
Lannes, Marshal Jean, Duc de, 166
Lapua, battle of (1808), 172
Lapua Movement (Finland), 308
Larka, General Andres, 306–7
Lassalle, General Antoine, 157, 166
Latvia: nationalism, 220–1, 235; revolutionary
 unrest (1906), 242–3; autocracy resumed,
 250; in First World War, 259; and Russian
 revolution, 271–2, 280; claims autonomy,
 272; under German occupation in First World
 War, 272; Soviet regime displaces provisional
 government (1918), 279–80; unknown in
 West, 281; post-First World War disorder,
 282–3; opposes German invasion army (1919),
 284–6; avoids Russian Civil War, 287; peace
 treaty with Russia (1920), 288; frontiers
 agreed, 289; recognized, 289; agricultural
 economy, 294; democratic government in,
 294; land redistribution, 295; minorities'
 status in, 295–6; trade balance, 298; inter-
 war economy, 305; anti-democratic
 government in, 307–8; non-aggression pact
 with Nazi German, 321; racial resettlement,
 329; Soviet Russia hardens policy on, 330–1,
 342–3; becomes Soviet Republic (1940), 343,
 380; Soviet deportations from, 347; Germans
 occupy in Second World War, 350; Jews
 exterminated, 351–2; German recruitment
 in, 360; borders changed, 380–1; under
 Soviet control, 381–3; song festivals, 394;
 moves to independence from Soviet Union,
 397–400, 402; EU membership, 402–3;

financial crisis (1995), 402; ethnic tensions, 404; membership of NATO, 405
Lauenberg, 223
League of Foreign Peoples of Russia (*Fremdvölker Russlands*), 261
League of Nations, 281, 293, 295, 299, 310–11, 313, 335
LeBlond, Alexandre, 132, 145
Lech, chief of the Polanie, 35
Ledocowski, Archbishop of Gniezno, 220
Lee, Robert, 12
Leeb, Field Marshal Wilhelm von, 349, 353
Leipzig, battle of (1813), 181
Lenin, Vladimir Ilich: returns to Russia, 266–7; in Finland, 268, 270; negotiates armistice with Germany, 270, 272; Decree of Peace (1917), 274; and German advance, 275; moves capital to Moscow, 275; accepts Finnish independence, 276; and German revolution, 279; and Civil War, 287; death, 303; New Economic Plan, 303
Leningrad *see* St Petersburg
Leo VI, Byzantine Emperor, 24
Leo XIII, Pope, 220
Leopold I, Holy Roman Emperor, 121, 124
Leopold, Prince of Bavaria, 274
le Queux, William: *The Great War in England in 1897*, 232, 246; *The Invasion of 1910*, 246
Leslie, Alexander, 103, 106
Lesnaya, battle of (1708), 134
Leuthen, battle of (1757), 150
Lewenhaupt, Count Carl, 134
Libau, 215, 255, 258
Lie, Trygve, 378
Lindh, Anna, 402
Lindisfarne, 21
Lindqvist, Sune, 19
Linköping: Synod of (1153), 34; Bloodbath of (1599), 93
Linnaeus, Carolus (Carl von Linné), 153
Lipski, Jozef, 317
List, Friedrich, 204
Lithuania: raids along Niemen and Dvina, 50; Christianized, 53–4; conflict with Teutonic Knights, 53–6, 63; religious differences in, 81, 235; forms Commonwealth with Poland, 89–91; and Russian domination, 235; in First World War, 261; and Russian revolution, 271; under German occupation in First World War, 272–3; declares independence, 273, 275; Taryba (National Council), 273; Mindaugas II elected, 278; post-First World War government, 279; and Polish claims on Vilnius, 288–9, 301–2, 311; recognized, 288–9; agricultural economy, 294; democratic government in, 294; land laws, 295; minorities' status in, 295–6; trade balance, 298; nationalist coup (1926), 300–1; inter-war economy, 305; political extremism

in, 305–6; agrees truce with Poland, 315; Germans agree to restore Vilnius to, 323; Soviet pressure on, 342–3; becomes Soviet Republic (1940), 343; Hitler's interest in, 344; Soviet deportations from, 347; reclaims independence in Second World War, 350; Jews exterminated, 351; resistance to Soviet control, 381–2, 384; Popular Front (*Sajūdis*) reforms, 394–5; claims independence from Soviet Union, 397–400, 402; political crisis (1991), 398–9; EU membership, 402; exports decline, 402; economic development, 404; membership of NATO, 405
Little Belt, 3
Litvinov, Maxim, 304, 311, 319
Livonia: and Holy Wars, 43–4, 47–8; land rights, 52; Plettenberg's status in, 82; Ivan IV invades, 87–8; Gustavus Adolphus occupies, 99–100; protests at Charles XI's reforms, 126; revolt against Sweden, 128; in First World War, 259
Livonian Order, 47, 56, 78, 82, 87
Lloyd George, David, 287, 291–2
Lohse, Heinrich, 346, 350
Loki (god), 30
London: Hanse activities in, 53
London Protocol (on Schleswig-Holstein), 221–2
longships, 20–1
Louis I, Emperor, 31
Louis XIV, King of France, 124–5
Louis XV, King of France, 153–4
Louis XVI, King of France, 154, 159–60
Louis XVIII, King of France, 182
Louis Ferdinand Hohenzollern, Prince, 370
Louis, King of Hungary and of Poland, 37
Louis Philippe, King of the French, 193, 198
Louisa Ulrika, Queen of Adolf Frederick of Sweden, 152
Louise (of Mecklenburg-Strelitz), Queen of Frederick William III, 161, 167, 169
Löwenstadt, 41
Lübeck: position, 7; as episcopy, 38; growth, 40–1; fire (1157), 41; as free city, 41, 224; as Hanse centre, 43, 58–60; trading privileges, 43; overland route to Hamburg, 62; attacks Denmark, 67–8, 71; and Swedish-Danish alliance (1534–5), 85; bank collapses, 175; bombed by RAF in war, 355–6; at war's end (1945), 373, 375
Lucas, Lieutenant Charles, VC, 210
Ludendorff, General Erich, 256–8, 266, 268, 273, 277–8, 282, 286
Lund: church property confiscated, 83; battle of (1676), 124–5; university, 125
Lüneburg: salt trade, 60
Lüneburg Heath, 373
Luther, Martin, 79–80, 82, 84
Lutheranism, 80–5, 92, 125

Lützen, battle of (1632), 96, 108–9
Lvov, Prince Georgi, 267–8, 271

Maasing, Colonel J., 321
Maastricht Treaty (1994), 401
MacDonald, Marshal Jacques Etienne Joseph, 179–80
MacMillan, Margaret, 291
Mäe, Hjalmar, 351, 360, 363
Magnus I (the Good), King of Norway, 32
Magnus II Eriksson, King of Sweden, 66–8
Malmö: raided by pirates, 62
Mannerheim, Baron Gustav, 259, 276–9, 282, 287, 289, 308–9, 312, 321, 334, 336, 354, 364–5
Mansfeld, General Peter Ernst, Count von, 101–2
Maret, Hugues, Duc de Bassano, 178–9
Margaret Leijonhuvud, (second) Queen of Gustav I of Sweden, 84
Margaret (Margrete) Valdemarsdotter, 68–71
Margrethe II, Queen of Denmark, 379
Maria Eleonore, Queen of Gustavus Adolphus, 108
Marie Antoinette, Queen of France, 154, 160
Mariehamn, Åland, 8
Marielyst, Denmark, 6
Marienburg: Teutonic Order in, 51–3
Marienwerder, 292
Marlborough, John Churchill, 1st Duke of, 132
Marshall Plan, 376
Masséna, Marshal André, 168
Masurian lakes, battle of the (1914), 257
Matwy, battle of (1666), 123
Maud, Queen of Norway, 244
Maximilian II, Holy Roman Emperor, 89
Maximilian, Duke of Bavaria, 107
Maximilian, Holy Roman Emperor, 79
Maximov, Lieutenant, 267
Mazeppa, Hetman Ivan, 134
Mazowiecki, Tadeusz, 392
Mecklenburg, Dukes of, 62
Medici, Lorenzo de' (the Magnificent), 61
Memel (Klaipėda), 289, 301, 306, 316–18, 367
Memling, Hans: The Last Judgement (triptych), 61
Meretskov, General K.A., 335, 362, 364
Metternich, Prince Clemens Lothar Wenzel, 187, 189, 198
Michael III, Byzantine Emperor, 23
Michael, Grand Duke of Russia, 191
Michael of Novgorod, 77
Michael Romanov, Tsar, 115
Michael Wisniowecki, King of Poland-Lithuania, 123
Michetti, Niccolo, 138
Mickiewicz, Adam, 191, 260
Mieroslawski, Ludwik, 194, 199–200
Mieszko I, Polish king, 36

Mieszko II, King of Poland, 36
Mikolajczýk, Stanislaw, 368–9, 385
Miloradovitch, Count M., 191
Milyukov, Paul, 167–8
Mindaugas II, King of Lithuania, 278
Mindaugas, Grand Prince of Lithuania, 44, 50
Mirabeau, Honoré Gabriel Riqueti, Comte de, 157
Mitau (Jelgava), 87, 122, 148, 283, 286
Mitterrand, François, 397
Molotov, Viacheslav M., 319–20, 322–3, 327, 330, 333–4, 342, 345–6
Moltke, General Helmuth, Count von, 224
Moltke, Helmuth (nephew of General Helmuth Moltke), 254, 256, 262
Montesquieu, Charles-Louis de Secondat, Baron de, 158
Montgomery, Field Marshal Bernard Law, 1st Viscount, 373–4
Moon Island, battle of (1917), 270
Moore, General Sir John, 181
Mörner, Count Gustav, 166
Mortier, Marshal Adolphe Eduard Casimir Joseph, 168
Moryson, Fynes, 1–4, 64
Mościcki, Ignacy, 315, 327, 329
Moscow: as centre of Russian empire, 77; Peace of (with Finland, 1940), 336, 341
Motz, Friedrich von, 188
Mountagu, Edward (later 1st Earl of Sandwich), 120
Mukden, battle of (1905), 240
Munich agreement (1938), 316
Murat, Marshal Joachim, 167, 179–80
Muscovy see Russia

Napier, Vice Admiral Sir Charles, 207–11, 264
Napoleon I (Bonaparte), Emperor of the French, 164–5, 167–71, 173–80, 182
Napoleon III, Emperor of the French, 207–8, 212–14, 218, 224
Narutowicz, Gabriel, 299
Narva (town), 7, 87–8, 347, 363, 366; Swedish victory over Russians (1700), 129–30
Narva, river, 78–9, 362, 363
Narvik, 263, 331–2, 337, 339
naval arms race (pre-1914), 246–7
Nazi Party: rise to power, 305; ideology, 315
Nelson, Vice Admiral Horatio, 1st Viscount, 162–4
Nepenin, Admiral A.I., 265
Neris, river, 13
Nesselrode, Charles Robert, Count, 184, 198, 213
Nestor, monk, 23–4
Netherlands: Peter the Great visits, 127; in French revolutionary wars, 157, 159; see also Dutch, the
Neva, river, 10–12

Ney, Marshal Michel, 179
Nicholas I, Tsar: accession and autocratic reign, 191–4, 215; and railway development, 196; on French republic of 1848, 198; and Frankfurt Parliament, 201; and Schleswig-Holstein crisis, 202; and Crimean War, 206–7, 209; death, 211
Nicholas II, Tsar: upbringing, 233; accession, 236; policy on Finland, 236, 243; autocratic rule, 237, 249; and Bloody Sunday (1905), 241; seeks western alliances, 244–7; and war with Japan, 244–5; accepts Duma, 249; at opening of widened Kiel canal, 252; and outbreak of First World War, 253–4; and Polish freedom, 260; abdicates, 266–7; proposed flight to Britain, 267–8; killed, 268
Nicholas Nicholaevich, Grand Duke of Russia, 246, 260, 263
Nicolson, Sir Arthur (later Baron Charnock), 248
Nicolson, Harold, 359
Niedra, Andrievs, 283
Niels, King of Denmark, 33
Nobel, Alfred, 226
Nordic Council: established (1952), 378
Nördlingen, battle of (1634), 110
Normandy landings (1944), 365
Norris, Admiral Sir John, 139–40, 142–3
Norse gods, 30
North Atlantic Treaty Organisation (NATO), 377, 405–6
North German Confederation, 224
Northern War, First (1655–8), 115–21
Norway: achieves independence (1035), 32; and Scandinavian disunity, 70; Charles XII's final campaign in, 141; Swedish ambitions on, 176, 180; Denmark surrenders to Sweden, 182–3; independence movement, 183–4; war in (1814), 184; Eidsvoll Constitution, 194; respect for Charles XIV Johann, 196; and Scandinavianism, 208; gains independence from Sweden, 243–4; mercantile fleet, 244; neutrality in First World War, 261–3; declines participation in Baltic bloc, 301; and shipment of Swedish iron ore in Second World War, 331–2; Germans invade and occupy (1940), 337–40; Sweden aids in Second World War, 359; Quisling followers in, 360; joins NATO, 377–8; rejects membership of EU (EEC), 401
Noske, Gustav, 279
Nöteborg (Orekhov; Schlüsselburg), 131; treaty of (1323), 49
Notke, Bernt, 74
Novgorod, 22, 32, 35, 41, 43, 48–50, 77, 98
Novosiltsov, Nicholas, 187
Nyklot, Prince of Abotrites, 39–40, 62
Nystad, Treaty of (1721), 143–4, 149
Ochab, Edward, 386

Odense, Diet of, 82
Oder, river, 6
Odin (god), 30
Öland, 8
Olav, King of Norway, 69–70
Oldenburg, 31, 33, 38, 175–6
Oleg, Prince of Novgorod, 23–5, 31
Oliva, Treaty of (1660), 121
Olivares, Gaspar de Guzmán, Count-Duke of, 102
Olof Skötkonung, Swedish king, 32
Ordyn-Naschokin, Afanasy, 121
Øresund (the Sound), 1–3; Denmark levies tolls, 71–2, 76, 94, 100, 110, 143, 189
Øresundforbindelsen (Sound Fixed Link), 2, 406
Orlov, Prince Andrei, 198
Orlov, Gregory, 148
Orthodox Church: in eastern Baltic, 34; in Russia, 233–5
Orzel (Polish submarine), 330, 338
Oscar I, King of Sweden, 195–7, 202, 208, 212–14, 216, 228
Oscar II, King of Sweden, 228, 243–4
Ösel (island), 111
Ostmark Verein, 220
Ottokar II, King of Bohemia, 47
Ottoman Empire: expansion into Europe, 59; Polish-Lithuanian conflict with, 115; thirty-year truce with Russia (1700), 129; war with Russia (1711), 137; peace treaty with Russia (1792), 158; in Crimean War (1854–5), 207–8
Oxe, Peder, 94, 110
Oxenstierna, Axel: as Gustavus Adolphus's Chancellor, 96–7; devises conscription system, 98; treaty with Danzig, 100; and war finances, 101; and Thirty Years War, 105, 107, 109–10; policy-making, 108–9; heads regency, 109–10; attacks Denmark, 111; understanding of Queen Christina, 112; villa, 114

Paasikivi, Juho, 290, 333–4, 364, 376–7
Paderewski, Ignace, 260
paganism, 30, 32–5
Paksas, Rolandas, 403–4
Palme, Olof, 379, 389–90
Palmerston, Henry John Temple, 3rd Viscount: and Schleswig-Holstein crises, 202–3, 223; on German fleet, 205; supports Turkey, 206; and Crimean War, 208, 212
Pappenheim, Gottfried Heinrich, Count zu, 109
Paris: peace congress and Treaty (1856), 214–15, 250; peace conference (1919), 281–2, 290–1; treaty (1947), 376
Parker, Admiral Sir Hyde, 162–4
Pärnu, Estonia, 220, 366, 404–5

Partnership for Peace programme, 405
Pascal, Blaise, 112
Pasch, Gustaf, 226
Paschal II, Pope, 33
Paskevich, Field Marshal Ivan, 193–4, 199, 206
Patkul, Johann von, 126, 128, 133
Päts, Konstantin, 275, 306–7, 330, 343
Paul, Tsar, 145, 147, 159, 161–3
Pawest (Hanse captain), 61
Peenemünde, 105–7, 361
Pénaud, Admiral Charles, 211
Pepys, Samuel, 120, 122
Peter I (the Great), Tsar: amber panels, 5; war with Sweden, 9; builds St Petersburg, 10–11, 49, 131; hostility to Sweden, 121, 127–8; on Great Embassy to western Europe, 126–7; character and manner, 127; in Great Northern War against Sweden, 129–34, 142–4; Narva defeat (1700), 130; Poltava victory, 135–7; expansionist policy in Baltic, 137–8, 140–1; develops navy, 140, 142; attacks Swedish coast, 142–3; administration and reforms, 144–5; gains from Nystad Treaty, 144; *Bronze Horseman* statue, 147, 191
Peter II, Tsar, 146
Peter III, Tsar, 146, 150
Peterhof: built, 145; in Second World War, 356–7
Petri, Laurentius, Archbishop of Uppsala, 85
Petri, Olaus, 83–5
Philippa, Queen of Eric VIII of Denmark, 71
Photius, Patriarch of Constantinople, 23
Piast family, 35–7
Pillau, 371–2
Pilsudski, Josef, 260, 288, 296, 299–300, 310–11, 315
Pinksner, Leon, 234
piracy, 33, 62–3
Pitt, William, the Younger, 164
plague (1708–10), 138–9
Plettenberg, Wolter von, 78–9, 81–2, 87
Pleve, Viacheslav, 237
Plunkett-Ernle-Erle-Drax, Admiral Sir Reginald, 320, 322
Pobedonostsev, Konstantin, 233–5, 240, 249
Põdder, General Ernst, 285
Poincaré, Raymond, 253, 267
Poland: geographical position, 6; settled, 35; access to Baltic, 36; Church in, 36–7; power of nobility in, 37; conflict with Teutonic Knights, 54–6, 58; rules 'Prussian' territories, 56–7; trade with Dutch, 64; religious variety in, 81; defends Lithuania against Ivan IV, 89; forms Commonwealth with Lithuania, 89–91; occupies Moscow (1610–12), 98; Sweden's war with (1620), 99; claims to Swedish throne, 109; conflicts with Russia, 115–16; detachment in Thirty Years War, 115; Sweden invades (1655), 116–21; and

Truce of Andrusovo, 121; elected monarchs, 123; Charles XII's activities in, 130–2; and Nystad peace settlement, 144; as Russian protectorate under Warsaw agreement, 144; constitution guaranteed (1768), 151–2; partitioned, 151–2, 160; new constitution (1791), 157–8; welcomes French Revolution, 157, 159; under Russian control, 158; revolt under Kosciuszko, 159; in Napoleonic wars, 167–8, 176; benefits from Tilsit Treaty, 169; Jews in, 169, 220, 296, 387, 404; Alexander I's policy on, 186–7; settlement in Treaty of Vienna, 187–8; insurrection (1830), 192–3; nationalism suppressed, 193–4; religious tensions, 193; and revolutions of 1848, 198–9; Prussian hostility to, 200; Tsar Nicholas threatens, 206; Alexander II's policy on, 218–19; rebels against Russian rule (1863–4), 218–20; land reform, 219, 295; Russian domination in, 219; Germanization, 220; civil unrest, 242; position in First World War, 260; frontiers determined (1945), 275, 368–70; claims Vilnius from Lithuania, 288–9, 301–2, 311, 315; war with Soviet Russia (1920), 288; 'Corridor', 291–2, 311, 316; independence under Versailles Treaty, 291; constitution of 1921, 294; agricultural economy, 295; political unrest, 299–300; inter-war economy, 305; relations with Nazi Germany, 310–11, 315–16; and German threat, 315–18, 323–4; Lithuania agrees truce with, 315; occupies Teschen, 316; mutual assistance pact with Britain, 318, 321–3; mistrust of Soviet Russia, 322; Nazi-Soviet pact agrees partition of, 323, 325, 327, 329; Germans invade and defeat, 325–6; atrocities and repression in, 328–9; wartime resistance and government in exile, 329–30; Home Army, 366, 368–9; Soviet army advances over, 367–8, 370; National Unity Government (1944), 369; resists Soviet domination, 384–8; dependence on Soviet goodwill, 388–9; Solidarity movement, 390–2, 396; democratic elections (1990), 392; votes for EU membership, 402–3; membership of NATO, 405; *see also* Danzig
Polanie tribe, 35
Polentz, George, Bishop, 80
Polish Democratic Society, 194
Poltava, battle of (1709), 135–6, 137
Pomerania: fertility, 13; stewards serve Eric VIII, 71; in Thirty Years War, 104, 106; Swedes gain and retain territory in (1648), 111, 171; Elector Frederick William attacks, 124; and Treaty of Nystad (1721), 143–4; Davout threatens, 176; Denmark acquires part, 182, 184; and Germanism, 221
Poniatowski, Prince Joseph, 168
Popieluszko, Jerzy, 391

Portugal: voyages and exploration, 64
Porvoo, Finland, 9, 185
Posen, Grand Duchy of, 188, 199–200
Poska, Jaan, 271
Potemkin, Prince Grigoriy, 147–8
Potsdam conference (1945), 375
Pound, Admiral Sir Dudley, 332–3
Poznań, 35–6, 386
Prague, Peace Treaty of (1866), 224
Pressburg, Treaty of (1806), 165
printing, 80, 83
Prinz Eugen (German heavy cruiser), 366, 371,
    373
Prittwitz, General Max von, 256
privateering: by Hanse, 61–2
Probert, Air Commodore Henry, 356
Protestantism: effect on wax trade, 59; in
    Germany, 85; in Thirty Years War, 101, 103,
    105–7; *see also* Lutheranism; Reformation
Prunskienė, Kazimira, 397–8
Prussia: Crusade against, 46–8; land rights, 52;
    Lutheranism in, 80–1; Ducal, 91; rise to
    power, 115, 149; conflict with Russia,
    149–50; gains territory in Poland, 151;
    revolutionary wars with France, 158–60; in
    Napoleonic wars, 164–7, 169, 180; acquires
    Pomerania, 184; and Treaty of Vienna, 187;
    and German Confederation, 188; *Zollverein*,
    188, 201, 204, 224; hostility to Poland, 200;
    and Schleswig-Holstein crises, 202–4, 222–3;
    develops navy, 203–5, 222, 224; peace treaty
    with Denmark (1850), 203; Polish subjects in,
    219; Jews in, 220; defeats Austria (1866),
    223–4
Pskov, 79
Putin, Vladimir, 12
Pytalovo (Abrene), 381
Pytheas, 17

Raczkiewicz, Wladyslaw, 329
Raczynski family, 199
Radziejowski, Michal Stefan, Cardinal-
    Archbishop, 130
Radziwill family, 199
Raeder, Grand Admiral Erich, 324, 337, 339
Ragnvald (Viking), 26–7
Rantzau, General Daniel, 89
Rantzau, General Johan, 83
Rapallo, Treaty of (1922), 303
Raštikis, General Stasys, 350
Rastrelli, Bartolommeo, 132, 145, 148
Rastrelli, Carlo-Bartolommeo, 132
Razumovsky, Alexei, 148
Reformation, 59, 79–83
Rehnsköld, Field Marshal Gustav, 129, 135
Rei, August, 306
Reid, Anna: *The Shaman's Coat*, 347
Reinsurance Treaty (1890), 230
Remnick, David: *Lenin's Tomb*, 395

Rennenkampf, General P.K., 255–7
Reric, 21, 28
Reuterholm, Count, 161
Reval *see* Tallinn
revolutions of 1848, 198
Ribbentrop, Joachim von, 313, 316, 318, 322–4,
    329, 340–1, 350, 354, 365
Ribe, Denmark, 27
Richelieu, Cardinal Armand Jean Duplessis,
    Duc de, 105–7, 110
Riga: founded and developed, 41, 43; financial
    support for Livonian Order, 78; Poles rule,
    87; privileges, 90; Gustavus Adolphus
    occupies, 99–100; shipbuilding and supplies,
    100, 122; Peter the Great visits, 126–7; falls to
    Russians (1710), 138; in First World War,
    258–9, 268–70; controlled by local soviet,
    272; Goltz attacks and captures, 284; industry,
    298; Soviet army attacks and captures (1944),
    366–7; Soviet repression in (1991), 399–400
Riga Latvian Association, 225
Roberts, Michael, 125
Rodda Bank, Lübeck, 175
Rokossovsky, Marshal Konstantin K., 368–70,
    385–6
Rokossovsky, Platon, 217
Roman Empire, 18, 30
Roon, General Albrecht von, 224
Roosevelt, Franklin D., 368–9
Rosenberg, Alfred, 346–7, 350–1
Rosenborg, Denmark, 94
Roskilde, Peace of (1658), 119, 121
Rossbach, battle of (1757), 150
Rostock, 40, 62, 162, 356
Royal Prussia (Polish), 56, 81, 90, 116, 118, 151
Rozdhestvensky, Admiral Z.P., 237–9
Rozen, Andrei, 192
Rügen, 6, 204
Rumbold, Sir Horace, 305
Rumiantsev, Field Marshal Nikolai, 175
Rundstedt, General Gerd von, 326
runic inscriptions, 26
Rurik (Russian warship), 232, 246–7, 265
Rurik, Varangian leader, 22
Rus (Swedish Vikings), 22–5
Russdorf, Grand Master von (of Teutonic
    Knights), 56
Russell, Lord John, 207
Russia (and Soviet Union): Swedish Vikings in,
    22–4; Swedish apprehensions of, 70, 78;
    expands under Ivan III, 77–8; conflict with
    Livonian Order, 78–9, 87; gains access to Baltic,
    78, 88; wars with Livonia and Estonia, 87;
    White Sea route to, 88, 131; rise to power, 115,
    149; wars with Poland-Lithuania, 115–18; peace
    settlements (1660–1), 121; Great Northern War
    against Sweden,
    129–36, 144; thirty-year armistice with Turks,
    129; war with Ottomans (1711), 137;

Russia (*continued*)
expansion along Baltic coast, 138; naval
development, 139–40; peace with Sweden
(1821), 143–5; royal succession, 145;
economic ties with Britain, 149; war with
Prussia (1757–9), 150; war with Sweden
(1788–90), 155–6; Jews in, 158; peace treaty
with Ottomans (1792), 158; western frontiers
advanced at Polish expense, 160; in anti-
Napoleon alliance, 164–5, 167–8; and Treaty
of Tilsit (1807), 168–9; British blockade of
(1808), 171; war with Sweden in Finland
(1808–9), 171–2; acquires Finland, 172;
leaves Continental System, 175; resumes war
against Napoleon, 176–7; Napoleon invades,
177–81; secret societies and revolutionary
movements, 191; and Polish insurrection
(1830), 192–3; opposes free port at Slite, 197;
and Schleswig-Holstein crisis, 202; western
apprehension of, 206; and Baltic actions in
Crimean War, 209, 213–14; agrees settlement
of Åland Islands (1856), 214; railways
developed, 215, 217, 231; serfdom abolished,
215; and Finnish famine, 225; alliance with
France, 230, 231–2; in Far East, 231; anti-
semitism and pogroms, 233–4, 248–9,
259–60, 296; nationalism, 233–5; Orthodox
Church in, 233–5; war with Japan (1904–5),
237–40; Nicholas II's enforced reforms,
241–2, 249; revolution (1905), 242; William
II of Germany seeks alliance with, 244–5;
convention with Britain (1907), 247–8;
autocracy resumed, 249–50; succession of
dumas, 249–50; and outbreak of First World
War, 253–5; and conduct of First World War,
255–8, 263–5, 267–70; Provisional
Government (1917), 266–7, 271; revolutions
of 1917, 266, 270; armistice with Germany
(1917), 270; renounces sovereignty over Baltic
territories, 275; Civil War (1918–21), 280–2,
287; peace treaties with Baltic republics, 288;
Churchill on enigma of, 302; co-operation
with Nazi Germany, 303, 311, 329, 345;
Lenin formulates New Economic Plan, 303;
Soviet Union formed, 303; resurgence of
trade, 304; membership of League of
Nations, 311; Soviet navy modernized,
314–15; and Nazi German threat, 319–20;
Red Army purged, 319; British military
mission in, 320–3; pact with Nazi Germany
(1939), 322–4, 394, 396; and Anglo-Polish
pact (1939), 323–4; in Fourth Partition of
Poland (1939), 325; occupies and represses
partitioned Poland, 327–8; wartime Soviet
pressure on Baltic republics, 330–1; Winter
War with Finland (1939–40), 334–6; expelled
from League of Nations, 335; Moscow Peace
Treaty with Finland (1940), 336; and German
aggression in Scandinavia, 342; takes over
Baltic republics, 342–4; Germans invade
(1941), 345–6, 348, 349; military campaign
against Germany, 351, 356–7, 361–3; British
Arctic convoys to, 355; bombing offensive
against Finland and Estonia (1944), 364;
westward advance to Berlin (1944–5), 366–7,
370–1; post–1945 dominance, 375; peace
agreements and treaties with Finland, 376–7;
controls Baltic republics, 380–4, 397; as
super-power, 389; Gorbachev's reforms in,
391; Communist regime declines and ends,
393, 395–6, 400; and Baltic republics' move to
independence, 397–8; Soviet Union
dissolved, 400, 402; troops leave Baltic states
(1993–4), 402
Russian Primary Chronicle, 23
Rüütel, Arnold, 395, 398, 403
Ryti, Risto, 335–6, 353–4, 364, 365

Sabe, August, 381
Sadowa (Königgrätz), battle of (1866), 223
Saimaa canal, Finland, 215–16
Saint Barthélemy, Caribbean, 231
St Petersburg (Petrograd; Leningrad): built,
10–11, 49, 131–2; described, 10–12, 147–9;
name changes, 12, 258, 303; Treaty of (1793),
158; Winter Palace burnt, 197; naval
development, 232; Palace Square massacre
('Bloody Sunday', 1905), 237, 241; and
revolutions of 1917, 266, 270–1; capital
transferred to Moscow, 275; British
blockade (1919), 283; besieged (1941–4),
352–3, 356–8, 362–3; anti-communist protests,
400
Salisbury, John Montague, 3rd Earl of, 53–4
Salisbury, Richard Neville, 2nd Earl of
(Warwick the Kingmaker), 61–2
salt: trade in, 60
Saltykov, Sergei, 150
Salvius, Johan Adler, 106, 111
Sami people, 15–16
Samogitia, 44, 48, 50, 55–6
Samsonov, General Alexander, 255–7
Sarajevo, 252–3
Saumarez, Admiral Sir James, 171, 180
Savonenkov, General G. M., 376
Saxons: drive to east, 38–9
Sazonov, Sergei D., 249
Scandinavianism, 208
Schaumann, Eugen, 237
Schleswig, 28–9
Schleswig-Holstein: Denmark acquires (1460),
73; crisis (1848–52), 201–4; Bismarck on,
221; renewed crisis (1863), 221–3; Danes
surrender to Austro-Prussian alliance, 223;
redetermined in 1920 peace settlement,
290–1
Schleswig-Holstein (German battleship), 324, 327,
372

Schlieffen, Alfred, Count von: Plan, 256; opposes occupation of Denmark, 261
Schliemann, Heinrich, 4
Schmidt, Augustus, 321
Schulenburg, Count Friedrich Werner von der, 342
Schwerin, 40
Scotland: acquires timber in Baltic, 100
Sedan, battle of (1870), 224
Sejm (Polish-Lithuanian Diet), 89–90, 123, 144, 151, 157, 294, 300
Semigallia, 122
Serbia, 252–4
Setus (people), 17
Seven Years War (Baltic, 1563–70), 88–9, 94
Seven Years War (1756–63), 149
Sheremetev, General B.P., 131
Sibelius, Jan, 236
Sienkiewicz, Henryk: *The Deluge*, 117
Sigismund I, King of Poland, 80–1
Sigismund II Augustus, King of Poland, 87, 89–90
Sigismund III, King of Poland, 92–3, 98–9, 101, 106
Sigtuna, Sweden, 27, 29
Sikorski, General Wladyslaw, 329, 368
Sirk, Artur, 306–7
Skåne: herring trade, 60
Škirpa, Kazys, 350
Skrzynecki, General, 192
slaves, 35
Slavs: Saxon hostility to, 38–9
Slite, Gotland, 197
Slovakia, 316
Smetona, Anatanas, 300, 305–6, 315, 331, 342, 344
Smigly-Rydz, Marshal Edward, 315, 321, 327
Smolensk, 79, 98
Smolina, Lake, battle of (1502), 79
Snellman, Johann, 217
Sniečkus, Antanas, 381, 383, 394
Solidarity movement (Poland), 390–2, 396
Sophia Magdalena, Queen of Gustav III of Sweden, 153
Sorbs (people), 17
Soult, Marshal Nicolas Jean de Dieu, 166
Sound, the *see* Øresund
Sound Dues (tolls), 1, 2, 71, 94, 189
Spartacus (Soviet destroyer), 280
Spinola, General Ambrogio, 101
Sprengtporten, Göran, 185
Spychalski, General, 387
Ståhlberg, Kaarlo, 287, 308
Stalin, Josef V.: mistrust of West, 319; Hitler's relations with, 322, 329; and pact with Nazi Germany (1939), 322–3; occupies partitioned Poland, 327; supplies Germany with oil, 328; meets Paasikivi's Finnish delegation, 333–4; and German invasion of Russia,
346–8; limited British wartime support for, 355; respects Finnish independence, 364; and Polish frontiers, 368–9; and Warsaw rising (1944), 369; and attack on Berlin, 370
Stalingrad, battle of (1942–3), 358
Stångebro, battle of (1598), 93
Stanhope, James, 1st Earl, 141
Stanileski, battle of (1711), 137
Stanislas Augustus, King of Poland, 152, 158, 160
Stanislaw Leszczyński, King of Poland, 130, 139
Stanislaw, Bishop of Cracow, 37
Stanislaw Poniatowski, King of Poland, 151
Starya Ladoga, 22
Starzynski, Stefan, 327
Stauning, Thorvald, 297
Steele, Lieutenant G., VC, 284
Stein, Karl, Baron von, 181
Steingell, General, 180
Stephen Batory, King of Poland-Lithuania, 90–2
Stettin: position, 12; Saxons advance on, 39; Treaty of (1560), 98; Gustavus Adolphus captures, 106; falls to Russian alliance (1713), 139; Lassalle captures, 157
Stockholm: position, 8; founded, 32; Bloodbath (1520), 74–5, 83; Storkyrkan, 74; Three Towers castle burnt down, 126; plague deaths, 139; fire (1835), 197; urban riot (1848), 198; Olympic Games (1912), 250
Stockholm Accord (1986), 389
Stolbova, Peace of (1617), 98
Stolypin, Peter A., 248–50
Störtebeker, Klaus, 63
Stralsund: growth, 40; Treaty of (1370), 68; siege of (1628), 102–4; Charles XII returns to from exile, 137, 139; falls to Danes (1715), 139; in Napoleonic wars, 167, 171–2, 175–6, 181; in German Confederation, 188
Strang, William (*later* Baron), 320
Strasdenhof armistice (1919), 285
Strindberg, August: *Miss Julie*, 227
Stucka, Peteris, 283
Sture, Nils, 92
Sture, Sten ('the Elder'), 73–4, 78
Sture, Sten ('the Younger'), 74–5
Sudetenland, 316
Suomenlinna *see* Sveaborg
Suomi people, 16
Svantopolk, Duke of Danzig, 48
Sveaborg (Suomenlinna), Finland, 9, 171, 209, 211–12
Svenskund, battle of (1790), 156
Svinhufvud, Pehr, 250, 275–6, 278–9, 308, 312
Sweden: lakes, 7; pre-Viking rulers, 19; Vikings, 22; Christianity introduced to, 32, 34; regional divisions, 32, 65; supports Christianizing of Estonia, 45; attacks Novgorodian settlements (1240), 48; occupies

Sweden (*continued*)
  south-western Karelia, 49–50; in Hanse trade,
  59; Riksråd (Council of the Realm), 66,
  72–3, 124; serfdom abolished (1335), 66;
  Black Death in, 67; wars with Denmark,
  67–8, 73–4, 88–9, 95, 97, 111, 118–20, 124–5,
  128, 139; invites Margaret of Norway to rule,
  69; and Russian threat, 70, 78; and
  Scandinavian disunity, 70; peasantry in, 73;
  Riksdag (parliament), 73, 75, 84, 141, 194,
  228; achieves independent kingdom status,
  76; Lutheranism in, 82–5, 92, 125; Church
  lands and properties, 83–4; conscript army,
  84–5, 98–9; established as hereditary
  monarchy, 84; alliance with Denmark (1534),
  85; fortresses developed, 86; occupies Reval,
  87; pays Denmark for recovery of Älvsborg,
  89, 97–8; captures Kexholm, 91; defeats in
  Poland (1605) and Russia (1610), 94; iron
  industry, 97; campaign against Russia
  (1604–14), 98; taxation, 98; in Thirty Years
  War, 103, 105–10; primacy in north, 111;
  colonial enterprises, 112, 231; land
  ownership, 113, 125; invades Poland (1655),
  116–20; and terms of Treaty of Copenhagen,
  121; reforms under Charles XI, 125–6; Great
  Northern War against Russia, 129–34, 142–3;
  Poltava defeat, 135–6; alliance against
  (1714–15), 139; plague in, 139; 'Caps' and
  'Hats' parties, 141, 143, 152–3; Peter I attacks
  coast, 142–3; signs treaties of peace
  (1719–20), 142; peace with Russia (1721),
  143–5; scholarship and cultural life, 152–3;
  Jews in, 153–4, 197, 296; naval development,
  154; war with Russia (1788–90), 155;
  neutrality in Napoleonic Wars, 162; in anti-
  Napoleon alliance, 164–7, 170–1; war with
  Russia in Finland (1808–9), 171–2; joins
  Napoleon's Continental System, 172, 174;
  loses Finland to Russia, 172; declares war on
  Britain (1810), 174–5; and Napoleon's
  invasion of Russia, 181–2; Norway
  surrendered to, 182–3; sells Pomerania to
  Prussia, 184; war in Norway (1814), 184;
  reform movement in, 195–6; technological
  developments, 196; supports Denmark in
  1848 crisis, 202; and Scandinavianism, 208;
  and Crimean War, 212; treaty with France
  and Britain (1855), 213; and Schleswig-
  Holstein Question (1863), 221–2; emigration
  from, 225; food shortages (1860s), 225;
  labour conditions, 226–7; railways and
  industrial development, 226–7; religious
  freedom in, 227; social order, 227;
  democratic development, 228; conscription
  and army training, 229; and Norwegian
  independence, 243; resents renewed
  Russification of Finland, 250; crisis over
  social versus defence expenditure (1914), 251;

neutrality in First World War, 251, 261–3;
  and British blockade in First World War, 262;
  trade with Germany in First World War, 263;
  universal suffrage, 263; and Lenin's return to
  Russia, 267; socialist militancy, 279;
  constitutional changes (1719–20), 141–5?;
  (1809), 194; (1921), 293; post-First World
  War labour unrest, 297; maintains neutrality,
  302; economic upsets (1920s–1930s), 304;
  navy strengthened, 314; neutrality and
  actions in Second World War, 331, 340–1;
  and supply of iron ore to Germany in Second
  World War, 331–2, 337, 339, 341; and
  Finland's Winter War (1939–40), 335–6;
  grants transit rights to German troops, 340,
  344, 358; supplies ball-bearings to Britain in
  Second World War, 341; pro-Allied
  sympathies in Second World War, 359–60;
  alarm at Finland's agreements with Soviet
  Union, 377; armed neutrality, 378; high
  standard of living and social welfare, 378–9;
  parliamentary reform, 379; and oil crisis
  (1973–4), 388; investigates Soviet submarine,
  389; economic recession (1992), 401; and
  membership of EU (EEC), 401; rejects euro
  currency, 402
Swedenborg, Emmanuel, 152
Swedish East India Company, 162
Swedish Intelligencer (London newspaper), 109
Swedish West Indies Company, 154
Sword Brothers (Knighthood of Christ in
  Livonia), 43–7

Tacitus, 4–5; *Germania*, 17–18
Tallents, Colonel Stephen, 285, 289
Talleyrand, Charles Maurice de, 187
Tallinn, Estonia (Reval): as port, 6–7; described,
  9–10; urbanized, 35; founded by Danes, 45;
  Sweden occupies (1561), 87; Russians besiege
  (1570–1), 88; Russians occupy (1710), 138; as
  Russian naval harbour, 140; Edward VII and
  Nicholas II meet at, 248; unemployment and
  labour unrest, 299; coup (1919), 303; in
  Second World War, 330, 349, 364, 366; hosts
  Olympic yachting (1980), 383; free from
  Soviet rule, 394, 395, 398, 400, 405
Tani, Agnolo, 61
Tannenberg, battles of: (1410), 55–6, 257; (1914),
  256–7, 260
Tanner, Väinö, 335
Tartu (Dorpat), 99, 133, 288
Tauroggen, Convention of (1812), 180
Tegetthof, Admiral Wilhelm von, 222
Teutonic Order of the Hospital of St Mary in
  Jerusalem: builds Hermann Keep, 7; in
  northern crusades and campaigns, 46–8, 51,
  54–7, 63; defeated by Alexander Nevsky,
  48–9; Mindaugas opposes, 50; at Marienburg,
  51; dominance in Hanse, 51–2, 56;

Tannenberg defeat (1410), 55–6; in Thirteen Years War with Poland, 58; attack pirates, 62–3; supported by Valdemar II of Denmark, 65; acquires Estonia from Denmark, 66; conflict with Muscovy, 78–9; divided over Lutheranism, 80–1
Third Coalition, 165
Thirteen Years War (Poland-Teutonic Knights, 1454–66), 58
Thirty Years War (1618–48), 100–10
Thomas, General Georg, 344
Thor (god), 30
Thorn, treaties of: (1411), 56; second (1466), 56, 81
Three Crowns Union: Charles X Gustav proposes, 119
Thugut, Franz Maria, Baron, 159
Tieshausen, Countess, 177
Tilly, Johann Tserklaes, Count von, 101, 107–8
Tilsit: Treaty of (1807), 168, 175–6; renamed Sovetsk, 375
timber: trade in, 59
Time of Troubles (1604–13), 98, 115
Times, The (newspaper), 213, 282
Timoshenko, Marshal Semyon K., 336, 347–8
Tirpitz, Admiral Alfred von, 246–7, 269
Tirpitz (German battleship), 350
Togo, Admiral Heihachiro, 239
Tõnisson, Jaan, 235, 243, 271, 301–2, 343
Tönning, 128
Topelius, Zachris, 225
Torstensson, Lennart, 110–11
Townsend, Charles, 2nd Viscount, 141
Trafalgar, battle of (1805), 165, 167
Trans-Siberian Railway, 231
Trezzini, Domenico, 131–2
Tributs, Admiral Vladimir, 349–50
Triple Alliance (Germany-Austria-Italy), 230
Trolle, Archbishop of Uppsala, 74, 83
Troppau Congress (1820), 190
Trotsky, Leon, 241, 267, 270, 274, 276, 279, 287
Tsarskoye Selo, 148; amber room, 5, 357; in Second World War, 356–7
Tschirschky, Heinrich von, 244
Tsushima, battle of (1905), 239–40, 245
Tubelis, Jonas, 305
Tukachevsky, Marshal Mikhail, 288, 303, 319
Turkey see Ottoman Empire
Turner, General, 286
Tyrgils Knutson, 49

Uesson, Anton, 299, 343
Ulmanis, Karlis, 279, 283, 285–6, 307–8, 342–3
Ulrika Eleonora, Queen of Sweden, 141–2
Uluots, Jüri, 351, 363
Umeå, 140
Undén, Östen, 377–8
Union of Toiling Peoples, The (Baltic republics), 343

United Gotland Travellers, 42
United States of America: naval development, 247; maintains relations with Finland, 355
V-1 and V-2 weapons (German), 361
Vācietis, Jakums, 279–80
Vadstena, Sweden, 67, 84
Valdemar I, King of Denmark, 40
Valdemar II, King of Denmark, 41, 45, 65
Valdemar IV ('Atterdag'), King of Denmark, 65–9
Valentin, Weit, 12
Valka, 272, 289, 366
Valmy, battle of (1792), 158
Värälä, Treaty of (1790), 156
Varangians, 22–6, 32
Varberg, Sweden, 88
Vasa (Swedish warship), 103–4
Vasaloppet (ski race), 75
Vasilevsky, Marshal Alexander M., 366–7
Vasily III, Tsar, 77, 79
Västerås, Diet of, 85
Vaxholm Fortress, 86
Vendel, Sweden, 19
Versailles, Treaty of (1919), 281–2, 289–92, 314
Veterans League (Estonia), 306–7
Victoria, Queen, 198, 207, 212
Vienna: siege (1683), 123; Congress and Treaty of (1815), 184, 187–9, 201
Viipuri see Vyborg
Vika-Freiberga, Vaira, 403
Vikings: voyages and trade, 20–1; in Russia, 22–4; in Byzantium, 24–6; in East, 26–9
Vilnius (Vilna): described, 13–14; in 1812, 178–9; Zionism in, 234; Poland claims, 288–9, 301, 315, 404; Poles seize (1920), 302, 311; Germans agree to restore to Lithuania, 323; Lithuania reoccupies after Soviet army enters, 331; Jews exterminated, 352; political crisis and counter-revolution (1991), 398–400
Visby, Gotland, 27, 41–3, 67
Vistula, river, 6, 13
Vitalien Brotherhood (Vitalienbrüder), 62, 70
Vivesholm, Gotland, 62–3
Viviani, René, 253
Vladimir, Prince of Kiev, 34
Voldemaras, Augustinas, 300–1, 305, 344
Voltaire, François Marie Arouet, 147
Voroshilov, Marshal Kliment E., 320
Vyborg (Viipuri): founded, 49; raided by pirates, 62; strengthened against Russian threat, 78; Russians occupy and gain, 138, 143; Napier attempts to attack, 209; in Winter War (1939–40), 336; Soviet Russia bombs (1944), 364; ceded to Soviet Union, 376
Vyshinsky, Andrei, 343
Vytautas, Grand Duke of Lithuania, 56

Wałęsa, Lech, 388, 390–1
Wall Street crash (1929), 304

Wallenrod, Grand Master of Teutonic Knights, 54

Wallenstein, Albrecht Wenzel von, Duke of Friedland, 101–6, 108, 110

Wallhof, battle of (1626), 99

Wannsee Conference (1942), 352

Warsaw: described, 13; as administrative centre, 90; Confederation of, 90; burnt by Swedes, 121; captured by Germans, 327; ghetto rising (1943), 329; rising (1944), 368–9, 385; destroyed on Hitler's orders, 369

Warsaw agreement (1715), 144

Washington Naval Conference (1921), 314

wax: trade in, 59

Wegner, Hans, 380

Weimar Republic, 293–4

Wellington, Arthur Wellesley, 1st Duke of, 170

Wends, 17, 30, 32, 39

Westerplatte, 324, 326

Westphalia, Peace of (1648), 111, 115

White Sea, 88, 315

Wichfeld, Monica de, 360

Wilhelm Gustoff (German liner), 371

William I, King of Prussia (*later* German Kaiser), 219, 223

William II, German Kaiser: naval development, 231; assertiveness in Baltic, 244; seeks alliance with Russia, 244–7; opens broadened Kiel Canal, 252; and outbreak of First World War, 253–4; and Nicholas II's proposed flight, 268; approves naval action in Baltic, 269; in Riga, 272; exile in Holland, 278; self-aggrandisement, 278

Willisen, General Wilhelm von, 200

Wilmot, Martha, 12

Wilson, Sir Robert, 12

Wilson, Woodrow, 260, 281, 290–1

Windau (Ventspils), 122

Wismar, 60, 62, 105

Witte, Sergei, 231, 239, 246

Wittenberg, 79–83, 85

Wittenberg, Field Marshal Arvid, 117

Wittenborg, Burgomaster of Lübeck, 67–8

Woermann, Ernst, 342

Wojtyla, Karol *see* John Paul II, Pope

Wolgast, battle of (1628), 104

Worms, Diet of (1521), 79, 82

Wrangel, Marshal Charles Gustav, 114, 202

Wrede, General Karl Philipp, 174

Wybickli, Joseph, 168

Wyszinski, Cardinal Stefan, 386, 390

Yalta Conference (1945), 370

Yaroslav the Wise, Grand Prince of Kiev, 26, 34

Yeltsin, Boris, 395, 400

Yeremenko, General Ivan, 367

Yorck von Wartenburg, General Johann David Ludwig, Count, 180

Yudenich, General Nikolai N., 281–2, 287

Zaionczek, General Joseph, 187

Zariņš, Karlis, 342

Zeligowski, General Lucijan, 288, 302, 404

Zemgal tribe (Semigallians), 17

Zhdanov, Andrei, 343

Zhukov, Marshal Georgi, 303, 347–8, 370, 373, 386

Zölloner, Grand Master of Teutonic Kinghts, 54

Zollverein see Prussia